The Genealogy Of The Existing British Peerage: With Brief Sketches Of The Family Histories Of The Nobility

Edmund Lodge

THE

GENEALOGY

OF THE EXISTING

BRITISH PEERAGE,

WITH BRIEF SKETCHES

OF THE FAMILY HISTORIES OF

THE NOBILITY.

BY EDMUND LODGE, ESQ.

NORROY KING OF ARMS, F.S.A., &c.

WITH ENGRAVINGS OF THE ARMS.

LONDON:
SAUNDERS AND OTLEY, CONDUIT STREET.
1832.

PREFACE.

The design and method of this volume has been already so fully explained in that which will perhaps be usually found to accompany it, under the title of "The Peerage of the British Empire as now existing," that scarcely any explanation of its design or contents will be here necessary. As the present state of the Peerage of the three kingdoms will form the matter of that volume, so will this before us offer to our view the earlier story of the Ancestors and Families of the Nobility of the present day—the commencement of a chain of information not less acceptable to the historical antiquary, than its later links may probably be found by the more light and careless reader.

EDMUND LODGE, Norroy.

College of Arms,
Dec. 6, 1831.

ABBREVIATIONS.

Hon.	Honourable.
b.	born.
m.	married.
unm.	unmarried.
d.	died.
P.C.	Privy Counsellor.
E.I.C.	East India Company.
K G.	Knight of the Garter.
K.T.	Knight of the Thistle.
K.P.	Knight of St. Patrick.
G.C.B.	Knight Grand Cross of the Bath.
K.C.B.	Knight Commander of the Bath.
C.B.	Companion of the Bath.
G.C.H.	Grand Cross of the Guelphs of Hanover.
K.C.H.	Knight Commander of the Guelphs of Hanover.

Communications for this work are requested to be addressed (POST FREE) to EDMUND LODGE, ESQ., Norroy King of Arms, Messrs. Saunders and Otley, Public Library, Conduit Street, London.

ARMS

OF THE

Peers, Peeresses, &c.

OF THE

United Kingdom.

THE KING

LONDON.

PUBLISHED BY SAUNDERS & OTLEY, CONDUIT STREET.

Mores & King, Sc 33 Ludgate Street.

ABBREVIATIONS.

Hon.	Honourable.
b.	born.
m.	married.
unm.	unmarried.
d.	died.
P.C.	Privy Counsellor.
E.I.C.	East India Company.
K G.	Knight of the Garter.
K.T.	Knight of the Thistle.
K.P.	Knight of St. Patrick.
G.C.B.	Knight Grand Cross of the Bath.
K.C.B.	Knight Commander of the Bath.
C.B.	Companion of the Bath.
G.C.H.	Grand Cross of the Guelphs of Hanover.
K.C.H.	Knight Commander of the Guelphs of Hanover.

Communications for this work are requested to be addressed (POST FREE) to EDMUND LODGE, ESQ., Norroy King of Arms, Messrs. Saunders and Otley, Public Library, Conduit Street, London.

ARMS
OF THE
Peers, Peeresses, &c.
OF THE
United Kingdom.

THE KING

LONDON.
PUBLISHED BY SAUNDERS & OTLEY, CONDUIT STREET.

4 LABELS OF DISTINCTION

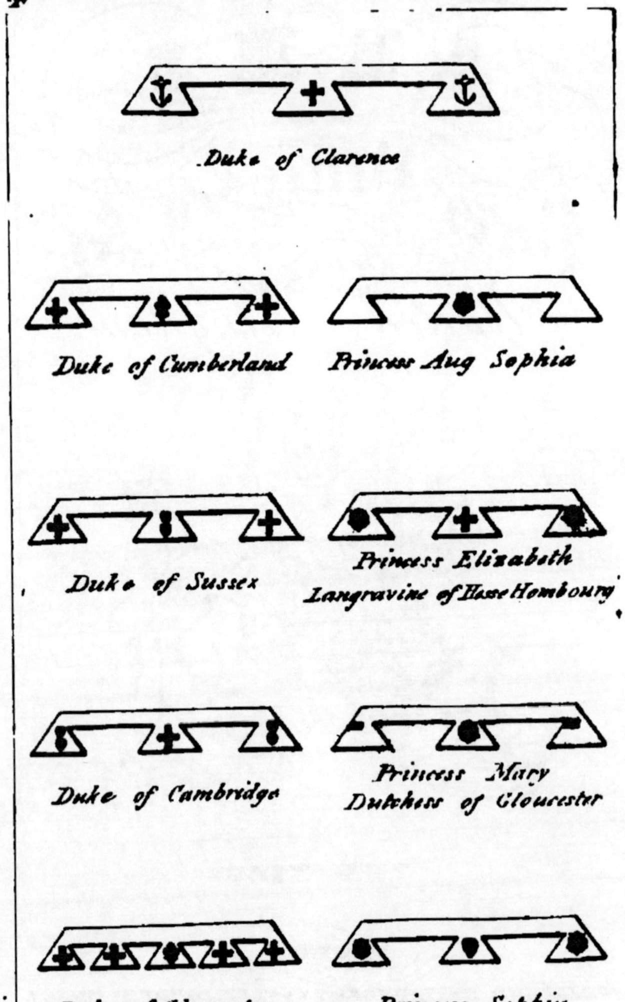

ENGLISH DUKES

NORFOLK

SOMERSET

RICHMOND

GRAFTON

BEAUFORT

S^T ALBANS

LEEDS

BEDFORD

[illegible] Ludgate Str.

6

ENGLISH DUKES

ENGLISH DUKES

NORTHUMBERLAND

WELLINGTON

BUCKINGHAM & CHANDOS

WINCHESTER

LANSDOWNE

STAFFORD

TOWNSHEND

SALISBURY

BATH

ABERCORN

HERTFORD

[illegible]

Morris & King Sc 35 Ludgate Street

ENGLISH MARQUESSES

BRISTOL

CLEVELAND

AILSA

BREADALBANE

WESTMINSTER

Morris & King sc

ENGLISH EARLS

11

12

ENGLISH EARLS

ENGLISH EARLS

B

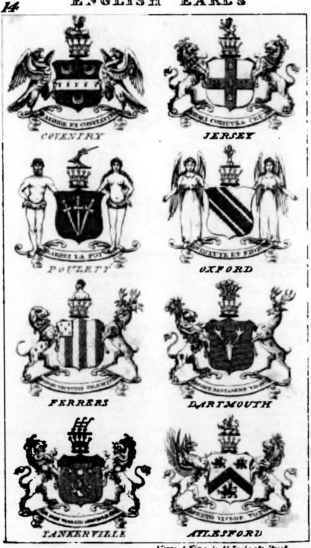

ENGLISH EARLS

Norris & King Sc. S. Ludgate Street.

BRISTOL

COWPER

STANHOPE

HARBOROUGH

MACCLESFIELD

POMFRET

WALDEGRAVE

ASHBURNHAM

A DEO ET REGE
HARRINGTON
PORTSMOUTH
WARWICK & BROOKE
BUCKINGHAMSHIRE
FITZWILLIAM
EGREMONT
HARCOURT
GUILDFORD

BATHURST
CLARENDON
ABERGAVENNY
TALBOT
GROSVENOR M. of WESTMINSTER
MOUNT EDGECUMBE
FORTESQUE
DIGBY

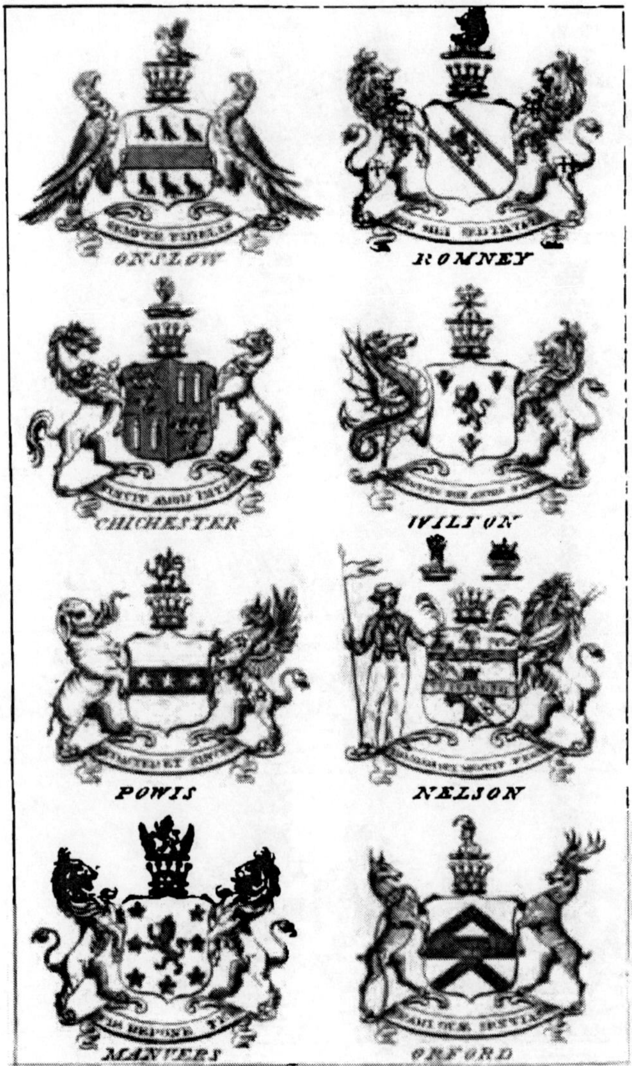
ONSLOW
ROMNEY
CHICHESTER
WILTON
POWIS
NELSON
MANVERS
ORFORD

ENGLISH EARLS

GREY

LONSDALE

HARROWBY

MULGRAVE

HAREWOOD

MINTO

CATHCART

VERULAM

ENGLISH EARLS

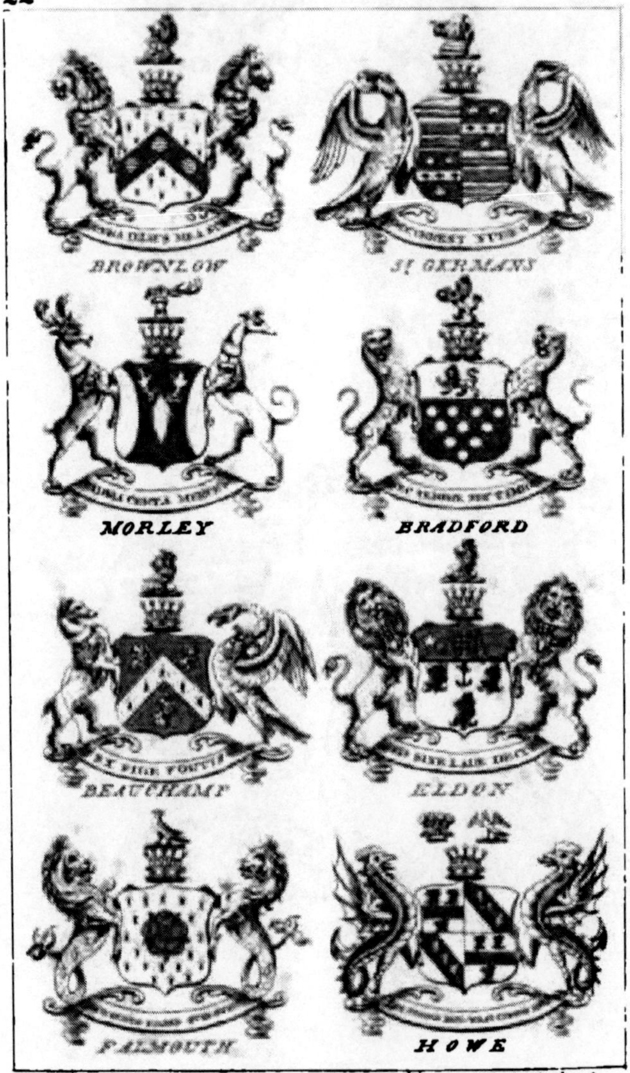

Morris & King Sc. 33 Ludgate Street.

SOMERS

STRADBROKE

AMHERST

DUDLEY

CAWDOR

MUNSTER

BURLINGTON

CAMPERDOWN

Morris & King, Sc. 35 Ludgate street.

LITCHFIELD

ENGLISH VISCOUNTS

ENGLISH VISCOUNTS

DUNCAN E of CAMPERDOWN

ST VINCENT

MELVILLE

SIDMOUTH

ANSON E. of LITCHFIELD

LAKE

GRANVILLE

EXMOUTH

Morris & King Sc 35 Ludgate Street

BERESFORD

COMBERMERE

GODERICH

[illegible] King [illegible] Ludgate Street

LE ROY LE VEUT
LE DESPENCER
DE CLIFFORD
JE LE TIENS
AUDLEY
CLINTON
DACRE
WILLOUGHBY D'ERESBY
STOURTON
WILLOUGHBY DE BROKE

ST JOHN
HOWARD OF EFFINGHAM
HOWARD DE WALDEN
PETRE
ARUNDELL
DEO DATE
DORMER
SPES MEA IN DEO
TEYNHAM

STAFFORD
BYRON
CLIFFORD
MIDDLETON
KING
MONSON
MONTFORT
SONDES

Morris & King Sc. Aldersgate Street.

FOLEY

DYNEVOR

WALSINGHAM

BAGOT

SOUTHAMPTON

GRANTLEY

RODNEY

CARTERET

Morris & King, Sc. 15 Ludgate Street.

GRENVILLE
THURLOW
AUCKLAND
LYTTELTON
SELSEY
DUNDAS
YARBOROUGH
CALTHORPE

ENGLISH BARONS

WILLOUGHBY D' ERESBY

[illegible]

ROLLE

CARRINGTON

BAYNING

BOLTON

WODEHOUSE

NORTHWICK

[illegible] Street

PARTA TUERI
LILFORD
RIBBLESDALE
PATIENTIA VINCES
ALVANLEY
VIVE UT VIVAS
ABERCROMBY
S^T HELENS
REDESDALE
ELLENBOROUGH
SUB CRUCE CANDIDA
ARDEN

BARHAM

[illegible]

CREWE

PONSONBY

GARDNER

MANNERS

GAMBIER

LYNEDOCH

Morris & King [illegible] Ludgate Street

ENGLISH BARONS

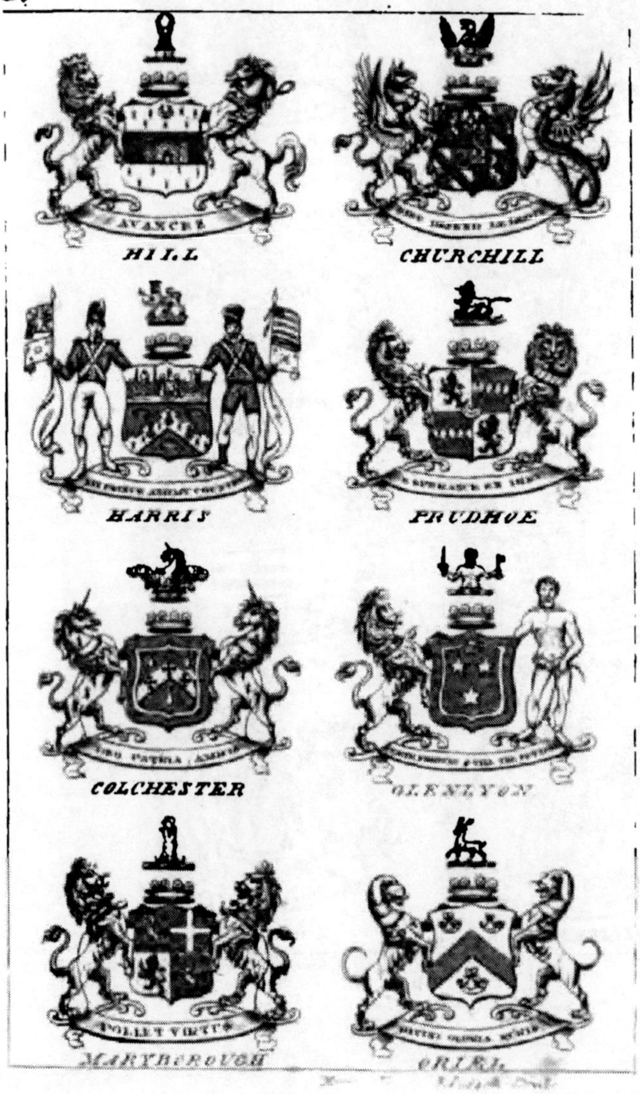

STOWELL

[illegible]

DELAMERE

FORESTER

BEXLEY

GIFFORD

FARNBOROUGH

DE TABLEY

ENGLISH BARONS

HEYTESBURY

DURHAM

SKELMERSDALE

WALLACE

WYNFORD

BROUGHAM

DOVER

PANMURE

Morris & Co

ENGLISH BARONS

OAKLEY

POLTIMORE

WENLOCK

MOSTYN

SEGRAVE

TEMPLEMORE

DINORBEN

DE SAUMAREZ

[illegible] Ludgate Street

COUN^TS OF MANSFIELD
COUN^SS DE GREY
VISC^SS CANNING
DE ROS
DE LA ZOUCH
GREY DE RUTHYN
HOWE
SANDYS

KEITH

RAYLEIGH

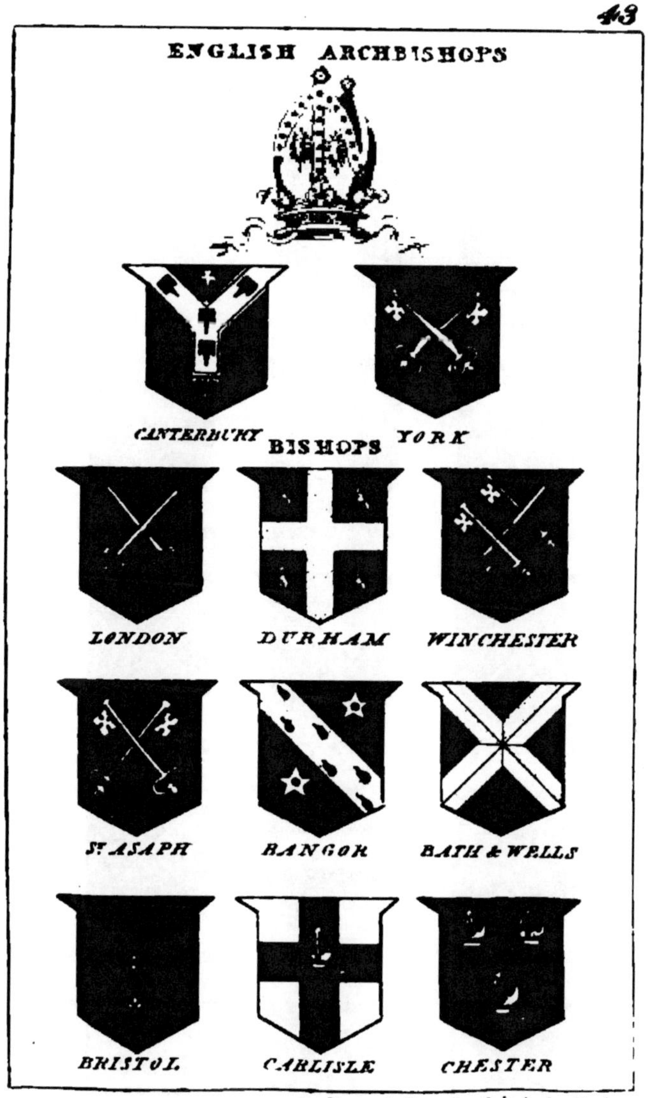
ENGLISH ARCHBISHOPS
CANTERBURY
YORK
BISHOPS
LONDON
DURHAM
WINCHESTER
St. ASAPH
BANGOR
BATH & WELLS
BRISTOL
CARLISLE
CHESTER

44

ENGLISH BISHOPS

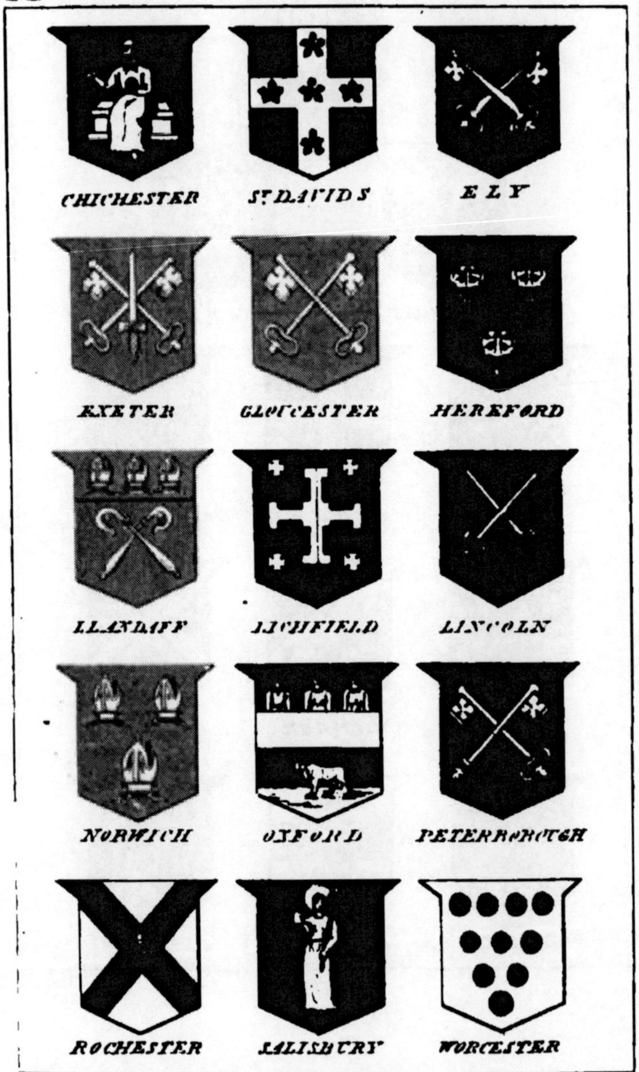

SODOR & MAN

BISHOPS OF THE COLONIES

BARBADOES

CALCUTTA

JAMAICA

QUEBEC

NOVA SCOTIA

Morris & Co.

46

SCOTCH DUKES

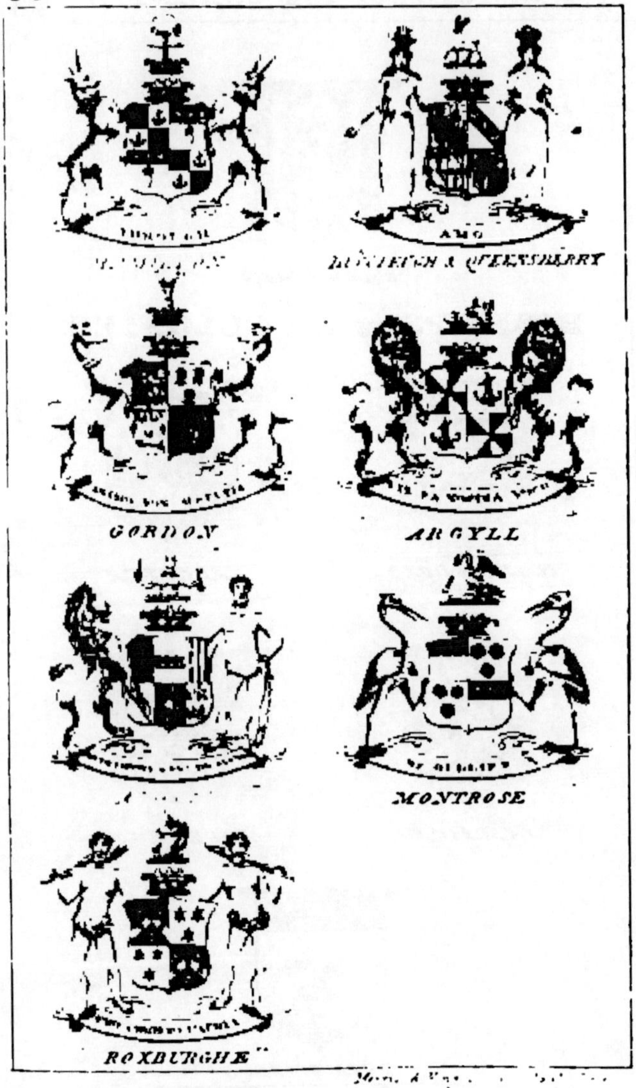

SODOR & MAN
BISHOPS OF THE COLONIES
BARBADOES
CALCUTTA
JAMAICA
QUEBEC
NOVA SCOTIA

Merry & King

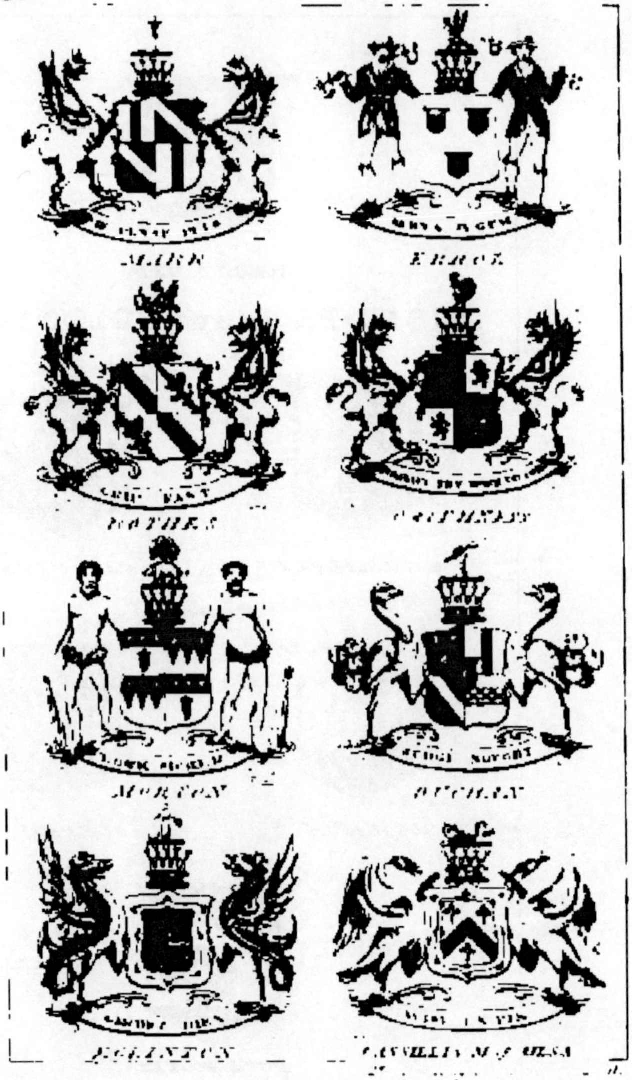
MARR
ERROL
ROTHES
MORTON
BUCHAN
EGLINTON

SCOTCH EARLS

MORAY

HOME

STRATHMORE

KELLIE

HADDINGTON

GALLOWAY

LAUDERDALE

KINNOULL

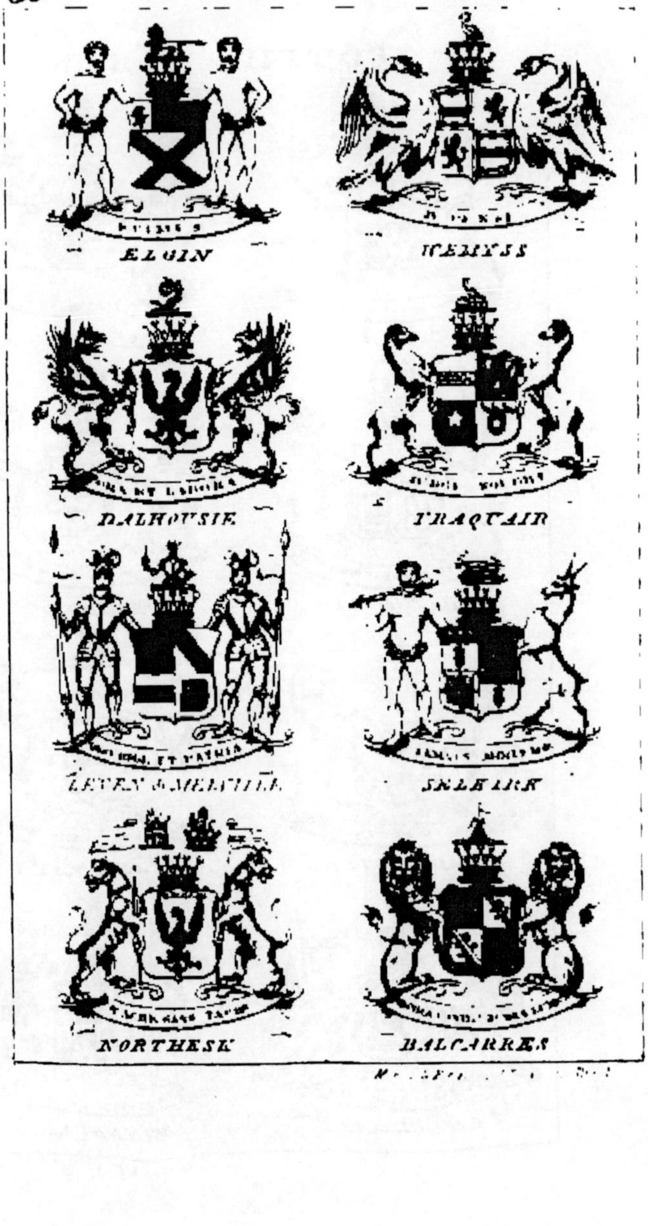
ELGIN
WEMYSS
DALHOUSIE
TRAQUAIR
LEVEN & MELVILLE
SELKIRK
NORTHESK
BALCARRES

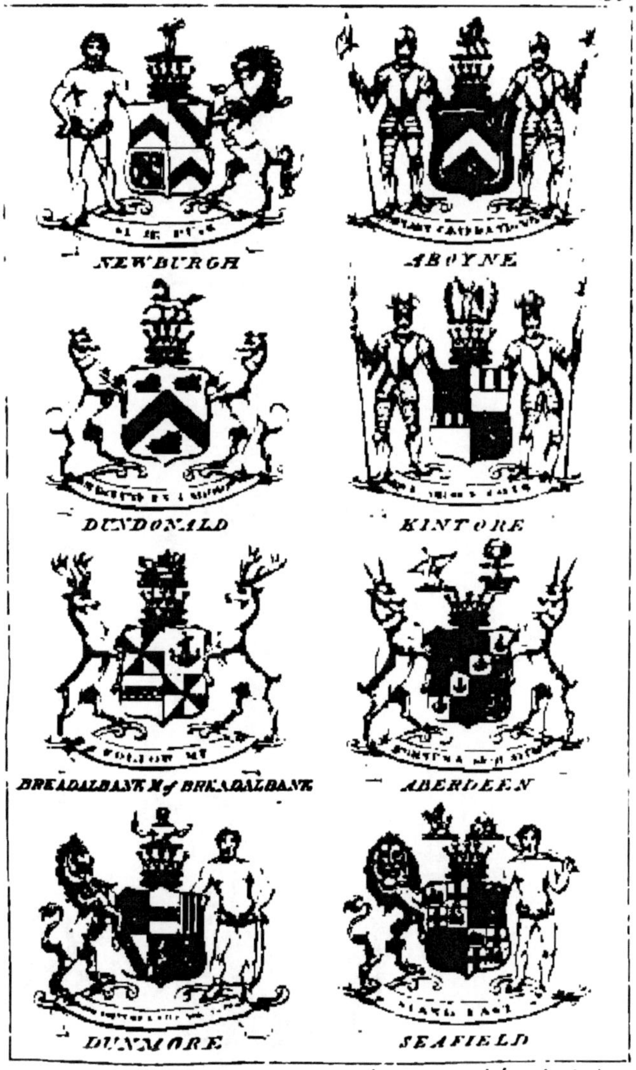
NEWBURGH
ABOYNE
DUNDONALD
KINTORE
BREADALBANE M of BREADALBANE
ABERDEEN
DUNMORE
SEAFIELD

FIRM
STAIR
ROSEBERY
GLASGOW
HOPETOUN
AVANCE
PORTMORE
A FIN
AIRLIE
I DARE
CARNWATH
STIRLING

FALKLAND

KENMURE

ARBUTHNOT

STRATHALLAN

SCOTCH BARONS

Morris & King Sc. 35 Ludgate Street

SCOTCH BARONS

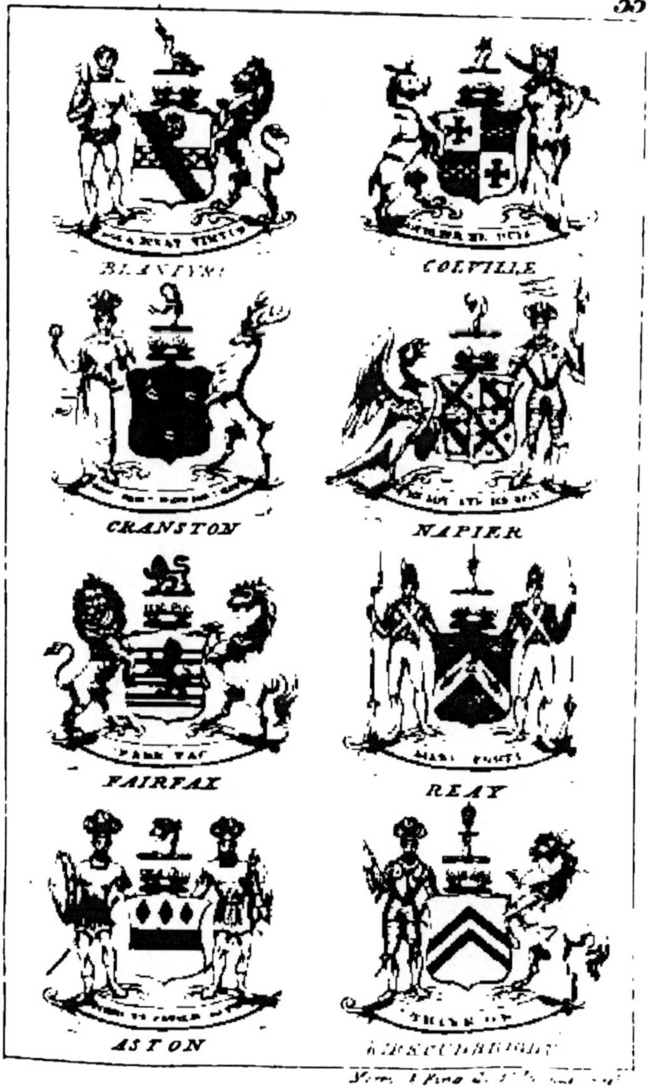

SCOTCH BARONS

SCOTCH PEERESSES

SUTHERLAND

LOUDOUN

DYSART

ORKNEY

[illegible]

LEINSTER

MARQUESSES

WATERFORD

DOWNSHIRE

DONEGAL

DROGHEDA

WELLESLEY

THOMOND

HEADFORT
SLIGO
ELY
LONDONDERRY
CONYNGHAM
WESTMEATH
ORMONDE
CLANRICARDE

Morris & King, Sc. Ludgate Street.

62 IRISH EARLS

ARRAN
COURTOWN
MILTOWN
CHARLEMONT
MEXBOROUGH
WINTERTON
HOWTH
KINGSTON

IRISH EARLS

VIVERE SAT VINCERE
SEFTON
RODEN
LISBURNE
TOUJOURS PRET
CLANWILLIAM
ALDBOROUGH
VIS UNITA FORTIOR
MOUNT CASHELL
LONGFORD
PORTARLINGTON

CARHAMPTON
MAYO
ANNESLEY
ENNISKILLEN
ERNE
CARYSFORT
KILKENNY
MOUNTNORRIS

IRISH EARLS

DESART
WICKLOW
CLONMEL
CLARE
LEITRIM
LUCAN
BELMORE
LLANDAFF

O'NEILL
BANDON
FORWARD
CASTLESTEWART
DONOUGHMORE
CALEDON
LOYAL EN TOUT
KENMARE
LIMERICK
CLANCARTY

IRISH EARLS

GOSFORD

ROSSE

NORMANTON

CHARLEVILLE

BLESSINGTON Ext.

BANTRY

GLENGALL

SHEFFIELD

Merrin & King Sc. 38 Ludgate Street.

IRISH EARLS

KILMOREY

[illegible]

LISTOWEL

DUNRAVEN

NORBURY

RANFURLY

70

IRISH VISCOUNTS

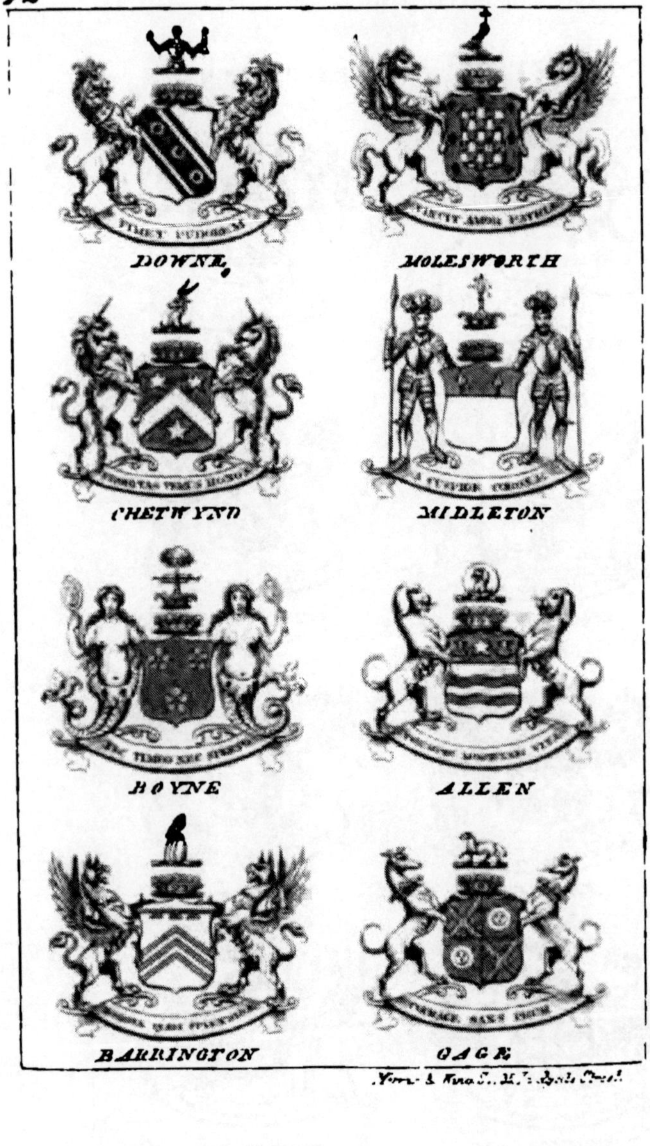
DOWNE
MOLESWORTH
CHETWYND
MIDLETON
BOYNE
ALLEN
BARRINGTON
GAGE

PALMERSTON
GALWAY
POWERSCOURT
ASHBROOK
MOUNTMORRES
DUNGANNON
SOUTHWELL
DE VESCI

IRISH VISCOUNTS

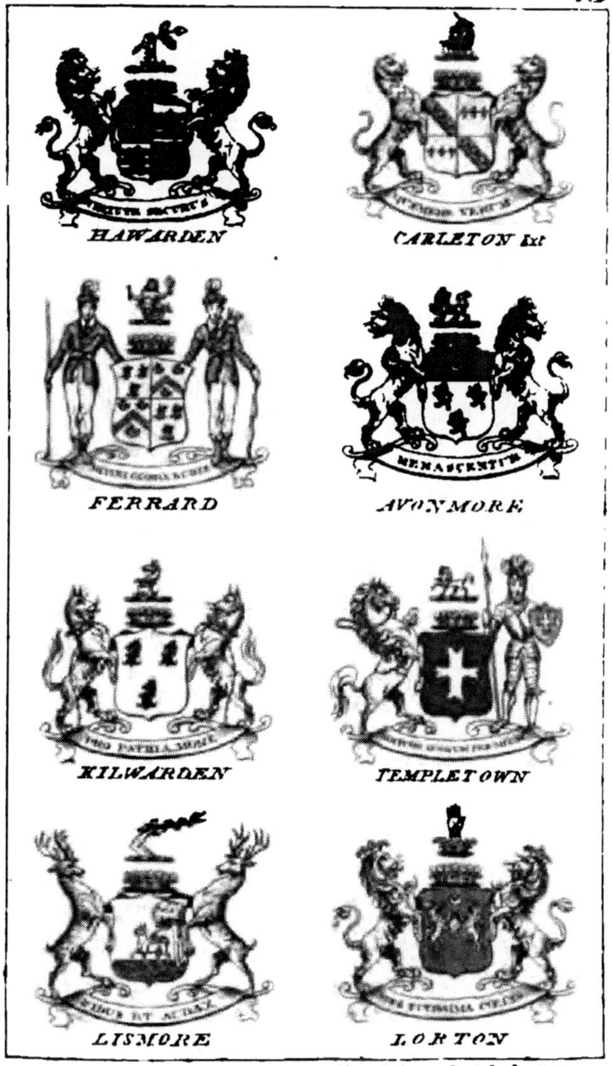
HAWARDEN
CARLETON Ext
FERRARD
AVONMORE
KILWARDEN
TEMPLETOWN
LISMORE
LORTON

FRANKFORT

GORT

CASTLEMAINE

GUILLAMORE

KINGSALE

DUNSANY

TRIMLESTOWN

LOUTH

BLAYNEY

CARBERY

AYLMER

FARNHAM

BRANDON
LISLE
NEWBOROUGH
MACDONALD
KENSINGTON
ONGLEY
MASSY
ROKEBY

MUSKERRY

RIVERSDALE

MUNCASTER

KILMAINE

CLONCURRY

CLONBROCK

WATERPARK

GRAVES

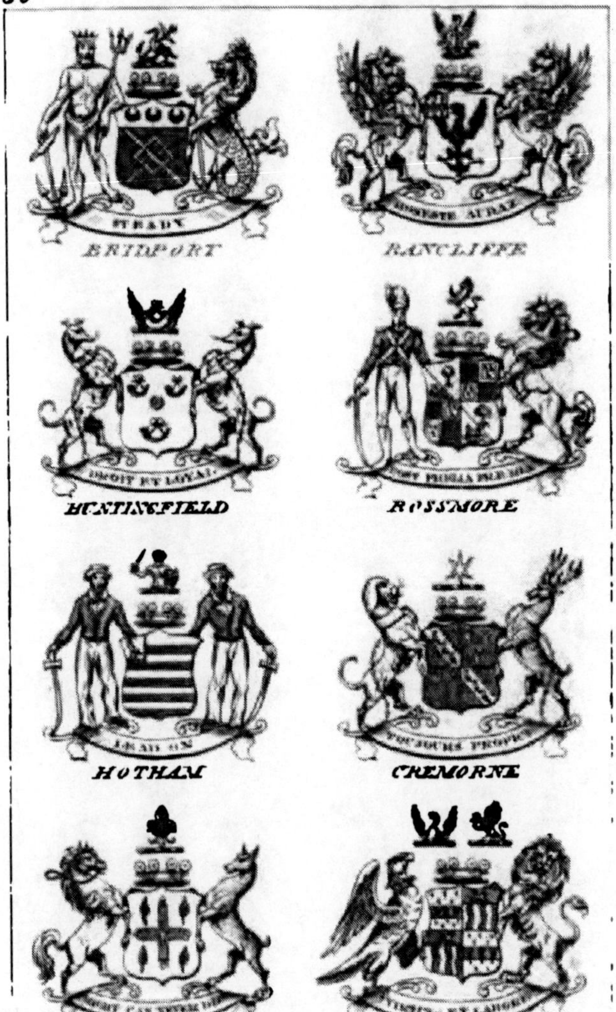
STEADY
BRIDPORT
RANCLIFFE
DROIT ET LOYAL
HUNTINGFIELD
ROSSMORE
HOTHAM
CREMORNE
NORWOOD
HEADLEY

TEIGNMOUTH
CROFTON
FFRENCH
HENLEY
VINCIT VERITAS
CASTLE COOTE
LANGFORD
DE BLAQUIERE
HENNIKER

PER VIAS RECTAS
DUFFERIN
VIVERE SAT VINCERE
VENTRY
WALLSCOURT
MOUNT SANDFORD
IN OMNIA PARATUS
DUNALLEY
HARTLAND
CLANMORRIS
ST VINCENT
RADSTOCK

NORBURY

NUGENT

ASHTOWN

CLARINA

RENDLESHAM

DECIES

GARVAGH

HOWDEN

DOWNES

BLOOMFIELD

85

ANTRIM

MASSEREENE

TALBOT & MALAHIDE

FITZGERALD & VESEY

IRISH ARCHBISHOPS

IRISH BISHOPS

IRISH BISHOPS

GENEALOGY.

THE KING AND ROYAL FAMILY.

From all the various lines of kings which from the earliest historical period have reigned in England, his present Majesty is lineally descended, and in his paternal line traces an ancestry to which no family in modern Europe can boast superior antiquity.

A long line of princes, who through the dark ages of Italian history held various offices and possessions in the northern parts of that troubled country, were the predecessors of the Marquises of Este, whose pedigree from the ninth century is accurately preserved. Azo, 4th Marquess of Este, having by marriage with Cunegunda, daughter of Guelph, 3d Duke of Lower Bavaria, and sister and heir of Guelph 4th, engrafted this ancient race upon a German stock of equal antiquity and larger dominion, left his possessions in Italy to his younger brother Fulco, whose male descendants became extinct in 1790, by the death of Hercules 3d, Duke of Modena, now represented in the female line by a prince of the Austrian family.

The house of Guelph, which thus became united to the paternal line of Este, loses the certainty of its pedigree in the remote ages to which it ascends; but in the 11th century, when Azo 4th, of Este, succeeded to the inheritance of his brother-in-law, had long been powerful and renowned. Guelph 5th, his son by Cunegunda, was father of Henry the Black, who married Wulfhilda, daughter and heir of Magnus Duke of Saxony on the Elbe. Their son, Henry the Proud, married Gertrude, daughter and heir of the Emperor Lothair, by Richenza, daughter and heir of Henry Duke of Saxony on the Weser, who united in his own person, and by marriage, the inheritance of the ancient Dukes of Saxony in all their various branches, and of the Saxon Emperors; being himself descended through twenty male generations, all reigning Kings, Princes, or Dukes of Saxony, from Hengist, King of the Saxons, whose successful descent upon the coast of Kent gave rise to the establishment of the Kings of his lineage in Britain.

KING AND ROYAL FAMILY.

In the person of HENRY the Lion, Duke of Saxony and Bavaria, son of HENRY the Proud, and Gertrude, heiress of Saxony, the house of ESTE attained a degree of power in the empire so formidable to the reigning Emperors, that by the promulgation of the ban of the empire, in the year 1180, his vassals were instigated to assert their independence; and after a life spent in military achievements and the display of prowess and heroism worthy of better success, he left at length to his posterity the possession of the Duchy of Brunswick only, while the present reigning houses of Saxony, Bavaria, Brandenburg, Mecklenburg, Wirtemburg, Anhalt, and the first line of Austrian princes rose on the ruins of their ancient inheritance. From HENRY the Lion descended in the 11th degree,

ERNEST, Duke of Brunswick, whose eldest son Henry was ancestor of the present reigning Duke of Brunswick; and his second son WILLIAM was grandfather of ERNEST, Elector of Hanover, whose marriage with the Princess Sophia, daughter of Frederick 5th, Elector Palatine, by the Princess Elizabeth, daughter of King James 1st, finally conducted the House of Brunswick to the throne of these realms.

But in a volume devoted to the elucidation of British genealogies, a slight sketch of the descent of the British Crown seems desirable. Our early history, like that of all other nations, is too much involved in the clouds of doubtful tradition, to permit us to lay much stress on that pedigree of the House of Tudor, which by claiming for it a descent from the ancient British kings, would place an heir of that race on the throne, in the person of Henry 7th, from whom all our subsequent monarchs have descended. But from CERDIC, one of the earliest Saxon invaders, and founder of the kingdom of Wessex in the sixth century, the Royal lineage is unequivocal.

EGBERT, the seventeenth King of Wessex, ninth in paternal descent from Cerdic, united under his sceptre, about the year 828, by inheritance or conquest, all the kingdoms of the Saxon Heptarchy, and transmitted the kingdom undivided through fourteen successions and seven generations in the male line, to EDMUND Ironside; on whose death, in 1017, Canute the Dane acquired the English Crown, his reign and that of his two sons forming an interruption to the line of Saxon Kings, which was temporarily restored under EDWARD the Confessor, the brother of Edmund Ironside, to be finally closed at his death in 1066. Edward the Confessor left no issue, but Edward, a son of Edmund Ironside, left a son, Edgar Atheling, and a daughter, Margaret; from the marriage of the latter with Malcolm 3d, King of Scotland, proceeded all the subsequent kings of Scotland, till the accession of James 6th, of Scotland to the English throne restored the true heir of this ancient and honoured line to the inheritance of his ancestors.

The disorders which had affected the succession towards the close of the Saxon dynasty, terminated in the introduction of a foreign race through the result of the battle of Hastings; and from thenceforth William the Conqueror must be considered as the stock of the Royal family.

WILLIAM I., surnamed the CONQUEROR, left three sons, 1 ROBERT, who succeeded him as Duke of Normandy, and died without surviving issue in 1134; 2 WILLIAM, his successor in the throne of England; 3 HENRY, who succeeded his brother William; and several daughters, one of whom,

ADELA, m. Stephen, Count of Blois, and had four sons; 1 William, Count of Blois; 2 Theobald, Count of Champagne; 3 STEPHEN, who residing at the English Court, found means to usurp the Crown on the death of his uncle King Henry 1st; 4 Henry, Bishop of Winchester.

WILLIAM 1st *d.* 9 Sept. 1087, and was succeeded in the throne by his 2d son,

WILLIAM II., who *d.* unmarried, 2 August, 1100.

HENRY I., his brother, who succeeded, had one son, William, who died before him, and an only daughter, MATILDA, to whom the nobles of England and Normandy swore fealty as the successor of her father, and who afterwards contested the crown with King Stephen; was herself crowned Queen in 1141, but again overpowered by Stephen, and compelled to retire to Anjou. She was first m. to Henry 4th, Emperor of Germany, by whom she had no issue; and secondly, to Geoffrey Plantagenet, Count of Anjou, by whom she was mother of HENRY, acknowledged by King Stephen as his successor. HENRY 1st d. 1 December 1135.

STEPHEN, the nephew of King Henry, being on the spot at his death, and enabled by the assistance of his brother, the Bishop of Winchester, to seize the crown, retained it through numerous vicissitudes of fortune; but was unable to transmit it to his descendants. He had two sons, who both died without issue. STEPHEN d. 25 Oct. 1154, when

HENRY II., son of the Empress Matilda, and grandson of King Henry 1st, peaceably ascended the throne, presenting the first example in our history of the triumph of hereditary right over temporary usurpation. Four of his sons lived to maturity, viz. 1 Prince HENRY, whom he caused to be crowned King, but who died in his father's lifetime; 2 RICHARD, who succeeded; 3 Geoffrey, Duke of Brittany, who died in his father's lifetime, leaving two children, Arthur Duke of Brittany, and Eleanor, both of whom should have successively inherited the crown after the death of their uncle King RICHARD, but were superseded by the usurpation of JOHN; they both d. unmarried.

HENRY 2nd d. 6 July 1189.

RICHARD I., his eldest surviving son, succeeded; he d. without issue, 6 April 1199, when

JOHN, taking advantage of the youth of Arthur, only son of his elder brother Geoffrey, obtained possession of the crown; to which his posterity at length acquired an hereditary right, by the extinction of Geoffrey's descendants. King JOHN d. 17 October 1216, and was succeeded by his eldest son,

HENRY III., who d. 16 Nov. 1272. His eldest son,

EDWARD I., succeeded him. By his first marriage with Eleanor of Castille, this King had but one surviving son, EDWARD, the first Prince of Wales of the Royal family of England; by his second marriage with Margaret of France he had two sons, Thomas de Brotherton, Earl of Norfolk, and Earl Marshal of England, from whom the office of Earl Marshal has lineally descended through female heirs to the present Duke of Norfolk; and Edmund Earl of Kent, whose male issue failed in his sons.

King EDWARD 1st d. 7 July 1307, and was succeeded by his eldest son,

EDWARD II., who was dethroned 13 January 1326, and murdered 21 September 1327. He was also succeeded by his eldest son,

EDWARD III. The conflicting claims of this King's numerous issue caused the long civil wars which disturbed the reigns of the subsequent kings of the house of Plantagenet; and though so well known to the British public, and more perhaps through the works of our immortal dramatic bard, than even by those of our best historians, must be shortly noticed in this lineal sketch of our royal race. King Edward had five sons who lived to maturity, viz.:—

1 Edward, Prince of Wales, the renowned Black Prince, whose only surviving issue was RICHARD, who succeeded his grandfather.

2 Lionel, Duke of Clarence. He left an only daughter,

Phillippa, *m.* to Edmund Mortimer, Earl of March, by whom she was mother of

Roger, Earl of March. He left a son, Edmund, Earl of March, who died without issue, and a daughter,

Anne, heiress of her brother. She married Richard, Earl of Cambridge, 2nd son of Edmund, Duke of York, 4th surviving son of King Edward 3rd, and thus, carrying into the house of York the hereditary rights of the Duke of Clarence, gave to that line a priority of claim through the female descent over the elder male line of Lancaster. By the Earl of Cambridge she had an only son,

Richard, Duke of York, father, besides several sons who died young, of the three following:

1 King EDWARD 4th.

2 George, Duke of Clarence, who being drowned in a butt of Malmsey in the reign of his brother EDWARD, left by Isabella, eldest daughter and co-heir of Richard Neville, Earl of Warwick, the celebrated king-maker, one son, Edward, Earl of Warwick, and one daughter, Margaret, Countess of Salisbury, who married Sir Reginald Pole; her eldest son Henry, Lord Montague, left two daughters, Catherine, married to Francis Hastings, Earl of Huntingdon, of which marriage the Marquis of Hastings is the representative; and Winifred, married first Sir Thomas Hastings, by whom she had no issue, and secondly, Sir Thomas Barrington; the lineal descendant and heir male of this marriage is Sir Fitzwilliam Barrington, Bart., who is consequently co-heir, with the Marquis of Hastings, of George Plantagenet, Duke of Clarence.

3 King RICHARD 3rd.

3 John of Gaunt, Duke of Lancaster; he married first the Lady Blanche, daughter of Henry, Duke of Lancaster, and at length sole heir of the house of Lancaster, descended from Edmund, 2nd son of King Henry 3d, by whom he had an only son, afterwards King HENRY 4th; he married secondly, Constance, daughter of Peter the Cruel, King of Castile, and had an only daughter, heiress to the throne of Castile, who married Henry 3d, King of Castile. By Catherine, daughter of Sir Payne Roet, and widow of Sir Otes Swinford, whom he afterwards married, John of Gaunt had a son,

John, surnamed Beaufort, legitimated by Parliament, and created Earl of Somerset; he had three sons: 1 Henry, Earl of Somerset, who died unmarried; 2 John, who succeeded his brother, and was created Duke of Somerset. He died without issue male. 3 Edmund, 2nd Duke of Somerset, who had two sons, Henry and Edmund, successively Dukes of Somerset; with the latter of whom, who was beheaded by King Edward 4th, in 1471, failed the legitimate male line of John Beaufort, Earl of Somerset, the legitimated son of John of Gaunt, Duke of Lancaster; but Henry, Duke of Somerset, his elder brother, left a natural son, Charles, who assumed the surname of Somerset, was created Earl of Worcester, and was ancestor of the present Duke of Beaufort.

John, Duke of Somerset, 2nd son, as above, of John Beaufort, Earl of Somerset, left an only daughter,

Lady Margaret Beaufort, *m.* first to Edmund Tudor, Earl of Richmond, eldest son of Owen Tudor (a supposed descendant of Cadwallader, King of Britain) by Catherine, daughter of Charles 6th, King of France, widow of Henry 5th and mother of Henry 6th, Kings of England; secondly, to Sir Henry Stafford; and thirdly, to Thomas Lord Stanley and Earl of Derby. By the two last she had no issue, but by Edmund Tudor, Earl of Richmond, she was mother of

King HENRY 7th.

[4 Edm]und, Duke of York. He left two sons,

1 Edward, [redacted] f York, who died without issue.
2 Richard, [redacted] ho *m.*, as before related, Anne, daughter of Roger Mor[redacted]h, grand-daughter of Phillippa, only daughter of Lionel, [redacted]e, and heiress of the rights of the line of Clarence; their [redacted]ard, who succeeded his uncle as Duke of York, was fa[redacted] King EDWARD 4.
5 Thomas of Wood[redacted]loucester, who left no surviving sons. His only daughter who [redacted]
Anne, *m.* first [redacted] Stafford without issue; secondly, to Edmund his[redacted]afford; and thirdly, to William Bourchier, Earl of E[redacted] marriage descended the family of Devereux, Earls of [redacted] their female heirs the present Duchess of Buckingh[redacted] an[redacted] From the second marriage, the line of Stafford, Du[redacted] of [redacted]n, of which, and of Thomas of Woodstock, Duke of Gl[redacted] present Lord Stafford is, through females, the lineal rep[redacted]

King EDWAR[redacted]rvived his eldest son the Black Prince, *d.* 21 June, 1377, and was su[redacted] grandson,

[redacted]CHARD I[redacted] son of the Black Prince; he *d.* 14 February 1400, [redacted]r 1399, by the Parliament, which passing over th[redacted]mer, Earl of March, by female descent from [redacted] of King Edward 3rd, declared the crown to [redacted] Gaunt, Duke of Lancaster, 3rd son of [redacted]

[redacted]d was succeeded by his eldest son,

[redacted]422, was succeeded by his only son,

[redacted]nd, having survived his only son Edward, [redacted]imate male line of John of Gaunt, Duke of L[redacted] 3rd. But the civil war which had raged thr[redacted]rtunate monarch's reign, had during his lifetime [redacted]eir of the rival house of York,

EDW[redacted]ed as above, in the female line, from Lionel, Duke of Clarence, secon[redacted] of King Edward 3rd. He *d.* 9 April 1482, leaving issue, besides several younger daughters,

1 King EDWARD 5th.
2 Richard, Duke of York, murdered in the Tower, with his elder brother.
3 Elizabeth, heiress of the House of York; who, transmitting her rights to her children, their final establishment on the throne produced the triumph of the lineal succession in the elder line through females, in preference to the junior male heirs; but it must be acknowledged that this settlement did not actually take effect till after the total extinction of the male line of Plantagenet. She *m.* King HENRY 7th, and by him, besides other issue, was mother of King HENRY 8th, and of Margaret, from whose marriage with James 4th, King of Scotland, descended JAMES 1st, and all the subsequent kings of Great Britain.

EDWARD V., succeeded his father, under the protectorate of his uncle Richard, Duke of Gloucester, and was by him murdered in the Tower; after which the Protector ascended the throne by the name of

RICHARD III., to the exclusion of his niece, the Princess Eliz
daughter of King Edward 4th; and lest even the plea of male inheritanc

a shadow of sanction to the usurpation of that [illegible] descent of which on the female heirs the house of York had so long [illegible] contended, to the exclusion also of Edward, Earl of Warwick, [illegible] of George, Duke of Clarence, next brother of King Edward 4th, and [illegible] ther of Richard. The usurpation and tyranny of this prince, who left no [illegible] issue, having alienated a large portion of the nation, the power of the Lan[illegible] rived, and the Battle of Bosworth, in which he lost his life, 22 Aug[illegible] nsferred the crown to the distant and scarcely legitimate scion of the [illegible] ter.

HENRY VII., the son, as above stated, of [illegible] of Richmond, by the Lady Margaret Beaufort, grand-daughter a[illegible] n Beaufort, Duke of Somerset, the legitimatized son of John of [illegible] ancaster. By his marriage with Elizabeth, eldest daughter of Ki[illegible] th, [illegible] finally closed the contest between the rival houses of York and [illegible] They had issue, besides other children who died in infancy, two sons and [illegible]

1 Arthur, Prince of Wales, who died in his f[illegible] without issue by his consort, Catherine, daughter of Ferdinand [illegible] King and Queen of Castille and Arragon, who afterwards became the [illegible] surviving brother,

2 Henry 8th.

3 Princess Margaret, *m.* to James 4th, King [illegible] whom she [illegible] mother of

James 5th, King of Scotland, killed at the b[illegible] 3, leaving an infant daughter and heir [illegible]

Mary Queen of Scots, who had no iss[illegible] of France; but by her second, [illegible] was mother of

James 6th, King of Scotland and 1[illegible]

4 Princess Mary, *m.* first to Louis [illegible] Charles Brandon, Duke of Suffolk. By [illegible] second she had two daughters:

1 Lady Frances Brandon, *m.* to Henry [illegible] f Suffolk, by whom she had three da[illegible]

1 Lady Jane Grey, proclaimed [illegible] of King Edward 6th; and beheaded [illegible] ord Dudley, by order of Queen Mary, [illegible] ssue.

2 Lady Catherine Grey, *m.* to Edward, E[illegible] e Protector, Edward, Duke of Somerset; by w[illegible] , Edward, Viscount Beauchamp, whose lineal heir is the [illegible] ss of Buckingham and Chandos.

3 Lady Mary Grey, who *m.* Henry Keyes, and *d.* without issue.

2 Lady Eleanor Brandon, who, by Henry Clifford, Earl of Cumberland, had an only daughter,

Margaret, *m.* to Henry Stanley, Earl of Derby, by whom she had issue.

King Henry 7th *d.* 22 April 1509, and was succeeded by his only surviving son,

HENRY VIII. To recite the numerous marriages of this monarch is not necessary to our purpose, as they eventually produced no change in the succession. By three different Queens, he left issue one son and two daughters, viz.:—King Edward 6th, Queen Mary, and Queen Elizabeth. The King *d.* 28 January 1547, and was succeeded by his only son,

EDWARD VI., who *d. unm.* 6 July 1553, and, notwithstanding his testament in favour of his cousin, the Lady Jane Grey, was succeeded by his eldest sister,

Queen MARY. She *m.* Philip 2nd, King of Spain, but dying without issue, 17 Nov. 1558, was succeeded by her sister,

KING AND ROYAL FAMILY.

Queen ELIZABETH; on whose death, 24 March 1503, the issue of King Henry 8th became extinct, and she was succeeded by the King of Scotland,

JAMES I, King of Great Britain, great grandson of the Princess Margaret, Queen of Scotland, eldest daughter of King Henry 7th, and the lineal heir to the throne on the extinction of the line of King Henry 8th. Besides several children, who died infants, the King had by his consort, ANNE, daughter of Frederick 2nd, King of Denmark, two sons and a daughter;

1 Frederick Henry, Prince of Wales, who *d. unm.* 16 November 1612.

2 King CHARLES 1.

3 Princess Elizabeth, who *m.* Frederick 5th, Elector Palatine and King of Bohemia, by whom she had a numerous issue, all of whom becoming Roman Catholics, or having died without issue before the Revolution of 1688, except her youngest daughter,

The Princess Sophia, the crown of Great Britain was, by the Act of Settlement in 1701, in default of the issue of King William and the Princess, afterwards Queen Anne, settled on this Princess, and the heirs of her body being Protestants. She is therefore now the stock of the royal house. She *m.* Ernest Augustus, Elector of Hanover, and *d.* 8 June 1714, only two months before Queen Anne, on whose death the crown of Great Britain would have descended to her. She had seven sons, who all *d. unm.* except King GEORGE 1st, and one daughter, Sophia-Charlotte, married to Frederick 1st, King of Prussia; of which marriage, the only issue that survived the period of infancy was Frederick-William 1st, King of Prussia, who *m.* his cousin, the Princess Sophia Dorothea, only daughter of King GEORGE 1st.

King James *d.* 6 April 1625, and was succeeded by his only surviving son,

CHARLES I, who *m.* HENRIETTA-MARIA, daughter of Henry 4th, King of France, and had, besides other children who died young,

1 King CHARLES 2nd.

2 King JAMES 2nd.

3 Princess Mary, *m.* to William 2nd, Prince of Orange and Stadtholder of Holland, by whom she had a posthumous son, King WILLIAM 3rd.

4 Henrietta Maria, *m.* to Philip, Duke of Orleans, brother of Louis 14th, King of France, by whom she had an only daughter,

Mary Anne, *m.* to Victor Amedeus, Duke of Savoy, and afterwards King of Sardinia. She left by him one son and two daughters:

1 Charles Emanuel 1st, King of Sardinia. His heir in direct male descent was Victor Emanuel, late King of Sardinia, who *d.* 10 January 1824, leaving four daughters; the eldest of whom, the Princess MARIA BEATRICE VICTORIA JOSEPHINE, wife of Francis 4th, Archduke of Austria and Duke of Modena, is the present representative of King Charles 1st.

2 Princess Maria Adelaide, *m.* to the Duke of Burgundy, Dauphin of France, grandson of Louis 14th, King of France, and great-grandfather of Charles 10th, the ex-king of France.

3 Princess Maria Louisa Gabriella, *m.* to Philip 5th, King of Spain, by whom she was mother of Louis, and Ferdinand 6th, Kings of Spain, neither of whom left issue.

King Charles was beheaded 30 January 1649, and was succeeded by his eldest son,

CHARLES II.; who *m.* CATHERINE, daughter of John 4th, King of Portugal, but *d.* without issue by her, 16 February 1685, and was succeeded by his only brother,

JAMES II. He was twice *m.*, first to Anne, daughter of Edward H

Clarendon, who *d.* before his accession to the throne; and secondly, to MARY, daughter of Alphonzo of Este, Duke of Modena; by both marriages he had a numerous issue, most of whom *d.* in infancy: the survivors were, by the first marriage, Queen Mary and Queen Anne; and by the second a son,

James Francis Edward, commonly called the Pretender, whose two sons, Charles Edward and Henry, *d.* without issue; the latter in July 1807, when the male line of the Royal House of Stewart became extinct.

King James was held to have abdicated the throne, by quitting the kingdom in 1688, and *d.* at St. Germains, in France, 16 Sept. 1701. He was succeeded on his abdication by his son-in-law and daughter,

WILLIAM III. and MARY II. The Queen *d.* 1 January 1695, and the King 19 March 1702; they had no issue; and the crown devolved on the King's decease upon

Queen ANNE, second daughter of JAMES 2nd; by George Prince of Denmark, her husband, she had several children, who all *d.* in very early age. The Queen *d.* without surviving issue, 12 Aug. 1714, and was succeeded, according to the Act of Settlement, by the nearest Protestant heir, the Elector of Hanover,

GEORGE I., *b.* 28 May 1660, *m.* 21 Nov. 1682, Sophia Dorothea, daughter of his uncle, George Duke of Brunswick Zell, whom he divorced 28 December 1694; she was *b.* 3 February 1666, and *d.* 13 November 1726. Their issue were

1 King GEORGE 2nd.

2 Princess Sophia Dorothea, *b.* 15 March 1687, *m.* 28 November 1706, Frederick William 1st, King of Prussia, and *d.* 29 June 1757.

King GEORGE 1st *d.* 22 June 1727, and was succeeded by his only son,

GEORGE II. *b.* 10 November 1683, *m.* 2 September 1705, WILHELMINA CAROLINE, daughter of John Frederick, Margrave of Brandenburg-Anspach, *b.* 1 March 1683, *d.* 1 December 1737. The King *d.* 25 October 1760, and having survived his eldest son, was succeeded by his grandson, GEORGE 3rd. The issue of King GEORGE 2nd and Queen Caroline were

1 Frederick-Lewis, Prince of Wales.

2 Anne, Princess Royal, *b.* 2 November 1709, *m.* 25 March 1734, William-Charles-Henry 4th, Prince of Nassau and Orange, Stadtholder of Holland, and *d.* 12 January 1759.

3 Princess Amelia-Sophia-Eleanora, *b.* 10 June 1711; *d.* unmarried, 31 October 1786.

4 Princess Elizabeth-Caroline, *b.* 10 June 1713; *d.* unmarried 28 December 1757.

5 Prince George-William, *b.* 13 November 1717; *d.* 17 February 1718.

6 Prince William-Augustus, *b.* 26 April 1721; created Duke of Cumberland 27 July 1726; *d.* unmarried, 31 October 1765.

7 Princess Mary, *b.* 5 March 1723; *m.* 18 May 1740, Frederick, Landgrave of Hesse-Cassel, and *d.* 14 January 1772.

8 Princess Louisa, *b.* 18 December 1724; *m.* 11 December 1743, Frederick 5, King of Denmark; and *d.* 9 December 1751.

FREDERICK-LEWIS, Prince of Wales, eldest son of King George 2nd, was *b.* 31 January 1707; *m.* 8 May 1736, Augusta, daughter of Frederick 2nd, Duke of Saxe-Gotha, who *d.* 8 February 1772; he *d.* 31 March 1751, during the lifetime of the King his father, having had issue,

1 Princess Augusta, *b.* 11 August 1737; *m.* 17 January 1764, Charles-William-Ferdinand, Duke of Brunswick-Wolfenbuttel, and *d.* 23 March 1813.

2 King GEORGE-WILLIAM-FREDERICK 3rd.

3 Prince Edward-Augustus, *b.* 14 March 1739; created Duke of York 1 April, 1760; *d.* unmarried 17 September 1767.

4 Princess Elizabeth-Caroline, *b.* 10 January 1741; *d.* unmarried 4 September 1759.

5 Prince William-Henry, *b.* 25 November 1743; created Duke of Gloucester, &c. 17 November 1764; *d.* 25 August, 1805, having *m.* 6 September 1766, Maria, daughter of Sir Edward Walpole, K.B., and widow of James, second Earl Waldegrave, who was *b.* 3 July 1739, *d.* 22 Aug. 1807. Their issue were,

1 Princess Sophia-Matilda, *b.* 29 May 1773.

2 Princess Caroline-Augusta-Maria, *b.* 24 June, 1774, and *d.* 14 March 1775.

3 Prince William-Frederick, the present Duke of Gloucester, for whom see *The Peerage Volume.*

6 Prince Henry-Frederick, *b.* 7 November 1745, created Duke of Cumberland, &c. 18 October 1766; *m.* 18 October 1771, Anne, daughter of Simon Luttrell, first Earl of Carhampton, and widow of Christopher Horton, of Catton-Hall, in Derbyshire, Esq.; *d.* 18 September 1790, without issue.

7 Princess Louisa-Anne, *b.* 19 March 1749; *d.* unmarried, 13 May 1768.

8 Prince Frederick-William, *b.* 24 May 1750; *d.* 29 December 1765.

9 Princess Caroline-Matilda, *b.* posthumous, 22 July 1751; *m.* 8 November 1766, Christian 7th, King of Denmark, and *d.* 10 May 1775, leaving issue.

GEORGE III. succeeded his grandfather, King George 2nd. As all the genealogical particulars relating to this illustrious Monarch and his descendants are stated at length in *The Peerage Volume*, it is unnecessary to repeat them here. His Majesty died, after a glorious reign of longer duration than that of any preceding British monarch, 29 January 1820, leaving by his Queen, Charlotte of Mecklenburg, a numerous issue, whose posterity we may justly hope will, under the blessing of Providence, flourish to adorn the British throne through many generations. The King was succeeded by his eldest son,

GEORGE IV., our late gracious Sovereign, who *d.* 26 June, 1830; and having survived his only child, the lamented Princess Charlotte of Wales, and his brother Frederick, Duke of York, was succeeded by his next brother,

WILLIAM IV., his present most excellent Majesty, whom may Heaven preserve!

THE PEERAGE.

ABERCORN, MARQUIS OF. (Hamilton.)

Peer of Great Britain, Scotland, and Ireland.

Sir Gilbert Hamilton, from whom this illustrious family, of which the Marquis of Abercorn is the chief, derive their descent, settled in Scotland before 1272. The Scotch genealogists describe him as son of William de Hameldun, so named from the place of his birth, the Manor of Hambledon, or Hamilton, in the Parish of Barkby, County of Leicester, a part of the inheritance of the Earls of Leicester, from whose grant the Hamiltons possessed it, and suppose this William to be the third son of Robert, 3rd Earl of Leicester. The English genealogists are silent upon this descent, which therefore remains problematical; and, if it be admitted, chronology requires that the above William de Hameldun, the father of Sir Gilbert, should be a descendant not of the 3rd, but of Robert, his father, the 2nd Earl of Leicester, who was son of Robert, Earl of Mellent, and 1st Earl of Leicester, son of Roger de Bellomont, one of the northern nobles, who accompanied William the Conqueror into England.

Sir John Hamilton, fourth in descent from Sir Gilbert, was father of Sir James, his eldest son, whose son James was the first Lord Hamilton; and of Thomas, his third son, ancestor of Lord Belhaven.

James, the 1st Lord Hamilton, *m.* Mary, eldest daughter of King James 2nd, and by her had a son, James, created Earl of Arran, whose son,

James, 2nd Earl, was declared, by Act of Parliament, on the death of King James V. to be next in succession to the crown, Regent of the Kingdom, and Tutor to the infant Queen; he was Duke of Chatelherault in France, and had four sons; 1 James, 3rd Earl, who *d.* without issue; 2 John, 1st Marquis of Hamilton, great grandfather of Anne, Duchess of Hamilton, who, on the extinction of his male line, carried the honours of her ancestors into the family of Douglas; 3 Lord David, who *d.* without issue; and 4,

Lord Claud, created Baron of Paisley, in the Peerage of Scotland, in 1587, *d.* in 1621; he also had four sons; 1 James, 1st Earl of Abercorn; 2 Claud, from whom descends the present Sir John Hamilton, Bart, (for whose family see the Peerage;) 3 Sir George, whose only son, James, *d.* unmarried; 4 Sir Frederick, ancestor of Viscount Boyne in Ireland.

James the eldest son of the first Lord Paisley, was created Baron of Abercorn in 1603, and in 1606, Earl of Abercorn, Baron of Paisley, Hamilton, Mountcastle, and Kilpatrick; he *d.* in his father's lifetime, 16 March, 1617, leaving five sons:

1 James, 2nd Earl, who was created a Peer of Ireland in 1616, by the ti[illegible] Lord Hamilton, Baron of Strabane, with remainder to the heirs male of his

and resigned this title in favour of his next brother in 1633; his male line failed in his only surviving son, GEORGE, 3rd EARL.

2 Claud, who became Lord Strabane on the resignation of his elder brother, and was father of the 3rd and 4th Lords Strabane; the 4th Lord was father of Claud, 5th Lord, who also succeeded as 4th EARL of ABERCORN, and was succeeded by his brother CHARLES, 5th EARL, on whose death, in 1701, the male line of Claud, 2nd Lord Strabane, became extinct.

3 Sir William Hamilton, who *d.* without issue.

4 Sir George: his five younger sons *d.* without issue male; James, his eldest son, was father of JAMES, 6th EARL, and of William Hamilton, of Chilston in Kent, from whom descends the present Sir Charles Hamilton, described in the Peerage.

5 Sir Alexander, created a Count of the empire, whose son Count Julius, left three sons and several daughters.

JAMES, 6th EARL, *d.* 28 Nov. 1734; he had nine sons, four of whom left issue, viz.: JAMES, 7th EARL, George, whose male line failed in 1793, Francis and Charles.

JAMES, 7th EARL, who *d.* 13 Jan. 1744, had, besides other issue, 1 JAMES, 8th EARL, who was created, in 1786, Viscount Hamilton of Hamilton, Co. Leicester, in the Peerage of Great Britain, with remainder, failing his issue male, to his nephew, John-James, son of John, his brother, and his issue male; he *d. unm.* 9 Oct. 1789; 2 John, father of JOHN-JAMES, who succeeded as 9th EARL of ABERCORN, and 2nd VISCOUNT HAMILTON, and was created MARQUIS of ABERCORN in 1790; his surviving issue are given in the Peerage; 3 George, Canon of Windsor, who has also left surviving issue: See *The Peerage Volume.*

JOHN-JAMES, 1st MARQUIS, was three times married; 1st to Catherine, eldest daughter of Sir Joseph Copley, Bart.; 2ndly to Cecil, daughter of his uncle, the Hon. and Rev. George Hamilton, Canon of Windsor, whom he divorced; and 3rdly to Lady Anne-Jane, eldest daughter of Arthur Saunders, 2nd Earl of Arran, and widow of Henry Hatton, Esq. By the 1st marriage he had issue:

1 Lady Harriet-Margaret, *b.* 1781, *d. unm.* 20 April, 1803.

2 Catherine-Constantia, *b.* 7 Oct. 1782, *d.* 23 May 1783.

3 Lady Catherine-Elizabeth, *b.* 10 Jan. 1784, *d.* 29 Feb. 1812, having *m.* 28 July 1805, George present Earl of Aberdeen, whose second wife is Frances, widow of James, Viscount Hamilton.

4 Lady Maria, *b.* 28 Feb. 1785, *d. unm.* 21 Jan. 1814.

5 James Viscount Hamilton, who *d.* 27 May 1814, leaving JAMES, the present MARQUIS, and other issue.

6 Lord Claude, *b.* 1 Nov. 1787, *d.* June 1808.

The Marquis *d.* 27 Jan. 1818, and, having survived his eldest son, was succeeded by his grandson

JAMES, the present and 2nd MARQUIS.

ABERCROMBY, BARON. (ABERCROMBY.)

Peer of the United Kingdom.

The family of Abercromby descends from Humphrey de Abercombie, who obtained a charter from King Robert Bruce in 1315. Sir Alexander Abercromby of Birkenbog, his lineal descendant, and supposed to be chief of the name, was created a Baronet of Nova Scotia in 1637; he was falconer to King Charles 1st, but took an active part on the side of the Covenanters in the civil war; his eldest son, Sir James, was ancestor of Sir George Abercromby, Bart., of Birkenbog, and from his younger son, Alexander, descended

George Abercrombie of Tullibody, Esq., who *m.* Mary, daughter of Ralph Dundas, of Manour, Esq., and *d.* 8 June 1800, having had issue

1 Sir Ralph, father of the present Peer.

2 Burnet, a Capt. in the E. I. C.'s service, who *d.* without issue 24 March 1792, aged 54.

3 Sir Robert, G.C.B., a Gen., Col. of the 75th foot, and Gov. of Edinburgh Castle, who *d.* 3 Nov. 1827.

4 Alexander, a Lord of Session by the title of Lord Abercromby, he *d.* 17 Nov. 1795.

5 Elizabeth, *m.* Alexander Joass, Esq.

6 Mary, *m.* James Edmonstone, of Newton, Esq.

7 Helen, *m.* Robert Bruce, of Kennett, a Lord of Session.

The gallant Sir Ralph Abercromby, K.B., a Lt. Gen. in the army, and Col. of the 2nd Reg. of Dragoons, after serving in the campaigns in Flanders in 1793 and 1794, was appointed Commander in Chief in the West Indies, and subsequently, in Ireland; he commanded in 1799 the first division of the Expedition to the Helder, and in 1801 that to Egypt, where he was mortally wounded in the glorious Victory of Alexandria; in consequence of which his widow was created a Baroness. She died in 1821, leaving the family described in *The Peerage Volume*, and was succeeded by her eldest son, the present Peer.

ABERDEEN, EARL OF. (Gordon.)

Peer of Scotland and of the United Kingdom.

This family is supposed to descend from Bertrand de Gourdon, who caused the death of King Richard 1st, by the shot of an arrow. From Patrick Gordon of Methley, who flourished in the reign of King James 1st, of Scotland, descended in the 8th degree, Sir John Gordon of Haddo, who, in reward for his active loyalty, was created a Baronet of Nova Scotia in 1642, and sealed his gratitude with his blood, being taken prisoner, after standing a siege in his house at Kelly, against the parliamentary forces under the Marquis of Argyll, on the 8th of May 1744, and beheaded at Edinburgh the 19th of July following. His second son, and eventual heir,

Sir George Gordon, was appointed Lord Chancellor of Scotland in 1682, and created in the same year Earl of Aberdeen, Viscount of Formantine, Lord Haddo, Methlie, Tarves, and Kellie, in the Peerage of Scotland; he *d.* 20 April 1720, and was succeeded by his only surviving son,

William, 2nd Earl, *d.* 30 March 1746, leaving, besides George, 3rd Earl, his successor, (for whom and his issue See *The Peerage Volume*,) and other sons who died unmarried, Alexander appointed in 1788, a Lord of Session, by the title of Lord Rockville, whose surviving issue are also stated in *The Peerage Volume*.

George, 3rd Earl, *d.* 13 Aug. 1801, and having survived his eldest son George Lord Haddo, was succeeded by his grandson,

George, the present and 4th Earl, who was created a Peer of Great Britain in 1814, by the title of Viscount Gordon of Aberdeen, in the Co. of Aberdeen.

ABERGAVENNY, EARL OF. (Neville.)

Peer of the United Kingdom.

Robert Lord of Raby, of a noble Saxon ancestry, married Isabel de Nevill, sister and heir of Henry Baron Nevill, and great grand-daughter of Gilbert de Nevill, Admiral of the Fleet to William the Conqueror. Their son Geoffrey assumed the name of Nevill, and was great grandfather of Ralph, summoned to Parliament as Baron Nevill in 1295. His numerous progeny flourished in great dignity, so that at one and the same period, namely, during the years 1470 and 1471, they reckoned among their various branches, the Duke of Bedford; the Marquis of Montagu, Earl of Northumberland; the Earl of Salisbury and Warwick, Baron Montacute and Monthermer; the Earl of Westmoreland, Baron Neville; and the Barons Latimer and Monthermer; the titles of Baron Furnival, and Baron Fauconberg, and Earl of Kent, had also been previously enjoyed by members of the same noble family; the only branch of which now existing in the Peerage is the Earl of Abergavenny.

Ralph, 4th Baron Nevill, great grandson of the first Lord, was created Earl of Westmoreland, which title continued in the male posterity of his eldest son till it was forfeited, together with the Barony of Nevill, by the attainder of Charles, 6th Earl of Westmoreland, in 1570.

Edward Nevill, 4th son of the 1st Earl of Westmoreland, (and brother of Richard Earl of Salisbury, father of the renowned Earl of Warwick,) married Elizabeth, coheir by her mother of the Barons Despencer and Burghersh, daughter and sole heir of RICHARD DE BEAUCHAMP, Earl of Worcester, son and heir of WILLIAM DE BEAUCHAMP, who was summoned to Parliament as Baron DE BERGAVENNY, in 1392, being seised of the Castle and lands of Bergavenny, whose Lords had been Peers of Parliament, by tenure from the reign of Henry 3rd. In right of Elizabeth his said wife, EDWARD NEVILL was summoned to Parliament in 1450, as Baron ABERGAVENNY. He died in 1476, and was succeeded by his son GEORGE, 4th LORD by writ, and 11th by tenure, who was succeeded in 1492 by his son,

GEORGE, 12th LORD, K.G., he *d.* in 1535, leaving two sons, HENRY, his successor, 13th LORD, who *d.* without issue male in 1587, and Sir Edward Nevill, father of

EDWARD, 14th LORD, who succeeded according to a decision of the House of Lords; while the Barony of Ledespencer (that of Berghersh not having been called out of abeyance) was adjudged to Elizabeth, wife of Sir Thomas Fane, and only daughter of the 13th LORD. The Barony of Abergavenny thus declared to be held by tenure, has since lineally descended to the heirs male. The 14th Lord, however, was never summoned to Parliament, having *d.* in 1589, while the case was under consideration; he was succeeded by his son,

EDWARD, 15th LORD, who *d.* in 1622; leaving two sons, 1 HENRY, his successor, and 2 Christopher, father of Richard, whose son George was father of 1 GEORGE, 21st LORD, and 2 Edward, whose son WILLIAM, succeeded as 24th LORD.

HENRY, 16th LORD, *d.* 1641, leaving two sons, JOHN, 17th LORD, who *d.* in 1660; and GEORGE, 18th LORD, who succeeded his brother, and was succeeded, in 1666, by his son GEORGE, 19th LORD, on whose death in 1695, the male issue of HENRY, 16th LORD, became extinct, and the title devolved upon

GEORGE, 20th LORD, descended from the second son of the 15th LORD; he *d.* in 1721, leaving issue, GEORGE, 21st LORD, who *d.* in 1723, and EDWARD, 23rd LORD, who *d.* in 1724, both without issue; the latter was succeeded by his Cousin,

WILLIAM, 24th LORD, he *d.* in 1744, when he was succeeded by his son,

GEORGE, 25th LORD, created in 1784, EARL OF ABERGAVENNY, and VISCOUNT NEVILL of Berling; he *d.* 10th Sept. 1785, and was succeeded by his son,

HENRY, the present and 2nd EARL.

ABINGDON, EARL OF. (BERTIE.)

Peer of England.

This is a branch of the family of the Earl of Lindsey. Montagu, 2nd Earl of Lindsey, was father, by his first marriage, of Robert, his successor, ancestor of the extinct Dukes of Ancaster, and of the present Earl of Lindsey; and by his 2nd marriage, with BRIDGET BSS. NORREYS OF RYCOTE, grand-daughter and heir of FRANCIS LORD NORREYS OF RYCOTE, and Earl of Berkshire, of

JAMES, who succeeded his mother, and was created Earl of ABINGDON in 1682;

he *d.* in 1699, leaving two sons, Montagu, the 2nd Earl, who *d.* without surviving issue in 1743, and James, father of

Willoughby, 3rd Earl, *b.* 28 Nov. 1692; *d.* 10 June 1760; having *m.* Aug. 1727, Anna-Maria, daughter of Sir John Collins, Knt., by whom, who *d.* 21 Dec. 1763, he had issue, 1 James, Lord Norreys, burnt in his bed at Rycote, 12 Oct. 1745; 2 Willoughby, 4th Earl; 3 Hon. Peregrine, *b.* 13 March 1741, a Capt. R. N., *d.* 20 Aug. 1790, having *m.* in the preceding May, Miss Hutchins; 4 Lady Elizabeth, *d.* 17 Aug. 1804, having *m.* Sir John Gallini, Knt., who *d.* 6 Jan. 1805; 5 Lady Jane, *d.* 25 Feb. 1791, having *m.* 29 Sept. 1760, Thomas Clifton, Esq.; 6 Lady Bridget, *d. unm.* 9 Dec. 1760; 7 Lady Anne; 8 Lady Eleonora, *d.* 19 April 1804, having *m.* 7 July 1766, Philip, Viscount Wenman of Ireland, who *d.* 26 March 1800, when that title became extinct; 9 Lady Mary, *b.* 12 Nov. 1746, *d.* 22 July 1826, having *m.* Miles Stapleton, of Clints, Co. of York, Esq.; 10 Lady Sophia, *d. unm.* 12 Oct. 1760.

Willoughby, 4th Earl, who succeeded, was father of Montagu, his successor, the present and 5th Earl.

ABOYNE, EARL OF. (Gordon.)

Peer of Scotland and of the United Kingdom.

His Lordship is descended from Lord Charles Gordon, 3rd son of George, 2nd Marquis of Huntley, ancestor to the Duke of Gordon, who was created Lord Gordon of Strathavon and Glenlivet, and Earl of Aboyne in 1660, in consideration of his faithful services in the Royal cause during the civil wars; he died in March 1681, and was succeeded by his eldest son, Charles, 2nd Earl, who was succeeded, in April 1702, by his only son,

John, 3rd Earl, he *d.* in Aug. 1732, having *m.* Grace, daughter of George Lockhart of Carnwath, who *m.* 2ndly, James, 9th Earl of Moray, by whom she was mother of the 10th Earl of Moray; she *d.* 17 Nov. 1738, leaving by the Earl of Aboyne three sons, the surviving issue of all of whom are stated in *The Peerage Volume*; they were, 1 Charles, 4th Earl; who succeeded his father, and was father of George the present and 5th Earl, created a Peer of the United Kingdom in 1815, by the title of Baron Meldrum, of Morven, Co. Aberdeen.

2 Hon. John Gordon, Lt.-Col. in the army, *b.* 19 June 1728, *d.* 30 Oct. 1778; having *m.* 18 May 1761, his Cousin Clementina, daughter of George Lockhart, Esq., of Carnwath, who *d.* 31 March 1803.

3 Hon. Lockhart Gordon, Judge Advocate General of Bengal, *b.* 1732, *d.* 24 March 1788; having *m.* 3 Oct. 1770, Hon. Catherine Wallop, daughter of John Viscount Lymington, eldest son of the 1st Earl of Portsmouth, who *d.* May 1813.

AILESBURY, MARQUIS OF. (Brudenell-Bruce.)

Peer of the United Kingdom.

Thomas, 1st Earl, the Marquis's father, was 4th son of George, 3rd Earl of Cardigan, by Lady Elizabeth Bruce, daughter of Thomas, 2nd Earl of Ailesbury, and 3rd Earl of Elgin in Scotland, and sister of Charles, 3rd Earl of Ailesbury and 4th of Elgin. Earl Charles was created Baron Bruce, of Tottenham, Co. Wilts, in 1746, with remainder to his nephew Thomas Bruce-Brudenell, who succeeded him, and was created in 1776 Earl of Ailesbury; he *d.* 19 April 1814, and was succeeded by his only surviving son, Charles, 2nd Earl, created in 1821 Marquis of Ailesbury, Earl Bruce, and Viscount Savernake.

AILSA, MARQUIS OF. (Kennedy.)

Peer of the United Kingdom and of Scotland.

His Lordship's first known ancestor was Duncan de Carrick, living in the 12th century; 5th in descent from him was Sir John of Dunure, who dropped the name of Carrick, and assumed that of Kennedy; his great-grandson Gilbert, obtained the title of Baron Kennedy, about the year 1452, and was grandfather of

David, 3rd Lord, who was advanced by King James 4th to the dignity of Earl of Cassillis in 1509. He fell in the battle of Flodden with his Royal Master, 9 Sept. 1513, and was succeeded by his eldest son, Gilbert, 2nd Earl, who died by the hand of an assassin, Hugh Campbell, Sheriff of the Co. of Ayr, 22 Dec. 1527, and was succeeded by his eldest Son,

Gilbert, 3rd Earl, *b.* in 1515. He was taken prisoner by the Lords Dacre and Musgrave in the Battle of Solway in 1542, and being committed to the custody of Cranmer, Archbishop of Canterbury, was, by the instructions of that venerable martyr, induced to embrace the reformed religion. He was released in 1545, and in 1558 was present as one of the eight Commissioners appointed by the Scottish Parliament at the marriage of Mary Queen of Scots to the Dauphin of France, to whom the Scottish deputies unanimously refused the Crown matrimonial. The Court of France appeared deeply mortified by this disappointment, and the Earl of Cassillis, with two others of the Commissioners, dying in one night, the 28th of November, at Dieppe, a report was raised that poison had been administered to them, which was farther countenanced by the death of a fourth Commissioner, Lord Fleming, at Paris, on the 15th of December following. The Earl left two sons, Gilbert, 4th Earl, his successor, and Sir Thomas Kennedy of Cullean, from whom the present Earl derives his descent.

Gilbert, 4th Earl, *d.* in 1576, leaving also two sons: 1 John, 5th Earl, who succeeded him, and *d.* without issue in 1615; 2 Gilbert, who, dying before his brother, was father of John, 6th Earl. He *d.* in 1668, and was succeeded by his only surviving son, John, 7th Earl; to whom, in 1701, succeeded his grandson, John, 8th Earl, only son of John, Lord Kennedy, the 7th Earl's eldest son, who died before him.

No Patent of creation exists either to the Barony of Kennedy or Earldom of Cassillis, and it is held by the law of Scotland, that titles of Honour, when not otherwise limited by patent, are hereditary in the heirs male of the first grantee; this principle being recognized by the House of Lords, on the petition of Sir Thomas Kennedy, on the death, in 1759, of John, 8th Earl, whereby the male descendants of Gilbert, 4th Earl, became extinct, he succeeded as 9th Earl; being the lineal descendant and heir male of Sir Thomas Kennedy of Cullean, 2nd son of Gilbert, 3rd Earl, and brother of the 4th Earl. Which Sir Thomas Kennedy of Cullean, was father of Sir Alexander, who left two sons; viz.:

1 John, father of Sir Archibald, created a Baronet of Nova Scotia in 1682, whose son, Sir John, was father of Thomas, 9th Earl, and David, 10th Earl, both of whom *d. unm.*; the latter in 1792, when the male issue of John, *eld.* son of Sir Thomas Kennedy of Cullean became extinct.

2 Alexander, father of Archibald Kennedy, collector of the customs at New York, he *d.* in 1763, leaving a son,

Archibald, who, on the decease of the 10th Earl, succeeded to the title; his marriage and issue are described in *The Peerage Volume.* He *d.* in 1794, and was succeeded by his *eld.* son,

Archibald, 12th Earl, who was created a Peer of the United Kingdom in 1806, by the title of Baron Ailsa of Ailsa; was farther advanced, in 1831, to the dignity of MARQUIS of AILSA, of the Isle of Ailsa, in the Co. of Ayr; and is the present Peer.

AIRLIE AND LINTRATHEN, EARL OF. (OGILVY).

Peer of Scotland.

Gilbert, a younger son of Gilibrede, Earl of Angus, obtained the lands of Ogilvie, from which he assumed his surname, and was living in 1207. From him descended, in the 6th degree, Sir Walter Ogilvy of Lintrathen, whose eldest son, Sir John, was father of Sir JAMES, 1st LORD OGILVY; and his 2nd son, Sir Walter, was ancestor of the Earls of Findlater and Seafield, and the Barons Banff, both now extinct in their male lines.

JAMES, created BARON OGILVY of Airly in 1491, was successively followed in direct paternal de[illegible]HN, 2nd LORD, and the 3rd, 4th, 5th, 6th, 7th, and 8th LORDS, all of t[illegible]AMES. The last was created EARL of AIRLY and LINTRATHEN in 16[illegible] with his three sons, greatly distinguished by their zeal in the Roy[illegible] during the civil wars of the years immediately ensuing. He was succeeded [illegible]dest son JAMES, 2nd EARL, and he by his son,

DAVID, 3rd EARL. He *d.* in 1717, leaving two sons, JAMES LORD OGILVY, who [illegible] succeeded him; [illegible] having engaged in the rebellion of 1715 was for[illegible] title, after the death of the 3rd Earl, remaining dormant during the [illegible] Lord Ogilvy; and

[illegible], who succeeded on the death of his brother without issue in 1731; [illegible], 1761, leaving also by Margaret, his wife, eldest daughter and co-heir [illegible] Ogilvy of [illegible] 67, two sons, viz.:

1. DAV[illegible] b. 17[illegible], attainted for taking part in the rebellion of [illegible] AIRLY after his father's death. He *d.* 3 March 1803, hav[illegible] Margaret, dau. of Sir James Johnstone of Westerhall, Bart., who was *b.* [illegible] taken at Culloden in April 1746, committed prisoner to Edinburgh [illegible] escaped in November following, and died in France in 1757. [illegible] Anne, daughter of James Stewart of Blairhall, who *d.* without [illegible] By his 1st marriage Lord Ogilvy, called Earl of Airly, had [illegible] Margaret, who *d.* 23 March 1775, having *m.* 26 Nov. 1769, Sir John [illegible] Balindean, Bart., and Lady Johanna; and one son DAVID, who should [illegible] been 7th EARL, *b.* 4 Dec. 1751, *d. unm.* 6 April, 1812.

2 WALTER, who should have been 8th EARL. On the death of DAVID, 7th EARL, his nephew, he claimed the title, but without success; he *d.* April 1819, and his marriage and surviving issue are described in *The Peerage Volume*; he was father of DAVID the present EARL, who was restored to the honours of his family by Act of Parliament, which received the Royal Assent 26 May 1826.

ALBEMARLE, EARL OF. (KEPPEL.)

Peer of England.

ARNOLD-JOOST VAN KEPPEL, heir of a junior branch of an ancient and noble family in Guelderland, and 12th in descent from Walter van Keppel, living in 1179, came to England with King William 3d, and was created, in 1696, Baron Ashford of Ashford in Kent, Viscount Bury in Lancashire, and EARL of ALBEMARLE in Normandy. He died in 1718, and was succeeded by his only son,

WILLIAM-ANNE, 2nd EARL, *b.* 5 June 1702, and *d.* 22 Dec. 1754; having *m.* 21 Feb. 1723, Lady Anne Lennox, 2nd daughter of Charles, 1st Duke of Richmond and Lennox, by whom, who *d.* 20 Oct. 1789, he had eight sons and seven daughters, of whom only the following survived the period of infancy.

1 GEORGE, his successor, the 3d EARL, father of the present EARL.

2 Hon. Augustus Keppel, an Admiral, who for his naval services was created Viscount Keppel of Elvedon, Co. Suffolk, in 1782; was afterwards appointed first Lord of the Admiralty, and *d. unm.* 3 Oct. 1786, when his title became extinct.

3 Hon. and Rt. Rev. Frederick, Lord Bishop of Exeter, *b.* 19 Feb. 1729, *d.* 27 Dec. 1777; having m. 13 Sept. 1758, Laura, daughter of Sir Edward Walpole, K.B. *b.* 1734, *d.* 27 July 1813; his issue by her will be found in *The Peerage Volume.*

4 Lady Caroline, *b.* 20 Aug. 1737, *d.* 11 Sept. 1769; having *m.* 24 Feb. 1759, Robert Adair, Esq. Surgeon-Gen. to the army, who *d.* 17 March 1790, nearly eighty years of age.

5 Lady Elizabeth, *b.* 15 Nov. 1739, *d.* 2 Nov. 1768; having *m* 7 June 1764, Francis, Marquis of Tavistock, eld. son of John, 4th Duke of Bedford, who *d.* 22 March 1767.

6 Hon. Henry, formerly an officer in the army.

ALDBOROUGH, EARL OF. (S[illegible]

Peer of Ireland.

ROBERT STRATFORD, Esq., 37th in lineal descent from Edward Stratford, who is said to have lived in the reign of Alfred, settled in Ireland about 16[illegible] [illegible] member of the Irish Parliament, for the Co. Wicklow. His grand[illegible]

JOHN, having served during many years in the Irish Parliament, [illegible] created Baron of Baltinglass in 1763, Viscount Aldb[illegible] of Belan [illegible] 1776, [illegible] Earl of ALDBOROUGH and Viscount Amiens 9 Feb. [illegible] July [illegible] Martha, daughter and co-heir of the Rev. Benjamin O[illegible] he had a numerous issue, of whom the present Earl and the Viscountess D[illegible] Powerscourt are the only survivors. The whole were[illegible]

1 EDWARD, 2nd EARL, his successor, who *d.* without issue [illegible] Jan. 18[illegible]; having m. 1st, 1765, Barbara, daughter and heir of Hon. Nichola[illegible] [[illegible] son of Thomas, 8th Earl of Pembroke,] who was *b.* July 17[illegible] *d.* [illegible] April 17[illegible]; 2ndly, 24 March 1788, Hon. Anne-Elizabeth Henniker, [illegible] Lord Henniker, she m. 2ndly, Dec. 1801, George Powe[illegible] *d.* 14 July 1802.

2 JOHN, 3rd EARL, who succeeded his brother, and *d.* 7 March 18[illegible], leaving by Elizabeth, daughter of the Rev. Frederick Hamilton, who survives, three daughters as stated in *The Peerage Volume.*

3 The Hon. and Rev. Francis Paul Stratford, *d.* 22 Jan. 1820, *unm.*

4 BENJAMIN O'NEALE, who succeeded his brother, and is the present and 4th EARL.

5 The Hon. Robert Stratford, a Capt. in the R.N., *d. unm.* 1778.

6 William, *d.* young.

7 Lady Hannah, *d. unm.* 24 Nov. 1801.

8 Lady Elizabeth, b. 1730, *d.* 12 June 1816; having *m.* Robert Tynte, Esq. of Dunlavan.

9 Lady Martha, *d.* 28 Sept. 1816, having *m.* Morley Saunders, Esq.

10 Lady Anne, *d.* July 1800; having *m.* George Powell, Esq., who *m.* 2ndly, Dec. 1801, Anne-Elizabeth, Countess Dowager of Aldborough, widow of the 2nd Earl.

11 Lady Grace, *d.* May 1803; having *m.* Rev. Hayes Queade.

12 Lady Emily, *m.* Richard, 3rd Viscount Powerscourt, and is now his widow.

13 Lady Harriet, *m.* Robert Hartpole, Esq., who *d.* 28 July 1791.

14 Lady Maria, and 15 Lady Letitia, both *d. unm.*

16 Lady Frances, *d.* May 1792; having *m.* William Holt, Esq.

ALLEN, VISCOUNT. (Allen.)

Peer of Ireland.

This family emigrated from England to Holland in 1580. The first who settled in Ireland was John Allen, who came to Dublin as factor for the Dutch; his son, Sir Joshua, was Lord Mayor of Dublin in 1673, and was father of

John, created Viscount Allen and Baron of Stillorgan in 1717; he *d.* 8 Nov. 1726, leaving three sons:

1 John, 2nd Viscount; *d.* 5 Sept. 1742, leaving a son John, 3rd Viscount, who *unm.* 25 May 1745.

2 Robert, who *d.* in 1741, without surviving issue male.

3 Richard; he *d.* in 1745, leaving John, 4th Viscount, who *d.* without issue 10 Nov. 1753; and Joshua, 5th Viscount, who succeeded his brother, and was father of the present and 6th Viscount.

ALVANLEY, BARON. (Arden.)

Peer of the United Kingdom.

His Lordship is said to be descended from Aylwyn de Arden, Sheriff of the Co. Warwick, in the reign of Edward the Confessor; and is 4th in descent from Sir John Arden, of Arden, Co. Chester, Knt., who *d.* in 1702. John Arden of Hawarden, Esq., his grandson, *m.* Sarah, daughter of Cuthbert, and sister and heir of Prescot Pepper, Esqs., of Pepper Hall and South Cawton, Co. York, and was father by her of John Arden, Esq., of Arden and Pepper Hall, and of

Richard-Pepper, Lord Chief Justice of the Common Pleas, created Baron Alvanley of Alvanley, Co. Chester, in 1801, and father of the present Peer.

AMHERST, EARL. (Amherst.)

Peer of the United Kingdom.

This family is of Saxon origin; from Hamo, Lord of Marourd, Sheriff of the Co. of Kent in the time of William the Conqueror, descended John Amherst of Amherst, Co. Kent, living in 1398, from whom the 9th in descent was

Jeffrey Amherst, Esq., of Riverhead, Co. Kent, who *d.* in 1750, leaving issue,

1 Sackville Amherst, Esq., *b.* 1715, *d. unm.* 12 Dec. 1763.

2 Jeffrey, 1st Lord.

3 John, Admiral of the Blue, *m.* Anne, daughter of Thomas Lindzee, Esq., and *d.* without issue, 12 Feb. 1778.

4 William, a General in the army, father of the present Lord. He *d.* 1781.

5 Elizabeth, *m.* the Rev. John Thomas.

Sir Jeffrey Amherst, K.B., the first Lord, was *b.* 29 Jan. 1717; he was commander of the British forces in North America from 1758 to 1764, and afterwards Commander-in-chief of the Army and a Field Marshal. He *m.* 1st, Jane, only daughter of Thomas Dalison, Esq., who *d.* 7 Jan. 1765; and 2ndly, 26 March 1767, Elizabeth, daughter of the Hon. George Cary, 2nd son of Lucius, 5th Viscount Falkland, she *d.* 22 May 1730. He was created, in 1776, Baron Amherst of Holmesdale, Co. Kent, which title became extinct on his death; and in 1778, Baron Amherst of Montreal,

Co. Kent, with remainder, failing his issue male, to his nephew William-Pitt Amherst. He *d.* without issue 3 Aug. 1797, and was succeeded by his nephew, the present and 2d LORD, who was created EARL AMHERST and Viscount Holmesdale in 1826.

ANGLESEY, MARQUIS OF. (PAGET.)

Peer of the United Kingdom.

His Lordship's ancestors derived their surname of Bayly from being anciently Bailiffs or Earls of a certain district in Scotland. Lewis Bayly, who came into England with King James 1st, was Bishop of Bangor; his great-grandson, Sir Nicholas Bayly, Bart., *m.* Caroline, daughter and heir of Thomas Paget, Esq., son of Henry, 2nd son of WILLIAM, 6th LORD PAGET, by whom he was father of HENRY, 10th LORD PAGET, created EARL OF UXBRIDGE.

SIR WILLIAM PAGET, K.G., was summoned to Parliament as Baron Paget de Beaudesert in 1550; his eldest son, HENRY, 2d LORD, *d.* in 1568; leaving an only daughter and heir, ELIZABETH, 3d BARONESS; she *d.* young in 1571, and was succeeded by her uncle, THOMAS, 4th BARON, 2nd son of the 1st LORD. He forfeited his honours by attainder, but his son WILLIAM, 5th LORD, was restored in blood; he *d.* 1629, and was succeeded by his son WILLIAM, 6th LORD, who had two sons; William, 7th Lord, and HENRY, father of Thomas Paget, whose only daughter and heir, Caroline, *m.* as above stated, Sir Nicholas Bayly, Bart.

WILLIAM, 7th LORD, *d.* in 1713; leaving an only son, HENRY, 8th LORD, created in 1711, during the lifetime of his father, Baron Burton of Burton, Co. Stafford, and having succeeded to the Barony of Paget, was farther advanced to the dignity of Earl of Uxbridge in 1714; he had an only son, Thomas Catesby, Lord Paget, who died in his father's lifetime, leaving but one surviving son, HENRY, who in 1743 succeeded his grandfather as 2d Earl of Uxbridge, and was the 9th LORD PAGET; on his death in 1769, the Barony of Burton and Earldom of Uxbridge became extinct, but the Barony of Paget devolved on Sir Henry Bayly, Bart., who assumed the name of Paget, eldest son of Sir Nicholas Bayly, Bart. and Caroline Paget. Which Sir Nicholas Bayly had issue by Caroline his wife, who *d.* 7 Feb. 1766,

1 Edward, who *d. unm*, 30 June 1753.

2 HENRY, mentioned above, who succeeded his father in the Baronetage, and became 10th Lord Paget; he assumed the name and arms of Paget by Royal sign manual, dated 29 Jan. 1770, and was created Earl of Uxbridge in 1784; his marriage and issue are described in *The Peerage Volume;* he *d.* 13 March 1812, and was succeeded by his eldest son, HENRY WILLIAM, the present Peer, created MARQUIS of ANGLESEY in 1815.

3 Nicholas Bayly, Esq. Colonel of the West Middlesex Militia, *d.* 7 June 1812, leaving a widow and ten children.

4 Thomas, and 5 Brownlow, died infants.

6 Paget Bayly, Esq., *b.* 1753, *d.* 15 Nov. 1804, having *m.* 25 Aug. 1791, Miss Colepepper, and had issue; 1 an only son, who *d.* 1 Nov. 1801; 2 Louisa-Augusta, *m.* April 1810, Sir Edward Perrott; 3 Rose-Maria, *m.* Dec. 1812, G. A. Coleman, Esq.

7 Mary, *d.* 20 Oct. 1790, having *m.* Stephen Metcalfe, of Sereby, Co. Lincoln, Esq.

8 Dorothy, *d.* 24 Feb. 1764, having *m.* Hon. George Forbes, afterwards 5th Earl of Granard.

9 Caroline, *d.* 1786; 10 Gertrude, *d.* 1761, both *unm.*

11 Louisa, *b.* 4 Dec. 1750, *m.* 6 April 1789, Captain Thomas Poplett, R.N.

ANNESLEY, EARL. (ANNESLEY.)

Peer of Ireland.

The Honourable Francis Annesley, 6th son of Francis, 1st Viscount Valentia, (ancestor by Arthur his eldest son, of the Earl of Mountnorris,) had three sons, of whom Francis, the eldest, only survived him; he *d.* in 1750, leaving 7 sons, of whom Francis, the eldest, and William, 6th son, left male issue.

The said WILLIAM, grandson of the Honourable Francis Annesley, was created Baron Annesley, of Castle-Wellan, in 1758, and VISCOUNT GLERAWLY, in 1766, and *d.* 12 Sept. 1770; having *m.* 16 Aug. 1738, Lady Anne Beresford, eldest daughter of Marcus Earl of Tyrone, and sister of the 1st Marquis of Waterford, by whom, who *d.* 12 May, 1770, he had issue;

1 FRANCIS-CHARLES, his successor, created EARL ANNESLEY 1789, with remainder, in default of issue male, to his brother Richard; *b.* 1740, and *d.* 19 Dec. 1802; having *m.* 8 Feb. 1766, Mary, daughter and co-heir of Richard Grove, Esq., by whom he had no issue: he left, however, an infant son, George De-la-poer, for whom his guardians disputed the title against his uncle Richard, but the young claimant *d.* at the Royal Military College at Sandhurst, before the case was decided.

2 Marcus, *d. unm.*

3 RICHARD, 2d EARL, who claimed the honours against his nephew, and obtained undisputed possession of them by his death; he was father of the present EARL, and his marriage and issue are described in *The Peerage Volume.*

4 Hon. and Very Rev. William Annesley, Dean of Downe, *b.* 3 March 1747, *d.* 11 June 1817; having *m.* the only daughter of John Digby, Esq., of Landestown, Co. Kildare, by whom he has left issue as stated in "*The Peerage.*"

5 Hon. Catherine, *d.* 23 Nov. 1770, having *m.* 14 July 1760, Arthur Saunders, 2nd Earl of Arran.

ANTRIM, COUNTESS OF. (MACDONNEL.)

Peeress of Ireland.

John Macdonald, Lord of the Isles, who died in 1388, 6th in descent from Somerled, King of the Isles, was father of 1 Donald, Lord of the Isles, ancestor of Lord Macdonald; and 2 John, whose descendants removed into the North of Ireland in the 15th century. His lineal representative,

Randal Macdonnel, was created Baron of Antrim 1619, and Viscount Dunluce and Earl of Antrim 1620. He had two sons; 1 Randal, 2nd Earl, created Marquis of Antrim 1644, which title became extinct on his death in 1682; 2 Alexander, 3d Earl, great-grandfather of

RANDAL-WILLIAM, 6th Earl, who obtained, in 1785, a renewed patent of the Earldom and Viscounty, with remainder, failing his issue male, to his daughters and their issue male. He was also created Marquis of Antrim in 1789, which title became extinct at his death; when he was succeeded in the Earldom by his eldest daughter, the present Countess.

ARBUTHNOT, VISCOUNT. (ARBUTHNOT,)

Peer of Scotland.

SIR ROBERT ARBUTHNOT, of Arbuthnot, Co. Kincardine, 1st Viscount, was lineally descended, in the 17th generation, from Hugo, the first of the family on record, who lived in the 12th century; and it is remarkable that with one only exception the inheritance was carried from father to son. The 1st Viscount *d.* in 16[illegible], and was succeeded by his eldest son,

Robert, 2nd Viscount, who besides other issue had two sons, Robert, his successor, and John, father of John, 6th Viscount. He *d.* in 1781; his eldest son,

Robert, 3d Viscount, *d.* in 1694; he was father of Robert, 4th Viscount, who *d. unm.* in 1710, and of John, 5th Viscount, who succeeded his brother, and *d.* without issue. He was succeeded by

John, 6th Viscount, son of John, 2nd son of the 1st Viscount; he *d.* 20 April 1791, and was succeeded by his son, John, 7th Viscount, father of John, the present and 8th Viscount, who succeeded in 1800.

ARDEN, BARON. (Perceval.)

Peer of Ireland and of the United Kingdom.

The present Peer is uncle to the Earl of Egmont. His father, John, 2d Earl of Egmont, *d.* 20 December, 1772, having *m.* 1st, Lady Catherine Cecil, 2nd daughter of James, 5th Earl of Salisbury, who *d.* 16 August 1752, leaving issue, John James, third Earl of Egmont, father of the present Earl: and he *m.* 2ndly, Catherine, 3d daughter of the Honourable Charles Compton, and sister of Charles, 7th, and Spencer, 8th, Earls of Northampton; which Lady was, in 1770, created a Peeress, by the title of Baroness Arden of Lohort Castle, Co. Cork, with remainder to her issue male. Her children by the Earl of Egmont, who lived to maturity, are given in *The Peerage Volume;* she *d.* 11 June 1784, and was succeeded by her eldest son, the present and 2nd Lord; who was also created a Peer of Great Britain in 1802, by the title of Baron Arden, of Arden, Co. Warwick.

ARGYLL, DUKE OF. (Campbell.)

Peer of Scotland and of Great Britain.

The first of this name on record is Gillespie Campbell, of Anglo-Norman origin, who *m.* Eva, heiress of the ancient Lords of Lochow: 9th in descent from them was Duncan, 1st Lord Campbell, whose second son, Sir Colin, was ancestor of the Earl of Breadalbane and the Countess of Loudoun.

Colin, 2nd Lord, grandson and successor of the 1st Lord, was created Earl of Argyll in 1457; he *d.* in 1492, and to him succeeded Archibald, 2nd Earl, who was killed at Flodden Field in 1513, leaving two sons, Colin, 3rd Earl, his successor, and Sir John, ancestor of Lord Cawdor.

Archibald, 4th Earl, son and successor of the 3rd Earl, *d.* in 1558, leaving issue, Archibald, 5th Earl, who *d.* without issue in 1575; and

Colin, 6th Earl, who succeeded his brother, and *d.* in 1584. Archibald, 7th Earl, his son, *d.* in 1638, and was succeeded by his son,

Archibald, 8th Earl, who was created Marquis of Argyll in 1641, but being attainted after the restoration of King Charles 2nd, in consequence of the share he had taken in the civil war, he was beheaded 27 May 1662, and all his honours forfeited. The other titles, except the Marquisate, were afterwards restored to his son,

Archibald, 9th Earl. He was also attainted for high treason, and beheaded 30 June, 1685; but an act of the Scottish Parliament, passed in 1689, rescinding his forfeiture, in consequence of which his titles descended upon his eldest son. His 2nd son, the Hon. John Campbell, was father of John, 4th Duke of Argyll.

Archibald, 10th Earl, who succeeded his father, was created Duke of Argyll, to him and his heirs male whatsoever; he *d.* in 1703, leaving two sons, 1 JOHN, 2nd DUKE, who was created Duke and Earl of Greenwich and Baron Chatham, in the Peerage of England, in 1705, which titles became extinct on his death without issue male in 1743; and 2 ARCHIBALD, 3rd DUKE, who *d.* without issue 15 April 1761, and was succeeded by his cousin,

JOHN, 4th DUKE, eldest son of John, 2nd son of the 9th Earl. He *m.* Mary, daughter of John, 2nd Lord Bellenden, and *d.* 9 November 1770, having had issue,

1 JOHN, his successor, 5th DUKE, father of the present DUKE.

2 Lord Henry, killed at the battle of Lanffeldt, 2 July 1747.

3 Lord Frederick, who *d.* without issue 8 June 1816, and his widow, daughter of Amos Meredith, Esq., was unfortunately burnt to death at Coomb-Bank, Kent, 25 July 1807.

4 Lord William, *d.* 5 September 1778; having *m.* 7 April 1763, Sarah, daughter of Ralph Izard, of Charles Town, South Carolina, Esq., *d.* 4 September 1784. Their surviving issue are stated in *The Peerage Volume.*

5 Lady Caroline, *m.* 1st, Charles, Earl of Aylesbury, and 2ndly, Field-Marshal the Right Hon. Henry Seymour Conway, brother to the 1st Marquis of Hertford. His Grace is also BARON SUNDRIDGE, of Coomb-Bank, Co. Kent; and Baron Hamilton, of Hambledon, Co. Leicester, in the Peerage of Great Britain. The former of these titles was conferred upon his father, JOHN, 5th DUKE, in 1766, with remainder, failing his issue male, to his brothers, the Lords Frederick and William Campbell; and the latter in 1776, upon his mother Elizabeth, 2nd daughter of John Gunning, Esq., relict of James, 6th Duke of Hamilton, and wife of JOHN, 5th DUKE OF ARGYLL.

ARRAN, EARL OF. (GORE.)

Peer of Ireland.

John Gore, Esq., of London, living in the 16th century, was grandfather of Sir Paul Gore, of Manor-Gore, Bart., who settled in Ireland, and had two sons; 1 Sir Ralph, ancestor of the extinct Earls of Ross; 2 Sir Arthur, also created a Bart. in 1662; whose great grandson,

Sir ARTHUR, 3rd Baronet, was created Baron Saunders and Viscount Sudley, of Castle Gore, in 1758, and Earl of the Islands of Arran, Co. Galway, in 1762. He *d.* 17 April 1773, having *m.* 16 March 1730, Jane, daughter and heir of Richard Saunders, Esq., of Saunders Court, and widow of William Worth, Esq., by whom he had issue,

1 ARTHUR SAUNDERS, 2nd EARL, his successor, who *d.* 8 October 1809, and was succeeded by his eldest son, ARTHUR SAUNDERS, the present and 3rd EARL.

2 Hon. Richard Gore, *b.* 1734, many years a Member of Parliament, *d.* 28 Dec. 1807, leaving an only son Arthur.

3 Hon. Paul Gore, *m.* Anne, daughter of Oliver Leonard, Esq.; his surviving issue are described in *The Peerage Volume.*

4 Lady Johanna, *m.* 1st, Philip Doyne, Esq., and 2ndly, Michael Daly, Esq.

5 Lady Elizabeth, *m.* 15 July 1764, Sir John Evans Freke, Bart., who *d.* 20 March 1777.

ARUNDELL, BARON. (ARUNDELL.)

Peer of England.

Roger de Arundel was a powerful Lord in the reign of William the Conqueror. Eighteenth in descent from him was,

Thomas, created Baron Arundell, of Wardour in 1605; for his services against the Turks, he had been created a Count of the Holy Roman Empire, by the Emperor Rudolph, in 1595; he *d.* in 1639, and was followed, in uninterrupted paternal descent, by Thomas, 2nd Lord, who *d.* in 1643; Henry, 3rd Lord, *d.* 1694; Thomas, 4th Lord, *d.* 1712; Henry, 5th Lord; and

Henry, 6th Lord, who succeeded his father in 1726, and *d.* in 1746, leaving three sons;

1 Henry, 7th Lord, who *d.* in 1756, and was succeeded by his son, Henry, 8th Lord, *b.* 11 April 1740, *m.* 31 May 1762, Maria Christina, only daughter and heir of Benedict Conquest, of Irnham, Co. Lincoln, Esq., who was *b.* in 1742, and *d.* 21 June 1813, and by her had two daughters, on whom as co-heirs devolved his claim to one moiety of the Barony of Fitzpayne, (created by writ in 1299,) of which his Lordship was co-heir with Lord Stourton; 1 Mary-Christina, *d.* 14 February 1805, wife of her cousin, James Everard Arundell, afterwards 9th Lord, by whom she was mother of the present Lord; 2 Eleanor Mary, wife of the present Lord Clifford. The 8th Lord *d.* without issue male, 4 December 1808, and was succeeded by his cousin and son-in-law, James Everard, 9th Lord.

2 Hon. Thomas Arundell *d.* without issue, 11 May, 1768, having *m.* 19 May 1760, Mary, eldest daughter of John Porter, Esq., who *d.* 14 September 1799.

3 Honourable James Everard Arundell, *b.* October, 1721, *d.* 20 March 1803, having *m.* 24 June 1751, Anne, daughter of John Wyndham, of Ashcombe, Co. Wilts, Esq., *b.* 1731, *d.* 10 April 1796; by whom he had issue, 1 Mary Wyndham, (for whom see *The Peerage Volume,*) wife of the Hon. Bartholomew Bouverie. 2 Catherine-Elizabeth, *b.* 2 January 1759, *d.* 27 December 1803; having *m.* 3 January 1792, Rear-Admiral George-Frederick Ryves, *b.* 8 September 1758, *d.* 20 May 1826, (having *m.* 2ndly, in 1806, Emma, daughter of Richard Robert Graham, Esq.) 3 James-Everard, 9th Lord, described with his issue in "*The Peerage;*" he *d.* 14 July 1817, and was succeeded by his eldest son, Everard, present and 10th Lord. 4 Thomas Raymond, *b.* 9 March 1765, *d.* 17 January 1829, having *m.* Elizabeth-Mary-Anne, daughter of Sir Edward Smythe, Bart.; his surviving issue by her are stated in *The Peerage Volume.*

ASHBROOK, VISCOUNT. (Flower.)

Peer of Ireland.

The ancestor of this family was William Flower, of Oakham, Co. Rutland, Sheriff of that county, 1382. The founder of the Irish branch was Sir George Flower, living in the reign of Elizabeth, great grandfather of William Flower, created Baron Castle Durrow 1733; he died 26 April 1746, leaving an only son,

Henry, 2nd Lord, created Viscount Ashbrook in 1751. He was succeeded in 1752 by his only son,

William, 2nd Viscount, father of William, the 3rd, and Henry-Jeffrey, the present and 4th Viscount: his issue are given in *The Peerage Volume.*

ASHBURNHAM, EARL OF. (Ashburnham.)

Peer of Great Britain.

The first of this family recorded, is Pius de Esburnham, whose grandson, Bertram, and great-grandson Philip, were beheaded by William the Conqueror for their attachment to Harold. From Philip the representation passed through twenty generations to the loyal, but unfortunate John Ashburnham, groom of the bedchamber to King Charles 1st, and grandfather of

JOHN, created BARON ASHBURNHAM of Ashburnham, Co. Sussex, in 1689; he *d.* 22 Jan. 1710, leaving two sons,

WILLIAM, 2nd LORD, and

JOHN, who succeeded his brother 16 June 1710, and was created, in 1730, Viscount St. Asaph in Wales, and Earl of Ashburnham in Sussex. He was three times *m.* but left only one surviving child,

JOHN, 2nd EARL, for whom and his issue see *The Peerage Volume.* He *d.* in 1812, and was succeeded by his only son, GEORGE, 3rd EARL, father of BERTRAM, present and 4th EARL.

ASHTOWN, BARON. (TRENCH.)

Peer of Ireland.

Lord Ashtown is a collateral branch of the Earl of Clancarty's family, but separated before the creation of either Peerage. Both families descend from Frederick Trench, who settled at Garbally in Ireland, and *d.* in 1669, leaving issue: 1 Frederick, ancestor of the Earl of Clancarty; and 2 John, Dean of Raphoe, grandfather of Frederick Trench, Esq. of Moate and Woodlawn, who is described, with his issue, in *The Peerage Volume.* His eldest son,

FREDERICK TRENCH, Esq. was created a Peer of Ireland in 1800, by the title of Lord Ashtown, Baron Ashtown of Moate, Co. Galway, with remainder to the heirs male of the body of his late father.

ASTON, BARON. (ASTON.)

Peer of Scotland.

The first of this family on record is Randall de Astona, living in the reign of Edward 1st: 11th in descent from him was

Sir Walter Aston, who had two sons:

1 Sir Edward, father of Sir WALTER, K. B., created, in 1627, BARON ASTON, of Forfar, with remainder to his heirs male for ever. His male line failed by the death of JAMES, 5th LORD.

2 William, from whom the succeeding Lords descended.

WALTER, 1st LORD, *d.* in 1639, and was followed in direct paternal descent by WALTER, 2nd LORD, distinguished for his loyal services during the great Civil War; he *d.* in 1678. WALTER, 3d LORD; WALTER, 4th LORD, who succeeded in 1714, and *d.* in 1746; and JAMES, 5th LORD, whose death, in 1751, terminated the male line of the 1st Lord.

William Aston, noticed above, second son of Sir Walter Aston, and uncle of the 1st Lord, was father of Edward Aston, of Milwich, Co. Stafford, and grandfather of another Edward, who *d.* in 1705, leaving two sons:

1 Walter, father of PHILIP, who succeeded in 1751 as 6th LORD, and *d. unm.* in 1755; and of WALTER, 7th LORD, who also *d. unm.* in 1763.

2 Edward, *d.* in 1738; his son WALTER succeeded his cousin as 8th LORD, and was father of WALTER HUTCHINSON, present and 9th LORD, who succeeded in 1805.

ATHLONE, EARL OF. (De Ginkell.)

Peer of Ireland.

Godart de Ginkell, of an ancient and noble family in Holland, came over to England with King William 3rd. He was Lieut.-gen. of the forces in Ireland, under that King; and for his important services against the Catholic army of King James 2nd, was created to the Irish Peerage in 1691, by the titles of Earl of Athlone, and Baron of Aghrim, Co. Galway. He had also large grants of the forfeited lands of William Dungan, Earl of Limerick, which being reversed by Parliament in 1695, the family retired to Holland, and no Earl of Athlone sat in the Irish House of Peers till the year 1795. He *d.* in 1703, leaving a numerous issue; of whom Godart, the eldest son, 2nd Earl, succeeded him; and Frederick-Christian, 2nd son, was father of Frederick-William, 5th Earl.

Godart, 2nd Earl, left two sons: Godart-Adrian, 3rd Earl, who *d.* in 1736; and Godart, 4th Earl, who *d.* in 1747, both *unm.*

Frederick-William, 5th Earl, son of Frederick-Christian, 2nd son of the 1st Earl, succeeded. He *d.* in 1756, leaving two sons:

1 Frederick-Christian-Renaud, 6th Earl, who *d.* in 1808, and is described with his issue in *The Peerage Volume*. He was succeeded by Frederick-William, 7th Earl, his eldest son, who dying without issue in 1810, was succeeded by his next brother, Renaud-Diedrich-Jacob, 8th Earl, father of George-Godart-Henry, the present and 9th Earl.

2 Arend-William, Baron de Reede-Lynden, *d.* 7 June, 1815; he *m.* 1st in 1768, Elwig-Adriana-Amarantha, Baroness of Lynden, by whom he left issue as stated in *The Peerage Volume*; and 2ndly, Wilhelmina-Henrietta, Baroness of Krusemark, by whom he had no issue.

ATHOLL, DUKE OF. (Murray.)

Peer of Scotland and Great Britain.

The first known ancestor of the Duke was Sir John de Moravia, *d.* about 1225; 9th in descent from him was

Sir William Murray of Tullibardine *d.* about 1511, whose 2nd surviving son, Sir Andrew, was ancestor of the Earl of Mansfield, and Sir William, the eldest son, was great-grandfather of Sir John Murray, created Baron Murray of Tullibardine in 1604, and Earl of Tullibardine, in 1606; he *d.* in 1609.

William, 2nd Earl, his son, *m.* Lady Dorothea Stewart, eldest daughter and heir of line, of John, 5th Earl of Atholl, [by patent 1357, to Sir John Stewart, eldest son of Sir James Stewart of Lorn, by Jane, Queen-dowager of Scotland, widow of King James 1st, and mother of King James 2nd.]

John, their son, was in consequence of his descent, empowered in 1629 to change his title to Earl of Atholl, and the title of Earl of Tullibardine was transferred to his uncle, Patrick, 3rd Earl, 3rd son of the 1st Earl, but on the death of his son James, 4th Earl of Tullibardine in 1670, it reverted to

John, 5th Earl of Tullibardine, 2nd Earl of Atholl, (son of John, 1st Earl of Atholl,) who succeeded his father in 1642, and was created Marquis of Atholl in 1676; he *m.* Lady Amelia-Sophia Stanley, 3rd daughter and at length sole heir of James, 7th Earl of Derby, and *d.* in 1703, leaving issue:

1 John, his successor, 1st Duke of Atholl.

2 Lord Charles, created Earl of Dunmore: he was ancestor of the present Earl of Dunmore.

3 Lord James; left two daughters.

4 Lord William, who became Lord Nairne in right of his wife, and was ancestor of the present Lord Nairne.

5 Lord Edward, who left issue.

6 Lady Amelia, *m.* Hugh, 10th Lord Lovat.

JOHN, 2nd MARQUIS, was created in 1703, DUKE of ATHOLL, and Marquis of Tullibardine; he *d.* in 1724, having had nine sons, from whom there is now no surviving issue, except the descendants of Lord George, the 5th son; the four younger sons may therefore be passed over. The five elder were:

1 John, Marquis of Tullibardine, a Colonel in the Dutch service, who was killed in the battle of Malplaquet, in 1709.

2 William, Marquis of Tullibardine. Being concerned in the rebellion of 1715, he was attainted, but escaped to the Continent, and continued in exile till he accompanied the young Pretender in his expedition into Scotland in 1745. He was taken prisoner after the decisive battle of Culloden, and committed to the Tower, where he *d. unm.*

3 JAMES, 2nd DUKE, to whom the honours devolved upon his father's death, in consequence of an Act of Parliament passed after the attainder of the Marquis of Tullibardine, in 1716.

4 Lord Charles, who was also concerned in the rebellion of 1715; taken prisoner at Preston, and tried by a court-martial as a deserter, being an officer upon half-pay in the King's service, and sentenced to be shot, but reprieved. He *d.* without issue in 1720.

5 Lord George, a Lieut.-general in the Pretender's army in 1745, was attainted by Act of Parliament, but escaped to the Continent, and *d.* in Holland in 1760, leaving three sons, the two younger of whom left no issue; the eldest was JOHN, the 3rd DUKE.

JAMES, 2nd DUKE, *b.* 1690, succeeded his father 14 Nov. 1724, to the exclusion of his elder brother; and on the death of James, 10th Earl of Derby in 1736, succeeded to the sovereignty of the Isle of Man, and to the Barony of Strange, as sole heir of the body of James, 7th Earl of Derby, through the Lady Amelia-Sophia Stanley, his grandmother. He *m.* 1st, in 1727, Jane, youngest daughter of Thomas Frederick, Esq., and widow of James Lannoy, Esq.; she *d.* 13 June, 1748, and he *m.* 2ndly, 7 June, 1749, Jean, daughter of John Drummond, of Megginch, by whom he had no issue. She survived him, and re-married Lord Adam Gordon, 4th son of Alexander, 2nd Duke of Gordon. The Duke *d.* 8 Jan. 1764, having had by his 1st marriage, besides one son, who *d.* an infant, two daughters, 1 Lady Jane, *m.* 3 March, 1747, John, 17th Earl of Crawford, and *d.* 10 Oct. following without issue; 2 Lady Charlotte, his only surviving child and heir. The DUKE *d.* 8 Jan. 1764, when the sovereignty of Man and the Barony of Strange devolved upon the Lady Charlotte his daughter, and his other titles upon his nephew,

JOHN, 3rd DUKE, being adjudged to him by a resolution of the House of Lords, 7 Feb. 1764, notwithstanding the attainder of his father, Lord George Murray. He was *b.* 6 May, 1729, and *d.* 5 Nov. 1774; having *m.* 23 Oct. 1753, his cousin Lady Charlotte, BARONESS STRANGE, only surviving daughter and heir of the 2nd DUKE, by whom, who was *b.* 1690, and *d.* 13 Oct. 1805, he had the following issue:

1 JOHN, 4th DUKE, his successor, father of the present Duke. He was created a Peer of Great Britain, in 1786, by the titles of EARL STRANGE, Baron Murray of Stanley, Co. Gloucester, and succeeded his mother, in 1805, in the Barony of Strange, created by writ in 1628. His Grace *d.* 29 Sept. 1830. His marriage, and surviving issue will be found in *The Peerage Volume.*

2 Lady Charlotte, *b.* 2 Aug. 1754, *d. unm.* 4 April, 1808.

3 Lord James, *b.* 5 Dec. 1757, *d.* April, 1770.

4 Lord George, *b.* 5 Jan. 1759, *d.* the same year.

5 Lord George, Bishop of St. David's, *b.* 30 Jan. 1761, *d.* 3 June 1803; having

11th LORD, succeeded. He *d.* in 1686, and was succeeded by his son JAMES, 12th LORD; to whom succeeded, in 1700, his son JAMES, 13th LORD. He *d.* in 1740, leaving two sons and one daughter, viz. JAMES, 14th LORD, his successor, who *d.* without issue in 1740; 2 JOHN-TALBOT, 15th LORD, on whose death also without issue, in 1777, the Irish Earldom of Castlehaven became extinct; 3 Elizabeth, *m.* to Philip Thicknesse, Esq. by whom she had issue,

GEORGE THICKNESSE, 16th LORD, who succeeded to this ancient Barony on the death of his uncle, and was father of the present and 17th LORD, who succeeded him in 1818.

AVONMORE, VISCOUNT. (YELVERTON.)

Peer of Ireland.

The Viscount descends from a family of the name of Yelverton, seated in the County of Norfolk; two brothers went from thence into Ireland, and settled there, one in the County of Tipperary, the other in the County of Cork; but their families are now united by intermarriages. The Viscount descends in the male line from the latter.

Walter Yelverton, Esq., *d.* Dec. 20, 1727, aged 50, and was buried at Castle Magnes, Co. Cork, leaving a son, Francis Yelverton, of Kanturk, Co. Cork, Esq., who *d.* 27 March 1746; by his wife Elizabeth, daughter of Jonas Barry, Esq., he was father of

BARRY, Lord Chief Baron of the Exchequer in Ireland, created in 1795, Lord Yelverton, Baron of Avonmore; and in 1800, VISCOUNT AVONMORE. He *d.* in 1805, leaving a daughter now living, Anna-Maria, dowager Lady Clanmorris, and three sons, all deceased; viz. 1 WILLIAM-CHARLES, his successor, 2nd VISCOUNT, father of BARRY-JOHN, the present and 3rd VISCOUNT, by whom he was succeeded in 1814; 2 the Hon. Barry Yelverton, *b.* 12 Nov. 1763, *d. unm.* May 1824; 3 the Hon. Walter-Aglionby Yelverton, *b.* 26 Jan. 1772, and *d.* 3 June 1824; his issue by Cecilia, daughter of George Yelverton of Bellisle, Co. Tipperary, Esq. will be found in *The Peerage Volume.*

AYLESFORD, EARL OF. (FINCH.)

Peer of Great Britain.

This family is a branch from that of the Earl of Winchilsea and Nottingham. The Hon. HENEAGE FINCH, 2nd son of Heneage, 1st Earl of Nottingham, and brother of Daniel, 2nd Earl of Nottingham and 7th Earl of Winchilsea, was bred to the bar; having been removed by King James 2nd from the office of Solicitor-general, he was one of the principal counsel who pleaded for the Seven Bishops, in June 1688. In 1703 he was created Baron Guernsey, and in 1714, EARL of AYLESFORD. He *d.* 22 July 1719, and was succeeded by his eldest son, HENEAGE, 2nd EARL; he *d.* 29 June 1757, leaving by his wife Mary, daughter and heir of Sir Clement Fisher, of Packington, Co. Warwick, Bart., an only son,

HENEAGE, 3rd EARL, *b.* 6 Nov. 1715, *d.* 9 May 1777; having *m.* 6 Oct. 1750, Lady Charlotte Seymour, daughter of Charles, 6th Duke of Somerset, who *d.* 15 Feb. 1805. Besides some surviving issue who are described in *The Peerage Volume*, and others who *d. unm.* the Earl left one daughter, Lady Charlotte, *b.* 13 May 1754, *d.* 9 July 1828, having *m.* 14 Aug. 1777, Henry, 12th Earl of Suffolk and Berkshire, who *d.* 7 March 1779, and three sons; 1 HENEAGE, 4th EARL, his successor, and father of HENEAGE, present and 5th EARL; 2 the Hon. Charles Finch, *b.* 4 June 1752, *d.* 17 Dec. 1819, having *m.* 28 Dec. 1778, Jane, eldest daughter and co-heir of Watkin Wynne of Voelas, Co. Denbigh, Esq., by whom, who *d.* Nov. 1811, he left the issue named in *The Peerage Volume*, and a younger daughter, Louisa, who *d.* in Dec. 1822, having *m.* 22 Jan. 1822, Ambrose St. Martin, Count d'Aiglie, Sardinian Minister in London; 3 the Hon. William-Clement Finch, of Albury, Co. Surrey, a Rear-Admiral, *b.* 27 May, 1753, *d.* Sept. 1794, having *m.* 2 Aug. 1789, Miss Brouncker, of St. Christopher's: his issue by her are stated in *The Peerage Volume.*

AYLMER, BARON. (AYLMER.)

Peer of Ireland.

This family is said to descend from a Saxon Duke of Cornwall named Aylmer. Sir Christopher Aylmer, who was created a Bart. of Ireland in 1662, *d.* in 1679, leaving two sons, of whom the eldest succeeded him, and was ancestor of Sir Matthew Aylmer, the 6th Bart., on whose death, in 1780, the late Lord Aylmer succeeded to the Baronetcy as heir male of the family; and MATTHEW, the younger, a Rear Admiral of the Red, distinguished for his naval services, was created BARON AYLMER, of Balrath, Co. Meath, in 1718. He *d.* in 1724, and was succeeded by his son,

HENRY, 2nd LORD, whose 4th son, the Hon. and Rev. John Aylmer, a Prebendary of Bristol, was father of the only existing collateral branch of this house, Admiral John Aylmer, who is *m.* and has a numerous family. His Lordship *d.* in 1754, and was succeeded by his eldest son, HENRY, 3rd LORD, to whom succeeded, in 1766, his only son,

HENRY, 4th LORD, who, by Catherine, 2nd daughter of Sir Charles Whitworth, and sister of the late Earl Whitworth, left issue, besides MATTHEW, the present and 5th LORD, his successor, and his surviving brother, the Hon. Capt. Aylmer, for whom see *The Peerage Volume*, 1 Henry, *b.* 14 May 1776, *d.* at Petersburgh June 1798; 2 Rose Whitworth, *b.* 5 Oct. 1779, *d.* in India in 1800; 3 James Thomas, *b.* 1785, *d.* in India in 1812; all *unm.*

BAGOT, BARON. (BAGOT.)

Peer of Great Britain.

Bagod, Lord of Bromley in Staffordshire, is recorded in the Doomsday-Book; and his descendants have continued seated there, and at Blythfield in the same county, from the time of the Conquest, when that ancient document was compiled, to the present period. The 16th in descent from this first ancestor on record was Sir Hervey Bagot, created a Bart. by King Charles 1st, and afterwards eminent for his loyalty in the wars of that monarch. His son, Sir Edward, Sir Walter, and another Sir Edward, carried the succession in direct descent to

Sir Walter Wagstaffe Bagot, Bart., *b.* 23 Aug. 1702, succeeded his father, Sir Edward, in May 1712, and *d.* 20 Jan. 1768, having *m.* 27 July 1724, Lady Barbara Legge, eldest daughter of William, 1st Earl of Dartmouth, by whom, who *d.* 29 Aug. 1765, he had the following issue:

1 Barbara, *b.* 29 March 1725, *m.* Ralph Sneyd, Esq. of Keele, Co. Stafford.

2 Edward, who *d.* an infant.

3 Anne, *b.* 28 Feb. 1727, *d. unm.* 30 Dec. 1812.

4 WILLIAM, his successor, created in 1780 BARON BAGOT of Blythfield, Co. Stafford. He is described with his issue, except such as have *d. unm.*, in *The Peerage Volume*, and was father of WILLIAM, the present and 2nd LORD.

5 Charles, *b.* 1 Sept. 1730, took the name and arms of CHESTER by Act of Parliament, in pursuance of the will of his cousin, Sir Charles-Bagot-Chester of Chichley, Co. Bucks, Bart. He *m.* 3 Oct. 1765, Catherine, daughter of the Hon.

Heneage Legge, one of the Barons of the Court of Exchequer, 2nd son of William, 1st Earl of Dartmouth; and *d.* 2 April 1792, leaving by her the following numerous issue: 1 Catherine, *b.* 16 Sept. 1766; 2 Louisa, *b.* 18 Nov. 1767; 3 Barbara, *b.* 28 Feb. 1769, *m.* John Drummond, Esq. Banker of Charing-Cross; (see *The Peerage Volume*, title Strathallan;) 4 Charles, *b.* 25 Oct. 1770; 5 Frances, *b.* 26 Oct. 1771, *m.* R. G. Braddyl. Esq.; 6 Anthony, *b.* 5 May 1773; 7 William, in holy orders, *b.* 27 May 1775; 8 Ann, *b.* 21 June 1776; 9 Mary, *b.* 24 June 1777, Countess-dowager of Liverpool, (see *The Peerage Volume*;) 10 Elizabeth, *b.* 19 July 1778; 11 John, a Major in the army, *b.* 3 Aug. 1779; 12 Henry, *b.* 28 Oct. 1780.

6 Walter, in holy orders, of Pipe Hall, and Rector of Blythfield and Leigh, Co. Stafford, *b.* 2 Nov. 1731, and *d.* in 1806, having been twice *m.*; 1st, 7 Sept. 1773, to Anne, daughter of Willi m Swinnerton, Esq., and 2ndly, to Mary, daughter of —— Ward, Esq. By his 1st marriage he had issue, 1 Ann, *b.* 12 June 1774; 2 Honora, *b.* 20 June 1775, *m.* the Hon. and Rev. Augustus Legge, (see *The Peerage Volume*, title Dartmouth,) 3 Egerton-Arden, in holy orders, *b.* 3 Jan. 1777; 4 Walter, *b.* 13 Feb. 1778, *d. unm.* 10 Jan. 1800; 5 Elizabeth, *b.* 25 May 1780, *m.* Joseph Phillamore, D.C.L.; 6 William, *m.* 28 Dec. 1820, Martha, daughter of Thomas Swinnerton, Esq.; 7 Louisa, *m.* 1804, Rev. R. Levett. By his 2nd marriage, the Rev. Walter Bagot had issue, 8 Hervey, Capt. R.N., *d.* 18 Jan. 1816; 9 Humphrey, killed in India; 10 Ralph, in holy orders; 11 Mary; 12 Caroline, *m.* 19 Aug. 1828, Edmund Robert Daniell, Esq. Bar.-at-law; 13 Charlotte, *m.* to the Rev. William Somerville, (see *The Peerage Volume*, title Somerville,) 14 Jane-Margaret, *m.* 5 Sept. 1826, Edward-Vaughan Williams, Esq., Bar.-at-law; 15 Agnes, *m.* 12 Oct. 1826, John Farquhar Fraser, Esq.

7 Frances, *b.* 3 Nov. 1732.

8 Richard, *b.* 13 Nov. 1733. He took the name of HOWARD by royal sign manual, and *d.* 12 Nov. 1818, having *m.* 20 March 1783, the Hon. Frances Howard, sister and heir of Henry, 12th Earl of Suffolk, only daughter of William, Viscount Andover, son of the 11th Earl of Suffolk; she *d.* 16 Sept. 1818. They have left an only daughter and heir, Mary, *m.* to the Hon. Col. Fulhe-Greville Upton, who has assumed the name of HOWARD. (See *The Peerage Volume*, title Templetown.)

9 Jane, *b.* 29 Sept. 1735, *d. unm.* Nov. 1816.

10 John, *d.* an infant.

11 Elizabeth, *b.* 17 Sept. 1738, *d. unm.* 7 July 1821.

12 Maria, *b.* 23 Nov. 1739, *d.* 21 March 1813, having *m.* Rowland Wingfield, of Preston Buckhurst, Co. Salop, Esq.

13 Lewis, *b.* 1 Jan. 1741, Lord Bishop of Bristol, and afterwards of Norwich, *d.* 4 June 1802, having *m.* 7 Oct. 1771, Mary, daughter of the Hon. Edward Hay, *b.* 25 July 1754, *d.* 17 Aug. 1799.

14 Catherine, *b.* 25 Feb. 1742, *d. unm.* 22 Feb. 1812.

15 Henrietta, *b.* 4 Feb. 1744, *d.* 25 Jan. 1825.

16 Thomas, *b.* 14 Feb. 1746, *d. unm.* at Naples.

BALCARRES, EARL OF. (LINDSAY.)

Peer of Scotland and of the United Kingdom.

The name of Lindsay is supposed to be derived from a manor of that name in Essex. Two brothers of the name obtained lands in Scotland, from King David 1st, and were ancestors of all the Lindsays of Scotland. From William de Lindsay, living in 1145, descended, in the 9th generation, Alexander, 2nd Earl of Crawford, whose 3rd son, Walter Lindsay of Edzell, was ancestor, in the 5th degree, of DAVID, created BARON LINDSAY of Balcarres, in 1633, whose son, Alexander, was farther created Earl of Balcarres and Lord Lindsay and Balneil in 1650. He *d.* in 1659, leaving issue CHARLES, 2nd EARL, who *d. unm.* in 1662; and

COLIN, 3rd EARL, who succeeded his brother, and *d.* in 1722, leaving also two sons, ALEXANDER, 4th EARL, who *d.* without issue in 1740; and JAMES, 5th EARL, for whom see *The Peerage Volume.* He *d.* in 1768, and was succeeded by his eldest son, ALEXANDER, 6th EARL; father of JAMES, present and 7th EARL, who succeeded him in 1825, and was created a Peer of the United Kingdom in 1826, by the title of BARON WIGAN, of Haigh Hall, Co. Lancaster.

BANDON, EARL OF. (BERNARD.)

Peer of Ireland.

The Earl is of English extraction. Francis Bernard, Esq. of Castle Mahon, Co. Cork, *d.* in 1660, and was grandfather of Francis Barnard of Castle Mahon, *b.* 1663, appointed Solicitor-general of Ireland in 1711, and a Judge of the Court of Common-Pleas in 1726, and *d.* in 1731. He was grandfather of

James Bernard, Esq. *b.* 8 Dec. 1729, *d.* 7 July 1790, having *m.* Esther, daughter of Percy Smyth, Esq., and widow of Robert Gookin, Esq., by whom he had issue:

1 Francis, 1st EARL, created Baron Bandon in 1793, Viscount Bandon in 1795, EARL of BANDON and Viscount Bernard in 1800; his marriage and issue are described in *The Peerage Volume.* He *d.* in 1830, and was succeeded by his eldest son, JAMES, the present and 2nd EARL.

2 Rose, *b.* 8 March 1758, *d.* 26 May 1810, having *m.* 1st, William, 1st Lord Riversdale, (see *The Peerage Volume,* title Riversdale,) and 2ndly, 18 Oct. 1792, James Millerd, Esq., who *d.* 23 July 1804.

3 Esther, *b.* 17 March 1759, *m.* 2 Dec. 1775, the late Sampson Stawell, Esq.

4 Mary, *d.* 14 Nov. 1825, having *m.* the late Sir Augustus Warren, Bart.

5 Charlotte, *b.* 1764, the present Viscountess Dowager Doneraile. (See *The Peerage Volume,* title Doneraile.)

6 Elizabeth, *m.* 1785, to the late Richard Acklom, Esq., by whom she was mother of the late Viscountess Althorpe. (See *The Peerage Volume,* title Spencer.)

BANGOR, VISCOUNT. (WARD.)

Peer of Ireland.

This family is of Norman origin. Bernard Ward, Esq., who settled in Ireland in 1580, was ancestor of Michael Ward, a justice of the King's Bench in Ireland; father of

BERNARD, 1st VISCOUNT, created Baron Bangor of Castle Ward, Co. Downe, in 1770, and VISCOUNT BANGOR, in Jan. 1781. He was *b.* 18 Aug. 1719, and *d.* 27 May 1781, having *m.* Dec. 1748, Lady Anne Bligh, eldest daughter of John, 1st Earl of Darnley, and widow of Robert Hawkins Magill, Esq.; she *d.* 7 Feb. 1789. Besides the daughters mentioned in *The Peerage Volume,* they had three sons, viz.:

1 NICHOLAS, 2nd VISCOUNT, *b.* Dec. 1749, and *d. unm.* 11 Sept. 1827, when he was succeeded by his nephew, EDWARD SOUTHWELL, the present and 3rd VISCOUNT.

2 The Hon. Edward, who *d.* in 1812, and is described with his marriage and issue in *The Peerage Volume.* He was father of the present VISCOUNT.

3 The Rt.-Hon. Robert, a Privy-Councillor in Ireland, *b.* 14 July 1754, *d.* 7 March 1831, having *m.* 1st, May 1782, Sophia Frances, 3rd daughter of Chapel Whaley, Esq., who *d.* Sept. 1793; and 2ndly, May 1797, Louisa Jane, 2nd daughter and co-heir of the Rev. Dr. Abraham Symes; she *d.* 18 Feb. 1811. He had issue by both marriages. (See *The Peerage Volume.*)

BANTRY, EARL OF. (WHITE.)

Peer of Ireland.

Sir Thomas White, of Rickmansworth, Co. Herts, Lord Mayor of London in 1655, was the first of this family who settled in Ireland. His great grandson, Simon White, Esq., *m.* 1760, Frances-Jane, daughter of Richard-Hedges Eyre, Esq., by whom, who *d.* 3 May 1816, he had issue; 1 RICHARD, present EARL, created Baron Bantry, of Bantry, Co. Cork, in 1797, Viscount Bantry in 1800, and EARL of BANTRY and Viscount Berehaven in 1816; 2 Simon, who is *m.* and has issue; 3 Hamilton, who *d.* 7 Dec. 1804, leaving issue; 4 Helen, late wife of Richard-Devonsher Newenham, Esq.; 5 Martha, wife of Michael-Goold Adams, Esq.; 6 Frances, wife of Gen. Edward Dunne.

BARHAM, BARON. (NOEL.)

Peer of the United Kingdom.

Baptist Noel, 4th Earl of Gainsborough, was 19th in paternal descent from Noel, who came over with William the Conqueror, and obtained lands in England. Lady Jane, the Earl's eldest surviving daughter, and heir of her brother, Henry, 6th Earl, on whose death, 9 April 1798, the title became extinct, was *b.* 1733, *d.* June 1811, having *m.* Gerard-Anne Edwardes, Esq., natural son of Lord Anne Hamilton, by whom she was mother of Sir Gerard-Noel Edwards, Bart., who has assumed the name of NOEL; father of the present Lord, by his marriage with Diana, daughter of Sir Charles Middleton, Bart., who was created BARON BARHAM, of Barham and Teston, Co. Kent, with remainder, failing his issue male, to his daughter Diana, wife of Sir Gerard-Noel Noel, Bart., and her issue male. He *d.* in 1813, and was succeeded by his daughter, the 1st Baroness.

BARRINGTON, VISCOUNT. (BARRINGTON.)

Peer of Ireland.

His Lordship's family was originally Norman, and bore the name of Shute. JOHN SHUTE, 1st Viscount, took the name and arms of Barrington, in consequence of succeeding to the estates of a junior branch of that ancient family, of Barrington Hall, Baronets. He was created VISCOUNT BARRINGTON, of Ardglass, Co. Down, and Baron Barrington, of Newcastle, Co. Dublin, in 1720, and *d.* in 1734; having *m.* Anne, daughter and co-heir of Sir William Daines, Knt., by whom he had issue:

1 WILLIAM-WILDMAN, 2nd VISCOUNT, who after passing through some subordinate ministerial offices, was appointed Secretary at War and Chancellor of the Exchequer in 1761, Treasurer of the Navy in 1762, and again Secretary at War in 1764, from which situation he retired in 1778, after serving the Crown thirty-four years; he *m.* 16 Sept. 1740, Mary, daughter and heir of Henry Lovell, Esq., widow of the Hon. Samuel Grimston, and *d.* 1 Feb. 1793, without surviving issue.

2 John, a Major-General, Governor of Berwick, and Commander of the British troops at the taking of Guadaloupe in 1758; he *d.* 2 April, 1764, having *m.* Elizabeth, daughter of Florentius Vassal, Esq., by whom he had issue,

1 WILLIAM-WILDMAN, 3rd VISCOUNT, who succeeded his uncle in the Peerage, and *d.* without issue 13 July 1801; having *m.* Miss Anne Murrell, who after his death *m.* 2ndly, Edward Thornycroft, Esq., and *d.* May 1816.

2 RICHARD, 4th VISCOUNT, who succeeded his brother, and *d.* without issue, Jan. 1814; having *m.* Susan, daughter of William Budder, Esq., who survives him.

3 GEORGE, in holy orders, the 5th VISCOUNT, who succeeded his brother in 1814, and was succeeded in 1829 by his eldest son, the present and 6th VISCOUNT.

4 Louisa, wife of Thomas Cooke, Esq.

3 Daines, a Welsh Judge and distinguished author, *d.* 14 March 1800.

4 Samuel, an Admiral, eminent for his naval services, *d. unm.* 16 Aug. 1800.

5 Shute, Lord Bishop of Llandaff, translated to Salisbury, and subsequently to Durham; he *d.* without issue 25 March, 1826; having *m.* 1st, 2 Feb. 1761, Lady Diana Beauclerk, only daughter of Charles, 2nd Duke of St. Albans, who *d.* in 1766; and 2ndly, 20 June 1770, Jane, only daughter of Sir Berkeley-William Guise, Bart., who *d.* Aug. 1807.

6 Sarah, *d.* 17 March 1759; having *m.* June 1746, Robert Price, of Foxley, Co. Hereford, Esq.

7 Anne, *m.* 1st, Jan. 1747, Sir Thomas Clarges, Bart., and 2ndly, Sir Roger Gilbert, Bart.

BATH, MARQUIS OF. (THYNNE.)

Peer of Great Britain.

Sir Geoffrey de Boteville, of considerable rank in Poitou, settled in England in the reign of King John, and was ancestor in the 10th degree of John de Boteville, called John of the Inn, from his mansion at Stretton, which gave rise to the surname of Thynne. His heir in the 7th generation was

SIR THOMAS THYNNE, Bart., created, in 1682, Baron Thynne, of Warminster, Co. Wilts, and VISCOUNT WEYMOUTH, Co. Dorset, with remainder, failing his issue male, to his brothers James and Henry-Frederick Thynne, and their heirs male respectively; he *d.* 28 July 1714, without surviving issue male, and his brother James having *d. unm.* in 1708, he was succeeded by THOMAS, 2nd VISCOUNT, his nephew, grandson and heir of his brother Henry-Frederick Thynne. The 2nd Viscount *d.* 12 Jan. 1751; having *m.* Lady Louisa Carteret, daughter of John Earl Granville, by whom he left two sons:

1 THOMAS, 2nd Viscount, created in 1789, MARQUIS of BATH; for his marriage and issue, see *The Peerage Volume;* he *d.* in 1796, and was succeeded by his eldest son, the present and 2nd MARQUIS.

2 Henry-Frederick, who being appointed by will heir to his grandfather, Earl Granville, took the name of Carteret, and was created Baron Carteret in 1784, with remainder, failing his issue male, to the 2nd, 3rd, 4th, and every other son of Thomas Viscount Weymouth, his elder brother, and their heirs male; he *d. unm.* in 1826, and was succeeded by his nephew, Lord George Thynne, 2nd son of the 1st Marquis of Bath, the present Baron Carteret.

BATHURST, EARL. (BATHURST.)

Peer of Great Britain.

This family existed at Bathurst in Sussex, before the wars of York and Lancaster.

Sir Benjamin Bathurst, Knight, was 4th in descent from Lawrence Bathurst of Cranebrook, Kent, living in the reign of King Henry 6th. He *d.* in 1704, leaving three sons; 1 ALLEN, 1st EARL; 2 Peter, whose male issue became extinct in 1803, by the death of his son, General Peter Bathurst; 3 Benjamin, of Sydney Park,

Gloucestershire, who left issue, besides other children, a daughter, Anne, *m.* to Charles Bragge, Esq., and mother by him of the Right Hon. Charles Bragge Bathurst, of Lydney Park, who *d.* in 1731; and a son, Henry, present Bishop of Norwich, who by Grace Coote, sister of the late Lord Castlecoote, has a numerous issue.

ALLEN, 1st EARL, was created Baron Bathurst of Battlesdon, Co. Bedford, in 1712, and EARL BATHURST, of Bathurst, Co. Sussex, in 1772; he *d.* 14 Sept. 1775, and was succeeded by his eldest surviving son, HENRY, 2nd EARL, who had been appointed Lord High Chancellor, and created Baron Apsley, of Apsley, Co. Sussex, in 1771; he *d.* in 1794, and was succeeded by his only son, HENRY, present and 3rd EARL.

BAYNING, BARON. (WILLIAM-POULETT.)

Peer of Great Britain.

The Hon. William Townshend, 3rd son of Charles, 1st Viscount Townshend, was Aid-de-Camp to King George 2nd, and Groom of the Bedchamber and Privy Purse to Frederick Prince of Wales; he was *b.* 9 June 1702, and *d.* 29 Jan. 1738; having *m.* 29 May 1725, Henrietta, daughter and sole heir of Lord William Powlett, (2nd son of Charles, 1st Duke of Bolton,) by his 2nd marriage with Anne, daughter and heir of Randolph Egerton, Esq., of Betley, Co. Stafford, by Anne, eldest daughter and co-heir of Henry Murray, Esq., by Anne, created Viscountess Bayning in 1674, and whose title became extinct, on her death without issue male, in 1698, 2nd daughter of Sir Paul Bayning, created Viscount Bayning in 1627, and sister and heir of Paul, 2nd Viscount, whose title became extinct in 1638.

CHARLES TOWNSHEND, the only surviving son of this marriage, was created, in 1797, BARON BAYNING, of Foxley, Co. Berks, and *d.* in 1810; having *m.* Annabella, sister and heir of Powlett Smyth, Esq. of Somborne, Hants, who assumed the name of Powlett, and daughter of the Rev. Richard Smyth, by Annabella, daughter and heir of William Powlett, Esq., the only son of the above-mentioned Lord William Powlett, by his first marriage with Louisa, daughter of the Marquess de Monpouillon, and younger son of the Duc de La Force, in France. Lord Bayning had issue by this marriage, besides some children who died young, and the daughters stated in *The Peerage Volume*, two sons, viz.: 1 CHARLES-FREDERICK POWLETT, his successor, 2nd LORD, who *d. unm.* in 1823; 2 HENRY, 3rd and present LORD, who succeeded his brother, and has assumed by Royal sign-manual the names of WILLIAM-POWLETT.

BEAUCHAMP, EARL. (PYNDAR.)

Peer of the United Kingdom.

Anne, daughter and co-heir of Richard, 2nd Lord Beauchamp of Powyck, *m.* Richard Lygon, of a family existing in the time of Richard 1st; 7th in descent from them was William Lygon of Madresfield, whose daughter and eventual heir Margaret *m.* Reginald Pyndar, Esq.; their son Reginald assumed the name and arms of Lygon, and was father of WILLIAM LYGON, created Baron Beauchamp of Powyk, Co. Worcester, in 1806, and EARL BEAUCHAMP and Viscount Elmley in 1815. He was father of WILLIAM-BEAUCHAMP, his successor, 2nd EARL, who *d. unm.* in 1823; and of JOHN-REGINALD, 3d and present EARL, who by Royal sign-manual resumed, in 1813, the paternal name of Pyndar only.

BEAUFORT, DUKE OF. (Somerset.)

Peer of England.

No family of the British Peerage traces a longer line of illustrious descent than that of Beaufort. The three sons of John of Gaunt, Duke of Lancaster, (4th son of King Edward 4th,) all bearing the name of Beaufort, were legitimated by Act of Parliament, with an exception against any claim to the Throne; Thomas Earl of Dorset and Duke of Exeter, who died without issue; and Henry, the well-known Cardinal Beaufort, Bishop of Winchester, and Lord Chancellor, were the two younger of these legitimated sons. John de Beaufort, created in 1397 Earl of Somerset, was the eldest, and was father of three successive Earls, Henry, John, and Edmund. The eldest died unmarried; and the second, having been created Duke of Somerset in 1443, was constituted by his cousin, King Henry 6th, Captain-General of the whole realm of France and Duchy of Normandy, and left an only daughter, Margaret, wife of Edmund Tudor, Earl of Richmond, and mother of King Henry 7th, who, in her right, claimed the Crown, as heir of the House of Lancaster.

Edmund, the 3rd son, Earl of Mortaigne and Marquis of Dorset, who succeeded his brother as Earl of Somerset, was likewise Regent of Normandy, and created Duke of Somerset. He was killed in the battle of St. Albans in 1455, leaving four sons, Henry, Edmund, John, and Thomas, the two eldest of whom were successively Dukes of Somerset, and all lost their lives, either valiantly supporting in the field the declining fortunes of the House of Lancaster, or falling by the hands of the executioner victims to the spirit of party vengeance, which in that period deluged the scaffolds with the best blood of the realm. With Edmund, the 4th Duke of Somerset, who was beheaded by King Edward 4, after the battle of Tewkesbury, expired the legitimate descendants of the 1st Earl of Somerset; but Henry, the 3rd Duke, left an illegitimate son,

Charles, to whom he gave the name of Somerset, and who obtained, from King Henry 7th, the Order of the Garter; he *m.* Elizabeth, sole daughter and heir of William Herbert, Earl of Pembroke, and 2nd Baron Herbert by writ (1461), and was created by patent, in 1506, Baron Herbert of Ragland, Chepstow, and Gower, and in 1514 Earl of Worcester; he *d.* in 1526. Henry, 2nd Earl, their son, inherited the Barony of Herbert by writ; he *d.* in 1549, and was succeeded by his eldest son, William, 3rd Earl, K.G. who *d.* in 1589. Edward, 4th Earl, K.G. succeeded his father, and was succeeded in 1628 by his son,

Henry, 5th Earl, who was created Marquis of Worcester in 1642; he was amongst the most conspicuous defenders of the Royal cause, in the civil wars of the reign of Charles 1st; assisting the King with large supplies both of men and money, and maintaining for four years, with 800 men, his Castle of Ragland, in the county of Monmouth, which was amongst the last places in England that surrendered to the Parliamentary forces, and obtained at last, in August 1646, an honourable capitulation from General Fairfax; in violation of which, however, he was taken into custody, and died a prisoner in December following. The Castle of Ragland was wholly destroyed, and injury to an immense amount was committed upon his property. He was succeeded by his eldest son, Edward, 2nd Marquis, also a distinguished Royalist. He was styled in his father's lifetime Earl of Glamorgan, to which title he is said to have been created by patent in 1644; he *d.* in 1667, and was succeeded by his only son,

Henry, 3rd Marquis, K.G., created Duke of Beaufort in 1682. On the elevation of William 3rd to the Throne, this noble Duke refused to take the oaths of allegiance, and consequently lived in retirement till his death in 1699, when he was succeeded by his grandson,

Henry, 2nd Duke, K.G., son of Charles, Marquis of Worcester, who *d.* in the

Esq., by whom, besides two sons and two daughters who *d. unm*, he had the three sons stated in *The Peerage Volume.*

4 Lovell Stanhope, Esq., under Secretary of State, *d. unm.* 1 Sept. 1783.

CHETWYND, VISCOUNT. (Chetwynd.)

Peer of Ireland.

This family, which takes its name from Chetwynd in Shropshire, flourished in that County from the reign of Henry III. to that of William III. Capt. John Chetwynd, of Mare and Rudge, Co. Stafford, had three sons, Walter John, and William-Richard. Walter, the eldest son, was created, in 1717, Viscount Chetwynd of Berehaven, Co. Cork, and Baron of Rathdown, Co. Dublin, with remainder to his issue male, failing which, to the issue male of his father; he *d.* without issue in 1735, and was succeeded by his next brother John, 2nd Viscount, who, dying also in 1767 without surviving issue male, was succeeded by his younger brother, William-Richard, 3rd Viscount; he *d.* in 1770, leaving three sons: 1 William, 4th Viscount; 2 Thomas, who *d. unm.*; 3 John, in holy orders, deceased; he left a son William Chetwynd, who was killed in an action against the Irish rebels, at Saintfield, in June 1796, and has left a widow and family, for whom see *The Peerage Volume.*

William, the eldest son, succeeded his father as 4th Viscount, 3 April 1770; was *b.* 25 Nov. 1721, and *d.* 12 Nov. 1791; having *m.* Susannah, youngest daughter of Sir Jonathan Cope, Bart., by whom, who *d.* 3 March 1790, he was father of his successor Richard, 5th Viscount. The latter *d.* in 1821, and was succeeded by his only surviving son, Richard-Walter, the present and 6th Viscount.

CHICHESTER, EARL OF. (Pelham.)

Peer of the United Kingdom.

The name of Pelham is taken from a Lordship so called in Hertfordshire, where this family are supposed to have resided before the Conquest; 12th in descent from Walter de Pelham, living in 1292, was Sir John Pelham, Bart., father of

1 Sir Thomas, created, in 1706, Baron Pelham of Laughton, Co. Sussex, which title became extinct in 1768, on the death of his son, Thomas Pelham-Holles, Duke of Newcastle; who had been created, in 1762, Baron Pelham of Stanmer, Co. Sussex, with remainder to his cousin, Thomas Pelham, Esq., and his issue male.

2 Henry, who *d.* in 1721, leaving a son Thomas, who, in consequence of the special limitation of the patent, succeeded as 2nd Lord, and was created Earl of Chichester in 1801; for his marriage and issue see *The Peerage Volume.* He *d.* in 1805, and was succeeded by his eldest son Thomas, 2nd Earl, father of Henry-Thomas, the present and 3rd Earl, who succeeded him in 1826.

CHOLMONDELEY, MARQUIS. (Cholmondeley.)

Peer of the United Kingdom and of Ireland.

Richard de Belward became possessed of the Lordship of Cholmondeley, shortly after the Conquest, by marriage with the heiress of the ancient Barons of Malpas; 13th in descent from this marriage was

Sir Hugh Cholmondeley, of Cholmondeley, Co. Chester, who, before he was lifetime of his father, the 1st Duke; he *d.* in 1714, leaving only two sons, HENRY, who *d.* without issue in 1745, and CHARLES-NOEL, successively DUKES of BEAUFORT.

CHARLES-NOEL, 4th DUKE, *d.* 28 Oct. 1756; having *m.* ELIZABETH, sister and heir of NORBORNE BERKELEY, BARON BOTTETOURT; to which ancient Barony she succeeded on the death of her brother, and transmitted it, in 1799, to her only son, HENRY, 5th DUKE, K.G., who is described at length with his issue in *The Peerage Volume*. He *d.* in 1803, and was succeeded by his eldest son, HENRY-CHARLES, the present and 6th DUKE, K.G.

BEDFORD, DUKE OF. (RUSSELL.)

Peer of England.

John Russell was Constable of Corfe Castle, Co. Dorset, in 1221; 8th in descent from him was JOHN RUSSELL, who entered into the service of King Henry 7th, as a Gentleman of the Privy Chamber, and rose to be Comptroller of the Household in that of King Henry 8th. He was created, in 1539, Baron Russell, of Cheneys, Co. Bedford, made a Knight of the Garter in the following year, and obtained considerable grants of land upon the dissolution of monasteries. He enjoyed many other high offices under this King, and was appointed one of the Council of administration during the minority of King Edward 6th, at whose coronation he acted as High Steward. In 1550 he was created EARL OF BEDFORD, and *d.* in 1554, and was succeeded by his only son,

FRANCIS, 2nd EARL, K.G., who *d.* in 1585; having had four sons, viz.

1 Edward Lord Russell, who *d.* without issue in his father's lifetime.

2 John Lord Russell, who also *d.* in his father's lifetime, having had one son, who *d.* before him, and two daughters, Elizabeth, who *d. unm.*, and Anne, who *m.* Henry, 5th Earl, afterwards Marquis of Worcester.

3 Francis, summoned to Parliament as Baron Russell, was killed in an accidental fray on the Scottish borders, only one day before his father's death, leaving an only son, EDWARD, 3rd EARL, who succeeded his grandfather, and *d.* without issue in 1627.

4 WILLIAM, Lord Deputy of Ireland, created in 1603 BARON RUSSELL of Thornhaugh; he *d.* in 1613, leaving two sons; 1 FRANCIS, his successor, 2nd LORD RUSSELL, of THORNHAUGH, who succeeded his cousin as 4th EARL; and 2 William, from whom a family of Russell seated at Speldhurst, in Kent, descended.

WILLIAM, 5th EARL, K.G., eldest son of the 4th Earl, succeeded his father in 1641; in 1694 he was created Marquis of Tavistock and DUKE of BEDFORD, and *d.* in 1700. He was father of William, the celebrated Lord Russell, who lost his life on the scaffold 21 July, 1683, but his attainder was annulled by Act of Parliament soon after the Revolution. He *m.* Lady Rachel Wriothesley, 2nd daughter and at length heir of Thomas, 4th Earl of Southampton, so distinguished for her conjugal affection, and left issue by her,

WRIOTHESLEY, 2nd DUKE, K.G. He was created BARON HOWLAND of Streatham in 1695, before his accession to the Ducal title, by the death of his grandfather. He *d.* in 1711, leaving two sons, successively Dukes of Bedford, WRIOTHESLEY, 3rd DUKE, who *d.* without issue in 1732, and

JOHN, 4th DUKE, K.G., who *d.* in 1771, and was succeeded by his grandson, FRANCIS, 5th DUKE, eldest son of Francis, Marquis of Tavistock, who died before his father; the 5th Duke *d. unm.* in 1802, and was succeeded by his brother JOHN, the present and 6th Duke.

BELHAVEN, BARON. (Hamilton.)

Peer of Scotland and of the United Kingdom.

Sir John Hamilton was created Baron Belhaven and Stenton in 1647, and in 1675 had his patent renewed, with remainder to John Hamilton, husband of his grand-daughter Margaret, (daughter of Sir Robert Hamilton, Bart., by Anne, his Lordship's 2nd daughter,) and the heirs male of his body, failing which, to the heirs male whatever of the said John Hamilton, who succeeded as 2nd Lord in 1679, and his male line failed on the death of John, 5th Lord, 25 Jan. 1777; when the title descended, according to the limitation of the patent, to

Robert, 6th Lord, grandfather of the present Peer, lineal descendant and heir male of William Hamilton of Wishaw, younger brother of James Hamilton of Barncleugh, grandfather of the 2nd Lord. He was descended from Thomas, 3rd son of Sir John Hamilton of Cadzow, and uncle of James, 1st Lord Hamilton, ancestor of the Marquis of Abercorn. He *d.* however in 1784, without having established his claim, but the Peerage was allowed by the House of Lords in 1799, to his son, William, 7th Lord, father of the present and 8th Lord, who succeeded him in 1814; and was created a Peer of the United Kingdom in 1831, by the title of Baron Hamilton of Wishaw, Co. Lanark.

BELMORE, EARL OF. (Lowry-Corry.)

Peer of Ireland.

Robert Lowry, Esq. was descended from an ancient Scotch family, which settled at Ahenis, Co. Tyrone, Ireland; he was father of Galbraith Lowry, Esq., who *m.* Sarah, daughter and co-heir of John Corry, Esq., and in consequence assumed the name of Corry. Armar, their son and heir, was created Baron Belmore of Castle Coole in 1681, Viscount Belmore in 1689, and Earl of Belmore in 1797; he *d.* in 1802, and was succeeded by his only son, Somerset, the present and 2nd Earl.

BERESFORD, VISCOUNT. (Beresford.)

Peer of the United Kingdom.

William-Carr Beresford, the illegitimate son of George, 1st Marquis of Waterford, was raised to the Peerage of the United Kingdom in 1814, for his eminent military services in the Peninsular War, by the title of Baron Beresford of Albuera and Dungarvon, Co. Waterford, and was advanced in 1823 to the dignity of Viscount Beresford, of Beresford, Co. Stafford, and is the present Viscount. His Lordship has a brother,

Vice-Admiral Sir John-Poo Beresford, Bart., K.C.B., M.P., *m.* 1st, Mary, daughter of Captain Anthony-John-Pye Molloy, R.N., she *d.* 1 July 1813; and 2ndly, 17 Aug. 1815, Harriet-Elizabeth, 3rd daughter of Henry Peirse, Esq., (by Hon. Charlotte-Grace Monson, 2nd daughter of John, 2nd Lord Monson,) who *d.* 27 Feb. 1825. He has issue by his 1st marriage one son, George; and by his 2nd,

2 Harriet-Charlotte, *b.* 28 June 1816,
3 Mary-Anne-Araminta, *b.* 5 Sept. 1817, *d.* 2 Aug. 1818.
4 Georgiana, *b.* 18 April 1819.
5 Henry, *b.* 27 Sept. 1820.
6 John, *b.* 28 Sept. 1821.
7 Mary-Anne, *b.* 1 Jan. 1824.

BERKELEY, EARL. (BERKELEY.)

Peer of England.

This very ancient family derives its origin from Harding, a Nobleman sprung from the Kings of Denmark, who accompanied William Duke of Normandy into England, and fought in the memorable battle of Hastings. His son, ROBERT, obtained, from King Henry 2nd, the Castle of Berkeley, and held it with the dignity of BARON of the realm, which was enjoyed by his descendants, by tenure of their castle of Berkeley, till THOMAS, 6th BARON BERKELEY, by tenure, was summoned to Parliament by writ in 1295. He was succeeded in 1321 by his son MAURICE, and he in 1326 by his son THOMAS, 3rd LORD, to whose custody the unfortunate King Edward 2nd was confided after his deposition; but exceptions being taken to the too great civility with which Lord Berkeley was supposed to treat his Royal prisoner, he was required to deliver up his charge, and also his Castle of Berkeley, to John Lord Maltravers and Sir Thomas Gournay, under whom the King was barbarously murdered. This Lord was succeeded by his son,

MAURICE, 4th LORD, who *d.* in 1368, leaving two sons, THOMAS, his successor, and James; the latter was father of JAMES, 6th LORD. The said THOMAS, eldest son, 5th LORD, and 10th by tenure, *m.* Margaret, daughter and sole heir of Warine, 2nd Baron Lisle, [by writ 1357,] and *d.* without issue male in 1416, leaving an only daughter Elizabeth, wife of Richard Beauchamp, 14th Earl of Warwick, between whose three daughters and co-heirs the Barony of Lisle is in abeyance, and the Barony of Berkeley [by writ 1295] would have been so, but that JAMES de Berkeley, nephew and heir male of the 10th Lord, claimed and was allowed the Barony by the tenure of his castle of Berkeley to which he was heir of entail; he was summoned in 1416. He *d.* in 1463; having *m.* Isabel, 2nd daughter at length and co-heir of Thomas Mowbray, 1st Duke of Norfolk, Baron Mowbray, [by writ 1295,] and co-heir of the Barony of Braose of Gower, [by writ 1299,] by Elizabeth, daughter and sole heir of John, 3rd Baron Segrave, [by writ 1264.] WILLIAM, their son and heir, was created Viscount Berkeley in 1481, Earl of Nottingham 1483, and Marquis of Berkeley 1488; he *d.* without issue in 1492, when these titles became extinct, but the Barony devolved on

MAURICE, his brother, 8th LORD. He *d.* in 1507, leaving two sons, MAURICE the 9th, and THOMAS the 10th LORD; the latter *d.* in 1532, and was succeeded by his son THOMAS, to whom, in 1534, succeeded his son HENRY, 12th LORD, who *d.* in 1613. Sir Thomas Berkeley, his eldest son, *d.* before his father, having *m.* Elizabeth, daughter and sole heir of George Cary, 2nd Lord Hunsdon, grandson and heir of William Cary, Esq., by Lady Mary, 2nd daughter and co-heir of Thomas Boleyn, Earl of Wiltshire and Ormond. GEORGE, 13th LORD, their son, succeeded his grandfather, and *d.* in 1658. His son,

GEORGE, 14th LORD, was created Viscount Dursley and EARL of BERKELEY, Co. Gloucester, in 1679; he *d.* in 1698, and to him in direct paternal descent have succeeded CHARLES, 2nd EARL, who *d.* in 1710; JAMES, 3rd EARL, K.G., who *d.* in 1736; AUGUSTUS, 4th EARL, who *d.* 1755; and FREDERICK-AUGUSTUS, 5th and late EARL, whose double marriage, as represented by himself and his Countess, failed of establishment, on a patient investigation by the House of Peers after the Earl's death in 1810; when THOMAS-MORTON-FITZ-HARDING, his eldest son, born after the acknowledged marriage of 1796, was declared to be the successor to his honours. The castle of Berkeley, however, devolved with other estates by the will of the late Earl to his first-born son, William-Fitz-Harding, called in his father's lifetime Viscount Dursley, who in 1831, was raised to the Peerage by the title of Baron Segrave, of Berkeley Castle, Co. Gloucester. See *The Peerage Volume*, under that title.

BERWICK, BARON. (Hill.)

Peer of Great Britain.

The paternal name of this family is Harwood. Thomas Harwood, of Tern Hall, near Shrewsbury, Esq., *m.* Elizabeth, widow of Richard Atcherley, Esq., and sister of the Right Hon. Richard Hill, by whom he was father of Thomas Harwood, Esq., who being one of the heirs of entail to the Baronetcy of Hill of Hawkestone, in right of his mother, assumed the name of Hill. He *m.* Susan-Maria, eldest daughter and co-heir of William Noel, Esq., Judge of the Common Pleas, by whom he had a son,

Noel-Hill, created in 1784 Baron Berwick, of Attingham, Co. Salop, whose marriage and issue will be found in *The Peerage Volume.* He *d.* in 1789, and was succeeded by his eldest son, Thomas-Noel, the present Lord.

BESBOROUGH, EARL OF. (Ponsonby.)

Peer of Ireland and of Great Britain.

John Ponsonby, Esq., of Hale, Co. Cumberland, was great-grandfather of Sir John, who settled in Ireland, and was father of Sir William, created an Irish Peer in 1721, by the title of Baron of Besborough, and advanced to the dignity of Viscount Duncannon in 1723. He *d.* in 1726, leaving two sons; 1 Brabazon, his successor; 2 Major-General Henry Ponsonby, who was killed in the battle of Fontenoy, 11 May 1745; his son, Chambre Brabazon, *d.* 20 Feb. 1762, having *m.* 1st, 26 Sept. 1746, Elizabeth, daughter and heir of Edward Clarke, Esq., 2ndly, 23 Oct. 1752, Louisa, daughter of John Lyons, Esq., and 3rdly, Mary, daughter of Sir William Barker, Bart.; he had a daughter by each marriage, and by his third was also father of a posthumous son, Chambre-Brabazon Ponsonby-Barker, Esq., for all of whom see *The Peerage Volume.*

Brabazon, 2nd Viscount, was created Earl of Besborough in 1739, and *d.* in 1758, leaving two sons,

1 William, 2nd Earl, his successor, for whose issue and marriage see *The Peerage Volume;* he *d.* in 1793, and was succeeded by his son, Frederick, the present and 3rd Earl.

2 The Right Hon. John Ponsonby, who *d.* 16 Aug. 1787; having *m.* 26 Sept. 1742, Lady Elizabeth Cavendish, 2nd daughter of William, 3rd Duke of Devonshire, by whom he had issue,

1 William-Brabazon, created Baron Ponsonby in the Peerage of the United Kingdom. See *The Peerage Volume,* title Ponsonby.

2 Catherine, who *d.* 23 Jan. 1827, having *m.* Richard, 2nd Earl of Shannon.

3 Right Hon. George, *b.* 5 March 1755, *d.* 8 July 1817; having *m.* 18 May 1781, Lady Mary Butler, eldest daughter of Brinsley, 2nd Earl of Lanesborough, by whom he has left a daughter, Elizabeth. See *The Peerage Volume.*

4 Frances, *b.* 18 Feb. 1757, who *d.* 25 May 1827, having *m.* Cornelius, 1st Lord Lismore.

5 Charlotte, *b.* 22 Dec. 1761, who *d.* 27 Aug. 1781, having *m.* 10 July 1780, Right Hon. Denis-Bowes Daly, deceased.

6 Henrietta, who is still living, and will be found in *The Peerage Volume.*

BEVERLEY, EARL OF. (Percy.)

Peer of Great Britain.

For the pedigree of this noble family, *see* the Duke of Northumberland. Algernon, 1st Earl, was the 2nd son of Hugh, 1st Duke of Northumberland, who was created Baron Louvaine of Alnwick, Co. Northumberland, in the Peerage of Great Britain, with remainder to Algernon Percy, his 2nd son, and the heirs male of his body. His Lordship succeeded the Duke his father in the Barony, in 1786, and was advanced to the dignity of Earl of Beverley, Co. York, in 1790; he *d.* in 1830, and was succeeded by his eld. son, George, the present and 2nd Earl.

BEXLEY, BARON. (Vansittart.)

Peer of the United Kingdom.

This is an ancient family originally from the Netherlands. Peter Vansittart, an eminent merchant, settled in England about 1675, and was great-grandfather of the present Peer.

Arthur, his 5th son, was verderer of Windsor Forest, he *d.* 16 Sept. 1760, having *m.* 23 May 1723, Martha, eldest daughter of Sir John Stonehouse, of Radley, Co. Berks, Bart., by whom he had, besides other children, four sons:

1 Arthur, of Shottesbrooke-house, Co. Berks, Esq., who was *b.* 15 Feb. 1727, and *d.* 12 Nov. 1804, leaving issue, by Anne, sister of Lord Coleraine; 1 Arthur, who *d.* 31 May 1829, having *m.* Caroline, 4th daughter of William, 1st Lord Auckland, by whom he has left a numerous issue; 2 Robert; 3 William, in holy orders, *m.* to Charlotte, daughter of General George Ward, and has issue,

2 Robert, *b.* 6 Dec. 1728, professor of civil law at Oxford, *d. unm.* 1789.

3 Henry, father of the present Lord.

4 George, *b.* 15 Sept. 1743, of Bisham Abbey, Co. Berks, *m.* Sarah, daughter of Sir James Stonehouse, Bart., and *d.* 21 Jan. 1825, having had issue; 1 George-Henry, a General in the army, *b.* July 1768, *d.* 4 Feb. 1824; having *m.* Oct. 1818, Anna-Maria Copson-Harris, only surviving child of Thomas Copson, Esq. of Shepey Hall, Co. Leicester, by whom he has left issue; 2 Edward, in holy orders, Rector of Taplow, took the surname of Neale by Royal sign manual, 1805; 3 Henry, Capt. R. N.; 4 Caroline-Anne, *m.* 22 Dec. 1792, Augustus-Henry East, Esq., 2nd son of Sir William East, Bart.; 5 Laura, *m.* 26 Nov. 1809, Fulwar Craven, of Chilton House, Esq. (see *The Peerage Volume*, title Craven); 6 Henrietta.

Henry Vansittart, Esq., the third son, father of the present Lord, was *b.* 3 June 1732. Having been Governor-General of Bengal, he set sail for India a second time in the Aurora frigate, which was lost in the Mozambique Channel about Jan. 1771, when all on board perished; he *m.* Amelia, daughter of Nicholas Morse, Esq., Governor of Bombay, by whom, who died 1 Aug. 1819, he left issue:

1 Henry, who *d.* 12 Oct. 1787, leaving a son, Henry Vansittart, Esq., *m.* in 1812, to Hon. Theresa Gleadowe-Newcomen, 2nd daughter of Charlotte, 1st Viscountess Newcomen, and the late Right Hon. Sir William Gleadowe-Newcomen, Bart., and widow of Sir Charles Turner, Bart, by whom he has one daughter.

2 Nicholas, the present Lord, created, in 1823, a Peer of the United Kingdom, by the title of Baron Bexley of Bexley, Co. Kent.

3 Sophia.

4 *Emilia*, who is deceased, having *m.* Edward Parry, Esq.

BLANTYRE, BARON. (STUART.)

Peer of Scotland.

His Lordship is of the same ancestry with the Earl of Galloway, being descended from Sir Thomas Stewart of Minto, 3rd son of Sir William of Dalswinton and Garlies, whose eldest son Sir Alexander was ancester of the Earl of Galloway. From Sir Thomas, WALTER, 1st LORD BLANTYRE, so created in 1606, was 4th in descent. He was succeeded in 1616, by his son WILLIAM, 2nd LORD; who *d.* in 1638, leaving two sons, WALTER, 3rd LORD, and ALEXANDER, 4th LORD. The latter was father of ALEXANDER, 5th LORD, who left issue, WALTER, 6th, and ROBERT, 7th LORDS. The 7th LORD *d.* in 1743, leaving three sons, successively LORDS BLANTYRE; viz. WALTER, WILLIAM, and ALEXANDER, the 8th, 9th, and 10th LORDS. LORD WALTER *d.* in 1751, LORD WILLIAM in 1776, both *unm.*; and ALEXANDER, 10th LORD, for whose marriage and issue see *The Peerage Volume*, in 1783, when he was succeeded by his eldest son, ROBERT-WALTER, 11th LORD, who *d.* in 1830, and was succeeded by his eldest surviving son, CHARLES, the present and 11th LORD, a minor.

BLAYNEY, BARON. (BLAYNEY.),

Peer of Ireland.

This family is said to trace its genealogy from the ancient Kings of Britain. SIR EDWARD BLAYNEY, who settled in Ireland in the reign of Elizabeth, was created BARON BLAYNEY of Monaghan in 1621. He *d.* in 1629, and was succeeded by his eldest son HENRY, 2nd LORD; father of EDWARD, 3rd, and RICHARD, 4th LORDS. The latter left also two sons, who successively inherited the title, viz. HENRY-VINCENT, 5th LORD, and WILLIAM, 6th LORD, who *d.* in 1705, and was succeeded by his son CADWALLADER, 7th LORD. He *d.* in 1733, leaving CHARLES-TALBOT, 8th LORD, who *d.* without surviving issue male; and Cadwallader, 9th LORD, succeeded his brother. For an account of his issue, &c. see *The Peerage Volume*; he was father of CADWALLADER-DAVIS, 10th LORD, and of ANDREW-THOMAS, the present LORD; he *d.* in 1775, and was succeeded by his eldest son, who dying *unm.* in 1784, was succeeded by his only brother, ANDREW-THOMAS, the present and 11th LORD.

BLOOMFIELD, BARON. (BLOOMFIELD.)

Peer of Ireland.

His Lordship is descended from the Bloomfields of Redwood Castle, an ancient family in the Co. of Tipperary. His grandfather, Benjamin Bloomfield, Esq., of Meelick, Co. Galway (younger brother of John Bloomfield, Esq., of Redwood), was father of

John Bloomfield, Esq., of Newport, Co. Tipperary, who *m.* Charlotte, eldest daughter of Samuel Waller, Esq., (by Anne Jocelyn, sister to Robert, Viscount Jocelyn, Lord Chancellor of Ireland), by whom, who *d.* 1 Feb. 1828, he had issue:

1 BENJAMIN, the present PEER, created Baron Bloomfield of Oakhampton and Redwood, Co. Tipperary, in 1825.

2 Anne, *m.* Thomas Ryder Pepper, Esq., of Loughton, Co. Tipperary.

3 Charlotte, *m.* the Very Rev. Thomas-B. Gough, Dean of Derry.

BOLINGBROKE, VISCOUNT. (St. John.)

Peer of Great Britain.

The Viscount is a branch of the family of Lord St. John. Sir Oliver St. John of Bletshoe, Co. Northampton, and Lydiard Tregoze, Co. Wilts, in right of his wife, *m.* Margaret, daughter of John, 3rd Lord Beauchamp of Bletshoe, and sister and sole heir of John, 4th Lord Beauchamp of Bletshoe; this John Lord Beauchamp and Margaret his sister were fourth in paternal descent from Roger Baron Beauchamp of Bletshoe, Chamberlain to King Edward 3rd, by his marriage with Sibil, sister and co-heir of William de Pateshul (who, though he survived his father, was never summoned to Parliament) and eldest daughter of John de Pateshul (who received summons as a Baron in 1342), by his wife Mabel, only daughter of William, Baron Grandison, summoned in 1299, and heir of her nephew Thomas, 4th Baron Grandison; who, as well as his predecessor, John, 3rd Baron, never received summons to Parliament. The above-mentioned Roger Baron Beauchamp of Bletshoe (to whom, and Sibil his wife, heiress of Pateshul and Grandison, Margaret, the wife of Sir Oliver St. John, was great-great-grand-daughter, and eventual heir), was summoned as a Baron of the Realm to all the Parliaments convened from 1363 to 1379, the year of his death; but none of his descendants ever received summons in right of the Barony thus created. Sir Oliver St. John *d.* in 1437, and Margaret Beauchamp, his widow, *m.* 2ndly, John Beaufort, Duke of Somerset, by whom she had a daughter, Margaret, wife of Edmund Tudor, Earl of Richmond, and mother by him of King Henry 7th. After the death of the Duke of Somerset, Margaret Beauchamp *m.* 3rdly, Lionel, Lord Welles, by whom she was mother of John Viscount Welles, who *m.* Princess Cecily, daughter of King Edward 4th. By Sir Oliver St. John she had two sons, Sir John St. John, Knt. the elder son, ancestor of Lord St. John, and

Oliver, the younger son; he was father of Sir John St. John, Knt., Chamberlain and executor to Margaret, Countess of Richmond and Derby, mother of King Henry 7th; who left a son, John, father of Nicholas St. John; whose elder son, Sir John, continued the family; and his second son, Oliver, was created, in 1620, Viscount Grandison of Limerick, in the Peerage of Ireland, with limitation failing his issue male to the issue male of his niece, Barbara (eldest daughter of his brother Sir John St. John), by Sir Edward Villiers her husband, elder brother of George Duke of Buckingham, the celebrated favourite of James 1st, and Charles 1st; and in 1626 was created a Baron in the Peerage of England, by the title of Baron Tregoze of Highworth, Co. Wilts. He *d.* without issue in 1630, when his English Barony became extinct; but his Irish Peerage devolved on his great-nephew William Villiers, and still exists in the Earl of Jersey, the male heir of the marriage of Barbara St. John and Sir Edward Villiers.

Sir John St. John, of Lydiard Tregoze, elder Brother of Oliver, 1st Viscount Grandison, and father of Barbara, on whose issue male that honour was entailed, was father also of Sir John St. John, created a Baronet in 1611. He had seven sons, three of whom, namely, William 2nd son, Edward 3rd son, and John 5th son, were killed in battle in the service of King Charles 1st; Oliver, the eldest son, *d.* in his father's lifetime, leaving one son, Sir John, who succeeded his grandfather, and *d.* under age and *unm.*; Nicholas, 4th son, *d.* before his nephew *unm.*; Henry, 7th son, *d.* without issue male, and Sir Walter, 6th son, succeeded his nephew in the Baronetage, and dying in 1708, was succeeded by his son

Sir Henry St. John, created in 1716 (after the attainder of Henry, Viscount Bolingbroke, his only son by his first wife Lady Mary, 2nd daughter and co-heir of Robert Rich, Earl of Warwick) Baron St. John, of Battersea, Co. Surrey, and Viscount St. John, with remainder to his issue male by Angelica, his second wife, daughter of George Pillesary, Treasurer of the Marines under Lewis 14th, King of France. His only surviving son by this marriage was John, 2nd Viscount St. John.

Henry, only son of the 1st Viscount St. John, by his 1st marriage, was the celebrated philosopher and statesman, who being then Secretary of State to Queen Anne, was created, in 1712, Baron St. John of Lydiard Tregoze, Co. Wilts, and Viscount Bolingbroke, Co. Lincoln, with remainder, failing his issue male, to Sir Henry St. John, his father, and his issue male. He was a zealous Tory, and one of the principal promoters of the Treaty of Utrecht; and, when the Whig Administration came into office on the accession of King George 1, was, while party feuds were at the highest, impeached, together with the Duke of Ormonde, the Earl of Oxford, and others, for his share in the negociations which terminated in the ratification of that treaty, and which were pronounced by Parliament to be treasonable. Having made a timely retreat into France, he eluded the extreme vengeance intended against him, but was attainted by Act of Parliament in 1715; he was however restored in blood in 1725, and *d.* without issue in 1751.

John, the only surviving son of Henry, 1st Viscount St. John, succeeded his father as 2nd Viscount St. John, and dying in 1749, was succeeded by his son, Frederick, 3rd Viscount St. John, who succeeded also to the title of Viscount Bolingbroke, on the death of his uncle Henry, 1st Viscount Bolingbroke. He will be found in the Peerage, together with his only surviving son, the Hon. Gen. Frederick St. John. He *d.* in 1787, and was succeeded by his eldest son, George-Richard, 3rd Viscount Bolingbroke and 4th Viscount St. John, father of Henry, the present Viscount, who succeeded him in 1824.

BOLTON, BARON. (Orde-Powlett.)

Peer of Great Britain.

John Orde, Esq., of East Orde and Morpeth, Co. Durham, father of Thomas, 1st Lord, is supposed to be descended from John Orde, living in that County in 1615, son of Gawen Orde of Fenwick, Co. Northumberland. The said John Orde, Esq., left three sons, viz.

1 William, whose male heirs are seated at Fenham Hall, Co. Northumberland.

2 Thomas, 1st Lord.

3 Sir John Orde, an Admiral, and Governor of Dominica, created a Baronet in 1790, and *d.* in 1824; leaving issue, Sir John-Powlett Orde, his successor, the present Baronet.

Thomas, the 2nd son, *m.* Jane-Mary, natural daughter of Charles, 5th Duke of Bolton, on whom her father entailed the principal part of his large estates, on failure of male heirs to his brother Harry, 6th Duke. The 6th Duke *d.* without issue male in 1794; in 1795 Mr. Orde assumed, by his Majesty's permission, the name and arms of Powlett, and in 1797, was created Baron Bolton of Bolton Castle, Co. York. He *d.* in 1807, and was succeeded by his eldest son William, the present and 2nd Lord.

BOSTON, BARON. (Irby.)

Peer of Great Britain.

His Lordship's grandfather, William, 1st Lord, was 5th in descent from Anthony Ireby, Esq., Master in Chancery in the reign of James 1st, of a family of great antiquity, and supposed to be descended from Sir William de Ireby, who was living in 1251. He was *b.* 8 March 1707, created Baron Boston of Boston, Co. Lincoln, in 1761, and *d.* 30 March 1775; having *m.* 26 Aug. 1746, Albinia, eldest daughter of Henry Selwyn, Esq., by whom, who *d.* 1 April 1769, he left issue:

1 Frederick, his successor, the 2nd Lord, father of George, the present and 3rd Lord, who succeeded him in 1825.

2 Augusta, late Lady Walsingham; *See* that title in *The Peerage Volume.*

3 Hon. William-Henry, *b.* 9 Sept. 1750, *d.* 17 May, 1830; having *m.* 25 Oct. 1781, Mary, youngest daughter and co-heir of Rowland Blackman, Esq.; by whom, who *d.* 30 July 1792, he had the issue stated in *The Peerage Volume.*

BOYNE, VISCOUNT. (Hamilton.)

Peer of Ireland.

Claude, 1st Lord Paisley, had besides other issue, James, his eldest son, 1st Earl of Abercorn, ancestor of the Marquis of Abercorn; and Sir Frederick Hamilton, his 4th son, father of Gustavus, the 1st Viscount, who distinguished himself in King William's army in the war of the Revolution in Ireland, particularly at the battle of the Boyne, where he commanded a regiment, one of six raised by himself. He attained the rank of Major General in the army, and was elevated to the Irish Peerage by King George 1st, in 1715, by the title of Baron Hamilton of Stackallan, Co. Meath, and was further created Viscount Boyne, in 1717. He *d.* in 1723, having had three sons, viz.

1 Frederick, who *d.* before his father, in 1715, leaving a son, Gustavus, 2nd Viscount, who succeeded his grandfather, and *d. unm.* in 1746.

2 Gustavus, who *d.* in 1735; he left two sons, Frederick and Richard, the 3rd and 4th Viscounts.

3 Henry, from whom there are still existing male descendants.

Richard, 4th Viscount, for whom, see *The Peerage Volume,* succeeded his brother in 1772, and *d.* in 1789; he was father of Gustavus, 5th Viscount, who was succeeded in 1816 by his eldest son, Gustavus, the present and 6th Viscount.

BRADFORD, EARL OF. (Bridgeman.)

Peer of the United Kingdom.

The Rev. Dr. John Bridgeman, descended in the 3rd generation from John Bridgeman, Esq., seated at Dean Magna, Co. Gloucester, about the beginning of the 16th century, was consecrated Bishop of Chester in 1619, which see he continued to hold till the suppression of Episcopacy under the Commonwealth, when the temporalities of his bishoprick were sequestered, and he retired to his son's house at Moreton in Shropshire, where he *d.* about 1658. Sir Orlando Bridgeman, his eldest son, was successively Lord Chief Baron of the Exchequer, Lord Chief Justice of the Common Pleas, and Lord Keeper of the Great Seal; he was created a Baronet in 1660, immediately after the Restoration, and *d.* in 1674.

His great-grandson, Sir Orlando Bridgeman, Bart., *d.* 25 July 1764, having *m.* 8 April 1719, Lady Anne Newport, 3rd daughter of Richard, 2nd Earl of Bradford, and eventually sole heir of her brother, Thomas, the 5th Earl, on whose death in 1762, his honors became extinct. Their son, Sir Henry, was *b.* 7 Sept. 1725, created in 1794 Baron Bradford, of Bradford, Co. Salop, and *d.* 5 June, 1800; having *m.* 12 June, 1755, Elizabeth, daughter and heir of John Simpson, Esq., who *d.* 6 March, 1806. Their eldest son, Henry-Simpson, *d.* in 1782, before his father's creation to the Peerage, at 25 years of age, *unm.*; Orlando, the eldest surviving son, succeeded his father, and was created in 1815, Viscount Newport and Earl of Bradford, both in the Co. of Salop; and *d.* in 1825, when he was succeeded by his eldest son, GEORGE-AUGUSTUS-FREDERICK-HENRY, the present and 2nd EARL, the remaining issue of the 1st BARON which lived to maturity, are stated in *The Peerage Volume.*

BRANDON, BARON. (CROSBIE.)

Peer of Ireland.

This Lordship's ancestors descended from the family of Crosbie, seated anciently at Great Crosbie in Lancashire, settled in Ireland in the time of Queen Elizabeth, when John Crosbie was consecrated Bishop of Ardfert and Aghadoe; he *d.* in 1621.

Sir Pierce Crosbie, the son of the Bishop's elder brother, having served as Colonel under Gustavus Adolphus, King of Sweden, in his German wars, was Gentleman of the Privy Chamber to King CHARLES 1st, and a Privy Counsellor; he was created a Baronet of Ireland; but dying without issue, in 1646, was succeeded in his estates by the sons of his uncle the Bishop of Ardfert. These were Sir Walter, created a Baronet of Scotland in 1630, whose male line is extinct, and Maurice, ancestor of

SIR MAURICE CROSBIE, created BARON BRANDON in the Peerage of Ireland in 1758; he *d.* in 1762, having *m.* Lady Anne Fitzmaurice, eldest daughter of Thomas Earl of Kerry, by whom, who *d.* 17 Dec. 1757, he had three sons, viz.: WILLIAM, his successor; John, who *d.* without issue in 1755; and Maurice, Dean of Limerick, for whom see *The Peerage Volume*, father of the present Peer.

WILLIAM, 2nd LORD, was created Viscount Crosbie of Ardfert in 1771, and Earl of Glandore in 1776. He *d.* 11 April 1781, having *m.* 1st, Lady Theodosia Bligh, 3rd daughter of John, 1st Earl of Darnley, who *d.* 20 May 1777, leaving an only son, John, 2nd EARL; and 2ndly, 1 Nov. 1777, Jane, daughter of Edward Vesey, Esq., and widow of John Ward, Esq., by whom, who *d.* Sept. 1787, he had no issue.

JOHN, 3rd LORD, and 2nd Earl of Glandore, son of William, 1st Earl, was *b.* 25 May 1753, and *d.* 23 Oct. 1815, having *m.* 26 Nov. 1777, the Hon. Diana Sackville, eldest daughter of George, 1st Viscount Sackville, sister to the Duke of Dorset, who was *b.* 8 July 1756, and *d.* 29 Aug. 1814. On his Lordship's death the titles of Earl and Viscount became extinct, and the Barony devolved on his cousin, the Rev. WILLIAM CROSBIE, only son of Maurice, Dean of Limerick, the present and 4th LORD.

BRAYBROOKE, BARON. (GRIFFIN.)

Peer of Great Britain.

His Lordship is head of the ancient family of Aldworth of Stanlakes, Oxon. His great-grandfather Richard Aldworth-Neville, Esq., who *d.* May 1738, assumed the name of Neville in consequence of his marriage with Catherine, who *d.* 1720, daughter and at length sole heir of Richard Neville, Esq. of Billingbear, Berks, great-grandson of Henry Nevill, next brother of Edward, 5th Lord Abergavenny of the family of Nevill, and heir of her brother Henry Neville-Grey, Esq., who *m.* Elizabeth, eldest co-heir of the Lords Griffin.

Anne, sister of the said Richard Neville, *m.* Richard Rainsford, Esq., and had an only daughter and heir, Anne, who *m.* James, 2nd Lord Griffin, by whom she had Edward, 3rd and last Lord Griffin, on whose death without issue, in 1742, the title became extinct, and two daughters, co-heirs to their brother; 1 Elizabeth, who *d.* without issue, having *m.* 1st, Henry Neville-Grey, Esq., above, and 2ndly, John, Earl of Portsmouth; 2 Anne, at length sole heir, who *m.* William Whitwell, Esq., by whom she was mother of JOHN-GRIFFIN WHITWELL, who took the surname of

Griffin, claimed and was allowed the Barony of Howard-de-Walden, and was created LORD BRAYBROOKE, Baron of Braybrooke, Co. Northampton, in 1788, with remainder, failing his issue male, to Richard Aldworth-Neville, Esq., afterwards 2nd Lord Braybrooke, and his issue male.

The first-mentioned Richard Aldworth-Neville, Esq., had by his said wife Catherine Neville, an only son Richard, who was *b.* 3 Sept. 1717, and *d.* 17 Feb. 1793, having *m.* Magdalen Calendrini, by whom, who *d.* in 1750, he was father of

RICHARD ALDWORTH-NEVILLE, Esq., appointed, as above, heir to the Barony of Braybrooke, to which he succeeded in 1797; see *The Peerage Volume*; and in 1798 assumed the name of Griffin only. He *d.* in 1825, and was succeeded by his eldest son, RICHARD, the present and 3rd LORD.

BREADALBANE, MARQUIS OF. (CAMPBELL.)

Peer of the United Kingdom, and of Scotland.

The Earl derives his pedigree from the House of Argyll. Duncan, 1st Lord Campbell, who *d.* in 1453, was father of, 1 Archibald, ancestor of the Duke of Argyll; 2 Sir Colin, who also had two sons: Sir Duncan, ancestor of the Earl of Breadalbane, and John, from whom the Countess of Loudoun descends. Fourth in descent from the above Sir Duncan was

Sir Robert Campbell of Glenorchy, who had two sons; 1 Sir John, father of the 1st Earl; 2 Colin, great-grandfather of the present Earl.

Sir JOHN CAMPBELL of Glenorchy, son of the above Sir John, was created Earl of Caithness, in the Peerage of Scotland, in 1677, and it being found that George Sinclair of Keiss, heir male of the last Earl, had a right to that dignity, Sir John Campbell was created, in 1681, EARL OF BREADALBANE and Holland, Viscount of Tay and Paintland, Lord Glenorchy, Benedaralock, Ormelie, and Weik, with the precedency of the former patent, remainder to whichever of his sons he may designate, and his heirs male, failing which to the heirs male of the body of the Earl, failing which to the nearest legitimate heirs male of the Earl, failing which to his nearest legitimate heirs whatever. Under this patent, Duncan, stiled Lord Ormelie, his eldest son, who survived him, was passed over; the Earl was succeeded, in 1716, by his second son, JOHN, 2nd EARL; and he, in 1752, by his son, JOHN, 3rd EARL, who *m.* Lady Amabel Grey, eldest daughter and co-heir of Henry, Duke of Kent, whose title of Marquess de Grey was entailed on Lady Jemima Campbell, the Earl's only daughter by Lady Amabel Grey. He *m.* a second wife, but died without surviving issue male in 1782, when the male heirs of the body of the 1st Earl became extinct; and the present EARL, the great-grandson and lineal heir male of Colin, 2nd son of Sir Robert Campbell of Glenorchy, succeeded as 4th EARL. He was created to the Peerage of the United Kingdom in 1806, by the title of Baron Breadalbane of Tamworth Castle, Co. Perth, and was farther advanced to the dignity of MARQUIS of BREADALBANE, and Earl of Ormelie in 1831.

BRIDPORT, BARON. (HOOD.)

Peer of Ireland.

Alexander Hood, of Mosterton in Dorsetshire, Esq. had issue:

1 Alexander, whose son, Samuel, was father of, 1 Arthur, Lieut. R.N. lost in a hurricane in the West Indies; 2 Alexander, Capt. R.N., who circumnavigated the globe with Capt. Cook, and was killed on board the Mars, 21 April 1798, in a successful action against the French ship l'Hercule. He left a son, now Sir Alexander Hood, Bart., who being in remainder to the title will be found in *The Peerage Volume.*

3 Sir Samuel Hood, Vice-Admiral and K.C.B., who, after a series of brilliant successes in the naval service, was created a Baronet in 1809, with remainder to his nephew Sir Alexander Hood, who succeeded him in 1814; he *m.* 6 Nov. 1804, the Hon. Mary-Frederica-Elizabeth Mackenzie, eldest daughter and co-heir of Francis Lord Seaforth, (whose title became extinct on his death in 1815.) Sir Samuel Hood *d.* without issue 24 Dec. 1814, and his widow re-married James Alexander Stewart, Esq., who in her right has assumed the additional name of Mackenzie. See *The Peerage Volume*, title Earl of Galloway.

2 The Rev. Samuel Hood, Vicar of Butleigh, Co. Somerset, and of Thorncombe, Co. Devon, who *m.* Mary, daughter of Richard Hoskins, Esq., and by her, who *d.* 10 Oct. 1766, had issue: 1 Samuel, 1st Viscount Hood, father of the present Viscount Hood, Lord Bridport's father; and 2 Sir Alexander Hood, celebrated in the naval history of his country, who rose to be Admiral of the Red, Vice-Admiral of Great Britain, and General of Marines; he was created in 1794, in consequence of his gallant conduct as second in command on the memorable 1st of June, Baron Bridport of Cricket St. Thomas, in the Peerage of Ireland, with remainder, failing his issue male, to Samuel Hood, 2nd son of his nephew Henry, (afterwards 2nd Viscount Hood,) eldest son of his brother Samuel, Baron (afterwards 1st Viscount) Hood, and his issue male; which failing to Alexander Hood, Capt. R.N. (father of Sir Alexander Hood, Bart.) and his issue male, remainder to Vice-Adm. Sir Samuel Hood, Bart., and his issue male. He was also created a Peer of Great Britain in 1796, by the title of Baron Bridport of Cricket St. Thomas, Co. Somerset, and Viscount Bridport in 1801. He *m.* 1st, in 1761, Mary, daughter of the Rev. Richard West, (by Maria Temple, sister of Richard, 1st Viscount Cobham,) she *d.* 12 Sept. 1786; and he *m.* 2ndly, 26 June 1788, Mary-Sophia, only daughter and heir of Thomas Bray, Esq., of Edmonton, Co. Middlesex, who *d.* 18 Feb. 1831, aged 85. The Viscount *d.* without issue 3 May 1814, when the Viscounty and English Barony became extinct, but the Irish Barony devolved on Samuel, the present Lord, 2nd son of Henry, now Viscount Hood.

BRISTOL, MARQUIS OF. (Hervey.)

Peer of the United Kingdom.

From Robert Fitz-Hervey, a Commander in the army of William the Conqueror, and younger son of Hervey Duke of Orleans, descended Harvey de Yuon, who *d.* in 1169; and whose descendants have all borne the name of Hervey; 17th in descent from him was John Hervey, created Baron Hervey of Ickworth, Co. Suffolk, in 1703; and Earl of Bristol in 1714. He *d.* in 1751, having *m.* Elizabeth, daughter and sole heir of Sir Thomas Felton, Bart., by Lady Elizabeth Howard, 2nd daughter and co-heir (with her sister, Lady Essex, wife of Edward Lord Griffin, whose issue failed in 1797) of James, 3rd Earl of Suffolk, and Baron Howard de Walden by writ; and by her had ten sons, of whom the five eldest, and Felton the ninth son, were married; the other four *d.* young or *unm.* The five eldest were,

1 John Lord Hervey, Lord Privy Seal and a Peer of Parliament by the title of Baron Hervey of Ickworth, who *d.* before his father in 1743, leaving four sons and four daughters; to the latter the title and precedency of an Earl's daughters were granted, by his Majesty's sign manual in 1753. The sons were, 1 George-William, 2nd Earl, who succeeded his grandfather and *d. unm.* in 1775; 2 Augustus-John, 3rd Earl, whose marriage with Miss Chudleigh, who afterwards, during his life, *m.* the Duke of Kingston, produced no issue, and he *d.* in 1779; 3 Frederick-Augustus, 4th Earl, and Bishop of Derry in Ireland, who, having succeeded his brother in 1779, became Baron Howard de Walden in 1797, by the extinction of the descendants of Lady Essex Howard, elder daughter and co-heir of the 3rd Earl of

Suffolk and Baron Howard de Walden, and *d.* in 1803; 4 The Hon. Gen. William Hervey, who *d. unm.* in 1815.

2 Thomas, Equerry to Caroline, Queen of GEORGE 2nd, who *d.* in 1775, leaving one son, William Thomas.

3 William, a Captain in the Navy, *d.* in 1776, leaving one daughter, Elizabeth, who *d. unm.*

4 Henry, who entered the army, but afterwards took orders, and became a Doctor in Divinity; he *m.* Catherine, eldest sister and heir of Sir Thomas Aston, of Aston, in Cheshire, Bart., and assumed the name of ASTON. He was father of Henry HERVEY-ASTON, Esq., father of Colonel Henry HERVEY-ASTON, who was unfortunately killed in a duel at Madras, 23 Dec. 1798: having *m.* 16 Sept. 1789, the Hon. Harriet Ingram-Shepherd, 4th daughter and co-heir of Charles, 9th and last Viscount Irvine, of Scotland, by whom, who *d.* 3 June, 1815, he has left one son, HENRY-CHARLES. See *The Peerage Volume.*

5 Charles, in holy orders, D.D., Prebendary of Ely, *d.* in 1783, having *m.* in 1743, Miss Martha-Maria Howard, of St. Edmondsbury, Co. Suffolk.

The 1st EARL's 9th son was Felton, also Equerry to Queen Caroline, and Groom of the Bedchamber to William Duke of Cumberland; he *d.* in 1775, leaving a son, Felton-Lionel, who *d.* in 1785; having *m.* Selina-Mary, daughter and heir of Sir John Elwell, Bart., by Selina, daughter of Peter Bathurst, Esq.; their issue, who now bear the names of BATHURST-HERVEY, will be found in *The Peerage Volume.*

FREDERICK-AUGUSTUS, the 4th EARL, *b.* 1 Aug. 1730, *d.* 8 July 1803; having *m.* Elizabeth, daughter of Sir Jermyn Danvers, Bart., who *d.* 16 Dec. 1800. JOHN-AUGUSTUS, Lord Hervey, the Earl's eldest son, *d.* before him 10 Jan. 1796; he *m.* Elizabeth, daughter of —— Drummond, Esq., by whom, who *d.* 4 Sept. 1818, he had an only daughter, Elizabeth-Catherine-Caroline, *b.* 1 Aug. 1780, *d.* 21 Jan. 1803; having *m.* 2 Aug. 1798, Charles-Rose Ellis, Esq., now Lord Seaford, by whom she had

Charles-Augustus Ellis, *b.* 5 July 1799, succeeded his great-grandfather, Frederick-Augustus, 4th Earl, as Baron Howard de Walden, 8 July 1803; and other issue. See *The Peerage Volume*, titles Lord Howard de Walden, and Lord Seaford.

The 4th EARL was succeeded in the Earldom by his eldest surviving son, FREDERICK-WILLIAM, created in 1826 MARQUIS of BRISTOL, and Earl Jermyn, of Horninghurst, Co. Suffolk.

BROUGHAM AND VAUX, BARON. (BROUGHAM.)

Peer of the United Kingdom.

The ancestors of this family were seated at Brougham, in Westmoreland, in the time of Edward the Confessor, and continued uninterruptedly Lords of the Manor of Brougham till the death of Thomas Brougham of Brougham, without issue, in 1607. From Peter Brougham, an uncle of this Thomas, descended a branch, of which the representative, John Brougham, was seated at Scales Hall, Co. Westmoreland, at Sir William Dugdale's Visitation in 1665; his grandson, John Brougham, regained possession of the ancient family demesne of Brougham, and was succeeded there by his nephew, Henry Brougham, who *d.* in 1783, leaving a son and heir,

Henry Brougham, Esq., of Brougham and Scales Hall, who *m.* Eleanor, only child of the Rev. James Syme, D.D., by Mary, sister of Robertson the historian; and *d.* 19 Feb. 1810, leaving issue,

1 HENRY, the celebrated Barrister and Member of Parliament, elevated to the dignity of Lord High Chancellor, and created BARON BROUGHAM and VAUX, of Brougham, Co. Westmoreland, in 1830, for whom see *The Peerage Volume.*

2 James, M.P. for Winchelsea.

3 Peter, *d. unm.*

4 John, *d.* Sept. 1829, having *m.* Margaret, daughter of James Rigg, Esq., by whom he has left issue.

5 William, a Barrister and Master in Chancery, M.P. for Southwark.

6 Mary.

BROWNLOW, EARL. (Cust.)

Peer of the United Kingdom.

Sir Peter Cust, of Pinchbeck, Co. Lincoln, who *d.* in 1338, was ancestor, in the 13th degree, of Sir Richard Cust, a zealous assertor of constitutional liberty under the government of King, Lords, and Commons. These principles becoming unsuited to the fanaticism of the period, he was excluded by Cromwell, when in the height of his illegal power, from the representation of the county of Lincoln in Parliament; he was, however, twice elected after the Restoration for the borough of Stamford. He was created a Baronet by King Charles 2nd in 1677, and *d.* in 1700. By his marriage with Beatrix, daughter and heir of Thomas Purey, of Kinton, Co. Lincoln, Esq., he had one son, Sir Purey Cust, who *d.* before him in 1699. At the period of the Revolution, Sir Purey raised at his own expense a troop of horse, and joining with other gentlemen to form a regiment, of which William, Earl of Devonshire, was chosen Colonel, they marched to receive King William on his landing in the west. This regiment was afterwards highly distinguished in the war in Ireland, and on his return from thence, Sir Purey was knighted by King William. He was twice *m.*, 1st, to Ursula, daughter and heir of Edward Woodcock, of Newtimber, Co. Sussex, Esq., and 2ndly, to Alice, daughter and co-heir of William Savile, of Newton, Co. Lincoln, Esq., by whom he had only one child that survived the period of infancy, Savile Cockayne Cust, Esq., who *d. unm.* in 1772. By his first marriage Sir Purey had a son,

Sir Richard Cust, who succeeded his grandfather in the Baronetcy. He *d.* in 1734, having *m.* Anne, daughter of Sir William Brownlow, Bart., and sole heir of her brother John, Viscount Tyrconnel, of the Kingdom of Ireland, by which marriage the mansion and estate of Belton, Co. Lincoln, was conveyed to his son and successor,

Sir John Cust; he was Clerk of the Household to Frederick Prince of Wales, and after his death was appointed to the same office in that of his son, afterwards King George 3rd. In 1761, and again in 1768, he was elected Speaker of the House of Commons; in which important office his unceasing attention to the extraordinary increase of the national business overpowered his constitution, and deprived his family of a valuable life, devoted to the service of his country. He *d.* 24 Jan. 1770, in the 52nd year of his age. He *m.* in 1743, Etheldred, daughter and co-heir of Thomas Payne, of Hough, Co. Lincoln, Esq., by whom, who *d.* 27 Jan. 1775, he had only one surviving son, viz.,

Sir Brownlow Cust, who was created, in 1776, Baron Brownlow of Belton, Co. Lincoln; for whom see *The Peerage Volume*. He *d.* in 1807, and was succeeded by his eldest son, John, 2nd Lord, who was created in 1815, Earl Brownlow, and Viscount Alford, and is the present Earl.

BUCCLEUCH AND QUEENSBERRY, DUKE OF. (Montagu-Douglas-Scott.)

Peer of Scotland and of England.

The ancestor of the House of Buccleuch was Richard le Scot of Murthockstoun, who was among the Barons that swore fealty to King Edward 1st, in 1296; from him Walter, 1st Lord Scott of Buccleuch, was 12th in descent. His son Walter,

2nd Lord, was created Earl of Buccleuch in 1619, and was father of Francis, 2nd Earl, who, dying without issue male in 1651, left two daughters, Ladies Mary and Anne, who successively inherited the title. Lady Mary m. Walter Scott, of Harden, and d. without issue in 1661, in the 13th year of her age.

Lady Anne, Countess of Buccleuch, was m. 20 April 1663, to James, Duke of Monmouth, natural son of King Charles 2nd, who, on the day of his marriage, was created, with Anne, his wife, Duke and Duchess of Buccleuch, and Earl and Countess of Dalkeith, with remainder to the heirs male of their bodies, remainder to the heirs whatever of their bodies succeeding to the estate and Earldom of Buccleuch. It is unnecessary here to follow the unfortunate Duke of Monmouth through his well-known history; his English titles were forfeited by his attainder, but the Scotch titles being conferred on him jointly with the Duchess, were inherited by her descendants: they had issue, 1 James, Earl of Dalkeith, who d. in 1705, during the lifetime of his mother, but was father of Francis, 2nd Duke; 2 Henry, created, in 1706, Earl of Deloraine in the Peerage of Scotland, which title became extinct in 1807, on the death of his grandson, Henry, 4th Earl.

Francis, 2nd Duke, succeeded his grandmother, in 1732, as Duke of Buccleuch, and was restored to the Earldom of Doncaster, and Barony of Tyndale. The Duke d. in 1751, having m. Lady Jean Douglas, eldest daughter of James, 2nd Duke of Queensberry, by whom he had a son, Francis, Earl of Dalkeith; who m. Lady Caroline Campbell, 2nd daughter and co-heir of John, 2nd Duke of Argyll and Greenwich, and d. in 1750, in the lifetime of his father, leaving, besides other issue, a posthumous daughter, Lady Frances, who is deceased, having m. Archibald, late Lord Douglas; and a son,

Henry, 3rd Duke, who succeeded his grandfather in 1751, and also succeeded, as heir of line, in right of his grandmother, on the death of William, 4th Duke of Queensberry, 23 Dec. 1810, to the titles of Duke of Queensberry, Marquis of Dumfriesshire, Earl of Drumlanrig and Sanquhar, Viscount of Nith, Torthorwald and Ross, and Lord Douglas of Kinmont, Middlebie, and Dornock; these titles having been surrendered by the 2nd Duke of Queensberry, who in 1706 obtained a new patent, granting them to him and his heirs of entail, male or female, succeeding to the property and estate of Queensberry, provided such heirs were descended from the body of William, 1st Earl of Queensberry. Henry, 3d Duke, m. (see *The Peerage Volume*) Lady Elizabeth Montagu, only daughter and heir of George, Duke of Montagu, 4th Earl of Cardigan, by Lady Mary, daughter, and at length sole heir, of John, Duke of Montagu; and by her was father of Charles-William, who succeeded him in 1812, 4th Duke of Buccleuch, and 6th of Queensberry; he d. in 1819, and was succeeded by his eldest son, Walter-Francis, the present Duke.

BUCHAN, EARL OF. (Erskine.)

Peer of Scotland.

James Stewart, 1st Earl of Buchan, in Scotland, under the grant of 1469, was 2nd son of Sir James Stewart, of Lorn, by Jane, Queen Dowager of Scotland, widow of King James I, and mother of King James II. His son Alexander, 2nd Earl, d. in 1505; and was succeeded by his son John, 3rd Earl, whose eldest son John, Master of Buchan, was killed in his father's lifetime, at the battle of Pinkie, in 1547; leaving an only daughter and heir, Christian, whose husband, Robert Douglas, brother of William, Earl of Morton, was in her right 4th Earl of Buchan; their son James, 5th Earl, who d. in 1601, left an only daughter, Mary, Countess of Buchan; she m.

James Erskine, 2nd son of John, 6th Earl of Marr; he became 6th Earl of Buchan, in right of his wife, on whose resignation he obtained a charter of the

Earldom, to him and MARY, COUNTESS of BUCHAN, his wife, remainder to the heirs male of their bodies, which failing to the nearest lawful heirs male and assignees whatever of the said 6th Earl. He was one of the Lords of the Bedchamber to King Charles I., and resided much in England, where he *d.* in 1640, having survived his Countess twelve years. JAMES, 7th EARL, their son, *d.* in 1664, and was succeeded by his only son, WILLIAM, 8th EARL, on whose death in 1695, the issue male of JAMES and MARY, 4th EARL and COUNTESS of BUCHAN, became extinct. The 8th EARL executed in 1677 a deed of entail, settling the reversion of the Earldom on HENRY ERSKINE, 3rd LORD CARDROSS, William, John, and Charles, his brothers, [sons of DAVID, 2nd LORD CARDROSS, only son of Henry, 3rd son of John, 6th Earl of Marr, and brother of JAMES, 6th Earl of BUCHAN,] and their heirs male respectively; remainder to William Erskine, 7th son of John, 6th Earl of Marr; [he died without issue;] Sir Charles Erskine, of Alva, Bart., and John, his elder brother, [the latter died without issue; sons of Sir Charles Erskine of Alva, 4th son of John, 6th Earl of Marr,] and their heirs male respectively, remainder to his nearest heirs male whatever, remainder to his heirs and assignees whatever.

JOHN, 6th Earl of Marr, father by his 1st *m.* of John, 7th Earl of Marr, ancestor of all the succeeding Earls, and by his 2nd, of James, 6th Earl of Buchan, and other sons mentioned above, had a grant of the Barony of CARDROSS to himself, his heirs and assigns, and assigned it accordingly after himself to Henry, his 3rd son, *mentioned above*, and his heirs male. This Henry, dying before his father, in 1628, DAVID, his only son, became 2nd LORD CARDROSS; he *d.* in 1671, leaving the four sons, HENRY, William, John, and Charles, mentioned in the entail; of whom HENRY succeeded him as 3rd LORD CARDROSS. William was ancestor of Sir John-Drummond Erskine, of Torrie, Bart., for whom, and others of his family, see *The Peerage Volume*; from John descends a numerous issue, described in *The Peerage Volume;* and Charles was killed in 1692, at the battle of Steinkirk, without issue. HENRY, 3rd LORD CARDROSS, his eldest son and successor, *d.* in 1693, leaving four sons, who all married and had issue; the male descendants of the three younger are extinct.

DAVID, the elder son, succeeded as 4th LORD CARDROSS, and became 9th EARL OF BUCHAN by the above entail. He strenuously opposed in his place in the Scotch Parliament that article of the union with England which gave to only sixteen Scotch Peers a right to sit and vote in future Parliaments as representatives of the whole number; and was afterwards a zealous supporter of the Hanoverian succession; he *d.* in 1745; having had seven sons, of whom only HENRY-DAVID, his successor, the 3rd son, 10th EARL OF BUCHAN, had issue. He was *b.* 17 April 1710, and *d.* 1 Dec. 1767; having *m.* 31 Jan. 1739, Agnes, 2nd daughter of Sir James Stewart of Goodtrees, Bart.; by whom, who *d.* 17 Dec. 1778, he had, besides three children, who *d.* young, the following issue:

1 Lady Anne-Agnes, *b.* 1739, *d. unm.* 5 Oct. 1804.

2 David, Lord Cardross, *b.* 12 June 1741, *d.* 4 Oct. 1747.

3 DAVID STEWART, 11th EARL, his successor, *b.* 12 June, 1742, and *d.* without issue, 19 April, 1829; having *m.* 15 Oct. 1771, Margaret, eldest daughter of William Fraser, Esq., grandson of the 11th Lord Saltoun; she was *b.* 24 April 1754, and *d.* 12 May 1819.

4 Hon. Henry, father of HENRY-DAVID, the present and 11th EARL, who succeeded his uncle; and of other issue, see *The Peerage Volume.*

5 Thomas, created a British Peer, by the title of Baron Erskine, of Restormel Castle; he *d.* in 1823, leaving issue. See *The Peerage Volume*, title Erskine.

6 Lady Isabella, *m.* 1st, 21 Jan. 1770, to William Leslie Hamilton, Esq., who *d.* 2 Oct. 1780; 2ndly, 23 April 1785, to John, 15th Earl of Glencairn, who *d.* without issue, 24 Sept. 1796, when his title became extinct. The Countess *d.* 17 May 1824.

For the descendants of Sir Charles Erskine, of Alva, Bart, the only substitute named, after the sons of David Lord Cardross, in the entail of 1677, from whom there exists surviving issue, see *The Peerage Volume*, titles Buchan, Rosslyn, and Marr.

BUCKINGHAM AND CHANDOS, DUKE OF. (Temple-Nugent-Brydges-Chandos-Grenville.)

Peer of the United Kingdom and of Ireland.

Sir Richard Temple, Bart., descended from Leofric, Earl of Mercia, who *d.* in 1057, and, through heiresses, from the Lords Cobham, [*by writ* 1313, *forfeited* 1619,] was distinguished for his military services in the wars of Queen Anne, under the Duke of Marlborough, and rose to be a Field Marshal, Lieutenant General of the Ordnance, and Colonel of the 10th regiment of Dragoons. He was also appointed Envoy Extraordinary, and Minister Plenipotentiary, from King George 1st to the Emperor Charles 6th, and was created Baron Cobham, of Kent, in 1714, and in 1718 Viscount and Baron Cobham, of Kent, with remainder, failing his issue, to his sisters, Hester, wife of Richard Grenville, Esq., and Christian, wife of Sir Thomas Lyttelton, Bart., and their issue male respectively. He *d.* without issue, 15 Sept. 1749, and was succeeded by his eldest sister, Hester, 2nd Viscountess, created in 1749 Countess Temple, with remainder to her issue male. She *d.* in 1752, having had, besides two sons who *d.* young, the following issue:

1 Richard, her successor, 2nd Earl Temple, K. G.; he was Keeper of the Privy Seal at the death of King George 2nd, and made a conspicuous figure as leader of the Opposition to Lord Bute's Administration, in the early part of the reign of George 3rd; he *d.* without issue 11 Sept. 1779.

2 The Right Hon. George Grenville, for whom see *The Peerage Volume;* he became Prime Minister in 1763, and *d.* in 1770; he was father of George, 3rd Earl, who having *m.* Mary-Elizabeth, daughter and heir of Robert, Earl Nugent, assumed by Royal Sign Manual, after succeeding his uncle in the Earldom, the additional surnames of Nugent and Temple. His father-in-law, Robert Nugent, who had been created, in 1766, Baron Nugent and Viscount Clare, which titles became extinct on his death in 1788, was also created, in 1776, Earl Nugent, in the Peerage of Ireland, with remainder to his said son-in-law, George Grenville, afterwards Earl Temple, who succeeded to the Irish Earldom on his death, 13 Oct. 1788; and was created Marquis of Buckingham in 1784. His Lady was created, in 1800, Baroness Nugent in Ireland, with remainder to her second son, Lord George Grenville-Nugent-Temple, who succeeded her in that title 16 March, 1812. The Marquis *d.* 11 Feb. 1813, and was succeeded by his eldest son Richard, the present Duke.

3 The Right Hon. James Grenville, who at various times enjoyed several offices under government, was *b.* 12 Feb. 1715, and *d.* 14 Sept. 1783, having *m.* 8 April 1740, Mary, daughter of James Smyth, Esq., by whom, who *d.* 14 Dec. 1757, he had two sons, viz. 1 James, *b.* 6 July, 1742, created Baron Glastonbury, 1767, and *d. unm.* 26 April 1825, when the title became extinct. 2 General Richard Grenville, who *d. unm.* 22 April 1823.

4 The Hon. Henry Grenville, Governor of Barbadoes, and afterwards Ambassador to the Porte, *b.* 1717, *d.* 22 April, 1784; having *m.* 11 Oct. 1757, Margaret-Eleonora, daughter of John Banks, Esq., by whom, who *d.* 19 June, 1793, he left an only daughter, Louisa, *b.* 10 Aug. 1758, *m.* Charles, 3rd Earl Stanhope, and *d.* 7 March, 1829.

5 Thomas, a Captain in the Royal Navy, was killed in command of the Defiance of 60 guns, in Vice Admiral Anson's victory over the French fleet off Cape Finisterre, 3rd May 1747.

6 Lady Hester, *b.* 1720, *m.* the Right Hon. William Pitt, afterwards Earl of Chatham, and was herself created Baroness Chatham in 1761; she was mother of the present Earl of Chatham, and of the late illustrious William Pitt.

Richard, the present Duke, who, in 1813, succeeded his father as 2nd Marquis, is 20th in paternal descent from Robert Grenville, living in the reign of Richard 1st, who was descended from Rollo, the 1st Duke of Normandy; having *m.* Lady Anna-Elizabeth Brydges, daughter and heir of James, 3rd and last Duke of Chandos, his Grace has assumed the additional surnames of Brydges and Chandos; he was created in 1822 Duke of Buckingham and Chandos, Marquis of Chandos, and Earl Temple of Stowe, with remainder of the said Earldom, failing the heirs male under the patent of 1749, to Anne-Eliza, his Grace's granddaughter, and the heirs male of her body.

Lord Lyttelton, and the other male descendants of William-Henry, 1st Baron Lyttelton and Westcote, see that title in *The Peerage Volume*, are in remainder to the titles of Viscount and Baron Cobham, being descended from Christian Lady Lyttelton.

BUCKINGHAMSHIRE, EARL OF. (Hobart.)

Peer of Great Britain.

Certain lands in the County of Norfolk are recorded to have passed through six generations of this family to Sir James Hobart, Attorney-General to King Henry VII.; he *d.* in 1507. Sir Henry Hobart, his great-grandson, Lord Chief Justice of the Common Pleas, was created a Baronet in 1611, and *d.* in 1625. He purchased the manor of Blickling in Norfolk, and built there a stately house; he left, besides other issue, two sons, Sir John, his successor, who *d.* without issue male, and Sir Miles Hobart, Knt., father of Sir John, who succeeded his uncle in the Baronetcy. Sir Henry, his son, succeeded him; being Member for Norwich in the Convention Parliament; he voted for the vacancy of the throne, and afterwards attended King William as Gentleman of the Horse in the battle of the Boyne; he was killed in a duel in 1699, leaving a son,

Sir John, created to the Peerage in 1728, by the title of Lord Hobart, Baron Hobart of Blickling, Co. Norfolk; and in 1746 advanced to the dignity of Earl of Buckinghamshire. He *d.* in 1756, having by two marriages had five sons, two of whom *d.* young; the other three were, 1 John, 2nd Earl, *b.* 17 Aug. 1723, succeeded 22 Sept. 1756, *d.* 3 Aug. 1793; having *m.* 1st, 15 July 1761, Mary-Anne, daughter and co-heir of Sir Thomas Drury, she *d.* 30 Dec. 1769; and 2ndly, 24 Sept. 1770, Caroline, daughter of William Conolly, Esq., who *d.* 26 Jan. 1817. His Lordship had three sons by his 2nd marriage, who all *d.* in their infancy; but he left daughters by both marriages, for whom see *The Peerage Volume*; he was succeeded by his next brother, 2 George, 3rd Earl, succeeded 3 Aug. 1793, *d.* 14 Nov. 1804; having *m.* 22 May 1757, Albinia, eldest daughter of Lord Vere Bertie, 3rd son of Robert, 1st Duke of Ancaster and Kesteven, by whom, who was *b.* 1738, and *d.* 11 March 1816, he was father of Robert, 4th Earl, his successor, who *d.* without issue male in 1816, of the Hon. George-Vere Hobart, father of George-Robert, the present and 5th Earl, and of other issue, for whom see *The Peerage Volume.* 3 Hon. Henry, who *d.* 10 May 1799; having *m.* 22 July 1761, Anne-Margaret, daughter of John Bristow, Esq., by whom, who *d.* 12 July 1788, he had issue, see *The Peerage Volume.*

BURLINGTON, EARL OF. (Cavendish.)

Peer of the United Kingdom.

Lord George-Augustus-Henry Cavendish, 2nd son of the marriage of William, 4th Duke of Devonshire, with Lady Charlotte Boyle, daughter and heir of Richard, 3rd Earl of Burlington in the Peerage of England (which title became extinct on his death in 1753), and 4th Earl of Cork, in the Peerage of Ireland; was created, in 1831, Earl of Burlington, and Baron Cavendish of Keighley, Co. York. His Lordship is uncle and presumptive heir of William Spencer, present Duke of Devonshire, is married, and has a numerous issue. See *The Peerage Volume.*

BUTE, MARQUIS OF. (Crichton-Stuart.)

Peer of Great Britain and of Scotland.

Seventh in descent from Sir John Stewart, Sheriff of Bute, a natural son of King Robert II. of Scotland, was Sir James Stuart, created a Baronet by King Charles I. in 1627. His active and efficient loyalty throughout the troubles of that unfortunate monarch, brought him into great difficulties and dangers; he, however, lived to witness the happy restoration of King Charles II., and, dying in London in 1662, was buried in Westminster Abbey. His son, Sir Dugald, was father of Sir James, created a Peer of Scotland in 1703, by the titles of Earl of Bute, Viscount of Kingarth, Lord Mountstuart, Cumra, and Inchmarnock. He *m.* Agnes, eldest daughter and heir of Sir George Mackenzie of Rosehaugh, and dying in 1710, was succeeded by his son James, 2nd Earl; to whom, in 1723, succeeded his eldest son

John, 3rd Earl, K.G. His Lordship, shortly before the death of Frederick Prince of Wales, was appointed one of the Lords of the Bedchamber to His Royal Highness; and having continued in the household of the Princess Dowager and the young Prince her son, acquired in a high degree the confidence of the latter, who soon after his accession placed Lord Bute at the head of the administration. This appointment, however, not proving popular, his Lordship, after concluding, in 1763, the treaty which terminated the seven years' war, retired from office, and never afterwards took any prominent part in politics. He was *b.* 25 May 1713, succeeded 28 Jan. 1723, and *d.* 10 March 1792; having *m.* 24 Aug. 1736, Mary, only daughter of Edward Wortley-Montagu, Esq. [eldest son of the Hon. Sidney Wortley-Montagu, 2nd son of Edward, 1st Earl of Sandwich,] which Lady was *b.* Feb. 1718, created to the British Peerage in 1761, by the title of Baroness Mountstuart, of Wortley, Co. York, with remainder to her issue male by the Earl of Bute; she *d.* 6 Nov. 1794, and was succeeded in her Barony by her eldest son. The Earl and Countess had issue,

1 Lady Mary, who *d.* 5 April 1824; having *m.* 7 Sept. 1761, James, Earl of Lonsdale, who *d.* 24 May 1802.

2 Lady Jane, *b.* April 1742, *d.* 28 Feb. 1828; having *m.* 1 Feb. 1768, George, Earl Macartney, who *d.* 31 March 1806, when his title became extinct.

3 John, his successor, the 1st Marquis.

4 Lady Anne, *b.* Aug. 1746, is deceased; having *m.* 2 July 1764, Hugh, Earl Percy, afterwards 2nd Duke of Northumberland, which marriage was dissolved in 1779.

5 Hon James Stuart-Wortley Mackenzie, who *d.* in 1818; his son James-Archibald is now Baron Wharncliffe; see that title in this volume.

6 Lady Augusta, *b.* Feb. 1749, *d.* 5 Feb. 1778; having *m.* 26 July 1773, Capt. Andrew Corbett.

7 Lady Caroline, *b.* May 1750, *d.* 20 Jan. 1813, late Countess of Portarlington; see that title in *The Peerage Volume.*

8 Hon. Frederick-Stuart, *b.* Sept. 1751, *d. unm.* 17 May 1802.

9 Hon. Sir Charles, K.B., who *d.* in 1801; his son Sir Charles is now Baron Stuart de Rothsay; see that title in this volume.

10 Hon. and Most-Rev. William, Lord Archbishop of Armagh, *b.* March 1755, *d.* 6 May 1822; having *m.* 3 May 1796, Sophia, daughter of Thomas Penn, Esq., who survives him; for whom and her issue, see *The Peerage Volume.*

11 Lady Louisa, living, see *The Peerage Volume.*

John, 4th Earl, who succeeded his father in 1792, had previously been created a British Peer in 1776, by the title of Baron Cardiff, of Cardiff Castle, Co. Glamorgan; in 1794 he succeeded to his mother's Barony of Mountstuart, and in 1796 was created Viscount Mountjoy, in the Isle of Wight; Earl of Windsor, Co. Berks; and MARQUIS OF BUTE, Co. Bute. He *d.* in 1814; having survived his eldest son, John, Lord Mountstuart. The latter *m.* Lady Elizabeth-Penelope Crichton, only daughter and heir of PATRICK, 5th EARL OF DUMFRIES, in the Peerage of Scotland, by whom he left two sons, see *The Peerage Volume*, who have both assumed the additional surname of Crichton; JOHN, the eldest son, succeeded his maternal grandfather as 6th EARL OF DUMFRIES in 1803; and his paternal grandfather as 2nd MARQUIS OF BUTE in 1814; and is the present MARQUIS.

WILLIAM, 7th LORD CRICHTON, in the Peerage of Scotland, succeeded his cousin ROBERT, 6th LORD, as heir male; he was created Viscount of Ayr, in 1622, and in 1633 EARL OF DUMFRIES, and Lord Crichton of Sanquhar, and Kumnock, all with remainder to his heirs male; WILLIAM, 2nd EARL, his son, had one son, Charles, Lord Crichton, who *d.* before him, leaving a son, WILLIAM, afterwards 3rd EARL; and four daughters, Penelope, Margaret, Mary, and Elizabeth. WILLIAM, 2nd EARL, surrendered all his honours, and obtained a new patent for them, with precedency according to the former patents, and with limitation to each of the children of Charles Lord Crichton, and the heirs of their bodies respectively, failing which, to the nearest heirs whatsoever of the said Charles Lord Crichton. The 2nd EARL *d.* in 1691; and WILLIAM, 3rd EARL, *d. unm.* in 1694; when he was succeeded by his eldest sister PENELOPE. She *m.* the Hon. William Dalrymple, 2nd son of John, 1st Earl of Stair, by whom she had WILLIAM, 5th EARL, and also Earl of Stair, who *d.* without surviving issue in 1768; and a daughter, Lady Elizabeth; she *m.* John Macdowall, Esq., and had issue,

PATRICK, who succeeded his uncle as 6th EARL, and assumed the name of Crichton; he was *b.* 15 Oct. 1726, and *d.* 7 April, 1803; having *m.* 12 Sept. 1771, Margaret, daughter of Ronald Crauford of Restalrig, Co. Edinburgh; by whom, who *d.* 5 May 1799, he had only one surviving child, Lady Elizabeth-Penelope, *m.* to John, Viscount Mountstuart, eldest son of JOHN, 1st Marquis of BUTE, by whom she was mother of JOHN, the present and 7th EARL, and 2nd MARQUIS of BUTE.

BYRON, BARON. (BYRON.)

Peer of England.

The first of his Lordship's immediate ancestors on record is Ralph de Buron, who held considerable estates in the Counties of Nottingham and Derby, in the reign of William the Conqueror; from this Ralph, descended in the 17th generation, JOHN, 1st LORD, who was created, in 1643, Baron Byron, of Rochdale, Co. Lancaster, with remainder, failing his issue male, to his brothers, Richard, William, Robert, Gilbert, and Philip, and their issue male. The first LORD *d.* without issue, in 1652, and was succeeded by his next brother,

RICHARD, 2nd LORD, who *d.* in 1679; and was succeeded by his son, WILLIAM, 3rd LORD; to whom succeeded, in 1695, his son WILLIAM, 4th LORD, he *d.* in 1736, leaving two sons,

1 WILLIAM, his successor, 5th LORD, *b.* 5 Nov. 1722, succeeded 8 Aug. 1736, *d.* 19 May, 1798, without surviving issue male; having *m.* 18 March 1747, Elizabeth, daughter and heir of Charles Shaw, Esq., by whom, who *d.* 5 July 1788, he had issue a son, William, who *d.* an infant in May 1749; another son, William, *b.* 27 October, 1749, and *d.* 22 June 1776; having *m.* Juliana-Elizabeth, 2nd daughter of the Hon. Admiral John Byron, his uncle, who *d.* 15 March, 1788, (having *m.* 2ndly, Sir Robert Wilmot, Bart.) *See* below. They had a son, William, who survived his

father, but *d.* in 1794, in the lifetime of his grandfather. The 5th LORD had also a daughter, Caroline, who is still living. See *The Peerage Volume.*

2 Hon. Admiral John Byron, *b.* 8 Nov. 1723, and *d.* 10 April 1786, having *m.* Aug. 1748, Sophia, daughter of John Trevannion, of Cachays, Co. Cornwall, Esq.; by whom he had two sons and three daughters:

1 John, *b.* 7 Feb. 1756, *d.* 2 Aug. 1791; having *m.* 1st, 1 June 1779, Lady Amelia D'Arcy, Baroness Conyers, daughter and heir of Robert, 4th Earl of Holdernesse, divorced 31 May 1779, from Francis, 5th Duke of Leeds; by whom, who *d.* 26 Jan. 1784, he had one daughter, Hon. Augusta-Mary, now living, the wife of George Leigh, Esq.; see *The Peerage Volume.* He *m.* 2ndly, 12 May 1785, Miss Catherine Gordon, by whom, who *d.* 6 Aug. 1811, he had one son, GEORGE-GORDON, 6th LORD, the celebrated Poet; who succeeded to the Peerage on the death of his great uncle, the 5th Lord, in 1798; and *d.* in Greece, without issue male, in 1824; his widow and only daughter will be found in *The Peerage Volume.*

2 Captain George-Anson Byron, R.N., for whom see *The Peerage Volume*, father of GEORGE-ANSON, present and 7th LORD, who succeeded his cousin in 1824.

3 Frances, *d.* 19 Oct. 1823; having *m.* General Charles Leigh, *d.* 7 Aug. 1815.

4 Juliana-Elizabeth, *d.* 15 March 1788; having *m.* 1st, Hon. William Byron, son of WILLIAM, 5th LORD—*See* above; and 2ndly, 23 Sept, 1783, the present Sir Robert Wilmot, Bart.

5 Charlotte-Augusta, *d.* 10 March 1824; having *m.* Vice-Admiral Christopher Parker, who *d.* 26 May 1804, [eldest son of the late Sir Peter Parker, Bart.]

3 Hon. and Rev. Richard, *b.* 28 Oct. 1724, *d.* 5 Nov. 1811; having *m.* 1768, Mary, daughter of Richard Farmer, Esq.; she was *b.* 1749, and *d.* 9 April 1827: for their issue see *The Peerage Volume.*

4 Hon. George, *b.* 22 April 1730, *d.* 6 May 1789; having *m.* Frances, daughter and co-heir of Elton Levett, Esq., by whom, who *d.* 13 June 1822, he had several children, all deceased, except one daughter, Isabella, for whom see *The Peerage Volume.*

CADOGAN, EARL. (CADOGAN.)

Peer of Great Britain.

The 1st of this family to whom the pedigree is traced is Thomas Cadogan, said to be lineally descended from Kehdlyn, Prince of Powis; 4th in descent from this Thomas, was

Henry Cadogan, Esq., who had two sons:

1 WILLIAM, who having served with great distinction as Lieutenant-General in the wars of Queen Anne, under the Duke of Marlborough, was afterwards Ambassador from her Majesty and King GEORGE I. to the Hague, and was finally appointed Commander-in-Chief of his Majesty's forces, Master-General of the Ordnance, and Colonel of the 1st Regiment of Foot-Guards. He was created Baron Cadogan, of Reading, Co. Berks, 1716; and BARON CADOGAN, of Oakley, Co. Bucks, Viscount Caversham, Co. Oxford, and Earl Cadogan, 1718; with remainder of the Barony, failing his issue male, to Charles Cadogan, his brother; he *d.* without male issue 1726, when the titles of Earl and Viscount, and the Barony of Cadogan, of Reading, became extinct.

2 CHARLES, 2nd LORD, succeeded his brother, as Baron Cadogan of Oakley. He also served in the wars under the Duke of Marlborough, and rose to the rank of General; he *d.* in 1776, and was succeeded by his only son, CHARLES-SLOANE, 3rd LORD, created in 1800 Viscount Chelsea, Co. Middlesex, and Earl Cadogan; he *d.* in 1807, and was succeeded by his eldest son, CHARLES-HENRY-SLOANE, the present and 3rd EARL; whose next surviving brother, the Hon. Captain George Cadogan, R.N., was created, in 1831, Baron Oakley, of Caversham, Co. Oxford.

CAITHNESS, EARL OF. (SINCLAIR.)

Peer of Scotland.

The family of St. Clair came into England with William the Conqueror; and this branch, with that of Herdmanstoun, paternal ancestors of Lord Sinclair, settled in Scotland in the 12th century.

William de St. Clair obtained the Manor of Rosslyn in the reign of King David I.; 7th in descent from him was Sir William, who *m.* Isabel, daughter and co-heir of Malise, Earl of Strathern, Caithness, and Orkney; their son Henry obtained the Earldom of Orkney, and was grandfather of WILLIAM, 3rd EARL, who surrendered his Earldom to the King, and had a grant, in 1455, of that of Caithness, which he resigned to WILLIAM, his son by a second marriage, (passing over another William, the only son of his first marriage, and from whom Lord Sinclair is maternally descended.

The above WILLIAM, 2nd EARL of CAITHNESS, in the Peerage of Scotland, who obtained a confirmation of the Earldom, to him and his heirs whatsoever, was killed in the battle of Flodden in 1513, and was succeeded by his eldest son, JOHN, 3rd EARL. He was killed in 1529, in an unsuccessful attempt to obtain possession of the Orkney Islands, to which he alleged a claim, and was succeeded by his only-surviving son,

GEORGE, 4th EARL; he *d.* in 1582, having had three sons, of whom two left issue, viz.: 1 John, Master of Caithness, ancestor of the succeeding Earls; and 2 George Sinclair, of Mey; from whom are descended many collateral branches of this noble family, and among them, SIR JOHN SINCLAIR, of Dunbeath, Bart. Sir John, 2nd son of this George Sinclair, of Mey, obtained the title of Baronet, which, after his decease without issue, devolved on the male heirs of his eldest brother, Sir William Sinclair, of Mey; from whom, through seven generations of Baronets, in direct male succession, descended SIR JAMES SINCLAIR, of Mey, who became 12th EARL of CAITHNESS in 1789.

John, Master of Caithness, eldest son of the 4th Earl, *d.* before his father in 1577, leaving three sons, viz.,

1 GEORGE, 5th EARL, who succeeded his grandfather.

2 Sir James Sinclair, of Murchill, father of another Sir James, whose son JOHN succeeded as 8th EARL of CAITHNESS in 1698.

3 Sir John Sinclair, of Greenland: he had five sons, of whom three elder and the youngest *d.* without issue; but James Sinclair, of Ratter, his 4th son, was great-grandfather of WILLIAM, who succeeded in 1765, as 10th Earl of Caithness, and established his claim to the Earldom before the House of Peers in 1772.

GEORGE, 5th EARL, *d.* in 1643; having survived his eldest son, William Lord Berriedale, and John, Master of Berriedale, the only son of the latter; the Master dying before his father in 1639, left also an only son, GEORGE, 6th EARL, he succeeded his great-grandfather, and *d.* without issue in 1676; having disposed of his estates, in consideration of his debts, to his principal creditor, Sir John Campbell, of Glenorchy, who in 1677 was created Earl of Caithness. But GEORGE, 5th EARL, had also a second son, Francis Sinclair, of Keiss, whose son, GEORGE, 7th EARL, succeeded in establishing his claim to the Earldom of Caithness, and Sir John Campbell, of Glenorchy, was in consequence created Earl of Breadalbane. The 7th EARL *d. unm.* in 1698; when the title devolved on the heir male,

JOHN, 8th EARL, grandson, *as shewn above*, of Sir James Sinclair, of Murchill, 2nd son of John, Master of Caithness, eldest son of the 4th EARL. He *d.* in 1705, and was succeeded by his son, ALEXANDER, 9th EARL, who *d.* without issue male in

1765, when the male line of Sir James Sinclair, of Murchill, became extinct, and the title devolved on the heir male of his younger brother, Sir John Sinclair, of Greenland.

William, 10th Earl, fourth in descent from the said Sir John, as *above* described, *d.* in 1779, and was succeeded by his son, John, 11th Earl, who *d. unm.* in 1789, when the male issue of John, Master of Caithness, failed.

The line of George Sinclair, of Mey, 2nd son of the 4th Earl, was next in succession, and his descendant, Sir James Sinclair, of Mey, made good his claim to the title; he *d.* in 1823, and was succeeded by his eldest son, Alexander, the present and 13th Earl.

CALEDON, EARL OF. (Alexander.)

Peer of Ireland.

His Lordship is of the same family with the Scotch Earl of Stirling, descended from the ancient Clan Macdonald. The name of Alexander was assumed from the Christian name of its founder, Alexander Macdonald, of Menstrie. This branch, on removing into Ireland, adopted into the family shield, the Canton, charged with the Harp of Ireland.

Nathaniel Alexander, Esq., his Lordship's grandfather, had three sons,

1 William, whose youngest son Robert has left issue male.

2 Robert, who had issue; 1 Nathaniel, D.D., present Bishop of Meath, *m.* to Miss Jackson; 2 Henry, *d.* 1818, having *m.* Miss Rivers; 3 Major-General William, deceased; 4 James, M.P., *m.* and has issue; 5 Josias-Dupré, East India Director, *m.* and has issue.

3 James, 1st Earl, father of the present Earl.

4 Eliza, wife of the late Josias Dupré, Esq.

James Alexander, Esq., the 3rd son, was created Baron Caledon, of Caledon, Co. Tyrone, in 1790, Viscount Caledon in 1797, and Earl of Caledon in 1800, all in the Peerage of Ireland; he was father of Dupre, the present and 2nd Earl, who succeeded him in 1802.

CALTHORPE, BARON. (Gough-Calthorpe.)

Peer of Great Britain.

The paternal name of this family is Gough. His Lordship's grandfather, Sir Henry Gough, 9th in descent from John Gough, living in Wales at the end of the 14th century, was created a Baronet in 1728; he *m.* Barbara, only daughter of Reynolds Calthorpe, Esq., and heir to her brother, Sir Henry Calthorpe, K.B., on whose death, Henry, her son, by Sir Henry Gough, assumed the name of Calthorpe; he was created, in 1796, Baron Calthorpe, of Calthorpe, Co. Norfolk; he had a numerous issue, of whom six *d.* young or *unm.*, besides Charles, 2nd Lord, who succeeded him in 1798, and *d. unm.* in 1807, having just attained his majority; and George, the present and 3rd Lord, who succeeded his brother. Two other sons and a daughter are now living, for whom see *The Peerage Volume.*

CAMDEN, MARQUIS. (Pratt.)

Peer of the United Kingdom.

The ancestors of the Marquis were anciently seated in Devonshire, and were of Careswell in that County, in the reign of Elizabeth. Sir Richard Pratt, who lost his estates in the Civil Wars, was grandfather of the Right Honourable Sir John Pratt, Chief Justice of the Kings Bench, father of the 1st Earl. Sir John *d.* in 1724, leaving a numerous issue by two marriages; of nine sons, seven *d.* without issue, the other two were, 1 John Pratt, of the Wilderness in Kent, Esq.; his heir, who *d.* in 1770, leaving a son John, who *d.* in 1797, and bequeathed all his property to the present Marquis. 2 Charles, 8th son, who having passed through the usual gradations of law offices, was, when Chief Justice of the King's Bench in 1765, created Baron Camden of Camden Place, Co. Kent, and was soon afterwards appointed Lord High Chancellor, but resigned the seals in 1770. In 1786, he was created Viscount Bayham, of Bayham Abbey, Co. Sussex, and Earl Camden, and *d.* in 1794. John-Jeffreys, his successor, the present Peer, was advanced in 1812 to the dignity of Marquis Camden, and at the same time created Earl of Brecknock in Wales.

CAMPERDOWN, EARL OF. (Duncan.)

Peer of the United Kingdom.

William Duncan, of a very ancient family seated at Lundie, Co. Angus, was great-grandfather of Alexander, who, by marriage with Helen Haldane, heiress of Gleneagles, was father of the distinguished Admiral, Adam Duncan, created, in 1797, in consequence of his splendid victory over the Dutch fleet off Camperdown, Viscount Duncan of Camperdown, and Baron Duncan of Lundie, Co. Forfar, in the British Peerage. He *d.* in 1804, and was succeeded by his eldest son, Robert Dundas, present and 2nd Viscount, advanced in 1831 to the dignity of Earl of Camperdown, of Lundie, Co. Forfar, and Gleneagles, Co. Perth.

CANNING, VISCOUNTESS. (Canning.)

Peeress of the United Kingdom.

Her Ladyship's father, Major-General John Scot, of Balcomie, the lineal descendant of a younger branch of the family of Scott, of Buccleuch, left, by his marriage with Margaret, 3rd daughter of the Right Honourable Robert Dundas, eldest brother of the 1st Viscount Melville, three daughters his co-heirs; 1 Henrietta, Duchess of Portland; 2 Lucy, who *d.* 3 Aug. 1798, wife of Francis, Dord Doune, now Earl of Moray; 3 Joan, the present Viscountess.

The late Right Hon. George Canning was son of George Canning, Esq., who *d.* 11 April 1771, eldest son of Stratford Canning, Esq., of Garvagh, and elder brother of Paul Canning, Esq., of Garvagh, father of the present Lord Garvagh. On his death, in consequence of the fatigues he incurred in administering the affairs of his high office of Prime Minister to George IV., his widow was created, in 1828, Viscountess Canning of Kilbraham, Co. Kilkenny, in the Peerage of the United Kingdom, with remainder to the heirs male of her body by her late husband, the Right Hon. George Canning, deceased.

CARBERY, BARON. (EVANS-FREKE.)

Peer of Ireland.

This noble family were originally seated in Carmathenshire, and are supposed to be descended from one of the ancient Princes of Wales. In the reign of James I. John Evans removed into Ireland, and was living in Limerick in 1628. His son, Col. George Evans, M.P. for Limerick, *m.* Anne, daughter of Thomas Bowerman, Esq., and was father of the Right Hon. George Evans, who served many years in Parliament, *m.* in 1679, Mary, daughter of John Eyre, Esq., and sister of John, 1st Lord Eyre, and *d.* at an advanced age, having refused the honour of the Peerage. He left three sons,

1 GEORGE, 1st LORD.

2 Eyre, father of Hampden-Evans, Esq., deceased, who being in remainder to the title, his widow and issue will be found in *The Peerage Volume.*

3 Thomas, *d.* 15 Sept. 1753; having *m.* Mary, daughter of Thomas Waller, Esq., grandson of the republican General Sir Hardress Waller; she *d.* in 1762. They had two sons, viz. 1 Eyre Evans, Esq. of Ashhill, who *d.* 5 April 1773, having *m.* Sept. 1756, Mary, only daughter and heir of Thomas Williams, Esq.; she *d.* 29 Nov. 1825, leaving a son, Eyre Evans, Esq. of Ashhill, Co. Limerick, and Miltown Castle, Co. Cork, and three daughters, for all of whom see *The Peerage Volume.* 2 Rev. Thomas-Waller Evans, who *d.* in 1796; having *m.* Catherine, only daughter of James Holdernesse D'Arcy, Esq., and heir to her brother, Colonel James D'Arcy; she *d.* in 1805, leaving Thomas D'Arcy Evans, Esq., of Bushy Island, Co. Limerick, and other issue, who are all described in *The Peerage Volume*, being in remainder to the title.

GEORGE, eldest son of the Right Hon. George Evans, was created, in 1715, BARON CARBERY, Co. Cork, in the Peerage of Ireland, with remainder, failing his issue male, to the issue male of his father; he *d.* in 1749, leaving two sons:

1 GEORGE, 2nd LORD, who *d.* in 1759, leaving also two sons, viz.:

1 GEORGE, 3rd LORD, his successor, who *d.* in 1783, and was succeeded by his only son, GEORGE, 4th LORD, *b.* 11 Feb. 1766, succeeded 26 May 1783, and *d.* 31 Dec. 1804; having *m.* 13 Aug. 1792, Susan, daughter and heir of Col. Watson, who *m.* 2ndly, George Freke Evans, Esq., and *d.* Oct. 1828.

2 JOHN, 5th LORD, *b.* 1738, succeeded his nephew in 1804, and *d.* 4 March 1807, without surviving male issue; having *m.* 15 April 1759, Emilia, 4th daughter of the very Rev. William Crowe, Dean of Clonfert, by whom, who *d.* 6 Jan. 1806, he had issue, besides one son, John-William, who *d. unm.* in the East Indies in 1805, aged 42, and a daughter, Emily Francis, who *d.* young, the two still living and married who are stated in *The Peerage Volume.*

2 The Hon. John Evans, of Bulgaden Hall, who *d.* in 1758, having *m.* Grace, only daughter of Sir Ralph Freke, of West Bilney, Co. Norfolk, and of Castle Freke, Co. Cork, Bart., and sole heir of her brother, Sir John Redmond Freke, Bart., by whom he had issue,

1 George, his successor, who *d.* without issue in 1769.

2 Sir John, who on succeeding to the estate of his uncle assumed the name and arms of FREKE; he was created a Baronet in 1768, and *d.* 20 March 1777; having *m.* Lady Elizabeth Gore, 2nd daughter of Arthur, 1st Earl of Arran, by whom he was father of SIR JOHN, who succeeded him in the Baronetcy in 1777, and his cousin the 5th LORD in the Peerage in 1807, and is the present and 6th LORD.

3 William, who *d.* Feb. 1796, leaving by his marriage with Elizabeth, daughter

of Richard Becher, Esq., a son John, who is deceased *unm.*, and three daughters, who all married, and are also deceased.

4 Ralph, who *m.* Elizabeth, daughter of Robert Woodcock, Esq., and left a son and daughter, both deceased.

CARDIGAN, EARL OF. (BRUDENELL.)

Peer of England.

The first of this family from whom the pedigree can be traced was William de Brudenell, living in the reign of Henry III.; 8th in descent from him was THOMAS BRUDENELL, created a Baronet by King James I. in 1611, and, in 1627, Baron Brudenell of Stanton-Wivill, Co. Leicester, by King CHARLES I.; to which unfortunate monarch he faithfully adhered during his wars with the Parliament; and on the triumph of the latter was committed to the Tower, where he relieved the tedium of a long confinement by making extracts and collections from the national records there deposited, most of which still remain in manuscript in the library of the Earl of Cardigan at Dean, in Northamptonshire. Soon after the Restoration, he was advanced by King CHARLES II., in 1661, to the dignity of EARL of CARDIGAN. He *d.* in 1664, and was succeeded by his son ROBERT, 2nd EARL. He *d.* in 1703, and Francis Lord Brudenell, his only son who survived the age of infancy, *d.* before him in 1698, leaving two sons, GEORGE, 3rd EARL, and the Hon. James Brudenell, from whom male issue still exists.

GEORGE, 3rd EARL, succeeded his grandfather, and *d.* in 1732; having *m.* Lady Elizabeth Bruce, daughter of Thomas, 2nd Earl of Ailesbury in the Peerage of England, and 3rd Earl of Elgin in Scotland, by whom he had four sons, viz.:

1 GEORGE, (BRUDENELL-MONTAGU,) 4th EARL, *b.* 26 July 1712, succeeded 5 July 1732; assumed the additional surname of MONTAGU after the death of his father-in-law in 1749; was created Duke of Montagu and Marquis of Monthermer, in 1766; and Baron Montagu, of Boughton, Co. Northampton, in 1786, with remainder to his grandson Henry-James Montagu-Scott, 2nd son of Henry, 3rd Duke of Buccleuch, by Elizabeth, his daughter; he *d.* 23 May 1790, having *m.* 7 July 1730, Lady Mary Montagu, 2nd daughter and at length sole heir of John, Duke of Montagu, *b.* 1712, *d.* 1 May 1775; they had one son John, Marquis of Monthermer, who *d.* before his father, and a daughter and heir Elizabeth, late Duchess of Buccleuch and Queensberry. On his death the titles of Duke and Marquis became extinct; the Barony of Montagu devolved, according to the Patent, on his grandson, Lord Henry-James Montagu-Scott, and the Earldom on his next brother,

2 JAMES, 5th EARL, *b.* 10 April 1725, created in 1780, Baron Brudenell of Deane, Co. Northampton, which title became extinct on his death; succeeded as EARL, 23 May 1790, *d.* 24 Feb. 1811; having *m.* 1st, 19 Nov. 1760, the Hon. Anne Legge, eldest daughter of George, Viscount Lewisham, son of William, 1st Earl of Dartmouth, who *d.* 12 Jan. 1786; and 2ndly, 28 April 1791, Lady Elizabeth Waldegrave, eldest daughter of John, 3rd Earl Waldegrave, *b.* 26 May 1758, and *d.* 23 June 1823.

3 The Hon. Robert Brudenell, who *d.* in 1768, father of ROBERT, present and 6th EARL, who succeeded his uncle in 1811.

4 Thomas, created Earl of Ailesbury, father of the present Marquis of Ailesbury.

CARLISLE, EARL OF. (Howard.)

Peer of England.

The Earl is descended from Lord William Howard, who *d.* Aug. 1640, 4th son of Thomas, 4th Duke of Norfolk, by his marriage with Elizabeth, daughter of Thomas, 4th Lord Dacre, of Gillesland, and co-heir of her brother George, 5th Lord, through whom the Earl is co-heir of the Barony of Dacre, of Gillesland, now in abeyance, and of which the Lords Petre and Stourton are joint co-heirs of the other moiety. Sir Philip, eldest son of Lord William Howard and Elizabeth Dacre, was grandfather of Charles Howard, created in 1661, Baron Dacre, of Gillesland, Co. Cumberland, Viscount Howard, of Morpeth, Co. Northumberland, and Earl of Carlisle; he *d.* in 1686, and was succeeded by his only surviving son, Edward, 2nd Earl; to whom, in 1692, succeeded his eldest son, (the only one who left issue,) Charles, 3rd Earl, father of

Henry, 4th Earl, who was *b.* in 1694, succeeded 1 May 1738, *d.* 2 Sept. 1758; having *m.* 1st, 27 Nov. 1717, Lady Frances Spencer, eldest daughter of Charles, 3rd Earl of Sunderland, who *d.* 27 July 1742; and 2ndly, 8 June 1743, the Hon. Isabel Byron, eldest daughter of William, 4th Lord Byron, who was *b.* 10 Nov. 1721, and *d.* 22 Jan. 1795. The Earl had issue by his 1st marriage,

1* Charles Viscount Morpeth, *d.* 9 Aug. 1741.

2* Robert Viscount Morpeth, *b.* 1724, and *d.* 20 Oct. 1743.

3 Lady Arabella, who *d.* 1746, having *m.* 1741, Sir Jonathan Cope, Bart.

4 Lady Diana, *d.* 18 March 1770, having *m.* 8 Jan. 1749, Thomas Duncombe, Esq.

By his 2nd marriage:

5 Lady Anne, *b.* in 1744, *d. unm.* 13 Oct. 1799.

6 Lady Frances, *b.* in 1745, *d.* 27 April 1808, having *m.* April 1768, John Radcliffe, Esq., who *d.* 21 Dec. 1783.

7 Lady Elizabeth, *b.* 1747, *d.* June 1813, having *m.* 1st, 16 Feb. 1769, Peter Delme, Esq., who *d.* 5 Sept. 1789; and 2ndly, 13 Jan. 1794, Capt. Charles Garnier, R.N., *d.* 16 Dec. 1796.

8 Frederick, his successor, 5th Earl, who was succeeded in 1825, by his eldest son, George, the present and 6th Earl.

9 Lady Juliana, who is living – see *The Peerage Volume.*

CARNARVON, EARL OF. (Herbert.)

Peer of Great Britain.

The Earl is descended from the family of the Earl of Pembroke and Montgomery. The Hon. William Herbert, a Major-Gen. in the army, 5th son of Thomas, 8th Earl of Pembroke and Montgomery, *d.* 31 March 1757, having *m.* Catherine-Elizabeth Tewes, of Aix-la-Chapelle, by whom he had issue:

1 William, *d.* young.

2 Henry, *b.* 1741, created, in 1780, Baron Porchester of High-Clere, Co. Southampton, and in 1793, Earl of Carnarvon: for his marriage, issue, &c. see *The Peerage Volume.* He *d.* in 1811, and was succeeded by his eldest son, Henry-George, the present and 2nd Earl.

3 Charles, *b.* 1743, *d.* 5 Sept. 1816, without issue, having *m.* July 1775, Lady Caroline Montagu, eldest daughter of Robert, 1st Duke of Manchester.

4 Catherine, *d.* young.

5 Georgiana, *b.* 1747, *d. unm.*

6 Robert, in holy orders, *b.* 1751, *d. unm.* 2 Feb. 1814.

CARNWATH, EARL OF. (Dalzell.)

Peer of Scotland.

Nisbet, in his heraldry, gives the following singular origin for the armorial bearings and surname of this family. A favourite and near kinsman of Kenneth II., King of Scotland, having been taken by the Picts and hanged upon a gibbet, the King being exceedingly grieved that the body of his friend should be so disgracefully treated by his enemies, proffered a great reward to any of his subjects who would undertake to rescue it; the enterprize, however, appeared so hazardous, that it was long before any one could be found to adventure it; till at length a valorous gentleman said to the King "Dal zell," which in the old Scottish language signifies "I dare;" and having successfully performed the exploit, took for his arms a naked man hanging on a gibbet, and for his name the word "Dalzell," both which his posterity bear to the present day. Nisbet, however, elsewhere says, that the name is local and taken from the Barony of Dalzell, in the county of Lanark, which he supposes this family to have lost by forfeiture, as it was granted by King David II., to Sir Malcolm Fleming, in 1343. From the period however designed by the above first questionable anecdote, numerous individuals of this name have signalized themselves, or are specified in various existing charters; and William de Dalzell, from whom the Earl is certainly descended, recovered the estate of his ancestors about 1406. But the earliest ancestor from whom the present family can regularly deduce their pedigree, is Robert Dalzell, of Dalzell, Co. of Lanark, who *d.* in 1552. Sir Robert Dalzell of Dalzell, his son, was engaged on the side of his unfortunate Sovereign in the battle of Langside, in which Queen Mary was totally defeated. Sir Robert Dalzell, of Dalzell, grandson of the last-mentioned Sir Robert, was created Baron of Dalzell in 1628, and Earl of Carnwath in 1639, and *d.* soon afterwards. He left two sons.

1 Robert, 2nd Earl, constant in his loyalty to King Charles I., whom he served in person in the field throughout the Civil Wars. Lord Clarendon imputes to the Earl's anxious zeal for the safety of his Royal Master, the loss of the battle of Nazeby, on the 14th of June 1645, for when the King was on the point of charging the enemy in person at the head of his guards, Lord Carnwarth suddenly siezed his bridle, and turning his horse's head, gave an impulse of doubt and alarm to the whole army, which ended in every one endeavouring to save himself. The Earl was succeeded before April 1646, by his son Gavin, 3rd Earl, who, also distinguished for his loyalty, was taken prisoner at the battle of Worcester, and detained some years in confinement; he *d.* in 1674, leaving two sons, James, 4th Earl, who *d.* without issue male in 1683, and John, 5th Earl, who succeeded his brother, and *d. unm.* in 1703, when the whole male line of the 2nd Earl became extinct.

2 John, whose son Sir Robert Dalzell, of Glenæ, was created a Baronet of Nova Scotia, in 1666, and *d.* in 1685; leaving three sons, of whom James, 2nd son, who was concerned in the Rebellion of 1715; and Thomas, 3rd son, both left issue male. Sir John of Glenæ, his eldest son and successor, was father of a younger son John, who left a son settled at St. Christopher's, and of his eldest son and heir,

Sir Robert, who succeeded as 6th Earl. He was also engaged in the Rebellion, and with his brother John, was taken prisoner at the battle of Preston; both were tried for their lives, the latter as a deserter, having once been a Captain in the army, but acquitted; the Earl was condemned and pardoned; but his titles remained forfeited by the attainder till restored in 1826. He *d.* in 1737, leaving two sons; viz.

1 Alexander, who should have been 7th Earl; he *d.* 3 April 1787; having *m.* Miss Elizabeth Jackson, by whom he had two daughters, see *The Peerage Volume*, and two sons both deceased, viz:

1 Richard, Lord Dalzell, *b.* 23 July 1753, *d.* 5 July 1782; having *m.* in 1775, Miss Elizabeth Johnston, by whom he has left a daughter Elizabeth—see *The Peerage Volume.*

2 ROBERT, who but for the attainder would have been 8th EARL, *b.* 7 Jan. 1755, *d.* 13 Feb. 1808, having *m.* 18 March 1785, Anne, daughter of David Armstrong, Esq., by whom, who *d.* 21 Feb. 1787, he had two surviving daughters, (for whom see *The Peerage Volume,*) and one son, JOHN, who should have been 9th EARL; he was *b.* 9 Aug. 1795, and *d. unm.* 10 Oct. 1814, when his eldest sister inherited his estate of Glenæ.

2 Robert, who *d.* in 1788, father of ROBERT-ALEXANDER, present and 10th EARL, on whom the representation of the Earldom devolved on the death of his cousin JOHN, 9th EARL, in 1814; he was restored to his honours by Act of Parliament, which received the Royal assent 26 May 1826.

CARRICK, EARL OF. (BUTLER.)

Peer of Ireland.

His Lordship is a younger branch of the Marquis of Ormonde's family. 8th in descent from John, 2nd son of Edmund, Earl of Carrick, and brother of James, 1st Earl of Ormonde, was SIR PIERCE BUTLER, of Lismallon, created in 1607 Bason Butler, of Lismallon, Co. Tipperary, and in 1629 VISCOUNT IKERRIN. He survived his son James, and was succeeded by his grandson PIERCE, 2nd VISCOUNT, father of

JAMES, 3rd VISCOUNT, who *d.* in 1688, leaving four sons, of whom only two had issue, viz.:

1 PIERCE, 4th VISCOUNT; he *d.* in 1710, and was succeeded by his only son, JAMES, 5th VISCOUNT, who dying in his 13th year, in 1712, was succeeded by his uncle,

2 THOMAS, 6th VISCOUNT, in holy orders, and Chaplain-General to the army in Flanders; he *d.* in 1720, leaving two sons,

JAMES, 7th VISCOUNT, who *d.* a minor in 1721, and

SOMERSET-HAMILTON, 8th VISCOUNT, who at three years of age succeeded his brother; he was created in 1748 EARL of CARRICK, Co. Tipperary, and *d.* 15 April 1774; having *m.* 18 May 1745, Lady Juliana Boyle, eldest daughter of Henry, 1st Earl of Shannon, by whom, who *d.* 22 Feb. 1804, he had issue,

and HENRY-THOMAS, 2nd EARL, for whom see *The Peerage Volume*; he *d.* in 1813,

1 was succeeded by his eldest son, SOMERSET-RICHARD, present and 3rd EARL.

2 Lady Margaret, *b.* 30 Jan. 1749, *d.* Jan. 1777, late Countess of Belmore. See *The Peerage Volume.*

3 } twins { Lady Henrietta, *b.* 15 Aug. 1750, *d.* 20 June 1785; late Viscountess Mountgarret. See *The Peerage Volume*, title Kilkenny.

4 } twins { Hon. Pierce Butler-Cooper, *b.* 15 Aug. 1750, *d.* 5 May 1826, having *m.* 24 Dec. 1774, Catherine, eldest daughter of Richard Roth, Esq.

CARRINGTON, BARON. (SMITH.)

Peer of Ireland and of Great Britain.

His Lordship's ancestor purchased the estate of Crophall Boteler, Notts, in 1622. Abel Smith, Esq., his grandfather, had two sons, Sir George, created a Baronet in 1757, grandfather of Sir Robert Howe Bromley, Bart., and

Abel Smith, Esq., an eminent Banker in Nottingham, who was *b.* in 1717, and *d.* 12 July 1788, having *m.* Mary, daughter of Thomas Bird, Esq., by whom, who *d.* 4 April 1780, he had the following flourishing issue:

1 Thomas, who *d.* before his father *unm.* in 1769.

2 Abel, who *d.* 22 Jan. 1779; having *m.* Sept. 1777, Elizabeth, daughter of —— Uppleby, Esq.; by whom he left one daughter, Mary, *b.* 4 Oct. 1778, *m.* 29 Nov. 1804, the Rev. John Sargent.

3 ROBERT, created, in 1796, BARON CARRINGTON, of Bulcot Lodge, in the Peerage of Ireland; and, in 1797, Baron Carrington, of Upton, Co. Notts, in the Peerage of Great Britain. He is the present Peer, is *m.*, and has issue; see *The Peerage Volume.*

4 Samuel, M.P., a Commissioner of the Lieutenancy for London, *b.* 14 April 1754, *m.* 2 Dec. 1783, Elizabeth-Frances, eldest daughter of the late Edmund Turnor, Esq., by whom he has issue:

1 Sophia, *b.* 14 Oct. 1784, *m.* 12 July 1803, William Dickenson, Esq.
2 Frances-Anne, *b.* 16 Dec. 1785, *m.* 18 April 1806, Claude George Thornton, Esq.
3 Mary, *b.* 1 April, 1787, *m.* 25 June 1811, Thomas Daniel, Esq.
4 Abel, M.P., *b.* 17 July 1788, *m.* 1st, 28 Aug. 1822, Lady Marianne Leslie-Melville, 4th daughter of Alexander, 10th Earl of Leven and Melville, who *d.* 22 March 1823; and he *m.* 2ndly, 12 July 1826, Frances-Anne, youngest daughter of the late General Sir Harry Calvert, Bart., G.C.B.; they have issue, a daughter, *b.* 15 Aug. 1827; a son, *b.* 30 Dec. 1829; a daughter, *b.* 3 July 1831.
5 Samuel-George, *b.* 19 July 1789, *m.* 4 July 1821, Eugenia, 3rd daughter of the Rev. Robert Chatfield, LL.D.; they have issue; 1 Samuel, *b.* 1822; 2 Frederick-Chatfield, *b.* 1823; 3 Rowland, *b.* 6 Dec. 1826; 4 A son, *b.* 24 Feb. 1829; 5 Eugenia-Maria, b. 15 Feb. 1831.
6 Caroline, *b.* 4 Aug. 1790, *d.* 17 Feb. 1816; having *m.* 13 July 1814, Major-General Thomas Carey, *d.* 9 Nov. 1825.
7 Lucy, *b.* 21 Oct. 1791, *d.* 25 March 1820.
8 Henry, *b.* 12 Dec. 1794, *m.* 14 July 1824, Lady Lucy Leslie-Melville, 2nd daughter of Alexander, 10th Earl of Leven and Melville; they have issue, 1 Henry-Abel, *b.* 7 March, 1826; 2 Robert-Melville.
9 Barbara, *b.* 12 July 1797.
10 Charlotte, b. 15 Aug. 1800, *m.* 19 Oct. 1825, Hon. Alexander Leslie-Melville.—See *Earl of Leven.*

5 George, a Commissioner of the Lieutenancy for London, *b.* 30 April 1765, *m.* 12 May 1792, Frances-Mary, daughter of the late Sir John-Parker Mosley, Bart., *b.* 19 Feb. 1770, by whom he has issue:

1 George Robert, M.P., *b.* 2 May 1793, *m.* 4 May 1818, Jane, eldest daughter of John Maberly, Esq., M.P.
2 Oswald, *b.* 7 July 1794, *m.* 18 March 1824, Henrietta-Mildred, eldest daughter of the Very Rev. Robert Hodgson, D.D., Dean of Carlisle. They have issue, 1 Isabella-Mary, *b.* 24 April 1825; 2 Oswald-Augustus, *b.* 21 Oct. 1826; 3 Eric-Carrington, *b.* 25 May 1828; 4 Laura-Charlotte, *b.* 2 Aug. 1829; 5 A son, *b.* 12 Aug. 1830.
3 John-Henry, *b.* 30 Oct. 1795.
4 Thomas-Charles, *b.* 19 March 1797.
5 Frances-Mary, *b.* 27 Nov. 1798, *m.* 30 April 1822, the Rev. Robert-Mosley Master.
6 Georgiana-Elizabeth, *b.* 7 June 1801, *d.* 17 Dec. 1828: having *m.* 30 Oct. 1824, the Rev. Edward Serocold-Pearce.
7 Edward-Peploe, *b.* 1 Feb. 1803, *m.* 23 March, 1824, Henrietta-Frances, daughter of Charles Bayley, Esq., Hon. East India Company's Civil S-

vice, Bengal; she *d.* 18 Dec. 1824, leaving a daughter, Mary-Anne-Bayley, *b.* 25 Nov. 1824.
8 Arthur, *b.* 22 June 1804.
9 Emily, *b.* 11 May 1806.
10 Catherine, *b.* 5 Aug. 1807; *m.* 10 Aug. 1830, Edward Wigram, Esq., 12th son of the late Sir Robert Wigram, Bart.
11 Edmund, *b.* 16 May 1809.
12 Mosley, *b.* 31 Oct. 1810.
13 Sophia-Sarah, *b.* 28 Aug. 1812.
14 Alfred, *b.* 5 Jan. 1815.
15 Augusta-Mary, *b.* 15 Oct. 1816.

6 John, M.P., *m.* 1st, 1 December 1793, Sarah, daughter of Thomas Boone, Esq., who *d.* 23 Sept. 1794, in child-bed of a daughter, which *d.* an infant; he *m.* 2ndly, 6 Jan. 1800, a daughter of Lieutenant-Colonel Tucker, after whose death he *m.* 3rdly, 1 May 1811, Emma, daughter of Egerton Leigh, Esq. He has issue:

by his 2nd marriage:

1 John Abel, M.P., *m.* 26 Dec. 1827, Anne, eldest daughter of the Rev. Sir Samuel Clarke Jervoise, Bart., by whom he has issue: 1 Jervoise, *b.* 3 Oct. 1828; 2 Dudley-Robert, *b.* 27 April 1830.
2 Martin-Tucker, M.P., *b.* 6 July 1803; *m.* 8 July 1831, Louisa, 3rd daughter of Sir Matthew White-Ridley, Bart., M.P.

by his 3rd marriage:

3 Emma, *b.* 14 Feb. 1812.
4 Caroline, *b.* 2 May 1813.
5 Henry, *b.* March 1816, *d.* young.

7 Elizabeth, *d.* 29 March, 1789; haviug *m.* William Manning, Esq.
8 Lucy.

CARTERET, BARON. (THYNNE.)

Peer of Great Britain.

John Granville was created in 1661 Baron Granville, of Kilkhampton and Bideford, Viscount Granville, of Lansdown, and Earl of Bath; he had one son, Charles, 2nd Earl, whose issue failed, in 1711, by the death of his son, William-Henry, 3rd Earl, when the titles became extinct; and two daughters, co-heirs to their nephew,

1 Jane, *m.* Sir William Leveson Gower, and was great-grandmother of Granville, 1st Marquis of Stafford, father of the present Marquis, and of Viscount Granville.

2 Grace, *m.* Sir George Carteret, Bart., created, in 1681, Baron Carteret; she was created, in 1714, Viscountess Carteret and Countess Granville; their issue male and all these titles became extinct in 1776, by the death of Robert, 3rd Earl, their grandson: he left five sisters, his co-heirs, of whom Lady Sophia, the youngest, *m.* William, 2nd Earl of Shelburne, created Marquis of Lansdowne; and

Lady Louisa, the 2nd, *m.* Thomas, 2nd Viscount Weymouth, by whom she was mother of Thomas, 1st Marquis of Bath, and of HENRY-FREDERICK, created, in 1784, BARON CARTERET, of Hawnes, Co. Bedford, with remainder, failing his issue male, to the 2nd, 3rd, 4th, and every other son of his brother Thomas, 1st Marquis of Bath; he was *b.* 17 Nov. 1735, assumed the name of CARTERET by Act of Parliament in 1776, and *d.* 17 June 1826, when his nephew, the present Lord, 2nd son of Thomas, 1st Marquis of Bath, and brother of the present Marquis, succeeded.

CARYSFORT, EARL OF. (Proby.)

Peer of Ireland and of the United Kingdom.

The first of this family on record is Randolph Proby, of Chester, living about 1580; ancestor in the sixth generation of Sir John Proby, K.B., a Lord of the Admiralty and Privy Counsellor, who was created in 1752 Baron Carysfort, of Carysfort, Co. Wicklow, in the Peerage of Ireland; he *d.* in 1772; having *m.* 27 Aug. 1750, the Hon. Elizabeth Allen, daughter of Joshua, 2nd Viscount, and sister and co-heir of John, 3rd Viscount Allen, by whom, who *d.* March 1783, he had issue one daughter, Elizabeth, *b.* 14 Nov. 1752, *d.* 19 March 1808; having *m.* Thomas-James Storer, Esq., who *d.* 10 Nov. 1792; and an only son, John-Joshua, 2nd Lord, who was advanced to the dignity of Earl of Carysfort in 1789, and created a Peer of the United Kingdom in 1801, by the title of Baron Carysfort, of Norman Cross, Co. Huntingdon. He *d.* in 1828, and was succeeded by his eldest surviving son, John, present and 2nd Earl.

CASTLEMAINE, VISCOUNT. (Handcock.)

Peer of Ireland.

William Handcock, of Twyford, Co. Westmeath, descended from a good family in Lancashire, was Knight of the Shire for Westmeath, in the first Parliament after the restoration of King Charles II.; he was great-grandfather of Richard, Dean of Achonry, father of William, the present Viscount.

His Lordship was created, in 1812, Baron Castlemaine, of Moydrum, Co. Westmeath, with remainder, failing his issue male, to his brother Richard and his issue male; and advanced to the dignity of Viscount Castlemaine in 1822.

CASTLE-STEWART, EARL OF. (Stuart.)

Peer of Ireland.

The founder of this family was Walter, younger brother of Andrew, 1st Lord Avandale, in Scotland, both legitimated sons of Sir James Stewart, 4th son of Mordoch, Duke of Albany, 3rd son of King Robert II. Andrew, eldest son of the above Walter, succeeded his uncle, as 2nd Lord Avandale, and was father of Andrew, 3rd Lord, and of Sir James, ancestor of the Earl of Moray. Andrew, 3rd Lord Avandale, exchanged that title for that of Ochiltree, and was great-grandfather of Andrew, 3rd Lord Ochiltree, a Gentleman of the Bedchamber to King James VI., General of the Ordnance, and Governor of Edinburgh Castle. He sold his Lordship of Ochiltree to his cousin, James Stuart, of Killeith, son of James, Earl of Arran, second son of Andrew, 2nd Lord Ochiltree, and resigned his title in his favour in 1615; in which year this James Stuart obtained from King James VI. a charter confirming him in all the honours and privileges of the Peerage, as formerly possessed by the said Andrew, Lord Ochiltree; he *d.* in 1659, leaving a grandson, his successor, William Lord Ochiltree, with whom his male issue expired in 1673. Andrew, 3rd Lord Ochiltree, having thus divested himself of that title, was created a Peer of Ireland in 1619, by the title of Lord Stuart, Baron of Castle-Stuart, Co. Tyrone, and *d.* in 1632, leaving three sons, viz.:

1 ANDREW, created a Baronet of Nova Scotia in 1637, succeeded his father as 2nd LORD CASTLE-STUART, and *d.* in 1639, leaving two sons, ANDREW, 3rd LORD, who *d.* without issue male in 1650, and JOSIAS, 4th LORD, who *d.* without issue in 1662.

2 JOHN, who succeeded his nephew as 5th LORD, *d. unm.* in 1684, from which time the title remained dormant till claimed, in 1774, by the late Lord.

3 Colonel Robert Stuart *d.* in 1662, leaving a son, ROBERT, who should have been 6th LORD, but he never assumed the title; he *d.* in 1684, leaving a son, ANDREW, who should have been 7th LORD; he had two sons, Robert, his heir, and Alexander, from whom there are male descendants. ROBERT, the eldest son, who should have been 8th LORD, *d.* in 1742, leaving a son,

ANDREW-THOMAS, 9th LORD, who in 1774 claimed the title of BARON CASTLE-STUART, to which the Irish House of Lords resolved that he was entitled. He likewise claimed the title of Lord Ochiltree, to which, in 1793, the House of Lords in England determined that he had not made out his right. He was created VISCOUNT-CASTLE-STUART in 1793, and further created, in 1800, Earl of Castle-Stuart. For his marriage, issue, &c. see *The Peerage Volume.* He *d.* in 1809, and was succeeded by his eldest son, ROBERT, present and 2nd EARL.

CATHCART, EARL OF. (CATHCART.)

Peer of the United Kingdom and of Scotland.

The name of Cathcart was assumed from a Barony in the County of Renfrew, in the reign of William the Lion. From a line of distinguished ancestors descended ALAN CATHCART, dignified with the title of LORD CATHCART, before the year 1450. Alan, Master of Cathcart, his eldest son, *d.* before him, leaving a son, JOHN, 2nd LORD, who succeeded his grandfather, and *d.* in 1535; having had, besides other issue, the four sons following:

1 Alan, Master of Cathcart, who *d.* before his father, leaving a son, ALAN, 3rd LORD.

2 Robert, killed at Flodden Field in 1513; he was ancestor of Sir John-Andrew Cathcart, Bart., and of John Cathcart, Esq., of Genoch, and his brother, the late Robert Cathcart, of Drum; see *The Peerage Volume.*

3 John, also killed at Flodden-field.

4 David, from whom are descended James Cathcart, Esq., of Carbiston, late Major of the 19th Dragoons, and his brother, Capt. Robert Cathcart, R.N.

ALAN, 3rd LORD, who succeeded his grandfather, was killed in the battle of Pinkie in 1547, leaving a son, ALAN, 4th LORD, who signalized himself in the army of King JAMES at the battle of Langside, in 1568; he *d.* in 1618, having survived his only son Alan, Master of Cathcart, who *d.* in 1603, leaving a son, ALAN, 5th LORD, who succeeded his grandfather, and was succeeded, in 1628, by his infant son ALAN, 6th LORD. He *d.* in 1709, and was succeeded by his son ALAN, 7th LORD, to whom, in 1732, succeeded his son CHARLES, 8th LORD, father of CHARLES, 9th Lord, who succeeded him in 1740, and, dying in 1776, was succeeded by his eldest son, WILLIAM-SCHAW, the present and 10th Lord, who in 1807 was created Viscount Cathcart, and Baron Greenock, in the Peerage of the United Kingdom, and in 1814 was advanced to the dignity of EARL CATHCART.

CAVAN, EARL OF. (Lambart.)

Peer of Ireland.

The first of this ancient family on record was Rodolph de Lambert, who came over from France with William the Conqueror, and was grandson of Lambert, Count of Mons and Louvaine. His descendents settled in Yorkshire and Northumberland, till Sir Oliver Lambart, 17th in descent from the above Rodolph, removed into Ireland in the reign of Elizabeth, was appointed Governor of Connaught in 1601, and in 1618 was created Baron of the County of Cavan. He *d.* in 1618, leaving a son, Charles, 2nd Lord, created in 1647 Earl of Cavan and Viscount Kilcoursie. On the breaking out of the great rebellion, he raised a regiment for King Charles's service, and was appointed Governor of the city of Dublin and Commander of his Majesty's forces in that city and suburbs; he was succeeded by his son, Richard, 2nd Earl, father of Charles, 3rd Earl; the latter had two sons:

1 Richard, 4th Earl, father of Ford, 5th Earl, who *d.* without issue male in 1772.

9 Henry, father of Richard, who succeeded as 6th Earl, and was succeeded in 1778, by his only son Richard-Ford-William, the present and 7th Earl.

CAWDOR, EARL. (Campbell.)

Peer of the United Kingdom.

His Lordship is a branch of the family of the Duke of Argyll, being descended from the Hon. Sir John Campbell, 3rd son of Archibald, 2nd Earl of Argyll, by his marriage with Muriel, daughter and heir of Sir John Calder, of Calder. One of their descendants *m.* the heiress of the Lorts of Stackpoole Court, Co. Pembroke, and with her got that seat and a good estate in Pembrokeshire.

Lieut.-Col. John Campbell, of the Royal Horse-Guards, was father of Pryce Campbell, his heir, and of Lieut.-Col. Alexander Campbell, father of the present Lieut.-Gen, Sir Henry-Frederick Campbell, K.C.B. & G.C.H., *b.* 1769, who by his marriage, 10 April 1808, with Emma, daughter of Thomas Williams, Esq., of Marlow, Co. Bucks, has issue; 1 Henrietta-Frances, *b.* 29 Jan. 1809; 2 George-Herbert-Frederick, *b.* 19 June 1811; 3 Frances-Augusta.

Pryce Campbell, Esq., of Cawdor Castle, Co. Nairne, and of Stackpoole Court, Co. Pembroke, was father of

1 John, created in 1796 Baron Cawdor, of Castlemartin, Co. Pembroke, and *d.* in 1821; when he was succeeded by his eldest son John-Frederick, present and 2nd Lord; created in 1827 Viscount Emlyn of Emlyn, Co. Carmarthen, and Earl Cawdor of Castlemartin, Co. Pembroke.

2 Admiral Sir George Campbell, G.C.B.; he *d.* 28 Jan. 1821, leaving no issue by his wife Eustachia, daughter of his uncle, Lieut.-Col. Alexander Campbell.

3 Sarah, *m.* to Thomas Wodehouse, Esq., brother of Lord Wodehouse; see that title in this Volume.

1 ANDREW, created a Baronet of Nova Scotia in 1637, succeeded his father as 2nd LORD CASTLE-STUART, and *d.* in 1639, leaving two sons, ANDREW, 3rd LORD, who *d.* without issue male in 1650, and JOSIAS, 4th LORD, who *d.* without issue in 1662.

2 JOHN, who succeeded his nephew as 5th LORD, *d. unm.* in 1684, from which time the title remained dormant till claimed, in 1774, by the late Lord.

3 Colonel Robert Stuart *d.* in 1662, leaving a son, ROBERT, who should have been 6th LORD, but he never assumed the title; he *d.* in 1684, leaving a son, ANDREW, who should have been 7th LORD; he had two sons, Robert, his heir, and Alexander, from whom there are male descendants. ROBERT, the eldest son, who should have been 8th LORD, *d.* in 1742, leaving a son,

ANDREW-THOMAS, 9th LORD, who in 1774 claimed the title of BARON CASTLE-STUART, to which the Irish House of Lords resolved that he was entitled. He likewise claimed the title of Lord Ochiltree, to which, in 1793, the House of Lords in England determined that he had not made out his right. He was created VISCOUNT-CASTLE-STUART in 1793, and further created, in 1800, Earl of Castle-Stuart. For his marriage, issue, &c. see *The Peerage Volume.* He *d.* in 1809, and was succeeded by his eldest son, ROBERT, present and 2nd EARL.

CATHCART, EARL OF. (CATHCART.)

Peer of the United Kingdom and of Scotland.

The name of Cathcart was assumed from a Barony in the County of Renfrew, in the reign of William the Lion. From a line of distinguished ancestors descended ALAN CATHCART, dignified with the title of LORD CATHCART, before the year 1450. Alan, Master of Cathcart, his eldest son, *d.* before him, leaving a son, JOHN, 2nd LORD, who succeeded his grandfather, and *d.* in 1535; having had, besides other issue, the four sons following:

1 Alan, Master of Cathcart, who *d.* before his father, leaving a son, ALAN, 3rd LORD.

2 Robert, killed at Flodden Field in 1513; he was ancestor of Sir John-Andrew Cathcart, Bart., and of John Cathcart, Esq., of Genoch, and his brother, the late Robert Cathcart, of Drum; see *The Peerage Volume.*

3 John, also killed at Flodden-field.

4 David, from whom are descended James Cathcart, Esq., of Carbiston, late Major of the 19th Dragoons, and his brother, Capt. Robert Cathcart, R.N.

ALAN, 3rd LORD, who succeeded his grandfather, was killed in the battle of Pinkie in 1547, leaving a son, ALAN, 4th LORD, who signalized himself in the army of King JAMES at the battle of Langside, in 1568; he *d.* in 1618, having survived his only son Alan, Master of Cathcart, who *d.* in 1603, leaving a son, ALAN, 5th LORD, who succeeded his grandfather, and was succeeded, in 1628, by his infant son ALAN, 6th LORD, to whom, in 17[illegible] He *d.* in 1709, and was succeeded by his son ALAN, 7th LORD, [illegible] 8th LORD, who succeeded [illegible] succeeded his [illegible] WILLIAM [illegible] him in 17[illegible] [illegible]

CHARLEMONT, EARL OF. (Caulfeild.)

Peer of Ireland.

Sir Toby Caulfeild, a distinguished soldier, settled in Ireland in the reign of Elizabeth, and, for his services against the rebels, had a grant of part of the estate of Con O'Neil, Earl of Tyrone, and was created, in 1620, Baron Caulfeild of Charlemont, Co. Armagh, with limitation to his nephew, William Caulfeild, (son of his brother James,) who succeeded his uncle in 1627, as 2nd Lord, and *d.* in 1640, leaving four sons; 1 Toby, 3rd Lord, murdered by Sir Phelim O'Neil in the rebellion of 1641; 2 Robert, 4th Lord, *d.* also in 1641, from taking too large a dose of opium; 3 William, 5th Lord, ancestor of the Earl; 4 Thomas, whose eldest son Willian was Chief Justice of the King's Bench in Ireland, and was ancestor of St. George-Francis Caulfeild, Esq., (for whom see *The Peerage Volume*,) the only collateral branch amongst many of this family which the editor has yet been able to trace to its origin.

William, 5th Lord, was created, in 1665, Viscount of Charlemont; he was succeeded by his son William, 2nd Viscount, who *d.* in 1726, and was succeeded by his son James, 3rd Viscount, who dying in 1734, left two sons; viz. James, 4th Viscount, and Francis, who was lost in Nov. 1775, with his Lady, their eldest daughter, and a female infant, in a tremendous storm which they encountered on their passage to Dublin, whither Mr. Caulfeild was returning from London to attend in the Irish Parliament, as representative for Charlemont; he *m.* Oct. 1760, Mary, only child and heir of John Lord Eyre; they left a daughter, Eleanor, who *d.* 2 April 1807, having *m.* the Hon. William-Forward Howard, afterwards 3rd Earl of Wicklow, see *The Peerage Volume*, title Wicklow, and a son, James, who has assumed the name of Eyre—see *The Peerage Volume*.

James, 4th Viscount, was created, in 1763, Earl of Charlemont, and *d.* in 1799, when he was succeeded by his eldest son, Francis-William, the present and 2nd Earl.

CHARLEVILLE, EARL OF. (Bury.)

Peer of Ireland.

John Moore, Esq., of Benenden, Co. Kent, in the reign of Queen Mary, left, besides other issue, two sons, Sir Edward, ancestor of the Marquis of Drogheda; and Sir Thomas Moore, who, settling in Ireland early in the reign of Queen Elizabeth, had large grants of lands in King's County, from the Crown, on certain conditions of rent and service. His heir and descendant in the fifth degree was John Moore of Croghan, Esq., created, in 1715, Baron Moore of Tullamore; he *d.* in 1725, leaving a son, Charles, who was created Earl of Charleville in 1758, and *d.* without issue in 1764, when his titles became extinct; and a daughter, Jane, who *d.* 11 Dec. 1766; having *m.* 17 Jan. 1724, William Bury, Esq., by whom she had five sons, viz. John, Charles, William, Richard, and Thomas; and four daughters, viz. Jane, Georgiana, wife of Richard, 4th Viscount Boyne, Mary, and Elizabeth.

John Bury, Esq., the eldest son, *b.* 1 Nov. 1725, *d.* 4 Aug. 1764; having *m.* Catherine, 2nd daughter and co-heir of Francis Sadleir, Esq., of Sopwell Hall, Co. Tipperary; by whom, who *m.* 2ndly, 6 Jan. 1766, Henry, 1st Lord Dunalley, (was mother by him of the present Lord Dunalley,) and *d.* 26 Feb. 1821, he left an only child, Charles-William, who succeeded to the estates of his great-uncle,

Charles Moore, Earl of Charleville; was created, in 1797, Baron Tullamore of Charleville Forest, King's Co.; Viscount Charleville in 1800, and, in 1806, Earl of Charleville of Charleville Forest, King's Co., and is the present Peer.

CHATHAM, EARL OF. (*Pitt.*)

Peer of Great Britain.

His Lordship is descended from John Pitt, Clerk of the Exchequer in the reign of Queen Elizabeth, whose eldest son, William, was ancestor of the late Lord Rivers; and his 3rd son Thomas, was grandfather of

Thomas, Governor of Fort St. George, and purchaser of the Pitt Diamond; he *d.* in 1726; leaving, by his marriage with Jane, daughter of James Innes of Reid Hall, Co. Moray, grandson of Sir Robert Innes of Innes, Bart., besides other issue, two sons; Robert, his heir, and Thomas, created Earl of Londonderry, in the Peerage of Ireland, which title became extinct with his male issue in 1764.

But it was in the reigns of George II. and III. that the name of Pitt acquired a lustre which will cease to shine only with the extinction of British history. Robert Pitt, of Boconnock, Co. Cornwall, Esq., eldest son of Governor Pitt, *d.* in 1727; having *m.* Harriott, sister of John Villiers, Earl Grandison, in Ireland; by whom he had two sons; 1 Thomas, who *d.* in 1760, leaving a son, Thomas, created in 1784, Lord Camelford, Baron of Boconnock, Co. Cornwall; which titles became extinct in 1804, by the death of his only son, Thomas, 2nd Lord Camelford; and 2

William Pitt, the illustrious statesman and popular minister, who having devoted his life to the service of his country, had the happiness of fostering those germs of talent in his younger son which were afterwards to spring up so precociously, and to bear such excellent fruit. Lady Hester, his wife, daughter of Richard Grenville, Esq., by Hester, Countess Temple, (see the title *Buckingham*, in this volume), was, on his resigning the seals of office in 1761, created Baroness Chatham of Chatham, Co. Kent, with remainder to her heirs male by the Right Hon. William Pitt; and he was himself, on being recalled to the administration as Lord Privy Seal, in 1766, created Viscount Pitt, of Burton Pynsent, Co. Somerset, and Earl of Chatham in Kent; he *d.* in 1778, leaving two sons, John, the present and 2nd Earl, who also succeeded to his mother's Barony in 1803; and the immortal William Pitt, who, after guiding the helm of State through the stormy period of the French Revolution, died in the discharge of his high duties as Prime Minister of the empire, from the inability of his constitution to support the exertions, and great anxiety of mind which the critical state of public affairs occasioned. "He lived a Commoner, and died in debt."

CHESTERFIELD, EARL OF. (Stanhope.)

Peer of England.

This noble family traces its pedigree from Sir Richard Stanhope, who had large possessions in the North, in the reign of Henry 3rd; 10th in descent from him was Sir John Stanhope, of Shelford, Co. Derby, father, by his 1st marriage, of Philip, 1st Earl, and by his 2nd, of John, ancestor of the Earl of Harrington.

Philip, the eldest son, was, in 1616, created Baron Stanhope of Shelford, Co. Notts., and in 1628, Earl of Chesterfield, Co. Derby; after endeavouring in his place in Parliament by every gentle expedient to prevent the eruption of a civil war, and after having urged in vain that the rabble which assaulted both the King and the House of Peers should be dispersed; finding that no parliamentary measures were likely to produce the desired effect, he retired into the country, and put himself and his sons in arms, hoping to aid the rest of the King's loyal subjects in reducing the rebels to obedience. He put a garrison into his house at Shelford under the command of his son Philip, who lost his life in its defence, when it was stormed by the Parliamentary forces. The Earl himself having taken possession of the City of Lichfield for the King, defended first the City, and then the Close, or Cathedral yard, to the last extremity, but was at length compelled to surrender, together with one of his sons, and the survivors of his party; he *d.* in 1656, after a long confinement. He had by his first marriage eleven sons, of whom John, the eldest, died young; and Henry Lord Stanhope, the 2nd, *d.* before his father; Charles, the 3rd son, *m.* but *d.* without issue in 1645; Edward, William, Thomas, Michael, and George, *d.* under age; Ferdinando, the 9th son, was a Colonel of Horse in the Royal army, was in the battle of Edgehill and other engagements, and was killed at Bridgford in Nottinghamshire in 1643; he was *m.*, but left only a daughter; Philip, 10th son, lost his life at Shelford, *unm.*; and Arthur, 11th son, was ancestor of the present Earl. The 1st EARL had also by his 2nd marriage, a 12th son, Alexander, ancestor of Earl Stanhope.

Henry Lord Stanhope, the 2nd son, *d.* in 1634; having *m.* Catherine, daughter and co-heir of Thomas, 2nd and last Lord Wotton, which lady being appointed governess to the Princess Mary, eldest daughter of King CHARLES I., went with her into Holland upon her marriage with the Stadtholder, and was very instrumental in supplying the King's troops with money, arms, and ammunition; she was created Countess of Chesterfield for life, by patent bearing date on the day of King CHARLES II.'s restoration, with the precedency of an Earl's daughters, for her daughters by Lord Stanhope; they had one son, PHILIP, who succeeded his grandfather as 2nd EARL; he was very serviceable in forwarding the restoration of the royal family, and *d.* at an advanced age in 1713. He was succeeded by his son PHILIP, 3rd EARL; who was succeeded, in 1726, by his son PHILIP-DORMER, 4th EARL, so celebrated for his accomplishments, and his literary, political, and oratorical talents; he *d.* without issue, in 1773, and his titles devolved on the heir male of

Arthur Stanhope, of Stoke in Nottinghamshire, 11th son of PHILIP, 1st EARL. He was father of Charles Stanhope, who had five sons, 1 Francis, who *d. unm.*; 2 Dr. Michael Stanhope, ancestor of the EARL; 3 Henry, *m.* but left two daughters only; 4 Charles, whose son Edwyn-Francis, *d.* in 1802, having *m.* Catherine, daughter and co-heir of John Brydges, Marquis of Carnarvon, son and heir of James, 1st Duke of Chandos, by whom, who was widow of William Berkeley Lyon, Esq., he was father of Admiral Sir Henry-Edwyn Stanhope, *b.* 21 May 1754, created a Baronet in 1807, and *d.* 20 Dec. 1814, having *m.*, Aug. 1783, Peggy, daughter of Francis Malbone, Esq., by whom, who was *b.* 9 Feb. 1761, and *d.* 8 Aug. 1810, he was father of the present Sir Edwyn-Francis Scudamore-Stanhope, Bart., and a daughter, for whom see *The Peerage Volume.*

Michael Stanhope, D.D., Canon of Windsor, the 2nd son of Charles Stanhope, Esq., *d.* in 1738, leaving four sons:

1 Arthur-Charles, who *d.* 9 March 1770; having *m.* 1st, in Nov. 1740, Mary, daughter of St.-Andrew Thornhaugh, Esq. who *d.* 18 March 1748; 2ndly, 25 Aug. 1750, Margaret, daughter and co-heir of Charles Headlam, Esq., who *d.* Jan. 1764; and 3rdly, 2 March 1767, Frances, daughter of —— Broade, Esq., who survives him, and is re-married to the Rev. Thomas Bigsby. By his 1st and 3rd marriages, Mr. Stanhope had no issue, but by his 2nd, he had Margaret, *b.* 10 June 1754, *d.* 7 Sept. 1811, having *m.* 26 Dec. 1776, the Rev. William Smelt; and one son, PHILIP, who, in 1773, succeeded as 5th EARL, and was father of the present EARL, his only son, who succeeded him in 1805.

2 Sir Thomas Stanhope, Capt. R.N., and Colonel of Marines, *d. unm.* 7 March 1770.

3 Ferdinand, who *d.* 11 Feb. 1790; having *m.* Mary, daughter of —— Philips,

Esq., by whom, besides two sons and two daughters who *d. unm*, he had the three sons stated in *The Peerage Volume.*

4 Lovell Stanhope, Esq., under Secretary of State, *d. unm.* 1 Sept. 1783.

CHETWYND, VISCOUNT. (CHETWYND.)

Peer of Ireland.

This family, which takes its name from Chetwynd in Shropshire, flourished in that County from the reign of Henry III. to that of William III. Capt. John Chetwynd, of Mare and Rudge, Co. Stafford, had three sons, Walter John, and William-Richard. WALTER, the eldest son, was created, in 1717, VISCOUNT CHETWYND of Berehaven, Co. Cork, and Baron of Rathdown, Co. Dublin, with remainder to his issue male, failing which, to the issue male of his father; he *d.* without issue in 1735, and was succeeded by his next brother JOHN, 2nd VISCOUNT, who, dying also in 1767 without surviving issue male, was succeeded by his younger brother, WILLIAM-RICHARD, 3rd VISCOUNT; he *d.* in 1770, leaving three sons: 1 WILLIAM, 4th VISCOUNT; 2 Thomas, who *d. unm.*; 3 John, in holy orders, deceased; he left a son William Chetwynd, who was killed in an action against the Irish rebels, at Saintfield, in June 1796, and has left a widow and family, for whom see *The Peerage Volume.*

WILLIAM, the eldest son, succeeded his father as 4th VISCOUNT, 3 April 1770; was *b.* 25 Nov. 1721, and *d.* 12 Nov. 1791; having *m.* Susannah, youngest daughter of Sir Jonathan Cope, Bart., by whom, who *d.* 3 March 1790, he was father of his successor RICHARD, 5th VISCOUNT. The latter *d.* in 1821, and was succeeded by his only surviving son, RICHARD-WALTER, the present and 6th VISCOUNT.

CHICHESTER, EARL OF. (PELHAM.)

Peer of the United Kingdom.

The name of Pelham is taken from a Lordship so called in Hertfordshire, where this family are supposed to have resided before the Conquest; 12th in descent from Walter de Pelham, living in 1292, was Sir John Pelham, Bart., father of

1 Sir Thomas, created, in 1706, Baron Pelham of Laughton, Co. Sussex, which title became extinct in 1768, on the death of his son, THOMAS PELHAM-HOLLES, Duke of Newcastle; who had been created, in 1762, BARON PELHAM of Stanmer, Co. Sussex, with remainder to his cousin, Thomas Pelham, Esq., and his issue male.

2 Henry, who *d.* in 1721, leaving a son THOMAS, who, in consequence of the special limitation of the patent, succeeded as 2nd LORD, and was created EARL of CHICHESTER in 1801; for his marriage and issue see *The Peerage Volume.* He *d.* in 1805, and was succeeded by his eldest son THOMAS, 2nd EARL, father of HENRY-THOMAS, the present and 3rd EARL, who succeeded him in 1826.

CHOLMONDELEY, MARQUIS. (CHOLMONDELEY.)

Peer of the United Kingdom and of Ireland.

Richard de Belward became possessed of the Lordship of Cholmondeley, shortly after the Conquest, by marriage with the heiress of the ancient Barons of Malpas; 13th in descent from this marriage was

Sir Hugh Cholmondeley, of Cholmondeley, Co. Chester, who, before he was twenty-one years of age, marched with one hundred and thirty men, raised at his father's expense, to assist in suppressing the rebellion in the North, headed by the Earls of Westmoreland and Northumberland, against Queen Elizabeth, for the restoration of the Roman Catholic religion. He *d.* in 1601, leaving, besides other issue, three sons, viz.:

1 Robert, created a Baronet in 1611, and Viscount Cholmondeley of Kells, in the Peerage of Ireland, in 1628; he was also, for his great services to King CHARLES I. in the Civil Wars, created, in 1645, Baron Cholmondeley of Wiche Malbank, Co. Chester, in the Peerage of England; and Earl of Leinster in Ireland, in 1646; he *d.* without issue 2 Oct. 1659, when all his titles became extinct.

2 Hugh, ancestor of the Marquis.

3 Thomas, ancestor of Lord Delamere.

Hugh, the 2nd son of Sir Hugh Cholmondeley, was father of ROBERT, created, in 1661, VISCOUNT CHOLMONDELEY of Kells, in the Peerage of Ireland; he *d* in 1681, leaving two sons:

1 HUGH, 2nd VISCOUNT, created, in 1689, Baron Cholmondeley, of Namptwich, Co. Chester, in the Peerage of England, with remainder, failing his issue male, to his brother George; also, in 1706, Viscount Malpas, and EARL CHOLMONDELEY, both in the Co. of Chester, with the same remainder. He *d. unm.* in 1725.

2 GEORGE, created, in 1714, BARON of NEWBURGH, Co. Wexford, in the Peerage of Ireland; and, in 1716, BARON of NEWBURGH, in the Isle of Anglesey, in the Peerage of Great Britain; he succeeded his brother as EARL CHOLMONDELEY, &c., and *d.* in 1733, when he was succeeded by his son,

GEORGE, 3rd EARL; he *d.* in 1770, having had two sons who lived to maturity, viz.:

1 George, Viscount Malpas, *b.* 27 Oct. 1724, *d.* before his father, 15 March 1764, having *m.* 19 Jan. 1747, Hester, daughter and heir of Sir Francis Edwardes, Bart., by whom, who *d.* Sept. 1794, he left issue:

1 GEORGE-JAMES, who succeeded his grandfather as 4th EARL in 1770, and was created, in 1815, Earl of Rocksavage and MARQUIS CHOLMONDELEY; he *d.* in 1827, and was succeeded by his eldest son, GEORGE-HORATIO, present and 2nd MARQUIS.

2 Hon. Hester, *b.* 19 Feb. 1755, *d.* 26 Nov. 1828; having *m.* 6 Sept. 1773, William-Clapcot Lisle, Esq., who *d.* before her.

2 Hon. and Rev. Robert, *b.* 2 Nov. 1727, *d.* 6 June 1804; having *m.*, 30 Nov. 1746, Mary, daughter of Arthur Woffington, Esq., by whom, who *d.* 4 April 1811, he left a son and a daughter, as stated in *The Peerage Volume.*

CHURCHILL, BARON. (SPENCER.)

Peer of the United Kingdom.

His Lordship is the 2nd surviving son of George, 4th Duke of Marlborough; he was created, in 1815, BARON CHURCHILL of Whichcote, Co. Oxford. For his pedigree, see the title *Marlborough* in this Volume; his marriage, issue, &c. are given in the *The Peerage Volume.*

CLANCARTY, EARL OF. (LE POER TRENCH.)

Peer of Ireland and of the United Kingdom.

This family is of ancient descent, and was formerly seated at La Tranche, in Poitou, from whence the name is derived. Frederick de la Trench, a Protestant nobleman, emigrated to England in 1574, and his grandson, Frederick, removed to Ireland. He *d.* in 1699, leaving two sons, viz.:

1 Frederick, whose son, Richard Trench, Esq., *m.* Frances, only daughter and heir of David Power, Esq., descended from the Barons de la Poer, by whom he was father of William-Power-Keating Trench, Esq., who was created, in 1797, Baron Kilconnel of Garbally; in 1801, Viscount Dunlo of Dunlo and Ballinasloe; and, in 1803, Earl of Clancarty, all in the Peerage of Ireland; his marriage, issue, &c. are described in *The Peerage Volume.* He *d.* in 1805, and was succeeded by his eldest son, Richard, the present and 2nd Earl, who was created a Peer of the United Kingdom in 1815, by the title of Baron Trench of Garbally, Co. Galway, and was father advanced, in 1823, to the rank of Viscount Clancarty.

2 John, Dean of Raphoe, great-grandfather of Lord Ashtown.

CLANMORRIS, BARON. (Bingham.)

Peer of Ireland.

His Lordship is of the same family with the Earl of Lucan; being 7th in descent from John, younger son of George Bingham, Esq., Governor of Sligo, whose eldest son, Sir Henry Bingham, created a Baronet in 1632, was ancestor of the Earl of Lucan. His father, John Bingham, Esq., was created, in 1800, Baron Clanmorris of Newbrook, Co. Mayo; for his marriage, issue, &c. see *The Peerage Volume.* He *d.* in 1821, and was succeeded by his eldest surviving son, (having lost his two first-born sons, Yelverton and Richard, in their childhood,) Charles-Barry, 2nd Lord, who *d.* in 1829, and was succeeded by his brother, Denis-Arthur, the present and 3rd Lord.

CLANRICARDE, MARQUIS. (De Burgh.)

Peer of Ireland and of the United Kingdom.

John de Burgh, Earl of Comyn, in Normandy, accompanied William the Conqueror into England; he *m.* Beatrix, *dau.* and heir of Ivo de Vesey, a Norman Noble, and by her had two sons. 1 Harlowen, ancestor of the Marquis of Clanricarde; 2 Eustace, Lord of Knaresborough, the reputed ancestor of the Viscount De Vesci.

Harlowen, the eldest son, *m.* Arlotte, mother of William the Conqueror, and *d.* before his father, leaving, by her, two sons:

1 Robert, called de Moreton, created, in 1068, Earl of Cornwall, of which Earldom his son William was dispossessed by King Henry I., in 1104.

2 Odo, Bishop of Bayeux, in Normandy, created Earl of Kent in 1067, and *d.* without issue in 1096.

William, the 2nd and last Earl of Cornwall of this family, had also two sons; 1 Adelm; and 2 John, who was father of Herbert de Burgh, Chief Justiciary of England, who makes so conspicuous and honourable a figure in the history of the reigns of King John and Henry III.; he was created Earl of Kent in 1226, and *d.* in 1243, leaving male issue, but none of them ever enjoyed his Earldom.

Adelm, the elder son, obtained from King Henry II., a grant of large domains in the province of Connaught, in Ireland; his son Richard, was lord of Connaught and Trim, and Lord Justice of Ireland, and *d.* in 1243; leaving two sons:

1 Walter, who *m.* Maud, daughter and heir of Hugh de Lacy, Earl of Ulster, and was, in her right, Earl of Ulster, which Earldom continued in his male descendants till they failed in 1333, by the death of his great-grandson William, 3rd Earl, whose

only daughter and heir, Elizabeth, *m.* Lionel, Duke of Clarence, 2nd son of King Edward III.; and was ancestor by him of King Edward IV., and the succeeding Kings of England.

2 William, father of Sir William de Burgh, whose 2nd son, Sir Edmund, was ancestor of the Earl of Mayo, and Lord Downes; and his eldest son, Sir William, or Sir Ulick, was ancestor in the fourth degree of Ulick de Burgh, created, in 1543, Baron of Dunkellin, Co. Galway, and EARL of CLANRICARDE, in the same county; he *d.* in 1544, and was succeeded by his son RICHARD, 2nd EARL, who was succeeded, in 1582, by his son,

ULICK, 3rd EARL. He *d.* in 1601, leaving, besides other issue,

1 RICHARD, his successor, 4th EARL; who was created, in 1624, Baron Somerhill, and Viscount Tunbridge, Co. Kent, in the Peerage of England, and farther advanced to the dignity of Earl of St. Albans; he was also created Baron of Immany, in the province of Connaught, and Viscount Galway, Irish honours, and, dying in 1636, was succeeded by his only son ULICK, 5th EARL; who was created, in 1645, Marquis of Clanricarde, in Ireland; he *d.* without issue male in 1657, when the title of Marquis of Clanricarde, together with the Irish titles which had been conferred upon his father, and all the English honours, became extinct; but the Earldom devolved on his Cousin.

2 Sir William de Burgh; left two sons, RICHARD, who succeeded as 6th EARL, and died without issue male in 1666; and WILLIAM, 7th EARL, who succeeded his brother; he *d.* in 1687, and was father of RICHARD, 8th EARL, who *d.* without issue; of JOHN, 9th, EARL; and of Ulick, created Viscount of Galway, who *d.* without issue in 1691.

JOHN, 9th EARL, succeeded his brother; he *d.* in 1722, and was succeeded by his son MICHAEL, 10th EARL, father of

JOHN-SMITH, 11th EARL, who was born 11 Nov. 1720, succeeded 29 Nov. 1726, and *d.* 21 April 1782, having *m.* in 1740, Hester, youngest daughter of Sir Henry Vincent, Bart., by whom, who *d.* 29 Dec. 1803, he was father of 1 HENRY, 12th EARL, his successor, for whom see *The Peerage Volume*; he was created, in 1785, Marquis of Clanricarde; the Lady Anne Paulet, his widow, is still living, but the Marquis *d.* without issue in 1797, when that title became extinct; 2 JOHN-THOMAS, 13th EARL, who succeeded his brother in the Earldom, and obtained, in 1800, a renewed patent of his Earldom, with remainder, failing his issue male, to his daughters and their issue male respectively; he was father of ULICK-JOHN, the present and 14th Earl, who succeeded him in 1808; was advanced to the dignity of MARQUIS of CLANRICARDE in 1825; and, in 1826, was created a Peer of the United Kingdom, by the title of Baron Somerhill of Somerhill, Co. Kent.

CLANWILLIAM, EARL OF. (MEADE.)

Peer of Ireland and of the United Kingdom.

This is a very ancient family of the County of Cork. Sir John Meade of Ballentobber, who *d.* in 1626, was grandfather of Sir John, created a Baronet in 1703; who was father of Sir Pierce and Sir Richard, successive Baronets; Sir Richard *d.* in 1744, and was succeeded by his only son Sir John, created in 1766, Baron Gilford, Co. Down, and Viscount Clanwilliam, Co. Tipperary, and advanced to the rank of EARL of CLANWILLIAM, in 1776, all in the Peerage of Ireland. For his marriage, issue, &c., see *The Peerage Volume*; he *d.* in 1800, and was succeeded by his eldest son, RICHARD, 2nd EARL, to whom, in 1805, succeeded his only son, RICHARD, the present and 3rd EARL; who was created, in 1828, BARON CLANWILLIAM, of Clanwilliam, Co. Tipperary, in the Peerage of the United Kingdom.

CLARE, EARL OF. (Fitz-Gibbon.)

Peer of Ireland and of Great Britain.

The Earl is a collateral branch of the Duke of Leinster's family. Thomas, 3rd Lord Offaley, *d.* in 1260, ; his only son, John, had issue, 1 Maurice, grandfather of the first Earl of Kildare, from whom the Duke of Leinster descends ; 2 Gilbert, ancestor of John Fitz-Gibbon, Esq., an eminent Barrister, who *d.* in 1780 ; he was father of John Fitz-Gibbon, the celebrated Lord High Chancellor of Ireland, who was created, in 1789, Baron Fitz-Gibbon, of Lower Connello, Co. Limerick ; in 1793, Viscount Fitz-Gibbon, of Limerick, Co. Limerick, and, in 1795, Earl of Clare ; all in the Peerage of Ireland ; and, in 1799, was farther created Baron Fitz-Gibbon, of Sidbury, Co. Devon, in the Peerage of Great Britain. His marriage, issue, &c., will be found in *The Peerage Volume* ; he *d.* in 1802, and was succeeded by his eldest son, John, present and 2nd Earl.

CLARENDON, EARL OF. (Villiers.)

Peer of Great Britain.

The Honourable Thomas Villiers, 2nd son of William, 2nd Earl of Jersey, *m.* Lady Charlotte Capel, eldest surviving daughter of William, 3rd Earl of Essex, and co-heir of her mother, Lady Jane Hyde, eldest surviving daughter and co-heir of Henry Hyde, the last Earl of Clarendon and Rochester ; which lady was entitled, on the death of the Earl of Clarendon, her grandfather, to use the name and arms of Hyde. Her husband was created, in 1756, Baron Hyde, of Hindon ; and in 1776, Earl of Clarendon. Frederick II., King of Prussia, at whose Court his Lordship had been many years Ambassador, granted to him, as a token of his esteem, the title of Count of the Kingdom of Prussia, and permission to bear his arms on the body of the Prussian eagle ; which marks of royal favour, King George III. permitted his Lordship to accept. The Earl *d.* in 1786, and was succeeded by his eldest son, Thomas, 2nd Earl, who, dying *unm.* in 1824, John-Charles, his next brother, the present and 3rd Earl succeeded. For a further account of the 1st Earl and all his issue, see *The Peerage Volume.*

CLARINA, BARON. (Massey.)

Peer of Ireland.

Col. Hugh Massy of Duntrileague, Co. Limerick, left seven sons, of whom Hugh the eldest, was created in 1776, Baron Massy ; and Eyre, the 6th son, having early entered the army, was engaged in the battle of Culloden in 1746, afterwards rose to the rank of General, and was, throughout his life, much employed in the wars abroad ; at length, in reward of his long and valuable services, he was created to the Peerage, in 1800, by the title of Baron Clarina of Elm Park, Co. Limerick, and *d.* in 1804, when he was succeeded by his only surviving son, Nathaniel-William, 2nd Lord, father of Eyre, the present and 3rd Lord, who succeeded him in 1810. For a further account of the 1st Lord and his issue, see *The Peerage Volume.*

CLEVELAND, MARQUIS OF. (VANE.)

Peer of the United Kingdom.

John Vane, Esq., of Tudeley, 12th in descent from Howell ap Vane, was father of Richard, from whom the Earl of Westmoreland descends, and of John Fane of Hadloe, Co. Kent, Esq., whose son and grandson, both Henry Fanes, successively inherited his estate; the latter was father and grandfather of the two Sir Henry Vanes who played such conspicuous parts in the great historical drama during the reign of King Charles I. and the succeeding interregnum. Sir George Vane, youngest son of the elder Sir Henry, surprised and took his father's castle of Raby, on behalf of the king, in 1645, with a party of royalist forces raised by himself. He was ancestor of the late Sir Henry Vane Tempest, Bart., whose daughter and heir is the present Marchioness of Londonderry, and of Sir Frederick-Fletcher Vane, Bart., of Hutton Hall, Cumberland.

Sir Henry Vane, the younger, was beheaded upon Tower-hill, 14 June 1662, soon after the restoration of King CHARLES II.; but his son CHRISTOPHER was created, in 1699, Baron Barnard, of Barnard's Castle, Co. Durham, and *d.* in 1723. His son, GILBERT, 2nd LORD, was father of

HENRY, 3rd LORD, who succeeded him in 1753, and was created, in 1754, Viscount Barnard, of Barnard's Castle, and EARL of DARLINGTON; he *d.* in 1758, having *m.* in 1725, Lady Grace Fitzroy, daughter of Charles Fitzroy Duke of Cleveland and Southampton, and co-heir of her brother William, 2nd and last Duke, by whom he left three sons: 1 HENRY, his successor, 2nd EARL; 2 The Hon. Frederick Vane, *b.* 26 June, 1732, *d.* 28 April 1801, having *m.*, 1st, Henrietta, daughter of Sir William Meredith, Bart., by whom he has left a daughter, *m.* 22 Feb. 1795 to Captain Metcalfe; and 2ndly, Aug. 1796, Jane, eldest daughter of Arthur Lysaght, Esq., who *d.* 7 April 1813; 3 The Hon. Capt. Raby Vane, R.N., *b.* 2 Jan. 1736, *d.* Oct. 1769; having *m.* 17 April 1768, a daughter of the late Bishop Eyre.

HENRY, 2nd EARL, *d.* in 1792, and was succeeded by his only son WILLIAM-HENRY, present and 3rd EARL, who was created MARQUIS of CLEVELAND in 1827, since which period he has quartered with the arms of Vane those of King Charles II., debruised by a baton sinister ermine; and has borne by royal grant the crest and supporters of Fitzroy Duke of Cleveland and Southampton.

CLIFDEN, VISCOUNT. (AGAR-ELLIS.)

Peer of Ireland and of Great Britain.

Charles Agar, Esq., of Yorkshire, (descended from a French Protestant family of the Comte Venaissin, who left their country during the wars of religion,) settled at Gowran in Ireland, and was father of

1 Henry.

2 James, whose son George, *b.* 18 April 1754, and created Baron Callan 1790, *d. unm.* 9 Oct 1815, when his title became extinct.

3 Ellis, *m.* 1st, Theobald, 7th Viscount Mayo, and 2ndly, Francis Birmingham, 21st Lord Athenry; she was created Countess of Brandon, and *d.* without issue in 1789, when the title became extinct.

Henry Agar, Esq., of Gowran, eldest son, *d.* 18 Nov. 1746; having *m.* 29 May 1733, Anne, daughter of Welbore Ellis, Lord Bishop of Meath, descended from the family of Ellis, who trace their possessions in Yorkshire to the time of the Conquest, and sister of Welbore, created, in 1794, BARON MENDIP, Co. Somerset, in the

Peerage of Great Britain, with remainder, failing his issue male, to Henry-Welbore Agar, 2nd Viscount Clifden in Ireland, John-Ellis Agar, and Charles-Bagenal Agar, sons of James, 1st Viscount Clifden in Ireland, eldest son of Henry Agar, Esq., by Anne Ellis, only sister of the said Lord, and their heirs male respectively; in default of which, to Welbore-Ellis Agar, Esq., and Dr. Charles Agar, Archbishop of Cashel, (afterwards Earl of Normanton, and Archbishop of Dublin,) 2nd and 3rd sons of the above-mentioned Henry Agar and Anne Ellis, and their heirs male respectively. This Welbore Ellis, 1st Lord Mendip, was born in 1713, and *d.* without issue 2 Feb. 1802; having *m.*, 1st, Elizabeth, daughter of the Hon. Sir William Stanhope, K.B., (2nd son of Philip, 3rd Earl of Chesterfield,) who *d.* 1 Aug. 1761; and 2ndly, Anne, daughter of George Stanley, Esq., who was *b.* in 1725, and *d.* 7 Dec. 1803. Anne, his sister, who was *b.* 26 Aug. 1707, *m.* 2ndly, after Mr. Agar's death, George Dunbar, Esq., and *d.* 14 April 1765, leaving, by her 1st husband Henry Agar, Esq., 1 James; 2 Welbore Ellis, who *d.* without issue in Oct. 1805; 3 Charles, Archbishop of Cashel, and afterwards of Dublin, and late Earl of Normanton; 4 The Rev. Henry Agar, not included in the limitation of the patent; he has left a son, Henry Agar-Ellis, Esq., who is *m.* in Bombay, and has issue.

James, their eldest son, was created, in 1776, Lord Clifden, Baron of Gowran, Co. Kilkenny, and, in 1781, Viscount Clifden, both in the Peerage of Ireland; he *d.* in 1789, leaving 3 sons, viz.:

1 Henry-Welbore, his successor, present and 2nd Viscount, who, in 1802, pursuant to the limitation of the patent, also succeeded his maternal uncle in the Barony of Mendip, in the Peerage of Great Britain, and assumed the name and arms of Ellis. For his marriage, issue, &c. see *The Peerage Volume.* George, his only son, was created a Peer of the United Kingdom in 1831, by the title of Baron Dover.

2 Hon. and Rev. John, *b.* 31 Dec. 1763, *d.* 3 Jan. 1797; having *m.* 11 March 1792, Hon. Harriet Flower, 3rd daughter of William, 2nd Viscount Ashbrook, who was *b.* 18 Nov. 1771, [*m.* 2ndly, 20 July 1798, Pryse-Loveden Pryse, Esq., M.P.] and *d.* 14 Jan. 1813.

3 Hon. Charles-Bagenal, *b.* 13 Aug. 1769, *d.* 16 June 1811; having *m.* 15 Nov. 1804, Anna-Maria, daughter of Thomas Hunt, Esq., by whom, who survives him, he had issue, besides his surviving son and heir, Thomas-James Robartes, Esq., stated in *The Peerage Volume;* an elder son, Charles, *b.* 18 Dec. 1805, who *d.* before him in 1809; and a posthumous son, Edward, *b.* 12 Sept. 1811, *d.* in 1818.

CLIFFORD, BARON. (Clifford.)

Peer of England.

William Fitzponz came into England with William the Conqueror, and was grandfather of Walter, who acquired the castle of Clifford by marriage, and assumed his family name therefrom; 5th in descent from him was Robert, summoned to Parliament by writ as Baron Clifford in 1299; grandfather of Roger, 5th Lord, who *d.* in 1390, leaving issue:

1 Thomas, 6th Lord, ancestor of the Earls of Cumberland, extinct in 1569, and whose Barony is now possessed by Lord De Clifford as heir general.

2 Sir Lewis Clifford, K.G., whose son William had issue: 1 Lewis, ancestor of the Cliffords of Kent; 2 John, ancestor in the 7th degree of

Sir Thomas Clifford of Ugbrooke, Co. Devon, who raised himself by his industry and abilities to great eminence in the state; he resumed, during the interregnum after the death of King Charles I., the profession of the Roman Catholic religion, and was one of the five statesmen who during the reign of Charles II. were denominated the cabal, from the initial letters of their names; (*viz.; Clifford, Ashley, Buckingham, Arlington, Lauderdale.*) Having served in various high offices of government, he held for a short time the distinguished post of Lord High Treasurer of the kingdom, and, in 1672, was created BARON CLIFFORD of Chudleigh, Co. Devon. He *d.* in 1673; and from him the title was inherited, in direct descent from father to son, by three Barons all named HUGH; the 2nd LORD *d.* in 1730; HUGH, 3rd LORD, in 1732, having had four sons, of whom HUGH the eldest son, his successor, and Thomas the youngest son, alone left issue. The latter was *b.* 22 Aug. 1732, and *d.* 18 June 1787; having *m.* 2 Feb. 1762, Hon. Barbara Aston, daughter of James, 5th Lord Aston, who *d.* 2 Aug. 1786. For their surviving issue, see *The Peerage Volume.*

HUGH, 5th LORD, *b.* 29 Sept. 1726, succeeded his father 26 March 1732, and *d.* 1 Sept. 1783; having *m.* 17 Dec. 1749, Lady Anne Lee, 5th daughter of George-Henry, 2nd Earl of Lichfield, who was *b.* Jan. 1731, and *d.* 9 Dec. 1802. They had issue, besides two daughters who *d. unm.* and two daughters now living, (see *The Peerage Volume,*) the four sons following:

1 HUGH-EDWARD-HENRY, 5th LORD, *b.* 2 July 1756, succeeded 1 Sept. 1783, and *d.* without issue 15 Jan. 1793; having *m.* May 1780, the Hon. Apollonia Langdale, youngest daughter and co-heir of Marmaduke, 4th and last Lord Langdale; she *d.* Dec. 1815.

2 CHARLES, 6th LORD, (see *The Peerage Volume,*) who succeeded his brother, and *d.* in 1831, when he was succeeded by his eldest son, HUGH-CHARLES, present and 7th LORD.

3 Hon. Robert-Edward, F.R. and A.S., *b.* 16 Oct. 1767, *d. unm.* 18 Feb. 1817.

4 Hon. Thomas-Edward, *b.* 5 Dec. 1774, *d.* 2 April 1817; having *m.* 17 Nov. 1807, Henrietta-Philippina, Baroness de Lutzow, by whom, who *d.* 20 Nov. 1822, he has left three daughters.

CLINTON, BARON. (TREFUSIS.)

Peer of England.

THEOPHILUS CLINTON, 4th Earl of Lincoln, and 11th BARON CLINTON, 11th in direct paternal descent from JOHN de CLINTON, the 1st Baron by writ 1299, and 16th from Osbert, the 1st Baron by tenure, had, besides seven daughters, a son, Edward, father of EDWARD, 5th EARL and 12th Lord, on whose death, without issue, in 1692, the Earldom devolved on Francis Clinton, 6th Earl, his cousin and heir male, and this Barony fell into abeyance, between his aunts, daughters of THEOPHILUS, 4th EARL and 11th LORD; of whom four *d. unm.* Lady Catherine, eldest daughter, *m.* George Booth Lord Delamere, and left an only daughter and heir, Vere, who *d. unm.* in 1717: the other two were,

Lady Arabella, 4th daughter, who *m.* Robert Rolle, Esq., and had by him a son, Samuel, father of MARGARET, 14th BARONESS, his only daughter and heir; and a daughter, Bridget, who, by Francis Trefusis, Esq., was great-great-grandmother of ROBERT-GEORGE-WILLIAM, 16th LORD; and

Lady Margaret, 5th daughter, who *m.* Hugh Boscawen, Esq., by whom she had a daughter and heir, Bridget, who, by marriage with Hugh Fortescue, Esq., was mother of HUGH, 13th LORD, in whose favour the King was pleased to terminate the abeyance in 1721; on his death in 1751, it again fell into abeyance, till, by the death, in 1760, of Margaret, his sister and heir,

MARGARET, 14th BARONESS, became sole heir of the Barony; she *m.* Robert, 2nd Earl of Orford, and *d.* in 1781, when her son GEORGE, 15th Lord, and 3rd Earl of Orford, succeeded; he *d.* 5 Dec. 1791; and in 1794 the sole heir,

ROBERT-GEORGE-WILLIAM TREFUSIS, 16th LORD, descended from an ancient family, seated at Trefusis, Co. Cornwall, claimed and was allowed the Barony.

His Lordship is also the eldest co-heir of the ancient Barony of Saye, by writ 1313, being heir-general of JOHN, 3rd LORD CLINTON, by his marriage with Idonea de Saye, eldest daughter of Geoffrey, 2nd Lord Saye, and co-heir of her niece Elizabeth, Baroness Saye; Joan, the other daughter, and at length co-heir of Geoffrey Lord Saye, *m.* Sir William Fiennes, and the present Lord Dacre is her heir-general, and the younger co-heir of the Barony of Saye.

CLONBROCK, BARON. (DILLON.)

Peer of Ireland.

His Lordship is of the same ancestry with Viscount Dillon, and the Earl of Roscommon, being descended from Sir James, younger son of Gerald Dillon, of Drumrany, whose eldest son, Sir Maurice, was ancestor of Viscount Dillon. Sir James was father of Sir Robert, who had issue: 1 Sir Richard, ancestor of the Earl of Roscommon, and of Sir Charles Dillon, Bart., of Lismullen, Co. Meath; 2 Gerald, ancestor of Luke Dillon, father of ROBERT, 1st LORD CLONBROCK, and of Luke Dillon, Esq., who *d.* in 1821, having *m.* Lady Margaret-Augusta de Burgh, 2nd daughter of John Smyth, 11th Earl of Clanricarde, by whom he has left issue.

ROBERT, 1st LORD, was created, in 1790, BARON CLONBROCK of Clonbrock, Co. Galway, and *d.* in 1795; when he was succeeded by his only son, LUKE, 2nd LORD, to whom, in 1826, succeeded his only-surviving son, ROBERT, the present and 3rd LORD.

CLONCURRY, BARON. (LAWLESS.)

Peer of Ireland and of the United Kingdom.

SIR NICHOLAS LAWLESS, created a Baronet in 1776, was also, in 1789, created BARON of CLONCURRY, Co. Kildare. He was sixth in descent from Walter Lawless, of Talbot Inche, Co. Kilkenny, who *d.* in 1627, and whose ancestor, Sir Hugh de Lawless, of Hoddesdon, Co. Herts, settled in Ireland in the reign of Henry II. The 1st LORD *d.* in 1799, and was succeeded by his only son, VALENTINE-BROWNE, present and 2nd LORD; who was also created in 1831 a Peer of the United Kingdom, by the same title of BARON CLONCURRY, of Cloncurry, Co. Kildare.

CLONMEL, EARL OF. (SCOTT.)

Peer of Ireland.

Thomas Scott, a Captain in King William's army, fell in battle in Ireland, in the war of the Revolution; his family settled in Ireland, and his grandson, John Scott, having passed through several of the subordinate Law Offices in Ireland, was appointed, in 1784, Lord Chief Justice of the King's Bench; in the same year was created Baron Earlsfort; advanced to the dignity of Viscount Clonmel of Clonmel, Co. Tipperary, in 1789, and to that of EARL of CLONMEL in 1793. He *d.* in 1798, and was succeeded by his only son, THOMAS, the present and 2nd EARL.

COLCHESTER, BARON. (ABBOT.)

Peer of the United Kingdom.

The Rev. John Abbot, D.D., Rector of All-Saints, in Colchester, was *b.* in Oct. 1717, and *d.* 29 April 1760, having *m.* Sarah, daughter of Jonathan Farr, Esq., who *m.* 2ndly, Jeremiah Bentham, Esq., and *d.* 27 Sept. 1800.

83

The Right Hon. Charles Abbot, their 2nd son, (John Farr, the eldest son, having *d.* in 1794 without issue,) was Speaker of the House of Commons from 1802 to 1817, when, retiring from public business, he was called to the House of Peers, by the title of Baron Colchester of Colchester, Co. Essex; he *d.* in 1829, and was succeeded by his eldest son, CHARLES, present and 2nd LORD.

COLVILLE, BARON. (COLVILLE.)

Peer of Scotland.

This family was of great consideration in England previous to the reign of King Stephen, when Richard de Colville removed to Scotland. Robert, his lineal heir male, killed at the battle of Flodden in 1513, was grandfather of Sir James, who had two sons, James and Alexander; James, the eldest son, was created, in 1609, BARON COLVILLE of Culross, with remainder to his heirs male whatsoever, and his issue male failing in his grandson, JAMES, 2nd LORD, who *d.* in 1640, the title devolved on his nephew, JOHN, of right 3rd LORD, son of his brother Alexander; but neither he nor his successors assumed the title, till it was claimed by, and allowed by the House of Lords in 1723 to, JOHN, of right 7th LORD, 4th in descent from JOHN, who should have been 3rd LORD.

JOHN, 7th LORD, was a Lieutenant-Colonel in the Army, and in the expedition to Carthagena, where he fell a victim to the epidemic disease so fatal to the British troops in that fruitless siege; he *d.* on board a transport in the harbour, in April 1741; five of his sons survived their infancy, and all were highly distinguished either in the military or naval service of their country; all, however, *d. unm.*, except ALEXANDER and JOHN, successive Lords Colville. ALEXANDER, 8th LORD, succeeded his father, but *d.* without issue in 1770, and was succeeded by his next surviving brother, JOHN, 9th LORD, father of JOHN, the present and 10th LORD, who succeeded him in 1811.

COMBERMERE, VISCOUNT. (STAPLETON-COTTON.)

Peer of the United Kingdom.

This family is supposed to be of Saxon origin. Sir Hugh Cotton was seated at Combermere in the reign of King John, and was ancestor of William, living there in the reign of Henry V.; 6th in descent from him was

Sir Robert Cotton, knighted at the restoration of King Charles II., and created a Baronet in 1677. He *m.* Hester, daughter and sole heir of Sir Thomas Salusbury, of Lewenney, Co. Denbigh, Bart.; and his son and successor, Sir Thomas, *m.* Philadelphia, daughter and sole heir of Sir Thomas Lynch, of Esher, Co. Surrey. Sir Robert, their eldest son, succeeded, but left no issue, and Sir Lynch, their 7th and last surviving son, succeeded his brother, and was father of

Sir Robert Salusbury Cotton, Bart., who *d.* in 1807; having *m.* in 1767, Frances, youngest daughter and co-heir of James-Russell Stapleton, Esq., of Boddryddon, Co. Denbigh; by whom, besides a daughter, Frances, who *d. unm.* in 1786, and his son and heir, Robert-Salusbury Cotton, Esq., who *d.* before him *unm.* in 1799, he had the following issue:

1 General Sir Stapleton Cotton, who succeeded him in the Baronetcy, and was created, in 1814, Baron Combermere of Combermere, Co. Chester, and, in 1826, VISCOUNT COMBERMERE, of Bhurtpore, in the East Indies, and of Combermere, Co. Chester; and is the present Peer, see *The Peerage Volume.* His Lordship assumed, in 1827, the additional surname of Stapleton.

2 The Rev. William Cotton.

3 Colonel Lynch Cotton, who *d.* in the East Indies in 1799; and whose widow is now the wife of the Hon. General Sir William Lumley. See *The Peerage Volume*, title Scarborough.

4 Frances, who *m.* 10 Jan. 1792, Robert, 11th Viscount Kilmorey, and *d.* 26 Nov. 1818.

5 Hester-Maria.

6 Sophia, *m.* 29 Dec. 1803, Sir Henry-Mainwaring Mainwaring, Bart.

CONYNGHAM, MARQUIS. (CONYNGHAM.)

Peer of Ireland and of the United Kingdom.

Lieutenant-General Henry Conyngham, descended from William, youngest son of William, 4th Earl of Glencairn, in Scotland, had, besides other issue,

1 HENRY, created Baron Conyngham of Mountcharles 1753, Viscount Conyngham 1756, Earl Conyngham 1780, and at the same time BARON CONYNGHAM, with remainder to his nephew, Francis-Pierrepont Burton, Esq.; he *d.* 3 April 1781, when all his titles became extinct, except the last-created Barony.

2 Mary, 3rd daughter; she *d.* in 1737, having *m.* Francis Burton, Esq., descended from Sir Edward Burton, knighted by King EDWARD IV., by whom she was mother of FRANCIS-PIERREPONT, 2nd LORD, who succeeded his uncle, and assumed the name of CONYNGHAM; he *d.* in 1787, (see *The Peerage Volume,*) and was succeeded by his eldest son, HENRY, present and 3rd LORD; he was created Viscount Conyngham, of Slane, Co. Meath, in 1789; Viscount Mountcharles, Co. Donegal, and Earl Conyngham, of Mountcharles, in 1797; MARQUIS CONYNGHAM, Earl of Mount-Charles, Co. Donegal, and Viscount Slane, Co. Meath, in 1816; also created, in 1821, Baron Minster, of Minster, Co. Kent, in the Peerage of Great Britain.

CORK AND ORRERY, EARL OF. (BOYLE.)

Peer of Ireland and of Great Britain.

Ludovick Boyle, living in the County of Hereford, in the reign of Henry III., was ancestor, in the 10th generation, of

SIR RICHARD BOYLE, who rose to great power, wealth, and dignity, in the service of Queen Elizabeth, King James I., and King Charles I., in Ireland. He was *b.* 3 Oct. 1566; created Baron Boyle of Youghall, Co. Cork in 1616, Viscount Dungarvan, Co. Waterford, and Earl of the County of Cork, in 1620; and lived to see his numerous issue flourishing in a state of extraordinary worldly splendour and dignity. Of his eight daughters, all esteemed Ladies of great piety and virtue, and ornaments to their sex, the youngest only died unmarried, the other seven all married Earls or their heirs-apparent; of his seven sons, two died young, and of the remaining five, four were raised to the honours of the Peerage. This great Earl's latter days were, however, clouded with heavy care and loss, by the breaking out of the great rebellion in Ireland in 1641, during the course of which himself and sons devoted their lives and fortunes to the service of their King and country. From his private resources he garrisoned and supplied with ammunition all his castles; at his own charge held the town and harbour of Youghall with two hundred English Protestants, well-armed and disciplined; and in the great battle of Liscarrol, where the Royal troops, under the command of his eldest son Viscount Dungarvan, and the Lord Inchiquin, were completely victorious, four of his sons were engaged, all were distinguished for their valour, and one of them, Lord Kinal meaky, lost his life. In the midst of these confusions the Earl *d.* 15 Sept. 1643, at his seat at Youghall. His five sons who survived their childhood were popularly distinguished as Richard, Earl of Cork, the rich; Lewis, Lord Kinalmeaky, the valiant; Roger, Earl of Orrery, the wise; Francis, Lord Shannon, the just; and Robert Boyle, the philosopher; it is, however, necessary here to give a more particular account of them.

1 RICHARD, 2nd EARL, *b.* 26 Oct. 1612, one of the Commanders in the battle of Liscarrol; he continued faithful to the King to the close of the civil war, and was, with all his brothers, active in promoting the restoration of King Charles II.; he *m.* Elizabeth, sole daughter and heir of Henry Clifford, 5th Earl of Cumberland, and Baron Clifford [by writ 1628;] she *d.* in 1690; he was created Baron Clifford of Lanesborough in 1644, and Earl of Burlington in 1663, both in the Peerage of England, and *d.* in 1697. Charles Viscount Dungarvan, their eldest son, should have succeeded his mother in the Barony of Clifford, by the writ of 1628, but he had been called to the House of Peers before her death, in 1689, and placed in his father's Barony of Clifford of Lanesborough, and never claimed the Barony by writ; he *d.* before his father, leaving two sons, of whom Henry, the younger son, was Chancellor of the Exchequer, and principal Secretary of State in the reign of Queen ANNE, and President of the Council under King GEORGE I.; he was created Baron Carleton of Carleton, Co. York in Oct. 1714, and *d. unm.* in 1725, bequeathing his house in Pall-Mall to Frederick Prince of Wales; his title became extinct. CHARLES, the elder son, succeeded his father as Baron Clifford by writ, and his grandfather as 3rd EARL of CORK and 2nd Earl of Burlington; he *d.* in 1704, and was succeeded by his only son, RICHARD, 4th EARL, K.G., who, in 1737, claimed and was allowed the Barony of Clifford, created by writ in 1628; he *d.* in 1753, without issue male, when the English titles of Earl of Burlington, and Baron Clifford of Lanesborough, became extinct; the Barony of Clifford by writ, was inherited by his only-surviving daughter, Lady Charlotte, Duchess of Devonshire, whose grandson, the present Duke of Devonshire, is also Baron Clifford; but the Irish titles devolved on the heir male, JOHN, 5th Earl of Orrery.

2 Lewis, *b.* 23 May 1619, created in 1628, Baron of Bandon Bridge, and Viscount Boyle of Kinalmeaky, with remainder to his father and his heirs male; he was killed in the battle of Liscarrol, 3 Sept. 1642, *unm.*, when his father, the 1st Earl of Cork, succeeded to his titles, which have since continued in the Earls of Cork.

3 ROGER, *b.* 25 April 1621, created in 1628, Lord Broghill, Baron of Broghill, Co. Cork. From the breaking out of the Rebellion of the Irish Catholics, in 1641, he was remarkable for the zeal and valour with which he resisted them; at the battle of Liscarrol he was taken prisoner, but rescued by his own men, and continued in arms till the death of King Charles I., when he retired to his seat, at Marston Bigot, in Somersetshire. Being afterwards in London, when a correspondence between him and King Charles II. had just been detected by the heads of the government, Cromwell, in a private interview, pointed out to him the danger in which he stood, and promised him his life only on condition of his joining the Parliament to put down the Irish rebels; this he undertook to do, and passing over to Ireland with Cromwell, continued in active service to the end of the war, and was afterwards closely connected with Cromwell till the usurper's death. He then lent his best assistance towards the restoration of King CHARLES II., and sent his brother, Lord Shannon, to invite his Majesty into Ireland. An opening had, however, by this time, been made for the King's return to England, but Lord Broghill's services were acknowledged by his creation, in Sept. 1660, to the title of EARL of ORRERY. He *d.* in 1679, leaving two sons, viz.:

1 ROGER, 2nd EARL of ORRERY, who *d.* in 1698, leaving also two sons,
1 LIONEL, 3rd EARL, who *d.* without issue in 1703, and CHARLES, 4th EARL, who succeeded his brother. He was celebrated, before his accession to the Peerage, for his literary dispute with the learned Dr. Bentley; and after-

wards entered on a military career, in which he rose to the rank of Lieutenant-General, served with distinction under the Duke of Marlborough in Flanders, and in particular led on his regiment with the utmost intrepidity at the battle of Malplaquet. He was created a Peer of Great Britain in 1711, by the title of Baron Boyle, of Marston, Co. Somerset. During the suspension of the Habeas Corpus Act in 1722, he was committed to the Tower on suspicion of high treason, which appearing utterly groundless on the strictest examination, he was liberated. He *d.* in 1730, leaving an only son, John, 5th Earl of Orrery, who also succeeded as 5th Earl of Cork.

2 Henry, whose son Henry was created Earl of Shannon, and was ancestor of the present Earl of Shannon.

4 Francis, who was created, in Sept. 1660, Viscount Shannon, Co. Limerick, which title became extinct in 1740, by the death of his grandson, Richard, 2nd Viscount.

5 The Hon. Robert Boyle, who, though the only one of his family not raised to the dignity of the Peerage, has left behind him a reputation superior to any title of honour, for his proficiency in learning, his discoveries in chemistry and natural philosophy, and, above all, for his solid virtues, unaffected piety, and Christian charity.

Roger, 5th Earl of Cork and Orrery, great-grandson of Roger, 1st Earl of Orrery, the 1st Earl of Cork's 3rd son, succeeded as Earl of Cork, and became the male representative of this distinguished family, on the death in 1753, of Richard, 4th Earl of Cork, and 3rd Earl of Burlington, great-grandson of Richard, 2nd Earl of Cork, the 1st Earl's eldest son. He was *b.* 2 Jan. 1707, and *d.* 22 Nov. 1762; having *m.* 1st, 9 May 1728, Lady Henrietta Hamilton, 3rd daughter of George, 1st Earl of Orkney, who *d.* 22 Aug. 1732; and 2ndly, 30 June 1738, Margaret, daughter and heir of John Hamilton, Esq., who *d.* 24 Nov. 1758. He had issue by both marriages as follows:

1 Charles, Viscount Dungarvan, *b.* 27 Jan. 1729, *d.* 16 Sept. 1759, having *m.* 11 May 1753, Susanna, daughter of Henry Hoare, Esq.; she *m.* 2ndly, 17 Feb. 1761, Thomas, 1st Earl of Ailesbury, was mother by him of Charles, 1st Marquis of Ailesbury, and *d.* 4 Feb. 1783. They had issue:

1 Hon. Henry, *b.* 19 Jan. 1754; *d.* 22 Dec. 1755.

2 Hon. Harriet-Frances, *d.* 3 Sept. 1793; having *m.* 18 Oct. 1777, the Right Hon. John O'Neill, afterwards 1st Viscount O'Neill.—See *The Peerage Volume*, title O'Neill.

2 Hamilton, 6th Earl, *b.* 3 Feb. 1730, succeeded 22 Nov. 1762, *d.* 17 Jan. 1764.

3 Lady Elizabeth, *b.* 7 May 1731, *d.* 16 Jan. 1800; having *m.* 4 March 1749, Sir Thomas Worsley, Bart., who *d.* 1768.

4 Edmund, 7th Earl, for whom see *The Peerage Volume;* he was *b.* in 1742, and dying in 1798, was succeeded by his eldest son, Edmund, the present and 8th Earl.

5 Lady Lucy, *b.* 27 May 1744, *d.* 18 March 1792, having *m.* 10 July 1765, George, 4th Viscount Torrington, who *d.* 14 Dec. 1812.

CORNWALLIS, EARL. (Mann.)

Peer of Great Britain.

Thomas Cornwallis, who *d.* in 1378, was father of John Cornwallis, seated at Brome, Co. Suffolk. 4th in descent from him was Sir John Cornwallis, appointed by King Henry VIII. Steward of the Household to his son, Prince Edward. He *d.* in that honourable office in 1544. His son, Sir Thomas Cornwallis, was Sheriff of the Counties of Norfolk and Suffolk, at the decease of King Edward VI., and bringing the forces of those counties to the aid of Queen Mary, was the principal means of securing the accession of that Princess to the Throne. He was also very instrumental in suppressing Sir Thomas Wyatt's rebellion, was of the Privy Council, and Comptroller of the Household to the Queen; but on the accession of Queen Elizabeth, was, on account of his religion, omitted on the appointment of her Council and Household; he *d.* in 1604, leaving two sons, viz.:

1 Sir William, who was knighted at Dublin in 1599, by Robert Devereux, Earl of Essex, on his expedition against the Irish rebels; he was father of FREDERICK, 1st LORD CORNWALLIS.

2 Sir Charles Cornwallis, Ambassador from King JAMES I. to the Court of Spain, and afterwards Treasurer of the Household to Henry Prince of Wales. He left male descendants.

FREDERICK, 1st LORD, was in the service of King CHARLES I., when Prince of Wales, and accompanied him in his journey into Spain. He was created a Baronet by that Monarch in 1627. He vehemently opposed the proceedings of the republican party in Parliament, during the Civil War was distinguished for his bravery in most of the principal engagements of the Royal troops, and at its close, his estate being sequestrated, he followed King CHARLES II. in his exile, and afterwards in his triumphant entry into London. In 1661, three days before that Monarch's coronation, he was created BARON CORNWALLIS of Eye, Co. Suffolk; and dying in 1662, was succeeded by his eldest son, CHARLES, 2nd LORD, to whom, in 1673, succeeded his son, CHARLES, 3rd LORD. His Lordship took to his second wife, the Lady Anne Scott, Duchess of Monmouth and Buccleuch, widow of James, Duke of Monmouth; his children by her bore the name of Scott, but all *d.* young or *unm.* By his 1st wife he was father of CHARLES, 4th LORD, who *d.* in 1722, leaving a numerous issue, both male and female; of nine sons, five *d. unm.*, the other four were,

1 CHARLES, (eldest son,) 5th LORD, and 1st Earl Cornwallis.

2 John, (4th son,) Equerry to Frederick Prince of Wales; he *d.* in 1768, leaving by his wife, Sarah, daughter of the Rev. Hugh Dale, only one surviving daughter, Sarah, wife of the Rev. Walter Earle.

3 Edward, (6th son,) a Lieut-general in the army, and Governor of Gibraltar; he *m.* Mary, daughter of Charles, 2nd Viscount Townshend, but *d.* without issue in 1776.

4 Frederick, (7th son, twin with Edward;) he was Bishop of Litchfield and Coventry, and was elected, in 1768, Archbishop of Canterbury. He *m.* Caroline, daughter of William Townshend, Esq., 3rd son of Charles, 2nd Viscount Townshend, and *d.* without issue in 1783.

CHARLES, 5th LORD, was created, in 1753, Viscount Brome, Co. Suffolk, and EARL CORNWALLIS; he *d.* in 1762, leaving three surviving sons, viz.

1 CHARLES, 2nd EARL, K.G. *b.* 11 Jan. 1739, created MARQUIS CORNWALLIS in 1792. Eminently distinguished as a General and a Statesman, his Lordship was actively employed in the service of his country nearly throughout the eventful reign of GEORGE III. In the American war, he held an important command which, after many brilliant successes, terminated in the defeat and capture of himself and the troops entrusted to his guidance. This reverse, however, was amply compensated by the laurels he reaped in the East, as Governor-general and Commander-in-chief in India; where, by his integrity, disinterestedness, and strict regard for public faith, as much as by his victories, he raised the reputation of the British name; and greatly ameliorated the condition of our Eastern empire by his judicious and efficient measures of improvement. In 1792 he returned to Europe, and was appointed Lord Lieutenant of Ireland in 1798, when the rebellion of that unhappy country demanded in its Governor military as well as political abilities. There also his administration was successful. He accepted a second time the high office of Governor-general of India, and died soon after his arrival there, universally respected and regretted, on the 5th of Oct. 1805. He *m.* 14 July 1768, Jemima-

Tullikens, daughter of James Jones, Esq., by whom, who *d.* 14 Feb. 1779, he had an only son and daughter, for whom see *The Peerage Volume.* He was succeeded by his son CHARLES, 3rd EARL, and 2nd MARQUIS, on whose death without issue male, in 1823, the Marquisate became extinct.

2 JAMES, Bishop of Lichfield and Coventry, *b.* 25 Sept. 1743, succeeded as 4th EARL 16 Aug. 1823, *d.* 20 Jan. 1824; having *m.* 30 April 1771, Catherine, 3rd daughter of Galfridus Mann, Esq., by whom, who *d.* 17 Sept. 1811, he was father of the present and 5th EARL, who assumed the surname of MANN only, by Royal sign-manual in 1814.

3 Admiral Sir William Cornwallis, G.C.B., Vice-Admiral of the United Kingdom, who greatly distinguished himself in many naval engagements. He was *b.* 20 Feb. 1744, and *d. unm.* 5 July 1819.

COURTOWN, EARL OF. (STOPFORD.)

Peer of Ireland and of Great Britain.

This family is said to derive its descent from Nicholas de Stockport, one of the eight Barons of the County Palatine of Chester, created by Hugh Lupus, Earl of Chester, in the reign of William the Conqueror. It is probable the family had been settled in that county before the Conquest; and certainly the estate of Saltersford, near Macclesfield, to this day in the possession of the Earl of Courtown, has belonged to his ancestors from time immemorial. The first of the family who settled in Ireland was James Stopford, Esq., an officer of rank in Cromwell's army, who acquired considerable estates in the city of Dublin, and the counties Meath, Westmeath, Wexford, Carlow, Kilkenny, and Kerry, and became seated at Tarah Hill, Co. Meath.

Fourth in descent from him was JAMES STOPFORD, created, in 1758, Baron of Courtown, Co. Wexford; and, in 1762, Viscount Stopford and EARL of COURTOWN. He *m.* 24 Feb. 1726, Elizabeth, only daughter of Dr. Edward Smyth, Lord Bishop of Down and Connor, and heiress of her brother, Edward Smyth, Esq., and *d.* 12 Jan. 1770, leaving, besides other issue, the three sons following:

1 JAMES, 2nd EARL, his successor, (see *The Peerage Volume;*) he was created to the British Peerage in 1796, by the title of Baron Saltersford of Saltersford, Co. Palatine of Chester; and dying in 1810, was succeeded by his eldest son, JAMES-GEORGE, the present and 3rd EARL.

2 The Hon. Lieut.-general Edward Stopford, *b.* in 1732, *m.* 1 Oct. 1783, Letitia, daughter of William Blacker, Esq., who survives him, and *d.* 22 Oct. 1794; leaving, besides the surviving issue described in *The Peerage Volume,* James, his 2nd son, a Lieut.-Colonel in the army, who *d.* 13 May 1823; and Thomas, 5th son, a Commander in the Navy, who *d.* 15 Oct. 1824, both *unm.*

3 The Hon. and Right-Rev. Thomas, Lord Bishop of Cork and Ross; he *d. unm.* 24 Jan. 1805.

COVENTRY, EARL OF. (COVENTRY.)

Peer of England.

John Coventry, Sheriff of London in 1416, son of William Coventry, of the city of Coventry, was ancestor of

Thomas Coventry, who, amongst other issue, had

1 Sir Thomas Coventry, who, having passed through the usual gradations of legal offices, became at length Lord Keeper of the Great Seal, and was created, in 1628, Baron Coventry of Aylesborough, Co. Worcester, and *d.* in 1640, leaving behind him a reputation of great ability and singular integrity in the discharge of his

important official duties; and also a very numerous and flourishing issue: of whom, Dorothy, his 5th and youngest daughter, the wife of Sir John Packington of Westwood, Co. Worcester, Bart., is said to be the authoress of that pious, and still popular work, "The Whole Duty of Man;" and John, the 2nd of his five sons, was father of Sir John Coventry, made Knight of the Bath at the coronation of CHARLES II.; who, having uttered in Parliament some words supposed to be personally offensive to that King, was attacked by some gentlemen of the Court, and, notwithstanding a most gallant defence made with his sword, and a flambeau snatched from his servant, was severely wounded in the face, which so highly incensed the House of Commons, that a bill of banishment, since called the Coventry Act, was immediately passed against the perpetrators of this malicious deed, including a clause barring the King's power of pardoning the offenders, and another, denouncing the punishment of death for the wilful maiming or wounding of any person. The 1st Lord was succeeded by his son and heir, Thomas, 2nd Lord, who left two sons; 1 George, 3rd Lord, father of John, 4th Lord, who *d.* in 1685, without issue; and 2 Thomas, 5th Lord, created, in 1697, Viscount Deerhurst, Co. Gloucester, and EARL of COVENTRY, with remainder failing his issue male to William, Thomas, and Henry, grandsons of Walter, brother of the 1st Lord, and their issue male. He *d.* in 1699, leaving two sons; 1 THOMAS, 2nd EARL, who was succeeded, in 1710, by his only surviving son, THOMAS, 3rd EARL; he *d.* at Eton College, aged ten years, in 1712, and was succeeded by his uncle, 2 GILBERT, 4th EARL, on whose death without issue male, in 1719, the whole male line of the 1st LORD failed, and the Barony became extinct; but the Earldom devolved on William Coventry, Esq., the first inheritor named in the limitations of the patent.

2 William, who left a family seated at Ridmarley, in Worcestershire, but whose issue male had failed before 1697.

3 Walter, whose son Walter was father of WILLIAM, Thomas, and Henry, mentioned above. The two latter left male issue; and WILLIAM, the eldest son, succeeded in 1719, according to the limitation of the patent, as 5th EARL of COVENTRY; he *d.* in 1751, and was succeeded by his son,

GEORGE-WILLIAM, 6th EARL, who was *b.* 26 April 1722, and *d.* 3 Sept. 1809; having *m.* 1st, 5 March 1752, the celebrated beauty, Maria Gunning, sister to Elizabeth, Duchess of Hamilton and Argyll, and daughter of John Gunning, Esq., of Castle-Coote, Co. Roscommon, by Bridget, daughter of Theobald, 6th Earl of Mayo; he *m.* 2ndly, 6 Sept. 1764, the Hon. Barbara St. John, 4th daughter of John, 10th Lord St. John, who was *b.* 19 Sept. 1737, and *d.* 28 Nov. 1800. His Lordship had issue by both marriages as follows:

1 Lady Elizabeth-Anne, who *d.* young in 1756.

2 Lady Mary-Alicia, *b.* 9 Dec. 1754, *d.* 8 Jan. 1784; having *m.* 25 June 1777, Sir Andrew Bayntun, Bart., who *d.* 12 Aug. 1816; this marriage was dissolved June 1783.

3 Lady Anne-Margaret, *b.* 18 March 1756, *m.* 1st, 20 Oct. 1778, Hon. Edward Foley, of FOLEY, who *d.* 22 June 1803; this marriage was dissolved in May 1787, and she *m.* 2ndly, 15 July 1788, Captain Samuel Wright.

4 GEORGE-WILLIAM, his successor, 7th EARL, for whom see *The Peerage Volume.* He *d.* in 1831, and was succeeded by his eldest son, GEORGE-WILLIAM, present and 8th EARL.

5 Hon. John, *b.* 20 July 1765, *d.* 12 Nov. 1829; having *m.* 1st, in 1788, Anne, daughter of —— Clayton, Esq.; and after her death, in Aug. 1809, Anna-Maria, 2nd daughter of Francis Eves, Esq., and widow of Ebenezer Pope, Esq., by whom who survives him, he had no issue. For his children by the 1st marriage, see *The Peerage Volume.*

6 Hon. Thomas-William, *b.* 24 Dec. 1778, *d.* April 1816; having *m.* Miss Clarke, by whom, who was *b.* 1783, and *d.* 14 Oct. 1806, he left, besides the surviving issue mentioned in the *The Peerage Volume*, Julia-Catherine, his 2nd daughter, who *d.* 9 Oct. 1826; having *m.* 25 Aug. 1825, Augustus Pococke, Esq.

COWLEY, BARON. (Wellesley.)

Peer of the United Kingdom.

His Lordship is the 7th, but 5th surviving and youngest son of Garrett, 1st Earl of Mornington, and brother of the Marquis Wellesley, Lord Maryborough, and the Duke of Wellington. He was created Baron Cowley of Wellesley, Co. Somerset, in 1828.

COWPER, EARL. (Cowper.)

Peer of Great Britain.

From John Cowper, Esq., of Strode, Co. Sussex, in the time of Edward IV., descended in the 5th degree, Sir William Cowper, created a Baronet in 1642; and afterwards imprisoned for his loyalty to King Charles I. at Ely House, in Holborn, with John, his eldest son. The latter *d.* under confinement, leaving one son, Sir William, who succeeded his grandfather and left two sons; 1 Sir William, 1st Earl; 2 Spencer Cowper, Esq., one of the judges of the Court of Common Pleas, who *d.* in 1728, leaving two sons, Major William Cowper and the Rev. Dr. John Cowper, Rector of Great Berkhampstead, in Hertfordshire, father of William Cowper, the poet, who *d. unm.* in 1800. It is also probable that Judge Cowper had a 3rd son, General Spencer Cowper, father of the late Henry Cowper, Esq., deputy-clerk of the House of Lords.

Sir William Cowper, eldest son and successor of the 2nd Baronet, Lord Keeper of the Great Seal, and afterwards Lord High Chancellor, was created, in 1706, Lord Cowper, Baron Cowper of Wingham, Co. Kent, and in 1718 Viscount Fordwich, Co. Kent, and Earl Cowper; he *d.* in 1723, and was succeeded by his eldest son William, 2nd Earl, to whom, in 1764, succeeded his only son George Nassau, 3rd Earl. This nobleman, residing much in Italy, was, by the Emperor Joseph II., created a Count of the Holy Roman Empire; he *d.* in 1789, leaving the issue stated in *The Peerage Volume*, and was succeeded by his eldest son, George-Augustus, 4th Earl, who *d. unm.* in 1799, and was succeeded by his next brother, Peter-Leopold-Louis-Francis, present and 5th Earl.

CRANSTOUN, BARON. (Cranstoun.)

Peer of Scotland.

This family was seated at Cranstoun, in the Counties of Edinburgh and Roxburgh, as early as 1170. The 1st male ancestor from whom his Lordship's pedigree is lineally traced is John Cranstoun, of Morriestoun, 1st Lord, so created in 1609; who *m.* Sarah, daughter and heir of John Cranstoun of Cranstoun, and *d.* in 1627 leaving issue by her; 1 John, 2nd Lord, who *d.* without issue, and 2 James, who *d.* before his brother, leaving a son William, 3rd Lord. Being in the army of King Charles II., his Lordship was taken prisoner at the battle of Worcester, committed to the Tower, and his estates sequestrated. He was succeeded by his son James, 4th Lord; and he by his son William, 5th Lord, who *d.* in 1727; having had seven sons, none of whom left issue male except James, his successor, and the Hon. George Cranstoun, 7th son; the latter *d.* 30 Dec. 1788, leaving the issue given in *The Peerage Volume*, by his marriage with Maria, daughter of Thomas Brisbane, Esq., who *d.* 27 Oct. 1807. James, the eldest son, 6th Lord, *d.* in 1773, leaving issue, 1 William, 7th Lord, who *d. unm.* in 1778; 2 James, 8th Lord, a Captain in the Navy, distinguished for his gallantry in the command of the *Belliqueux*, 64 guns, in the engagements under Sir Samuel Hood and Lord Rodney, in 1782, and the *Bellerophon*, under Admiral Cornwallis in 1795; he *d.* without issue in 1796; 3 Charles, who *d.* in Nov. 1790; having *m.* Miss Elizabeth Turner, by whom, who *d.* 22 Feb. 1781, he left one son, James-Edmund, who succeeded his uncle as 9th Lord; for his marriage, issue, &c. see *The Peerage Volume*; he *d.* in 1818, and was succeeded by his only son James-Edward, the present and 10th Lord.

CRAVEN, EARL. (Craven.)

Peer of the United Kingdom.

John Craven, of Appletreewick, in Craven, Co. York, was father of

1 Henry, whose son Robert had three sons; Sir William, Sir Thomas, ancestor of the Earl, and Sir Anthony.

2 William, whose son, Sir William Craven, Lord Mayor of London in 1611, left also three sons; William, 1st Lord; John, created Baron Craven of Ryton, which title became extinct on his death in 1650, and Thomas.

William Craven, the eldest son of the Lord Mayor, was created Baron Craven, of Hampstead Marshall, Co. Berks, in 1626, with remainder, failing his issue male, to his brothers and their issue male. He was one of the commanders of the forces sent into Germany to the assistance of Gustavus Adolphus, King of Sweden, after whose death his Lordship entered into the service of the Elector Palatine, for whose mother, Elizabeth, Queen Dowager of Bohemia, and daughter of King James I., he professed a romantic and constant attachment. He was taken prisoner in a total defeat of the Elector's army by the Imperial troops in 1737, and afterwards entered into the service of the States General of Holland, who received and protected the Queen and her family in their exile; his Lordship was thus not personally engaged in the wars of King Charles I., but assisted him with considerable supplies, for which, and his attendance upon King Charles II. after his father's death, his estates were confiscated by the Parliament. On the Queen of Bohemia's retiring into England after the Restoration, she is supposed to have privately accepted of Lord Craven for her 2nd husband; she, however, *d.* in London in 1662, and his Lordship never entered publicly into the marriage state. In 1663 he was created Viscount Craven of Uffington, Co. Berks, and Earl Craven, Co. York, with a new creation of the Barony of Craven, remainder, failing his issue male, (his brothers having died without issue,) to his 2nd cousins, Sir William Craven of Lenchwyke, and his brother, Sir Anthony Craven. Sir William Craven dying also without issue male, his Lordship obtained a new creation of the Barony in 1665, with remainder, failing the issue male of Sir Anthony Craven, to Sir Thomas Craven, elder brother of Sir Anthony. His Lordship *d.* in 1697, when the titles of Earl and Viscount, and the Baronies of 1626 and 1663, became extinct, Sir Anthony Craven having *d.* before him, without issue; and the Barony of 1665 devolved on William Craven, son and heir of

Sir William, only son of the above Sir Thomas; which Sir William *d.* in 1695, having had, besides other issue, three sons;

1 William, 2nd Lord, who *d.* in 1711, leaving two sons; 1 William, 3rd Lord; 2 Fulwar, 4th Lord, who succeeded, upon the death of his brother, without issue, in 1739, and *d.* also without issue in 1764, when the line of the 2nd Lord became extinct.

2 John, father of William, 5th Lord, who *d.* without issue in 1769; and of John, whose only son William succeeded his uncle as 6th Lord; see *The Peerage Volume*. He *d.* in 1791, and was succeeded by his eldest son William, 7th Lord,

who was created, in 1801, Viscount Uffington, Co. Berks, and EARL of CRAVEN, Co. York; he *d.* in 1825, and was succeeded by his eldest son, WILLIAM, present and 2nd EARL.

3 Charles, whose son, the Rev. John Craven, of Chilton House, Co. Wilts, *d.* 19 June 1804, leaving, by his marriage with Catherine, daughter of James Hughes, Esq., Fulwar Craven, Esq., now of Chilton House, and other issue: see *The Peerage Volume.*

CREMORNE, BARON. (DAWSON.)

Peer of Ireland.

Thomas Dawson, Esq., removed from the County of York to Ireland in the reign of Queen Elizabeth; 4th in descent from him was Richard Dawson, Esq., of Dawson's Grove, Co. Monaghan, father of THOMAS, 1st LORD, and of Richard, on whose son, Richard Dawson, Esq., grandfather of the present LORD, the Barony was entailed.

THOMAS, 1st LORD, was created Baron Dartrey in 1770, Viscount Cremorne in 1785, and afterwards, in 1797, BARON CREMORNE, of Castle Dawson, Co. Monaghan, with remainder, failing his issue male, to his nephew, Richard Dawson, Esq., son of Richard, his brother. The Viscount was *b.* 25 Feb. 1725, *d.* 1 March 1813; having *m.* 1st, 15 May 1754, Lady Anne Fermor, 6th daughter of Thomas, 1st Earl of Pomfret, *b.* 1733, *d.* 1 March 1769; and, 2ndly, 8 May 1770, Philadelphia-Hannah, daughter of Thomas Freame, Esq., *b.* 1740, *d.* 14 April 1826. His Lordship leaving no surviving issue by either marriage, the titles of Viscount Cremorne and Baron Dartrey became extinct on his death, and the Barony of Cremorne devolved on his great-nephew, RICHARD-THOMAS, 2nd LORD, son of the above Richard Dawson, Esq., and father of RICHARD, the present and 3rd LORD, who succeeded him in 1827. See *The Peerage Volume.*

CREWE, BARON. (CREWE.)

Peer of the United Kingdom.

His Lordship's paternal name is Offley. John Offley, Esq., whose ancestors had possessed the Manor of Madely, Co. Stafford, since 1237, *m.* Anne, daughter and heir of John Crew, Esq., of a family of equal antiquity, and which had been formerly ennobled. John, their eldest son, assumed the name of Crewe, and *d.* in 1752; leaving by his marriage with Anne, daughter of Richard Shuttleworth, Esq., 1 JOHN CREWE, Esq., created, in 1806, BARON CREWE of Crewe, Co. Chester; he *d.* in 1829, and was succeeded by his only son, JOHN, present and 2nd LORD.

2 Major-General Richard Crewe, *b.* 27 Sept. 1749, *d.* 17 June 1814; having *m.* Milborough, daughter of Samuel Allpress, Esq., by whom he left issue, 1 Richard, *b.* 1783, *m.* 1815, Frances, daughter of J. Hare, Esq., and has issue. 2 John-Frederick, *b.* 1788, *m.* 28 June 1819, the Hon. Harriet Smith, daughter of Lord Carrington, and has issue. 3 Rev. Willoughby, *m.* July 1816, Catherine, daughter of J. Hervey, Esq. 4 Emma, *m.* 1815, John-Pusey Edwardes, Esq., of Jamaica.

3 Sarah, *d.* June 1814; having *m.* Obadiah Lane, Esq.

4 Elizabeth, widow of Dr. John Hinchcliffe, Lord Bishop of Peterborough, who *d.* 11 Jan. 1794.

5 Frances, *m.* Dec. 1776, General John-Watson Tadwell-Watson.

CROFTON, BARON. (Crofton.)

Peer of Ireland.

His Lordship is paternally descended from the family of Lowther, and of the same ancestry with the Earl of Lonsdale.

His maternal ancestor, John Crofton, Esq., Auditor-General of Ireland in the reign of Queen Elizabeth, was of an ancient family seated at Crofton in Cumberland; his great-grandson, Sir Edward Crofton, of Mote, was created a Baronet in 1661, and *d.* in 1675. His son, Sir Edward, was father of Sir Edward, 3rd Baronet, his successor, and of Oliver, whose son, Sir Oliver, succeeded as 5th Baronet, and *d.* in 1780, when the Baronetage became extinct. Sir Edward, the 3rd Baronet, *d.* in 1739, leaving a son, Sir Edward, 4th Baronet, who *d.* in 1746, without issue; and a daughter, Catherine, heir to her brother: she *m.* Marcus Lowther, Esq. of Kilrue, Co. Meath, who, on the death of his brother-in-law, took the name and arms of Crofton, and was created to the Baronetage in 1758. Their eldest son, Sir Edward, for whom see *The Peerage Volume*, *d.* 30 Sept. 1797, while a patent was preparing for raising him to the Peerage; but his widow, Anne, daughter of Thomas Croker, Esq., was created, 1 Dec. 1797, Baroness Crofton, of Mote, Co. Roscommon; she *d.* in 1817, and having survived her eldest son, the Hon. Sir Edward Crofton, Bart., was succeeded by his son Edward, the present Lord.

DACRE, BARON. (Brand.)

Peer of England.

Thomas de Multon, summoned to Parliament in 1307, *d.* 1313; leaving an only daughter and heir, Margaret, married to

Ralph de Dacre, who was summoned to Parliament by the title of Baron Dacre, in 1321; their three sons, William, Ralph, and Hugh, were the 3rd, 4th, and 5th Lords; the last was succeeded, in 1383, by his son William, 6th Lord; to whom succeeded his son Thomas, 7th Lord. He *d.* in 1457, leaving Joan, only child of his son Thomas, heir to the Barony; she married

Richard Fiennes, co-heir of the Barony of Saye, and in her right 8th Lord Dacre; their son, Sir John Fiennes, *d.* in his father's lifetime; having married Alice, eldest daughter, and at length co-heir of Henry, 5th Baron Fitz-Hugh, by writ 1321, and co-heir of one moiety of the Barony of Marmion, by writ 1313, by whom he was father of Thomas, who succeeded his grandfather as 9th Lord Dacre. He *d.* in 1534, having survived his eldest son Thomas, whose son Thomas succeeded as 10th Lord; he was executed in 1541, in his 24th year, for murder, as having been one of a party engaged in shooting deer in Sir Nicholas Pelham's park, when an affray took place, in which one of the park-keepers was unfortunately killed, but not by the Lord Dacre, who was even in a distant part of the park at the time. His title was forfeited, but his two children, Gregory and Elizabeth, were restored in blood in 1559. Gregory, who thus became 11th Lord, *d.* without issue in 1594; and in 1604

Margaret, his sister and heir, wife of Sampson Lennard, Esq., claimed and was allowed the Barony. She *d.* in 1611, and was succeeded by her son, Henry Lennard, 13th Lord. His son, Richard Lennard, 14th Lord, succeeded him in 1616, and *d.* in 1630, leaving two sons; 1 Francis, 15th Lord, father of Thomas, 16th Lord, who succeeded him in 1662, and in 1674 was created Earl of Sussex, which title became extinct on his death in 1715, when the Barony fell into abeyance, between his two daughters and co-heirs, but emerged in 1741, on the death, without

issue, of the elder daughter Barbara, when her sister ANN succeeded to the dignity.
2 Richard, whose grandson and heir, Richard-Barrett Lennard, Esq., *m.* the above ANN, 17th Baroness; by whom he had THOMAS-BARRETT, 18th LORD. The Baroness *m* 2ndly, Henry Roper, 8th Lord Teynham, to whom she was 3rd wife, and by whom she had Charles Roper, father of TREVOR-CHARLES, 19th LORD, and of GERTRUDE, 20th Baroness; and 3rdly, the Hon. Robert Moore, 6th son of Henry, 3rd Earl of Drogheda. She was succeeded, in 1755, by her eldest son, THOMAS-BARRETT LENNARD, 18th LORD; he, in 1786, by his nephew,

TREVOR-CHARLES ROPER, 19th LORD; and he, in 1794, by his sister,

GERTRUDE, 20th Baroness, wife of Thomas Brand, Esq., and mother of THOMAS, the present and 21st LORD, who succeeded her in 1819.

His Lordship is co-heir with Lord Clinton, of the ancient Barony of Saye, and co-heir of the Barony of Fitshugh, also of one moiety of the Barony of Marmion.

DALHOUSIE, EARL OF. (RAMSAY.)

Peer of Scotland and of the United Kingdom.

Simon de Ramsay settled in the Lothians under King David I.; from him descended Alexander Ramsay, of Dalhouse, a celebrated warrior, for whose important services against the English, King David II. injudiciously bestowed upon him the office of Sheriff of Teviotdale, then held by Sir William Douglas, of Liddisdale. Douglas, in revenge, attacked Ramsay when in the exercise of his judicial functions in the church at Hawick, and carrying him prisoner to the castle of Hermitage, left him to perish with famine in a dungeon. His representative, in the 12th generation, was GEORGE, created in 1619, BARON RAMSAY OF DALHOUSIE; to whom succeeded in 1629,

WILLIAM, his son, and 2nd LORD, created in 1633, EARL OF DALHOUSIE, and Lord Ramsay of Kerington. He *d.* in 1674, leaving two sons:

1 GEORGE, 2nd EARL; to whom. in 1675, succeeded his son, WILLIAM, 3rd EARL, father of GEORGE, 4th EARL, who succeeded him in 1682, and *d. unm.* in 1696; and of WILLIAM, 5th EARL, on whose death in 1710, the male line of the 2nd Earl became extinct.

2 John, whose son WILLIAM, succeeded in 1710, as 6th EARL, and *d.* in Oct. 1739.

George, Lord Ramsay, eldest son of the 6th Earl, *d.* in May 1739, in his father's lifetime; having *m.* Jane, 2nd daughter of the Hon. Harry Maule, brother of James, 4th Earl of Panmure; by whom he had two sons; 1 CHARLES, who succeeded his grandfather as 7th EARL, and *d. unm.* in 1764; 2 GEORGE, 8th EARL, who succeeded his brother in 1782, became possessed, in life-rent, with remainder to his second son, of the large estates of the Earl of Panmure, in virtue of a settlement made by his uncle, William, last Earl of Panmure, who *d.* in that year. His marriage, issue, &c., are described in *The Peerage Volume*; he *d.* in 1787, and was succeeded by his eldest son, GEORGE, present and 9th EARL, who was created in 1815, Baron Dalhousie of Dalhousie Castle, Co. Edinburgh, in the Peerage of the United Kingdom; and the Hon. William Maule, his 2nd son, brother of the present Earl, and successor to the Panmure estates, was created in 1831, Baron Panmure.

DARNLEY, EARL OF. (BLIGH.)

Peer of Ireland and of England.

GERVASE CLIFTON, 1st LORD CLIFTON of Layton Bromswold, summoned to Parliament by writ in 1608, *d.* in 1618, leaving a daughter and sole heir, Catherine, who *m.* Esme Stuart, Duke of Richmond; their 2nd son George, Lord Aubigny, left a daughter, Catherine, wife of Henry O'Brien, son and heir of Henry, Earl of Thomond; she became at length heir to her grandmother, and in 1674 claimed and was allowed the Barony, which had been dormant since the death of the 1st Lord; Catherine, her sole daughter and heir, *m.* Edward Hyde, 3rd Earl of Clarendon, and *d.* in the lifetime of her mother, leaving one only surviving daughter and heir, THEODOSIA, Baroness Clifton, wife of John Bligh, Esq., grandson of John Bligh, who settled in Ireland in Cromwell's time, and was supposed to be a descendant of an ancient family of that name in Yorkshire. He was created, in 1721, Baron Clifton of Rathmore, Co. Meath, in 1723 Viscount Darnley of Athboy, and in 1725 Earl of Darnley, in the Peerage of Ireland. He *d.* in 1728; leaving two sons, 1 EDWARD, 2nd EARL, who inherited his mother's English Peerage in 1722; succeeded his father in 1728, and *d. unm.* in 1747; 2 JOHN, 3rd EARL, who succeeded his brother, and died in 1781, leaving the issue described in *The Peerage Volume.* He was succeeded by his eldest son, JOHN, 4th EARL, to whom, in 1831, succeeded his eldest son, EDWARD, present and 5th EARL.

DARTMOUTH, EARL OF. (LEGGE.)

Peer of Great Britain.

The family of Legge is said to originate in Italy. This branch was seated at Legg's Place, near Tunbridge, for many generations before Thomas Legge, who lived there in the reign of Edward III., and was ancestor, in the 5th degree, of William Legge, Esq., Groom of the Bedchamber to King CHARLES I., in all whose battles he fought with distinguished gallantry, and on the night after the first battle of Newbury, when attending the King in his bedchamber, received from him, in memorial of his services in that day's fight, the hanger the King had himself worn in it, the handle of which was an agate set in gold; it was preserved as an heir-loom in the family, till their house at Blackheath was robbed in 1693, when it was lost with other valuable property. Mr. Legge remained to the last with his royal master, who desired the Duke of Richmond to report of him to the Prince of Wales, that he was the faithfulest servant ever prince had. After the King's death, he narrowly escaped condemnation for high treason, but being by an act of grace permitted to go abroad, speedily joined King CHARLES II., and was again taken prisoner at the battle of Worcester, and would this time have inevitably forfeited his life for his loyalty, but that his wife contrived to convey to him the clothes of an old woman, in which he escaped from prison. After the Restoration, the King informing him of the message he had received through the Duke of Richmond from his royal father, offered him an Earldom preparatory to the coronation, but Mr. Legge, pleading his small income and large family, declined the honour. He however obtained several grants of lands in England and Ireland, and in the sunshine of royal favour the circumstances of his family so far improved, that, in 1682, his eldest son, GEORGE, was enabled to accept a Peerage, and was created Baron DARTMOUTH, of Dartmouth, Co. Devon, with remainder, failing his issue male, to his brother, William Legge, and his issue male. His Lordship was father of WILLIAM, 2nd LORD, who succeeded him in 1691, and was created, in 1711, Viscount Lewisham, Co. Kent, and Earl of Dartmouth, Co. Devon: he *d.* in 1750, having had, besides other issue, the three sons following;

1 George, Viscount Lewisham, who *d.* before his father in 1732, leaving a son, WILLIAM, 2nd EARL.

2 Hon. Heneage Legge, one of the Barons of the Exchequer, who *d.* in 1759, and his only son, Heneage Legge, Esq., *d.* in 1827.

3 The Right Hon. Henry-Bilson Legge, Chancellor of the Exchequer in 1754, and again, from 1757 to 1762; he *d.* in 1764, having *m.* Mary, daughter and sole heir of Edward, 4th Lord Stawell, who, after that title had become extinct by the

death of her father, in 1755, was created Baroness Stawell, in 1760; she *d.* in 1780, and was succeeded by their only son, the Right Hon. HENRY-STAWELL-BILSON, 2nd BARON STAWELL, *b.* 22 Feb. 1757, on whose death, 25 Aug. 1820, the title became extinct; he *m.* 1 July 1779, the Hon. Mary Curzon, 2nd daughter of Asheton, 1st Viscount Curzon, who was *b.* 11 Feb. 1760, and *d.* 19 Sept. 1804; leaving an only daughter, Mary, Lady Sherborne, see *The Peerage Volume.*

WILLIAM, 2nd EARL, succeeded his grandfather, and *d.* in 1801, leaving the family described in the Peerage; he was succeeded by his eldest son, GEORGE, 3rd EARL, K.G., father of WILLIAM, the present and 4th EARL, who succeeded him in 1810.

DE BLAQUIERE, BARON. (DE BLAQUIERE.)

Peer of Ireland.

Anthony de Blaquiere, a French noble of Guienne, *m.* Elizabeth de Montiel, and by her had a son, Florence, who settled at Loreze, Languedoc, and was father of John, who took refuge in England, on the revocation of the edict of Nants, in 1685; he *m.* Mary Elizabeth, daughter of Peter de Verennes, and *d.* in 1753, leaving a son, JOHN, who was created a Baronet in 1784, and BARON DE BLAQUIERE of Ardkill, Co. Londonderry, in 1800. For his marriage and issue, see *The Peerage Volume;* he *d.* in 1812. He was succeeded by his eldest son, JOHN, the present and 2nd LORD.

DECIES, BARON. (HORSLEY DE-LA-POER-BERESFORD.)

Peer of Ireland.

The Most Rev. WILLIAM DE-LA-POER BERESFORD, 1st BARON, Lord Archbishop of Tuam, his Lordship's father, was 3rd son of Marcus, 1st Earl of Tyrone, and brother of George, 1st Marquis of Waterford. He was created, in 1812, BARON DECIES, Co. Waterford; and *d.* in 1819, leaving the issue stated in the Peerage, and having had several other children, who *d.* young. His Grace was succeeded in the Peerage by his eldest son, JOHN, present and 2nd LORD, who having *m.* the daughter and heir of Robert Horsley, Esq., of Bolam House, Co. Northumberland, has assumed the additional name of Horsley.

DE CLIFFORD, BARON. (SOUTHWELL-CLIFFORD.)

Peer of England.

ROBERT DE CLIFFORD, 1st BARON, summoned to Parliament in 1299, *d.* in 1314, leaving two sons, successive Barons, viz.: ROGER, 2nd LORD, and ROBERT, 3rd LORD. The latter *d.* in 1344, leaving also two sons, who both inherited the title, viz., ROBERT, 4th LORD, who *d.* under age in 1357, and ROGER, 5th LORD, who *d.* in 1390, and was succeeded by his son, THOMAS, 6th LORD; he *d.* in 1392, and was followed by a line of Barons in direct paternal descent, viz.: JOHN, 7th LORD, K.G., who *d.* in 1422; THOMAS, 8th LORD, who *d.* in 1454; JOHN, 9th LORD, who *d.* in 1461, having forfeited his honours by attainder; but HENRY, 10th LORD, his son, was restored in blood, and *d.* in 1523; HENRY, 11th LORD, K.G., his son, was created Earl of Cumberland in 1525, and *d.* in 1542; HENRY, 12th LORD, and 2nd Earl of Cumberland, *d.* in 1569; and GEORGE, 13th LORD, and 3rd Earl, *d.* in 1605. With him ended this long continued male line; he left an only daughter, who succeeded him in the Barony; LADY ANNE, m. 1st, to Richard Sackville, Earl of Dorset, by whom she had two daughters, the Ladies Margaret and Isabella; and, 2ndly, to Philip, Earl of Pembroke, by whom she had no issue; she d. in 1675. Isabella, wife of James, Earl of Northampton, her 2nd daughter, d. in 1661, leaving one only surviving child, the Lady Alathea, who d. without issue in 1678; when the issue of Margaret, wife of John Tufton, Earl of Thanet, her eldest daughter, became sole heirs to the Barony, which was of right inherited by her four sons, NICHOLAS, JOHN, RICHARD, and THOMAS, all successively Earls of Thanet; RICHARD, d. in 1684, and THOMAS TUFTON, 18th LORD, and 6th Earl of Thanet, her 4th son, claimed, and was allowed the Barony, in 1691; he d. in 1729, leaving five daughters his co-heirs, amongst whom the Barony fell into abeyance; which the Crown terminated in 1734, in favour of MARGARET, wife of Thomas Coke, Earl of Leicester, the 3rd daughter, who d. without issue 1775. In 1776, the King again called the Barony out of abeyance, in favour of EDWARD SOUTHWELL, 20th LORD, son and heir of Edward Southwell, Esq., by Catharine, daughter and heir of Edward Watson, Viscount Sondes, by Catherine, eldest daughter and co-heir of THOMAS, Earl of Thanet, 18th LORD.

Which Edward Southwell, Esq., father of the 20th Lord, was 10th in descent from Robert, eldest son of John Southwell, M.P. for Lewes, in the time of HENRY VI.; whose 2nd son, John, was ancestor of Viscount Southwell.

EDWARD, 20th LORD, d. in 1777, and was succeeded by his son, EDWARD, 21st LORD; in the event of whose decease without issue, the Barony will again fall into abeyance between the heirs of his three deceased sisters, for whom see *The Peerage Volume.*

DE DUNSTANVILLE, BARON. (BASSET.)

Peer of Great Britain.

This family acquired distinction soon after the Conquest, and has, in its different branches, been raised to four several Baronies. The present Peer is 12th in descent from Sir William Basset, living in the reign of King Henry VIII.

His father, Francis Basset, Esq., d. Nov. 1769, having m. 19 Oct. 1756, Margaret, 3rd daughter of Sir John St. Aubyn, Bart., by whom, who d. 19 Oct. 1768, he had issue; 1 FRANCIS, present LORD, created a Baronet in 1779, raised to the Peerage, in 1796, by the title of BARON DE DUNSTANVILLE of Tehidy, Co. Cornwall, and afterwards, in 1797, created Baron Basset of Stratton, Co. Cornwall, with remainder, failing his issue male, to his daughter, Frances Basset, and the heirs male of her body; 2 Margaret, wife of John Rogers, Esq.; 3 The Rev. John Basset, who d. 20 May 1816, leaving a son, John, a Barrister-at-Law; 4 Cecilia; 5 Mary.

DE GREY, COUNTESS. (HUME-CAMPBELL.)

Peeress of the United Kingdom.

John Lucas was created, in 1644, Baron Lucas of Shenfield, with remainder to his brothers and their heirs male; the title became extinct in 1705, by the death of Thomas, 3rd Lord, his nephew; but the 1st Lord left an only daughter and heir, Mary, wife of Anthony Grey, 11th Earl of Kent. She was created Baroness Lucas of Crudwell, Co. Wilts, with remainder of the dignity of Baron Lucas aforesaid, to her heirs male by the Earl of Kent, failing which the title not to be suspended, but to be enjoyed by such of the daughters and co-heirs, if any shall be, as other indivisible inheritances, by the common law of this realm, are usually possessed by. She *d.* in 1700, and was succeeded by her son and heir, Henry Grey, 12th Earl of Kent, created, in 1706, Viscount Goderich of Goderich Castle, Co. Hereford, Earl of Harold, Co. Bedford, and Marquis of Kent; also, in 1710, Duke of Kent, and in 1740, Marquis de Grey, with remainder, failing his issue male, to Lady Jemima Campbell, only daughter of Lady Amabel Grey, his eldest daughter by her marriage with John, 3rd Earl of Breadalbane, and her heirs male. He *d.* 5 June 1740, when all his titles became extinct, except those of Marquis de Grey and Baron Lucas, which were inherited by his grand-daughter, LADY JEMIMA CAMPBELL, Countess of Hardwick, mother of AMABEL, the present Countess, who, on her death in 1797, (when the title of Marquis De Grey became extinct,) succeeded to the Barony, and was created, in 1816, COUNTESS DE GREY of Wrest, with remainder, failing her issue male, to her sister, Mary-Jemima, widow of Thomas Robinson, 2nd Baron Grantham, and her issue male.

DELAMERE, BARON. (CHOLMONDELEY.)

Peer of the United Kingdom.

His Lordship is a younger branch of the Marquis Cholmondeley's family. 13th in descent from Richard de Belward, the patriarch of this family, was Hugh Cholmondeley, Esq., who had issue: Hugh, ancestor of the Marquis Cholmondeley, and Thomas, (his 3rd son,) great-grandfather of

Thomas Cholmondeley, Esq., of Vale Royal, Cheshire, who *d.* 2 June 1779; having *m.* Dorothy, 2nd daughter and co-heir of Edmund Cowper, Esq., of Overleigh, Cheshire, by whom, who *d.* 25 May 1786, he had issue:

1 Hesther, *b.* 9 July 1766, *d.* 30 Sept. 1802; having *m.* 11 June 1789, John Drummond, Esq.—See *The Peerage Volume*, title Strathallan.

2 THOMAS, the present Peer, created, in 1821, BARON DELAMERE of Vale Royal, Co. Chester.

3 Charles, *b.* 6 June 1770, *m.* 13 Jan. 1794, Caroline-Elizabeth, 3rd daughter and co-heir of Nicholas Smyth, Esq., by whom, who *d.* 3 Dec. 1818, he had issue: 1 Rev. Charles-Cowper, *b.* 28 Sept. 1795, *m.* 22 June 1822, Mary, daughter of the late Reginald Heber, Esq., and sister of the late Bishop of Calcutta; they have issue. 2 Hugh, *b.* 1 July 1797; 3 Thomas, *b.* 9 Sept. 1801; 4 Caroline-Henrietta, *b.* 18 April 1803. *m.* 23 Jan. 1823, Thomas Hibbert, jun., Esq.; 5 Georgiana-Charlotte, *b.* 9 Dec. 1804; 6 George-James, *b.* 21 June 1807, Lieut. 51st foot; 7 Hesther-Mary, *b.* 1 Nov. 1808; 8 Anna-Maria-Emma, *b.* 13 Jan. 1810.

4 Essex, *b.* 18 Oct. 1771.

5 Dorothy, *b.* 20 June 1776, *m.* 14 Sept. 1795, Thomas Parker, Esq.

DELAWARR, EARL. (WEST.)

Peer of Great Britain.

From the writ of summons to Parliament to THOMAS, 1st BARON WEST, in 1342, this Barony has continued in his heirs in the direct male line through seventeen generations.

The 1st LORD *d.* in 1343, and was succeeded by his son, THOMAS, 2nd LORD, who *d.* in 1386. THOMAS, his son, 3rd LORD WEST, *d.* in 1405; having *m.* Joan, daughter of ROGER, 3rd BARON DELAWARR, (who was grandson and heir of ROGER, the 2nd LORD DELAWARR, son and heir of ROGER, 1st Lord DELAWARR, summoned to Parliament by writ in 1299,) and sister and heir of JOHN, 4th LORD, and THOMAS, 5th and last LORD, of the male line of La Warr; the latter *d.* in 1426.

THOMAS, 3rd LORD WEST, and Joan Delawarr, his wife, had two sons, 1 THOMAS, who succeeded as 4th LORD WEST, and *d.* without issue; and 2 REGINALD, 5th LORD WEST, who succeeded his brother in 1415, and his uncle, in 1426, as 6th BARON DELAWARR; he *d.* in 1451, and was successively followed by his son, grandson, and great-grandson, RICHARD, 7th LORD, who *d.* in 1476; THOMAS, 8th LORD, K.G.; and THOMAS, 9th LORD DELAWARR and 8th LORD WEST; and these two Baronies have ever since continued united in the male descendants of THOMAS, 3rd LORD WEST, and Joan Delawarr; although, on the death of THOMAS, 9th LORD, K.G. without issue, in 1554, there were two daughters living of Sir Owen West, his next brother, who, according to the present rules of succession to Baronies by writ, would have been preferred to WILLIAM, 10th LORD, son of Sir George West, younger brother of Owen West. Mary, the eldest daughter, and at length sole heir of the said Owen West, *m.* 1st, Sir Adrian Poynings, and 2ndly, Sir Richard Rogers; she left three daughters, whose descendants still exist.

THOMAS, 8th LORD DELAWARR, and 7th LORD WEST, K.G., *d.* in 1525, leaving the five sons following, viz.:

1 THOMAS, 9th LORD, K.G. above mentioned, who *d.* without issue in 1554.

2 William, who *d.* before his brother without issue.

3 Sir Owen, who *d.* in 1551, leaving, as above mentioned, two daughters, Mary and Anne; the latter *d. unm.* and Mary, the elder daughter, became his sole heir, but did not succeed to the Baronies.

4 Sir George, who *d.* in 1538, leaving two sons: 1 WILLIAM, 10th LORD, who succeeded his uncle to the exclusion of the daughters of Sir Owen, the elder brother; 2 Sir Thomas West, who *d.* in 1622, leaving an only daughter and heir.

5 Leonard West, ancestor in the 7th degree of James Roberts-West, Esq., now of Alscot House, Co. Warwick; for whom see *The Peerage Volume.*

WILLIAM, 10th LORD, having attempted to poison his uncle, the 9th LORD, was disabled by Act of Parliament from succeeding him in title and estate, but was subsequently, in 1579, created Baron Delawarr by patent, and took his seat in the House of Peers as junior Baron; he was restored in blood; and *d.* in 1595, when he was succeeded by his son, THOMAS, 11th LORD, who claimed and was allowed the ancient Baronies of DELAWARR and WEST, and took his seat accordingly. He *d.* in 1602, and was followed in uninterrupted lineal succession, by THOMAS, 11th LORD, who *d.* in 1618: HENRY, 12th LORD, *d.* 1628: CHARLES, 13th LORD, *d.* 1687: JOHN, 14th LORD, *d.* 1723: and JOHN, 15th Lord; this last was created, in 1761, Viscount Cantalupe and EARL DELAWARR; he *d.* in 1776, and was succeeded by his son, JOHN, 2nd EARL, who *d.* in 1777, leaving three sons: 1 WILLIAM-AUGUSTUS, his successor, 3rd EARL, who *d. unm.* in 1783; 2 JOHN-RICHARD, 4th EARL, who succeeded his brother, and *d.* in 1795; he was father of GEORGE-JOHN, the present and 5th EARL; 3 The Hon. Frederick West, for whom see *The Peerage Volume.*

DENBIGH, EARL OF. (FEILDING.)

Peer of England and of Ireland.

His Lordship derives his origin from the ancient Counts of Hapsburgh, in Germany, from whom the Emperors of Germany, of the House of Austria Hapsburg, were also descended. Sir Geoffrey, a younger son of Geoffrey, Count of Hapsburg, served under King Henry III, and, settling in England, assumed the surname of Feilding. 4th in descent from him was Sir William Feilding, of Lutterworth, Co. Leicester, who lost his life fighting on behalf of King Henry VI., at the battle of Tewkesbury, in 1471, having *m.* Agnes, daughter and heir of John St. Liz, a branch from the noble family of St. Liz, formerly Earls of Northampton and Huntingdon. 6th in descent from them was

SIR WILLIAM FEILDING, created in 1620, Baron Feilding of Newnham Padox,

Co. Warwick, and Viscount Feilding; and, in 1622, Earl of the County of Denbigh. He adhered stedfastly to King Charles I. in his civil wars, and proved himself a stout and valiant soldier in numerous engagements, till being mortally wounded in a sharp skirmish with the enemy, near Birmingham, in April 1643, he *d.* within a few days. He *m.* Mary, daughter of Sir George Villiers, and sister of the celebrated George Villiers, 1st Duke of Buckingham of that name, by whom he left two sons:

1 Basil, 2nd Earl, who, unswayed by the loyal principles of his father, connected himself with the leaders of the great rebellion, and held a considerable command in the Parliamentary army; he gave up his commission, however, in 1645, and from that time remained in retirement till the period of the restoration; in which, weary of fluctuations and democratic rule, he heartily concurred. He was created, in 1664, in respect of his descent, from the ancient and noble family of that name, Baron St. Liz, with remainder, failing his issue male, to the heirs male of his father; he *d.* in 1675, without issue.

2 George, created Baron Feilding of Lecaghe, and Viscount Callan, in Ireland, in 1619; and, in 1622, Earl of Desmond, in Ireland, in reversion after the death of Sir Richard Preston, then Earl of Desmond; he *d.* in 1655, leaving five sons, none of whom had issue male, except William, the eldest son, ancestor of the present Earl; and the Hon. and Rev. John Feilding, D.D., from whom male descendants still exist. Of this brauch was the celebrated author and magistrate, Henry Feilding, Esq.

The Earl was succeeded by his eldest son and heir, William, 2nd Earl of Desmond, who also succeeded to all the honours of his uncle, Basil, 2nd Earl of Denbigh; he *d.* in 1685, and was succeeded by his son, Basil, 4th Earl of Denbigh and 3rd Earl of Desmond, who *d.* in 1717; leaving issue, besides his eldest son, William, 5th Earl, a 2nd son, Charles, who *d.* in 1746, leaving two sons; William, a Colonel in the army, who *d. unm.*, and Charles, a Captain in the R.N., who *d.* 11 Jan. 1783, having *m.* 29 Feb. 1772, Sophia, 3rd daughter of the Hon. William Finch, and sister of George, 9th Earl of Winchilsea; by whom, who *d.* in 1748, he left issue, the present Captain Charles Feilding, R.N., for whom see *The Peerage Volume.*

William, 5th Earl, who succeeded his father, and *d.* in 1755, was father of Basil, 6th Earl, his successor; he *d.* in 1800, and having survived his only son, William-Robert, Viscount Feilding, who *d.* in 1799, leaving several children, (see *The Peerage Volume,*) was succeeded by his eldest grandson, William-Basil-Percy, the present and 7th Earl of Denbigh, and 6th Earl of Desmond, in Ireland.

DERBY, EARL OF. (Smith-Stanley.)

Peer of England.

The original surname of this noble family was Aldelegh, or Audley. Adam or Alan de Audley, who flourished in the reign of King Henry I., was father of

1 Lydulph, ancestor of Nicholas de Audley, summoned to Parliament in 1297, whose heir-general is the present Lord Audley.

2 Adam, whose son William took the name of Stanley from his seat Stanley, in Derbyshire; 4th in descent from him was Sir William de Stanley, who becoming possessed in right of his wife of the Bailiwick of Wyrall Forest, assumed on account of it the armorial bearings still used by his descendants—three stags' heads on a bend. His grandson, Sir William Stanley, was father of Sir William, his eldest son, ancestor in direct lineal descent of the present Sir Thomas Stanley, Bart., of Hooton, Co. Chester; and of Sir John Stanley, his 2nd son, K.G., who, in memory of his marriage with the heiress of Lathom, assumed the present family crest of an eagle prey-

ing upon an infant in its cradle. He was Lord Lieutenant of Ireland, and was much in favour with King Henry IV., whom he had assisted in acquiring the Crown, and from whom he obtained, on the forfeiture of Henry Percy, Earl of Northumberland, a grant of the Isle of Man in fee. He *d.* in 1414. His eldest son, Sir John Stanley, was father of

THOMAS, 1st LORD STANLEY, K.G., summoned to Parliament by writ in 1456. From John, his younger son, is descended the present Sir John Thomas Stanley, of Alderley Park, Co. Chester, Bart. THOMAS, his eldest son and heir, 2nd LORD, K.G., *m.* 1st, Eleanor, daughter of Richard Neville, Earl of Salisbury, and sister to the famous Richard Neville, Earl of Warwick; and 2ndly, Margaret, daughter and heir of John Beaufort, 3d Earl of Somerset, (See the Royal Genealogy,) widow of Edmund Tudor, Earl of Richmond, and mother of King Henry VII., on whose head the Lord Stanley had himself the gratification of placing the royal crown found on the field of Bosworth, after the great battle in which King Richard lost his life, 22 Aug. 1485. His Lordship was, in the October of the same year, created Earl of Derby, which Earldom had merged in the Crown on the accession of HENRY IV., having been a part of the inheritance of the Royal house of Lancaster. The Earl was likewise made Lord High Constable of England for life. He *d.* in 1504. He had several sons, of whom two only left issue:

1 George, Lord Stanley and Strange, who *d.* before him.

2 Sir Edward Stanley, who commanded the rear of the English army at Flodden, 9 Sept. 1513, and by the force of his archers first compelled the Scots to open their ranks, thus leading to the memorable victory of that bloody field, in which King JAMES IV. and so large a portion of his nobility lost their lives. For his important service on this occasion he was summoned to Parliament as Lord Monteagle; his male line failed in 1581, by the death of his grandson, William, 3rd Lord, whose only daughter and heir carried the Barony into the family of Parker, Baron Morley, and it is now in abeyance between the representatives of her two granddaughters.

George, Lord Stanley, K.G., eldest son of the 1st Earl, *m.* Johanna, daughter and sole heir of John, 8th Lord Strange of Knockyn, [by writ 1299,] co-heir of the Barony of Mohun, [by writ 1299;] he was summoned to Parliament, in her right, by writ, in 1482, as Baron Strange of Knockyn, and *d.* in his father's life-time, in 1497, leaving issue: 1 THOMAS, 2nd EARL, whose male line failed in 1736; 2 Sir James, ancestor of the present Earl.

THOMAS, his son and heir, 2nd EARL of Derby, succeeded to the Earldom and Baronies, and *d.* in 1521; he was succeeded by his son EDWARD, 3rd EARL, K.G., so celebrated for his magnificence and liberality, that Camden says, "that with Edward Earl of Derby's death, the glory of hospitality seemed to fall asleep;" he is also reported by Hollingshed and Stow to have fed, twice a-day, three score and odd poor persons, and all comers thrice a-week, on appointed days; besides giving, on every Good Friday, to two thousand seven hundred persons, meat, drink, and money. He *d.* in 1574, and his funeral was as splendid as his manner of living; he was succeeded by his son and heir HENRY, 4th EARL, K.G., who *d.* in 1592, leaving two sons, FERDINANDO, 5th EARL, his successor, and WILLIAM, 6th EARL. The 5th EARL *d.* without issue male in 1594, when the Baronies of Strange of Knockyn and Stanley, and his moiety of the Barony of Mohun, fell into abeyance between his three daughters and co-heirs. He was succeeded in the Earldom by WILLIAM, 6th EARL, his brother and heir male, whose son and heir JAMES, 7th EARL, K.G., was summoned to Parliament by writ, 1628, in his father's life-time, as BARON STRANGE, on the presumption that that Barony still accompanied the Earldom, which not being the fact, this writ created a new Barony in fee; his Lordship succeeded his father as 7th Earl in 1642. He gave numerous proofs of his valour and loyalty throughout the civil war, especially at the memorable fight in Wigan-lane, 26 Aug. 1651, from which, notwithstanding the immense disproportion between his small band of resolute followers and the enemy to whom he was opposed, and notwithstanding several wounds he himself received in the encounter, he made his way, with the residue of his men, to join King Charles II. in time to take part, on Sept. 3, in the battle of Worcester; here he was taken prisoner, and, notwithstanding quarter for his life had been given him, was beheaded at Bolton, Oct. 15 following. While the Earl was thus unfortunate in his loyal efforts, his illustrious wife, Charlotte de la Tremouille, daughter of Claude, Duc de Thouars, Peer of France, by Charlotte, daughter of William I., Prince of Orange, by Charlotte, daughter of Louis, Duc de Montpensier, of the Royal House of Bourbon, already distinguished by her gallant defence of Lathom House against the Parliamentary forces in 1644, was holding the Isle of Man with a courage and fidelity worthy of a happier result; and when at length the total destruction of the Royal army at Worcester, and the execution of her gallant Lord, left her without hope of assistance, she yielded with reluctance to the necessity of a surrender, and retained, says Hume, "the glory of being the last person in the three kingdoms, and in all their dependent dominions, who submitted to the victorious commonwealth." Charles, 8th Earl, their son and heir, *d.* in 1672, leaving two sons; 1 William-George-Richard, 9th Earl, his successor, who *d.* without issue male, in 1702, when the Barony of Strange, by writ of 1628, fell into abeyance between his two daughters and co-heirs, Henrietta and Elizabeth; the latter *d. unm.* in 1714, when the Barony devolved on her sister, who *d.* in 1718, leaving, by John, Lord Ashburnham, an only daughter and heir, Anne, who *d. unm.* in 1732; 2 James, 10th Earl, who succeeded his brother in the Earldom, and his niece, Anne Ashburham, in the Barony of Strange. On his death in 1736, without issue, the male descendants of Thomas, 2nd Earl, eldest son of George, Lord Stanley and Strange, son of the 1st Earl, became extinct, and the Barony of Strange, with the sovereignty of the Isle of Man, devolved on the heir-general, James Murray, 2nd Duke of Atholl, grandson and heir of John, 1st Marquis of Atholl, by the Lady Amelia-Sophia, 3rd daughter, and now, by the extinction of descendants from all his other children, sole heir of the body of James, 7th Earl.

The Earldom was inherited by the heir male, Sir Edward Stanley, Bart., of Bickerstaff, 6th in descent from Sir James, younger son of George, Lord Stanley and Strange. George, eldest son of this Sir James, was father of Henry Stanley, Esq., and grandfather of Sir Edward, created a Baronet in 1627; which Sir Edward had several sons, of whom Sir Thomas, the eldest son, was ancestor of the present Earl; and Henry, the 2nd son, was great-grandfather of Charles Stanley, who left several daughters, some of whom are still living, and one son, the Rev. James Stanley, whose widow is living, (see *The Peerage Volume*,) with issue, the second collateral branch of this noble family.

Sir Thomas, the 2nd Baronet, eldest son of Sir Edward, had two sons: 1 Sir Edward, his successor, father of Sir Thomas, whose son, Sir Edward, 4th Baronet, became the 11th Earl of Derby; 2 Peter, great-grandfather of James Stanley, Esq., whose widow is also living, and who was father of Edward Stanley, Esq., of Crosshall, Co. Lancaster, head of the first collateral branch of the family. See *The Peerage Volume*.

Edward, the 11th Earl of Derby, who succeeded, in 1736, on the extinction of the male line of the elder branch, had three sons; the two younger he lost in their infancy, and the elder, James, improperly styled Lord Strange, *d.* before him in 1771; having *m.* Lucy, 2nd daughter and co-heir of Hugh Smith, Esq., of Weald Hall, Essex, and, in consequence, assumed the additional name of Smith. The Earl *d.* 24 Feb. 1776, and was succeeded by his grandson, Edward, present and 12th Earl, who also, in respect of his mother's inheritance, bears the name of Smith, as does his eldest son, Edward, Lord Stanley.

DE ROS, BARON. (FITZGERALD-DE-ROS.)

Peer of England.

The present LORD is the eldest son of Lord Henry Fitzgerald, (3rd son of James, 1st Duke of Leinster,) by Charlotte, late Baroness de Ros, the only daughter and heir of the Hon. Capt. Robert Boyle, R.N., [6th son of Henry, 1st Earl of Shannon,] who assumed the name of Walsingham, and *d.* in Oct. 1779; by his marriage, 17 July 1759, with Charlotte, who *d.* 1790, 2nd daughter and co-heir [with her elder sister Frances, wife of William-Anne Holles, 4th Earl of Essex, and mother of the present Earl of Essex,] of Sir Charles Hanbury-Williams, K.B., by

Lady Frances Coningsby, daughter, and at length sole heir of Thomas, Earl of Coningsby, by

Lady Frances Jones, daughter and at length sole heir of Richard, Earl of Ranelagh, by

The Hon. Elizabeth Willoughby, daughter, and at length sole heir of

Francis, Lord Willoughby of Parham, son and heir of William, Lord Willoughby of Parham, by

Lady Frances Manners, 2nd daughter, and at length co-heir [with her elder sister, Lady Bridget, wife of Robert Tyrwhitt, of Kettleby, Esq.] of John, 4th Earl of Rutland, 2nd son, and at length heir of HENRY, 2nd EARL of RUTLAND, and 14th BARON ROOS, great-grandson of Sir Robert Manners, by Eleanor, daughter, and at length heir of THOMAS, 10th BARON ROOS.

This Barony was created by writ of summons, in 1264, to Robert, Lord De Roos, whose five preceding ancestors had been Barons, by tenure of their Barony of Roos, in Holderness, from the reign of Henry I. He *m.* Isabel, daughter and heir of William de Albini, Lord of Belvoir Castle, and *d.* in 1285. He was followed by his son and grandson, the 2nd and 3rd LORDS, both WILLIAMS; the latter *d.* in 1343, leaving two sons, successive Barons, WILLIAM, 4th LORD, who *d.* in 1352, and THOMAS, 5th LORD, who succeeded his brother; he *d.* in 1384, and was also successively followed by his two sons, JOHN, 6th LORD, who *d.* in 1393, and WILLIAM, 7th LORD, who *d.* in 1414, leaving also two sons, JOHN, 8th LORD, who *d.* under age in 1421, and THOMAS, 9th LORD, who *d.* in 1431. THOMAS, 10th LORD, his son, succeeded; he was attainted in 1461, and his son EDMUND, 11th LORD, though he obtained, in 1485, a reversal of the attainder, was never summoned to Parliament; he *d.* without issue in 1508, when the Barony fell into abeyance between his three sisters, but emerged, on the death of the two younger without issue, in the person of

GEORGE MANNERS, 12th LORD, son and heir of Sir Robert Manners, by Eleanor de Roos, the elder sister; he *d.* in 1513. THOMAS, his son and heir, 13th Lord, K.G., was created Earl of Rutland, and dying in 1543, left two sons, HENRY, 2nd Earl, and Sir John Manners, whose grandson, John, became 8th Earl of Rutland. HENRY, 2nd Earl of Rutland, and 14th LORD, K.G., the eldest son, *d.* in 1563, leaving also two sons:

1 EDWARD, 3rd Earl and 15th LORD, K.G., who dying in 1587, left an only daughter and heir, his successor in this Barony, ELIZABETH, wife of William Cecil, Lord Burghley, eldest son of the 1st Earl of Exeter, and afterwards himself 2nd Earl of Exeter; their only son, WILLIAM CECIL, succeeded his mother in 1591, as 17th LORD, and obtained a confirmation of the Barony in 1616, but *d.* without issue before his father and grandfather, in 1618, when the Barony returned to the House of Rutland.

2 John, 4th Earl, who, as heir male, succeeded his brother in the Earldom; he *d.* in 1588, leaving the following issue:

1 Roger, 5th Earl of Rutland; *d.* without issue in 1612.

2 FRANCIS, who succeeded his brother as 6th Earl of Rutland, and his cousin, WILLIAM CECIL, as 18th Baron Roos, K.G.; he *d.* without male issue in 1632, when the Barony devolved on his only daughter and heir, Katherine, widow of George Villiers, 1st Duke of Buckingham of that family, and mother of GEORGE, the 2nd Duke, and 20th BARON ROOS, who succeeded his mother in the Barony in 1666, and *d.* without issue in 1687, when this Barony fell into abeyance.

3 George, 7th Earl of Rutland, who as male heir succeeded his brother in the Earldom, and *d.* without issue in 1641, when the male heirs of the 2nd Earl of Rutland becoming extinct, the Earldom devolved on JOHN, 8th Earl, grandson of Sir John Manners, 2nd son of THOMAS, 1st Earl of Rutland, and 13th Baron Roos.

4 Lady Bridget, wife of Robert Tyrwhitt, of Kettleby, Esq., whose heir general is Sir Henry Hunloke, Bart.

5 Lady Frances, wife of William, Lord Willoughby of Parham, whose co-heirs, as shown above, are the Earl of Essex and the present LORD.

The Barony having thus fallen into abeyance, on the death, without issue in 1687, of GEORGE VILLIERS, 2nd Duke of Buckingham, 20th LORD, heir general of FRANCIS, 6th Earl of Rutland and 18th LORD, between the representatives of the Ladies Bridget and Frances, the two sisters and co-heirs of the said 6th Earl, so remained till 9 May 1806, when the King was pleased to terminate the abeyance in favour of Charlotte, the late BARONESS, on whose death in 1831, HENRY-WILLIAM, the present LORD, her eldest son, succeeded.

DESART, EARL OF. (CUFFE.)

Peer of Ireland.

The family of Cuffe, from which sprang Henry Cuffe, the unfortunate Secretary of Robert Devereux, Earl of Essex, who, in 1601, suffered death for his participation in his master's rebellion, originated in Somersetshire. Maurice Cuffe, of the same family, settled at Ennis, Co. Clare, and *d.* in 1638, leaving issue, Joseph Cuffe, Esq., of Castle Inch, Co. Kilkenny, who *d.* in 1679; he was grandfather of JOHN, created in 1733, BARON OF DESART, Co. Kilkenny, who *d.* in 1749. He left several sons, of whom, JOHN, 3rd but eldest surviving son, 2nd LORD, *d.* without issue male in 1767; OTWAY, the 4th son, 3rd LORD, was created Viscount Desart in 1781, and EARL OF DESART and Viscount Castle-Cuffe, in 1793, and *d.* in 1804, when he was succeeded by his son, JOHN-OTWAY, 2nd EARL, who dying in 1820, was succeeded by his infant son, JOHN-OTWAY-O'CONNOR, present and 3rd EARL; and the Hon. and Rev. Hamilton Cuffe, 6th son, was father, besides other children who *d.* young, of John-Otway Cuffe, Esq., of Williamstown House, Co. Meath, the only collateral heir to the title; of Nichola-Sophia, who *d.* 9 June 1825, widow of Thomas Freeman, Esq., of Shirehampton; and of Lucy Susannah, living *unm.*

DE SAUMAREZ, BARON. (SAUMAREZ.)

Peer of the United Kingdom.

The original name of this family, and which is still borne by the senior branch, is De Saumarez. Its ancestor accompanied William the Conqueror from Normandy into England, and finally settled in the Island of Guernsey.

Matthew Saumarez, Esq., 3rd son of Matthew de Saumarez, of Saumarez in Guernsey, Esq., *m.* 1st, Susannah, daughter of Thomas Dumaresq, of the Island of

Jersey, Esq ; and 2ndly, Carteret, daughter of James le Marchant, Esq. ; and had issue :

by his 1st marriage,

1 Susannah, who *m.* Henry Brock, Esq.,

by the 2nd marriage.

2 Philip, a Lieutenant in the R.N., deceased.

3 John *m.* Judith, daughter of William Brock, Esq.

4 Sir James, G.C.B., the present Peer, (see *The Peerage Volume,*) created a Baronet in 1801, and BARON DE SAUMAREZ, of the Island of Guernsey, in 1831.

5 Sir Thomas, Knt., a Lieut.-general in the army, *m.* Harriet, daughter of William Brock, Esq.

6 Richard Saumarez, Esq., Surgeon, F.R. and A.S., President and Honorary Member of various philosophical societies, and Author of several Philosophical works.

7 Nicholas, late Collector-general of the revenues of Ceylon.

8 Anne, *m.* Isaac Dobree, Esq..

9 Charlotte, *m.* the Rev. Nicholas Dobree.

10 Mary.

11 Carteret, *m.* Peter Listron, Esq.

DE TABLEY, BARON. (LEICESTER.)

Peer of the United Kingdom.

The family of O'Byrne claims descent from the ancient chieftains of Ireland- Sir Gregory Byrne, of Timoge, Queen's County, created a Baronet in 1671, was grandfather of Sir John Byrne, 2nd Baronet, who *d.* in 1742 ; having *m.* in 1728, Meriel, widow of Fleetwood Legh, Esq., and daughter and heir of Sir Francis Leicester, Bart., (13th in descent from Sir Nicholas Leicester, living in 1276 ;) she was *b.* 25 Nov. 1705, and *d.* in 1740 ; their son

Sir Peter Byrne, Bart., succeeding to the estates of his maternal grandfather, assumed the name of Leicester ; he was *b.* Dec. 1732, and *d.* 12 Feb. 1770 ; having *m.* Katherine, 3rd daughter and co-heir of Sir William Fleming, Bart., by whom, who *d.* 8 Dec. 1786, he had issue :

1 Sir JOHN-FLEMING LEICESTER, created BARON DE TABLEY of Tabley House, Co. Chester, in 1826 ; he *d.* in 1827, and was succeeded by his eldest son, the present and 2nd LORD.

2 Henry-Augustus, who *d.* 18 July 1816 ; having *m.* 16 Feb. 1791, Letitia-Sophia, 2nd daughter of Nicholas-Owen Smyth-Owen, Esq., who survives him ; he had by her a numerous issue, of whom only one son, Charles, survives.

3 Charles, who *d.* June 1815 ; having been twice married, 1st, 24 Jan. 1792, to Mary, 2nd daughter of Philip Egerton, Esq., who *d.* 3 April 1797 ; 2ndly, in 1798, to Louisa-Harriet, daughter of Nicholas-Owen Smyth-Owen, Esq., (and sister of Mrs. Henry Leicester,) who survives him ; he left, besides other issue, the Rev. Frederick Leicester, *m.* in July 1828, to the Dowager Lady de Tabley.

4 Katherine, *m.* 1st, Rev. Christopher Atkinson ; and 2ndly, Rev. Thomas Jee, Vicar of Thaxted, Essex.

DE VESCI, VISCOUNT. (VESEY.)

Peer of Ireland.

His Lordship is descended from Eustace, younger son of John, Earl of Comyn, whose eldest son, Harlowen, was ancestor of the Marquis of Clanricarde. The above Eustace was great-grandfather of William, who *m.* Beatrice, daughter and heir of Ivo, Lord De Vesci, whereupon he assumed the name and arms of Vesey. The first of the family who settled in Ireland, was William Vesey, Esq., in the reign of Elizabeth, grandfather of John, Lord Archbishop of Tuam, whose younger son, John, was grandfather of Baroness Fitz-Gerald and Vesey, and his elder son, Thomas, Bishop of Ossory, created a Baronet in 1698, was father of John-Denny, who was created Baron Knapton in 1750, and *d.* in 1761. His only son, Thomas, 2nd Lord, was created Viscount de Vesci, of Abbey Leix, Queen's County, in 1776, and was father of John, the present and 2nd Viscount, who succeeded him in 1804.

DEVON, EARL OF. (Courtenay.)

Peer of England.

Of this illustrious family, the first who settled in England was Reginald de Courtenay, who came over from France in the reign of Henry II.

Reginald de Courtenay, in common with the ancient Counts of Boulogne, who bore the same arms as the house of Courtenay, viz. Or, three torteaux; and from whom proceeded Godfrey I. and Baldwin I., Kings of Jerusalem, claimed his descent from Pharamond, founder of the French Monarchy. His immediate ancestor was Athon, who, about the year 1000, fortified the town of Courtenay, in Gastinois, in the Isle of France, and from thence took his surname. Josceline de Courtenay, his son and heir, had two sons; of whom, Josceline, the younger, engaging in the crusades, became Count of Edessa, and was father and grandfather of two Joscelines, Counts of Edessa, who, like himself, were celebrated in the history of the crusades. Milo, the elder son of Athon, was father of Reginald, who was also a crusader; he had a daughter and heir, Elizabeth, *m.* to Peter, youngest son of Louis VI., King of France, who assumed the name and arms of Courtenay, and was father, by her, of Peter, Emperor of Constantinople, whose male line failed in his grandchildren; and of other sons, of whom Robert continued the princely line of Courtenay in France, now extinct.

The said Reginald de Courtenay who came into England, married, Hawyse, daughter and heir of Robert de Abrincis, hereditary Sheriff of Devonshire, Baron of Oakhampton, and Governor of the Castle of Exeter, which title and offices he afterwards held in right of his said wife. His son, Robert de Courtenay, *m.* Mary, daughter of William de Redvers, Earl of Devonshire, and in 1293 Hugh de Courtenay, the great-grandson of the said Robert Courtenay and Mary Redvers, became the representative of the Redvers family. This Hugh Courtenay was summoned to Parliament, as a Baron, in 1299, and in 1335 was allowed the Earldom of Devon in consequence of his descent from the former Earls. He *d.* in 1340, and was succeeded by his son Hugh, 2nd Earl, who *d.* in 1377; having *m.* Margaret, daughter of Humphrey de Bohun, Earl of Hereford and Essex, by the Lady Elizabeth, daughter of King Edward I., by whom he had six sons: viz. 1 Sir Hugh Courtenay, K.G., summoned as a Baron to Parliament; he *d.* before his father, in 1374, leaving Hugh, his son and heir, who *d.* before his grandfather, in 1377. 2 Sir Edward, from whom the succeeding Earls descended; he likewise *d.* before his father, but left two surviving sons. 3 William, successively Bishop of Hereford and London, and Archbishop of Canterbury; he *d.* in 1396. 4 Humphrey, *d.* young. 5 Sir Peter Courtenay, K.G., distinguished as a Privy Counsellor of King Edward III., and companion in arms of the Black Prince; he *d. unm.* in 1409. 6 Sir Philip, of Powderham Castle, Co. Devon, from whom, in the direct male line, the present Earl descends; and through whom, to the present day, he inherits Powdersham and other lands which were settled by the 2nd Earl, on himself and his issue male.

Sir Edward Courtenay, 2nd son of Hugh, the 2nd Earl, left two sons: 1 Edward, 3rd Earl; 2 Sir Hugh Courtenay, of Haccomb.

Edward, the 3rd Earl, succeeded his grandfather, and *d.* in 1419; he was succeeded by his son Hugh, 4th Earl; and he, in 1422, by his son, Thomas, 5th Earl; the latter *m.* Lady Margaret Beaufort, 2nd daughter of John, 1st Earl of Somerset, and by her had three sons, and two daughters, who became the co-heirs of their brothers. The Earl sided with the house of Lancaster, in the civil wars, and *d.* in 1458, leaving his allegiance to that house as a fatal legacy to his three sons, namely;

1 Thomas, 6th Earl, taken prisoner at the battle of Towton, and beheaded at York, by order of King Edward IV., 3 April 1461; and, after his death, attainted by Act of Parliament, together with King Henry VI., the Queen, the Prince of Wales, and fourteen other Peers; the titles of all the other Lords, except the Earl of Devonshire, were restored in, or before, the reign of King Henry VII. He *d. unm.*

2 Henry, who, but for this attainder, would have succeeded as 7th Earl; he also was attainted and beheaded at Salisbury, 4th March 1466, *unm.*

3 John, who, on the temporary restoration of Henry VI. in 1470, was restored to the Earldom of Devon. He was killed in the battle of Tewkesbury, 4 May 1471, and *d. unm.*, when the male line of Edward, 3rd Earl, failed.

Sir Hugh of Haccomb, the 2nd son of Sir Edward Courtenay, and brother of Edward the 3rd Earl, left two sons; Edward, his heir, who *d.* without issue, and Sir Hugh of Boconnoc, who also lost his life in the battle of Tewkesbury. His son and heir, Sir Edward Courtenay, the then heir male of his house, was implicated in the Duke of Buckingham's conspiracy for setting the Earl of Richmond upon the throne, and was attainted in 1484; he escaped, however, to Brittany, where the Earl of Richmond then was; and, landing with him that same year in Wales, was present at the battle of Bosworth, which transferred the crown to Richmond by the name of Henry VII. Sir Edward's attainder was immediately reversed, but not that of the 6th Earl of Devon, the chief part of whose estates were conferred on him, which would otherwise have been inherited by that Earl's heirs general; and Sir Edward was created Earl of Devonshire in 1485, and honoured garter. In 1497 he held the city of Exeter for Henry VII. against Perkin Warbeck, and *d.* in 1509, leaving a son, Sir William, who *m.* the Princess Katherine, youngest daughter and co-heir of King Edward IV., and sister of the Queen consort. He was attainted in 1502, on suspicion of holding a treasonable correspondence with his wife's kinsman, Edmund De la Pole, Earl of Suffolk, a Yorkist, who had fled into Flanders; and he was detained a prisoner till the death of King Henry VII. Henry VIII. liberated him as soon as he came to the throne; and as, in consequence of the attainder, he could not legally inherit his father's Earldom, he was, on the 10th May, 1511, created Earl of Devon, by a new patent. He did not, however, long enjoy his honors and the King's favor, but *d.* of a fever on the 9th June following: leaving one son, Henry, K G., 11th Earl of Devon, in the order of succession. He inherited his father's Earldom of the creation of 1511, and having the following year obtained a reversal of his father's attainder, inherited also the Earldom of 1485. He was created Marquis of Exeter in 1525, and in 1532 declared by King Henry VIII. next heir to the crown; a short-lived honour, as in the following year his Lady stood sponsor to the Princess, afterwards Queen Elizabeth, whom her father declared his successor immediately upon her birth, in default of his own male issue. He fell, however, under the displeasure of that jealous tyrant, towards the close of his reign; and, after presiding in Westminster Hall, at the trial and condemnation of the Lords D'Arcy and Hussey, for high treason, in 1538, he was himself tried for his life in the same place, in the December following, on a charge of conspiring to raise Cardinal Reginald Pole to the throne, found guilty, beheaded upon Tower Hill, 9 Jan. 1539 and attainted. He left an only son, Edward, who was prevented from inheriting his father's honours by the Marquis's attainder; though only twelve years of age at his father's death, he was committed to the Tower, and continued a prisoner throughout the reign of King EDWARD VI. Queen Mary, who is supposed to have entertained an affection for him, released him immediately upon her accession, and created him Earl of Devon, with remainder to his "heirs male for ever," by patent dated 3 Sept. 1553; the same year he was restored in blood by Act of Parliament, but as the attainder of his father was never reversed, he did not succeed to any of his honours. Queen Mary, jealous of an imagined attachment between the Marquis and her sister, the Princess Elizabeth, threw them both into the Tower upon an accusation of being privy to Sir Thomas Wyat's rebellion, but released them on her marriage with King Philip, and the Earl of Devon, fearful of again falling under the royal displeasure, quitted his country. and *d. unm.* at Padua, 4 Oct. 1556.

In this unfortunate nobleman ended the splendour, interrupted by so many misfortunes, of the illustrious house of Courtenay, and with him failed the male descendants of Edward, the 2nd son of Hugh, the 2nd Earl, and the three intermediate sons of the said 2nd Earl having died without issue, the heirs male of this last Earl, on whom, by the patent of 1553, the Earldom was entailed, must be sought for in the issue of Philip, his 6th and youngest son.

This Sir Philip Courtenay of Powderham Castle, was ancestor of a line, which, during the troubles and prosperity of the elder branch, had flourished in respectability, though not in splendour, in the privacy of their Devonshire retirement, through six generations. Sir William Courtenay, the proprietor of Powderham Castle, at the death of Edward Earl of Devon in 1556, would, according to the construction recently given to the patent of 1553, have succeeded him in the title of Earl of Devon; he *d.* in 1557, and was succeeded by his son Sir William Courtenay, to whom in 1630 succeeded his son Francis. He *d.* in 1638, and was succeeded by his son Sir William, to whom the dignity of a Baron was offered in April 1689, but which he appears to have declined. He was created a Baronet, but not affecting that title, as conscious of the much higher dignities which of right pertained to him, never took out his patent; he was, however, always styled Baronet in the commissions sent him by the King. He *d.* in 1702, and Francis, his eldest son, having *d.* before him, he was succeeded by his grandson,

Sir William Smyth, 2nd Baronet, who *d.* in 1735, leaving two sons, viz.;

1 SIR WILLIAM, his successor, who was created, in 1762, VISCOUNT COURTENAY, of Powderham Castle, Co. Devon, and *d.* only ten days after his elevation to the Peerage, when he was succeeded by his only son, WILLIAM, 2nd VISCOUNT, who *d.* in 1788, leaving, besides the ten daughters described in *The Peerage Volume*, all married, and three who *d. unm.*, an only son, WILLIAM, present and 3rd VISCOUNT, to whom the Earldom of Devon was adjudged under the patent of 1553 by the House of Lords, 15 March 1831, and who, though only the 2nd Earl who has borne the title under that patent, is the 9th who has been entitled to it, and the 20th of his family in hereditary succession from the 1st Earl. His sisters have assumed the title and rank of Earl's daughters, their father having been unquestionably entitled to that dignity.

2 Henry-Reginald, who *d.* in 1763; having *m.* Lady Catherine, daughter of Allan, 1st Earl Bathurst, by whom he had two sons, both in holy orders; William, the eldest son, *d. unm.* in Nov. 1783, and Henry-Reginald, Bishop of Exeter, the younger, *d.* 9 June 1803; he *m.* 26 Jan. 1774, Lady Elizabeth Howard, eldest daughter and co-heir of Thomas, 2nd Earl of Effingham, and by her left two sons, 1 William Courtenay, Esq., heir-presumptive to the earldom, and 2 The Right Hon. Thomas-Peregrine Courtenay.—See *The Peerage Volume*.

DEVONSHIRE, DUKE OF. (CAVENDISH.)

Peer of England.

This family was founded by Robert de Gernon, a noble Norman, who came into England with William the Conqueror: 6th in descent from him was Roger de Gernon, who acquired by marriage the Lordship of Cavendish, and his issue, in consequence, assumed that name. Sir John Cavendish, his eldest son, appointed Lord Chief Justice of the King's Bench by King Edward III., in 1365, was beheaded in the reign of Richard II. by some rebels, in an insurrection in the County of Suffolk in 1381, the animosity of the mob being chiefly directed against the lawyers, and more especially against the Lord Chief Justice, whose son, John Cavendish, being the Esquire of the Body to the King, had, a very short time preceding, dispatched the rebel Wat Tyler in Smithfield, after he had been struck from his horse by the Lord Mayor. 4th in descent from this John Cavendish, the son, was Sir William Cavendish, a confidential attendant on Cardinal Wolsey, under whose patronage he laid the foundation of a large augmentation of his fortune, which was afterwards greatly forwarded in the service of the Kings HENRY VIII. and EDWARD VI., from both of whom he obtained considerable grants of abbey and other ecclesiastical lands. Sir William married to his 3rd wife, (having had daughters only by his two former marriages,) Elizabeth, daughter of John Hardwick, Esq., and co-heir of her brother James Hardwick of Hardwick, Co. Derby, who had been married at fourteen years of age to Alexander Bailey, of Bailey, Co. Derby, by whom she was shortly after left a widow, his large estates being settled upon her and her heirs. In complaisance to her, Sir William Cavendish sold his property in Suffolk and other parts, and purchased estates in the county of Derby, where he commenced, near his wife's paternal mansion of Hardwick, the building of the noble house of Chatsworth, which was completed by her after his death; she *m.* 3rdly, Sir William St. Loe, of Tormarton in Gloucestershire, Grand Butler of England, by whom she had no issue, but whose large estates were also settled on herself and her children: and 4thly, George Talbot, K.G., 6th Earl of Shrewsbury, and Earl Marshal of England, by whom also she had no issue; but he having children by a former marriage, she procured the union of her youngest daughter with Gilbert his son and heir, the 7th Earl of Shrewsbury, and of Henry her eldest son with the Lady Grace his daughter. Sir William had by her, besides Henry Cavendish, Esq., his eldest son and heir, who *d.* without issue in 1616, and three daughters all matched into the noblest families of the kingdom, two other sons, viz.:

1 WILLIAM, 1st EARL.

2 Sir Charles Cavendish, of Welbeck Abbey, Co. Nottingham, who *d.* in 1617; leaving by his 2nd marriage with Catherine, afterwards Baroness Ogle, daughter and at length sole heir of Cuthbert, 7th Baron Ogle by writ 1461, a son, William, K.G., created in 1620 Baron Ogle of Bothal, and Viscount Mansfield, Co. Nottingham; also Baron Cavendish of Bolsover, and Earl of Newcastle-upon-Tyne, in 1628; succeeded to his mother's Barony of Ogle in 1629, was farther created Marquis of Newcastle, Co. Northumberland, in 1643; was signally active in the cause of CHARLES I., under whom, and subsequently under King CHARLES II., after the Restoration, he held several offices of high trust and honour, and was finally, in 1664, created Earl of Ogle and Duke of Newcastle, both Co. Northumberland. He *d.* in 1676, leaving one son, Henry, 2nd Duke, on whose death, in 1691, all his honours became extinct except the Barony of Ogle by writ, which fell into abeyance between his three daughters and co-heirs.

WILLIAM, the 2nd son of Sir William Cavendish, was created Baron Cavendish, of Hardwick, Co. Derby; he was one of the first adventurers who planted colonies in Virginia and the Island of Bermudas; in 1616 he obtained a large increase to his already considerable fortune, by the death of Henry, his elder brother, whom he succeeded in the whole of his estates, and was created EARL of DEVONSHIRE, in 1618; he *d.* in 1625, and was succeeded by his son WILLIAM, 2nd EARL, who *d.* in 1628, leaving, besides his eldest son and successor, WILLIAM, 3rd EARL, a 2nd son, Lieut.-general Charles Cavendish, who after many gallant achievements in the Royal army during the Civil War, was killed in an action against Cromwell in 1643, in the 24th year of his age. WILLIAM, 3rd EARL, after attending the King's Parliament at Oxford, and supplying him with money, retired beyond the seas, where he remained till the mandate of the victorious Parliament compelled him to return. He *d.* in 1684, and was succeeded by his son,

WILLIAM, 4th EARL, K.G.; he was the intimate friend of William Lord Russel, who suffered death in the reign of CHARLES II., was himself a strenuous supporter of the Protestant religion against the encroachments of Popery under that King and JAMES II., and exerted himself to the utmost to secure the accession of WILLIAM III., and the settlement of the constitution on the principles of Protestantism and liberty. He was created Marquis of Hartington, Co. Derby, and DUKE of DEVONSHIRE, in 1694, and dying in 1707, was succeeded by his eldest son, WILLIAM, 2nd DUKE, K.G., who *d.* in 1729, leaving, besides his successor, William, 3rd Duke, a younger son, Lord Charles Cavendish, a well known Member of the Royal Society, and a Trustee of the British Museum; he was father of Henry and Frederick Cavendish, Esqs., both of whom *d. unm.*, the latter in 1812, and the former, a celebrated philosopher and chemist, in 1810, leaving behind him a name, of which a competent judge, the late Sir Humphrey Davy, has declared, that it will remain imperishably illustrious in the annals of science, and be an immortal honour to his house, to his age, and to his country.

WILLIAM, 3rd DUKE, K.G., *d.* in 1755, and was succeeded by his son WILLIAM, 4th DUKE, K.G., who *d.* 2 Oct. 1764; having *m.* 28 March 1748, Lady Charlotte Boyle, only daughter and heir of Richard, 3rd Earl of Burlington, 4th BARON CLIFFORD, and 4th Earl of Cork, in Ireland, great-grandson and heir of Richard, 1st Earl of Burlington, by Elizabeth, sole daughter and heir of HENRY CLIFFORD, 5th Earl of Cumberland, who had been summoned to Parliament by writ in 1628, in the lifetime of his father, Francis, 4th Earl of Cumberland, as BARON CLIFFORD, under the presumption that the ancient Barony of Clifford, by writ 1299, was vested in the 4th Earl of Cumberland; but the right to this Barony, now possessed by Lord de Clifford, proving to be in the heirs general of George, 3rd Earl of Cumberland, elder brother of the 4th Earl, this writ of 1628, constituted a new Barony in fee to the 1st Lord, which was claimed by and allowed in 1737, to Richard, 3rd Earl of Burlington, 4th LORD CLIFFORD, as his heir general. On the death of this Earl without issue male, in 1753, his Irish titles devolved on the heir male, Roger, Earl of Orrery, and 5th Earl of Cork; the other English titles became extinct, but the Barony of Clifford by writ descended to his daughter CHARLOTTE, Duchess of Devonshire; she *d.* 8 Dec. 1754, leaving, by the Duke, the following issue;

1 WILLIAM, 5th DUKE, K.G., see *The Peerage Volume:* he succeeded his mother in the Barony, and his father in 1764 in the Dukedom, and *d.* in 1811, when he was succeeded by his only son, WILLIAM-SPENCER, present and 6th DUKE, K.G.; in case of whose death without issue, the Barony of Clifford would fall into abeyance between his two sisters, the Countess of Carlisle and the Viscountess Granville.

2 Lord Richard, *b.* 19 June 1751, *d. unm.* 7 Sept 1781.

3 Lady Dorothy, *d.* in 1794, having *m.* the late Duke of Portland.

4 Lord George-Augustus-Henry, now heir presumptive to the Dukedom, and created in 1831, Earl of Burlington, &c.; see title *Burlington*.

DIGBY, EARL. (Digby.)

Peer of Great Britain and of Ireland.

This family, under the name of Tilton possessed a large estate in Leicestershire in the reign of King Henry II.; in that of Henry III. they removed to Digby, Co. Lincoln, and assumed that name. Robert de Digby, living in the time of Edward III., was grandfather of Everard Digby, who, with three brothers, all lost their lives in the battle of Towton, in 1440, fighting for King Henry VI. This Everard Digby left seven sons, who all fought resolutely at Bosworth, on the side of King Henry VII. Sir Everard, the eldest of these seven sons, was ancestor of a family long seated at Tilton, Co. Leicester; Sir Edward, 4th in descent from him, was executed in 1605, as a conspirator in the Gunpowder Plot; he was father of the well-known Sir Kenelm Digby, whose sons left no male issue.

Sir Simon Digby, the 2nd son of the Everard killed at Towton field, was ancestor in the fourth generation of Sir George Digby of Coleshill, Co. Warwick, father of

1 Sir Robert, father of Robert, 1st Lord Digby, in the Peerage of Ireland, and ancestor of the Earl.

2 John, created Baron Digby of Sherborne 1618, and Earl of Bristol 1622. He was Ambassador in Spain at the time of the journey thither of King Charles I., then Prince of Wales, and after his return home, he and the Duke of Buckingham mutually accused each other as the cause of failure in the Prince's object. He *d.* in 1653, and was succeeded by his son George 2nd Earl, K.G., who as Lord Digby took so conspicuous a part in the troubles of the reign of King Charles I., and was during his exile the chief counsellor of Charles II., till he lost his offices in the Royal service by openly reconciling himself to the church of Rome. He *d.* in 1676, and was succeeded by his son John, 3rd Earl, on whose death, in 1698, his honours became extinct.

Sir Robert, eldest son of Sir George Digby, *d.* in 1618; having *m.* Lettice, created Baroness Offaley for life, daughter and heir of Gerald, Lord Offaley, who *d.* before his father Gerald, 11th Earl of Kildare; Robert, their eldest son, was created Baron Digby, of Geashill, King's County, in the Peerage of Ireland, in 1620; he *d.* in 1642, and was succeeded by his son Kildare, 2nd Lord; he *d.* in 1661, leaving three sons, Robert, Simon, and William, successive Lords. Robert, 3rd Lord, *d.* in 1676, *unm.*; Simon, 4th Lord, in 1685, without issue male; and William, 5th Lord, in 1752, having had four sons; of whom the two elder, John and Robert, *d.* before him, *unm.*; Edward, the 3rd son, also *d.* before him, but was ancestor of the Earl; and Wriothesley, the 4th son, *d.* in 1767, leaving, besides two surviving daughters, for whom see *The Peerage Volume*, two sons, Wriothesley Digby, of Mereden, Co. Warwick, Esq., who *d.* in 1827, and the Rev. Noel Digby, Rector of Brixton, Isle of Wight, who *d.* in 1830; also two daughters deceased, viz. Mary, the wife of the late Hon. Hugh Somerville, see that title in *The Peerage Volume*, and Elizabeth, wife of the late William Mills, Esq.; she *d.* in 1828.

The Hon. Edward Digby, 3rd son, but after the death of his brothers heir apparent of the 5th Lord, *d.* also before his father, 2 Oct. 1746; having *m.* 10 July 1729, Charlotte, daughter of Sir Stephen Fox, and sister of the 1st Earl of Ilchester, by whom, who *d.* Nov. 1778, he had one daughter, Charlotte, who *d. unm.*, and the six sons following, all raised to the title and precedency of sons of a Baron.

1 Edward, 6th Lord, who succeeded his grandfather in Dec. 1752, and *d. unm.* 30 Nov. 1757.

2 Henry, 7th Lord Digby, in the peerage of Ireland; he was created, in 1765, Baron Digby of Sherborne, Co. Dorset, with remainder, failing his issue male, to

the issue male of his father, the Hon. Edward Digby; and was afterwards created, in 1790, Viscount Coleshill, Co. Warwick, and EARL DIGBY, Co. Lincoln. He was father of EDWARD, the present and 2nd EARL, who succeeded him in 1793.

3 The Hon. Admiral Robert, *b.* 1732, *d.* 25 Feb. 1814; having *m.* 19 Aug. 1784, Eleanor, daughter of Andrew Elliott, Esq., and widow of —— Jauncy, Esq.; she *d.* 28 July 1830.

4 The Hon. and Very Rev. William, LL.D., Dean of Durham, who *d.* 18 Sept. 1788; having *m.* 14 April 1766, Charlotte, daughter of Joseph Cox, Esq., by whom, who *d.* 27 June 1798, he had three sons and five daughters. William-Sheffield, his 2nd son, *d.* in Dec. 1793; and Julia, his 2nd daughter, *d.* in Nov. 1807, having *m.* Sir John-Henry Newbolt, who *d.* in 1825. His eldest son, Vice-Admiral Henry Digby, and his remaining issue, are described in *The Peerage Volume.*

5 The Hon. Colonel Stephen, *b.* 10 May 1742, is deceased; having *m.* 1st, 1 Oct. 1771, Lady Lucy-Fox-Strangways, 4th daughter of Stephen, 1st Earl of Ilchester, who was *b.* 15 Dec. 1748, and *d.* 16 Aug. 1787; and 2ndly, 6 Jan. 1790, Charlotte-Margaret, eldest daughter of Sir Robert Gunning, Bart., who was *b.* 5 Jan. 1759, and *d.* in 1794; his 2nd son, by the 1st marriage, Capt. Stephen-Thomas Digby, R.N., *d.* 9 April 1820; his surviving issue, by both marriages, are described in *The Peerage Volume.*

6 The Hon. and Rev. Charles, *b.* 22 April 1743, *d.* 10 Sept. 1811; having *m.* 5 Jan. 1775, Priscilla, daughter of William Mellior, Esq., by whom, who *d.* 15 Oct. 1811, he had one daughter—see *The Peerage Volume.*

DILLON, VISCOUNT. (DILLON-LEE.)

Peer of Ireland.

His Lordship derives his descent from Logan (3rd son of O'Neal, Monarch of Ireland of the blood Royal of Herimon) surnamed Dilune or Delion, (the Valiant) who having killed in single combat his kinsman Coleman, King of Timoria, in Hibernia, passed over into France, where he obtained in marriage the daughter and heir of the Duke of Aquitaine, by which marriage he and his posterity became Princes of Aquitaine, till they were dispossessed by King Henry II. of England, in 1172, when Thomas Dillon, Duke of Aquitaine, was killed in battle, and his sons Henry and Thomas were brought while infants into England. Sir Henry Dillon, the eldest son, attended King John into Ireland in 1185, where he obtained by grant divers lands, thence called "Dillon's Country," which name was changed, by the statute of 34th Henry VIII., for that of the Barony of Kilkenny West. 8th in descent from the above Sir Henry, called "Premier Dillon," was Gerald Dillon of Drumrany, living in the 14th century, whose younger son, Sir James, was ancestor of the Earl of Roscommon and Lord Clonbrock; and from Maurice, his eldest son, descended in the 6th degree, SIR THEOBALD DILLON, created, in 1622, VISCOUNT DILLON of Castello Dillon. He *d.* in 1624, leaving eight sons, of whom the two eldest were ancestors of all the succeeding Viscounts, viz.:

1 Christopher, *d.* before his father, leaving, besides other sons,

  1 LUCAS, who succeeded his grandfather, and *d.* in 1629, at nineteen years of age, leaving an infant son and heir, THEOBALD, 3rd VISCOUNT, who *d.* in 1630.

  2 THOMAS, who succeeded his nephew as 4th VISCOUNT, and at his death left only one survivor of six sons, THOMAS, who succeeded him as 5th VISCOUNT, and *d.* in 1674 without surviving issue.

  3 Theobald, who left a son, LUCAS, 6th VISCOUNT; he succeeded his cousin in 1674, and *d.* without issue in 1682, when the whole male line of Christopher, eldest son of the 1st Viscount, became extinct.

2 Lucas, whose son, Robert, was father of

THEOBALD, 7th VISCOUNT. He was outlawed in 1690, in consequence of his adherence to King JAMES II.; he *d.* in 1691, and although his successor obtained a reversal of the outlawry, the Viscounts have generally, as well as the junior branches of the family, resided abroad, and been distinguished in the military service of foreign sovereigns. The 7th Viscount, besides several other sons, was father of the two following:

1 HENRY, 8th VISCOUNT, who *d.* in 1713, leaving one son, RICHARD, 9th VISCOUNT; he *d.* in 1737, without issue male.

2 Arthur, a Lieut.-General in the French service; he *d.* in 1732, leaving, besides other issue, among whom was a son, Arthur, Archbishop of Thoulouse, the following:

1 CHARLES, 10th VISCOUNT, who *d.* without surviving issue in 1741.

2 HENRY, 11th VISCOUNT, who *d.* 3 Nov. 1787; having *m.* 26 Jan. 1745, Lady Charlotte LEE, eldest daughter and at length heir of George-Henry, 2nd Earl of Lichfield, *b.* 1720, *d.* 11 June 1794, leaving, besides other issue, for whom see *The Peerage Volume*, CHARLES, 12th VISCOUNT, who established his claim to the title before the House of Lords in Ireland, in 1788. He was father of HENRY-AUGUSTUS, who succeeded him in 1813, and is the present and 13th VISCOUNT.

DINORBEN, BARON. (HUGHES.)

Peer of the United Kingdom.

The Rev. Edward Hughes, of Kinmel Park, in the Counties of Flint and Denbigh, *m.* Mary, 2nd daughter and co-heir of the Rev. Robert Lewis, of Llystulas Co. Anglesey; by whom he had issue,

1 Margaret, *b.* 2 July 1766, *m.* Owen Williams, of Temple House, Co. Bucks, Esq., M.P.

2 WILLIAM LEWIS-HUGHES, Esq., created in 1831 BARON DINORBEN of Kinmel Park, Co. Denbigh, the present Peer.

3 Hugh-Robert, Banker in the City of Chester, Major of the Royal Chester Local Militia, *b.* 27 April 1774, *m.* Barbara, eldest daughter of J. B. Sparrow, Esq., of Red Hill, Co. Anglesey, and has issue; 1 Mary-Anne; 2 Margaret-Grace; 3 Harriet; 4 Anne-Barbara.

4 Anne, *b.* 26 Oct. 1775, *m.* June 1799, the late Sir Robert Williams, Bart., who *d.* 1 Dec. 1830.

5 James, *b.* 12 Nov. 1778.

6 Martha, *b.* 13 Nov. 1780, *m.* Cyn Lloyd, Esq., brother of Lord Mostyn.

7 Mary-Hester, *b.* 8 Aug. 1787.

DONEGAL, MARQUIS OF. (CHICHESTER.)

Peer of Ireland and of the United Kingdom.

His Lordship's first known ancestor was Walleran de Cirencester, (said to be descended from a brother of Robert de Cirencester, Bishop of Exeter, who *d.* in 1150,) 13th in descent from Walleran was

Sir John Chichester, of Raleigh, Co. Devon, father of, 1 John, ancestor of Sir Arthur Chichester, of Raleigh, Bart.; 2 Arthur, created Baron Chichester of Belfast, 1612, which title became extinct by his death, without issue, in 1624; 3

EDWARD, created VISCOUNT CHICHESTER of Carrickfergus, Co. Antrim, in 1625, and *d.* in 1648, leaving two sons:

1 ARTHUR, 2nd VISCOUNT, created during his father's lifetime, in 1647, EARL of

DONEGAL, with remainder to the issue male of his father; he *d.* in 1674, without surviving male issue.

2 John, father of 1 ARTHUR, who succeeded his uncle as 2nd EARL; and was succeeded, in 1697, by his son, ARTHUR, 3rd EARL; and 2 John, from whom male descendants exist.

ARTHUR, 3rd EARL, *d.* in 1706, leaving issue, 1 ARTHUR, 4th EARL, who *d. unm.* in 1756; 2 John, who *d.* in 1746; he was father of

ARTHUR, 5th EARL, created in 1790, Baron Fisherwick, Co. Stafford, in the Peerage of Great Britain; and advanced in 1791, to the dignities of Earl of Belfast and MARQUIS of DONEGAL in the Peerage of Ireland. He *d.* in 1799, leaving issue, 1 GEORGE-AUGUSTUS, the present and 2nd MARQUIS; and 2 Lord Spencer-Stanley Chichester, whose eldest son, Arthur, was created, in 1831, Baron Templemore—see that Title,

DONERAILE, VISCOUNT. (ST. LEGER.)

Peer of Ireland.

The Viscount's ancestor, Sir Richard Aldworth, Knt., settled in Ireland in the reign of Queen ELIZABETH, and held the Manors of Newmarket and Ballyhooly, Co. Cork, of which he obtained a patent of confirmation from King JAMES I. His grandson, Sir Richard Aldworth, of Newmarket, Knt., was appointed Provost Marshal and Vice-President of Munster; he was grandfather of Richard Aldworth, of Newmarket, Esq., who *m.* the Hon. Elizabeth St. Leger, only daughter of Arthur, created, in 1703, Viscount Doneraile, and sister and heir of Hayes, 4th Viscount, whose titles became extinct by his death in 1767; and by her was father of ST. LEGER-ALDWORTH, Esq., who, succeeding to the estates of his maternal uncle, Hayes, 4th Viscount Doneraile, assumed the name of ST. LEGER, and was created, in 1776, Baron Doneraile; and, in 1785, VISCOUNT DONERAILE, Co. Cork. He *d.* 15 May 1787, leaving by his marriage with Mary, eldest daughter of Redmond Barry, Esq., who *d.* 2 March 1778, the numerous issue stated in *The Peerage Volume*. He was succeeded by his eldest son, HAYES, 2nd VISCOUNT, who *d.* in 1819, and was succeeded by his only surviving son, HAYES, present and 3rd VISCOUNT.

DONOUGHMORE, EARL OF. (HELY-HUTCHINSON.)

Peer of Ireland and of the United Kingdom.

The family of Hely or O'Healy, of Donoughmore, Co. Cork, descended, according to the ancient Irish genealogists, from the M'Carthys, Princes of Desmond, forfeited large possessions from its adherence to the cause of JAMES II. in 1689. The Earl's grandfather, Francis Hely, Esq., of Gortroe, Co. Cork, (son of John Hely of Gortroe,) *m.* the daughter of Christopher Earbury, Esq., and was father of the Right Hon. John Hely, Secretary of State for Ireland, who *d.* in 1794; having assumed the name of Hutchinson in consequence of his marriage with Christian, daughter of Lorenzo Nixon, Esq., of Murray, Co. Wicklow, and niece and heiress of Richard Hutchinson, Esq., of Knocklofty, Co. Tipperary; which Lady was created BARONESS DONOUGHMORE of Knocklofty, in 1783, and *d.* in 1788; when she was succeeded by her eldest son, RICHARD, created in 1797, Viscount Donoughmore of Knocklofty, and in 1800, Viscount Suirdale and EARL of DONOUGHMORE, all with remainder to the heirs male of his mother Christian, Baroness Donoughmore, deceased; and, in 1821, he was farther created a Peer of the United Kingdom by the title of Viscount Hutchinson of Knocklofty, Co. Tipperary, with the same limitation. He *d.* in 1825, and was succeeded in all his honours by JOHN, the present and 2nd EARL, his next brother, who, in consequence of his gallantry in the battle of Alexandria, in Egypt, where, on the death of Sir Ralph Abercromby, the command in chief of the British forces devolved on him, had been created, in 1801, Baron Hutchinson of Alexandria and Knocklofty, Co. Tipperary, in the Peerage of the United Kingdom.

DORCHESTER, BARON. (CARLETON.)

Peer of Great Britain.

This family had existed for fifteen generations in the North of England, before the reign of CHARLES I., when Lancelot Carleton, Esq., of Brampton-foot, Cumberland, settled in the Co. of Fermanagh, Ireland, and was great-grandfather of General Guy Carleton, who having greatly distinguished himself by his military services, particularly in the American war, was, in 1786, created LORD DORCHESTER, Baron of Dorchester, Co. Oxford; he *d.* in 1808, having survived his five eldest sons, Guy, Thomas, Christopher, William, and Launcelot; the two first *d. unm.*, the 4th and 5th *d.* young, and the Hon. Lieut.-Colonel Christopher Carleton, the 3rd son, who was *b.* 23 July 1775, *d.* 4 Feb. 1806; having *m.* 9 June 1797, Priscilla-Martha, daughter of William Belford, Esq., by whom, who *d.* 29 Oct. 1815, he left an only son,

ARTHUR-HENRY, who succeeded his grandfather as 2nd LORD, was *b.* 20 Feb. 1805, and *d. unm.* 3 June 1826.

George, Charles, and Dudley, the 1st LORD's 6th, 7th, and 8th sons, are likewise deceased; the two latter *d. unm.*, and the Hon. Lieut.-Colonel George Carleton, *d.* in 1814; his widow survives—see *The Peerage Volume*. His eldest son, Guy, *d.* young, 8 Sept. 1811, and GUY, his 2nd and only surviving son, is the present and 3rd LORD, having succeeded his cousin, Arthur-Henry, 2nd Lord, in 1826.

DORMER, BARON. (DORMER.)

Peer of England.

Geffrey Dormer, of West Wycombe, Co. Bucks, the first of this family on record, was ancestor in the 6th degree of

Sir Robert Dormer, created a Baronet 10 June 1615, and BARON DORMER, of Wenge, Co. Bucks, on the 30th of the same month, and *d.* in 1616, having had three sons:

1 Sir William, who *d.* before him, leaving a son Robert, who at the age of six years succeeded his grandfather as 2nd LORD, and was created, in 1628, Viscount Ascott, and Earl of Carnarvon; he was a valiant soldier and excellent commander in the armies of CHARLES I., and eminently distinguished for his sense of honour and justice; he was killed in the first battle of Newbury, 20 Sept. 1743, to the great loss of the royal cause. He left an only son, CHARLES, 3rd Lord, and 2nd Earl of Carnarvon, who *d.* without surviving issue male, in 1709, when the Earldom and Viscounty became extinct.

2 Anthony, of Grove Park, Co Warwick. He left four sons, none of whom had issue: ROWLAND, his eldest son, surviving his cousin Charles, 2nd Earl of Carnarvon, succeeded him as 4th LORD DORMER, and *d. unm.* in 1712, being the last male of his father's issue.

3 Robert Dormer, of Peterley, Co. Bucks. Charles, his eldest surviving son, succeeded him at Peterley, and dying in 1677, was succeeded by his eldest son, CHARLES, who also succeeded his cousin as 5th LORD, and *d.* in 1728. He had nine

sons, of whom the two eldest were successive Lords; 1 Charles, his successor, 6th Lord, who *d.* in 1761; and 2

John, 7th Lord, who succeeded his brother, and *d.* in 1785, leaving three surviving sons:

1 Charles, 8th Lord, his successor, who *d.* in 1804, leaving, besides other issue, (for whom see *The Peerage Volume*,) Charles, 9th Lord, who *d. unm.* in 1819, and John-Evelyn-Pierrepont, 10th Lord, who succeeded his brother, and on whose death without issue in 1826, the male descendants of the 8th Lord failed.

2 Hon. John Dormer, a General in the Austrian service; he *d.* in 1795, leaving one son, Joseph-Thaddeus, present and 11th Earl, who succeeded his cousin in 1826.

3 Hon. James, *b.* 27 May 1735, *d.* 7 June, 1817; having *m.* Mary, daughter of Patrick Purcel, Esq., by whom he had issue:

1 James, *b.* 16 Feb. 1765, *d.* 10 March 1810; having *m.* Miss Fitzherbert, by whom, who is deceased, he has left issue.—See *The Peerage Volume.*
2 Anne, *b.* 22 Jan. 1767, and now living *unm.*
3 Robert, *b.* 1768, *d.* 12 Dec. 1823, leaving a widow, but no issue.
4 Mary, *b.* 1772, *d. unm.* 8 Jan. 1831.

DORSET, DUKE OF. (Sackville-Germain.)

Peer of Great Britain.

Herbrand de Sackville, who came into England with William the Conqueror, and settled at Buckhurst, in Sussex, was ancestor in the 14th generation of John Sackville, of Chiddingleigh, Co. Sussex, who *d.* in 1557, possessing extensive estates in various counties. He *m.* Anne, 2nd daughter of Sir William Boleyn, Knt., and sister of Thomas, Earl of Wiltshire and Ormond, whose daughter, Anne, was mother of Queen Elizabeth. He was father by her of Sir Richard Sackville, who having lived in great honour, held several important offices under King Edward VI., Queen Mary, and, in the early part of her reign, Queen Elizabeth, and greatly increased his possessions, *d.* in 1556, and was succeeded by his son,

Thomas, afterwards Lord Buckhurst and Earl of Dorset, K.G. He stood high in the favour of Queen Elizabeth, his kinswoman, was created by her Baron of Buckhurst, Co. Sussex, in 1567; and continued throughout his life faithfully and with ability to serve her Majesty, and King James, her successor, as all his descendants, Earls and Dukes of Dorset, have done by their respective sovereigns, holding the highest offices of trust and dignity under the government, and supporting the Crown and Constitution throughout all difficulties, with what has been termed the hereditary talent of the House of Sackville; till, at the close of the last century, the death of the 3rd Duke left his honours and estates to an infant. Thomas, 1st Earl, Lord Treasurer, was created by Queen Elizabeth, Baron Buckhurst in 1567, and by James I. in 1603, Earl of Dorset. He *d.* in 1608, and was succeeded by his son Robert, 2nd Earl, father of Richard and Edward, successively 3rd and 4th Earls. The 3rd Earl *d.* without surviving issue male, in 1624; and the 4th Earl, K.G., his brother, was succeeded, in 1652, by his son Richard, 5th Earl. He *d.* in 1677, having *m.* Frances, daughter of Lionel Cranfield, 1st Earl of Middlesex, and at length heir of Lionel, 3rd Earl, her brother, whose titles became extinct on his death in 1674, by her he was father of Charles, his successor, 6th Earl, K.G., who during his father's lifetime had been created, in 1675, Baron Cranfield of Cranfield, Co. Bedford, and Earl of Middlesex; he *d.* in 1706, and was succeeded by his son,

Lionel, 7th Earl, K.G., created Duke of Dorset in 1720; he *d.* in 1763, leaving three sons:

1 CHARLES, 2nd DUKE, his successor, who *d.* without issue in 1769.

2 Lord John-Philip, who *d.* in 1765, leaving a son, JOHN-FREDERICK, who succeeded his uncle as 3rd Duke, and *d.* 19 July, 1799; he *m.* 4 Jan. 1790, Arabella-Diana, daughter of Sir Charles Cope, Bart., who *d.* in Aug. 1825, having *m.* 2ndly, Charles, late Earl Whitworth; he left issue by her, GEORGE-JOHN-FREDERICK, 4th DUKE, his successor, who *d. unm.* 14 Feb. 1815, a few months after attaining his majority, and two daughters, the Countesses of Plymouth and Delawarr, co-heirs to their brother.

3 LORD GEORGE, so remarkable for his military and political career, in both which he was honourable and unfortunate; he assumed by Act of Parliament in 1770, the surname of Germain, having succeeded by the wills of Sir John Germain, of Drayton, Bart., and the Lady Betty, his widow, to their noble property in Northamptonshire. He was created, in 1782, Baron of Bolebrook, Co. Sussex, and VISCOUNT SACKVILLE of Drayton, Co. Northampton; and *d.* in 1785, when he was succeeded by his eldest son, CHARLES, 2nd VISCOUNT, who likewise succeeded to the Dukedom on the death of his young cousin, and is the present and 5th DUKE, and K.G.

DOUGLAS, BARON. (DOUGLAS.)

Peer of Great Britain.

His Lordship is, by paternal descent, of the illustrious House of Stewart; and, in common with its royal and other noble branches, traces his pedigree from Alexander, 6th Lord High Steward of Scotland; this Alexander was ancestor, through his eldest son, James, of the Kings of Scotland, whose male line ended in James V.; and through his 2nd son, Sir John of Bonkill, of the House of Lennox, which succeeded to the throne of Great Britain. From Sir James, the 4th son of Sir John of Bonkill, the 12th in descent was

Sir John Stewart, of Grandtully, Bart.; he *d.* 14 June 1764; having *m.* 1st, 13 Jan. 1725, Elizabeth, eldest daughter of Sir James Mackenzie, by whom he was father of Sir John, and great-grandfather of the present Sir John-Archibald Stewart of Grandtully, Bart.; 2ndly, 4 Aug. 1746, Lady Jane Douglas, only daughter of James, 2nd Marquis of Douglas, and sister and heir of Archibald, Duke of Douglas; she was *b.* 17 March 1698, and *d.* 22 Nov. 1753; the only surviving issue of this marriage was ARCHIBALD, the late Peer, who, on succeeding to the estates of his uncle the Duke of Douglas, assumed the name and arms of DOUGLAS; he was created, in 1790, BARON DOUGLAS of Douglas Castle, Co. Lanark, and *d.* in 1827, when he was succeeded by his eldest son, ARCHIBALD, present and 2nd LORD. Sir John *m.* 3rdly, the Hon. Helen Murray, 6th daughter of Alexander, 4th Lord Elibank, who *d.* 28 Dec. 1809.

DOVER, BARON. (AGAR-ELLIS.)

Peer of the United Kingdom.

The Hon. GEORGE AGAR-ELLIS, only son and heir of Henry-Welbore, present and 2nd Viscount Clifden, was created a Peer in 1831, by the title of BARON DOVER of Dover, Co. Kent.

DOWNE, VISCOUNT. (BURTON-DAWNAY.)

Peer of Ireland and of Great Britain.

Sir Payan Dawnay, of Dawnay Castle, in Normandy, came into England with WILLIAM the Conqueror, and was ancestor of John, living in the reign of EDWARD I.; 13th in descent from whom was Sir Christopher Dawnay, who, in reward for his loyalty and services, was created a Baronet by King CHARLES I. in 1642; he *d.* without issue, and was succeeded in title and estate by his brother, SIR JOHN, created in 1680, VISCOUNT Dawnay of the County of DOWNE; he *d.* in 1695, and was succeeded by his only son, HENRY, 2nd VISCOUNT, who *d.* in 1741; his eldest son, John, *d.* before him, leaving two sons, HENRY-PLEYDELL, 3rd VISCOUNT, who succeeded his grandfather, and *d. unm.* in 1760; and JOHN, 4th VISCOUNT, who succeeded his brother, and *d.* in 1780; he *m.* Laura, only daughter and heir of William Burton, Esq., of Luffenham, Co. Rutland, and by her had two daughters, both deceased *unm.*, and the four sons stated in *The Peerage Volume*; of whom JOHN-CHRISTOPHER, the eldest son, succeeded him as 5th VISCOUNT, has assumed the additional name of BURTON, was created, in 1796, Baron Dawnay of Cowick, Co. York, in the Peerage of Great Britain, and is the present Peer.

DOWNES, BARON. (BURGH.),

Peer of Ireland.

Dives Downes, Esq., of East Haddon, Co. Northampton, who. *d.* in 1629, was grandfather of Dives Downes, Lord Bishop of Cork and Ross, who *d.* in 1709; leaving issue by his marriage with Catherine Fitzgerald, sister of Robert, 19th Earl of Kildare,

1 Robert Downes, Esq., of Donnybrook, who *d.* 25 June 1754; father of WILLIAM, 1st LORD, *b.* 1751, created in 1822, BARON DOWNES, with remainder, failing his issue male, to his cousin, Sir Ulysses Burgh, K.C.B.; he *d. unm.* 2 March 1826.

2 Anne, *m.* Thomas Burgh, Esq., of Bert, Co. Kildare, grandson of Ulysses Burgh, Bishop of Ardagh, descended from the noble family of Burgh, of which the Marquis of Clanricarde is the head; she had issue by him, 1 Margaretta, created Viscountess Ferrard, (*see* title Ferrard); 2 Thomas, who *d.* in June 1810, having *m.* Anne, only daughter of David Aigoin, Esq., by whom he was father of SIR ULYSSES BURGH, the present and 2nd Lord, who succeeded his cousin in 1826.

DOWNSHIRE, MARQUIS OF. (HILL.)

Peer of Ireland and of Great Britain.

The first certain ancestor of this family was Sir Moyses Hill, who went to Ireland with the army under the Earl of Essex, in the reign of Queen Elizabeth, and settled at Hillsborough; his great grandson,

The Right Hon. Michael Hill, *m.* Anne, daughter and heir of Sir John Trevor, of Brinkinalt, Co. Denbigh, Master of the Rolls and Speaker of the House of Commons, and *d.* in 1699, leaving issue by her: 1 TREVOR, 1st VISCOUNT; 2 Arthur, 1st Viscount Dungannon, grandfather of the present Viscount Dungannon.

Trevor Hill, Esq., eldest son, was created, in 1717, Baron Hill of Kilwarlin, and Viscount Hillsborough, both in the County of Down. He *d.* in 1742, and was succeeded by his son Wills, 2nd Viscount, created in 1751, Viscount Kilwarlin and Earl of Hillsborough; in 1756 he was created a Peer of Great Britain, by the title of Lord Harwich, Baron of Harwich, Co. Essex, and farther advanced to the dignities of Viscount Fairford, Co. Gloucester, and Earl of Hillsborough, in 1772; in 1789 he was also created Marquis of Downshire, in the Peerage of Ireland. He *d.* in 1793, and was succeeded by his son Arthur, 2nd Marquis; to whom, in 1801, succeeded his eldest son, Arthur-Blundell-Sandys-Trumbull, the present and 3rd Marquis.

DROGHEDA, MARQUIS OF. (Moore.)

Peer of Ireland and of the United Kingdom.

The Marquis's ancestor came into England from France, soon after the Conquest; the family were settled at Moore Place, Co. Kent, as early as the reign of Henry II. Thomas Moore, living in the reign of Edward II. was ancestor, in the 11th generation, of John Moore, of Benenden Place, Co. Kent, living in 1519, who had issue, 1 Sir Edward, who settling in Ireland, was father of Garrett, 1st Viscount Moore; 2 Sir Thomas, from whom descended, in the 5th degree, John, Lord Moore of Tullamore, father of Charles, Earl of Charleville, on whose death, without issue, in 1764, his titles became extinct; and of Jane, who, by marriage with William Bury, Esq., was grandmother of the present Earl of Charleville.

Sir Garrett Moore, of Mellefont, rendered distinguished assistance to the government of Queen Elizabeth, in quelling the Irish rebellion, and received at Mellefont the submission of the Earl of Tyrone; he was created Baron Moore, of Mellefont, in 1616, and, in 1621, Viscount Moore of Drogheda; he *d.* in 1627, and was succeeded by his eldest surviving son, Charles, 2nd Viscount, who, after performing several signal services against the Irish Catholics, in their great rebellion in the reign of Charles I., was killed in an engagement at Postlester, Co. Meath, in 1643; and was succeeded by his eldest son, Henry, 3rd Viscount; who, though he continued his services, and materially assisted in the suppression of the rebellion after all hope of retrieving the royal cause had been abandoned, had his estate sequestered by Parliament, for his known loyal dispositions, and was reduced to great distress, when his house and park, and 300 acres of land adjoining, was released to him, for the maintenance of himself and family. King Charles II., after the restoration, created him, in 1661, Earl of Drogheda. He *d.* in 1675; leaving, besides other issue, two sons, viz. Charles, 2nd Earl, who *d.* without issue in 1679; and Henry, 3rd Earl, distinguished for his services to King William in Ireland, at the time of the Revolution. He *d.* in 1714, having only a few days survived his eldest son, Charles, Lord Moore. The latter left two sons; 1 Henry, 4th Earl, who succeeded his grandfather, and *d.* without surviving issue in 1727; 2

Edward, 5th Earl, who succeeded his brother; he was *b.* in 1701, and was lost, with his 4th son, the Hon. and Rev. Edward Moore, on his passage from London to Dublin, 28 Oct. 1758; he *m.* 1st, 22 April 1727, Lady Sarah Ponsonby, 3rd daughter of Brabazon, 1st Earl of Besborough, who was *b.* 4 March 1711, and *d.* 19 Jan. 1737; and 2ndly, 30 Sept. 1737, Bridget, daughter of William Southwell, Esq., brother of Thomas Lord Southwell, who *d.* 27 July 1761; and had issue,

by the 1st marriage:

1 Henry, Viscount Moore, *b.* 1 May 1728, *d.* before his father, in Aug. 1752.

2 Charles, 6th Earl, who succeeded.

3 Hon. Ponsonby, *b.* 29 June 1730, *d.* 10 Aug. 1819; having *m.* 1st, 24 Nov. 1768, the Hon. Elizabeth Moore, 3rd daughter of Stephen, 1st Viscount Mountcashel, who was *b.* 7 Sept. 1736, and *d.* Aug. 1777; and 2ndly, 3 April 1781, Catherine, eldest

daughter of Frederick Trench, Esq., and sister of Lord Ashtown; by whom, who survives him, he had a son, Edward, who *d.* an infant in 1782; and a daughter, Mary, who was *b.* in 1783, and *d. unm.* in March 1804; besides five surviving sons and one daughter, who, with their marriages and issue, are described in *The Peerage Volume.*

4 Lady Sarah, *m.* 13 Aug. 1748, William Pole, Esq.

5 Hon. and Rev. Edward, *b.* 29 Dec. 1736, Chaplain to the House of Commons, lost with his father, 28 Oct. 1758.

By the 2nd marriage:

6 Hon. Robert, who *d.* in 1831; for his surviving widow and daughter, see *The Peerage Volume.*

Charles, 6th Earl, who succeeded his father, and was created Marquis of Drogheda in 1791; also, in 1801, Baron Moore of Moore Place, Co. Kent, in the Peerage of the United Kingdom.

DUCIE, BARON. (Reynolds-Moreton.)

Peer of Great Britain.

His Lordship's paternal name is Reynolds.

Edward Moreton, Esq., *m.* Elizabeth, only daughter and heir of Robert Ducie, Esq., and niece and heir of William Viscount Ducie, in the Peerage of Ireland; which title became extinct in 1690. Their son, Matthew, was created Lord Ducie, Baron of Moreton, Co. Stafford, in 1720, and was father of

1 Matthew, 2nd Lord, who obtained, in 1763, a renewed patent, creating him Baron Ducie, of Tortworth, Co. Gloucester, with remainder to the issue male of his sister Elizabeth; he *d.* without issue, 27 Dec. 1770.

2 Elizabeth, (eldest daughter); she *m.* 1st, Richard Syms, Esq.; and 2ndly, 5 Feb. 1730, Francis Reynolds, Esq., who *d.* 8 Aug. 1773; by her 2nd marriage she had two sons, Thomas, and Francis, successively Lords Ducie, who, on the death of their uncle, Matthew, 1st Lord of the new creation, assumed the name of Moreton.

Thomas, 2nd Lord of the new creation was *b.* 26 Oct. 1733, succeeded 27 Dec. 1770, and *d.* 11 Sept. 1785; having *m.* 11 Feb. 1774, Margaret, daughter of Sir John Ramsden, Bart, who *d.* 9 May 1786. His Lordship leaving no issue, was succeeded by his brother, Francis, 3rd Lord, father of the present and 4th Lord, who succeeded him in 1808.

DUDLEY, EARL OF. (Ward.)

Peer of the United Kingdom.

From Simon Warde, living in 1391 descended in the 12th degree, Humble, created in 1644, Baron Ward of Birmingham, Co. Warwick; he *d.* in 1670; having *m.* Frances Sutton, Baroness Dudley, grandaughter and heir of Edward, 9th Lord Dudley, from the writ of summons to his ancestor, John Sutton de Duddeley, in 1342; they had two sons,

1 Edward, 2nd Lord Ward, and 11th Lord Dudley, whose male issue failed in 1740.

2 William, whose grandson, John, succeeded as 6th Lord Ward, was created Viscount Dudley and Ward, and was grandfather of the present Earl.

Edward, 2nd Lord Ward, succeeded his father in 1670, and to the ancient Barony of Dudley, on the death of his mother, in 1697; he *d.* in 1701; having survived his son William, who *d.* in 1692, leaving issue, 1 Edward, 3rd Lord; 2 William, 5th Lord; 3 Frances, who *d.* in 1737; having *m.* William Lea, Esq.

EDWARD, 3rd LORD, succeeded his grandfather, and *d.* in his minority, in 1704; having *m.* Diana, daughter of Thomas Howard, Esq.; by whom, who *d.* in the 23rd year of her age, in 1709, he had a posthumous son, EDWARD, 4th LORD; who dying *unm.* in 1731, was succeeded by his uncle WILLIAM, 5th LORD; he *d. unm.* in 1740, when the Barony of Dudley devolved on Ferdinando-Dudley Lea, Esq., son of his sister Frances, and on his death, in 1757, fell into abeyance between his five sisters and co-heirs.

The Barony of Ward fell to the male heir, JOHN, 6th LORD, grandson of William, younger son of the 1st Lord; this William *d.* in 1713, leaving an only son, William, who, at his death in 1720, left two sons, JOHN, 6th LORD; and the Rev. William Ward, who *d.* 21 July, 1758; having *m.* Elizabeth, daughter of John Hawkes, Esq., by whom he left a son, Humble, and a daughter, Frances, late wife of the present Earl Ferrers.

JOHN, 6th LORD, having succeeded as Baron Ward, on the death of William, his cousin, was, after the death of Ferdinando-Dudley Lea, Baron Dudley, created VISCOUNT DUDLEY AND WARD, in 1763; he *d.* in 1774, leaving two sons; 1 JOHN, his successor, 2nd VISCOUNT, who *d.* in 1788, without issue; 2 WILLIAM, 3rd VISCOUNT, father of JOHN-WILLIAM, who succeeded him in 1823, was created Viscount Ednam of Ednam, Co. Roxburgh, and EARL OF DUDLEY of Dudley Castle, Co. Stafford, in 1827, and is the present Peer.

DUFFERIN AND CLANEBOYE, BARON. (BLACKWOOD.)

Peer of Ireland.

Hans Stevenson, Esq., of Killyleagh, *m.* Anne, daughter and heir of James Hamilton, Esq.; [eldest son of Archibald Hamilton, Esq., next brother of James, created Viscount Claneboye, which title became extinct in 1675, on the death of Henry, 3d Viscount Claneboye, and 2nd Earl of Clanbrassil;] their son, James Stevenson, Esq., was father of DORCAS, created in 1800, BARONESS DUFFERIN and CLANEBOYE of Killyleagh and Ballyliedy; mother of the present Peer, by her marriage with Sir John Blackwood, Bart., of Ballyliedy, descended from John Blackwood, Esq., of an ancient family in Scotland, who went over to Ireland in the 17th century, and settled in the Co. of Down.

DUFFUS, BARON. (DUNBAR.)

Peer of Scotland.

Kenneth, 3rd Earl of Sutherland, 5th in descent from Freskin, the first of the family of Sutherland who settled in Scotland, had two sons: 1 William, 4th Earl, ancestor, through the family of Gordon, of the Countess of Sutherland; 2 Nicholas, from whom the 9th in descent was ALEXANDER SUTHERLAND, created BARON DUFFUS, in 1650, whose only son

JAMES, 2nd LORD, was father of

1 KENNETH, 3rd LORD, by whose attainder in 1715, the Peerage was forfeited; he *d.* in 1734, and his only son, ERIC, who should have been 4th LORD, *d.* in 1768; the latter left one son, JAMES, 5th LORD, to whom the title was restored by Act of Parliament, in 1826, and on whose death, in 1827, the issue male of the 3rd LORD failed.

2 James, who *m.* Elizabeth, daughter and heir of Sir William Dunbar, of Hempriggs, Bart., assumed the name of DUNBAR, and was created a Baronet, in 1706; their only son

Sir William Dunbar of Hempriggs, *d.* 1792; having *m.* 1st, in 1744, Elizabeth, only Daughter of Alexander Dunbar, Esq., by whom he had no issue male; 2ndly, Jean, daughter of David Sinclair, Esq., by whom he had no surviving issue; and 3rdly, Henrietta, daughter of Hugh Rose, Esq., of which marriage the present Peer, who succeeded on the death of his cousin, in 1826, is the only son.

DUNALLEY, BARON. (Prittie.)

Peer of Ireland.

The founder of this family in Ireland was Henry Prittie, Esq., who obtained Dunalley Castle, by grant from King Charles II., and was ancestor, through four generations of his own name, of Henry Prittie, created in 1800, Baron Dunalley of Kilboy, Co. Tipperary, father of Henry, present and 2nd Lord, who succeeded him in 1801.

DUNBOYNE, BARON. (Butler.)

Peer of Ireland.

Theobald Butler, 4th in descent from Herveius Fitzwalter, the patriarch of this noble family, was father of 1 Edmund, Earl of Carrick, ancestor of the Marquis of Ormonde, and the Earls of Kilkenny, Glengall, and Carrick; 2 Thomas le Botiller, who *m.* Sinolda le Petit, daughter and heir of William, Lord Dunboyne; from this marriage descended Edmund, created in 1541 Baron of Dunboyne, Co. Meath; he *d.* in 1566; his son and successor James, 2nd Lord, *d.* in 1624, having had issue:

1 John, who *d.* in his father's life-time, and was father of Edmund, 3rd Lord, whose son James, 4th Lord, succeeded him in 1641; being implicated in the rebellion of that unfortunate period, he was outlawed, and dying without issue, the male line of John, eldest son of the 2nd Lord, failed in him.

2 Pierce, grandfather of Pierce, who was also outlawed, and, on the death in 1800 of whose great-grandson, the Rev. Dr. John Butler, who but for the outlawries would have been 12th Lord, the male descendants of Pierce, 2nd son of the 2nd Lord became extinct;

3 James, whose male issue failed in the third generation;

4 Edward great-grandfather of James Butler, Esq., of Cragnagowra, Co. Clare, who *d.* in 1784, leaving an only son James, the present and 13th Lord, who having petitioned the King, and having proved his pedigree to the satisfaction of the Law Officers of the Crown in Ireland, to whom the petition was referred, obtained, in virtue of his Majesty's warrant, a reversal of the outlawries, in the Court of King's Bench in Dublin, in Michaelmas term 1827.

DUNDAS, BARON. (Dundas.)

Peer of Great Britain.

Uchtred, a younger son of Gospatrick, Earl of Northumberland, ancestor by his eldest son, Gospatrick, of the extinct Earls of Dunbar, and of the Earl of Home; was progenitor of the family of Dundas, who assumed their surname from the lands of Dundas, granted to Helias, son of Uchtred, by the chief of his family.

John de Dundas, of Fingask, living in 1342, was father of James, who *d.* in 1436; from whose eldest son, James, his Lordship descends; and whose 2nd son, Sir Archibald, was ancestor of James Dundas, Esq., of Dundas, and, by a junior branch, of Viscount Melville. 7th in descent from James, the eldest son, was

Thomas Dundas, Esq., of Fingask, whose eldest son, Thomas, was father of Charles Dundas, Esq., M.P. for Berks; and whose 2nd son, Sir Lawrence, was created a Baronet in 1762, and *d.* in 1781; he was father of SIR THOMAS, created, in 1794, BARON DUNDAS of Aske, Co. York; he *d.* in 1820, and was succeeded by his eldest son, the present and 2nd LORD.

DUNDONALD, EARL OF. (COCHRANE.)

Peer of Scotland.

Alexander Blair, a younger son of John Blair, of Blair, *m.*, about the year 1600, Elizabeth, daughter and sole heir of William Cochrane, of Cochrane, a gentleman of an ancient family in the County of Renfrew, and thereupon assumed the name and arms of Cochrane. SIR WILLIAM COCHRANE, their son, was created, in 1647, Baron Cochrane of Dundonald, with limitation to the heirs male of his body, and subsequently, in 1669, EARL of DUNDONALD, Lord Cochrane of Paisley and Ochiltree, with remainder to the heirs male of his body, failing which, to the eldest heirs female of his body without division, and the heirs male of such heirs female, bearing the name and arms of Cochrane. The Earldom, however, has continued in the heirs male of the 1st EARL. This nobleman, in his old age, was accused before the Privy Council of Scotland, though without any ill consequences, of having, in the year 1679, kept a chaplain about his son, Lord Cochrane, then dying, who prayed for the success of the rebels in the west—those Covenanters who, in the same year, routed the dragoons of Captain Graham, of Claverhouse, afterwards the celebrated Viscount Dundee; and who himself, so inviolably faithful to James VII. in his misfortunes, was, in the commencement of that Prince's reign, deemed unfit to be trusted with the secrets of his Council, because he had married a daughter of this very Lord Cochrane. The Earl *d.* in 1686; he had two sons, William Lord Cochrane, and John, both of whom having been ancestors to succeeding Earls, their pedigree will be successively traced.

William, Lord Cochrane, *d.* before his father in 1679, leaving, besides other issue, two sons, viz.:

1 JOHN, 2nd EARL, who succeeeded his grandfather, and *d.* in 1690, leaving issue, 1 WILLIAM, 3rd EARL, who *d. unm.* in 1705; and JOHN, 4th EARL, who succeeded his brother, and *d.* in 1720, leaving one son, WILLIAM, his successor, 5th EARL. He *d. unm.* in 1725, when the male line of the 2nd Earl became extinct.

2 WILLIAM, *d.* in 1717; he had one son, THOMAS, who succeeded as 6th EARL, and *d.* in 1737, leaving two sons, of whom the youngest *d. unm.* in 1748, and the eldest, WILLIAM, 7th EARL, succeeded his father. He was a Captain in the 17th regiment of foot, and was killed at the siege of Louisbourgh, in America, in 1758; he *d. unm.*, and with him ended the male issue of William, Lord Cochrane, eldest son of the 1st EARL.

Sir John Cochrane, of Ochiltree, 2nd son of the 1st EARL, was grandfather, by his son William, of THOMAS, 8th EARL, who succeeded in 1758, and was father of several sons, described in *The Peerage Volume*, besides others who *d.* young. He *d.* in 1778, and was succeeded by his eldest son, ARCHIBALD, 9th EARL, to whom, in 1831, succeeded his eldest son THOMAS, the present and 10th EARL.

DUNGANNON, VISCOUNT. (HILL-TREVOR.)

Peer of Ireland.

The Viscount is a younger branch of the family of the Marquis of Downshire. The Right Hon. Michael Hill *d.* in 1699; having *m.* Anne, daughter and heir of

Sir John Trevor, of Brinkinalt, Co. Denbigh, and had two sons, 1 Trevor, 1st Viscount Hillsborough, great-grandfather of the Marquis of Downshire; 2 ARTHUR, who, succeeding to the estates of his maternal grandfather, assumed the name and arms of TREVOR, was created in 1766, Baron Hill of Olderfleet, Co. Antrim, and VISCOUNT DUNGANNON, Co. Tyrone, and *d.* in 1771. His only son, the Hon. Arthur Trevor, was *b.* 24 Dec. 1738, and *d.* before his father, 21 June 1770; he was father of the present Viscount by his marriage 27 Feb. 1762, with Hon. Letitia Morres, eldest daughter of Henry, 1st Viscount Mountmorres; she *d.* 7 Dec. 1801, having *m.* 2ndly, Randall-William, 1st Marquis of Antrim, father by her of the present Countess of Antrim.

DUNMORE, EARL. (MURRAY.)

Peer of Scotland and of the United Kingdom.

The Earl is a branch of the family of the Duke of Atholl. Lord Charles Murray, 2nd son of John, 1st Marquis of Atholl, was created, in 1686, EARL of DUNMORE, Viscount of Fincastle, Lord Murray of Blair, Moulin, and Tillemot, and *d.* in 1710; he was father of JOHN, 2nd EARL, who *d. unm.* in 1752, and of WILLIAM, 3rd EARL. This nobleman was engaged in the rebellion of 1745, and in April 1746 surrendered himself to justice; he was tried in December following, pleaded guilty, and immediately received his Majesty's pardon. He succeeded his brother in 1752, and *d.* in 1756, when he was succeeded by his eldest son JOHN, 4th EARL, to whom, in 1809, succeeded his son GEORGE, present and 5th EARL.

DUNRAVEN, EARL. (WYNDHAM-QUIN.)

Peer of Ireland.

The family of Quin is of very ancient Irish extraction, and possessed large territories before the invasion of the English under King HENRY II. From James Quin of Kilmallock, Co. Limerick, the Earl's first certain ancestor on record, descended in the 5th degree, Sir Valentine-Richard Quin, created a Baronet of Great Britain in 1781; Baron Adare of Adare, Co. Limerick, in 1800; Viscount Mount-Earl, Co. Limerick, in 1816; and Earl of Dunraven and Mount-Earl, and Viscount Adare, in 1822. He *d.* in 1824, and was succeeded by his son WINDHAM-HENRY, the present and 2nd EARL, who, having *m.* Caroline, daughter and sole heiress of Thomas Wyndham of Dunraven Castle, Co. Glamorgan, assumed the additional name of Wyndham in 1815.

DUNSANY, LORD. (PLUNKETT.)

Peer of Ireland.

His Lordship is descended from John Plunkett of Bewley, in the reign of King Henry III., whose eldest son, John, was ancestor of Lord Louth, and his younger son, Richard, was grandfather of

Sir Christopher Plunkett, who, by marriage with Joan, heiress of the Lordships of Killeen, Dunsany, and Gerardstown, had issue: John, Lord Killeen, ancestor of the Earl of Fingall, and CHRISTOPHER, 1st LORD DUNSANY, who was followed in uninterrupted succession, from father to son, through the eight following generations: by JOHN, 2nd LORD; JOHN, 3rd LORD; EDWARD, 4th LORD; ROBERT, 5th LORD; CHRISTOPHER, 6th LORD; PATRICK, 7th LORD; CHRISTOPHER, 8th LORD;

and Patrick, 9th Lord. Edward, son of the latter nobleman, *d.* before his father, leaving two sons, Christopher, 10th Lord, who *d. unm.* in 1688, and Randall, 11th Lord, who *d.* in 1735, and was succeeded by his son Edward, 12th Lord; to whom, in 1781, succeeded his son Randall, 13th Lord, who, in 1791, claimed and was allowed his seat in the House of Lords, which had not been demanded by any Lord Dunsany since the outlawry, in 1691, of Randall, 11th Lord, which however had been reversed by the articles of the treaty of Limerick. His Lordship *d.* in 1821, and was succeeded by his eldest son Edward-Wadding, present and 14th Lord.

DURHAM, BARON. (Lambton.)

Peer of the United Kingdom.

"No earlier owners of the Manor of Lambton are on record, than the ancient and honourable family which still bears the local name," says Surtees, in his history of the Co. of Durham. From Robert de Lambton, Lord of Lambton, who *d.* in 1350, the present Lord is 16th in lineal descent.

Major-General John Lambton, his Lordship's grandfather, *m.* Lady Susan Lyon, daughter of Thomas, 8th Earl of Strathmore, and *d.* in 1794, leaving by her, William-Henry Lambton, Esq., his Lordship's father. He *d.* in 1797, leaving issue, by Lady Anne Villiers, who survives him, and is now the widow of her 2nd husband, the Hon. Charles-William Wyndham:

1 John-George, the present Peer, created in 1828, Baron Durham of the City of Durham, and of Lambton Castle, Co. Palatine of Durham.

2 William-Henry, *b.* 27 March 1793, *m.* 28 Jan. 1824, Henrietta, 2nd daughter of Cuthbert Ellison, Esq., by whom he has four children.

3 Frances-Susan, *b.* 6 Sept. 1794, *m.* 1st, 6 Aug. 1811, the Hon. Colonel Frederick Howard—see *The Peerage Volume*, title Carlisle; he *d.* 20 June 1815; and she *m.* 2ndly, 16 June 1819, Lieut.-Col. Henry-Frederick-Compton Cavendish.—See *The Peerage Volume*, title Devonshire.

4 Henry-William, *b.* 3 Aug. 1795, *d.* 23 Nov. 1826.

5 Hedworth, *b.* 26 March 1797.

DYNEVOR, BARON. (Rice.)

Peer of Great Britain.

His Lordship is of a very ancient Welch family. From Sir Rice ap-Thomas, Fitz-Urian, K.G., in the reign of King Henry VII., the 9th in descent was George Rice, Esq., his Lordship's father.

William, 1st Baron Dynevor, 1st Earl and 2nd Lord Talbot, *m.* Feb. 1734, Mary, daughter and heir of Adam de Cardonnell, Esq., by whom, who *d.* 5 April 1787, he had an only daughter, Lady Cecil; he was created Baron Dynevor of Dynevor, Co. Carmarthen, with remainder, failing his issue male, to his daughter Cecil, and her issue male. On his death in 1782, the Earldom became extinct; the Barony of Talbot devolved on his nephew, John Chetwynd, 3rd Lord, in whose favour the Earldom was revived, and the Barony of Dynevor on his daughter,

Lady Cecil Talbot, 2nd Baroness, wife of the above George Rice, Esq., by whom she was mother of George Talbot, her successor, the present and 3rd Lord.

DYSART, COUNTESS. (TOLLEMACHE.)

Peeress of Scotland.

WILLIAM MURRAY, (descended from Patrick, 3rd son of Sir David Murray of Tullibardine, whose eldest son, William, was ancestor of the Duke of Atholl,) was created EARL of DYSART; ELIZABETH, his eldest daughter and heir, had the Patent renewed, with the former precedence, to herself and such of her issue as she might nominate, and the heirs of such nominee, the eldest always succeeding without division if a female. The COUNTESS *m.* 1st, Sir Lionel Talmash, Bart., (descended from a family seated at Bentley, Co. Suffolk, in the reign of King JOHN,) and 2ndly, John, Duke of Lauderdale; by the 2nd marriage, she had no issue; but by the 1st, was mother of LIONEL, 3rd EARL, who succeeded her in 1697, and *d.* in 1727; Lionel, Lord Huntingtower, his only son, *d.* before him in 1712, leaving one son,

LIONEL, 4th EARL, who was *b.* June 1707, succeeded his grandfather 3 Feb. 1727, and *d.* 10 March 1770: having *m.* 22 July 1729, Lady Grace Cartaret, 2nd daughter of John, 1st Earl Granville, by whom, who *d.* 23 July 1755, he had, besides other children who *d.* young,

1 Lionel, Lord Huntingtower, *b.* 1730, *d.* 26 June 1731.

2 Lionel, Lord Huntingtower, *d.* an infant.

3 LIONEL, 5th EARL, his successor, who was *b.* 1736, and *d.* 22 Feb. 1799; having *m.* 1st, 2 Oct. 1760, Charlotte, daughter of Sir Edward Walpole, K.B., who *d.* 5 Sept. 1789; and 2ndly, 29 April 1791, Magdelena, daughter of Edward Lewis, Esq.; she *d.* 2 Feb. 1823.

4 WILBRAHAM, 6th EARL, who succeeded his brother; he was *b.* Oct. 1739, and *d.* 9 March 1821; having *m.* 4 Feb. 1773, Anna-Maria, eldest daughter of David Lewis, Esq., *b.* 1745, *d.* 14 Sept. 1804.

5 Hon. George, *b.* in 1745, was killed by falling from the mast-head of the Modeste, man-of-war, Oct. 1760.

6 Hon. John, Capt. R.N., *b.* 1750, killed at New York in a duel, 25 Sept. 1777; he *m.* Lady Bridget Henley, daughter of Robert, 1st Earl of Northington, and widow of the Hon. George Fox-Lane, only son of Lord Bingley; by whom, who *d.* 13 March 1796, he had an only son,

Lionel-Robert, Ensign 1st foot guards, who was killed by a shell before Valenciennes, 14 July 1793, *unm.*

7 Hon. William, also in the naval service; he was lost in the Repulse frigate, in a hurricane in the Atlantic, 16 Dec. 1776.

8 Lady Frances, *b.* 1737, *d. unm.* 18 Dec. 1807.

9 LADY LOUISA, *b.* 1745; she succeeded to the family honours on the death of her brother Wilbraham, 6th Earl, and is the present COUNTESS; for her Ladyship's marriage and issue, see *The Peerage Volume.*

10 Lady Jane, *b.* 1750, *d.* 28 Aug. 1802; having *m.* 1st, 23 Oct. 1771, John-Delap Halliday, Esq., who was *b.* 29 Sept. 1749, and *d.* 24 June 1794; she *m.* 2ndly, 4 March 1802, George-David Ferry, Esq., who survives. By her 1st marriage her Ladyship had three sons and one daughter, viz.:

1 Vice-Admiral John-Richard Delap, who has assumed the name of TOLLEMACHE; he *m.* 28 Feb. 1797, Lady Elizabeth Stratford, eldest daughter of John, 3rd Earl of Aldborough, and has issue:

1 Elizabeth-Jane-Henrietta, *b.* 8 Dec. 1797; *m.* 1st, 5 Aug. 1817, Christian-Frederick-Charles-Alexander-James Johnstone, Esq.; this marriage was dissolved 1826, and she *m.* 2ndly, James-Thomas, Lord Brudenell—see *The Peerage Volume*, title Cardigan.

2 Emily, *d.* 6 Dec. 1821, having *m.* Charles-Tyrwhitt Jones, Esq., who was *b.* 24 March 1801.

3 Louisa-Charlotte, *b.* 19 July 1801, *d.* 4 Feb. 1822.
4 Jane, *b.* 19 Aug. 1802, *d.* 13 Feb. 1822; having *m.* 7 June 1820, George Finch, Esq.
5 Marcia, *b.* 29 Jan. 1804.
6 John-Jervis Tollemache, Esq., of Tilstone Lodge, Cheshire; *b.* 7 Dec. 1805, *m.* Georgina, daughter of Thomas Best, Esq., by Lady Emily Stratford, 3rd daughter of John, 3rd Earl of Aldborough; they have issue.
7 Wilbraham-Spencer, *b.* 3 Oct. 1807.
8 Mary-Anne, *b* 29 Dec. 1809; *m.* 6 Sept. 1827, Hubert de Burgh, Esq.
9 Selina; *m.* 7 Dec. 1829, William Locke, Esq., Jun., of Norbury Park.
10 Charlotte.
11 William-Augustus, *b.* 23 Nov. 1817.
12 Georgina.

2 William Halliday, Esq., *d.* 10 April 1805.

3 Francis-Alexander Halliday, Esq., Com. R.N., *m.* 17 March 1801, Anne, youngest daughter of the Rev. H. White, by whom he has issue:
1 Lionel, *b.* 5 March 1803.
2 Frances-Louisa, *b.* 26 April 1806.
3 Lewis-Alexander, *b.* 14 Dec. 1808.
4 Georgina-Elizabeth, *b.* 20 March 1809.
5 Francis-Augustus, *b.* 28 May 1811.
6 Emily-Anne, *b.* 14 Oct. 1813.
7 George-Richard, *b.* 9 Oct. 1816.

4 Charlotte, *d.* Aug. 1826; having *m.* 1793, Henry-Wolseley, Esq.

EGLINTOUN, EARL OF. (MONTGOMERIE.)

Peer of Scotland and of the United Kingdom.

Roger de Montgomerie, who came into England with William the Conqueror, was Earl of Arundel, Chichester, and Shrewsbury, and gave his name to the town and County of Montgomerie in Wales. Robert de Montgomerie, supposed to be his grandson, settled in Scotland, and obtained from Walter, the High Steward of Scotland, the manor of Eglisham, in the County of Renfrew, which is still possessed by the Earl of Eglintoun. 6th in descent from him was John de Montgomerie of Eglisham, who, in 1388, made prisoner, at the battle of Otterbourn, the celebrated Henry Lord Percy, commonly called Hotspur. He *m.* Elizabeth, daughter and sole heir of Sir Hugh de Eglintoun, with whom, besides other considerable property, he obtained the Baronies of Eglintoun and Ardrossan, which also are still in possession of the Earl of Eglintoun. His grandson, SIR ALEXANDER, was created LORD MONTGOMERY about the year 1448. ALEXANDER, eldest son of the 1st LORD, *d.* before his father, leaving two sons; ALEXANDER, 2nd LORD, who succeeded his grandfather; and Robert, whose grandson Sir Hugh Montgomery, was created in 1622, to the Peerage of Ireland, by the title of Viscount Montgomery of Great-Ardes, Co. Down; Hugh, son of the Viscount, was advanced in 1661, to the dignity of Earl of Mount-Alexander in the same County, and both titles became extinct in 1758. To ALEXANDER, 2nd LORD, succeeded his son HUGH, 3rd LORD, created in 1507, EARL of EGLINTOUN; he *d.* in 1545. His two eldest sons *d.* before him; John, Master of Eglintoun, the 2nd, was killed, in 1520, in an affray in the streets of Edinburgh, between the Earls of Arran (with whom were the Montgomeries) and Angus, and their partisans; his eldest son Archibald, Master of Eglintoun, also *d.* before his grandfather, and HUGH, his 2nd son, succeeded as 2nd EARL. He *d.* in 1546, and was succeeded by his son HUGH, 3rd EARL, a zealous partisan of Queen Mary, on whose behalf he was engaged at Langside. He *d.* in 1585, leaving the two sons and two daughters following: 1 HUGH, his successor, 4th EARL, who was killed in a feud with the Cunninghams in 1586, leaving an only child HUGH, 5th EARL, then in his infancy, who, while still a minor, was affianced to the Lady Gabriela Stewart, sister of Ludowick, Duke of Lennox, and second cousin paternally to King James VI., which Lady, however, *d.* before the marriage, and the EARL *m.* his cousin, Margaret Montgomerie, and *d.* without issue in 1612; 2 Robert, who *d.* in 1596; he was father of the said Margaret, his only child, who, after the Earl's death, *m.* Robert, 6th Lord Boyd, and *d.* without issue; 3 Lady Margaret, *m.* to Robert, 1st Earl of Wintoun, by whom she had issue; 4 Lady Agnes, *m.* to Robert, 4th Lord Semphill, by whom she had issue.

HUGH, 5th EARL EGLINTOUN, resigned his Earldom, and, in 1611, had a new grant of it, with the former precedency, to him and to the heirs male of his body, failing which, to Sir Alexander Seton, Thomas Seton, and John Seton, 3rd, 4th, and 5th sons of Robert, 1st Earl of Wintoun, by Lady Margaret Montgomerie, his aunt; and the heirs male of their bodies respectively, which failing, to his heirs male whatsoever.

The present Earl is paternally descended from one of the two considerable Norman families in England of the name of Saye. Secher de Saye emigrated to Scotland in the reign of David I., and called his lands Saytoun, from whence his posterity derived their surname of Seton. In the 7th generation, Margaret, a daughter and heir, carried the estate by marriage to Alan de Wintoun, supposed to be a collateral of the same house; their only son, Sir William Seton, had two sons; 1 Sir John, who *d.* in 1441; 2 Alexander, who, by marriage with Elizabeth de Gordon, was ancestor of the Duke of Gordon.

Sir John, the eldest son, was grandfather of George, 1st Lord Seton; 7th in descent from whom was Robert, 6th Lord Seton, and 1st Earl of Wintoun, who *m.* the above-mentioned Lady Margaret Montgomerie, eldest daughter of HUGH, 3rd EARL of EGLINTOUN, and by her had five sons, viz.:

1 Robert, 2nd Earl of Wintoun, who *d.* without issue.

2 George, 3rd Earl of Wintoun, who continued the line of Earls of Wintoun, forfeited in 1716, and extinct in 1726, by the death of James, 3rd Viscount Kingston, the last male descendant of the 3rd Earl of Wintoun.

3 ALEXANDER, who assumed the name of Montgomerie, and became, in pursuance of the patent above recited, 6th EARL of EGLINTOUN.

4 Sir Thomas Seton, ancestor of the Setons of Olivestob.

5 Sir John Seton, who left an only daughter, *m.* to Alexander Menzies, of Coulterallers.

ALEXANDER, 6th EARL, popularly called Gray Steel, on account of his intrepid courage, was a ruling Elder of the General Assembly of the Church of Scotland in 1642, when the solemn league and covenant was resolved on; and in the following year had a command in the Scottish army, which was sent to the assistance of the English Parliament. However, when the fatal tragedy had been consummated in England by the murder of the King, the Earl, like many other Noblemen of his principles in Scotland, by no means desired the abolition of Royalty; and when, in 1650, CHARLES II. came to Scotland, the Earl of Eglintoun was appointed his Master of the Horse. In the following year, raising forces in the West for the King's service, he was surprised by a party of English horse, and sent prisoner first to Hull, and afterwards to Berwick, where he remained in confinement till the Restoration. He *d.* in 1661, leaving five sons; of whom, HUGH, the eldest, succeeded him, and became 7th EARL; James, 3rd son, was ancestor of the present Earl; and Robert, 5th son, after commencing his career in politics and war on the side of the English Parliament, repaired to the standard of King CHARLES II., and was Major-General of the Horse at the battle of Worcester, where he was wounded and taken prisoner. He was confined in the castle of Edinburgh, from whence he escaped in 1659, went abroad to the King, and returned with him at the Restoration; he left male issue.

Hugh, 7th Earl, was a staunch Royalist in the civil war, and commanded a troop of horse raised by himself, in the King's army, at the battle of Marston Moor, where his father was engaged on the opposite side; he *d.* in 1669, and was succeeded by his son, Alexander, 8th Earl; to whom, in 1701, succeeded his son, Alexander, 9th Earl; he *d.* in 1729, leaving two sons, Alexander, 10th, and Archibald, 11th Earls; the latter succeeded his brother in 1769, and *d.* without male issue in 1796, when the male line of the 7th Earl became extinct. He left two daughters, of whom Lady Susanna, the youngest, *b.* 20 May 1788, *d. unm.* 16 Nov. 1805; and Lady Mary, the eldest, wife of the late Lord Montgomerie, is the mother of the present Earl, and now *m.* to Sir Charles Montolieu-Lamb, Bart.—See *The Peerage Volume.*

By the death of the 11th Earl, and the extinction of the male line of the 7th Earl, the title devolved on the representative of Colonel James Montgomerie, of Coylsfield, 3rd son of the 6th Earl. He was father of Hugh, and grandfather of Alexander Montgomerie, both of Coylsfield; the latter *d.* 28 Dec. 1783, having *m.* Lillias, daughter of Sir Robert Montgomerie, Bart., heiress of the branch of Montgomerie, of Skelmorly, descended from the 2nd son of the 1st Lord Montgomerie; by whom, who *d.* 18 Nov. 1783, he had the following issue:

1 Hugh, who succeeded as 12th Earl, and was created in 1806, Baron Ardrossan of Ardrossan, Co. Ayr, in the Peerage of the United Kingdom; he *d.* in Dec. 1819; he had two sons, who both *d.* before him: Archibald, Lord Montgomerie, the eldest, having *m.* Lady Mary, daughter and heir of the 11th Earl, by whom he had a son and heir, which *d.* the day of its birth, 18 Dec. 1803; another son and heir, Hugh, *b.* 24 Jan. 1811, who became Lord Montgomerie on the death of his father, 4 Jan. 1814, and *d.* before his grandfather, 13 July 1817; and Archibald-William, the present and 13th Earl, who succeeded his grandfather. The Earl's 2nd son was the Hon. Robert Montgomerie, a Lieutenant R.N., who *d.* at Port Royal, in Jamaica, in Jan. 1799, *unm.* The Earl had also two daughters, for whom see *The Peerage Volume.*

2 Alexander Montgomerie, Esq., of Annick Lodge, in the naval service of the East India Company; he *d.* 8 July 1802, having *m.* Elizabeth, daughter of Dr. Taylor, by whom he had the issue described in *The Peerage Volume*, besides Thomas and Archibald, his 4th and 5th sons, who are both deceased *unm.*

3 Archibald Montgomerie, Esq., of Stair, in the civil service of the East India Company; he *d.* 5 Jan. 1831, having *m.* Miss Maria Chantry, by whom he had two elder sons, Alexander and Archibald, both officers in the Bengal military service, and both deceased. Also two surviving sons, William and Edmund, the former in the East India Company's civil service.

4 Lieutenant-General James Montgomery, *b.* 1756, *d.* April 1829; having *m.* 1810, Harriet-Isabella, daughter of Thomas Jackson, Esq.

5 Frances, *m.* 1753, James Ritchie, Esq.; they are both deceased.

6 Lillias, *m.* John Hamilton, Esq.; they are both deceased.

7 Margaret, *m.* 1772, John Dalrymple-Hamilton, Esq., who *d.* 12 Feb. 1796; he was great uncle of Sir Hew Dalrymple-Hamilton, Bart., of North Berwick.—See *The Peerage Volume*, title Stair.

EGMONT, EARL OF. (Perceval.)

Peer of Ireland and of Great Britain.

Robert de Ivery, supposed to have sprung from a younger son of Eudes, Duke of Brittany, was amongst the most powerful Barons who accompanied William the Conqueror into England, and obtained from that Prince considerable estates in Somersetshire and elsewhere; he *d.* in Normandy in 1083. Ascelin, his eldest son, sometimes called Gonel de Perceval, and, from the violence of his temper and actions, surnamed Lupus, or the Wolf, was continually in rebellion against Robert Duke of Normandy, and Henry I. King of England, and at war with his fellow-nobles; he at one time held out his castle of Breherval, by his own resources alone, against the united power of the King of France and the Duke of Normandy, with all the force they could raise, until, wearied with the tediousness and disgusted with the difficulties of the siege, they agreed to a treaty with Ascelin; he *d.* in 1119. William Gonel de Perceval, his son, surnamed Lupellus, or the Lesser Wolf, from whence the surname of Luvel, and at length Lovell, was assumed by his descendants, immediately on coming to his inheritance, joined with Waleran, Earl of Mellent and Leicester, in rebellion against King Henry I.; and after the defeat of Turold in Normandy, narrowly escaped being taken; by exchanging, however, his arms for the dress of one peasant, and giving his shoes to another, for providing him a passage over the river Seine, he reached his castle of Ivery in safety, and found means to reconcile himself to the King. From this time he resided chiefly in England, and fortified his Castle of Kary, in Somersetshire, against King Stephen. On his death his five sons divided his inheritance; they were,

1 Walleran, Lord of Ivery, and Chief Butler of Normandy; he succeeded to all his father's possessions in that Duchy, and transmitted them to his descendants, who flourished in direct male succession of great and eminent men, till the line terminated, in the 15th century, in heiresses, who have carried the inheritance of Ivery, by repartition amongst their co-heirs, into many of the most illustrious princely houses of Europe.

2 Ralph Lovell, Baron of Castle Kary; he inherited the principal part of his father's English possessions, but *d.* without issue.

3 Henry Lovell, who added his brother's inheritance to his own share, and succeeded as Baron of Castle Kary; in which he was followed by eight successive Barons, his descendants to the sixth generation; Richard, the last of them, received summons to Parliament, by writ in 1438, and *d.* in 1351, having survived his son James, and his grandson Richard; Muriel, sister of the latter, became heir to her grandfather, and carried the Barony into the family of St. Maur, from whence it passed by an heiress to that of Zouche of Harringworth, amongst the co-heirs of which it is still in abeyance.

4 William Lovell, who for his share of the inheritance obtained the Manor of Tichmarsh, in Northamptonshire, and was also Lord of Minster Lovell, in Oxfordshire. John Lord Lovell, of Tichmarsh, his descendant in the direct male line through four generations, was summoned to Parliament in 1299, and transmitted the honour also in uninterrupted descent to his great grandson, John Lord Lovell, who *d. unm.* in 1361, and was succeeded by his brother, another Lord John. This latter *m.* Maud, grand-daughter and heir of Robert, 2nd Lord Holland, by writ 1314, and the united Baronies descended in uninterrupted male succession through other four generations to Francis, Lord Lovell and Holland, K.G., who was created Viscount Lovell in 1483; in 1487 he was killed in the battle of Stoke, in support of Lambert Simnel, the counterfeit Duke of York, against King Henry VII., and being attainted, all his honours were forfeited, including, besides those of Lovell and Holland, the Baronies of Deincourt and Grey of Rotherfield, inherited from his grandmother; he left two sisters, his co-heirs, married into the families of Stapleton, of Carlton, which still exists in male descent, and Norres, which was attainted in the next generation. The male line of this branch inherited, however, another Peerage, that of Morley, created by writ in 1299, and centering in Alianore, daughter and heir of Robert de Morley, the 6th Baron, who *m.* William Lovell, 2nd son of William, 7th Baron Lovell, of Tichmarsh, and uncle of Francis Viscount Lovell; he was summoned to Parliament in her right in 1469, and left a son, Henry, who *d.* without issue in 1489; and a daughter, Alice, heir to her brother, who, by marriage with Henry Parker, carried the Barony of Morley into the family of Parker, in which it continued till 1686, when, together with that of Monteagle, which the Parkers, Barons Morley, inherited from the Courtenay family, it fell into

abeyance between the aunts and co-heirs of the last Lord. But the male descendants of Alice Lovell, by her marriage with Henry Parker, continued to flourish till they finally failed in 1740, by the death of Sir Philip Parker à Morley Long, Bart., whose sister and heir, Catherine, *m.* JOHN, 1st EARL of EGMONT.

5 Richard; he received for his share of the inheritance some lands in Somersetshire, and took the name of Perceval, which has been ever since borne by his descendants; he went with King Richard to the holy wars, and returned thence in consequence of being disabled, by the loss of a leg, in battle against the Saracens. Richard his son was with him in the Holy Land, and having succeeded to his patrimony, left three sons: 1 Robert de Perceval, who settled in Ireland, and was summoned to the Irish Parliament in 1285; he left two sons, Richard and Robert, successive Barons; the latter left one son, Thomas, 4th Lord Perceval, on whose death, in 1312, the title became extinct; 2 Hugh, of whom nothing farther is known; 3 John de Perceval, who possessed the chief part of the family inheritance in Somersetshire; he *d.* in 1281.

The 13th in descent from him was Richard Perceval, who settled in Ireland in the reign of King James I., sold a part of his ancient patrimony, and with the proceeds bought to great advantage considerable property in the County of Cork, including the castles of Canturk and Lohort. Sir Philip, his youngest son and eventual heir, took a distinguished part in the military and political events of the troublous times in which his lot was cast; during which he lost property, according to a minute specification submitted to government by his son, to no less an amount than £248,004. 9s. 1d. In the first eruption of the rebellion, he vehemently opposed the Irish Catholics, but being sent for by the King into England to assist at the conferences for the pacification of that unhappy kingdom, he became involved in English politics, and took his seat in Cromwell's Parliament. Here he soon became obnoxious to the ruling party, and saw every thing verging either to tyranny or democracy, till finally, worn out by the anxiety the ruin of the country and of his private affairs created, he *d.* in London in 1647. John, his eldest son, was created a Baronet in 1661, and was grandfather of

Sir John Perceval, Bart., created in 1715, Baron Perceval of Burton, Co. Cork; in 1722, Viscount Perceval, of Kanturk, in the same county; and, in 1733, EARL of EGMONT. He *d.* in 1748; having *m.* as mentioned above, Catherine, daughter of Sir Philip Parker à Morley, by whom he was father of JOHN, 2nd EARL, created in 1762, a Peer of Great Britain, by the title of BARON LOVELL and HOLLAND of Enmore, Co. Somerset. He *d.* 20 Dec. 1772; having *m*, 1st, Lady Catherine Cecil, 2nd daughter of James, 5th Earl of Salisbury, by whom he had issue, JOHN, 3rd EARL, his successor, the Hon. Edward Perceval, who was *b.* 19 April 1744, and *d.* 13 Feb. 1829; having *m.* 25 July 1775, Sarah, daughter of John Howarth, Esq., by whom, who *d.* 30 April 1808, he had the three daughters stated in *The Peerage Volume*, and one other daughter, Catherine, twin with Mary, who *d.* 28 April 1824, aged 46. The Earl had also by his first marriage one daughter, Lady Catherine, *b.* 20 Feb. 1746, *d.* June 1782, wife of the first Lord Newborough. He *m.* 2ndly, 26 Jan. 1756, Catherine, 3rd daughter of the Hon. Charles Compton, and sister to Charles and Spencer, late Earls of Northampton, by whom, who was created, in 1770, a Peeress of Ireland, by the title of Baroness Arden of Lohort Castle, Co. Cork, and *d.* 11 June 1784; he was father of Charles-George, present Baron Arden, and other issue. See Arden.

His Lordship was succeeded by his eldest son, JOHN-JAMES, 3rd EARL, who was *b.* 23 Jan. 1738, and *d.* 25 Feb. 1822; having *m.* 4 June 1765, Isabella, only daughter and heir of Lord Nassau Powlett, (3rd son of Charles, 2nd Duke of Bolton,) by whom, who was *b.* in 1738, and *d.* 8 Sept. 1821, he was father of JOHN, the present and 4th EARL.

EGREMONT, EARL OF. (WYNDHAM.)

Peer of Great Britain.

ALGERNON SEYMOUR, Duke of Somerset and Earl of Northumberland, was created in 1749, Baron of Cockermouth and Earl of Egremont, both in the County of Cumberland, with remainder, failing his issue male, to his nephews, Sir Charles Wyndham, Bart., and Percy Wyndham, and their issue male. The Duke was succeeded in this Earldom, in 1750, by Sir CHARLES, his eldest nephew, 2nd EARL.

His Lordship is of a Saxon family, seated, soon after the conquest, at Wyndham, Co. Norfolk. From Ralph de Wyndham, living in the reign of King Edward I., the 8th in descent was

Sir John Wyndham, of Orchard Wyndham, Co. Somerset, a Cadet of the House; whose 2nd son, Edmond, was father of Sir Thomas Wyndham, of Kentsford, of whom it is related, that shortly before his death, in 1636, he called his children together, emphatically warned them that they were likely to see cloudy and troublesome times, and added, "I command you to honour and obey our gracious Sovereign, and in all times to adhere to the Crown; and although the Crown should hang upon a bush, I charge you forsake it not." Most of his sons engaged in the service of King CHARLES I., and Colonel Francis Wyndham, his 4th son, Governor of Dunstar Castle, is memorable for conducting King CHARLES II., after the battle of Worcester, to his house at Trent; after the restoration he was created a Baronet; which title became extinct in 1719, by the death of his last male descendant, Sir Francis Wyndham, of Trent, Bart.

John, the eldest son of Sir John Wyndham, of Orchard Wyndham, *d.* in his father's lifetime, leaving an only son, Sir John, who succeeded his grandfather, and afterwards to the estates of Felbrigg, &c. in Norfolk, on the extinction of the senior line of the house; he had nine sons, three of whom *d. unm.*, the others were,

1 John, who succeeded to his estates in Somersetshire, and was father of Sir William, created a Baronet in 1661.

2 Thomas, ancestor of the Wyndhams, of Felbrigg, Co. Norfolk, from whom proceeded the late Right Hon. William Wyndham.

3 Humphrey, ancestor of the Wyndhams, of Dunraven Castle, Co. of Glamorgan, whose heir female has carried that estate by marriage to the present Earl of Dunraven.

4 Sir Hugh Wyndham, of Silton, one of the Barons of the Exchequer; he was three times married, but *d.* in 1684, without surviving issue male.

5 Sir Wadham Wyndham, appointed in 1660, one of the Judges of the King's Bench; he was ancestor of the Wyndhams of Norrington, Dinton, Salisbury, and Spargrove.

6 Sir George, from whom the Wyndhams of Cromer descend.

Sir William Wyndham, 1st Baronet, was father of Sir Edward, his successor, and grandfather of Sir William Wyndham, Bart., who in 1708, *m.* Lady Catherine Seymour, sister of the above-mentioned ALGERNON, Duke of Somerset, 1st EARL of EGREMONT, and was father by her of, 1 CHARLES, 2nd EARL, 2 Percy, who, inheriting the estate of Henry, 8th Earl of Thomond, who had married his maternal aunt, the Lady Elizabeth Seymour, and whose titles became extinct by his death in 1741, assumed the name and arms of O'Brien, and was created Earl of Thomond, and Viscount Ibrickan, which titles became extinct by his death in 1774, *unm.*

CHARLES, 2nd EARL, succeeded to the titles on the death of his uncle, the 1st EARL in 1750, and *d.* in 1763, when he was succeeded by his eldest son, GEORGE-O'BRIEN, the present and 3rd EARL.

ELDON, EARL OF. (Scott.)

Peer of the United Kingdom.

This venerable and highly-respected nobleman is the younger brother of Lord Stowell, and has worked his way through the labours of the law to the first honours of the land, and to a reputation, both as an indefatigable and upright judge, and as an honest politician, which will last as long as the records of British history. On being appointed, in 1799, Lord Chief Justice of the Common Pleas, he was created Baron Eldon of Eldon, Co. Durham. In 1801 he was appointed Lord High Chancellor; and, with an interruption of fourteen months only, in the years 1806 and 1807, retained the custody of the great seal till the year 1827. In 1821 he was farther created Viscount Encombe of Encombe, Co. Dorset, and Earl of Eldon, Co. Durham.

ELGIN AND KINCARDINE, EARL OF. (Bruce.)

Peer of Scotland.

Robert de Bruys, of Clackmannan, is styled by King David II. his cousin. Sir David Bruce, of Clackmannan, 6th in direct male descent from him, had amongst other issue,

Edward Bruce, of Blairhall (his 2nd son) who had three sons;

1 Robert, of Blairhall, whose male line is extinct.

2 Edward, created in 1603, Lord Bruce of Kinloss, with remainder to his heirs male whatever; he *d.* in 1611, and was succeeded by his eldest son, Edward, 2nd Lord, who was killed in a duel by Sir Edward Sackville, afterwards Earl of Dorset, in 1613, *unm.*; Thomas, 2nd son of the 1st Lord, 3rd Lord Bruce of Kinloss, was created in 1633, Earl of Elgin, with remainder to his heirs male whatever; in 1641 he was also created a Peer of England, by the title of Baron Bruce of Whorlton, Co. Cork, and *d.* in 1663. Robert, 2nd Earl, his son, was created in 1664, Baron Bruce of Skelton, Co. York, Viscount Bruce of Ampthill, Co Bedford, and Earl of Aylesbury, Co. Buckinghamshire; he *d.* in 1685, and was succeeded by his son, Thomas, 3rd Earl; to him succeeded in 1741, Charles, his son, 4th Earl, on whose death in 1747, the issue male of the 1st Lord Bruce of Kinloss, failed, and the above-mentioned English honours became extinct; he had been created in 1746, Baron Bruce of Tottenham, Co. Wilts, with remainder to his nephew, Thomas Brudenell, 4th son of his sister Elizabeth, by George, 3rd Earl of Cardigan, who assumed the name of Bruce, succeeded to the Barony, and was father of the present Marquis of Ailesbury.

3 Sir George Bruce of Carnock, who *d.* in 1625, leaving two sons;

- 1 George, whose eldest son, Sir Edward Bruce, was created in 1647, Earl of Kincardine, and Lord Bruce of Torry, to him and his heirs male; he *d.* without issue, and was succeeded by his brother Alexander, 2nd Earl, who *d.* in 1680, and his issue male failed on the death in 1705, of his son, Alexander, 3rd Earl.
- 2 Robert, father of Alexander, who succeeded his cousin as 4th Earl, and was father of Robert, Alexander, and Thomas, the 5th, 6th, and 7th Earls; the two former left no issue male, and the latter was succeeded in March 1740, by his son William, 8th Earl, who dying in Sept. the same year, was succeeded by his son,

Charles, 9th Earl of Kincardine. He succeeded also in 1747, as 5th Earl of Elgin, and dying in 1771, was succeeded by his son Thomas, the present Earl.

ELIBANK, BARON. (Murray.)

Peer of Scotland.

From John de Moravia, probably the son of William, taken prisoner with King David II. in 1346, descended in the 6th generation, Andrew Murray of Blackbarony, who had issue; 1 John, ancestor of Sir Archibald Murray of Blackbarony, Bart.; 2 Gideon, a Lord of Session, and Treasurer Depute of Scotland; having been charged by James Stuart, Lord Ochiltree, with offences committed in this latter office, a day was appointed for his trial, which he took so much to heart, that he abstained for several days from food, and *d.* in consequence, 28 June 1621. He was father of Sir Patrick Murray of Elibank, created a Baronet of Nova Scotia in 1628, and Baron Elibank in 1643. He *d.* in 1649, and was succeeded by his son, Patrick, 2nd Lord, who was succeeded in 1661, by his son, Patrick, 3rd Lord, and he in 1687, by his son Alexander, 4th Lord, who *d.* in 1736, leaving five sons; viz.:

1 Patrick, 5th Lord, who *d.* in 1778, without issue.

2 George, 6th Lord, an Admiral in the R.N.; he succeeded his brother in 1778, and *d.* without issue male, 12 Nov. 1785; having *m.* in Jan. 1760, Lady Isabel Mackenzie, daughter and heir of George, 3rd Earl of Cromartie, by whom, who was *b.* 30 March 1725, and *d.* 28 Dec. 1801; he had the two daughters stated in *The Peerage Volume*, who succeeding to the noble estates of the Cromartie family, have assumed the name of Mackenzie.

3 The Hon. and Rev. Gideon Murray, D.D., Prebendary of Lincoln and Durham, Vicar of Gainsborough, Co. Lincoln, and Rector of Carlton, Co. Nottingham; he *d.* 21 June 1776, leaving two sons;

- 1 Alexander, who succeeded his uncle as 7th Lord, and *d.* in 1820, when he was succeeded by his son, Alexander, 8th Lord, who dying in 1830, was succeeded by his eldest son, Alexander-Oliphant, present and 9th Lord.
- 2 David Murray, Esq., who was *b.* 10 May 1748, and *d.* 8 May 1794; having *m.* 8 Oct. 1783, Elizabeth, 5th daughter and co-heir of the Hon. Thomas Harley of Oxford, by whom, who was *b.* April 1763, and *d.* 9 July 1824, he left the issue described in *The Peerage Volume.*

4 The Hon. Alexander Murray, who rendered himself very conspicuous by his vehemence on the popular side, in the contested election for Westminster in 1750, and was afterwards imprisoned in Newgate with circumstances of great severity, by the House of Commons; he *d. unm.* in 1777.

5 The Hon. General James Murray; he greatly distinguished himself in 1759-60, in the war then carrying on in America against the French; and afterwards, in 1781, in the government of Minorca, when that Island was invaded by an overpowering force of French and Spaniards. He *d.* 18 June 1794; having *m.* 1st, Cordelia, daughter of John Collier, Esq., who *d.* 26 June 1779, without issue; and 2ndly, Anne, daughter of Abraham Whitham, Esq., by whom he had the issue described in *The Peerage Volume.*

ELLENBOROUGH, BARON. (Law.)

Peer of the United Kingdom.

His Lordship is descended from a family that has long been seated at Askham, Co Westmoreland.

His grandfather, Edmund Law, Lord Bishop of Carlisle, was *b.* in 1703, and *d.* 14 Aug. 1787; having *m.* Mary, daughter of John Christian, Esq.; by whom, who *d.* in 1762, he had issue,

1 John, Lord Bishop of Elphin, who *d.* without issue, 19 March 1810, having *m.* Anne, daughter of —— Wallace, Esq., and widow of —— Tomlinson, Esq.; she *d.* 13 March 1813.

2 Mary, who *m.* the Rev. James-Stephen Lushington; he *d.* in June 1801.

3 Ewan Law, Esq., *d.* 24 April 1829; having *m.* Henrietta-Sarah, eldest daughter of the Most Rev. William Markham, Lord Archbishop of York, by whom he had issue;

1 Harriette.

2 Maria-Anne, *b.* 5 July 1788, *m.* 13 Aug. 1810, Sir George Clerk, Bart, M.P.

3 Rev. Edward, *b.* 7 Aug. 1790.

4 William-John, a Barrister-at-Law, a Commissioner of Bankrupts, and a Commissioner of the Insolvent Debtor's Court; *m.* Charlotte, daughter of Robert Sympson, Esq., by whom he has issue; 1 Edmund; 2 Ewan-Robert; 3 Charlotte-Elizabeth; 4 Emma-Henrietta; 5 William-George; 6 Cecilia-Maria; 7 A daughter, *b.* 27 Aug. 1826; 8 A daughter, *b.* 9 Oct. 1828; 9 A son, *b.* 10 April 1830; 10 A daughter *b.* 27 Sept. 1831.

5 Elizabeth-Frederica, *b.* 28 May 1794, *m.* 30 April 1816, the Rev. P. G. Crofts.

6 George-Ewan, *b.* 28 Oct. 1796, Assistant Secretary to the East India Government at Calcutta, *d.* there 6 Oct. 1820.

7 Cecilia-Anne, *m.* 1 Oct. 1824, the Rev. John Barlow.

4 Edward, created in 1802, Baron Ellenborough of Ellenborough, Co. Cumberland, on his appointment as Lord Chief Justice of the King's Bench; he *d.* in 1818, and was succeeded by his eldest son, Edward, 2nd and present Lord.

5 Joanna, *d.* 4 Jan. 1823; having *m.* 21 May 1772, Sir Thomas Rumbold, Bart. who *d.* 9 Nov. 1791.

6 Thomas, *m.* Miss Anne Curtis of South Carolina, and has a daughter.

7 The Right Rev. George-Henry, Lord Bishop of Bath and Wells, widower, 27 Sept. 1826, of Jane, eldest daughter of General Adeane; by whom he has had issue,

1 Anne.

2 Joanna, *m.* July 1807, Alexander, Powell, Esq., of Hurdcott House, Co. Wiltshire.

3 Augusta, *b.* 1789, *d.* 5 May 1822, having *m.* 28 May 1812, the Rev. James Slade, Prebendary of Chester.

4 Rev. James-Thomas, Chancellor of the Diocese of Lichfield and Coventry, Prebend of Lichfield, and Master of St. John's Hospital, Lichfield, *m.* 16 Dec. 1820, Lady Henrietta-Charlotte Grey, eldest daughter of George-Harry, 6th Earl of Stamford and Warrington, and has issue.

5 Jane, *m.* 1822. the Rev. —— Harkness.

6 George, *b.* 24 Aug. 1794, *d.* 30 Dec. 1811.

7 The Venerable Henry, Chancellor and Archdeacon of the Diocese, and Prebendary of Wells.

8 Rev. Robert-Vanburgh, Prebendary of Chester, *b.* 29 Sept. 1799; *m.* 3 Nov. 1829, Sidney-Dorothea, daughter of the late Colonel Davison, and has issue, a daughter, *b.* 7. Aug. 1830.

9 Margaret, *b.* 7. March 1803.

ELPHINSTONE, BARON. (Elphinstone.)

Peer of Scotland.

This family was existing at Elphinstone as early as 1250; Sir William Elphinstone, living in 1399, was great-grandfather of Alexander, created Baron Elphinstone, in 1509; he fell at the battle of Flodden, so fatal to the King and Nobility of Scotland, 9 Sept. 1513; and was succeeded by his son Alexander, 2nd Lord, who was slain at the battle of Pinkie, 10 Sept. 1547. He was succeeded by his son, Robert, 3rd Lord, who *d.* in 1602, leaving 3 sons, viz. 1 Alexander, his successor, 4th Lord; 2 George, a priest, Rector of the Scottish College at Rome; 3 James, created Lord Balmerinoch in 1604; he had been Secretary of State to King James in Scotland, before his accession to the throne of England, and in that capacity surreptitiously obtained the King's signature to a letter to the Pope, expressing his regard for the Papacy; which afterwards coming to the King's knowledge, his Lordship was tried, at St. Andrew's, for high treason, in 1609, convicted, and sentenced to be beheaded; his life, however, was spared, and he *d.* a prisoner in his own house at Balmerinoch, in 1612. He left two sons: John, 2nd Lord Balmerinoch; and James, created Lord Coupar in 1607, with remainder, failing his heirs male, to the male heirs of his father; he *d.* in 1669, without issue, and was succeeded by his nephew John, 3rd Lord Balmerinoch. John, 2nd Lord Balmerinoch, was restored in blood after the death of his father, and fell himself into equal trouble; being tried and capitally convicted, in 1634, for abetting and dispersing a petition to King Charles I., declared to be a seditious libel, and concealing the author; he was pardoned, however, but continued inveterately hostile to the King, assisting with all his ability in the rebellion, till his death in 1650. John, 3rd Lord Balmerinoch, his son and heir, succeeded to an estate ruined by his father's expenditure on behalf of the covenanters, and still further reduced after the restoration, by fines imposed for his own compliance under the usurpation, and for nonconformity; he succeeded to the title and estates of his uncle Lord Coupar in 1669, and *d.* in 1704, when he was succeeded by his only surviving son John, 4th Lord Balmerinoch, who *d.* in 1736; he was succeeded by his eldest son John, 5th Lord, who dying without issue, 5 Jan. 1746, was succeeded by his only surviving brother, Arthur, 6th and last Lord Balmerinoch; he had been engaged in the rebellion of 1715, had obtained a pardon at the earnest intercession of his father, so late as the year 1733; and was again engaged in the army of the Pretender, when he succeeded to the title of Lord Balmerinoch by the death of his brother, and was taken prisoner a few weeks afterwards, at the battle of Culloden. He was attainted of high treason, tried, condemned, and on the 18 Aug. 1746, beheaded on Tower Hill; his titles would have been forfeited, but with him ended this branch of the house of Elphinstone, which had been remarkable for so many vicissitudes of fortune.

Alexander, 4th Lord Elphinstone, elder brother of the 1st Lord Balmerinoch, *d.* in 1648, having sided with the Parliament in the civil wars; he had, besides other issue, two sons: 1 Alexander, 5th Lord, his successor, who *d.* without surviving issue male, in 1649, leaving an only daughter and heir, Lillias; 2 James, whose son Alexander, 6th Lord, succeeded his uncle as heir male; *m.* his cousin Lillias, the heir of line, and *d.* in 1654: having so strongly evidenced his loyalty as to be excepted from Cromwell's act of grace and pardon. He left two sons; Alexander, who succeeded him as 7th Lord, and *d.* without issue in 1669; and John, 8th Lord. The latter had thirty-six children by his wife, Lady Isabel Maitland, eldest daughter of Charles, 3rd Earl of Lauderdale, but all the sons *d. unm.* except Charles, 9th Lord; who *d.* in 1757; and was succeeded by his eldest surviving son,

Charles, 10th Lord, who *d.* 2 April 1781; having *m.* in 1735, Lady Clementina Fleming, only child of John, 6th Earl of Wigton, by whom, who was *b.* in 1719, and *d.* 1 Jan. 1799, he had issue:

1 John, 11th Lord, his successor, who *d.* in 1794, and was succeeded by his eldest son, John, 12th Lord; he *d.* in 1813, and was succeeded by his only child, John, present and 13th Lord.

2 Hon. Charles, who was lost in the Prince George of 90 guns, in 1758, when that vessel was burnt on the passage from England to Gibraltar.

3 Hon. William, who having *m.* Elizabeth, eldest daughter of William Fullerton, of Carstairs, Co. Lanark, and heiress of her uncle, John Fullerton, of Carberry, Co. Edinburgh, has assumed the additional name of Fullerton; his issue are described in *The Peerage Volume.*

4 Hon. Lockhart, *d.* young.

5 Hon. George, created Viscount Keith, *see* that title; he *d.* in 1823.

6 Hon. Eleonora, *b.* 1749, *d.* 4 Feb. 1800; having *m.* 7 May 1777, the Right Hon. William Adam, Chief Commissioner of the Scotch Jury Court, Lord-Lieutenant of Kinross-shire.

7 Hon. Clementina, *d.* 31 Aug. 1822; having *m.* 31 March 1785, James, Lord Perth, who was *b.* 24 Sept. 1744, created Baron Perth in 1797, and *d.* 2 July 1800. when the title became extinct; they left an only daughter, the Hon. Clementina Drummond, now wife of Lord Willoughby de Eresby.

ELY, MARQUIS OF. (Loftus.)

Peer of Ireland and of the United Kingdom.

Edward Loftus, Esq., of Swineshead, Co. York, had two sons:

1 Robert, whose son Adam, Lord High Chancellor of Ireland, was created in 1622, Viscount Loftus of Ely. He was succeeded by his son Edward, 2nd Viscount, whose son Arthur, 3rd Viscount, dying without surviving issue male, in 1725, the title became extinct.

2 Adam, Archbishop of Dublin in 1567, and Lord Chancellor of Ireland in 1578; he *d.* in 1605; leaving a son, Sir Dudley Loftus, of Rathfarnham, who *d.* in 1616; leaving, besides other issue, 1 Sir Adam, grandfather of Sir Adam, created in 1685, Viscount Lisburne and Baron of Rathfarnham; he was killed before Limerick, at which siege he commanded a regiment in King William's army, in 1691; and dying without issue, his titles became extinct; 2 Nicholas, grandfather of

Nicholas, created in 1751, Baron Loftus of Loftus Hall, and in 1756, Viscount Loftus of Ely; he *d.* in 1763, leaving, besides other issue:

1 Nicholas, 2nd Viscount, created Earl of Ely in 1766, whose son Nicholas, 2nd Earl, succeeded him 23 Oct. 1766, and *d.* without issue in 1769, when the Earldom became extinct.

2 Henry, 4th Viscount, created in 1771, Earl of Ely; he *d.* without issue in 1783, when his title became extinct.

3 Elizabeth, *d.* in 1754; having *m.* 31 Dec. 1736, Sir John Tottenham, of Tottenham Green, Co. Wexford, created a Baronet in 1780, and *d.* in 1787; their son, Sir Charles, on succeeding to the estates of his uncle Henry, Earl of Ely, assumed the name of Loftus; he was created, in 1785, Baron Loftus of Loftus Hall, Co. Wexford; in 1789, Viscount Loftus of Ely; in 1794, Earl of Ely; in 1800, Marquis of Ely; and in 1801 was farther advanced to the dignity of a Peer of the United Kingdom, by the title of Baron Loftus of Long Loftus, Co. York. His Lordship *d.* in 1806, and was succeeded by his son John, present and 2nd Marquis.

ENNISKILLEN, EARL OF. (COLE.)

Peer of Ireland and of the United Kingdom.

This was a family of rank in the County of Hants, in the reign of William the Conqueror. The 1st of his Lordship's ancestors who settled in Ireland was Sir William Cole of Enniskillen, living in 1611; 4th in descent from whom was JOHN COLE, Esq., of Florence Court, created in 1760, BARON MOUNTFLORENCE; he *d.* in 1767, and was succeeded by his eldest son, WILLIAM-WILLOUGHBY, 2nd LORD, created in 1776, Viscount Enniskillen, and in 1789, EARL OF ENNISKILLEN; he *d.* in 1803, and was succeeded by his eldest son, JOHN-WILLOUGHBY, present and 2nd EARL, who, in 1815, was created a Peer of the United Kingdom, by the title of Baron Grinstead of Grinstead, Co. Wilts.

ERNE, EARL OF. (CREIGHTON.)

Peer of Ireland.

This name was originally assumed from the Barony of Crichton, Co. Edinburgh. William de Crichton, living about 1240, was ancestor of the Viscounts of Frendraught in Scotland, extinct in 1698, and of John Creighton, Esq., of Crum Castle, Co. Fermanagh; whose son Abraham commanded a regiment in King WILLIAM's service in the battle of Aghrim; and David, son of Abraham, distinguished himself in the same war, by his gallant defence of his family-seat, Crum Castle, against King JAMES's army of 6000 men. This David died in 1728, and ABRAHAM, his son, was created in 1768, BARON ERNE of Crum Castle, Co. Fermanagh; he *d.* in 1772, and was succeeded by his eldest son, JOHN, 2nd LORD; who was created in 1781, Viscount Erne, and in 1789, EARL OF ERNE; he *d.* in 1828, and was succeeded by his eldest son, ABRAHAM, present and 2nd EARL.

ERROL, EARL OF. (HAY.)

Peer of Scotland and of the United Kingdom.

William de Haya, a branch of the Anglo-Norman family of Hay, settled in Scotland at the end of the 12th century; he was butler to Kings MALCOLM IV. and WILLIAM the Lion, and had two sons: 1 William, ancestor to the Hereditary Constables of Scotland, and Earls of Errol; 2 Robert, ancestor to the Marquis of Tweeddale.

The office of Hereditary Constable of Scotland, granted in 1314, to Sir Gilbert Hay, the 4th in direct male descent from the 2nd William de Haya, mentioned above, descended through five more generations to WILLIAM HAY of Errol, who was created EARL OF ERROL in 1543. His son NICHOLAS 2nd EARL, *d.* in 1470, and was succeeded by his son, WILLIAM 3rd EARL; he *d.* in 1506, leaving issue:

1 WILLIAM, his successor, 4th EARL: slain with his Royal Master at the battle of Flodden, 9 Sept. 1513. He was succeeded by his son WILLIAM, 5th EARL, who *d.* without surviving issue male, but left a daughter, Lady Jane, who *m.* the 7th Earl.

2 Thomas Hay, of Logyalmond; he was father of GEORGE, 6th EARL, to whom succeeded his son,

Andrew, 7th Earl; he m. Lady Jane Hay, daughter and heir of the 5th Earl, and d. in 1585; leaving by her two sons:

1 Francis, 8th Earl; adhering to the Popish religion, he entered into a treasonable correspondence with the court of Spain, with a view to the restoration of that faith in Scotland; was brought to trial, convicted of repeated acts of treason, but pardoned after a short confinement: entered into rebellion again, and conjointly with the Earl of Huntley, defeated a royal army of 700 men, under the Earl of Argyll, at Glenlivat, in 1594; but on the King's advancing against them, the two Earls besought and obtained permission to go abroad; and the Earl of Errol being once more pardoned, in 1596, returned home, and henceforth continued a peaceable and loyal subject till his death, in 1631. He was succeeded by his eldest son, William, 9th Earl.

2 George Hay, of Killour, father of Sir Andrew, and grandfather of Sir John Hay, of Killour, who succeeded as 11th Earl.

William, 9th Earl, d. in 1636, and was succeeded by his only son, Gilbert, 10th Earl, who was Colonel of horse in the "engagement" for the rescue of King Charles I., in 1648, and raised a regiment for the service of Charles II. He d. without issue in 1674; having, in 1666, obtained a charter, settling the Earldom, together with the office of High Constable, on himself, and the heirs male or female of his body, which failing to the heirs he should appoint, under which clause the present Earl inherits, which failing to the heirs male and of tailzie, which failing to his heirs male for ever. He was succeeded, according to his own appointment, by his next heir male, John, 11th Earl, grandson of George Hay, of Killour, 4th son of Andrew, 7th Earl; he d. in 1704, leaving three sons: Charles, 12th Earl, who d. without issue in 1717; James and Thomas, who also d. without issue; and 2 daughters, Lady Mary, who succeeded her brother, and d. without issue in 1758; and

Lady Margaret, who m. James, 5th Earl of Linlithgow, and 4th of Callendar, attainted in 1715; by whom she had an only daughter and heir,

Lady Anne Livingstone, m. to William Boyd, 4th Earl of Kilmarnock, by whom she had James, who succeeded his great-aunt, as 14th Earl of Errol.

His Lordship derives his paternal descent from Robert, surnamed Boyd, from the fairness of his complexion, son of Simon, the brother of Walter, 1st High Steward of Scotland: (from whom sprang the Royal House of Stuart:) 10th in descent from him, was Robert Boyd, of Kilmarnock, who was created a Peer of Parliament by the title of Lord Boyd, in 1459; in 1460 he was appointed one of the Council of Regency during the minority of James III., and in 1466, Governor of the Kingdom of Scotland, till the Sovereign came of age. In 1469, however, the King's mind being alienated from himself and family, he had recourse to arms, but was overpowered; his brother Alexander was taken and beheaded, but the Lord Boyd himself escaped to England, and d. at Alnwick in 1470; his estates and honours being forfeited. He left two sons:

1 Thomas, who, during the continuance of his father's power, was m. to the Princess Mary, eldest daughter of James II., with whom he had the Earldom of Arran; on the suppression of his father's rebellion, he escaped into Denmark, and from thence wandering into England and other countries, he found an early death and an obscure tomb. James, Earl of Arran, his only son, d. young in 1484.

2 Alexander, to whose son Robert, the title of Lord Boyd was restored in 1536. His son,

Robert, 5th Lord, was a supporter of Queen Mary, and, as well as his son and successor, Thomas, 6th Lord, was in her army at the defeat at Langside. The 6th Lord d. in 1611; his son Robert, Master of Boyd, d. before him, leaving two sons: 1 Robert, 7th Lord, who d. in 1628, and his only son, Robert, 8th Lord, d. without issue, in 1640; 2 Robert, 8th Lord, who, as a steady adherent of King Charles I., was compelled to submit to a fine for the recovery of his estate; he d. in 1654, and was succeeded by his only son,

William, 10th Lord Boyd, created, in 1661, Earl of Kilmarnock; he *d.* in March 1692, and was succeeded by his son William, 2nd Earl, who *d.* in May the same year. William, 3rd Earl, his son, succeeded, and was so zealous in the cause of the House of Hanover, that when the rebellion of 1715 broke out, he joined the King's army at the head of 500 volunteers, and brought with him in arms, in the same cause, his son William, Lord Boyd, though but eleven years of age. The same Lord Boyd having, in 1717, succeeded his father as 4th Earl, unfortunately in his maturer years adopted contrary principles, and joining the Pretender's army in 1745, was taken prisoner at Culloden, attainted, and beheaded on Tower-hill, together with the Lord Balmerinoch, 18 Aug. 1746. His honours were forfeited, but he *m.* the Lady Anne Livingstone, through whom, as above stated, the Earldom of Errol passed to his son,

James, Lord Boyd, 14th Earl of Errol, celebrated for the extraordinary size of his stature and the symmetrical proportions of his figure, his manly grace and strength, and the accomplishments of his mind as well as of his person. Horace Walpole, in adverting to the Coronation of George III., makes the following remarkable observation concerning this nobleman: "One there was, the noblest figure I ever saw, the High Constable of Scotland, Lord Errol; as one saw him in a space capable of containing him, one admired him; and it added to the energy of his person, that we considered him acting so considerable a part in the very hall where so few years ago one saw his father, Lord Kilmarnock, condemned to the block." He *d.* in 1778, leaving three sons and several daughters; the latter are described in *The Peerage Volume.* Of the sons, the Hon. Capt. James Hay, the youngest, of the East India Company's naval service, was drowned in passing ashore, in a boat, from his ship, the *Henry Dundas*, lying in the Thames, 19 May 1797, *unm.*; George, 15th Earl, the eldest son, succeeded his father, and *d.* in 1798 without issue; and William, 16th Earl, succeeded his brother; he *d.* in 1819, leaving a numerous issue, described in the *The Peerage Volume*, and was succeeded by his eldest surviving son, William-George, the present and 17th Earl, and 21st hereditary Lord High Constable of Scotland. He was created in 1831, a Peer of the United Kingdom, by the title of Baron Kilmarnock of Kilmarnock, Co. Ayr.

ERSKINE, BARON. (Erskine.)

Peer of the United Kingdom.

The Hon. Thomas Erskine, 3rd son of Henry-David, 10th Earl of Buchan, and uncle of the present Earl of Buchan, having distinguished himself beyond his cotemporaries by his eloquence at the English bar, was, on being appointed Lord High Chancellor, created in 1806, Baron Erskine of Restormel Castle, Co. Cornwall; he *d.* in 1824, and was succeeded by his eldest son David-Montagu, the present and 2nd Lord.

ESSEX, EARL OF. (Capel-Coningsby.)

Peer of England.

His Lordship is descended from an ancient family, Lords of the Manor of Capel, Co. Suffolk, for many generations before John Capel, Esq., of Stoke Neyland in that County, whose 2nd son, Sir William, was Lord Mayor of London in 1503, and ancestor, in the 6th degree, of Arthur Capel, created in 1641, Baron Capel of Hadham, Co. Hertford. From the first indication of a civil war, he devoted himself and his fortunes, in the senate and in the field, to the service of the Crown; and at length, when all the other garrisons were lost, and all the royal armies dispersed, his Lordship, joining his forces with those of George Goring, Earl of Norwich, and Sir Charles Lucas, for the purpose of making a last effort for the rescue of the King, was besieged in Colchester, which he vigorously defended for ten weeks, till, after suffering the utmost extremities of famine, they were compelled to surrender, under articles, it is true, for the town, but for themselves to the mercy of the conquerors. Mercy they found not; Sir Charles Lucas and Sir George Lisle were shot upon the spot, notwithstanding the spirited remonstrances of the Lord Capel. He was himself reserved for no better fate; but being committed to the Tower, he lived to learn the iniquitous execution of his royal master, and being shortly after brought before the tribunal, miscalled the High Court of Justice, was condemned to suffer death, and was decapitated in Old Palace Yard, Westminster, 9 March 1648-9; leaving behind him a reputation on which Lord Clarendon remarks, "That whoever shall after him deserve best of the English nation, he can never think himself undervalued when he shall hear that his courage, virtue, and fidelity is laid in the balance with, and compared to that of the Lord Capel." Sir Henry Capel, his second son, was created in 1692, Baron Capel of Tewkesbury, Co. Gloucester; but dying without issue in 1696, at Dublin Castle, in the exercise of the office of Lord Lieutenant of Ireland, the title became extinct.

ARTHUR, 2nd LORD, eldest son of the first Lord Capel of Hadham, was created in 1661, Viscount Malden, Co. Essex, and Earl of Essex. He was of the popular party in the Parliamentary struggles of the reign of CHARLES II.; was accused in 1683 of high-treason, with the Lord Russell, and committed to the Tower, where he was found a few days afterwards, with his throat cut: a mysterious transaction, which, though much investigated, has never been satisfactorily elucidated. ALGERNON, 2nd EARL, his only surviving son and successor, *d.* in 1692, and was succeeded by his only son WILLIAM, 3rd EARL, to whom, in 1743, succeeded his only son WILLIAM-ANNE, 4th EARL; he *m.* Frances, eldest daughter and co-heir (*with her sister Charlotte, wife of the Hon. Capt. Robert-Boyle Walsingham, and mother of the present Baroness De Ros,*) of Sir Charles Hanbury Williams, by Lady Frances Coningsby, daughter and co-heir of Thomas, Earl Coningsby, and co-heir by her mother, of the Barony of Roos; by whom his Lordship had the issue enumerated in *The Peerage Volume*, and one daughter, Frances, which *d.* an infant in 1759. He was succeeded, in 1799, by his eldest son, GEORGE, present and 5th EARL, who having succeeded to the estates of the Earl Coningsby, has assumed the additional surname of Coningsby.

EXETER, MARQUIS OF. (CECIL.)

Peer of the United Kingdom.

This family springs from Robert Sitsilt, who assisted in the conquest of Glamorganshire in 1091; 17th in lineal descent from him was WILLIAM CECIL, the 1st and great LORD BURLEIGH, K.G., Treasurer to Queen Elizabeth, who was created Baron Burleigh, Co. Northampton, in 1571, and *d.* in 1598, leaving two sons; 1 THOMAS, 2nd LORD, ancestor of the present Marquis; 2 Robert, created Earl of Salisbury, ancestor of the Marquis of Salisbury.

THOMAS, 2nd LORD, K.G., was created EARL of EXETER in 1605, and *d.* in 1622, leaving, besides other issue, the three sons following:

1 WILLIAM, 2nd EARL, K.G.; he *m.* 1st, Lady Elizabeth Manners, only daughter and heir of Edward, 3rd Earl of Rutland and Baron Roos, to which Barony her Ladyship succeeded on the death of her father in 1587, and transmitted it, on her death in 1591, to her only son William, 16th Lord Roos, who dying without issue before his father and grandfather in 1618, the Barony returned to the house of Rutland. The Earl took a second wife, but had no male issue by her, and, on his death in 1640, was succeeded by the son of his next brother.

2 Sir Richard Cecil, *d.* in 1633, leaving a son DAVID, who succeeded his uncle as 3rd EARL.

3 Sir Edward Cecil, a distinguished general, was created in 1625, Baron Cecil of Putney, and in 1626, Viscount Wimbledon, Co. Surrey; he *d.* in 1638, without surviving issue male, and his titles became extinct.

DAVID, 3rd EARL, *d.* in 1643, and was followed by his descendants to the 4th generation, in uninterrupted succession from father to son, all named John; the 4th EARL *d.* in 1678; the 5th in 1700; the 6th in 1721; and JOHN 7th EARL, in 1722, when he was succeeded by his brother BROWNLOW, 8th EARL; he *d.* in 1754, leaving two sons; 1 BROWNLOW, 9th EARL, his successor, who *d.* without issue in 1793; 2 Thomas-Chambers, who *d.* in 1777, leaving an only son,

HENRY, 10th EARL, created in 1801 MARQUIS of EXETER; he *d.* in 1804, and was succeeded by his eldest son BROWNLOW, present and 2nd MARQUIS.

EXMOUTH, VISCOUNT. (PELLEW.)

Peer of the United Kingdom.

His Lordship's father, Samuel Humphrey, 3rd son of George Pellew, Esq., of Hushing, Co. Devon, *m.* Constance, daughter of Edward Langford, Esq., and by her, who (after his death, *m.* 2ndly Mr. Woodis, and) *d.* 31 Jan. 1812, had issue; 1 Samuel-Humphry, a widower, with one son Samuel; 2 SIR EDWARD PELLEW, whose naval services have so honourably earned the rank to which he has attained; he was created a Baronet in 1796; advanced to the Peerage by the title of Baron Exmouth of Cannonteign, Co. Devon, in 1814; and further created VISCOUNT EXMOUTH aforesaid, after his gallant attack upon Algiers in 1816; 3 Admiral Sir Israel Pellew, K.C.B., also distinguished for his naval services; he was *b.* 25 Aug. 1759, *m.* Mary-Ellen, daughter of George Gilmore, Esq., and by her had an only son Edward, a Captain in the Life Guards, *b.* 15 July 1793, killed in a duel at Paris, with Lieutenant Walsh of the same regiment, 6 Oct. 1819; 4 Catherine, late wife of Charles-Louis, Count Jegerskjold, of Sweden, deceased; 5 Jane, late wife of Lieutenant Spriddle, R.N., deceased.

FAIRFAX, BARON. (FAIRFAX)

Peer of Scotland.

This family is of Anglo Saxon origin, and was settled at Torchester, Co. Northumberland, at the Conquest. Richard Fairfax was seated in Yorkshire in 1205, where his descendants continued to flourish through several generations. Richard, living in 1401, was father of William, (eldest son,) ancestor in the 5th degree of Sir Thomas Fairfax of Walton, created in 1629, Viscount and Baron Fairfax of Emely, Co. Tipperary, in the Peerage of Ireland, which titles became extinct in 1772, by the death of Charles-Gregory, 8th Viscount, his last male descendant; and of Sir Guy, (3rd son,) from whom descended in the 4th degree, SIR THOMAS FAIRFAX of Denton, employed by Queen Elizabeth in diplomatic affairs, especially in her intercourse with the King of Scotland; and afterwards created a Peer of Scotland, by the title of Baron Fairfax of Cameron, in 1627; four of his younger sons were killed in arms abroad in the year 1621, two in the Palatinate, one at Rochelle, and one in Turkey. His 2nd son, the Hon. and Rev. Henry Fairfax, was father of the 4th LORD; and his eldest son, FERDINANDO, 2nd LORD, succeeded him in 1640; taking arms in support of the Parliament, he was, in the beginning of the civil war, appointed General for the County of York, which County he represented in Parliament; he was very successful in his military career, but his fame was entirely eclipsed by that of his eldest son, THOMAS, 3rd LORD, who succeeded him in title and estate in 1647, and was the celebrated Parliamentary General. He defeated the Royal troops in many engagements, especially in the decisive battle at Naseby. He besieged and took the City of Colchester, the last which resisted the Republican arms, and shortly after refusing to sit in judgment upon his Sovereign, and declining to command the army destined to act against Scotland, after that kingdom had declared for King CHARLES II., he retired from public life to his seat in Yorkshire. After the death of Cromwell, he joined the promoters of the Restoration, and being again returned to Parliament, was one of the Committee appointed to wait upon the King at the Hague, and invite him into England; he then returned to his retirement, and *d.* in 1671. The Lady Fairfax, his wife, who rendered herself so remarkable at the trial of King CHARLES, by exclaiming, when the words in the impeachment, "All the good people of England," were read, "No, not the hundredth part of them;" was Anne, daughter and co-heir of Horace, Lord Vere of Tilbury, by whom he had no male issue; he was succeeded by

HENRY, 4th LORD, son, as before mentioned, of Henry, 2nd son of the 1st LORD; he *d.* in 1688, leaving besides other issue, two sons;

1 THOMAS, 5th LORD, who *d.* in Jan. 1710, and was father of THOMAS, 6th LORD, who *d.* in Feb. 1782; and of ROBERT, 7th LORD, who *d.* 15 July 1793.

2 Hon. Henry, who *d.* in 1708; and was father of William Fairfax, Esq. This gentleman having undertaken the management of some large estates in Virginia, which had devolved on his cousin, the 6th Lord Fairfax, acquired property himself in New England and settled there; he *d.* in 1757; leaving two sons, of whom BRYAN, the younger son, in holy orders, alone survived the 7th LORD, after whose death he came to England, and having made good his claim to the title as 8th LORD, before the House of Lords, returned to America, where he and his family have since continued to reside.

FALKLAND, VISCOUNT. (CARY.)

Peer of Scotland.

Adam de Carey was 1st Lord of Castle Carey, Co. Somerset, in the 13th century: the 7th in descent from him was Thomas Cary, who had two sons,

1 Sir John, grandfather of HENRY, 1st VISCOUNT.

2 William, whose male issue became extinct in 1765; he *m.* the sister of Queen Anne Bullen, and was father by her of Henry, Lord Hunsdon, K.G., created Baron Hunsdon of Hunsdon, Co. Herts., in 1559; he *d.* in 1596, leaving, besides other issue, the three sons following, viz.:

1 George, 2nd Lord Hunsdon, K.G. he *d.* without male issue, in 1603.

2 John, 3rd Lord, who *d.* in 1617, and was succeeded by his son Henry, 4th Lord, created in 1621, Viscount Rochford, and in 1628, Earl of Dover: and *d.* in 1668, when he was succeeded by his only son, John, 2nd Earl of Dover, on whose death, in 1677, without issue male, the Earldom became extinct, but the Barony devolved on the heir male, as below.

3 Sir Edmund; he had besides other issue, two sons, Sir Robert, and Ferdinand, whose son William, was father of the last Lord Hunsdon. Sir Robert, his eldest son, was father of, 1 Horatio, whose son Robert, became 6th Lord, on the extinction of the male line of the 3rd Lord, and *d.* without issue in 1692; 2 Ernest, father of Robert, 7th Lord, who was so unprepared for the remote dignity which awaited him, that on his accession to the Peerage, he was pursuing the humble occupation of a weaver; he also *d.* without issue, in 1702. The next and last heir male of this family, was then found

in the person of Ferdinand-William, grandson of Ferdinand younger son of Sir Edmund Cary; he succeeded as 8th Lord Hunsdon, and on his death without issue, in 1765, the title became extinct.

4 Robert, created in 1622 Baron Cary of Leppington, Co. York, and in 1626 Earl of Monmouth; he *d.* in 1639, leaving two sons; Henry, his successor, 2nd Earl of Monmouth, on whose death in 1661, the title became extinct; and Thomas, who having been Groom of the Bedchamber to King Charles I., and having zealously served him throughout the civil wars, took his afflicting death so much to heart, that he fell sick and *d.* very shortly afterwards, in 1648-9.

Sir Henry, son of Sir Edward Cary, and grandson of the Sir John Cary mentioned above, was created Viscount Falkland in 1620; he *d.* in 1633, and was succeeded by his son Henry, 2nd Viscount, who makes so conspicuous a figure in the early history of the civil war. The increasing troubles of the times drew him from domestic retirement, and a course of intense study, in which he had become a proficient in classical and ecclesiastical learning, to place him in the vortex of political and even military activity; resigning his whole soul to the promotion of his country's good, he entered ardently into the war, when that first object of his desires was no longer to be obtained by milder measures, and was among its noblest victims; he was killed in the first battle of Newbury, 20 Sept. 1743, in the 34th year of his age. He was followed in regular succession from father to son by his descendants to the fourth generation, viz.: Henry, 3rd Viscount, he *d.* in 1663; Anthony, 4th Viscount, *d.* in 1694; Lucius-Henry, 5th Viscount, *d.* in 1730; and Lucius-Charles, 6th Viscount. The latter *d.* in 1785, having survived his only son, Lucius-Ferdinand, who *d.* in 1780, leaving two sons; 1 Henry-Thomas, 7th Viscount, who succeeded his grandfather, and *d. unm.* in 1796; and 2 Charles-John, who succeeded his brother as 8th Viscount, and being unfortunately killed in a duel in 1809, was succeeded by his eldest son, Lucius, present and 9th Viscount Falkland.

FALMOUTH, EARL OF. (Boscawen.)

Peer of the United Kingdom.

His Lordship's ancestors assumed their surname from the Lordship of Boscawen-Rose, Co. Cornwall, which they possessed in the reign of King John. From Henry Boscawen, living in 1292, the inheritance passed through thirteen generations to

Hugh Boscawen, Esq., created Baron of Boscawen-Rose and Viscount Falmouth, both in the County of Cornwall, in 1720, he *d.* in 1734; having had eight sons, viz.:

1 Hugh, his successor, 2nd Viscount; he was *b.* in 1707, and *d.* without issue 4 Feb. 1782; having *m.* 6 May 1736, Hannah-Catherine-Maria, daughter of Thomas Smith, of Worplesdon, Co. Surrey, Esq., and widow of Richard Russell, Esq.

2 Charles, *b.* 12 June 1710, *d.* young.

3 The Hon. Admiral Edward Boscawen, who first distinguished himself in the naval service of his country at the age of 18, in Admiral Vernon's squadron in the West Indies, and from that period to the end of his life, a continued train of successes brought his gallantry and abilities conspicuously before the country. He was *b.* 19 Aug. 1711, and *d.* 10 Jan. 1761; having *m.* Dec. 1742, Frances, daughter of William-Evelyn Glanville, of St. Clere, Co. Kent, Esq., by whom, who *d.* 26 Feb. 1805, he had issue, besides two elder sons who *d. unm.*, 1 George-Evelyn, 3rd Viscount, who succeeded his uncle, and *d.* in 1808; when he was succeeded by his eldest son Edward, present and 4th Viscount, who, in 1821, was created Earl of Falmouth; 2 Frances, *b.* 7 March 1746, *d.* 14 July 1801, having July 1773, the Hon. Admiral John Leveson-Gower, brother to Granville, 1

quis of Stafford, who *d.* 15 Aug. 1792; 3 Elizabeth, *b.* 28 May 1747, *d.* 15 June 1828, having *m.* HENRY, 5th Duke of Beaufort, K.G.

4 The Hon. General George Boscawen, *b.* 1 Dec. 1712, *d.* 3 May 1775; having *m.* July 1743, Anne, daughter of John-Morley Trevor, Esq., by whom he had issue the two sons stated in *The Peerage Volume*, and two daughters, the Hon. Anne Boscawen, *b.* Oct. 1744, Maid of Honour to Queen Charlotte, who *d.* 14 Feb. 1831; and Charlotte, *b.* May 1747, *d.* July 1829.

5 The Hon. Major-General John Boscawen, *b.* Jan. 1714, *d.* 30 April 1767; having *m.* Dec. 1748, Thomasina, daughter of Robert Surman, Esq., by whom, who *d.* 17 Jan. 1750, he had a son, Colonel William-Augustus-Spencer Boscawen, who was *b.* 7 Jan. 1750, and *d.* 13 June 1828; having *m.* Mary-Anne, daughter of —— Hughes, Esq. by whom, who *d.* 21 Sept. 1821, he left the issue described in *The Peerage Volume.*

6 Hon. William-Frederick, *d. unm.* in the service of the East India Company.

7 Hon. Henry, *d. unm.*

8 Hon. and Rev. Nicholas, D.D., Dean of St. Burien in Cornwall, a Prebendary of Westminster, and Chaplain to the King; he was *b.* 16 Aug. 1723, and *d.* 4 July 1793; having *m.* Jane, daughter of —— Woodward, Esq., and widow of —— Hatton, Esq., by whom, who *d.* Jan. 1797, he had one son, Nicholas.—See *The Peerage Volume.*

FARNBOROUGH, BARON. (LONG.)

Peer of the United Kingdom.

This family is of considerable antiquity in the County of Wilts, where it has flourished in numerous branches. John Long, Esq., of Netheravon, was grandfather of Samuel, who settled in Jamaica in 1655; his only son, Charles Long, Esq. of Longville, Jamaica, *d.* in 1723, leaving three sons, viz.:

1 Samuel, who having *m.* Mary, 2nd daughter and co-heir of Bartholomew Tate, Esq., his representatives (three daughters and co-heirs of his eldest son, Robert Long, who *d.* in 1779) are co-heirs with the present Lord Zouche of that Barony. His 2nd son, Edward Long, Esq., Chief Judge of the Vice-Admiralty Court, Jamaica, left a numerous family, of whom Edward-Beeston, eldest son, was father of Henry-Lawes Long, Esq., who *m.* in 1822, Lady Catherine Walpole, sister of the Earl of Orford; and Elizabeth, youngest daughter, *m.* in 1801, the late Lord Henry-Thomas Howard-Molyneux-Howard, brother to the Duke of Norfolk.

2 Charles of Saxmundham, who *d.* in 1780; he was father of Charles Long, Esq., who *m.* his cousin Jane, sister of the present Lord, and *d.* in 1813, without surviving issue; and of Dudley Long, Esq., who assumed the name of North, *m.* the Hon. Sophia Anderson-Pelham, sister of Lord Yarborough, and *d.* in 1829.

3 Beeston Long, Esq., of Carshalton, Co. Surrey; he was *b.* in 1710, and *d.* 21 Jan. 1783; having *m.* 24 Jan. 1745, Susannah, daughter and heir of Abraham Croft, Esq., who *d.* in 1780; they had the following issue:

1 Samuel, *d.* 19 Oct. 1807; having *m.* 22 Dec. 1787, Lady Jane Maitland, 4th daughter of James, 7th Earl of Lauderdale; she *m.* 2ndly, 5 Nov. 1808, Lieut.-General Sir William Houston, G.C.B.; by Mr. Long she had issue:

1 Lieut.-Colonel Samuel, 1st Foot-Guards, *b.* 18 May 1799; *m.* 1st, 18 April 1825, the Hon. Louisa-Emily Stanley, 3rd daughter of Edward, Lord Stanley, and grand-daughter of the Earl of Derby, who was *b.* 1 June 1805, and *d.* 11 Dec. 1825; he *m.* 2ndly, Sydney, 2nd daughter of Arthur Atherley, Esq.

2 Charles-Maitland, *b.* 16 Aug. 1803.

3 Mary, *b.* March 1805.

2 Beeston Long, Esq., a Bank Director; he was *b.* in 1757, and *d.* 8 Aug. 1820; having *m.* 10 July 1786, Frances-Louisa, eldest daughter of Sir Richard Neave, Bart., by whom he had the following issue:
  1 Beeston, *b.* 23 July 1787, *d.* 28 Feb. 1803.
  2 Frances-Louisa, *b.* 18 June 1788, *d.* 27 April 1800.
  3 Catherine-Mary, *b.* 15 Aug. 1789, *d.* 9 April 1808.
  4 Samuel-Henry, *b.* 27 Jan. 1791, *d.* 14 Feb. 1792.
  5 A son, *b.* 19 June 1792, *d.* an infant.
  6 Harriet, *b.* 9 Dec. 1793, *d.* 26 Nov. 1800.
  7 Caroline-Jane, *b.* 20 Sept. 1795, *d.* 29 Sept. 1824.
  8 Amelia-Anne, *b.* 8 Aug. 1798.
  9 Maria, *b.* 24 March 1800; *m.* 9 Sept. 1823, Henry-Seymour Montagu, Esq., a Commissioner of Stamps.
  10 William, *b.* 8 Oct. 1802; *m.* 20 Oct. 1830, Eleonora-Charlotte, sister of Sir Edward Poore, Bart., of Rushall, Wilts.
  11 Rosa, *b.* 15 Sept. 1805, *d.* 11 Nov. 1817.
  12 Charles-Beeston, *b.* 20 Jan. 1808, *d.* 3 April 1809.

3 The Right Hon. Sir Charles Long, G.C.B., created in 1826, Baron Farnborough, of Bromley-Hill Place, Co. Kent, the present Peer.

4 George, killed at the storming of Trincomalee.

5 The Rev. William Long, a Canon of Windsor.

6 Richard, *d. unm.*

7 Sarah, *d.* 18 July 1817; having *m.* 23 April 1774, Sir George-William Prescott, Bart., *d.* 22 July 1801.

8 Jane, *m.* 26 Dec. 1786, her cousin, Charles Long, Esq., eldest son of Charles, elder brother of Beeston Long, Esq., above.

9 Susannah, *d.* 12 June 1815; having *m.* 1 Nov. 1787, Rev. George Chamberlain.

FARNHAM, BARON. (Maxwell.)

Peer of Ireland.

His Lordship is of the same ancestry with the Earls of Nithsdale in Scotland, forfeited in 1716. Sir John Maxwell, 4th in descent from Marcus, the son of Unwin, who obtained estates in Scotland from King David I., was ancestor of John Maxwell, whose 2nd son Robert, was Dean of Armagh in the reign of Queen Elizabeth, and great-grandfather of

John Maxwell, Esq., created Baron Farnham of Farnham, Co. Cavan, in 1756; he *d.* in 1759; having *m.* Judith, daughter and heir of James Barry, Esq., by whom he had three sons:

1 Robert, 2nd Lord, created Viscount Farnham in 1760, and Earl of Farnham in 1763; he *d.* 16 Nov. 1779, without surviving issue male, when the Earldom and Viscounty became extinct.

2 Barry, 3rd Lord, created Earl of Farnham, and Viscount Maxwell in 1785, and *d.* 7 Oct. 1800; he was father of John-James, 4th Lord, and 2nd Earl, on whose death, 24 July 1823, the Earldom and Viscounty again became extinct.

3 Henry, Bishop of Meath, father of John, the present and 5th Lord, who succeeded to the Barony on the death of his cousin.

FERRARD, VISCOUNT. (Skeffington-Foster.)

Peer of Ireland.

.. s Lordship's grandfather, Anthony Foster, Esq., Lord Chief Baron of the Ex-..., ..e in Ireland, was *b.* 12 Dec. 1705, and *d.* 3 April 1778; having *m.* 1st, 25 ... 1736, Elizabeth, daughter of William Burgh, Esq., who *d.* 30 July 1744; ... 29 July 1749, Catherine, daughter of Thomas Burgh, Esq. By his first marriage he was father of

1 Margaret, *b.* 1737, *d.* 16 March 1792; having *m.* the Hon. and Right Rev. ...ry Maxwell, Lord Bishop of Meath, by whom she was mother of the present Lord Farnham.

2 The Right Hon. John Foster, who was created Baron Oriel in the Peerage ... England in 1821, and *d.* in 1828; having *m.* Margaretta, daughter of Thomas ...gh, Esq., of Bert, Co. Kildare, and aunt of Lord Down; she was created in ...0, Baroness Oriel of Collon, Co. Louth, and in 1797 Viscountess Ferrard, both in the Peerage of Ireland, and *d.* in 1824; when she was succeeded by her only surviving son, Thomas-Henry, present and 2nd Viscount; who also succeeded his ...ther, in 1828, as 2nd Baron Oriel. He *m.* Lady Harriet Skeffington, Viscountess Massereene, by whom, who *d.* in 1831, he had several children; John, their eldest son, succeeded his mother, and is the present and 10th Viscount Massereene.

3 The Right Rev. William, Lord Bishop of Clogher, *d.* 1796; having *m.* Catherine-Letitia, daughter of Rev. Henry Leslie, D.D. Their issue are:

1 John Leslie, M.P., *m.* 19 Aug. 1814, Hon. Letitia, youngest daughter of Right Hon. James Fitz-Gerald, and of Catherine, Baroness Fitz-Gerald; and has issue, 1 Catherine-Letitia, *b.* 19 May 1817, deceased; 2 William-Leslie; 3 John-Vesey-Fitz-Gerald; 4 A daughter, *b.* in 1826.

2 Rev. William, *m.* 18 Dec. 1821, Catherine, daughter of the late John Hamilton, Esq. and niece of the Earl of Longford.

3 Henry, late Commander R.N.

4 Catherine, *m.* William-Drummond Delap, Esq.

5 Anna, *m.* Jonas Stowell, Esq.

6 Henrietta, *m.* 1810, Count Jerome de Salis.

7 Elizabeth. 8 Letitia.

FERRERS, EARL. (Shirley.)

Peer of Great Britain.

The 1st of his Lordship's ancestors on record is Sasuvalo, an Anglo-Saxon, who ...ssed large estates immediately after the Conquest. 6th in descent from him ... Henry, who assumed the name of Shirley, from his estate, and was ancestor in ...th degree of Sir George, created a Baronet in 1611, and *d.* in 1622.

Sir Henry Shirley, Bart., his son, *m.* Dorothy, 2nd daughter of Robert Devereux, Earl of Essex, the unfortunate favourite of Queen Elizabeth, and co-heir ... brother Robert, 3rd Earl of Essex, and 11th Baron Ferrers of Chartley, on ... death in 1646, the Barony of Ferrers of Chartley fell into abeyance, which was ...ated by the Crown in 1677, in favour of Sir Robert Shirley, grandson and ... Sir Henry and Lady Dorothy Shirley, and son of Sir Robert Shirley, Bart., ... Cromwell for his loyalty, *d.* in the Tower. Sir Robert ... of Chartley, was created in 1711, Viscount Tamworth, ...rrers, and had thirteen sons, of whom, 1 Robert, Vis... son, *d.* before his father, leaving Elizabeth, his sole daughter and heir, who m. James Compton, 5th Earl of Northampton; and her daughter, Lady Charlotte, carried the Barony of Ferrers of Chartley into the family of the Marquis Townshend. WASHINGTON, 2nd EARL, also d. without issue male in 1729; HENRY, 3rd EARL, d. unm. in 1745; LAURENCE (10th son) was father of LAURENCE, 4th EARL, WASHINGTON, 5th EARL, and ROBERT, 6th EARL; and George, 13th son, was grandfather of Evelyn-John Shirley, Esq., of Eatington Park, Warwickshire, M.P.; for all his surviving descendants see *The Peerage Volume.*

The Hon. Lawrence Shirley, 10th son of the 1st Earl, and grandfather of the present Earl, was *b.* 26 Sept. 1693, and *d.* 27 April 1743; having *m.* Anne, 4th daughter of Sir Walter Clarges, Bart, and by her had the five sons following:

1 LAWRENCE, who succeeded his uncle as 4th EARL; he *m.* 16 Sept. 1752, Mary, youngest daughter of Amos Meredith, Esq.; from whom he was separated, and she was allowed a separate maintenance by Act of Parliament. After his Lordship's decease, she *m.* 2ndly, Lord Frederick Campbell, 3rd son of John, 4th Duke of Argyll, and was unfortunately burnt to death 25 July 1807. His Lordship being liable to sudden starts of passion, much resembling madness, in one of these shot Mr. Johnson, his steward; his Peers adjudged him guilty of murder, and he suffered death accordingly on 5 May 1760, leaving no issue.

2 WASHINGTON, 5th EARL, *d.* without issue 1 Oct. 1778; having *m.* Anne, daughter of —— Elliott, Esq., who *d.* in 1791.

3 ROBERT, 6th EARL, who *d.* in 1787, and was succeeded by his eldest son, ROBERT, 7th EARL, *b.* 21 Sept. 1756, *d.* 2 May 1827; having *m.* 1st, 13 March 1778, Elizabeth, daughter of John Prentiss, Esq., who *d.* 14 Sept. 1799; and 2ndly, 28 Sept. 1799, Elizabeth, youngest daughter of Wrightson Mundy, Esq., who *d.* 22 Feb. 1827. He had issue by his 1st marriage, Robert-Sewallis, Viscount Tamworth, *b.* 9 Nov. 1778, *d.* 6 June 1824, having *m.* 5 Aug. 1800, the Hon. Sophia-Caroline Curzon, VISCOUNTESS-DOWAGER TAMWORTH, eldest daughter of Lord Scarsdale. The Earl dying without surviving issue, was succeeded by his only brother, WASHINGTON, the present and 8th EARL.

4 Walter, in Holy Orders, *b.* 28 Sept. 1725, *d.* 7 April 1786; having *m.* 27 Aug. 1766, Henrietta-Maria, daughter of John Philips, Esq., who *d.* 15 Dec. 1792, leaving the issue stated in *The Peerage Volume.*

5 Admiral Thomas, *b.* 6 April 1733; *m.* 1st, 30 March 1773, the widow of Sir Stephen Anderson, Bart.; 2ndly, 6 Nov. 1809, Anne, daughter of —— Hele, Esq. The Admiral *d.* 6 April 1814, and his widow re-married Colonel John Tuffnell.

FEVERSHAM, BARON. (DUNCOMBE.)

Peer of the United Kingdom.

Alexander Duncombe, of Drayton, Bucks, had, besides other issue,

1 Sir Charles, Lord Mayor of London 1709, *d. unm.* in 1711, leaving very considerable estates, in the North and West of England, to the sons of his brother and sister.

2 Anthony, whose only son Anthony, inherited his uncle's property in the West, and was created in 1747, Lord Feversham, which title became extinct on his death in 1763, without issue male; his only daughter, Anne, *m.* Jacob, 2nd Earl of Radnor.

3 Mary, *m.* Thomas Browne, Esq., who took the name of Duncombe; they had issue, Mary, wife of John, Duke of Argyll and Greenwich, and

Thomas, heir to his uncle's estates in Yorkshire; he *d.* in 1746, leaving i-

1 Thomas, *d.* 25 Nov. 1779, without surviving issue male, having been th

married. His daughter, and at length sole heir, Anne, m. Robert Shafto, of Whitworth, Co. Durham, Esq.; Charlotte, his widow, m. 2ndly, Thomas, 2nd Earl Onslow.

2 Charles-Slingsby Duncombe, Esq., *d.* 11 Sept. 1803; having m. Isabel, daughter of —— Soleby, Esq., by whom, who *d.* 18 April 1800, he had three sons:

1 Charles, present Lord, created in 1826, Baron Feversham, of Duncombe Park.

2 Thomas, m. Emma, eldest daughter of the Right Rev. Dr. John Hinchcliffe, late Lord Bishop of Peterborough, and has issue:

1 Thomas-Slingsby Duncombe, Esq., M.P.
2 Rev. Henry.
3 Emma, m. Henry-Hay-Dawkins, Esq.
4 Frances.
5 Harriet.
6 Edward.
7 George.

3 Slingsby, m. and has issue.

FIFE, EARL. (Duff.)

Peer of Ireland and of the United Kingdom.

Macduff, Thane of Fife, was created Earl of Fife by Malcolm Canmore. The Earldom vested, in the 13th generation, in Isabel, only daughter of the 12th Earl, who having no issue by either of her three marriages, resigned it to the King, and obtained a renewed patent, with remainder after herself, to Robert, Duke of Albany, 3rd son of King Robert II,, and brother of her 2nd husband Walter Stuart. Upon the attainder of Murdoch, Duke of Albany, son of the above Robert, in 1425, the Earldom was forfeited, and afterwards annexed to the Crown by Act of Parliament, although the male descendants of Hugo, 2nd son of Gillmichael, 4th Earl, still exist. The Earl of Wemyss is his heir male.

William, son of William Duff, Esq. of Dipple, descended from the ancient Earls, though the precise line cannot be traced, was created to the Peerage of Ireland, in 1735, by the title of Baron Braco of Kilbride, Co. Cavan, and in 1759 was further created Earl of Fife and Viscount Macduff. He *d.* in 1763, and was succeeded by his son James, 2nd Earl, who was created in 1790, Baron Fife, in the Peerage of Great Britain, and *d.* without issue in 1809, when the English Barony became extinct, and the Irish Earldom devolved on his brother, Alexander, 3rd Earl, father of James, present and 4th Earl, by whom he was succeeded in 1811, and who was created a Peer of the United Kingdom in 1827, by the title of Baron Fife, Co. Fife.

FINGALL, EARL. (Plunkett.)

Peer of Ireland and of the United Kingdom.

John Plunkett, of Bewley, in the reign of Henry III., had two sons; 1 John, ancestor of Lord Louth; 2 Richard, whose son, Sir Christopher Plunkett, m. Joan, daughter and heir of Sir Lucas Cusack, Lord of Killeen, Dunsany, and Gerardstown; John, their eldest son, Lord Killeen, was father of Christopher Lord Killeen, and grandfather of Edmond, summoned to Parliament in 1486 as Baron Killeen, of Killeen Castle, Co. Meath, from whom the Earl descends in the 10th generation; and their younger son, Christopher, was 1st Lord Dunsany, and ancestor of the present Lord Dunsany.

Edmund, 1st Baron, *d.* in 1510; John, his son, 2nd Lord, in 1550; and was succeeded by his son, Patrick, 3rd Lord, father of Christopher, 4th Lord, who *d.* without issue male, and of JAMES, 5th LORD, who succeeded his brother, and dying in 1595, was succeeded by his son, CHRISTOPHER, 6th LORD, who *d.* in 1613.

LUKE, 7th Lord, who succeeded his father, was created EARL of FINGALL, and *d.* in 1637, had four sons, of whom the male issue of the 2nd and 3rd sons are extinct; CHRISTOPHER, the eldest son, succeeded him; and George, the 4th son, was grandfather, by his eldest son James, of ROBERT, 6th EARL. CHRISTOPHER, 2nd EARL, *d.* in 1649, and was successively followed by his son, grandson, and great-grandson, in direct descent, viz.: LUKE, 3rd EARL, who *d.* in 1682; PETER, 4th EARL, who *d.* in 1717; and JUSTIN, 5th EARL, on whose death in 1734, without issue, the male line of the 2nd Earl failed.

ROBERT, 6th EARL, son of James Plunkett, the eldest son of George, youngest son of the 1st EARL, succeeded; he *d.* in 1738, and was succeeded by his son, ARTHUR-JAMES, 7th EARL, who, besides ARTHUR-JAMES, present and 8th EARL, his successor, and the daughter stated in *The Peerage Volume*, had two sons, in the Austrian military service; Captain Luke, killed in Italy in 1794, and Colonel William, who *d.* 24 March 1806, and a son, Robert, who *d. unm.* May 1823. The 7th Earl *d.* in 1793; and the present Earl was created Baron Fingall, of Woolhampton Lodge, Co. Berks, in the Peerage of the United Kingdom, in 1831.

FITZ-GERALD AND VESCY, BARONESS. (FITZ-GERALD.)

Peeress of Ireland.

John Vesey, Lord Archbishop of Tuam, who *d.* in 1716, had two sons; Thomas, Lord Bishop of Ossory, father of John, 1st Lord Knapton, grandfather of the present Viscount de Vesci; and John, Archdeacon of Kilfenora, whose son, the Rev. Henry Vescy, *d.* in 1774, leaving issue:

1 John, who *d.* without issue in 1779, leaving his estates to his sisters.

2 Mary, *m.* James Irvine, Esq., by whom she had a daughter, Mary, *m.* to Lieut.-Colonel Poole Hickman Vesey.

3 CATHERINE, *m.* to the Right Hon. James Fitz-Gerald, and created in 1826, Baroness Fitzgerald and Vescy, of Clare and Inchicronan, Co. Clare.

FITZ-WILLIAM, EARL. (FITZ-WILLIAM.)

Peer of Ireland and of Great Britain.

The ancestor of this noble house was William Fitz-Godric, whose son and heir, William Fitzwilliam, gave the surname to his descendants. 18th in lineal male descent from this William Fitz-William, was WILLIAM Fitz-William, Esq., of Milton, Co. Northampton, created in 1620, BARON FITZ-WILLIAM, of Lifford, Co. Donegal, in the Peerage of Ireland; he *d.* in 1644, and was succeeded by his son, WILLIAM, 2nd LORD, who *d.* in 1658. To him succeeded his son, WILLIAM, 3rd LORD, created in 1716, Viscount Miltown, Co. Westmeath, and EARL FITZ-WILLIAM, Co. Tyrone; he *d.* in 1719, and was succeeded by his son, JOHN, 2nd EARL, to whom followed in 1726, his son WILLIAM, 3rd EARL. The latter was created in 1742, Lord Fitz-William, Baron of Milton, Co. Northampton, and in 1746, Viscount Milton and EARL FITZWILLIAM, of Norborough, Co. Northampton, all in the Peerage of Great Britain; he *d.* in 1756, leaving, besides the present and 4th EARL, his successor, who has enjoyed the honours of the Peerage longer than any nobleman now living, the two surviving daughters noticed in *The Peerage Volume*, and the Lady Amelia, who *d.* young, three daughters, Anne, Henrietta, and Dorothy, and one son, George, who have all *d. unm.*

FITZ-WILLIAM, VISCOUNT. (Fitz-William.)

Peer of Ireland.

His Lordship is known to be of the family of Earl Fitz-William, though the precise line of his descent is not ascertained. This branch of the family is said to have settled in Ireland in the reign of King John. Sir Thomas Fitz-William of Merion, Co. Dublin, was created, in 1629, Baron Fitz-William of Thorn Castle, and Viscount Fitz-William of Merion, both in the County of Dublin; and having with his two sons, Oliver and William, both afterwards Viscounts Fitzwilliam, been eminently serviceable to King Charles I. in the civil war, he obtained a patent to be drawn up in the 20th year of that King's reign, creating him an Earl in the English Peerage; but the great seal not being then in the King's possession, the patent never took effect. His eldest son and successor, Oliver, 2nd Viscount, was, however, after the restoration, created by King Charles II., in 1663, Earl of Tyrconnel, in the Peerage of Ireland; but this title became extinct by his death in 1667, when William, his brother, succeeded as 3rd Viscount; he *d.* in 1680, and was followed successively by his son, grandson, and great-grandson, in direct paternal descent, viz. Thomas, 4th Viscount; he *d.* in 1704; Richard, 5th Viscount, *d.* in 1743; and Richard, 6th Viscount; the latter *d.* in 1776, and was succeeded by his eldest son, Richard, 7th Viscount, who was followed, in 1816, by his next surviving brother John, present and 8th Viscount.

FOLEY, BARON. (Foley.)

Peer of Great Britain.

The first of this family on record is Edward Foley, of Stanbridge, Co. Worcester, whose son Richard *d.* in 1657. The latter was father of Thomas Foley, Esq., who had two sons: 1 Thomas, created Baron Foley of Kidderminster, Co. Worcester, in 1711, which title became extinct on the death of his son Thomas, 2nd Lord, in 1766; 2 Paul, great-grandfather of Thomas Foley, Esq., in whose favour the Peerage was revived. He was *b.* 10 Aug. 1716, created Baron Foley, of Kidderminster, Co. Worcester, in 1776, and *d.* 14 Nov. 1777; having *m.* 28 March 1740, Hon. Grace Granville, daughter and co-heir of George, Lord Lansdowne, by whom, who *d.* 1 Nov. 1769, he had issue:

1 Thomas, his successor, 2nd Lord, for whom see *The Peerage Volume*; he *d.* in 1793; having had, besides his eldest son, Thomas, present and 3rd Lord, and the surviving daughter stated in *The Peerage Volume*, two sons, William-Charles, and Charles, successively his heirs-apparent, who both *d.* young before him.

2 Hon. Grace, *b.* 17 Jan. 1744, *d.* 9 Jan. 1813; having *m.* 21 May 1774, James Hamilton, last Earl of Clanbrassil, *b.* 13 Aug. 1729, *d.* 6 Feb. 1798.

3 Hon. Edward, *b.* 16 March 1747, *d.* 22 June 1803; having *m.* 1st, 20 Oct. 1778, Lady Anne-Margaret Coventry, 2nd daughter of George-William, 6th Earl of Coventry, *b.* 18 March 1756, from whom he was divorced in May 1787, and she *re-m.* 15 July 1788, Capt. Samuel Wright. He *m.* 2ndly, 21 March 1790, Eliza-Maria, daughter and heir of John Hodgetts, Esq., by whom, who *d.* 9 July 1805, he had the issue stated in *The Peerage Volume.*

4 Hon. Andrew, *d.* 29 July 1818; having *m.* 1773, Elizabeth, only daugher and heir of Boulter Tomlinson, Esq., [by Sarah, daughter of Thomas Foley, Esq., and half-sister of Thomas, 1st Lord], *d.* 22 July 1811; for their issue see *The Peerage Volume.*

5 Hon. Mary, *b.* 8 Feb. 1750, *m.* Richard Clerke, Esq.

6 Hon. Elizabeth, *b.* 13 Oct. 1756, *d. unm.* 13 Oct. 1776.

7 Hon. Anne, *b.* 9 May 1760, *d.* 9 Dec. 1794; having *m.* 12 Sept. 1776, Sir Edward Winnington, Bart., who was *b.* 14 Nov. 1749, and *d.* Jan. 1805.

FORBES, BARON. (Forbes.)

Peer of Scotland.

This ancient family descends from John de Forbes, possessed of the lands of Forbes, in the reign of William the Lion. Alexander de Forbes defended the Castle of Urquhart in 1304, with such obstinacy against King Edward I., that the King, on taking it, put all the garrison to the sword; but this family was continued by the delivery of Alexander's wife of a posthumous son, Alexander, who was killed at the battle of Duplin in 1382; and had also a posthumous son, Sir John, whose eldest son was Alexander, 1st Lord, from whom the present Peer is 12th in descent; and his 2nd son was William, ancestor of the Lords Forbes of Pitsligo in Scotland, which title was forfeited by the accession of Alexander, 4th Lord, to the rebellion of 1745; his only son, John, Master of Pitsligo, dying without issue in 1781, the line became extinct.

Alexander, 1st Lord, *d.* in 1448, and was succeeded by his son, James, 2nd Lord, who had three sons: 1 William, 3rd Lord, his successor; 2 Duncan, ancestor of the present Sir John Stuart Forbes, of Pitsligo, Bart., and other existing families; 3 Patrick, ancestor of Sir John Forbes, of Craigievan, Bart, and of the Earl of Granard: *see* that title.

William, 3rd Lord, also left three sons: 1 Alexander, 4th Lord, who taking up arms to revenge the death of King James III., displayed the bloody shirt of the murdered monarch to incite the people to join him; but after the defeat of the Earl of Lennox at Tillymoss, he submitted to James IV.; 2 Arthur, 5th Lord, who succeeded, on his brother's death without issue; and dying also without issue himself, was succeeded by his youngest brother; 3 John, 6th Lord. His Lordship was, in 1536, committed to the Castle of Edinburgh, with his eldest son, John, Master of Forbes, on an accusation of high treason, and afterwards tried on an indictment, charging both father and son of conspiracy to murder the King, by the shot of a culverin, in Aberdeen, and of other treasonable acts, all comprised within the one charge of aiding the King's English enemies; the father was fully exculpated and released, after a tedious confinement, but the son was convicted and executed in 1537; he *d. unm.*; and the 6th Lord was succeeded by his 2nd son, William, 7th Lord; he *d.* in 1593, and was succeeded by his eldest son, John, 8th Lord. His eldest son, John, 9th Lord, entered into a religious order abroad, and *d.* without issue; he was succeeded by his brother, Arthur, 10th Lord; to whom succeeded his son, grandson, and great-grandson, Alexander 11th Lord, William 12th Lord, and William 13th Lord. The latter succeeded his father in 1691, and *d.* in 1716, leaving, besides other issue; 1 William, his successor, 14th Lord, who *d.* in 1730, leaving an only son, Francis, 15th Lord, who *d.* in his 13th year, in 1734; 2 James, who succeeded his nephew as 16th Lord. He was succeeded, in 1761, by his only son, James, 17th Lord, father of James-Ochoncar, present and 18th Lord, his successor.

FORESTER, BARON. (Forester.)

Peer of Great Britain.

Cecil Forester, Esq., his Lordship's grandfather, was great-grandson of Sir William Forester, of Dothill, by his marriage with Lady Mary Cecil, daughter of

James, 3rd Earl of Salisbury. He *m.* Anne, daughter and co-heir of Robert Townshend, Esq., by whom, who *d.* 24 May 1825, he was father of

1 Cecil-Weld, created in 1821, Baron Forester of Willey Park, Co. Salop; he *d.* in 1828, and was succeeded by his eldest son, John-George-Weld, present and 2nd Lord.

2 Francis Forester, Esq., who *m.* Lady Louisa-Catherine-Barbara Vane, daughter of the Marquis of Cleveland, by whom, who *d.* in 1821, he has issue.

FORTESCUE, EARL. (Fortescue.)

Peer of Great Britain.

His Lordship's ancestor, Sir Richard Le-Forte, is said to have assumed his family name and motto, from having, with his shield, preserved the life of William the Conqueror, at the battle of Hastings. Sir Adam, a son of Sir Richard, settled at Wriston, Co. Devon, where Adam Fortescue was seated in the reign of King Edward I. 6th in descent from him was Sir John Fortescue, Lord Chief Justice in the reign of King Henry VI., whose son Martin had two sons; 1 John, from whom descended, in the 5th degree, Hugh Fortescue, Esq.; 2 William, ancestor of Viscount Clermont.

The said Hugh Fortescue, Esq. *m.* 1st, Bridget, only daughter and heir of Hugh Boscawen, Esq., and co-heiress of the Barony of Clinton; and 2ndly, Lucy, daughter of Matthew, Lord Aylmer; by his 1st marriage he had one son, Hugh, 1st Lord, summoned to Parliament as Baron Clinton, and created in 1746, Earl Clinton, and Baron Fortescue of Castle Hill, Co. Devon, with limitation of the Barony to his half-brother, Matthew, and his issue male; he *d.* 2 May 1751, when the Earldom became extinct, the Barony of Clinton fell again into abeyance, and that of Fortescue devolved on Matthew, 2nd Lord, only son of Hugh Fortescue, Esq. by his 2nd marriage; he *d.* in 1785, and was succeeded by his son Hugh, the present Earl, who was created in 1789, Viscount Ebrington, Co. Gloucester, and Earl Fortescue.

FRANKFORT, VISCOUNT. (De Montmorency.)

Peer of Ireland.

Reymond Morres, Esq., father of the 1st Viscount, was younger brother of Harvey, 1st Viscount Mountmorres; he *d.* Aug. 1784, leaving issue, by his wife, Elizabeth, only daughter and heir of Francis Lodge, Esq.,

1 Lodge-Evans Morres, Esq., created in 1800, Baron Frankfort, of Galmoye, Co. Kilkenny, and in 1815, Viscount Frankfort de Montmorency; he resumed the ancient family name of De Montmorency in 1815, and dying in 1822, was succeeded by his only son, Lodge-Reymond, present and 2nd Viscount.

2 Eleanor, *d.* 1819; having *m.* 27 March 1762, Robert Browne, Esq., who is deceased.

3 Frances *m*, Andrew Prior, Esq.

4 Elizabeth, *m.* Ephraim Hutchinson, Esq.

5 Rev. Reymond, deceased; having *m.* Mary-Eyre, daughter and heir of Edward D'Alton, Esq., by whom he left issue,

1 Lieutenant-Colonel Reymond-Harvey de Montmorency, *d.* at Naples in 1827; having *m.* Letitia, daughter of the Rev. Narcissus-Charles Proby, by whom he left issue; 1 Hervey-Francis, *b.* 20 July 1802; 2 Reymond-Harvey, Lieutenant 65th regiment, *b.* 26 Aug. 1808, *m.* at Agra, 8 Oct. 1830,

Anna-Matilda, 3rd daughter of Henry Revell, Esq., late of Round-Oak, Surrey.

2 Lieutenant Edward D'Alton, R.N., *m.* 1802, Mary-Anne, only child of John Peat, Esq., by whom, he has had four elder children, deceased; and 1 Jane; 2 Elizabeth; 3 Adelaide; 4 William, *b.* 21 May, 1818.

3 Elizabeth, *m.* Captain Molesworth.

FFRENCH, BARON. (FFRENCH.)

Peer of Ireland.

His Lordship is paternally descended from Sir Theophilus Ffrench, who accompanied WILLIAM the Conqueror to England. The original settlement of the family in Ireland, was in the County of Wexford, whence they removed to Galway about 1425. Peter-Martin French, Esq., of Cloher, Co. Galway, living in 1579, was father of Oliver Ffrench, Esq., who had two sons; 1 Sir Oliver, who signed the capitulation of Galway to Cromwell's forces in 1652, he *d.* without issue; 2 Jasper, who built the Castle of Cloher, now called Castle Ffrench, in 1635. Sir Charles Ffrench of Castle Ffrench, great-grandson of this Jasper, was created a Baronet in 1779, and his widow, Dame Rose Ffrench, daughter of Patrick Dillon, Esq., descended from the same ancestry as the Earls of Roscommon, was elevated to the Peerage in 1798, by the title of Baroness Ffrench of Castle Ffrench, Co. Galway, and *d.* in 1805, when she was succeeded by her only son, THOMAS, 2nd LORD, to whom in 1814, succeeded his eldest son, CHARLES, present and 3rd LORD.

GAGE, VISCOUNT. (GAGE.)

Peer of Ireland and of Great Britain.

This family is of Norman extraction. Gaga or Gage, accompanied William the Conqueror to England, and obtained from him lands in the forest of Dean, Co. Gloucester; he was ancestor of John Gage, living in the reign of King Henry IV.; 4th in descent from whom was Sir John Gage, K.G., eminent in the service of King HENRY VIII., and of his daughter Queen Mary; he *d.* in 1555. His grandson, Sir John Gage of Firle, was created a Baronet in 1622, and *d.* in 1633, leaving four sons, of whom, Thomas the eldest, succeeded him, and Sir Edward 3rd son, ancestor of the present Sir Thomas Gage of Hengrave, Baronet, was created a Baronet in 1662.

Sir Thomas, the eldest son, was great-grandfather of Sir Thomas Gage, 8th Baronet, who in 1720, was created VISCOUNT GAGE of Castle Island, Co. Kerry, and Baron of Castlebar, Co. Mayo; his Lordship *d.* in 1754, leaving two sons:

1 WILLIAM-HALL, his successor, 2nd VISCOUNT, who *d.* without surviving issue, in 1791; having been created in 1780, Baron Gage of Firle, Co. Sussex, in the Peerage of Great Britain, which title became extinct on his death; and in 1790, Baron Gage of High-Meadow, Co. Gloucester, also in the Peerage of Great Britain, with remainder in default of issue male to his nephew, Henry Gage, Esq.

2 General Thomas Gage, who *d.* in 1788, see *The Peerage Volume*, leaving besides the issue there described, HENRY, his eldest son, who succeeded his uncle as 3rd VISCOUNT, and in consequence of the limitation of the British Barony in 1790, succeeded to that also; he *d.* in 1808, and was succeeded by his eldest son, HENRY-HALL, present and 4th VISCOUNT.

GALLOWAY, EARL. (Stewart.)

Peer of Scotland and of Great Britain.

Alan Fitz Fleald, a noble Norman, came into England in the suite of William the Conqueror. He had three sons; 1 William, ancestor of the Fitz-Alans, Earls of Arundel; 2 Walter, who settled in Scotland, and obtained the office of Lord High Steward; 3 Simon, ancestor of the family of Boyd, now represented by the Earl of Errol. Alexander, 6th High Steward of Scotland, great-grandson of Walter, *d.* in 1283, leaving two sons; 1 James, from whom sprung the Kings of Scotland, extinct in the male line in King James V.; 2

Sir John Stewart of Bonkyll; he was killed at the battle of Falkirk, 22 July 1298, leaving seven sons; the issue of Sir Hugh and Sir Robert, the two youngest sons, has not been ascertained, the five elder sons were,

1 Sir Alexander, from whom descended the extinct Earls of Angus.

2 Sir Alan, grandfather of Sir Alexander, who had two sons; 1 Sir John, founder of the Royal House of Lennox-Stuart, extinct in Cardinal York, in 1807; 2 Sir William of Jedworth, if this latter was not a descendant from Sir John of Jedworth below.

3 Sir Walter Stewart of Dalswinton, whose great grand-daughter and heir, *m.* the ancestor of the Earl of Galloway.

4 Sir James, whose grandson, Sir John, had issue; 1 Robert, founder of the extinct House of Lorn; 2 Sir James, who *m.* Jane, Queen Dowager of Scotland, widow of King James I., and mother of King James II.; and was ancestor of the Earls of Atholl and Buchan, both extinct in the male line, but from a legitimated son of the latter, the Earl of Traquair descends; 3 Alexander, ancestor of Sir John-Archibald Stewart of Grandtully, Bart., and of Lord Douglas.

5 Sir John of Jedworth, killed at Halidon Hill, 19 July 1333, by some supposed to be grandfather, by his son John, of the Sir William whose pedigree is otherwise deduced above.

This Sir William Stewart of Jedworth, was father of John, who *m.* the great grand-daughter and heir of Sir Walter Stewart of Dalswinton above, and had, besides other issue; 1 Sir Alexander, 6th in descent from whom was Alexander, 1st Earl of Galloway, ancestor in the 6th generation of the present Earl; 2 Thomas, ancestor of Lord Blantyre.

Sir Alexander Stewart of Garlies, was created Lord Garlies in 1607, and Earl of Galloway in 1623; he *d.* in 1649, having had two sons; 1 Alexander, Lord Garlies, who *d.* before him in 1638, leaving one son, Alexander, Lord Garlies, who also *d.* before his grandfather in 1642. 2 James, his successor, 2nd Earl. He was father of Alexander, 3rd Earl, who succeeded him in 1671; and left, besides other issue, Alexander, 4th Earl, who *d. unm.*, and James, 5th Earl; the latter succeeded his brother in 1694, and *d.* in 1746, when he was succeeded by his son Alexander, 6th Earl; he *d.* in 1773, having had six sons, of whom Alexander and James, the two eldest, *d. unm.* before him; John, 3rd son, succeeded as 7th Earl; George, a Lieutenant in the army, was killed at Ticonderago, in 1758; William, *d.* young, and Keith, 6th son, *b.* in 1739, *d.* 5 May 1795; having *m.* 13 May 1782, Georgiana-Isabella, daughter of — Simha d'Aguilar, Esq., by whom, who *m.* 2ndly, 16 Feb. 1797, Captain Richard Fitzgerald, he had the two sons mentioned in *The Peerage Volume*, and two others; viz.: Archibald-Keith, eldest son, *b.* Feb. 1783, unfortunately drowned when a midshipman on board Lord Bridport's flag-ship, 23 June 1795; and Edward-Charles, 4th son, *b.* 22 April 1792, also a Midshipman in the R.N., lost in Admiral Troubridge's flag-ship, the Blenheim, in the Indian seas in 1807.

John, 7th Earl, was created in 1796, a Peer of Great Britain, by the title of

Baron Stewart of Garlies, in the Stewartry of Kirkcudbright. Where so many are deserving of panegyric, it is difficult to particularise, yet is it equally, if not more difficult, to pass unnoticed a character so eminent for every domestic, patriotic, and Christian virtue, as this nobleman has left on record; he *d.* in 1806; and his widow, Anne, daughter of Sir James Dashwood, Bart., survived him till 1830, when she *d.* at the advanced age of 88, having lived to see one hundred and thirty-seven of her own descendants, namely, sixteen children, eighty-six grand-children, and thirty-five great-grandchildren. GEORGE, Viscount Garlies, their eldest son, succeeded his father, and is the present and 8th EARL.

GALWAY, VISCOUNT. (MONCKTON-ARUNDEL.)

Peer of Ireland.

The Viscount is said to be descended from Simon Monckton of Monckton, Co. York, in 1326; ancestor of Thomas Monckton, living in the reign of King Henry VI., from whom the 9th in descent was JOHN MONCKTON, Esq., created in 1727, VISCOUNT GALWAY, and Baron of Killard, Co. Clare; he *d.* in 1751, having *m.* 1st, Lady Elizabeth Manners, 3rd daughter of John, 2nd Duke of Rutland, whose sister, Lady Frances, (the Duke's 2nd daughter,) *m.* Richard Arundel, 2nd son of John Lord Arundel of Trerice, (which title became extinct in 1768.) The Viscount was father, by Lady Elizabeth, of WILLIAM, 2nd VISCOUNT, who assumed the name of Arundel pursuant to the will of his maternal aunt, and was grandfather of the present Viscount; of Lieut.-General Robert Monckton, who *d.* Governor of New York, in 1782, *unm.*, and of two children, who *d.* infants; he *m.* 2ndly, Jane, only daughter of Henry Westenra, Esq., by whom he had the two sons and one daughter stated in *The Peerage Volume*, and one other son Henry, killed in America.

WILLIAM, 2nd VISCOUNT, eldest son and successor of the 1st Viscount, *d.* in 1772, and was followed successively, by his two sons, HENRY-WILLIAM, 3rd VISCOUNT, who *d.* without issue in 1774, and ROBERT, 4th VISCOUNT, who was succeeded in 1810, by his eldest son, WILLIAM-GEORGE, present and 5th VISCOUNT.

GAMBIER, BARON. (GAMBIER.)

Peer of the United Kingdom.

Nicholas Gambier, his Lordship's great-grandfather, was a French Protestant, who took refuge in England on the revocation of the edict of Nantz; James, his son, was father of, 1 John, father of the present Lord; 2 Vice-admiral James Gambier, father of Sir James, who, besides other issue, has William, his eldest son, widower of the late Countess-Dowager of Athlone.

John Gambier, Esq., the eldest son, *b.* 15 June 1723, *d.* 5 April 1782, leaving issue, by his wife, Deborah Stiles of Bermuda, who *d.* in 1766,

1 Samuel, *b.* 1752, *d.* 11 May 1813; having *m.* Jane, 4th daughter of Daniel Matthew, Esq., by whom he left issue:

- 1 Mary, *d.*; having *m.* 14 Aug. 1813, Thomas Parry, Esq.
- 2 Henrietta-Maria.
- 3 Emily-Jane, *m.* 12 Sept. 1816, Edward-Morant Gale, Esq., who *m.* 1st, 16 June 1798, ——, daughter of Gore Townshend, Esq.
- 4 Charles-Samuel, *b.* 1790.
- 5 Captain Robert, R.N., *b.* 1791, *m.* 27 Oct. 1815, Caroline-Gore, 4th daughter of Major-General Browne, by whom, who *d.* 10 March 1827, he had, 1 Rosina; 2 Adeline; 3 Georgiana; 4 Charles.
- 6 Louisa.

7 Edward-John, *b.* 1794.
8 Captain George-Cornish, R.N., *b.* 1795.
9 Frederick, *b.* 1796.
10 Caroline-Penelope, *m.* 14 Nov. 1819, James Gordon Murdoch, Esq.
11 Sophia-Rose, *b.* 19 Oct. 1800, *m.* 30 May 1822, Rev. William-Wollaston Pym.
12 Francis-Shie, *b.* 22 May 1802, *d.* July 1813.
13 Frances-Anne, *m.* 1 July 1824, George-Stephen Butler, Esq.
14 Samuel-James, *b.* 1807, *m.* 8 April 1830, Maria-Rowlands, eldest daughter of Captain Rowland Money, R.N.

2 Admiral Sir James Gambier, whose distinguished naval services have procured him the honour of the Peerage, to which he was raised in 1807, by the title of Baron Gambier of Iver, Co. Buckingham, and is the present Peer.

3 Mary, *d.* 20 Feb. 1825; having *m.* Admiral Samuel Cornish, *b.* 1740, *d.* 3 April 1816.

4 Susanna, *m.* Richard Sumner, Esq.

5 Harriet, *m.* Rev. Lascelles Iremonger, Prebendary of Westminster, *d.* 6 Feb. 1830.

6 Margaret, *d.* 6 Nov. 1818; having *m.* William-Morton Pitt, Esq., M.P.

GARDNER, BARON. (Gardner.)

Peer of Ireland and of the United Kingdom.

Theophilus Gardner of Coleraine, Co. Londonderry, was father of Captain William Gardner, who commanded a company in the army of King William III., in defence of the city of Londonderry; he was grandfather of the gallant Admiral, Sir Alan Gardner; created a Baronet in 1794; and for eminent services created to the Irish Peerage, by the title of Baron Gardner of Uttoxeter, in 1802; in 1806 he was also created Baron Gardner of Uttoxeter, Co. Stafford, in the Peerage of the United Kingdom; and, dying in 1808, was succeeded by his eldest son, Alan-Hyde, 2nd Lord, also a distinguished Admiral: a warrant was issued for his creation to the dignity of a Viscount of the United Kingdom, and was published in the Gazette, but his Lordship dying 27 Dec. 1815, before the patent had passed the Great Seal, it never took effect. He was succeeded by his infant son, Alan-Legge, the present and 3rd Lord, the issue of his second marriage, whose right was confirmed by a vote in the House of Lords on an appeal from Henry-Fenton Gardner, otherwise Jadis, the son of the 2nd Lord's divorced wife by Mr. Jadis.

GARVAGH, BARON. (Canning.)

Peer of Ireland.

This family originated in England, and had been seated at Foxcote, in Warwickshire, since the marriage, in the time of Henry VI., of Thomas Canning, with the heiress of the Le-Marshalls; the elder branch still continues there represented by Francis Canning, Esq., 12th in descent from the said Thomas Canning. George Canning, Esq., son of Richard Canning, Esq., of Foxcote, having removed into Ireland in the time of Queen Elizabeth, settled at Garvagh, Co. Londonderry, and *d.* in 1646; he was ancestor in the 4th degree of Stratford Canning, Esq., of Garvagh, his Lordship's grandfather; he had three sons, 1 George, who *d.* before him, 11 April 1771, father of the late Right Hon. George Canning, whose widow is the present Viscountess Canning; 2 Paul, who succeeded his father at Garvagh, and *d.* in

Nov. 1784, leaving by his marriage with Jane, 2nd daughter of Conway Spencer, Esq., and sister of the late General Sir Brent Spencer, G.C.B., who was *b.* in 1753, and *d.* 24 Oct. 1825, an only surviving son, the present Peer; created in 1818, BARON GARVAGH of Garvagh, Co. Londonderry; 3 Stratford, who *d.* in May 1787, leaving besides other issue, the present Right Hon. Sir Stratford Canning, G.C.B., and M.P., who *m.* 3 Sept. 1825, Eliza-Charlotte, eldest daughter of James Alexander, Esq., of Somerhill, Kent, M.P.

GIFFORD, BARON. (GIFFORD.)

Peer of the United Kingdom.

Robert Gifford, Esq., a native of the city of Exeter, where his mother *d.* at the advanced age of 88, 1 Dec. 1828, worked his way by his legal talents and political integrity to the dignity of the Peerage, to which he was elevated by the title of BARON GIFFORD of St. Leonard's, Co. Devon, in 1824. He *d.* Master of the Rolls in 1826, and was succeeded by his minor son, ROBERT-FRANCIS, the present and 2nd LORD.

GLASGOW, EARL OF. (BOYLE.)

Peer of Scotland and of the United Kingdom.

This family was seated at Kelburn, Co. Ayr, as early as the reign of King Alexander III.; 7th in descent from John Boyle of Kelburn, who was killed in the battle of Bannockburn, in 1488, was DAVID BOYLE of Kelburn, created Lord Boyle of Kelburn, Stewartoun, Cumbra, Largs, and Dalry, in 1699; and farther created in 1703, EARL of GLASGOW, Viscount of Kelburn, and Lord Boyle of Stewartoun, Cumbraes, Finnick, Largs, and Dalry. His Lordship, on the alarm of invasion by the Pretender in 1715, raised, and throughout the ensuing rebellion, maintained at his own expense, a regiment of 1000 men for the service of the Government. He *d.* in 1733, and was succeeded by his eldest son, JOHN 2nd EARL, who *d.* in 1740, leaving, besides JOHN, 3rd EARL, his successor, and other issue, his 3rd son, the Hon. Patrick Boyle of Shewalton, who *d.* 26 Feb. 1798; having *m.* 1st, Agnes, daughter of William Mure, Esq., who *d.* 27 June 1758, without issue; and he *m.* 2ndly, Elizabeth, daughter of Alexander Dunlop, Esq., by whom he had, besides the issue stated in *The Peerage Volume*, two other sons and two daughters, who all *d.* in their youth *unm.*

JOHN, 3rd EARL, *d.* in 1775; and his eldest son, John Lord Boyle, *b.* 26 March 1756, having *d.* young, he was succeeded by his only surviving son, GEORGE, the present and 4th EARL; he left also two daughters, Lady Elizabeth, who was *b.* in 1759, and *d.* 15 Feb. 1801; having *m.* Sir George Douglas, Bart. of Springwood Park, who *d.* 4 June 1821; and Lady Jane-Mary, who *d.* *unm.* 30 Aug. 1823. The present EARL was created in 1815, BARON ROSS of Hawkstead, Co. Renfrew, in the Peerage of the United Kingdom.

GLENGALL, EARL OF. (BUTLER.)

Peer of Ireland.

His Lordship is a collateral branch of the Marquis of Ormonde's family. James 3rd son of James, 3rd Earl of Ormonde, was great-grandfather of

Thomas Butler, Esq., of Caher, who had two sons; 1 Thomas, created Baron of

Caher, Co. Tipperary, in 1543, which title became extinct on the death of his only son, Edmund, 2nd Lord, in 1560; 2 Pierce, father of

Theobald Butler, Esq., in whose favour the Peerage was revived in 1583; he *d.* in 1596, having had six sons, of whom the three elder were,

1 Thomas, 2nd Lord, who *d.* without issue male in 1627.

2 Pierce, father of Thomas, 3rd Lord; his issue male failed in 1676, on the death of Pierce, 4th Lord, grandson and successor of the 3rd Lord, being the son of his only son Edmund, who *d.* before him.

3 Edmund, father of Theobald, 5th Lord, and ancestor, by a younger son, of the present Lord.

Theobald, 5th Lord, who succeeded on the extinction of the line of the 1st Lord's 2nd son, *d.* in 1700; he was succeeded by his son Thomas, 6th Lord, father of James, 7th Lord, who succeeded him in 1744, and *d.* without issue in 1786; and of Pierce, 8th Lord, in whom failed the line of Theobald, 5th Lord. He *d.* without issue 10 June 1788; when the title devolved on James, 9th Lord, son of Richard Butler, Esq., of Ballynahinch, grandson of the above Edmund, by a younger son; he was in India at the time of his predecessor's death, and dying in July 1788 before the news of his elevation reached him, never bore the title; he was succeeded by his son Richard, 10th Lord, who was created in 1816, Earl of Glengall and Viscount Caher, Co. Tipperary; he *d.* in 1819, and was succeeded by his only son Richard, present and 2nd Earl.

GLENLYON, BARON. (Murray.)

Peer of the United Kingdom.

Lord James Murray, the 2nd son of John 4th Duke of Atholl, was created in 1821, Baron Glenlyon of Glenlyon, Co. Perth, and is the present Peer.

GODERICH, VISCOUNT. (Robinson.)

Peer of the United Kingdom.

This noble Peer, the Right Hon. Frederick-John Robinson, formerly Chancellor of the Exchequer, and, since his elevation to the Peerage, First Lord of the Treasury in 1827, was created, in April 1827, Viscount Goderich of Nocton, Co. Lincoln. He is younger brother of Lord Grantham, and 2nd son of Thomas, 2nd Lord Grantham, by Lady Mary-Jemima Yorke, sister and heir of the Countess de Grey, and 2nd daughter of Philip, 2nd Earl of Hardwicke, by Lady Jemima Campbell, grand-daughter and sole heir of Henry Grey, Duke of Kent, and 12th Earl of Kent, who had been created in 1706, Viscount Gooderich of Gooderich Castle, Co. Hereford, Earl of Harold, and Marquis of Kent. The Duke *d.* in 1740, when the titles of Marchioness de Grey and Baroness Lucas devolved on his grand-daughter, and all his other titles became extinct.

GORDON, DUKE OF. (Gordon.)

Peer of Scotland and of Great Britain.

The Duke's paternal name is Seton, and his Grace is a collateral branch of the Earl of Eglintoun's family.

The territory of Gordon, in Berwickshire, was granted in the reign of King David II., to an Anglo-Norman settler, who assumed from it his surname, and was ancestor of Adam de Gordon, killed at the battle of Halidon-Hill in 1333, leaving two sons;

1 Sir Alexander, great-grandfather of Sir Adam, who left an only daughter and heir, Elizabeth; 2 William, ancestor of the Viscounts of Kenmure.

Sir Alexander Seton, younger brother of Sir John, ancestor of the extinct Earls of Wintoun, and of the Earl of Eglintoun, *m.* Elizabeth, daughter and heir of Sir Adam de Gordon. Their son, ALEXANDER, was created EARL of HUNTLEY in 1450, with remainder to his issue by the said Elizabeth, his 3rd wife, remainder to his heirs whatever; by his 1st marriage he had no issue; by his 2nd he had one son, Alexander, ancestor of the Setons of Touch; the issue of the 3rd marriage assumed the name of Gordon, and in their male descendants the Earldom has since remained.

ALEXANDER, 1st EARL, *d.* in 1470, and was succeeded by his son, GEORGE, 2nd EARL, who *d.* in 1502; he had, besides other issue, the daughter and three sons following; 1 ALEXANDER, his successor, 3rd EARL; 2 Adam, who, in right of his wife, Elizabeth, sister and heir of John, 9th Earl of Sutherland, whose surname he assumed, was the 10th Earl, and ancestor of all the succeeding Earls of Sutherland; 3 Sir William, ancestor of the Gordons of Gicht, he was slain at Flodden in 1513; 4 Lady Catherine, *m.* at the desire of King JAMES IV. to Perkin Warbeck, professing to be the Duke of York, son of EDWARD IV., King of England.

ALEXANDER, 3rd EARL, commanded, in conjunction with the Lord Home, the left wing of the Scottish army at the battle of Flodden, and was one of the few Scottish nobles who escaped the carnage of that disastrous field. He *d.* in 1524, having survived his eldest son, John Lord Gordon, whose son GEORGE succeeded his grandfather as 4th EARL. During the reign of James V. this Earl commanded the forces employed against the English with alternate success; he completely defeated an army under Sir Robert Bowes, at Haddenrig, in 1542, taking the commander and six hundred men prisoners, and after greatly annoying for some time the large army of the Duke of Norfolk, was himself taken prisoner at the battle of Pinkie, 10 Sept. 1547; and having rebelled against the government of the Queen Mother, in consequence of several personal injuries, was defeated and killed by the royal forces in the battle of Corrichie, 28 Oct. 1562, and two of his sons, Sir John, and Adam, afterwards Sir Adam, were made prisoners; the former was beheaded, the latter pardoned on account of his youth, and lived to be an active and successful partizan of Queen MARY in the subsequent troubles of her reign. The Earl was succeeded by his son, GEORGE, 5th EARL, who being delivered up to the government by his father-in-law, the Duke of Chatelherault, to whom he fled after his father's defeat, he was convicted of high treason, and sentenced to execution, but finally pardoned. He subsequently signed the bond to support the authority of JAMES VI., but joined the association in favour of Queen MARY, and was in the North raising forces for her service, when the battle of Langside compelled him to submit to the Regent Moray in 1569; after whose murder, in 1570, he obtained from the Queen the commission of Lieutenant-General of the Kingdom, and raised forces with a view to her restoration, but was again obliged to submit, upon articles of indemnity. He *d.* in 1576, and was succeeded by his son, GEORGE, 6th EARL, who following in his father's steps, was repeatedly in rebellion, sometimes successful, but frequently obliged to submit, and as frequently pardoned by King JAMES, who, notwithstanding these political offences, was much attached to him, and considered him a good and loyal subject. He was created MARQUIS of HUNTLEY in 1599, and *d.* in 1636; he had, besides other sons, GEORGE, his successor, 2nd MARQUIS, and John, created in 1627, Viscount of Melgum and Lord Aboyne, but burnt to death in 1630, in the house of Sir James Crichton, at Frendraught, when those titles became extinct.

GEORGE, 2nd MARQUIS, a firm supporter of the Crown throughout the civil wars, was taken prisoner in Dec. 1647, tried, condemned, and beheaded at Edinburgh, 22 March 1649, for levying war against the Parliament on behalf and for the rescue of the King. He had five sons: 1 George Lord Gordon, who was killed serving under the Marquis of Montrose, at the battle of Alford, in 1645, *unm.*; 2 LEWIS, his successor, 3rd MARQUIS; 3 Lord James, who succeeded his father in the title of Viscount of Aboyne, to which the Marquis had been created in 1632, with a special limitation, on his accession to the title of Marquis, of this of Aboyne, to his son James, who, for having zealously served the King in several engagements, was declared a traitor by the Parliamentary government in 1543, and obliged to fly the kingdom; but returning with Montrose, in all whose successes he participated, he escaped again to France, after the defeat of Philiphaugh, and died there in a passion of grief, on hearing the news of the murder of King Charles I., early in Feb. 1649; 4 Charles, created Earl of Aboyne in 1660, ancestor of the present Earl of Aboyne, who is now the nearest collateral of this noble house; 5 Lord Henry, who was many years in the military service of the King of Poland.

LEWIS, 3rd MARQUIS, *d.* in 1653, and was succeeded by his only son, GEORGE, 4th Marquis, in whose favour the act of forfeiture against his grandfather, the 2nd Marquis, was rescinded in 1661, and his estates restored; he was created by patent in 1684, with remainder to the heirs male of his body, DUKE OF GORDON, Marquis of Huntley, Earl of Huntley and Enzie, Viscount of Inverness, Lord Badenoch, Lochaber, Strathaven, Balmore, Auchindoun, Garthie, and Kincardine. At the Revolution he held out the Castle of Edinburgh for King JAMES, and when it was no longer tenable, surrendered on capitulation, and made his submission to King WILLIAM, but through the course of that reign was always subject to the suspicions of the government, and frequently in custody. He *d.* in 1716, and was succeeded by his only son, ALEXANDER, 2nd DUKE, who in 1715 had joined the standard of the Pretender; but capitulating after the battle of Sheriffmuir, he was not prosecuted by the government; he *d.* in 1728, having *m.* the Lady Henrietta Mordaunt, daughter and eventually heir of Charles, the celebrated General, Earl of Peterborough and Monmouth, by whom he was father of COSMO-GEORGE, his successor, 3rd Duke; he *d.* in 1752, leaving three sons:

1 ALEXANDER, 4th DUKE, his successor.

2 Lord William Gordon, late Ranger of the Green Park; *b.* 15 Aug. 1744, and *d.* 1 May 1823; having *m.* 1 March 1781, the Hon. Frances-Ingram Shepherd, who survives him, (see *The Peerage Volume,*) by whom he left an only daughter, Frances-Isabella-Kerr, *b.* 6 March 1782, *d. unm.* 2 Sept. 1831.

3 The notorious and unfortunate Lord George Gordon, who, after the part he took in the riots in London in 1780, was committed to the Tower, and tried on a charge of high treason, but acquitted. He *d. unm.* 1 Nov. 1793.

The Barony of Beauchamp of Bletsho, created by writ in 1363, was carried into the family of St. John, by the marriage of Margaret, daughter and heir of John Beauchamp, (great-grandson and heir of ROGER, the 1st BARON,) with Sir Oliver St. John. On the death of John, 2nd Lord St. John, of Bletsho, in 1596, this Barony devolved on his only daughter,

ANNE, who *m.* William, Lord Howard, son and heir apparent of Charles, 1st Earl of Nottingham, by whom she had an only daughter and heir,

ELIZABETH; she *m.* JOHN, 5th LORD MORDAUNT of TURVEY, and 1st Earl of Peterborough, in whose family these Baronies continued till the death in 1814, of CHARLES-HENRY, 5th Earl of Peterborough, and 3rd of Monmouth, when they devolved on his half-sister, LADY MARY-ANASTATIA-GRACE MORDAUNT, who dying in 1819, was succeeded by

ALEXANDER, 4th Duke of Gordon, (son and heir of Cosmo, 3rd Duke of Gordon, eldest son of Alexander, 2nd Duke, by Lady Henrietta, daughter of Charles, 3rd Earl of Peterborough, and 1st of Monmouth.) The Duke had been created, in 1784, Earl of Norwich and Baron Gordon, of Huntley, Co. Gloucester, in the Peerage of Great Britain, and *d.* in 1827, when all his titles devolved on his only surviving son, the gallant General GEORGE, Marquis of Huntley, present and 5th DUKE.

GORMANSTON, VISCOUNT. (PRESTON.)

Peer of Ireland.

His Lordship's first known ancestor was Philip de Preston, living in the 13th century. 4th in descent from him was Sir Robert Preston, who in the reign of EDWARD III. was Lord of the Manor of Preston, in Lancashire, and going over into Ireland, was constituted a Baron of the Exchequer; his son, Sir Christopher, was father of SIR ROBERT, created in 1478, Baron of the Naas, Co. Kildare, and VISCOUNT of GORMANSTON, Co. Meath, being descended from an heiress of the family of Laundress, which formerly bore those titles. He *d.* in 1503, and his son and successor, WILLIAM, 2nd VISCOUNT, in 1532. JENICO, 3rd VISCOUNT, his son, *d.* in 1569, leaving, besides other issue, two sons: 1 CHRISTOPHER, 4th VISCOUNT, his successor; 2 Martin, ancestor in the 8th degree of John Preston, Esq., created in 1800, Baron Tara, of Bellinter, Co. Meath, which title became extinct on his death in 1821.

CHRISTOPHER, 4th VISCOUNT, *d.* in 1600; he was father of, 1 JENICO, 5th VISCOUNT; 2 Thomas, created Viscount Tara in 1650, which title also became extinct in 1674, on the death of his grandson, Thomas, 3rd Viscount.

JENICO, 5th VISCOUNT, *d.* in 1637, and was succeeded by his son, NICHOLAS, 6th VISCOUNT, father of, 1 JENICO, his successor, 7th VISCOUNT, who was outlawed for his adherence to King JAMES II., and *d.* in 1691, without issue male, leaving an only daughter, Mary, the wife of her cousin, the 9th Viscount; 2 Nicholas, who left issue, JENICO, 8th VISCOUNT, who succeeded his uncle, and *d.* without issue, and ANTHONY, 9th VISCOUNT, who succeeded his brother, and *d.* in 1716, leaving by his marriage with his cousin above-mentioned, an only son, JENICO, 10th VISCOUNT, who *d.* in 1757. He had, besides other issue, 1 ANTHONY, his successor, 11th VISCOUNT; 2 The Hon. James Preston, who *m.* Purefoy, 2nd daughter of Sir Willoughby Aston, Bart., by whom, who *d.* in 1792, he left the issue stated in *The Peerage Volume.*

ANTHONY, 11th VISCOUNT, *d.* 15 Dec. 1786; having *m.* Honnetta, daughter of Lieutenant-General John Robinson, of which marriage, JENICO, the present and 12th VISCOUNT, is the only issue; the Viscountess re-married the late Lieutenant-General Christopher Jeaffreson, and *d.* 6 Feb. 1826.

GORT, VISCOUNT. (VEREKER.)

Peer of Ireland.

This branch of the family of Vereker in Brabant settled in Ireland early in the 17th century. John Vereker, Esq. of Roxborough, Co. Limerick, who *d.* in 1671, was ancestor in the 4th degree of

Thomas Vereker, Esq., who, by his marriage with Juliana, eldest daughter of Charles Smyth, Esq., and sister of JOHN-PRENDERGAST, 1st VISCOUNT, had issue: 1 CHARLES, present VISCOUNT; 2 John, *m.* to Elizabeth, daughter of George Black, Esq.; 3 Elizabeth, wife of Henry d'Esterre, Esq.; 4 Maria, wife of Arthur Ormsby, Esq.; 5 Harriet, wife of Ralph Westropp, Esq.; 6 Julia, wife of Frederick Lloyd, Esq.

JOHN-PRENDERGAST SMYTH, Esq. was created in 1810, Baron Kiltarton, Co. Galway, with remainder, failing his issue male, to his nephew, the Right Hon. Charles Vereker, and his issue male; and advanced to the dignity of Viscount Gort, of Limerick, in 1816, with the same limitation.

He *d.* in 1817, and was succeeded by his nephew, Charles Vereker, Esq., the present and 2nd Viscount, who was most honourably distinguished in 1798, by his gallant opposition at Coloony to the French force sent to invade Ireland.

GOSFORD, EARL OF. (Acheson.)

Peer of Ireland.

The Earl is of an ancient Scotch family. Sir Archibald Acheson, of Gosford, Co. Haddington, Secretary of State in Scotland, who was created a Baronet of Nova Scotia in 1628, and *d.* in 1634, was ancestor in the 5th generation of Sir Archibald, 6th Baronet, created in 1776, Baron Gosford of Market Hill, Co. Armagh, and in 1785 Viscount Gosford; he *d.* in 1790, and was succeeded by his only surviving son, Arthur, 2nd Viscount, created Earl of Gosford in 1806; he *d.* in 1807, and was succeeded by his eldest son, Archibald, the present and 2nd Earl.

GOWER, BARON. (Leveson-Gower.)

Peer of Great Britain.

George-Granville, Earl Gower, eldest son of George-Granville, 2nd Marquis of Stafford, was summoned to his father's Barony of Gower, of Sittenham, Co. York, in 1826.—See *The Peerage Volume*, title Stafford.

GRAFTON, DUKE OF. (Fitz-Roy.)

Peer of England.

Anne Villiers, only daughter and heir of William, 2nd Viscount Grandison, of Ireland, and wife of Roger Palmer, Esq., created Earl of Castlemaine, in the Peerage of Ireland, was created by King Charles II. in 1670, Baroness of Nonsuch, Co. Surrey, Countess of Southampton, and Duchess of Cleveland, Co. York, with remainder to Charles Fitz-Roy and George Fitz-Roy, her natural sons by that King. The Earl of Castlemaine *d.* in 1705; and the Duchess afterwards, in the same year, *m.* Robert Feilding, Esq., and *d.* in 1709, without issue by either of her husbands; but leaving by King Charles the following issue:

1 Anne Palmer-Fitz-Roy, *m.* to Thomas Lennard, Baron Dacre, created in 1674, Earl of Sussex; he *d.* without issue male in 1715, when the Earldom became extinct.

2 Charles Fitz-Roy, *b.* June 1662, called Earl of Southampton, as heir apparent to his mother, after her creation in 1670 to the Ducal title; he was himself created, in 1674, Baron of Newbury, Co. Berks, Earl of Chichester, Co. Sussex, and Duke of Southampton. He succeeded as Duke of Cleveland on the death of his mother, in 1709, and *d.* in 1730, when he was succeeded by his only surviving son, William, 2nd Duke of Cleveland and Southampton, on whose death in 1774, without issue, all these titles became extinct; but the Lady Grace Fitz-Roy, one of his sisters and co-heirs, having *m.* Henry, 1st Earl of Darlington, her grandson William-Henry, 3rd Earl of Darlington, was in 1827 created Marquis of Cleveland, and has since quartered the arms, and borne the crest and supporters, of Fitz-Roy, Duke of Cleveland and Southampton.

3 Henry Fitz-Roy, *b.* 20 Sept. 1663, was created in 1672 Baron Sudbury, Viscount Ipswich, and Earl of Euston, all in the county of Suffolk, and further created Duke of Grafton, Co. Northampton, in 1675.

4 George Fitz-Roy, created in 1674, Baron of Pontefract, Co. York, Viscount Falmouth, Co. Cornwall, and Earl of Northumberland; and in 1683, Duke of Northumberland. He *d.* without issue in 1716, when these titles became extinct.

5 Charlotte Fitz-Roy, *m.* to Edward Lee, Earl of Lichfield, so created in 1674.

6 Barbara Fitz-Roy, a nun.

HENRY, 1st DUKE of GRAFTON, was killed at the siege of Cork, where he commanded King WILLIAM'S army in 1690. He *m.* in 1672, LADY ISABELLA BENNET, daughter and heir of HENRY BENNET, created in 1664, Baron Arlington of Arlington, Co. Middlesex; and further in 1672, Viscount Thetford, Co. Norfolk, and Earl of Arlington, Co. Middlesex, with remainder, failing his issue male, to the heirs of his body. The Earl *d.* in 1685, when he was succeeded by the Duchess of Grafton, his daughter, on whose death in 1723, her son, CHARLES, succeeded to her titles, having previously, in 1690, succeeded his father as 2nd DUKE of GRAFTON. He *d.* in 1757, having survived all his five sons. George, Earl of Euston, the 2nd son, *d.* in 1747, without issue; having *m.* in 1741, Lady Dorothy Boyle, daughter of Richard, Earl of Burlington and Corke, who *d.* in 1742. Lord Augustus, the 3rd son, *d.* before his elder brother; being in the naval service, he commanded the Orford man-of-war in the attack upon Carthagena, in Feb. 1741, and fell under the effects of fatigue in that unhealthy climate in May following. He left two sons; AUGUSTUS-HENRY, who, after the death of his uncle, was styled Earl of Euston, and succeeded his grandfather as 3rd DUKE; and Charles, created in 1781, Lord Southampton. He was grandfather of the present Lord Southampton.

AUGUSTUS-HENRY, 3rd DUKE, *d.* in 1811, and was succeeded by his eldest son, GEORGE HENRY, present and 4th DUKE.

GRANARD, EARL OF. (FORBES.)

Peer of Ireland.

His Lordship is a younger branch of the family of Lord Forbes, and is descended from Hon. Patrick, 3rd son of James, 2nd Lord Forbes; he was great-grandfather of William Forbes, Esq. of Corse, whose 4th son, Sir Arthur Forbes, settled in Ireland at Castle Forbes, Co. Longford, was created a Baronet of Nova Scotia in 1628, and *d.* in 1632, when he was succeeded by his son SIR ARTHUR, who was created in 1675, Baron of Clanehugh, and Viscount Granard, Co. Longford; and in 1684, EARL of GRANARD. From his Lordship to the present Earl, the Peerage has been uninterruptedly inherited in direct descent from father to son; the succession has been as follows: the 1st EARL *d.* in 1696; ARTHUR, 2nd EARL, *d.* in 1734; GEORGE, 3rd EARL, *d.* in 1765; he left, besides the 4th EARL, a second son, the Hon. Admiral John Forbes, who *d.* in 1796, leaving by Lady Mary Capel, 4th daughter of William, 3rd Earl of Essex, who *d.* in 1782, the two daughters described in *The Peerage Volume.* GEORGE, 4th EARL, *d.* in 1769; and GEORGE, 5th EARL, in 1780, when he was succeeded by his eldest son GEORGE, present and 6th EARL, who was created a Peer of the United Kingdom in 1806, by the title of Baron Granard of Castle Donington, Co. Leicester.

GRANTHAM, BARON. (WEDDELL.)

Peer of Great Britain.

William Robinson was Lord Mayor of York in 1581, as was his son William in the reign of JAMES I.; and William, his grandson, was High Sheriff for the County in the reign of CHARLES I. Sir Metcalfe Robinson, eldest son of the latter, was created a Baronet soon after the restoration, and three times represented the City of

York in Parliament, he *d.* without issue in 1689, and the Baronetcy was revived in 1690, in favour of Sir William, his nephew and heir, who was of the Convention Parliament, High Sheriff of the County at the Revolution, and member for the City of York in eight successive Parliaments. Sir Tancred, his 2nd son, who succeeded his elder brother, Sir Metcalfe, was twice Lord Mayor of York and a Rear-Admiral; he left posterity, but the Baronetcy, on the death of his grandson, Sir Norton Robinson, in 1792, devolved on Lord Grantham.

Thomas Robinson, Esq., the younger brother of Sir Tancred, after a long course of diplomatic services, was for a short period in the reign of George II. Secretary of State, and being personally agreeable to the King, afterwards filled the situation of Master of the Wardrobe till his Majesty's death. In 1761, he was created Baron Grantham of Grantham, Co. Lincoln, and *d.* in 1770, when he was succeeded by his eldest son Thomas, 2nd Lord. He *m.* Lady Mary-Jemima Yorke, sister of the Countess De Grey, and 2nd daughter and co-heir of Philip, 2nd Earl of Hardwicke, by Lady Jemima Campbell, Marchioness De Grey, grand-daughter and heir of Henry Grey, Duke of Kent; by whom he left two sons, Thomas-Philip, his successor, present and 3rd Lord, who has assumed the name of Weddell, and is heir presumptive to the Countess De Grey; and Frederick-John, created in 1827, Viscount Goderich; a third son, Philip, *d.* in infancy.

GRANTLEY, BARON. (Norton.)

Peer of Great Britain.

His Lordship is descended from Egbert Conyers, of the Norman family of that name, whose son Roger, marrying Margaret, only daughter and heir of Richard Norton, of Norton, Co. York, assumed her name. 6th in descent from them was Richard Norton, of Norton, Esq., who, in 1569, joined with the Earls of Northumberland and Westmoreland in that rebellion against Queen Elizabeth, in which they proposed to restore the ancient religion of the country. It was soon suppressed by the Queen's forces, and many of the principal malcontents were convicted of treason and attainted. Among them were this Richard Norton and his brothers, Christopher, Marmaduke, and Thomas. 7th in descent from him was Sir Fletcher Norton, of Grantley, who was bred to the bar, and having served the office of Attorney-General to the King, was elected in 1769, Speaker of the House of Commons, which honourable office he continued to fill till, in 1782, he was created a Peer by the title of Lord Grantley, Baron of Markenfield, Co. York. He was *b.* 23 Jan. 1716, and *d.* 1 Jan. 1789; having *m.* 21 May 1741, Grace, daughter of Sir William Chapple, who was *b.* in 1708, and *d.* 30 Oct. 1803; they had issue, besides two sons, who *d. unm.*,

1 William, 2nd Lord, *b.* 19 Feb. 1742, *d.* without surviving issue, 12 Nov. 1822; having *m.* 27 Sept. 1791, Anna-Margaretta, daughter of Jonathan Midgeley, Esq., who *d.* 23 April 1795.

2 Hon. Fletcher, a Baron of the Exchequer in Scotland, father of Fletcher, the present and 3rd Lord, who succeeded his uncle in 1822; and of the other issue stated in *The Peerage Volume.*

3 Hon. Grace, *d.* 13 Nov. 1813, Countess of Portsmouth.

GRANVILLE, VISCOUNT. (Leveson-Gower.)

Peer of the United Kingdom.

Lord Granville Leveson-Gower, the 2nd son of Granville, 1st Marquis of Stafford, and half-brother of the present Marquis, was created in 1815, Viscount

Granville of Stone Park, Co. Stafford, and is the present Peer. His Lordship's father, the late Marquis of Stafford, was grandson of John, 1st Lord Gower, son of Sir William Gower, Bart., by Lady Jane Granville, eldest daughter of John, 1st Earl of Bath, and Viscount Granville, and co-heir of her nephew William-Henry, 3rd Earl of Bath. *See* the titles Stafford, Carteret, and Lansdown.

GRAVES, BARON. (Graves.)

Peer of Ireland.

James Graves, Esq., descended from a good family in Yorkshire, was father of, 1 Samuel Graves, Esq., whose eldest son, Thomas, has left male issue seated at Castle Dawson, in Ireland; and his younger son John, reckoned among his sons four Admirals and one Captain in the R.N.; 2 Rear-Admiral Thomas Graves, of Thankes, Co. Cornwall, whose son Thomas, also an Admiral, led the van of the British fleet in the glorious victory of the 1st of June 1794, and received a wound in his arm. He was immediately created Lord Graves, Baron of Gravesend, Co. Londonderry. He *d.* in 1802, leaving issue,

1 Thomas-North, 2nd Lord, on whose melancholy death in 1830, his eldest son, William-Thomas, present and 3rd Lord, succeeded.

2 Hon. Peere-Williams Graves, *d. unm.*

3 Hon. Elizabeth-Anne, *d.* 12 Feb. 1803; having *m.* 22 Dec. 1802, William Bagwell, Esq.

4 Hon. Anne-Elizabeth, *d.* 11 Sept. 1823; having *m.* 15 Jan. 1803, Sir Thomas Hare, Bart.

5 Hon. Margaret-Anne, *m.* Nov. 1802, Capt. Christopher-John-Williams Nesham, R.N.

GRAY, BARON. (Gray.)

Peer of Scotland.

His Lordship is of the same family with Earl Grey, though the connexion cannot be distinctly traced. A younger son of the Greys of Northumberland settled in Scotland, as early as the 12th century, and was ancestor of Sir Andrew, who joined Robert Bruce in 1306; 4th in descent from him was Sir Andrew Gray, of Broxmouth, created Lord Gray in 1445; Andrew, his son and successor, 2nd Lord, *d.* in 1469; he had two sons, viz.:

1 Patrick, Master of Gray, *d.* before his father, leaving a son, Andrew, who succeeded his grandfather as 3rd Lord.

2 Andrew, ancestor of Sir William Gray of Pittendrum, and through him of the 9th and succeeding Lords Gray.

Andrew, 3rd Lord, *d.* in 1514; his two eldest sons were, 1 Patrick, 4th Lord, who *d.* without issue male; 2 Gilbert, father of Patrick, who succeeded his uncle as 5th Lord. He was taken prisoner at the rout of Solway, by Dacre and Musgrave, and committed to the custody of the Archbishop of York, but soon admitted to ransom. He was one of the first Scotch noblemen who countenanced the Reformation, and joined the association in support of James VI. in 1567. He *d.* in 1582, and was succeeded by his eldest son Patrick, 6th Lord, to whom, in 1609, succeeded his son Patrick, 7th Lord, who *d.* in 1612. His son and successor, Andrew, 8th Lord, *d.* in 1663, without surviving issue male; and his eldest daughter, Anne, having *m.* William Gray, eldest son of Sir William Gray, of Pittendrum, he made, in 1639, a resignation of his honours into the hands of King Charles I., from whom he obtained a renewed charter of the Peerage to himself, with remainder to William Gray, (eldest son of Sir William Gray of Pittendrum,) husband of Anne, his eldest daughter, and the heirs male of their marriage; failing which, to the nearest heirs male whatever of Sir William Gray of Pittendram.

This Sir William Gray descended from Andrew, 2nd son of the 2nd LORD, *d.* in 1648, in consequence of the troubles of the Royal family and the country, and of his own share in them, having been imprisoned in the Tolbooth of Edinburgh, for corresponding with the Marquis of Montrose, and heavily fined. He left two sons:

1 William, *m.* as above mentioned, to Anne, eldest daughter of the 8th LORD, and in her right was Master of Gray; he commanded a regiment chiefly raised at his own charge, in the Royal army at the battle of Worcester; and was killed in a duel by the Earl of Southesk, in 1660, in the lifetime of his father-in-law, but had survived Anne, his wife, by whom he was father of PATRICK, 9th LORD, whose only daughter and heir, Marjory, *m.* her cousin, John Gray.

2 Robert, whose son, JOHN, 10th LORD, *m.* the said Marjory daughter and heir of the 9th Lord; which PATRICK, 9th LORD, having no issue male, surrendered his honours into the hands of Queen ANNE, and obtained a new patent, with the former precedency, settling the Barony on John Gray, husband of his daughter Marjory, and the heirs male or female, without division, of their marriage, which failing, to the nearest heir male of himself, the said PATRICK LORD GRAY; he *d.* in 1711, and was succeeded by his son-in-law, John, 10th LORD; he *d.* in 1724, and was succeeded by his eldest son, JOHN, 11th LORD, to whom in 1738, succeeded his son, JOHN, 12th LORD, who *d.* in 1782, having had issue,

1 Hon. Andrew Gray, *d. unm.* 23 Mary 1767.
2 CHARLES, 13th LORD, his successor, *b.* in 1752, *d. unm.* 18 Dec. 1786.
3 WILLIAM-JOHN, 14th LORD, *b.* March 1754, succeeded his brother and *d.* also *unm.* 12 Dec. 1807.
4 FRANCIS, present and 15th LORD.
5 Hon. Jean, *d.* 19 Feb. 1786, having *m.* Francis, 10th Earl of Moray.
6 Hon. Helen, *d.* 29 July 1775; having *m.* 1 Oct. 1765, William Stirling, Esq.
7 Hon. Margaret Gray, *d. unm.* 12 July 1806.
8 Hon. Barbara Gray, *d. unm.* 5 Oct. 1794.
9 Hon. Elizabeth, *b.* 1755, *d.* 24 Aug. 1787; having *m.* in 1771, Sir Philip Ainslie, who was *b.* 1728, and *d.* 19 May 1802.
10 Hon. Anne, *d.* 10 Sept. 1802; having *m.* 30 Dec. 1776, George Paterson, Esq.

GRENVILLE, BARON. (GRENVILLE.)

Peer of England.

The Right Hon. WILLIAM-WYNDHAM GRENVILLE, 3rd son of the Right Hon. George Grenville, brother of George, 1st Marquis of Buckinghom, and uncle of the present Duke of Buckingham, having been Speaker to the House of Commons, and Secretary of State, was created in 1790, BARON GRENVILLE of Wotton-under-Bernewood, Co. Bucks, and is the present Peer. His Lordship was for a short time First Lord of the Treasury in 1806-7.

GREY, EARL. (GREY.)

Peer of the United Kingdom.

This family is supposed to have come into England from Normandy, with William the Conqueror, and settled in Northumberland, from whence a younger branch emigrated to Scotland in the 12th century, and founded the family of Lord Gray.

Sir John Grey, living in 1372, was father of Sir Thomas, who had two sons:

1 John, Earl of Tankerville in Normandy, *m.* Joan, eldest daughter and co-heir of Edward Lord Cherleton of Powis; his male line failed in 1552, and Lord Scarsdale, as his heir general, is eldest co-heir of the Barony of Cherleton of Powis.

2 Sir Thomas; 4th in descent from him was

Sir Ralph Grey, who had two sons,

1 Sir Ralph, father of William, created Baron Grey of Werke, which title became extinct in 1706, by the death of his grandson Ralph, 4th Lord, whose elder brother, Ford, 3rd Lord, had been created in 1695, Viscount Glendale and Earl of Tankerville; he *d.* without issue male, in 1701, leaving an only daughter, Lady Mary, *m.* to Charles Bennet, Lord Ossulston, who was created Earl of Tankerville, and was ancestor of the present Earl of Tankerville.

2 Sir Edward Grey of Howick, from whom the 5th in descent was Sir Henry Grey of Howick, created a Baronet in 1746. His eldest son, Sir Henry Grey, Bart., *d. unm.* in 1808. His younger son, General Sir Charles Grey, K.B., was created in 1801, Baron Grey of Howick, Co. Northumberland; and in 1806, Earl Grey, and Viscount Howick; he *d.* in 1807, and was succeeded by his eldest son, Charles, present and 2nd Earl.

GREY DE RUTHYN, BARONESS. (Rawdon-Hastings.)

Peeress of England.

Roger de Grey, younger son of John, 3rd Baron Grey de Wilton, *see* Earl of Stamford, was summoned, by writ 1324, as Baron Grey of Ruthyn; he *d.* in 1353, and was succeeded by his son Reginald, and he, in 1388, by another Reginald, his son, who *d.* in 1440, having survived his eldest son, Henry, whose son Edmund succeeded his grandfather as 4th Lord; he was created Earl of Kent in 1465, and *d.* in 1488, and the Barony continued merged in the Earldom, through George, 2nd Earl, his son, who *d.* in 1504, and whose two sons, Richard, who *d.* in 1523, without issue, and Henry, who *d.* in 1562, were successively 3rd and 4th Earls, though the latter, was from his poverty, unable to use any title of honour; Henry, his eldest son, who *d.* before him, leaving three sons, Reginald, who succeeded his grandfather, and *d.* in 1572; Henry, 6th Earl, who *d.* in 1615, and Charles, 7th Earl, who *d.* in 1625; till the death, without issue, in 1639, of Henry, 8th Earl of Kent, and 11th Lord, son of the 7th Earl; when the Earldom devolved on his cousin and male heir, Anthony Grey, ancestor of the extinct Duke of Kent and the Countess de Grey, and the Barony on his only sister,

Susan, wife of Sir Michael Longueville, by whom she had a son and heir, Charles, 13th Lord, who claimed and was allowed the Barony in 1640; he *d.* in 1643, leaving a daughter and heir,

Susan, *m.* to Sir Henry Yelverton, Bart.; she *d.* in 1676, leaving two sons, Sir Charles, 15th Lord, who *d.* without issue in 1679, and Henry, 16th Lord, who was created Viscount Longueville in 1690, and *d.* in 1704. Talbot, 17th Lord, his son and successor, was created in 1717, Earl of Sussex; he *d.* in 1731, leaving two sons, 1 George-Augustus, 18th Lord, and 2nd Earl of Sussex, who *d.* without issue in 1758, and 2

Henry, 4th Viscount, 3rd Earl, and 19th Lord, *b.* 7 July 1729, succeeded 8 Jan. 1758, *d.* 22 April 1799, without issue male; having *m.* 1st, Hester, daughter of John Hall, Esq., *b.* 1735, *d.* 11 Jan. 1777; by whom he had one daughter, Lady Barbara, wife of Edward-Thoroton Gould Esq.; 2ndly, 29 Jan. 1778, Mary, daughter of John Vaughan, Esq., *d.* 6 June 1796. On the Earl's death his other honours became extinct, but this Barony devolved on HENRY-EDWARD GOULD, 20th LORD, his grandson.

Lady Barbara Yelverton, only daughter and heir of the 3rd Earl of Sussex, 19th LORD GREY of RUTHYN, was *b.* 19 June 1760, and *d.* 8 April 1781; having *m.* in Oct. 1775, Edward-Thoroton Gould, Esq., who *d.* 15 Feb. 1830. They had a daughter, Mary, wife of the Hon. and Rev. Frederick Powis, (see *The Peerage Volume,*) and an only son, HENRY-EDWARD, 20th LORD, who assumed the name of Yelverton, and *d.* in 1810, leaving his infant daughter, BARBARA, present BARONESS, his heir; her Ladyship is now the wife of George-Augustus-Francis Rawdon-Hastings, 2nd Marquis of Hastings.

GUILFORD, EARL OF. (NORTH.)

Peer of Great Britain.

Robert North, who *d.* in 1470, was father of Thomas North, Esq., of Walkringham, Co. Notts, which Thomas, was grandfather of Edward, 1st Lord North, summoned to Parliament in 1554, and high in the favour and confidence of King HENRY VIII., from whom he received considerable grants of land. He continued to hold office under EDWARD 6th and Queen MARY, although he was one of the Council who signed the letter to that Queen, wherein they acknowledged the Lady Jane Grey for the lawful Sovereign. He *d.* in 1564, and was succeeded by his son Roger, 2nd Lord North, to whom, in 1600, succeeded his grandson Dudley, (son of John, his eldest son;) this Dudley, 3rd Lord North, was succeeded, in 1666, by his son, Dudley, 4th Lord North, he *d.* in 1677; leaving, besides other issue, the two sons following:

1 Charles, summoned to Parliament as Baron Grey of Rolleston, in 1673, succeeded his father, in 1677, as 5th Lord North, and *d.* in 1690, when he was succeeded by his son, William, 6th Lord North, and 2nd Lord Grey of Rolleston; he entered the army, and rose to the rank of Lieutenant-General, having served under the Duke of Marlborough in all his campaigns; in the battle either of Hochstet or Blenheim, he had his right hand shot off; he *d.* without issue in 1734, when the Barony of Grey of Rolleston became extinct; but that of North devolved on FRANCIS, 3rd BARON GUILFORD.

2 SIR FRANCIS NORTH, who having with the highest reputation passed through various gradations of legal offices, was appointed, in 1682, Lord Keeper of the Great Seal, and in 1683, was created BARON GUILFORD, of Guilford, Co. Surrey. Steady in his loyalty to the Crown, yet firm in his disapprobation of the unprincipled men and measures of his times, the uneasiness of his mind, after he accepted the custody of the Great Seal, hastened his end, and he *d.* in 1685, leaving behind him an exalted character for learning, integrity, and Christian piety, which is admirably pourtrayed in the memoirs of his life written by Mr. Roger North, his brother. He was succeeded by his son, FRANCIS 2nd LORD, to whom, in 1729, followed his son,

FRANCIS, 3rd LORD, who also succeeded in 1734, as 7th Lord North, and was created EARL of GUILFORD, in 1752. He *d.* in 1790, leaving two sons, Frederick, Lord North, and Brownlow, Bishop of Winchester, father of the present EARL; and was succeeded by his eldest son. FREDERICK, 2nd EARL, K.G., better known as Lord North, having held the reins of Government for twelve years as Prime Minister, while bearing his father's second title. His administration was unfortunate, and, after a vain effort for its support by a most unpopular coalition with his vehement opponent, Charles Fox, it sunk at length before the rising brightness of Mr. Pitt's talents; and this truly admirable Nobleman retired to grace, with his wit, cheerfulness, and virtues, the domestic hearth. He *d.* in 1792, leaving three sons, successively EARLS of GUILFORD, who all *d.* without surviving issue male; they were, 1 GEORGE-AUGUSTUS, 3rd EARL, who had the misfortune to lose four successive heirs apparent by two marriages, in their earliest infancy, and has left three surviving daughters, amongst whom, on his death in 1802, the ancient Barony of North fell into abeyance. 2 FRANCIS, 4th EARL; he *d.* without issue in 1817, and his Countess is also deceased. 3 FREDERICK, 5th EARL, who *d. unm.* in 1827, when the Rev. FRANCIS NORTH, eldest son of Brownlow, late Lord Bishop of Winchester, succeeded and is the present, and 6th EARL.

GUILLAMORE, VISCOUNT. (O'GRADY.)

Peer of Ireland.

The Right Hon. Standish O'Grady, Lord Chief Baron of the Exchequer in Ireland, was created a Peer of Ireland in 1831, by the titles of Baron O'Grady of Rockbarton, and Viscount Guillamore of Caher Guillamore, in the County of Limerick.

HADDINGTON, EARL. (HAMILTON.)

Peer of Scotland and of the United Kingdom.

From the Hamiltons of Innerwick, a branch of the ancient family of Hamilton, afterwards Dukes of Hamilton, of which the Marquis of Abercorn is the present male representative, descended SIR THOMAS HAMILTON of Priestfield, who being bred to the bar, was admitted Advocate in 1587, and appointed a Lord of Session in 1592, by the title of Lord Drumcairn; he was afterwards Lord Clerk Register of Scotland and Secretary of State, and was raised to the dignity of the Peerage in 1613, by the title of Lord Binning and Byres. Being subsequently Lord President of the Court of Session, he was, in 1619, advanced to the rank of EARL of Melrose, and in 1627, changed that title for HADDINGTON, by patent, retaining the former precedence. He *d.* in 1637, and was succeeded by his eldest son, THOMAS, 2nd EARL; siding with the Covenanters in the civil war, he was appointed Colonel of one of their regiments, and was killed in 1640, by the explosion of a considerable magazine of gunpowder in the castle of Dunglass, which, demolishing one of the castle walls, buried him and numerous other persons in its ruins. He left two sons, 1 THOMAS, 3rd EARL, who *d.* without issue in 1645; and 2 JOHN, 4th EARL, who was succeeded, in 1669, by his only son CHARLES, 5th EARL. He *m.* Margaret, in her own right Countess of Rothes, eldest daughter of John, Duke of Rothes, and by her, who *d.* in 1700, had two sons, John and Thomas. John, the eldest son, succeeding to the Earldom of Rothes, resigned that of Haddington, which was re-granted to his brother THOMAS, 6th EARL of HADDINGTON. The Earl of Rothes had eight sons; and dying in 1722, was succeeded by his eldest son John, 9th Earl, of Rothes, who *d.* in 1767, and was succeeded by his son, John, 10th Earl, on whose death in 1773, his sister, Jane-Elizabeth, became Countess of Rothes; but his uncle, the Hon. Andrew Leslie, 8th son of the 8th Earl of Rothes, became heir male and representative of the 1st Earl of Haddington. He *d.*, however, in 1776, and as all his brothers, the eldest only excepted, had done, he *d. unm.*, and the Earl of Haddington again became the heir male of his house.

THOMAS, 6th EARL, succeeded his father, according to the new arrangement of the entail, in 1685. He zealously supported the Treaty of Union; on the breaking out of the rebellion of 1715, assumed arms in defence of the house of Hanover, and was wounded, and had a horse shot under him at the battle of Sheriffmuir. He afterwards became remarkable for his zeal in planting his estate with forest trees, and the great improvements he effected by that means at Tyninghame; he *d.* in 1735. Charles, Lord Binning, his eldest son, *d.* before him, in 1733, leaving three surviving sons, viz.:

1 Thomas, who succeeded his grandfather as 7th Earl; he *d.* in 1794, and was succeeded by his only surviving son, Charles, 8th Earl, who, in 1827, was created a Peer of the United Kingdom by the title of Baron Melros of Tyninghame, Co. Haddington, and *d.* in 1828, when he was succeeded by his only son, Charles, present and 9th Earl.

2 Hon. George Hamilton, who, succeeding to the large estates of his maternal grandfather, George Baillie, Esq., of Jerviswood, Co. Lanark, and of Mellerstain, Co. Roxburgh, assumed the name of Baillie. He was *b.* in 1723, and *d.* 16 April 1797, having *m.* Miss Elizabeth Andrews, who *d.* 24 April 1799. Besides two daughters, Grizel, who *d. unm.* 18 Oct. 1800, and Rachel, who *d. unm.* 9 Jan, 1797; they left a third daughter, Elizabeth, and two sons, who are all, with their marriages and issue, described in *The Peerage Volume.*

HAMILTON AND BRANDON, DUKE OF. (Hamilton-Douglas.)

Peer of Scotland and of Great Britain.

The first ancestor on record of the illustrious House of Douglas, appears to be Theobald the Fleming, to whom the lands of Douglas were granted in 1160.

Archibald, his grandson, was father of 1 William, who continued the line; 2 Andrew, ancestor of the Earl of Morton.

Sir William Douglas, surnamed The Hardy, son of the above William, swore fealty to King Edward I. in 1291, but was in arms against him as governor of Berwick, when Edward invaded Scotland in 1296. He was then compelled to surrender the town upon capitulation, and again swore fealty to Edward; he however joined Sir William Wallace the following year, for which his estate was laid waste, and his wife and children carried off. Having afterwards himself made his submission to Edward, he was sent to England, and *d.* at York in 1302. He left three sons, the good Sir James, Hugh, of whom, though he succeeded to the family possessions, little mention is made, and Archibald, who carried on the line.

Of the good, and it may be added the great, Sir James Douglas, it is impossible to speak sufficiently in so concise a history as the present. This illustrious Patriot, the companion and friend of King Robert Bruce, is to be traced in all the signal actions of this eventful time. In the decisive battle of Bannockburn he took a prominent part, and a variety of minor engagements, besides the surprise of the English garrison in Douglas Castle, the taking of Roxburgh Castle and the town of Berwick by escalade, bear witness to his military talents and valour; and Scotland being cleared of the English invasions, England itself was destined to record his prowess. In 1319, he routed the Archbishop of York at Mitton, near Boroughbridge; in 1322, forced the English camp at Byland in Yorkshire, and put its defenders to flight; and in another invasion, when he headed 20,000 men, he, with two hundred horsemen, forced his way in the night to the Royal tent, in the English camp at Stanhope Park, and narrowly missed securing the person of King Edward III. Robert Bruce on his death-bed, in 1329, requested Douglas to carry his heart to Jerusalem, and deposit it in the sepulchre of our Saviour. Sir James set out with his precious charge, but, passing through Spain, could not resist the temptation of joining in battle with the Moors on behalf of Alphonzo XI., King of Castile and Leon; seeing the enemy wavering and about to give way, he threw the casket which contained the heart of his Royal master towards them, exclaiming, "Pass thou onward, as thou wert wont—Douglas will follow thee or die!" The Moors rallied, and, overwhelmed by superior numbers, Sir James Douglas fell, and his body, together with the heart of the King, were re-conveyed to Scotland. He *d.* in 1330, *unm.*; but an illegitimate son, Archibald, finally carried on the line of Earls of Douglas.

He was succeeded by his next brother, Hugh, who *d.* without issue; but Archibald, his younger brother, became Regent of Scotland in the minority of David II., and, in pursuance of the war with England, led an army to Halidon Hill, where his forces were totally defeated, and himself mortally wounded, living only long enough to be made prisoner; he *d.* in 1333. William, his son, obtained the family estates in 1342, by the resignation of his uncle Hugh. With hereditary hostility to the English, he fed the war upon the borders, and, in April 1356, concluded a truce with the Earl of Northampton, Lord Warden of the Marches, to continue till Michaelmas, that he might have time to go on a pilgrimage; in passing through France, he was present in aid of King John at the battle of Poictiers, and being wounded, was carried off the field by his attendants. In the following February he was created Earl of Douglas, and continued to make war, generally with success, upon the English on the borders, till his death in 1384. He was twice married; 1st, to Lady Margaret Marr, sister and heir of Thomas, 13th Earl of Marr, by whom he had a son, James, 2nd Earl of Douglas and 15th Earl of Marr, and a daughter, Lady Isabel, who inherited the Earldom of Marr on the death of her brother. The Earl, before his second marriage, appears to have made a settlement of the Earldom of Douglas, failing the issue male of his son, the 2nd Earl, upon Archibald, the illegitimate son of the good Sir James Douglas. He married 2ndly, Lady Margaret Stewart, Countess of Angus, sister and heir of Thomas, 3rd Earl of Angus, and relict of the above-mentioned Thomas, 13th Earl of Marr, by whom he had an only son, GEORGE, who, on his mother's resignation, obtained a grant of the Earldom of Angus in 1389, and was the 1st EARL of ANGUS of this family.

James, his eldest son, Earl of Douglas and Marr, succeeded; Fordun calls him "Miles acerrimus et Anglis semper infestissimus;" he made an incursion as far as the gates of York, and, with the rest of his spoil, brought off in one of his skirmishes the banner of Henry (Hotspur) Lord Percy, which he proposed to elevate on the pinnacle of his castle. This brought Percy with a large force after him, and the battle of Otterbourn ensued, 19 Aug. 1388; the utmost exertions of valour were displayed on both sides, and Douglas fell mortally wounded, "thanking God that few of his ancestors had died in chambers;" but his victory was complete, and Hotspur made prisoner. He *m.* Margaret, eldest daughter of King Robert II., but had no surviving issue by her; the Earldom of Marr devolved on his sister, that of Douglas, by the already mentioned settlement, probably, on Archibald Douglas the Grim, Lord of Galloway, the illegitimate son of the good Sir James. This Earl himself left two illegitimate sons, William, ancestor of the house of Queensberry, and Archibald, of the Douglases of Cavers.

Pity it is that our limits utterly preclude a digression on the various fortunes of this powerful and warlike family under the descendants of Archibald the Grim, 3rd Earl of Douglas; sometimes seated at the summit of the political system, with all but the regal title, swaying the destinies of the kingdom; sometimes suffering under the axe of the executioner. The title passed, in an incredibly short space of time, through seven inheritors.

Archibald, 3rd Earl of Douglas, *d.* in 1401, leaving two sons, Archibald, 4th Earl, and James, 7th Earl. Archibald, 4th Earl, *d.* in battle in France, in 1424, and was succeeded by his only son, Archibald, 5th Earl, who *d.* in 1439; leaving two sons, William, 6th Earl, and David his brother, both beheaded in 1440, when the elder was but seventeen years of age. James, 7th Earl, 2nd son of the 3rd Earl, succeeded, and *d.* in 1443, leaving six sons, all cut off without posterity, viz. 1 William, 8th Earl, killed in 1452, receiving his first wound from the hand of King James II.;

2 James, 9th and last Earl; 3 Archibald, Earl of Moray; 4 Hugh, Earl of Ormond; 5 Sir John Douglas, Lord of Balvenie; 6 Henry, a priest.

At length the whole inheritance was lost, through the necessity under which James II. found himself, in 1455, of deciding, by force of arms, whether himself or his too powerful subject, whom he had offended beyond hope of reconciliation, should rule the kingdom. The haughty rebel, James, 9th Earl of Douglas, at the head of 40,000 men, bade defiance to an equal number of the royal troops; but his arrogance offended his principal supporters; the Lord Hamilton set the example of desertion; a panic spread, and suddenly Douglas found himself in front of the King's army, with his own hereditary forces only; he fled with precipitation, and escaped imprisonment and death, but his titles and estates were declared forfeited, nor did James disband his troops till every portion of the Douglas domains were in his possession; thus, as with a stroke of magic, sunk for ever the power of this great family. Taken prisoner in his old age, after thirty years of exile, in an attempt to re-establish himself by force of arms, James III., in pity to his misfortunes, merely condemned him to the religious retirement of Lindores Abbey: the Earl, muttering, "He who may no better be must be a monk," submitted; and dying there in 1488, with him closed the line of his grandfather, Archibald the Grim, 3rd Earl of Douglas.

To return to George, 1st Earl of Angus of this family, the true continuator of the line; he was taken prisoner at the battle of Homildon in 1402, and *d.* the same year in England. He left two sons; 1 William, 2nd Earl, who *d.* in 1437, and was succeeded by his only son, James, 3rd Earl, who *d.* without issue by his wife, Lady Johanna Stewart, 3rd daughter of King James I.; 2 George, who succeeded his nephew as 4th Earl, and *d.* in 1462. He was succeeded by his only son, Archibald, 5th Earl, surnamed "Bell the Cat," from the well-known incident of the bridge of Lauder:

"I mean that Douglas, fifth of yore,
"Who coronet of Angus bore,
"And when his blood and heart were high,
"Did the third James in camp defy,
"And all his minions led to die,
"On Lauder's dreary flat."

When age and infirmities had grown upon him, he accompanied James IV. in his fatal expedition to England in 1513; and, remonstrating against the imprudence of joining battle with the English army at Flodden, was answered by the King, "Angus, if you are afraid, you may go home." The affront was unpardonable; the Earl left the field with tears of indignation, but commanded his two eldest sons, with all his followers, to abide the event; they fell in the battle with 200 gentlemen of their name, and the Earl *d.* in the following year. His two sons killed at Flodden were,

1 George, Master of Angus, father of Archibald, 6th Earl, and of Sir George, whose eldest son, David, succeeded as 7th Earl; and his 2nd son, James, Earl of Morton, after being many years Regent of Scotland, in the minority of James VI., suffered death upon the scaffold in 1581, for a supposed participation in the murder of King Henry, before the commencement of his Regency; he *d.* without issue.

2 Sir William Douglas, of Glenbervie, father of Sir Archibald, and grandfather through him of William, 9th Earl, and of James, ancestor of the late Sylvester Lord Glenbervie, so created in 1800, and whose title became extinct by his death without surviving issue in 1823; Harriet, the widow of his only son, the Hon. Frederick-Sylvester-North Douglas, who *d.* without issue in 1819, is now the wife of Lieutenant-Colonel Henry-Hely Hutchinson; see *The Peerage Volume*, title Donoughmore. The said James Douglas was also ancestor, through a younger son of his grandson Robert Bishop of Dumblane, of William Douglas, Esq., of Brigton.

Under Archibald, 6th Earl, grandson and heir of the 5th Earl, the house of

Angus nearly succeeded to the power and splendour of the former Earls of Douglas; he m. Margaret of England, Queen Dowager of Scotland, widow of King James IV. and mother of James V., in whose minority he was continually struggling against the authority of the Regent Duke of Albany, and finally overthrew it in 1526, by declaring the King's majority at the age of fourteen years; from thenceforth he himself governed in James's name for two years, when the young King making his escape, issued a proclamation of forfeiture against Angus and his family, and levied an army to put it in execution, and the Earl was obliged to retire into England; but on James's death, in 1542, he returned to Scotland, and obtained a reversal of the sentence of forfeiture; he was mainly instrumental in obtaining the victory of Ancrum-muir against the English, and fought with very different fortune in the battle of Pinkie in 1547; he d. in 1556, without issue male, leaving by the Queen Dowager an only daughter, Lady Margaret, wife of Matthew Stewart, Earl of Lennox, mother of Henry Lord Darnley, in her right Lord Douglas, and grandmother through him of James I. King of Great Britain. David, 7th Earl, succeeded his uncle, and d. in 1558; he was succeeded by his only son, Archibald, 8th Earl, who after the execution of his uncle, the Regent Morton, was twice in rebellion, and once attainted, but obtained a revocation of the act of attainder. He succeeded to the Earldom of Morton, and d. in 1588, without surviving issue.

The title of Angus then passed to William, 9th Earl, son of Sir Archibald, and grandson of Sir William Douglas, of Glenbervie, the 2nd son of the 5th Earl; notwithstanding a counter claim set up by James VI. as heir of line, which was decided in favour of the heir male. He d. in 1591, leaving several sons, of whom the two eldest were, William, his successor, 10th Earl, and Sir Robert, created a Baronet of Nova Scotia in 1625, ancestor of the present Sir Robert Douglas, of Glenbervie, Bart.

William, 10th Earl, engaged with the Earls of Errol and Huntley in a treasonable correspondence with the King of Spain, for the purpose of restoring the Roman Catholic religion in Scotland, but was pardoned; and retiring some years afterwards to a monastery in France, d. there in 1611, leaving, besides other issue, William, 11th Earl, 1st Marquis of Douglas, his successor, and Sir James, created in 1641, Lord Mordingtoun; his title descended uninterruptedly, from father to son, to Charles, 5th Lord, who, in total lack of landed property, did not assume it; he entered into the rebellion of 1745, and being taken prisoner, was put upon his trial as Charles Douglas, Esq.; but pleading his Peerage, and proving his title to it, the trial was put off, and never resumed. He was the last male of his family, and his only daughter assuming the title after his death, it expired with her in 1791.

William, 11th Earl, was created Marquis of Douglas, and Baron of Abernethy and Jedburgh Forest, in 1633; he joined Montrose after his victory of Kilsyth in 1645, but escaped from the rout at Philiphaugh, and soon afterwards capitulated with the ruling powers. He d. in 1660, having, amongst other issue, had the three sons following:

1 Archibald Earl of Angus, d. before his father in 1655, leaving two sons, James, who succeeded his grandfather as 2nd Marquis, and Archibald, created Earl of Forfar, which title became extinct by the death of Archibald, 2nd Earl, his only son, of the wounds he received in the King's army in 1715, at the battle of Sheriffmuir, where he was made prisoner.

2 William, who was created Earl of Selkirk, succeeded as Duke of Hamilton, in right of the Duchess Anne, his wife, and was ancestor of the present Duke.

3 George, created in 1675, Earl of Dunbarton, which title became extinct on the death of his only son, George, 2nd Earl.

James, 2nd Marquis, d. in 1700, and was succeeded by his only surviving son, Archibald, 3rd Marquis; he was created Duke of Douglas in 1703, and d. without issue in 1761, when the Dukedom became extinct, and a contest arose for the other titles, between the Duke of Hamilton, as heir male, and the present Lord Douglas, as the reputed son of Sir John Stewart, of Grandtully, Bart., by the Lady Jane, only sister of the Duke of Douglas. The titles were adjudged to the Duke of Hamilton, now become chief of this illustrious house; but the estates passed to Archibald Stewart, Esq., as nephew and heir of line of the Duke of Douglas, and he was created in 1790, Baron Douglas of Douglas Castle, which Peerage is now enjoyed by his son Archibald, the 2nd Lord.

Sir James Hamilton, 6th in descent from Sir Gilbert, the first of the family of Hamilton, who settled in Scotland, and whose pedigree is given under the Marquis of Abercorn, was created Lord Hamilton in 1445, and appears to have possessed considerable power and influence. It was an affront offered by the haughty Earl of Douglas to this nobleman, that caused him to return to his allegiance to James II., and produced the defection in one night of all the other chiefs composing the rebel army, and the consequent total overthrow of the Douglas family. He *d.* in 1479, having *m.* Mary, eldest daughter of King James II., and widow of Thomas Boyd, Earl of Arran, by whom he had one son, James, created Earl of Arran in 1503; he was in France, commanding the Scotch troops sent to the aid of Louis XII., when King James IV. was killed at Flodden, and returning immediately to Scotland, was a competitor, though unsuccessfully, with the Duke of Albany for the Regency; he *d.* in 1529, and was succeeded by his eldest son, James, 2nd Earl.

James, 2nd Earl, was declared by Act of Parliament, on the death of King James V., in 1542, to be next in succession to the Crown, Regent of the kingdom, and tutor to the infant Queen. One of the first statutes passed under his regency, was an Act allowing the reading of the Bible in the vulgar tongue. The failure of the treaty of marriage with England, which led to a destructive war between the two nations, induced the Scotch to send the young Queen to France for her education, in 1548; and on this occasion the Regent had the title of Duke of Chatelherault conferred upon him. In 1554, he resigned the regency into the hands of Mary of Lorraine, the Queen-mother. He opposed the marriage of the Queen with Lord Darnley, and thereby so much offended the new King, that he was forced to fly into France, in 1565, and to remain there till recalled by Mary in 1569, with the commission to act against her rebel subjects and the Regent Moray, as Lieut.-General of the kingdom for her; but Moray getting possession of his person, committed him to the Castle of Edinburgh, where he remained till the Regent's death. He afterwards submitted to the Regent Morton, and *d.* in 1574. He left four sons, viz. 1 James, 3rd Earl, who *d.* without issue in 1609; 2 John, 1st Marquis of Hamilton; 3 Lord David, who *d.* without issue in 1611; and 4 Lord Claud, Baron of Paisley, ancestor of the Marquis Abercorn, which family, on the extinction of the elder male line of Hamilton, in 1651, by the death of William, 2nd Duke of Hamilton, became the male representatives of this illustrious house.

Lord John Hamilton was banished by the Regent Morton, after the death of his father, the Duke of Chatelherault, for his fidelity to Queen Mary; but, entering Scotland with other banished noblemen, in 1685, collected a force sufficient to besiege the King in Stirling Castle; an accommodation was then agreed upon, and all acts enforced against the house of Hamilton and their partisans were rescinded. Lord John was created Marquis of Hamilton in 1599, and *d.* in 1604, when he was succeeded by his only son, James, 2nd Marquis, K.G., created a Peer of England in 1619, by the titles of Baron Ennerdale, Co. Cumberland, and Earl of Cambridge, and *d.* in 1625. He left two sons, 1 James, his successor, 1st Duke of Hamilton; 2 William, created in 1639, Earl of Lanark, Lord Machanshire and Polmont, and succeeded his brother as 2nd Duke.

James, 3rd Marquis, K.G., obtained in 1643 a patent, creating him Duke of Hamilton, Marquis of Clydesdale, Earl of Arran, Lanark, and Cambridge, Lord Aven, Polmont, Machanshire, and Ennerdale, remainder to the heirs male of his body; which failing, to his brother William, Earl of Lanark, and the heirs male of his body; which failing, to the eldest heir female of the 1st Duke of Hamilton; which failing, to his nearest heirs whatsoever, bearing the name and arms of Hamilton. With the consent of CHARLES I., he led a body of 6000 men to the assistance of Gustavus Adolphus in Germany, landed at the mouth of the Oder in Aug. 1631, contributed greatly to the victory of Leipsic, but being recalled, quitted the Swedish army in Sept. 1632, shortly before the battle of Lutzen, where Gustavus fell in the arms of victory. Owing to the rivalship between him and the Marquis of Montrose, he was imprisoned by the King during a part of the civil war; but being released in April 1646, by the surrender of Mount St. Michael, in Cornwall, to the forces of the Parliament, he hastened to afford what assistance he could to the Royal cause, but his efforts were greatly neutralized by his zeal for the Presbyterian profession, while the King would acknowledge no other national religion than the episcopal. He commanded the forces sent by the Scotch nobility for the relief of the King in 1648, but being defeated at Preston, surrendered, in August that year, to the Parliamentary General. He was spared to witness the murder of his Sovereign, and soon after, by his heroic death, set the seal to that fidelity which had been sometimes, though unjustly, considered equivocal. He was beheaded 9 March 1649. He had three sons who all *d.* young, as did his eldest daughter; two younger daughters survived him, viz., LADY ANNE, afterwards DUCHESS of HAMILTON, and Lady Susan, *m.* to John, 7th Earl of Cassilis. He was succeeded by his brother WILLIAM, Earl of Lanark, the 2nd DUKE; the Earl of Lanark made his escape from Oxford in Dec. 1643, when his brother was arrested and joined the Scotch Covenanters; he was one of the Commissioners sent by Parliament to treat with the King at Newark in 1646; but his endeavours towards conciliation were vain. When his brother marched into England for the rescue of the King in 1648, he was appointed Commander-in-Chief of the army in Scotland; and after the death of CHARLES I., went abroad to wait upon CHARLES II.; he raised a troop of horse to assist the King on his expedition into England, and received his death wound in the battle of Worcester, of which he *d.* a few days afterwards, 12 Sept. 1651, in the 35th year of his age. He also left no issue male, but had five daughters, four of whom lived to marry.

The titles according to the terms of the patent of 1643, reverted to LADY ANNE, eldest daughter of JAMES, 1st DUKE, the elder of these two brothers; she *m.* LORD WILLIAM DOUGLAS, whose pedigree has been deduced above, 2nd son of WILLIAM, 1st MARQUIS of DOUGLAS, and himself created in 1646, Earl of Selkirk, Lord Daer and Shortcleuch; he assumed on his marriage the surname of HAMILTON, and in 1660, he was created Duke of Hamilton for life; in 1688, he resigned the titles of Earl of Selkirk, Lord Daer and Shortcleuch, to King JAMES VII., who bestowed them by patent on his 3rd son, Lord Charles Hamilton, with remainder to all his younger sons and their issue male. In 1689, he was chosen President of the Convention Parliament at Edinburgh, which declared the throne vacant, and tendered the Crown to the Prince and Princess of Orange. He *d.* in 1694; his Duchess survived him till 1716, but made a surrender of her titles, in 1698, in favour of her eldest son. The male issue of the 3rd DUKE and DUCHESS were,

1 JAMES, 4th DUKE.

2 Lord-William, who *d.* in France without issue.

3 Lord Charles, Earl of Selkirk; he *d.* in 1739, without issue.

4 Lord John, created a Peer of Scotland, in 1697, by the titles of Earl of Ruglen, Viscount Riccartoun, and Lord Hillhouse, with remainder to the heirs whatsoever of his body; he succeeded his brother Charles as 3rd Earl of Selkirk, and *d.* in 1744, without surviving issue male; his only child, who left issue, was Lady Anne, his eldest daughter, who succeeded as Countess of Ruglen; she *m.* William Douglas, 2nd Earl of March, and *d.* in 1748, leaving an only son, who succeeded her as Earl of Ruglen, William, 4th Duke of Queensberry, on whose death without issue in 1810, this Earldom became extinct.

5 Lord George, created a Peer of Scotland in 1696, by the titles of Earl of Orkney,

Viscount of Kirkwall, and Baron of Dechmont, with remainder to the heirs whatsoever of his body; he *d.* in 1737, without issue male, and was succeeded by his eldest daughter, Anne, who carried the Earldom of Orkney, by marriage, to the Irish family of O'Brien, Earl of Inchiquin; she was grandmother of the present Countess of Orkney.

6 Lord Basil, whose grandson and heir, Dunbar, succeeded as 4th Earl of Selkirk, on the death of his great uncle, John, Earl of Selkirk and Ruglen, and was grandfather of the present and 6th Earl of Selkirk.

7 Lord Archibald, *b.* 1673, and *d.* 5 April 1754, having *m.* 26 Sept. 1719, Lady Jane Hamilton, 5th daughter of James, 6th Earl of Abercorn, she *d.* 6 Dec. 1753, leaving three sons, viz.:

1 Charles Hamilton, Esq. *b.* 29 Oct. 1721, *d.* 10 Sept. 1771; having *m.* Katherine, youngest daughter of Colonel De Fresne, by whom he left the daughter Mary, noticed in the *The Peerage Volume.*

2 The Rev. Frederick Hamilton, *b.* 25 Dec. 1728, *d.* 19 Feb. 1811; having *m.* Miss Daniel, by whom, who *d.* Nov. 1805, he had besides the Countess Dowager of Aldborough, noticed in *The Peerage Volume*, an only son, Robert who *d. unm.* 19 Nov. 1809.

3 The Right Hon. Sir William Hamilton, K.B., so well known for his Neapolitan Mission, in its political effects, and in his indefatigable exertions, in bringing to light the buried treasures of antiquity, and in his philosophical investigations of the phenomena attendant on the eruptions of Mounts Vesuvius and Etna.

James, 4th Duke, K G., as Earl of Arran, attended that Convention Parliament of which his father was the President, and therein delivered his opinion, that the surest way to heal the existing evils of the nation was, to address his Majesty to return from France, and call a free Parliament for the security of religion and property; saying, "I can distinguish between his Popery and his person, I dislike the one, but have sworn and do owe allegiance to the other." He was twice committed to the Tower on suspicion of conspiring for the restoration of the abdicated family, but was discharged without prosecution. He continued to support the interests of the House of Stuart, and was a determined opponent of the Treaty of Union, till, suddenly abandoning his opposition, the measure was unexpectedly carried; it is stated that this change of conduct was produced by representations from the Pretender, of his desire that his sister should be gratified in this particular. He was in 1711, created a Peer of Great Britain, by the title of Baron Dutton, Co. Cheshire, and Duke of Brandon, Co. Suffolk. His Grace lost his life in a very tragical manner, 15 Nov. 1712, in a duel with Lord Mohun, in which both parties were killed. He left three sons:

1 James, 5th Duke, his successor.

2 Lord William, *d.* 11 July 1734; having *m.* 30 April 1733, Frances, only daughter and heir of Francis Hawes, of Purley Hall, Berks, by whom, who *m.* 2ndly, William, 2nd Viscount Vane, and *d.* 31 March 1788, he had no issue.

3 Lord Anne, *d.* 25 Dec. 1748; having *m.* Oct. 1742, Anna-Charlotte-Maria, daughter and heir of Charles Powell, of Penybank, Co. Caermarthen, Esq., by whom, who *d.* 26 June 1791, he had two sons:

1 James, *b.* 18 Jan. 1746, *d.* 22 Jan. 1804; having *m.* 29 July 1767, Lucy, daughter of Sir Richard Lloyd, widow of Sir John Barker, Bart, by whom, who *d.* in Sept. 1790, he had an only son, James, who *d. unm.* 13 March 1802, and one daughter, stated in *The Peerage Volume.*

2 Admiral Charles-Powell Hamilton, he *d.* in 1825; his widow survives, and, with her issue, will be found in *The Peerage Volume.*

James, 5th Duke, *d.* 1 March 1743; having *m.* 1st, 14 Feb. 1723, Lady Anne Cochrane, eldest daughter of John, 4th Earl of Dundonald; by whom, who *d.* 14 Aug. 1724, he had one son, James, 6th Duke. He *m.* 2ndly, in 1727, Elizabeth, 4th daughter of Thomas Strangways, Esq., of Melbury, Co. Dorset, who *d.* without issue 3 Nov. 1729; and 3rdly, 23 July 1737, Anne, daughter and co-heir of Edward Spencer, of Rendlesham, Co. Suffolk, Esq., by whom he was father of ARCHIBALD, 9th DUKE, who succeeded his nephew, DOUGLAS, 8th DUKE, and *d.* in 1819, when he was succeeded by his eldest son, ALEXANDER, present and 10th DUKE.

JAMES, 6th DUKE, was *b.* in 1724, and *d.* 18 Jan. 1758; having *m.* Elizabeth, 2nd daughter of John Gunning, of Castle Coote, Co. Roxburgh, Esq., who was created a Peeress of Great Britain, 4 May 1766, by the title of Baroness Hamilton of Hameldon, Co. Leicester, with remainder to her issue male; she *m.* 2ndly, John, 5th Duke of Argyll, by whom she was mother of George-William, 6th Duke of Argyll, and present and 3rd Lord Hamilton; she *d.* 20 Dec. 1790, and was succeeded in her Barony by her eldest surviving son, DOUGLAS, 8th DUKE; their Graces had two sons:

1 JAMES-GEORGE, 7th DUKE, was *b.* 18 Feb. 1755, and outgrowing his strength, *d.* in his 15th year, 7 July 1769, and was succeeded by his brother;

2 DOUGLAS, 8th DUKE, *b.* 24 July 1756, obtained his summons to Parliament as Duke of Brandon, (which had hitherto been denied to his predecessors,) by a decision of the House of Lords in 1782; he *d.* without issue 2 Aug. 1799; having *m.* 5 April 1778, Elizabeth-Anne, 4th daughter of Peter Burrell, Esq., and sister of Peter, 1st Lord Gwydir, from whom he was separated, and she *m.* 2ndly, 19 Aug. 1800, Henry, 1st Marquis of Exeter. The Duke was succeeded by his uncle, Lord Archibald Hamilton, and in the Barony of Hamilton, by his half-brother, George-William, present Duke of Argyll.

HARBERTON, VISCOUNT. (POMEROY.)

Peer of Ireland.

This family is of Norman origin. Ralph de Pomeroy came into England at the Conquest, and settled in Devonshire. The branch from which the Viscount descends was seated at Engesdon, in Devonshire, in the reign of King James I.

The Very Rev. Arthur Pomeroy, Dean of Cork, came into Ireland in 1672, and was grandfather of ARTHUR POMEROY, Esq., created in 1783, Baron Harberton of Carbery, Co. Kildare; and in 1791, VISCOUNT HARBERTON; he *d.* in 1798, and was succeeded by his eldest son, HENRY, 2nd VISCOUNT, who *d.* without surviving issue in 1829, and was succeeded by his next brother, ARTHUR-JAMES, present and 3rd VISCOUNT.

HARBOROUGH, EARL OF. (SHERARD.)

Peer of Great Britain and of Ireland.

Schirrard, from whom this family derive their surname, held great possessions in Cheshire and Lancashire in the reign of William the Conqueror.

The 18th in descent from him was SIR WILLIAM SHERARD, created in 1627, BARON SHERARD, of Le Trim, in Ireland; he *d.* in 1640, leaving seven sons, the four younger all *d. unm.*: the three elder were,

1 BENNET, his successor, 2nd LORD, who *d.* in 1700, and was succeeded by his only surviving son, BENNET, 3rd LORD, created in 1714 Baron Harborough of Harborough, Co. Leicester, with remainder, failing his issue male, to his uncle Philip Sherard, and his issue male; in 1718 Viscount Sherard of Stapleford, Co. Leicester; and in 1719 EARL of HARBOROUGH, the latter also with remainder to his said uncle; he *d.* without issue in 1732, when the title of Viscount Sherard

became extinct; those of Earl and Baron of Harborough, and the Irish Barony, devolved on his cousin, Philip Sherard, grandson of his said uncle Philip.

2 Philip, on whom and his issue male the Earldom and Barony of Harborough were entailed; he *d.* in 1695, leaving issue: 1 Bennet, who *d.* in 1701, and was father of PHILIP, 2nd EARL; and 2 Philip, ancestor of a family of Sherards, seated at Carr-Coulston, Co. Notts.

3 George, ancestor of the Sherards of Glatton; his representative, the Rev. Philip-Castell Sherard, *d.* aged 46, in Nov. 1814, leaving issue.

PHILIP, 2nd EARL, *d.* in 1750, leaving, besides other issue,

1 BENNET, 3rd EARL, who *d.* without surviving issue male, 24 Feb. 1770; having *m.* 1st, 27 June 1748, Lady Elizabeth Verney, eldest daughter of Ralph, Earl Verney, who *d.* 7 June 1756; 2ndly, 3 July 1757, Frances, daughter of William Noel, Esq., by whom, who *d.* 15 Sept. 1760, he had the daughter Lady Frances Morgan, noticed in *The Peerage Volume*; he *m.* 3rdly, 31 March 1761, Margaret, daughter of Thomas Hill, Esq., (and half-sister of Noel, 1st Lord Berwick;) she *d.* 1 Feb. 1768; and his Lordship *m.* 4thly, 8 Oct. 1768, Elizabeth, eldest daughter of Sir Thomas Cave, Bart., who *d.* 5 March 1797.

2 ROBERT, 4th EARL, *b.* 21 Oct. 1719, *d.* 21 April, 1799, having *m.* 1st, Catherine, eldest daughter of Edward Hearst, Esq., who *d.* 5 Feb. 1765; and 2ndly, 10 Jan. 1767, Jane, daughter of William Reeve, Esq., by whom, who *d.* 9 Nov. 1770, he was father of PHILIP, 5th EARL, and of Lady Lucy Pusey, for whom see *The Peerage Volume.* His Lordship *m.* 3rdly, 25 May 1772, Dorothy, daughter of William Roberts, Esq., who *d.* 16 Sept. 1781.

PHILIP, 5th EARL, who succeeded his father, *d.* in 1807, and was succeeded by his only son, PHILIP, present and 6th EARL.

HARDWICKE, EARL OF. (YORKE.)

Peer of Great Britain.

PHILIP, 1st EARL, K.G., was the only son of Philip Yorke, of Dover, Attorney-at-law, who *d.* 18 June 1721. He was appointed Lord Chief Justice, and was created in 1733, Baron Hardwicke of Hardwicke, Co. Gloucester; in 1737 he was nominated Lord High Chancellor; and in 1754 was created Viscount Royston, and EARL of HARDWICKE; he *d.* in 1764, leaving five sons, viz.:

1 PHILIP, 2nd EARL, *b.* 9 Dec. 1720, *d.* 16 May 1790: having *m.* 22 May 1740, Lady Jemima Campbell, 2nd Marchioness Grey, only daughter of John, 3rd Earl of Breadalbane, and heir of her grandfather, Henry, Duke of Kent; by whom, who was *b.* 9 Oct. 1723, and *d.* 11 Jan. 1797, he had the two daughters stated in *The Peerage Volume.*

2 Charles, who was appointed Lord High Chancellor, but *d.* suddenly while the patent of his creation to the Barony of Morden was in progress, in Jan. 1770; he left PHILIP, the present and 3rd EARL, K.G., who succeeded his uncle, and the other issue described in *The Peerage Volume.*

3 Sir Joseph, was a Field-Marshal in the army, and created Baron Dover in 1788, but dying without issue 2 Dec. 1792, the title became extinct.

4 The Hon. John Yorke, *b.* 27 Aug. 1728, *d.* 4 Sept. 1801; having *m.* 1 Jan. 1762, Elizabeth, daughter of Reginald Lygon, Esq., (sister of William, 1st Earl Beauchamp,) by whom, who *d.* 17 July 1766, he had an only daughter, Jemima, *b.* 5 June 1763, *d.* 14 July 1804, having *m.* 18 Nov. 1784, the Right Hon. Reginald Pole-Carew; who *m.* 2ndly, 4 May 1808, the Hon. Caroline-Anne Lyttelton, 2nd daughter of William-Henry, 1st Lord Lyttelton.

5 The Hon. and Right Rev. James, Lord Bishop of Ely, *b.* 9 March 1730, *d.* 26 Aug. 1808; having *m.* 29 June 1762, Mary, daughter of the Right Rev. Isaac

Madocks, Lord Bishop of Worcester, by whom, who was *b.* 14 Sept. 1743, and *d.* 30 Dec. 1823, he had, besides two sons and a daughter, who *d. unm.*, the following issue:

1 Margaret, *b.* 11 June 1763, *d.* 3 July 1800; having *m.* 10 May 1788, the Rev. Thomas Waddington, D.D., who was *b.* in 1763, and *d.* 18 June 1815.

2 Joseph Yorke, Esq., of Forthampton Court, Co. Gloucester, who was *b.* 5 May 1765, and *d.* 9 Dec. 1830; having *m.* 17 Nov. 1800, Catherine, daughter of James Cocks, Esq., brother of Charles, 1st Lord Somers; by whom, who was *b.* 18 July 1780, and *d.* 3 March 1830, he left the issue stated in *The Peerage Volume.*

3 The Rev. Philip Yorke, *b.* 24 Feb. 1771, *d.* 29 May 1817; having *m.* 4 Dec. 1797, the Hon. Anna-Maria Cocks, 4th daughter of Charles, 1st Lord Somers, by whom, who survives him, he has left the issue stated in *The Peerage Volume.*

4 Elizabeth, *b.* 27 Nov. 1772, *d.* 11 Feb. 1802; having *m.* 10 April 1797, John Buller, Esq.

HAREWOOD, EARL OF. (Lascelles.)

Peer of the United Kingdom.

That this family is of long standing in the County of York, appears from Roger de Lascelles having been summoned to Parliament in 1295 and 1296; he *d.* about 1297, without male issue, and the Barony fell into abeyance between his four daughters and co-heirs.

The Earl's direct ancestor is John de Lascelles of Hindershelf, Co. York, living in 1315.

The 9th in descent from him was Daniel Lascelles, Esq., of Stank, who *d.* in 1734, leaving, besides other issue, two sons, Henry and Edward. Henry was father of Edwin Lascelles, Esq., who was created, in 1790, Baron Harewood, of Harewood Castle, Co. York, and *d.* without issue 25 Jan. 1795, when the title became extinct.

Edward, youngest son of Daniel Lascelles, Esq., was Collector of the Customs at Barbadoes, and *d.* there in 1747. Edward Lascelles, his son, was created Baron Harewood of Harewood, Co. York, in 1796, and *d.* in 1820, when Henry, his eldest son, present and 2nd Lord, succeeded.

HARRINGTON, EARL OF. (Stanhope.)

Peer of Great Britain.

This nobleman is a branch of the Earl of Chesterfield's family. Sir John Stanhope, of Shelford, was father of

1 Philip, 1st Earl of Chesterfield, who had twelve sons, of whom Arthur, 11th son, was ancestor of the present Earl of Chesterfield, and Alexander, 12th son, was father of James, 1st Earl Stanhope, to whose titles of Viscount and Baron Stanhope, the Earl of Harrington is in remainder.

2 Sir John Stanhope, of Elvaston, great-grandfather of William Stanhope, Esq., who, having distinguished himself by his diplomatic talents, especially in some difficult negociations with the Spanish Court under Philip V, was created in 1729, Baron Harrington, Co. Northampton, and in 1742, Viscount Petersham, Co. Surrey, and Earl of Harrington. He *d.* in 1756, and was succeeded by his eldest son, William, 2nd Earl; who was *b.* 18 Dec. 1719, and *d.* 1 April 1779; he was suc-

ceeded by his eldest son, CHARLES, 3rd EARL, who *d.* in 1829, leaving the issue described in *The Peerage Volume*, and was succeeded by his eldest son, CHARLES, present and 4th EARL.

HARRIS, BARON. (HARRIS.)

Peer of the United Kingdom.

His Lordship is grandson of the late Rev. George Harris, of Brasted, Co. Kent, who, by his marriage with Sarah, daughter of George Twentyman, Esq., who *d.* 1792, was father of the gallant General SIR GEORGE HARRIS, G.C.B., distinguished for his brilliant success in the conquest of the Mysore in 1799, when he commanded in chief. He was created in 1815, Baron Harris of Seringapatam and Mysore, in the East Indies, and of Belmont, Co. Kent; and *d.* in 1829, when his eldest son, WILLIAM-GEORGE, present and 2nd LORD, succeeded.

HARROWBY, EARL. (RYDER.)

Peer of the United Kingdom.

Richard Ryder, of the Cloisters, West Smithfield, mercer, was son of Dudley Ryder, of Bedworth, Co. Warwick, and father of Sir Dudley Ryder, who was appointed Lord Chief Justice of the Court of King's Bench in 1754; a warrant for his elevation to the Peerage was signed by the King, 24 May 1756, but he *d.* on the following day, before the completion of the patent. NATHANIEL, his only son, was created in 1776, BARON HARROWBY of Harrowby, Co. Lincoln; he *d.* in 1803, and was succeeded by his eldest son, DUDLEY, 2nd LORD, who was created in 1809, Viscount Sandon of Sandon, Co. Stafford, and EARL of HARROWBY, Co. Lincoln, and is the present Peer.

HARTLAND, BARON. (MAHON.)

Peer of Ireland.

This family claims its descent from the ancient Princes of Munster. Nicholas Mahon, Esq., distinguished for his loyalty in the civil wars, *d.* in 1680; he was great-grandfather of MAURICE MAHON, who was created in 1800, BARON HARTLAND of Stokestown, Co. Roscommon, and was succeeded in his title in 1819, by his son, THOMAS, present and 2nd LORD.

HASTINGS, MARQUIS OF. (RAWDON-HASTINGS.)

Peer of the United Kingdom and of Ireland.

Paulyn Rawdon had a grant from William the Conqueror of estates in Yorkshire, part of which are still in the Marquis's possession; his descendant George Rawdon, Esq., was created a Baronet of England in 1665, settled in Ireland, and was great-grandfather of

SIR JOHN RAWDON, 4th Baronet, who was created in 1750, Baron Rawdon of Moira, and in 1761, Earl of Moira, Co. Down, both in the Peerage of Ireland. His Lordship was *b.* in 1720, and *d.* 20 June 1793; having *m.* 1st, 10 Nov. 1741, Lady

Helena Perceval, 4th daughter of John, 1st Earl of Egmont, by whom, who *d.* 11 June 1746, he had two daughters, Ladies Catherine and Helena, for whom see *The Peerage Volume;* by his 2nd marriage, 23 Dec. 1746, with the Hon. Anne Hill, only daughter of Trevor, 1st Viscount Hillsborough, who *d.* 1 Aug. 1751, he had no issue; and he *m.* 3rdly, 26 Feb. 1752, LADY ELIZABETH HASTINGS, 16th BARONESS HUNGERFORD, &c., eldest daughter of Theophilus, 9th Earl of Huntingdon, and Baron Hungerford, &c., and sole heir of her brother FRANCIS, 10th Earl of Huntingdon, Baron Hungerford, &c., by whom, who *d.* 12 April 1808, he was father of FRANCIS, his successor, and the other issue stated in *The Peerage Volume.*

FRANCIS, 2nd Earl, was created Baron Rawdon, of Rawdon, Co. York, in the Peerage of England, in 1783; succeeded his father as Earl of Moira in 1793, and his mother as Baron Hungerford, &c. in 1808; was created in 1816, Viscount Loudoun, Earl of Rawdon, and MARQUIS of HASTINGS, and *d.* in 1826. He *m.* the Lady Flora-Mure Campbell, Countess Loudoun, (*see* that Title,) by whom, who survives him, he had issue, besides the daughters noticed in *The Peerage Volume*, Francis-George-Augustus, Lord Rawdon and Mauchlane, *b.* 22 Jan., *d.* 13 Feb. 1807; and an only surviving son, GEORGE-AUGUSTUS-FRANCIS, present and 2nd MARQUIS, who, by his recent marriage with the Lady Barbara Yelverton, Baroness Grey de Ruthyn, may probably, in the next generation, add another ancient Barony to those already merged under the coronet of Hastings.

William Baron BOTREAUX, summoned to Parliament by writ in 1368, *m.* Isabel, eldest of the two daughters and co-heirs of John, 3rd Baron MOELS; his Barony and the moiety of the Barony of Moels, was inherited by his great-grand-daughter Margaret, daughter and sole heir of William, 3rd Lord Botreaux; she *m.* Robert, 2nd Baron HUNGERFORD, (by writ 1426,) son and heir of Walter, 1st Lord Hungerford, by Catherine, co-heir of the other moiety of the Barony of Moels, being the daughter and sole heir of Sir Thomas Peverell, by Margaret, daughter and co-heir of Sir Thomas Courtenay, by Muriel, 2nd daughter and co-heir (with her sister Isabel mentioned above,) of John, 3rd Baron MOELS.

Robert, 2nd Baron Hungerford, had, by Margaret, Baroness Botreaux, his wife, a son and heir, Robert, 5th Baron Botreaux, and 3rd Baron Hungerford, who was also summoned to Parliament in 1445, as Baron MOLINES, in right of his wife Alianore, daughter and heir of William, Lord Molines. Thomas, their son, left an only daughter and heir, Mary, who *m.*

Edward, 2nd Lord HASTINGS, son and heir of William Lord Hastings, summoned to Parliament by writ in 1461. George, Baron Botreaux, Hungerford, Molines, and Hastings, their son and heir, was created Earl of Huntingdon in 1529. Francis, his son, 2nd Earl of Huntingdon, *m.* Katherine, eldest daughter and co-heir of Henry Pole, Lord MONTAGU; they had two sons, Henry, 3rd Earl, K.G., who *d.* without issue in 1595; and George, 4th Earl, who succeeded his brother, and was succeeded in 1604, by his grandson and heir, Henry, 5th Earl. He *m.* Elizabeth, 3rd daughter and co-heir of Ferdinando, 5th Earl of Derby and 6th Baron STANLEY, also 16th Baron Strange, being heir of George Stanley, son and heir apparent of Thomas, 1st Earl of Derby, and himself summoned to Parliament as Lord Strange, in right of his wife Joanna, daughter and sole heir of John, 11th Lord Strange of Knockyn, grandson and heir of John, 9th Lord Strange, by Maude, 3rd daughter and co-heir of John, 2nd Lord Mohun. Through the descendants of this 5th Earl and Elizabeth Stanley, the Baronies of Botreaux, Hungerford, Molines, and Hastings, continued merged in the Earldom of Huntingdon till the death of Francis, 10th Earl, in 1789, when they were inherited by Elizabeth, his sister and sole heir, grandmother, as before shown, of the present Marquis; who is also, by the intermarriages related above, co-heir of the Baronies by writ of Strange of Knockyn (1299), Stanley (1456), and Montagu (1533), heir of one moiety and co-heir of the other moiety of the Barony of Moels (by writ 1299), and co-heir of one moiety of the Barony of Mohun (by writ 1299).

His Lordship is also the eldest co-heir of George, Duke of Clarence, next brother of King Edward IV., and of the families of Neville, Earl of Warwick, and of Montagu, Earl of Salisbury, being heir general of Francis, 2nd Earl of Huntingdon, by his marriage with Katherine, eldest daughter and co-heir of Henry Pole Lord Montagu, son and heir of Sir Richard Pole, K.G., by Margaret Plantagenet, Countess of Salisbury, sister and heir of Edward, Earl of Warwick, and daughter of George, Duke of Clarence, by Isabel, daughter and at length sole heir of Richard Neville, Earl of Warwick, (in right of his wife Anne, heir of her brother Henry, Duke of Warwick, and co-heir of her mother Isabel, Baroness Despencer and Burghersh,) son of Richard Nevill, Earl of Salisbury, by Alice, daughter and sole heir of Thomas Montagu, Earl of Salisbury.

HAWARDEN, VISCOUNT. (MAUDE.)

Peer of Ireland.

Eustace de Montealto, the progenitor of this family, came into England from Italy at the period of the Conquest, and for his services, under the conduct of Hugh Lupus, Earl of Chester, had a grant of the castle and lordship of Hawarden, Co. of Flint. His descendant, Robert Maude, Esq., settled in Ireland, and *d.* there in 1685; he was grandfather of

Robert Maude, Esq., created a Baronet of Ireland in 1705, father of

1 Sir Thomas, who was created Baron de Montalt in 1776, and *d.* without issue in 1777, when the title became extinct.

2 SIR CORNWALLIS, who succeeded his brother in the Baronetcy, and was created Baron de Montalt in 1785, and VISCOUNT HAWARDEN of Hawarden, Co. Tipperary, in 1793. He *d.* in 1803, leaving by three marriages, besides one daughter by his 2nd marriage, and two daughters by his 3rd marriage, who *d.* young, the numerous issue described in *The Peerage Volume*; among whom are two sons, 1 THOMAS-RALPH, his successor, 2nd Viscount, who *d.* without issue in 1807; 2 CORNWALLIS, present and 3rd VISCOUNT, who succeeded his brother.

HAWKE, BARON. (HARVEY-HAWKE.)

Peer of Great Britain.

The gallant Admiral SIR EDWARD HAWKE, K.B., who was raised to the Peerage in reward of his naval services, was son of Edward Hawke, Esq., Barrister-at-Law, by Elizabeth, relict of Colonel Ruthven, and daughter of Nathaniel Bladen, Esq. His Lordship was *b.* 11 March 1716, created in 1776, Baron Hawke of Towton, Co. York, and *d.* 17 Oct, 1781; by his marriage with Catherine, daughter and heir of Walter Brooke, Esq., who *d.* 28 Oct. 1756, he was father of MARTIN BLADEN, 2nd LORD, his successor, who *d.* in 1805, and was succeeded by his eldest son EDWARD, 3rd LORD, who, in consequence of his marriage with the daughter and heir of Stanhope Harvey, Esq., assumed the name of Harvey; he *d.* in 1824, and was succeeded by his eldest son, EDWARD-WILLIAM, present and 4th LORD.

HEADFORT, MARQUIS OF. (TAYLOR.)

Peer of Ireland and of the United Kingdom.

This family descends from Thomas Taylor, Esq., who was of Battle in Sussex, and whose grandson, Thomas Taylor, removed to Ireland in 1660. He was father of Sir Thomas Taylor, created a Baronet of Ireland in 1704, and whose grandson, Sir Thomas, 3rd Baronet, was created Baron of Headfort in 1760, Viscount Headfort in 1762, and Earl of Bective of Bective Castle, in 1766. He *d.* in 1795, and was succeeded by his eldest son, Thomas, who was created in 1800, Marquis of Headfort, and *d.* in 1829, when Thomas, his eldest son, present and 2nd Marquis, succeeded. He was created in 1831, Baron Kenlis of Kenlis, or Kells, Co. Meath, in the Peerage of the United Kingdom.

HEADLEY, BARON. (Allanson-Winn.)

Peer of Ireland.

This family derives its descent from George Wynne of London, Draper to Queen Elizabeth, who obtained a patent of arms in 1604. George Winn, Esq., his grandson, who was High Sheriff of Lincoln in 1657, and a zealous adherent to the Royal cause, was created a Baronet in 1660; he left, besides other issue, Edmund, his successor, from whom the present Sir Edmund-Mark Winn, of Nostell, Co. York, Bart., is 4th in descent, and

George, 2nd son, grandfather of Sir George Winn, Baron of the Exchequer in Scotland, who assumed the additional name of Allanson in 1775, on succeeding to the estates of his maternal cousin, Charles Allanson, Esq.; was created a Baronet of England in 1776, and Lord Headley, Baron Allanson and Winn of Aghadoe, Co. Kerry, in 1797. He *d.* in 1798, and was succeeded by his eldest son, Charles, present and 2nd Lord.

HENLEY, BARON. (Eden.)

Peer of Ireland.

Sir Morton Eden, K.B., who, after a long course of diplomatic services at most of the German Courts, including those of Berlin and Vienna, and afterwards at the Court of Madrid, was, in 1799, created Baron Henley of Chardstock, was the 5th son of Sir Robert Eden, Bart., who *d.* 25 June 1755, and brother of William, 1st Lord Auckland. He *d.* in 1830, and was succeeded by his eldest surviving son, Robert-Henley, present and 2nd Lord.

HENNIKER, BARON. (Henniker-Major.)

Peer of Ireland.

John Henniker, Esq,, (son of John Henniker, an eminent merchant,) *m.* Anne, daughter and co-heir of John Major, Esq., of Worlingworth Hall, Co. Suffolk, who was created a Baronet in 1765, with remainder to his said son-in-law. He succeeded to the Baronetcy in 1781 was created in 1800, Baron Henniker, of Stratford upon Slaney, Co. Wicklow, and *d.* 18 April 1803; having had, besides other issue,

1 John, 2nd Lord, his successor, *b.* 19 April 1752, *m.* 27 April 1791, Emily, daughter of Robert Jones, Esq., who *d.* 18 Dec. 1819. His Lordship *d.* without issue 5 Dec. 1821, and was succeeded by his nephew the present Peer.

2 Major, who *d.* in 1789, leaving issue, John-Minet, the present and 3rd Lord, who succeeded his uncle, and has assumed the additional surname of Major, and others described in *The Peerage Volume.*

3 The Hon. Sir Brydges Trecothick Henniker, created a Baronet in 1813, and *d.* in 1816; for his widow and surviving issue, see *The Peerage Volume.*

HEREFORD, VISCOUNT. (Devereux.)

Peer of England.

This ancient and noble family derive their surname from Evereux, a town in Normandy; the first of them who settled in England was Robert, youngest son of Walter, Earl of Rosmar, who assisted at the battle of Hastings.

Sir Walter Devereux, K.G., 12th in descent from the above Robert, having *m.* Ann, daughter and sole heir of Edmund, 5th Baron Ferrers of Chartley, was summoned to Parliament in her right as Baron Ferrers of Chartley, and *d.* in 1485. Their son John, 7th Baron, *m.* Cecily, sister and at length heir of Henry Bourchier, Earl of Essex, and Baron Bourchier, great-grand-daughter of William Bourchier, Earl of Ewe, by his marriage with Anne Plantagenet, widow of Edmund, 5th Earl of Stafford, and daughter and heir of Thomas (son of King Edward III.) Duke of Gloucester and Earl of Buckingham, by Eleanor, daughter and heir of Humphrey de Bohun, Earl of Hereford, Essex, and Northampton.

Walter, K.G., son of John, 7th Baron Ferrers of Chartley, and Cecily Bourchier, became in right of his mother 8th Baron Bourchier, and was created Viscount of the County of Hereford in 1550; he had, besides other issue, two sons: 1 Sir Richard Devereux, who *d.* before his father, leaving a son Walter, 2nd Viscount; 2 Sir Edward Devereux, of Castle-Bromwich, Bart., ancestor of the present Viscount.

Walter, 2nd Viscount, K.G., was created Earl of Essex in 1572, and *d.* in 1576, in Ireland, whither he had been sent with the title of Earl Marshal, to repress the Irish rebels, but in fact because the Earl of Leicester was jealous of the favour Queen Elizabeth expressed towards him. He was succeeded by his eldest son, Robert, 3rd Viscount, 2nd Earl of Essex, K.G., the celebrated favourite of Queen Elizabeth. Brave and acomplished, but vehement and imprudent, the short and brilliant career of this distinguished nobleman, with its early catastrophe, is too well known to need relating here. He was attainted and beheaded 25 Feb. 1601, in the 34th year of his age, in consequence of his rash attempt to excite the citizens of London to rebellion; and to the inconsolable affliction of the Queen, who but a short time survived the fatal event. His only son Robert, 4th Viscount, and 3rd Earl of Essex, was restored in blood and honours in 1603. His unfortunate marriage at the age of fourteen, with Lady Frances Howard, eldest daughter of Thomas, 1st Earl of Suffolk, who, after a series of disgraceful intrigues, was divorced from him, and *m.* Robert Kerr, Earl of Somerset, the unworthy favourite of King James I., (*See* title Lothian,) led to his secession from Court, and, except two campaigns in the Palatinate, where he commanded a regiment raised by himself, he lived in retirement till the breaking out of the great Civil War. He then accepted the command of the Parliamentary army, and lived only long enough to see and heartily to desire the remedy of evils he had assisted to produce; the republicans, to whom noble birth and aristocratical privileges were highly unacceptable, made ungrateful returns to the services of the Earl of Essex, and he resigned his command, in consequence of the self-denying ordinance in April 1645. He *d.* in 1646, when the Earldom of Essex became extinct; the Baronies of Ferrers of Chartley, and Bourchier fell into abeyance between his two sisters, Lady Frances, wife of William Seymour, Duke of Somerset, whose heir general is the present Duchess of Buckingham and Chandos; and Lady Dorothy, wife of Sir Henry Shirley, Bart., and mother of Sir Robert Shirley, in whose favour the abeyance of the Barony of Ferrers was terminated in 1677; her heir-general is the present Marquis Townshend, co-heir with the Duchess of Buckingham of the Barony of Bourchier. The title of Viscount Hereford devolved on the heir male, Sir Walter Devereux, son and heir of Sir Edward Devereux, younger son of the 1st Viscount.

This Sir Edward Devereux of Castle Bromwich, was created a Baronet in 1612, and *d.* in 1622, leaving, besides other issue, the two sons following;

1 Sir Walter, who succeeded as 5th Viscount Hereford; and was succeeded by his son Leicester, 6th Viscount, who *d.* in 1676, leaving two sons: Leicester, 7th Viscount, the eldest, *d.* at nine years of age, in 1683, and was succeeded by his brother, Edward, 8th Viscount, on whose death in 1700, without issue, the male posterity of the 5th Viscount became extinct.

2 Sir George Devereux, whose eldest son, George Devereux, Esq., of Sheldon Hall, Co. Warwick, had seven sons, the two eldest of whom were,

1 Price, who *d.* in 1666, before his father, leaving a son Price, who succeeded in 1700, as 9th Viscount Hereford, he *d.* in 1740, and was succeeded by his only son, Price, 10th Viscount, the last male descendant of his grandfather; he *d.* in 1748.

2 Vaughan Devereux, Esq. of Nantaribba, Co. Montgomery; he *d.* in 1700, leaving a son Arthur, father of

Edward 11th Viscount; he *d.* in 1760, leaving two sons, Edward, his successor, 12th Viscount, who *d.* without issue in 1783; and George, 13th Viscount, who succeeded his brother, and was succeeded in 1804 by his only son, Henry, present and 14th Viscount.

HERTFORD, MARQUIS OF. (Seymour-Conway.)

Peer of Great Britain.

The Marquis is a collateral branch of the family of the Duke of Somerset. Francis, 1st Lord Conway, his immediate ancestor, was 4th son of Sir Edward Seymour, Bart., whose eldest son, by a former marriage, Sir Edward, was father of Edward, 9th Duke of Somerset.

Sir Edward Seymour, the father, took for his second wife, Letitia, daughter of Francis Popham of Littlecote, Co. Wilts, Esq.; whose aunt, Frances Popham, was wife of Edward, 2nd Viscount Conway, and mother of Edward, 3rd Viscount, created in 1679, Earl Conway; whose titles of Earl Conway, Viscount Conway of Conway Castle, Co. Carnarvon, (1627,) Baron Conway of Ragland, Co. Warwick, (1625) in the Peerage of England, and Viscount Killultagh, Co. Antrim, in the Peerage of Ireland, (1626,) became extinct by his death without issue in 1683; he devised his estates to the sons in succession of the said Sir Edward Seymour, Bart., of Bury Pomperoy, Co. Devon, by Letitia Popham, his wife, cousin of the Earl, on express condition of their assuming the name of Conway. He was accordingly succeeded by Popham Seymour, Esq., afterwards Conway, the eldest son of this marriage, who *d.* of a wound received in a duel in the 24th year of his age, 1699; and was succeeded by

Francis, his next brother, who also assumed the name of Conway; he was created Baron Conway of Ragland, Co. Warwick, in March 1703, and in June the same year, Baron Conway of Killultagh, Co. Antrim, in the Peerage of Ireland; he *d.* in 1732, leaving two sons, Francis, 2nd Lord, and the Right Hon. Henry Seymour-Conway, who having served in the army with reputation through the several gradations of military rank, and commanded the British forces in Germany in 1761, during the absence of the Marquis of Granby, rose at length to the station of Field-Marshal, and *d.* in 1795, aged 75.

Francis, 2nd Lord, K.G., eldest son and successor, was created in 1750, Viscount Beauchamp and Earl of Hertford; and in 1793 Marquis of Hertford, and Earl of Yarmouth, Co. Norfolk; he *d.* 14 June 1794, having *m.* 29 May 1741, Lady Arabella Fitz-Roy, 4th daughter of Charles, 2nd Duke of Grafton, who was *b.* 19 July 1726, and *d.* 10 Nov. 1782; they had seven sons, of whom two only *d. unm.*, Lord Henry in 1830, and the Hon. and Rev. Edward Seymour-Conway, in 1785, in his 29th year; the other five sons having all had issue, will be found in *The Peerage Volume;* his Lordship had also six daughters, viz:

1 Lady Anne *b.* 1 Aug. 1744, *d.* 4 Nov. 1784; having *m.* 15 Feb. 1766, Charles, 1st Marquis of Drogheda.

2 Lady Sarah-Frances, *b.* 27 Sept. 1747, *d.* 18 July 1770; having *m.* 3 June, 1766, Robert Stewart, Esq., afterwards 1st Marquis of Londonderry.

3 Lady Gertrude, *b.* 9 Oct. 1750, *d.* Sept. 1793; having *m.* 10 Feb. 1772, George Mason-Villiers, 2nd Earl Grandison of Ireland, who *d.* July 1800, when the title became extinct.

4 Lady Frances, *b.* 4 Dec. 1751, *d.* 11 Nov. 1820, having *m.* 22 May 1775, Henry, Earl of Lincoln, eldest son of Henry, 2nd Duke of Newcastle.

5 Lady Elizabeth, *b.* 3 March 1754, *d. unm.* 21 March 1825.

6 Lady Isabella-Rachel, *b.* 25 Dec. 1755, *d.* 16 May 1825; having *m.* 9 Oct. 1785, George Hatton, Esq.

Francis, 2nd Marquis, K.G., succeeded his father, and *d.* in 1822, when he was succeeded by his only son, Francis-Charles, present and 3rd Marquis. K.G.

HEYTESBURY, BARON. (A'Court.)

Peer of the United Kingdom.

This family is of Norman origin. Sir Francis de Court, or A'Court, Lord of the Manors of Tuderly and Lockerly, Co. Southampton, and possessor of lands in France and Lombardy, was employed by King Henry IV., in many foreign embassies. From him descended, in the male line, Pierce A'Court, of Ivy Court, Co. Wilts, Esq., who *m.* Elizabeth, daughter, and at length heir of William Ashe, Esq., of Heytesbury, Co. Wilts. William-Ashe A'Court, Esq., their son, *d.* 2 Aug. 1781; having *m.* Annabella, daughter and co-heir of Thomas Vernon, Esq., of Twickenham Park, by whom he had an only son, Sir William-Pierce-Ashe A'Court, created a Baronet in 1795; he *d.* in 1817, leaving issue,

1 Sir William A'Court, Bart., his successor, created in 1828, Baron Heytesbury of Heytesbury, Co. Wilts, the present Lord; who has been long employed in distinguished diplomatic missions.

2 Letitia, *d.* 20 Jan. 1810; having *m.* the Hon. William Eliot, now Earl of St. Germans.

3 Annabella, *m.* 15 May 1805, Richard Beadon, Esq., son of the late Bishop of Bath and Wells.

4 Maria, *m.* 7 Nov. 1811, the Hon. Philip-Pleydell Bouverie. See *The Peerage Volume*, title Radnor.

5 Caroline, (twin with Maria,) *m.* 28 Nov. 1817, Stewart Crawford, Esq., M.D.

6 Captain Edward-Henry A'Court, R.N., M.P.

7 Lieutenant-Colonel Charles-Ashe A'Court, *m.* 10 May 1815, Mary, only daughter of Abraham Gibbs, Esq., and has issue.

HILL, BARON. (Hill.)

Peer of the United Kingdom.

This is an ancient and distinguished family in the county of Salop, of which Hugh Hill or Hull, of Hull and Wlonkeslowe, lived in the reign of King Edward II.

Rowland Hill of Hawkestone, 11th in descent from him, was created a Baronet in 1727, with several remainders, and was father of Sir Richard, the 2nd Baronet, and of Sir John, 3rd Baronet, father of the present distinguished nobleman, who, in consideration of his important military services was created Baron Hill, of Almarez and of

Hawkestone, Co. Salop, in 1814; and again, in 1815, was created Baron Hill of Almarez, and of Hawkestone and Hardwicke, Co. Salop, with remainder, failing his issue male, to the issue male of his late brother John Hill, of Hawkestone, Esq., deceased.

HOLLAND, BARON. (Vassall.)

Peer of Great Britain.

Henry, 1st Lord, was younger brother of Stephen, 1st Earl of Ilchester, and his heirs male are in remainder to that title. Profuse and dissipated in his youth, after squandering his patrimony, and spending some years abroad to extricate himself from his embarrassments, Mr. Fox returned to his native country, took his seat in Parliament, and soon displayed his oratorical abilities as the political opponent of William Pitt, the celebrated Earl of Chatham. Sometimes in office, but more frequently in opposition, Mr. Fox, however, laid the foundation of wealth and greatness for his family; he *m.* 2 May 1744, Lady Georgiana-Caroline Lennox, eldest daughter of Charles, 2nd Duke of Richmond, who was *b.* 27 March 1723, created in 1762, Baroness Holland of Holland, Co. Lincoln, and *d.* 24 July 1774. Mr. Fox was himself created in 1763, Baron Holland of Foxley, Co. Wilts, and *d.* 1 July 1774, leaving three sons, viz.:

1 Stephen 2nd Lord, his successor, who, on his death, 26 Dec. 1774, was succeeded by his only son, Henry-Richard, the present and 3rd Earl, who has assumed the name of Vassall only.

2 The late Right Hon. Charles-James Fox, so greatly distinguished for his eloquence and his powerful opposition to the Administration of Mr. Pitt, his hereditary rival. He held office for a short time between the years 1770 and 1774, and again as Secretary of State under Lord Rockingham, in 1782, and in the coalition Administration with Lord North, in 1783; but the star of Pitt now rose upon the horizon, and Fox continued in opposition till it had sunk for ever; he then for a few months held the reins of Government in conjunction with Lord Grenville, till his death, 13 Sept. 1806. His widow survives him without issue. See *The Peerage Volume.*

3 The Hon. General Henry-Edward Fox, *b.* 4 March 1755, *d.* 18 July 1811; having *m.* 14 Nov. 1786, Marianne, 2nd daughter of William Clayton, Esq., by whom who was *b.* 5 Nov. 1763, and *d.* 15 Oct. 1808, he left the issue noticed in *The Peerage Volume.*

HOME, EARL. (Home.)

Peer of Scotland.

Elgiva, daughter of King Ethelred, *m.* Uthred, Earl of Northumberland; their daughter and heir, Algatha, *m.* Maldred, whose son by her, Cospatrick, Earl of Northumberland, retired, on the Norman conquest, into Scotland. He left three sons; of whom, Dolphin, the eldest, Lord of Raby, in England, was ancestor of the Nevills, extinct Earls of Westmoreland, &c., and now Earls of Abergavenny; and Cospatrick, the youngest, who with his descendants are styled Earls, was great-grandfather of Waldave, Earl of Dunbar, which title was borne by his male heirs till it was forfeited in 1435, by George, 11th Earl, whose male descendants became extinct in the reign of Queen Mary.

Patrick, 2nd son of the 3rd Earl Cospatrick, and brother of Waldave, 1st Earl of Dunbar, was father of William, who by Ada, his wife, daughter of Patrick, Earl of Dunbar, became possessed of the lands of Home, from which his descendants took their name. 5th in descent from them, was Sir Thomas Home of Home, whose eldest son, Sir Alexander, carried on the elder line of the family; and his second son, Sir David Home, of Wedderburn, was father of, 1 George, whose son Sir David, was ancestor, by his eldest son David, of Sir David Home, of Wedderburn and Polwarth, Bart.; and by his second son, Alexander, was great-grandfather of George Home, created in 1604, Baron Home and Berwick, and in 1605, Earl of Dunbar, with remainder to his heirs male; he *d.* without issue male, in 1611, and the title has not since been successfully claimed; and 2 Sir Patrick Home, ancestor in the 6th degree of Patrick Home, created Lord Polwarth in 1690, and in 1697 Earl of Marchmont, with remainder to his heirs male; these titles have been dormant since the death, in 1794, of his Lordship's grandson, Hugh, 3rd Earl of Marchmont, no heir having yet been able to substantiate his claim.

Sir Alexander, eldest son of Sir Thomas Home, was grandfather of Sir Alexander, created Lord Home, in 1473, and *d.* about 1490; Alexander, Master of Home, his eldest son, *d.* before him, leaving two sons, 1 Alexander, 2nd Lord, and John Home, of Whiteriggs, ancestor, in the 6th degree of direct paternal descent, of James, 3rd Earl.

Alexander, 2nd Lord, eldest son of the Master of Home, succeeded his grandfather; he was a nobleman of considerable political importance, and had the chief guidance of affairs in the reign of James IV., whose constant favour he enjoyed; amongst his memorable actions, a pilgrimage to Canterbury is recorded; he *d.* in 1506. His two eldest sons were: 1 Alexander, 3rd Lord, who, with the Earl of Huntley, led the van of the Scottish army at Flodden, dispersed the English force opposed to him, and was one of the few Scottish nobles who escaped the carnage of that disastrous day; he afterwards joined the party of the Queen-mother and her husband, Angus, and embraced the English interest in opposition to the Regent Albany; he made his peace, however, in March 1516, and venturing to Court in the following September, upon the strength of a treaty with the Regent, was arrested, tried, and executed for high treason, 8 Oct. 1516, leaving no male issue; 2 George, 4th Lord, succeeded his brother, and obtained a restoration of his honours and estates; he *d.* 22 Sept. 1547, of a wound received in a skirmish with the English, the day preceding the battle of Pinkie, and was succeeded by his eldest son, Alexander, 5th Lord, who was taken prisoner in the same skirmish in which his father received his mortal wound. His Lordship, after his liberation, became a warm supporter of the Reformation, and of young James, on his first elevation to the throne, in opposition to his mother; he led six hundred followers, on behalf of the King, to the battle of Langside, and is said to have decided the fortune of the day by the superiority of his border spearmen over the less practised warriors to whom they were opposed; he was wounded in the face and leg in the conflict. His Lordship afterwards withdrew his support from the Regent Moray, and held out the castle of Edinburgh for the Queen against the King's arms; but was compelled to surrender in May 1573, and was convicted of treason in Parliament, in October following, but it appears was not executed, for he *d.* 11 Aug. 1575. He was succeeded by his only son, Alexander, 6th Lord, who was created in 1605, Earl of Home, with remainder to his heirs male whatever; his issue male failed in 1633, on the death of James, 2nd Earl, his son, when the titles devolved on

James, 3rd Earl, descended from the above John Home, of Whiteriggs. He joined the association in favour of King Charles I. in 1641, and the engagement to attempt that Monarch's rescue in 1648; on the latter occasion he had the command of the Berwickshire regiment of foot. He *d.* in 1666, leaving three sons, successive Earls, viz.: Alexander, 4th Earl, who *d.* in 1674; James, 5th Earl, who *d.* in 1687, both without issue; and Charles, 6th Earl, who *d.* in 1706, leaving three sons, viz.:

1 Alexander, 7th Earl, his successor.

2 The Hon. James Home, of Ayton, who forfeited his estate for engaging in the rebellion of 1715; he *d.* 6 Dec. 1764, having *m.* Janet, daughter of Zerubabel Haig,

Esq., by whom who *d.* 21 Oct, 1777, he was father of Marion, the 2nd wife of ALEXANDER, 9th EARL of HOME, and of Mrs. Hunter.—See *The Peerage Volume.*

3 The Hon. George, who *d.* 20 Sept. 1777, and his widow in Oct. 1795; leaving two daughters, the eldest of whom survives, and Betty, the younger, *d.* 14 Jan. 1819, having *m.* James Murray, Esq.

ALEXANDER, 7th EARL, was committed prisoner to the Castle of Edinburgh, on suspicion, on the breaking out of the rebellion in 1715, in which his brother was involved, and was released only on the expiration of the Act for suspending the Habeas Corpus Act; he *d.* in 1720. Of his six sons, two only, successive Earls of Home, survived the age of infancy; he was succeeded by his eldest surviving son, WILLIAM, 8th EARL, who was efficiently active in the service of the government during the rebellion of 1745; he *d.* without issue in 1761, and was succeeded by his brother, ALEXANDER, 9th EARL, a Clergyman of the Church of England, who was succeeded in 1786, by his only surviving son, ALEXANDER, present and 10th EARL.

HOOD, VISCOUNT. (HOOD.)

Peer of Great Britain and of Ireland.

This family of naval heroes, so conspicuous in the annals of King George III., descends from a respectable ancestry in the county of Dorset, where the Hoods possessed a considerable landed property at the period of the civil wars. Alexander Hood, of Mosterton, Co. Dorset, *m.* Elizabeth, daughter of the Rev. Mr. Beach, and, besides a son, Arthur, in holy orders, who *d. unm.*, had the two sons following:

1 Alexander, who by his wife, Anne Way, was father of Samuel Hood, Esq., of Kingsbury Co. Dorset; he *m.* Anne, daughter of James Bern, Esq., of Westbury, Co. Wilts, by whom he had three sons, viz.:

- 1 Arthur, Lieutenant of the Pomona, lost in a hurricane in the East Indies.
- 2 Captain Alexander Hood, R.N., killed in action on board the Mars, 21 April 1796, leaving issue the present Sir Alexander Hood, Bart.
- 3 The late distinguished Vice-Admiral Sir Samuel Hood, Bart., who *d.* without issue in 1814.

2 The Rev. Samuel Hood, Vicar of Thorncombe, Co. Devon, who, by Mary, daughter of Richard Hoskins, Esq., was father of two sons, who both attained the honours of the Peerage, for a long series of the most brilliant and successful naval services:

- 1 Admiral Sir Samuel Hood, K.B., created in 1782, BARON HOOD of Catherington, in the Peerage of Ireland; Susannah, his wife, daughter of Edward Lindzee, Esq., was created Baroness Hood of Catherington, Co. Hants, in the Peerage of Great Britain, in 1795, and *d.* in 1806, when she was succeeded by her eldest son, the present Viscount. His Lordship also was advanced to the British Peerage in 1796, by the title of VISCOUNT HOOD of Whitley, Co. Warwick, and *d.* in 1816, when he was succeeded by his only surviving son, HENRY, who in 1806 had succeeded his mother as 2nd Baron Hood, of Catherington, and is the present and 2nd VISCOUNT. His numerous issue are described in *The Peerage Volume*, of whom Samuel, his second son, succeeded, in 1814, his great uncle, Alexander, Viscount Bridport, as 2nd Baron Bridport, in the Peerage of Ireland.—*See* that title.
- 2 Admiral Sir Alexander Hood, K.B., created Baron Bridport in the Peerage of Ireland in 1794, with remainder to his great nephew, Samuel Hood, above mentioned, and his issue male, and other remainders; he was also created Baron Bridport in the Peerage of Great Britain, in 1796, and Viscount Bridport in 1801, which latter titles became extinct on his death in 1814.

HOPETOUN, EARL OF. (Hope.)

Peer of Scotland and of the United Kingdom.

John de Hope is said to have come into Scotland from France, in the retinue of Magdalen, Queen of James V.; he was grandfather of Henry, a considerable merchant, whose eldest son, Thomas, continued the line in Scotland, and his younger son, Henry, was ancestor of the opulent family of Hope of Amsterdam, of which descends Henry-Thomas Hope, Esq., M.P., of Deepdene, Co. Surrey.

Thomas, the eldest son, was bred to the bar, and living to see two of his sons, Sir John Hope of Craighall, and Sir Thomas Hope of Krese, on the Bench, while he was himself still an Advocate, he had the privilege granted him by the Court of Session, of wearing his hat while pleading, it being judged unbecoming that a father should appear uncovered before his children. He was created a Baronet in 1628, and *d.* in 1646. Sir John, his eldest son, was ancestor of Sir John Hope of Craighall, the present Baronet, and undoubted chief of this family.

Sir James Hope, of Hopetoun, the 6th son, was also a Lord of Session, and was grandfather of Charles, created, in 1703, Earl of Hopetoun, Viscount Aithrie, and Lord Hope, by Patent, with remainder to the heirs male of his body, failing which, to the heirs female of his body; he *m.* Lady Henrietta Johnstone, only daughter of William, 1st Marquis of Annandale, whose male line became extinct in 1793; and his titles are claimed by John-James Johnstone-Hope, Esq., eldest son of Sir William and Lady Anne Johnstone-Hope, heir of line of this marriage. They had, besides other issue, the two sons following:

1 John, 2nd Earl.

2 The Hon. Charles Hope-Weir, *b.* 8 May 1710, *d.* 30 Dec. 1791; he *m.* 1st, 26 July 1733, Catherine, only daughter and heir of Sir William Weir, Bart., who was *b.* 1 Dec. 1716, and *d.* 5 Dec. 1743; he *m.* 2ndly, 20 March 1746, Lady Anne Vane, eldest daughter of Henry, 1st Earl of Darlington; this marriage was dissolved in 1757, and she re-married the Hon. Gen. George Monson, 3rd son of 1st Lord Monson, and *d.* 14 Sept. 1776; he *m.* 3rdly, 2 April 1766, Helen, daughter of George Dunbar, Esq., who *d.* 18 Sept. 1794. He had issue by each marriage, and his numerous descendants are described in *The Peerage Volume.* His sons, besides two named Charles, who *d.* infants, were,

1 William, *b.* 17 May 1736, *d.* 8 Sept. 1811; having *m.* 5 Jan. 1775, Sophia, daughter of Joseph Corrie, Esq., by whom, who survived him, he had four elder children, who have *d. unm.*, besides the four stated in *The Peerage Volume.*

2 John *b.* 7 April 1739, *d.* 21 May 1785; having *m.* 2 June 1762, Mary, only daughter of Eliab Breton, Esq., by whom, who was *b.* 1742, and *d.* 25 June 1767, he left three sons: 1 Charles, Lord President of the Court of Session; 2 Lieut.-General Sir John Hope, G.C.H.; and 3 the late Vice-Admiral Sir William Johnstone-Hope, G.C.B., both highly distinguished in the military or naval service.

3 Brig.-General Henry, *b.* 1746, *d.* without issue, 13 April 1789, having *m.* Sarah, daughter of the Rev. —— Jones; she *d.* April 1792.

4 Capt. Charles Hope, R.N. *d.* 10 Sept. 1808; having *m.* Susan-Anne, daughter of Admiral Herbert Sawyer, who *d.* 10 July 1802, leaving, besides the issue described in *The Peerage Volume*, a second daughter, Anne, who was *b.* 1790, and *d.* 4 Oct. 1825; having *m.* 18 Feb. 1820, Captain Charles-Sibthorpe-John Hawtayne, R.N.

5 Rear-Admiral Sir George Johnstone-Hope, K.C.B., who *d.* in 1818; his marriages and issue are described in *The Peerage Volume.*

The 2nd Earl *d.* in 1781, leaving a numerous issue, see *The Peerage Volume*, of whom JAMES, his eldest surviving son; 3rd EARL, succeeded him. He was created in 1809, Baron Hopetoun of Hopetoun, Co. Linlithgow, in the Peerage of the United Kingdom, with remainder, failing his issue male, to the issue male of John, 2nd Earl of Hopetoun, his father; whose second son, the Hon. SIR JOHN HOPE, G.C.B., was created in 1814, for his eminent military services, particularly in the Peninsular War, BARON NIDDRY of Niddry, Co. Linlithgow, in the Peerage of the United Kingdom; and on the death of the 3rd Earl, his half-brother, 29 May 1816, succeeded as 4th Earl of Hopetoun, in Scotland, and as BARON HOPETOUN in the Peerage of the United Kingdom; he *d.* 27 Aug. 1823, and was succeeded by his eldest son JOHN, present and 5th EARL.

HOTHAM, BARON. (HOTHAM.)

Peer of Ireland.

Sir John de Trehouse, ancestor of this ancient family, obtained from William the Conqueror the Manor of Hotham in Yorkshire, from which his descendants afterwards sook their surname. The 20th in lineal descent from him was Sir John Hotham, created a Baronet in 1621; he, and his eldest son Sir John Hotham, Knt., were beheaded by the republican party for their adherence to the royal cause in 1643.

Sir Beaumont Hotham, Bart., grandson of Charles, 2nd son of the 1st Bart., had five sons; viz.,

1 Sir Charles Hotham, Bart., who *d.* in 1794, without male issue; Henrietta-Gertrude, his only daughter, *d.* 1816.

2 The Rt. Rev. Sir John Hotham, Bart., Bishop of Clogher, who succeeded his brother; he was *b.* 16 March 1734, and *d.* 3 Nov. 1795; having *m.* 11 April 1765, Susan, daughter of Sir Herbert Mackworth, Bart., by whom he left the issue noticed in *The Peerage Volume.*

3 Admiral WILLIAM HOTHAM, who was *b.* 8 April, 1736, and, for his important naval services created in 1797, BARON HOTHAM, of South Dalton, with remainder, failing his issue male, to the issue male of his father, Sir Beaumont Hotham, Bart. His Lordship *d. unm.* 2 May 1813.

4 BEAUMONT, 2nd LORD, *b.* 16 Aug. 1737, succeeded his brother, and *d.* 4 March 1814; having *m.* 6 June 1767, Susannah, 2nd daughter of Sir Thomas Hankey, Knt., and widow of James Norman, Esq., by whom, who *d.* 15 Nov. 1811, he had, besides the issue described in *The Peerage Volume* as the uncles and aunts of the present Peer, an elder son, Beaumont, who *d.* before him, and was father of Beaumont, the present Lord, and his brother Capt. George-Frederick Hotham, R.N. His Lordship was succeeded by his grandson BEAUMONT, the present and 3rd LORD.

5 General George Hotham, *b.* 18 Jan. 1741, *d.* 7 Jan. 1806; having *m.* Diana, 9th daughter of Sir Warton Pennyman, Bart., by whom, who *d.* 17 July 1817, he had, besides Diana, late Lady Edward O'Brien, who *d.* in 1810—see *The Peerage Volume,* title Thomond—and Harriet, who *d.* in 1828, wife of Sir Giffin Wilson, his two youngest daughters, the issue described in *The Peerage Volume.*

HOWARD OF EFFINGHAM, BARON. (HOWARD.)

Peer of England.

LORD WILLIAM HOWARD, K.G., 9th son of Thomas, 2nd Duke of Norfolk, was created in 1554 BARON HOWARD of EFFINGHAM, Co. Surrey. He was much favoured by King HENRY VIII., till his niece, Catherine Howard, that Monarch's fifth Queen, was executed for treason, when the Lord William, and many other of her relatives, were tried and convicted of misprision of treason, and condemned to forfeiture and perpetual imprisonment, but he was soon after pardoned. He held offices of high trust and honour throughout the reigns of EDWARD VI. and Queen MARY, and also in the reign of ELIZABETH, to the close of his life in 1573. He left, besides other issue, two sons, CHARLES, 2nd LORD, his successor, and Sir William Howard, ancestor of the present Lord.

CHARLES, 2nd LORD, K.G., was Lord High Admiral of England, and Commander of that fleet which defeated and destroyed the armada sent by Spain for the invasion of England in 1588; for this great achievement he was created Earl of Nottingham in 1596. He lived to a great age in the utmost splendour and magnificence, keeping seven houses, all in the state becoming his high rank, his expenses being provided by the profits, very considerable at that period, of his office of Admiral. He served the state in many other important situations, and enjoyed, in a high degree, the favour of Queen ELIZABETH; this he probably in some measure owed to the dignity of his person, which was remarkable. He *d.* in 1624, having had three sons who lived to maturity; viz., 1 William, summoned to Parliament in the lifetime of his father, but *d.* before him in 1615, without issue male; having *m.* Anne, only daughter and heir of John, Lord St. John of Bletsho, heiress of the Barony of Beauchamp of Blethsho by writ, which their only daughter, Elizabeth, carried by marriage to the Earls of Peterborough; 2 CHARLES, 3rd LORD, 2nd Earl of Nottingham, who succeeded his father, and *d.* without issue in 1642; 3 CHARLES, 4th LORD and 3rd Earl of Nottingham, who succeeded his brother and *d.* also without issue in 1681, when the Earldom of Nottingham, and the male line of Charles, 2nd Lord Howard of Effingham, became extinct.

This Barony devolved on the heir male of Sir William Howard, 2nd son of the 1st Lord; his grandson, Charles, was father of FRANCIS, 5th LORD Howard of Effingham, who succeeded the Earl of Nottingham in the Barony; and of George Howard, whose son, Lieut.-General Thomas Howard, was father of

1 Sir George Howard, K.B.; he *d.* 16 July 1796; having *m.* 1st, in 1747, Lady Anne Wentworth, 2nd daughter of Thomas, 1st Earl, and sister and co-heir of William, 2nd Earl of Strafford, by whom, who *d* 27 April 1771, he had an only surviving daughter, Anne, who *d.* 2 Aug. 1784; she *m.* 20 April 1780, General Richard Vyse, who *d.* 30 May 1825; Sir George *m.* 2ndly, 21 May 1776, Elizabeth, daughter of Peter Beckford, Esq., and widow of THOMAS, 8th LORD, and 2nd Earl of Effingham, who *d.* without issue by him 12 Oct. 1791.

2 Henry Howard, Esq., of Arundel, for whom see *The Peerage Volume*; he was father of KENNETH-ALEXANDER, the present and 11th LORD.

FRANCIS, 5th LORD, who succeeded on the death of CHARLES, 3rd Earl of Nottingham, *d.* in 1695, leaving two surviving sons; 1 THOMAS, 6th LORD, his successor, who *d. unm.* in 1725; 2 FRANCIS, 7th LORD, who succeeded his brother, and was created in 1731, Earl of Effingham, Co. Surrey; he *d.* in 1743, and was succeeded by his eldest son,

THOMAS, 8th LORD, and 2nd Earl of Effingham; he *d.* 19 Nov. 1763; having *m.* 14 Feb. 1745, Elizabeth, daughter of Peter Beckford, Esq.; she *d.* 12 Oct. 1791, having *m.* 2ndly, in 1776, Sir George Howard K.B. *See above.* The Earl had issue by her,

1 THOMAS, 9th LORD and 3rd Earl, *b.* 13 Jan. 1747, *d.* 15 Nov. 1791; having *m.* 14 Oct. 1765, Catherine, daughter of Metcalfe Proctor, Esq., who *d.* 15 Oct. 1791; they had no issue.

2 RICHARD, 10th LORD and 4th Earl, who succeeded his brother; he was *b.* 21 Feb. 1748, and *d.* also without issue 11 Dec. 1816; having *m.* 14 June 1785, a daughter of John March, Esq., *d.* 7 March 1827.

3 Lady Elizabeth, *b.* 10 Nov. 1750, *d.* 31 Oct. 1815; having *m.* 26 Jan. 1774, the Right-Reverend Henry-Reginald Courtenay, Lord Bishop of Exeter, who *d.* 9 June 1803; see *The Peerage Volume,* title Devon.

4 Lady Anne, widow of Lieut.-Colonel Christopher Carleton; see *The Peerage Volume.*

5 Lady Maria, widow of Guy, 1st Lord Dorchester; see *The Peerage Volume*
6 Lady Frances-Herring, *b.* 22 May 1755, *d.* 16 June 1796.

On the death of RICHARD, 10th LORD, and 4th Earl of Effingham, in 1816, that Earldom became extinct, and the Barony devolved upon Major-General SIR KENNETH-ALEXANDER HOWARD, the present and 11th LORD, descended, as above shown, from George Howard, Esq., younger brother of the 5th Lord, and 2nd son of Charles, grandson of Sir William Howard, 2nd son of the 1st Lord Howard of Effingham.

HOWARD DE WALDEN, BARON. (ELLIS.)

Peer of England.

Lord Thomas Howard, K.G., 2nd son of Thomas, 4th Duke of Norfolk, was summoned to Parliament by writ in 1597, as BARON HOWARD DE WALDEN, and created in 1603, Earl of Suffolk; he *d.* in 1626, and was succeeded by his son THEOPHILUS, 2nd LORD, and Earl of Suffolk, to whom, in 1640, succeeded his eldest son, JAMES, 3rd LORD, and Earl of Suffolk; on his death without issue male, in 1706, the Earldom devolved on George Howard, his brother and heir male, and the Barony fell into abeyance between his two daughters and co-heirs, 1 Essex, wife of Edward, Lord Griffin, and 2 Elizabeth, wife of Sir Thomas Felton.

In 1784, the Crown terminated the abeyance in favour of the elder co-heir, JOHN-GRIFFIN WHITWELL-GRIFFIN, Esq., son of William Whitwell, Esq., by Anne, grand-daughter and heir of Edward, Lord Griffin, and Lady Essex Howard, his wife. He was summoned to Parliament as BARON HOWARD DE WALDEN, and was created in 1788, Baron Braybrooke, with a special limitation; on his death, 25 May 1797, the issue of Lady Essex Howard became extinct, and the Barony devolved on the heir general of Sir Thomas Felton, by Lady Elizabeth Howard, the youngest co-heir, whose daughter and heir, Elizabeth, *m.* John Hervey, 1st Earl of Bristol; their eldest son, John, *d.* before his father, and FREDERICK-AUGUSTUS, his son and eventual heir, 4th Earl of Bristol, inherited the Barony, which descended, on his death in 1803, to his great-grandson and heir general, the present LORD; who is son of Charles Rose Ellis, Esq., now Lord Seaford, by his marriage with the Hon. Elizabeth-Catherine-Caroline Hervey, only daughter and heir of John-Augustus, Lord Hervey, eldest son of the 4th Earl of Bristol.

The next heirs to the Barony, after his Lordship's brother, are the present Earl of Bristol and his family.

HOWDEN, BARON. (CRADOCK.)

Peer of Ireland and of the United Kingdom.

General SIR JOHN CRADOCK, G.C.B., was created to the Peerage of Ireland in 1819, by the title of BARON HOWDEN of Grimston and Spaldington, and of Cradockstown, Co. Kildare; and in 1831, was further created Baron Howden of Howden and Grimston, Co. York, in the Peerage of the United Kingdom.

His Lordship claims his descent from Caradoc, and the ancient Princes of Wales. He is the only son of his Grace John Cradock, Lord Archbishop of Dublin, who *d.* 11 Dec. 1778, by Mary, daughter of William Blaydwin, Esq., and widow of Richard St.-George, Esq.; she *d.* 15 Dec. 1819.

HOWE, EARL. (Curzon-Howe.)

Peer of the United Kingdom.

His Lordship is a branch of the family of Lord Scarsdale. Sir Nathaniel Curzon, Bart., *m.* Sarah, daughter of William Penn, Esq., of Penn, Co. Bucks, and was father of Sir Nathaniel Curzon, Bart., who *m.* Mary, daughter and co-heir of Sir Ralph Assheton of Middleton, Co. Lancaster, Bart., and *d.* in 1758, leaving issue; Nathaniel, 1st Lord Scarsdale and Assheton, created Baron Curzon of Pennhouse, Co. Bucks, in 1794; and Viscount Curzon in 1802. He *d.* in 1820; leaving issue —see *The Peerage Volume.* His eldest son, the Hon. Penn-Assheton Curzon, *d.* before him, having *m.* Charlotte-Sophia, Baroness Howe—*see* that title below; by whom he left a son and heir, Richard-William-Penn Curzon, who succeeded his grandfather, and is the present and 2nd Viscount. His Lordship has assumed the additional name of Howe by Royal sign-manual, and was created Earl Howe in 1821.

HOWE, BARONESS. (Waller.)

Peeress of Great Britain.

The family of Howe has long been seated in the Counties of Somerset and Wilts. The will of John How of Stanligth, in the Diocese of Bath and Wells, dated 1529, is witnessed by his relation Henry How.

John How, great-grandson of this Henry, had, besides other issue, two sons; Sir Scrope How, Knt., and John, whose son John was created in 1741, Baron of Chedworth, Co. Gloucester, in the Peerage of Great Britain, which title became extinct in 1804, on the death of his grandson, John, 4th Lord.

Sir Scrope How, Knt., eldest son of John How, Esq., was created in 1701, Baron of Clenawley, Co. Fermanagh, and Viscount Howe, in the kingdom of Ireland. He *d.* in 1712, and was succeeded by his only son Edmund Scrope, 2nd Viscount. who *d.* in 1735; he was father of

1 George-Augustus, 3rd Viscount, who *d. unm.* 6 July 1758.

2 Richard, 4th Viscount, K.G., the gallant and successful Admiral; a series of brilliant naval services were rewarded in 1782, with a Peerage of Great Britain, by the title of Viscount Howe of Langar, Co. Nottingham; and he was further created in 1788, Baron Howe of Langar, aforesaid, and Earl Howe, with remainder of the Barony, failing his issue male, to his daughters and the heirs male of their bodies respectively. His Lordship *d.* 5 Aug. 1799, when the Earldom and English Viscounty became extinct, the Irish titles devolved on his next brother, William, 5th Viscount, and the English Barony on his eldest daughter, the present Baroness.

3 William, who succeeded his brother as 5th Viscount; he *m.* Frances, 4th daughter of the Right Hon. William Conolly, of Castletown, Co. Kildare, who *d.* 31 Aug. 1817; and the Viscount *d.* without issue 12 July 1814, when the Irish titles also became extinct.

HOWTH, EARL OF. (St. Lawrance.)

Peer of Ireland.

This ancient family is of English extraction. Sir Armoricus Tristram obtained the lands and Barony of Howth in the 12th century, and having defeated an army of invading Danes on St. Lawrance's day, changed his name, according to a vow made to that Saint, on condition of his obtaining the victory, for that of St. Lawrance, which has been ever since borne by his descendants.

From Sir Amoricus, 1st Baron, by tenure from King Henry II., the Barony descended uninterruptedly from father to son, through fourteen generations, whose names it would be tedious to enumerate, and whose dates of succession are rarely preserved, to Sir Robert St. Lawrance, K.G., 15th Lord by tenure, summoned to Parliament in 1461; he was succeeded by his son Nicholas, 16th Lord, who *d.* in 1526. His son,

Christopher, 17th Lord, who *d.* in 1542, had three sons, Edward, Richard, and Christopher, who successively inherited the Peerage.

From Christopher, 20th Lord, who *d.* in 1589, the title again descended uninterruptedly from father to son, through Nicholas, 21st Lord, who *d.* in 1606; Christopher, 22nd Lord, in 1619; Nicholas, 23rd Lord, in 1643; William, 24th Lord, in 1671; Thomas, 25th Lord, in 1727; William, 26th Lord, in 1748; to Thomas, 27th Lord, who was created Viscount St. Lawrance and Earl of Howth in 1767; he was *b.* 10 May 1730, and *d.* 20 Sept. 1801; having *m.* 17 Nov. 1750, Isabella, 3rd daughter of Sir Henry King, Bart., and sister of Edward, 1st Earl of Kingston, by whom, who was *b.* 2 Aug. 1729, and *d.* 20 Oct. 1794, he had the issue noticed in *The Peerage Volume*, and his successor, William, 2nd Earl, father of Thomas, the present and 3rd Earl, and 29th Baron of Howth.

HUNTINGDON, EARL OF. (Hastings.)

Peer of England.

This ancient and noble family derives its name from the port of Hastings, in Sussex, of which Robert de Hastings, the first in their pedigree, is said to have been Portgreave, and Steward to William the Conqueror. From an elder branch of his descendants, which became extinct in the male line in 1390, sprang the Earls of Pembroke of this name, Barons Hastings by writ, and Bergavenny by marriage.

The 11th in descent from Robert de Hastings, in the junior male line, was Sir William de Hastings, K.G., summoned to Parliament as Baron Hastings, of Ashby de la Zouche, in 1461, the staunch supporter of King Edward IV. and the House of York, and beheaded by the tyrant Richard, in 1483, as too loyal to acquiesce in his intended usurpation. Edward, Lord Hastings, his son, *d.* in 1507; having *m.* Mary, daughter and sole heir of Thomas Hungerford, Baron Botreaux, Hungerford, and Molines, and was father by her of George, Baron Botreaux, Hungerford, Molines, and Hastings, created Earl of Huntingdon, in 1529; he *d.* in 1544.

Francis, 2nd Earl, K.G., his son, *d.* in 1560, leaving three sons:

1 Henry, 3rd Earl, K.G., who *d.* without issue in 1595.

2 George, 4th Earl, who succeeded his brother, and *d.* in 1604; his male posterity became extinct by the death of Francis, 10th Earl, in 1789.

3 Sir Edward, from whom the present Earl is 6th in descent.

The 4th Earl was succeeded by his grandson, Henry, 5th Earl, son of Francis Lord Hastings, who *d.* before his father. The 5th Earl *d.* in 1643; he was succeeded by his son, Ferdinando, 6th Earl, who *d.* in 1655, and was followed by his son, Theophilus, 7th Earl, who *d.* in 1701, leaving two sons, successive Earls; George, who *d.* in 1705, and Theophilus, 9th Earl, who *d.* in 1746; and was succeeded by his son, Francis, 10th Earl, with whom terminated the male line of the 4th Earl. He *d.* in 1789, when the Baronies of Botreaux, Hungerford, Molines, and Hastings, devolved on Elizabeth, his sister and heir, whose grandson and heir is the present Marquis of Hastings.

The Earldom, the inheritance of the heir male, fell to the descendant of Sir Edward Hastings, 3rd son of the 2nd Earl. Sir Henry Hastings, his son, *d.* in 1619; his son, Henry Hastings, of Humberston, Co. Leicester, a zealous loyalist, who was taken prisoner by the Parliamentary forces, confined at Leicester, and compelled to pay above £2000 for the redemption of his estate, *d.* in 1656. His 3rd son, Richard, continued the line, and was father of Henry Hastings, Esq., who *d.* in 1786, leaving two sons, viz. 1 the Rev. Theophilus Hastings, who *d.* without issue in 1804; 2 Lieut.-Colonel George Hastings, who *m.* in 1769, Miss Sarah Hodges, and *d.* in 1802, leaving one surviving son, Hans-Francis, 12th Earl.

On the death of Francis, 10th Earl, the Rev. Theophilus-Henry Hastings, elder brother of George, father of the 12th Earl, was living, and should have been 11th Earl, but he *d.* in 1804, without having claimed the title, and the heir of this dignity remained unascertained till Hans-Francis, the late and 12th Earl, was summoned to Parliament, 14 Jan. 1819, having proved his descent from the said Edward Hastings, 3rd son of Francis, 2nd Earl, and the extinction of all the intervening male descendants.

HUNTINGFIELD, BARON. (Vanneck.)

Peer of Ireland.

This family is of Dutch lineage, and his Lordship's ancestors appear upon record as Magistrates in the Dutch Provinces, for nearly three centuries.

Sir Joshua Vanneck, an eminent merchant in London, was created a Baronet in 1751, and was father of Sir Joshua Vanneck, 3rd Baronet, who was created in 1796, Baron Huntingfield, of Heveningham Hall, Co. Suffolk. He *d.* in 1816, and was succeeded by his eldest son Joshua, present and 2nd Lord.

ILCHESTER, EARL OF. (Fox-Strangways.)

Peer of Great Britain.

The Right Hon. Sir Stephen Fox, Knt., son of William Fox, Esq., of Farley, Co. Wilts., was Lord of the Treasury in the reigns of King Charles II., James II., and William III., and first projector of Chelsea Hospital; he *d.* in 1716, and was father of Stephen, created Baron of Ilchester, Co. Somerset, and Baron of Woodford Strangways, Co. Dorset, in 1741; and in 1747, Lord Ilchester and Stavordale, and Baron of Redlynch, Co. Somerset, with remainder, failing his issue male, to his brother Henry, afterwards 1st Baron Holland; also in 1756, Earl of Ilchester, with the same remainder. He *m.* in March 1734, Elizabeth, only daughter and heir of Thomas Horner, Esq., of Mells Park, Dorsetshire, by Susannah, sister and heir of Thomas Strangways, Esq., of Melbury, Co. Dorset; and in consequence assumed the name and arms of Strangways. He was *b.* in 1704, and *d.* 29 Sept. 1776; by his said wife, Elizabeth, only daughter and heir of Thomas Horner, Esq., who was *b.* in 1720, and *d.* 15 Nov. 1792, he was father of Henry-Thomas, 2nd Earl, and other issue. The 2nd Earl *d.* in 1802, and was succeeded by his eldest son Henry-Stephen, present and 3rd Earl.

JERSEY, EARL OF. (Child-Villiers.)

Peer of England and of Ireland.

This noble family is of Norman origin, and came into England with William the Conqueror. Sir Nicholas de Villers, a renowned warrior, who was seated at Brokesby, in Leicestershire, followed King Edward I., in the Crusades, and in commemoration of them assumed the Cross of St. George, charged with five escallop shells, for his coat of arms, which has been ever since borne by his descendants. 6th in descent from him, was Sir John Villiers of Brookesby, in Leicestershire, who, in 1487, was distinguished for his valour at the battle of Stoke, against Lambert Simnel and the Earl of Lincoln, when he commanded some forces raised by himself in aid of King Henry VII.; he was Esquire of the body to that King, and a Knight of the Bath. His grandson, Sir George Villiers, who *d.* in 1606, was father of five sons.

1 Sir William, created a Baronet in 1619, which title became extinct with his male line on the death of his grandson in 1711.

2 Sir Edward, ancestor of the present Earl.

3 John, created Viscount Villiers of Stoke, and Viscount Purbeck, but *d.* in 1657, without legitimate issue.

4 The celebrated George Villiers, Duke of Buckingham, K.G., who by the graces of his person and address, rose to a height of power perhaps never possessed by any other British subject, and enjoyed the favour and confidence of two successive Sovereigns, to a degree of which history can probably present no rival instance. In 1616, he was created Baron of Whaddon, and Viscount Villiers; in 1617, Earl of Buckingham, with remainder, failing his issue male, to his brothers, John and Christopher; Marquis of Buckingham, in 1618, and Duke of Buckingham and Earl of Coventry, in 1623; in 1618, he was appointed Lord High Admiral of England. Nothing could exceed the attachment expressed towards him by King James I., which the Duke repaid with that familiarity and even disrespect which, perhaps was rather agreeable than otherwise to the King; certain it is at least, that it never diminished his influence, while to the Prince, afterwards Charles I., his conduct was respectful and submissive, a proof that the Duke understood the characters of both Monarchs, and knew how to shape his conduct to suit their respective foibles. "He was of a noble nature," says the Earl of Clarendon, "and generous disposition;" his personal courage was fully displayed in the command of the armament with which he made a descent upon the Isle of Rhé, although the expedition turned out unfortunately; and upon the whole, though he certainly took care of his own fortunes, and promoted his relatives to places of profit and honour, it does not appear, notwithstanding that he was represented by the Parliament as the public grievance of the nation, that any very serious misdemeanour can be laid to his charge; which is certainly a favourable circumstance in weighing the character of an individual unexpectedly exalted so far above his original sphere, honourable as that doubtless was, and exposed to such great temptations. He was assassinated when preparing to embark on a new expedition to Rochelle, in 1628, aged 36 years; he had married Lady Katherine Manners, daughter and sole heir of Francis, 6th Earl of Rutland, whom she afterwards succeeded as Baroness de Ros; and by her left a son and successor, George, 2nd Duke of Buckingham, and she was afterwards delivered of a second son, Lord Francis Villiers; who, engaging with the Earl of Holland in 1648, to raise some forces for the rescue of King Charles, fell in the 20th year of his age, in a skirmish with the rebels near Kingston-upon-Thames, resting his back against an elm, after his horse had been killed under him, and fighting most valiantly against a hopeless superiority of numbers. His brother, the Duke, who was but just returned from his travels, was also in the fight, and behaved with great gallantry; but finding all lost, had the good fortune to escape to London, from whence he joined the Prince of Wales in Holland. He was received with great favour by the Prince, who now soon became King, and continued with him till after the battle of Worcester, in which he fought at the King's right hand with exemplary valour; and having secured his Majesty's retreat, was himself taken prisoner with the Earls of Derby and Lauderdale, and many gentlemen, but contrived to escape while they were employed in plundering his noble associates; he again reached Holland in safety, and soon after rejoined the King. Returning afterwards to England, he married the daughter and sole heiress of Thomas Lord Fairfax, notwith-

standing which alliance, he was again taken up as a malignant and committed to the Tower in Aug. 1758, but released in July 1759; and on the 4th of May 1660, had the whole of his estates restored to him by a resolution of both Houses of Parliament; on the King's triumphant entry into London on the 29th of the same month, he rode with General Monk bareheaded before his Majesty. From this time his credit at Court became nearly as great as that of his father had been before him; but his talents, though more versatile, were not equal to sustaining the favour he had acquired, and gradually losing the affections of the King, he lost also the respect of the people, and having survived his Royal Master little more than two years, died almost in poverty in a cottage in Yorkshire, in 1687, a striking example of the mutability of fortune. He left no issue, and all his titles expired with him, except that of Baron De Ros, which fell into abeyance.

5 Christopher, created Baron Villiers of Daventry, Co. Northampton, and Earl of Anglesey in Wales, in 1623; he *d.* the following year, leaving one son, Charles, his successor, 2nd Earl, who *d.* without issue in 1659, when his titles became extinct.

Having thus slightly touched upon the extraordinary fortunes of that branch of the House of Villiers, so highly distinguished under the title of Buckingham, the history of the family must revert to Sir Edward, the second son of Sir George Villiers, and elder brother of the 1st Duke of Buckingham; he was not included in the reversion of that title, but married Barbara, eldest daughter of Sir John St.-John, and niece of Oliver St.-John, created Viscount Grandison in Ireland, with remainder to the heirs male of this Barbara; they had four sons, of whom William, John, and George, were successively Viscounts Grandison, and the male line of the latter failed in 1766, on the death of his grandson and successor, John, 5th Viscount, who had been created Earl Grandison in 1721, which title became extinct, and the Viscounty devolved on the Earl of Jersey, descended from

Sir Edward, 4th son of Sir Edward Villiers, and Barbara St.-John, who, engaging heartily in the King's cause during the civil wars, served in several engagements against the Parliamentary forces, and was wounded in the battle of Newbury; he however survived the interregnum, and was, after the Restoration, appointed to the household of King CHARLES II., and his Lady was governess to the Princesses Mary and Anne, afterwards Queens of Great Britain.

SIR EDWARD VILLIERS, their eldest son, was created in 1691, Viscount Villiers, of Hoo, and Baron Villiers, of Dartford, both in the County of Kent; and EARL of the island of JERSEY in 1697; he *d.* in 1711, and was succeeded by his eldest son, WILLIAM, 2nd EARL, who *d.* in 1721, leaving two sons: 1 WILLIAM, his successor, 3rd EARL, and 2 Thomas, created Earl of Clarendon, father of the present Earl of Clarendon. WILLIAM, 3rd EARL, succeeded in 1776, as 6th Viscount Grandison, in Ireland, and *d.* in 1769, when he was succeeded by his only-surviving son, GEORGE-BUSSY, 4th EARL, father of GEORGE, the present and 5th EARL, who succeeded him in 1805; and having *m.* Lady Sarah Fane, eldest daughter of the Earl of Westmoreland, and grandaughter and heir of Robert Child, Esq., the banker, has assumed the additional name of Child by his Majesty's license.

KEITH, BARONESS. (MERCER-ELPHINSTONE.)

Peeress of Ireland and of the United Kingdom.

George Keith, the late Viscount, her Ladyship's father, was 5th son of Charles, 10th Lord Elphinstone, and great uncle to the present Lord Elphinston; he *m.* 1st, Jane, eldest daughter and co-heir of Colonel William Mercer, grandson of the 2nd Lord Nairne, and by her had an only daughter, the present Baroness. He was created in 1797, Baron Keith, of Stonehaven Marischal, in the Peerage of Ireland, with remainder to his only daughter, MARGARET MERCER, and her issue male; and was further created Baron Keith, of Stonehaven Marischal, Co. Kincardine, in the Peerage of the United Kingdom, in 1801; and in 1803, BARON KEITH of Banheath, Co. Dumbarton, in the Peerage of the United Kingdom, with remainder, failing his issue male, to his only daughter, MARGARET MERCER, and her issue male. His Lordship m. 2ndly, Hester-Maria, eldest daughter and co-heir of Henry Thrale, Esq., by whom he had a second daughter—see *The Peerage Volume*. In 1814, he was advanced to the dignity of Viscount Keith, which title, with the Barony of 1801, became extinct on his death in 1823; when his eldest daughter, the present Baroness, succeeded to the Barony of 1803, and to the Irish Peerage.

KENMARE, EARL OF. (BROWNE.)

Peer of Ireland.

His Lordship's family were of note in Lincolnshire in the reigns of King Edward VI. and Queen Mary. Sir Valentine Browne, of Crofts, Auditor-General of Ireland, *d.* 1567. Sir Valentine Browne, 4th in descent from him, was created in 1689, by James II., after his abdication, Baron of Castlerosse, and Viscount Kenmare, which titles were borne by his descendants, though not legally recognised till VALENTINE, 5th VISCOUNT, and 4th in descent from the 1st Viscount, had them granted to him in 1798; he was afterwards advanced to the dignity of Earl of Kenmare and Viscount Castlerosse, in 1801, and *d.* in 1812; he was father of VALENTINE, the present and 2nd EARL, his successor.

KENMURE, VISCOUNT. (GORDON.)

Peer of Scotland.

The territory of Gordon, in Berwickshire, appears to have been granted during the reign of David I. to an Anglo-Norman settler, who assumed from it the surname of Gordon. Richard and Adam de Gordon, his sons, are the first of this name on record; Alicia, great-grandaughter and heir of Richard, *m.* Adam, grandson and heir of Adam, and their son Adam re-united the family estates.

His son, Sir Adam, had two sons; 1 Sir Alexander, whose male line failed in 1402, when the lands of Gordon were carried into the family of Seton by the marriage of the heiress, from whom the present Duke of Gordon descends; 2 William, of whom the present Viscount is the male representative; the 7th in descent from him was

Sir James Gordon, of Lochinvar, who had two sons:

1 John, father of 1 Sir Robert, whose son JOHN was created, in 1633, VISCOUNT KENMURE, and Baron of Lochinvar, with remainder to his heirs male whatever; his male issue failed in 1629, by the death of his only son, JOHN, 2nd VISCOUNT; 2 James, father of JOHN, who succeeded as 3rd VISCOUNT, and of ROBERT, 4th VISCOUNT, who both *d. unm.*, the 3rd Viscount in 1643, and the 4th Viscount, who suffered many hardships on account of his loyalty, and was excepted from Cromwell's act of grace and pardon, in 1663.

2 William, great-grandfather of ALEXANDER, 5th VISCOUNT, who went to King JAMES VII. at St. Germains after his abdication, but was not well received by his Majesty; he *d.* in 1698, and was succeeded by his son WILLIAM, 6th VISCOUNT. His Lordship, on the breaking out of the rebellion in 1715, set up the standard of the Pretender at Lochmaben, and took the chief command of the rebel forces in the south of Scotland; marching with them into England, he was taken prisoner in the defeat at Preston, attainted, and beheaded, after trial before his Peers, in Feb. 1716. His son JOHN, who, but for the attainder, would have been 7th VISCOUNT, *d.* in

1769, leaving, besides other issue, JOHN, the present VISCOUNT, to whom the titles were graciously restored under King GEORGE IV., by Act of Parliament, in 1824.

KENSINGTON, BARON. (EDWARDES.)

Peer of Ireland.

Francis Edwardes, Esq., of a very ancient family in Wales, m. Lady Elizabeth, only daughter of Robert, 5th Earl of Warwick, of the family of Rich, and 2nd Earl of Holland; and his son WILLIAM, 1st LORD, inherited the estates of that family in 1721, on the death of his first cousin, Edward-Henry, 7th Earl of Warwick; and was created BARON KENSINGTON in 1776: he *d.* in 1801, and was succeeded by his only son, WILLIAM, present and 2nd LORD.

KENYON, BARON. (KENYON.)

Peer of Great Britain.

This is an ancient family in Lancashire, of which Jordan Kenyon was Lord of Kenyon, in the parish of Winwick, in the time of Henry III. His Lordship's immediate ancestors removed into Flintshire early in the last century. SIR LLOYD KENYON, father of the present LORD, was bred to the Bar, and after passing with honour through the subordinate legal offices, was appointed in 1788, Lord Chief Justice of the Court of King's Bench. His profound legal erudition, his inflexible integrity, his spirit and firmness in the administration of justice, and, above all, his unprecedented zeal in the cause of morality and virtue, have acquired for him a character, which will always be considered as one of the fairest ornaments of the English Bench; he was created in 1788, on his appointment as Chief Justice, Lord Kenyon, Baron of Gredington, Co. Flint; and having survived his eldest son, the Hon. Lloyd Kenyon, whose death affected him so deeply that it is supposed to have accelerated his own, was succeeded, in 1802, by his eldest surviving son, GEORGE, the present and 2nd LORD.

KILKENNY, EARL OF. (BUTLER.)

Peer of Ireland.

His Lordship is a younger branch of the Marquis of Ormonde's family. RICHARD, 2nd son of Pierce, 8th Earl of Ormonde, was created in 1550, Baron of Kells, Co. Meath, and VISCOUNT MOUNTGARRET, Co. Wexford; he *d.* in 1571, and was followed in the direct line of paternal descent by EDMUND, 2nd VISCOUNT; RICHARD, 3rd VISCOUNT; EDMUND, 4th VISCOUNT; and RICHARD, 5th VISCOUNT; the latter was outlawed, and lost his estate and seat in Parliament, by his adherence to King JAMES II. at the Revolution, and *d.* in 1707; EDMUND, his successor, 6th VISCOUNT, was restored in blood and honours in 1721, and *d.* in 1735, leaving three sons, successive Viscounts: RICHARD, 7th VISCOUNT, who *d.* without issue in 1736; JAMES, 8th VISCOUNT, who *d.* also without issue in 1749; and EDMUND, 9th VISCOUNT, who *d.* in 1750, and was succeeded by his only son, EDMUND, 10th VISCOUNT; he *d.* in 1778, leaving three sons; 1 EDMUND, his successor, 11th VISCOUNT; 2 The Hon. and Rev. Richard Butler, who *d.* in 1795; 3 The Hon. Simon Butler, who *d.* 19 May 1797; having *m.* 18 Jan. 1795, Eliza, second daughter of Edward Lynch, Esq., by whom, who *d.* 27 Feb. 1800, he was father of Edward-Lynch Butler, Esq.

EDMUND, 11th VISCOUNT, *d.* in July 1793, and was succeeded by his eldest son, EDMUND, 12th VISCOUNT, who was created EARL of KILKENNY in Dec. 1793, and is the present Earl.

KILMAINE, BARON. (BROWNE.)

Peer of Ireland.

Sir Anthony Brown was made a Knight of the Bath at the Coronation of King Richard II. His descendant, Sir Anthony Browne, was created Viscount Montagu in 1554, which title became extinct in 1797, by the death of Mark-Anthony, 9th Viscount.

A branch of the same family settled in Ireland in the time of Queen Elizabeth, of which John Browne, Esq., of the Neale, Co. Mayo, was created a Baronet of Nova Scotia, in 1632. He was father of Sir George, his successor, and of John, from whom the Marquis of Sligo is descended. Sir George, 2nd Baronet, was great-grandfather of SIR JOHN BROWNE, Bart., who was created in 1789, Baron Kilmaine of the Neale, Co. Mayo; he *d.* in 1794, and was succeeded by his eldest son, JAMES-CAULFEILD, 2nd LORD, father of JOHN-CAVENDISH, the present and 3rd LORD, who succeeded him in 1825.

KILMOREY, EARL OF. (NEEDHAM.)

Peer of Ireland.

This family is descended from William de Nedeham, Lord of Staunton, Co. Chester, in 1102, and has long been seated at Shenton, Co. Salop. SIR ROBERT NEEDHAM, of Shenton, created in 1625, VISCOUNT KILMOREY, Co. Clare, *d.* in 1627; his son ROBERT, 2nd VISCOUNT, *d.* in 1653, leaving, besides other issue, ROBERT, 3rd VISCOUNT, his successor, who *d.* without issue in 1657, and CHARLES, 4th VISCOUNT; the latter *d.* in 1660, leaving also two sons, ROBERT, 5th VISCOUNT, who *d. unm.* in 1668, and THOMAS, 6th VISCOUNT, who was succeeded by his son, ROBERT, 7th VISCOUNT; he left three sons: 1 ROBERT, 8th VISCOUNT, he *d.* an infant in 1717; 2 THOMAS, 9th VISCOUNT, he *d.* without issue in 1768; 3 JOHN, 10th VISCOUNT, he *d.* in 1791, and was father of ROBERT, 11th VISCOUNT, his successor, who *d.* without issue in 1818, and of FRANCIS, who succeeded his brother, was created in 1822, EARL of KILMOREY, and Viscount Newry and Morne, and is the present Peer.

KING, BARON. (KING.)

Peer of Great Britain.

PETER, 1st LORD KING, was son of Jerome King, a tradesman of the City of Exeter, but of good family in the County of Somerset, by a sister of the great John Locke. He was appointed Lord Chief Justice of the Common Pleas in 1714, and was constituted Lord High Chancellor in 1725, when he was also created LORD KING, Baron of Ockham, Co. Surrey; he *d.* in 1734. His four sons, JOHN, 2nd LORD, who *d.* without issue in 1740; PETER, 3rd LORD, who *d. unm.* in 1754; WILLIAM, 4th LORD, who *d. unm.* in 1767; and THOMAS, 5th LORD, who *d.* in 1779, successively inherited the title; the last was father of PETER, 6th LORD, his successor, who was succeeded in 1793, by his eldest son, PETER, present and 7th LORD.

KINGSALE, BARON. (De Courcy.)

Peer of Ireland.

This noble family claims a direct male descent from Charlemagne, who was ancestor in the 6th degree of Charles, Duke of Lorraine, father of, 1 Otho, Duke of Lorraine, who *d.* without issue; 2 Louis, founder of the line of Langraves of Thuringia in Germany, extinct in 1248; 3 Charles, by some called Hugh, father of Wigerius, father of

Baldricus, who coming into Normandy, in the time of Duke Richard 2nd, was surnamed Teutonicus, from his German origin. He had six sons, of whom Nicholas, the eldest, was ancestor of the Warrens, Earls of Warren and Surrey, and of the Mortimers, Earls of March and Ulster; and Robert, 3rd son, Lord of Courcy in Normandy, was father of

Richard de Courcy, who accompanied William the Conqueror to England, and besides many other Lordships had that of Stoke, Co. Somerset, from which his descendants took the title of Barons of Stoke Courcy. The 4th in descent from him was John, Baron of Stoke Courcy, who, serving King Henry II. in his Irish wars, conquered the province of Ulster, and was created Earl of Ulster, but having fallen under the displeasure of King John, was deprived of his Earldom, and confined in the Tower of London for a year, during which time it was that Philip Augustus, King of France, proposed to refer to the arbitration of single combat the disputes subsisting between the French and English Crowns, and named his champion; to meet whom King John thought no subject of his of sufficient strength and valour except the imprisoned Earl of Ulster; he spurned, however, the proposal, alleging the ingratitude of the King for his past services; but was at length prevailed on, for the honour of the nation, to take up the Frenchman's gauntlet. So great, however, was his strength, and so superior his stature, that the French champion, at the last charge of the trumpets, set spurs to his horse and fled, leaving the victory to the Earl of Ulster. King Philip, desirous of seeing some proof of the Earl's reputed strength, an helmet of excellent proof was laid on a block of wood, which the Earl cleft asunder, and with the same blow struck so deep into the wood, that no person present but himself could withdraw his sword. The King would now have restored his Earldom, which was held back by Hugh de Lacy, who refused to surrender it, and King John could only accede to the Earl the permission to repair to Ireland to reconquer it for himself; at the same time granting to him and his heirs male the privilege of appearing covered in the presence of the Kings of England, which the Barons of Kingsale exercise to this day. Contrary winds prevented his succeeding in fifteen several attempts to cross the seas to Ireland; and Myles, his son and heir, being unable to recover his father's Earldom, was created in 1181, Lord Kingsale, Baron Courcy of Courcy, and Baron of Ringrone, all in the County of Cork; he *d.* in 1223; and was succeeded by his son Patrick, 2nd Lord; and he by his son Nicholas, 3rd Lord, father of Edmund, 4th Lord, and John, 5th Lord; the latter was killed in battle in the island of Inchiduiny, Co. Cork, against the Irish chieftain, Daniel Moel Mac Carty, in the year 1295. He was followed without interruption by seven generations of Barons in direct parental descent to Nicholas, 12th Lord, who *d.* in 1474; his two eldest sons were,

1 James, 13th Lord, his successor, who *d.* in 1491, leaving one son, Edmund, 14th Lord, who *d.* without issue.

2 David, 15th Lord, who, besides other issue, had two sons, viz.

- 1 John, 16th Lord; he *d.* in 1535, and was succeeded by his only son Gerald, 17th Lord, who *d.* without issue male in 1599.
- 2 Edmund, father of Edmund Oge De Courcy, and grandfather of

John, 18th Lord; he *d.* in 1628; leaving, besides other issue, Gerald, his successor, 19th LORD, who *d.* without issue male in 1642; PATRICK, 20th LORD; and David, whose son Miles was father of JOHN, 25th LORD.

PATRICK, 20th LORD, *d.* in 1663, leaving, besides other issue,

1 JOHN, his successor, 21st LORD; he *d.* in 1667, leaving two sons: PATRICK, 22nd LORD, who *d.* at nine years of age, in 1669; and ALMERICUS, 23rd LORD, who asserted in presence of King WILLIAM III. the privilege of his ancestors of appearing before the Kings of England with their heads covered, which has since been frequently claimed and exercised by his successors. He *d.* without issue in 1719.

2 Miles, father of GERALD, 24th LORD, who succeeded his cousin, and *d.* without issue male in 1759; when the male line of the 20th Lord became extinct.

JOHN, 25th LORD, *d.* in 1776; and was succeeded by his eldest son JOHN, 26th LORD, on whose death in 1822, his eldest surviving son THOMAS, present and 27th LORD, succeeded.

KINGSLAND, VISCOUNT. (BARNEWALL.)

Peer of Ireland.

This ancient family came from Bretagne in the suite of William the Conqueror; and in the time of King HENRY II. Sir Michael de Barneval settled in Ireland, where by his sword he obtained large possessions under the banners of Richard de Clare, surnamed Strongbow, Earl of Pembroke. 13th in descent from him was Ulphram de Barneval, whose two elder sons were,

1 Sir Christopher; he had two sons: 1 Sir Nicholas, Lord Chief Justice of the Common Pleas in Ireland, ancestor of Sir Robert Barnewall, Bart., of Crickstown Castle, Co. Meath, the elder branch of this noble family; 2 Robert, who was created Baron of Trimlestown, Co. Meath, in 1461, and was ancestor of the present Lord Trimlestown.

2 John. From him descended

NICHOLAS BARNEWALL of Turvey, who was created in 1646, VISCOUNT Barnewall of KINGSLAND, Co. Dublin, and Baron of Turvey, Co. Dublin; he *d.* in 1663, leaving two sons:

1 HENRY, 2nd VISCOUNT, ancestor of all the succeeding Viscounts previous to the present Lord.

2 The Hon. Francis Barnewall, father of Nicholas Barnewall, Esq., of Begg's Town and Wood's Park, Co. Meath, father of Matthew Barnewall, Esq., and grandfather through him of Matthew, the present and 6th Viscount.

HENRY, 2nd VISCOUNT, *d.* in 1688, and was succeeded by his eldest son NICHOLAS, 3rd VISCOUNT; he *d.* in 1725, leaving two sons: 1 HENRY-BENEDICT, 4th VISCOUNT, who *d.* without issue in 1740; 2 George, whose son GEORGE succeeded as 5th VISCOUNT, and *d.* in 1800, when the male line of the 2nd VISCOUNT became extinct.

KINGSTON, EARL OF. (KING.)

Peer of Ireland and of the United Kingdom.

This is an ancient family, formerly of Yorkshire, of which Sir John King passed into Ireland, in the reign of Elizabeth. Sir Robert King, his son, was father of Sir John, created in 1660, Baron Kingston of Kingston, Co. Galway, which title became extinct in 1761, by the death of his grandson, James, 4th Lord; and of

Sir Robert, created a Baronet in 1682, whose descendant, Sir Robert, 4th Bart., was created Baron Kingsborough, which title became extinct on his death in 1755; he was succeeded in the Baronetcy by his brother

Sir Edward, 5th Bart., who was created in 1764 Baron Kingston of Rockingham, in 1766, Viscount Kingsborough, and in 1768 Earl of Kingston, all in the Peerage of Ireland; he *d.* in 1797, and was succeeded by his eldest son, Robert, 2nd Earl, father of George, the present and 3rd Earl, who succeeded him in 1799, and was created in 1821, Baron Kingston of Michelstown, Co. Cork, in the Peerage of the United Kingdom; and of Robert-Edward, the present Viscount Lorton.

KINNAIRD, BARON. (Kinnaird.)

Peer of Scotland and of the United Kingdom.

Radulphus, patriarch of this family, had a charter from King William the Lion, of the Barony of Kinnaird, in Perthshire, from which his descendants took their surname.

Sir George Kinnaird, 16th from him, was created Baron Kinnaird, of Inchture; he *d.* in 1689, leaving six sons, of whom Patrick, the eldest, succeeded as 2nd Lord, and George, the youngest, was ancestor of the present Lord.

Patrick, 2nd Lord, *d.* in 1701, leaving two sons: 1 Patrick, 3rd Lord; he *d.* in 1715, and was succeeded by his only son Charles, 4th Lord, who *d.* without issue in 1728; 2 Charles, 5th Lord, who succeeded his nephew, and *d.* in 1758, without issue, when the male line of the 2nd Lord, eldest son of the 1st Lord, became extinct; and the four succeeding sons of the 1st Lord having *d.* without issue, the title devolved on the heir male of George, 6th and youngest son of the 1st Lord.

George, son of the said Hon. George Kinnaird, was father of Charles, 6th Lord, who succeeded on the death of the 5th Lord, and *d.* in 1767; when he was succeeded by his eldest son George, 7th Lord, to whom, in 1805, succeeded his eldest son, Charles, 8th Lord; he *d.* in 1826, and was succeeded by his eldest son, George-William-Fox, present and 9th Lord.

KINNOUL, EARL OF. (Drummond-Hay.)

Peer of Scotland and of Great Britain.

The Hays of Scotland are a branch of the Anglo-Norman Hays, who came into England with William the Conqueror; and of which family William de Haya settled in Lothian towards the close of the 12th century; he had two sons, 1 William, and 2 Robert, ancestor of the Marquis of Tweeddale.

William, the eldest son, was father of David de Haya, who had two sons: 1 Gilbert, ancestor of the Hereditary Constables of Scotland, and Earls of Errol, both which dignities are enjoyed by the present Earl of Errol, as heir-general of the last male descendant from the 1st Earl; and 2 William, whose descendant,

Peter Hay, of Melginch, had two sons: 1 Peter, his successor at Melginch, and ancestor of the Earl of Kinnoul; and 2

Sir James Hay, of Kingash, who accompanied King James I. into England, and was through life high in the favour of that Monarch and of King Charles I.; from the latter he obtained a grant of the Island of Barbadoes, and by the former he was created Baron Hay of Sawley, Co. Cumberland, in 1615, Viscount Doncaster in 1618, and Earl of Carlisle in 1622. He was a fine gentleman and accomplished courtier; preferred pleasure to business, and is chiefly remarkable for having squandered in the most profuse magnificence and sumptuous profligacy the vast sums obtained from the liberality of his Prince; he *d.* in 1636, leaving an only son, James, who, with his titles, inherited no other property than the island of Barbadoes; he *d.* without issue in 1660, when all his titles became extinct.

Peter Hay, of Melginch, the eldest son, was father of

1 Patrick, ancestor of the Hays of Pitfour.

2 George, appointed Lord High Chancellor of Scotland in 1622, and created in 1633, Earl of Kinnoul, Viscount of Dupplin, and Baron Hay of Kinfauns, with remainder to his heirs male for ever; he *d.* in 1635, and was succeeded by his only surviving son George, 2nd Earl; who was succeeded in 1644, by his only son William, 3rd Earl, a zealous loyalist, who was twice taken prisoner by the rebels, but escaped with his life; he *d.* in 1677, leaving two sons, who both *d.* without issue: 1 George, 4th Earl, *d.* 1687, and 2 William, 5th Earl, who obtained, in 1704, a charter limiting the honours to himself for life; failing him, to Thomas, Viscount of Dupplin, and the heirs male of his body, which failing, to his heirs of tailzie and provisions succeeding him in the lands and Barony of Dupplin; he *d.* in 1709, when the issue male of the first Earl became extinct.

3 Peter, whose great-grandson, Thomas Hay, was created in 1697, Viscount of Dupplin, to him and the heirs male of his body, which failing, to his heirs of entail; he succeeded in 1709 as 6th Earl, and *d.* in 1719; he was father of

George, 7th Earl, who was created in 1711, a Peer of Great Britain by the title of Baron Hay of Pedwardine, Co. Hereford; he *d.* in 1758, leaving, besides other issue, the three sons following:

1 Thomas, 8th Earl, *b.* in 1710, *d.* 12 Dec. 1787, having *m.* 12 June 1741, Constantia, only daughter and heir of John Kyrle Ernle, Esq., of Whetham, Co Wilts, and Much Marele, Co. Hereford; she *d.* 15 July 1753, having brought his Lordship an heir, *b.* 12 Aug. 1742, *d.* an infant.

2 Robert, Lord Archbishop of York, who *d.* in 1776; for his issue, see *The Peerage Volume*; he was father of Robert-Auriol, who succeeded his uncle as 9th Lord, and *d.* in 1804, when Thomas-Robert, his eldest son, present and 10th Earl succeeded.

3 The Hon. Edward, who was *b.* 14 June 1722, and *d.* 21 Oct. 1779; having *m.* 1st, 8 Oct. 1752, Mary, daughter of Peter Flower, Esq., by whom, who was *b.* 27 Oct. 1727, and *d.* 11 Oct. 1775, he had the surviving issue noticed in *The Peerage Volume*, and several others deceased; he *m.* 2ndly, 24 Jan. 1779, Mary-Harborn, daughter of —— Barnwell, Esq.

KINTORE, EARL OF. (Keith-Falconer.)

Peer of Scotland.

The Falconers of Halkertown, Lords Falconer, derive their descent from Ranulphus, who obtained from King William the Lion, the office of King's Falconer, from which his descendants took their surname. Sir Alexander Falconer, a Lord of Session, who had the honour of being superseded in that office in 1649 for what was then termed malignancy, and was reinstated at the Restoration, was created in 1647, Baron Falconer of Halkertown, with limitation to his heirs male whatever; he *d.* in 1671, and was succeeded by his only son, Alexander, 2nd Lord, to whom, in 1684, succeeded his only son, David, 3rd Lord; he *d.* in 1724, when the issue male of the first Lord became extinct, and the title devolved on the male heir of Sir David Falconer, his next brother, in whose male descendants it has since continued.

This Sir David, brother of the 1st Lord, left two sons:

1 Sir Alexander, created a Baronet in 1671; he was father of Alexander, 4th Lord, who *d.* without issue in 1727.

2 Sir David Falconer of Newton, a Lord of Session; he was father of David, 5th Lord, ancestor in the 5th degree of the present Earl.

The family of Keith, Earl Marischal, of which Alexander Keith, Esq., of Dunottar and Ravelstown, is the male representative, derive their descent from Robert, a chief of the Catti, who emigrating from Germany, was signally serviceable to King Malcolm II., against the Danes, and was created heritable Marshal of Scotland.

His descendant, Sir William Keith, was created Earl Marischal in 1442, which title was forfeited by the attainder of George, 10th Earl, in 1715.

Sir John Keith, 3rd son of William, 6th Earl Marischal, was created in 1677, Earl of Kintore, and Lord Keith of Inverary and Keith Hall, with remainder to the heirs male of his body, and of the body of George, 8th Earl Marischal, his brother, which failing, to the heirs female of his body; he *d.* in 1714, and was succeeded by his only son, William, 2nd Earl, who *d.* in 1718, leaving issue:

1 John, 3rd Earl, who *d.* in 1758, without issue.

2 William, 4th Earl, who *d.* also without issue, 1761.

3 Lady Catherine-Margaret Keith, *m.* to David, 5th Lord Falconer.

The Earldom, on the death of the 5th Earl, devolved, according to the provisions of the patent, on George, 10th Earl Marischal, grandson and heir of George, 8th Earl Marischal, brother of the 1st Earl of Kintore; he had been attainted for joining in the Rebellion of 1715, and his estates and titles forfeited; but having taken refuge in Prussia, where he was received with distinction, and employed as his Prussian Majesty's Ambassador at Madrid, he had there an opportunity of performing signal service to the English Government, and obtained his pardon, together with an act of Parliament enabling him to inherit any real or personal estates notwithstanding his attainder, but without any provision for the inheritance of titles of honour; when, therefore, he became, by the extinction of the male heirs of the 1st Earl, 5th Earl of Kintore, that title in fact remained dormant till his death in 1778; he ended his days in Prussia, enjoying the full confidence and favour of Frederick the Great. He was the last male descendant of the 8th Earl Marischal, and the title of Kintore accordingly devolved on the heir female of the 1st Earl of Kintore.

David, 5th Lord Falconer, by his marriage with Lady Catherine-Margaret Keith, daughter of the 2nd Earl of Kintore, had, besides other issue, the three sons following:

1 Alexander, 6th Lord, who succeeded his father in 1751, and *d.* without issue in 1762.

2 William, 7th Lord, who settled in Holland; succeeded his brother, and *d.* at Groningen in 1776, leaving three sons: 1 Anthony-Adrian, his successor, 8th Lord, who, on the death of the Earl Marischal, 5th Earl of Kintore, succeeded as 6th Earl; 2 William, killed in battle at Quebec; 3 the Hon. Charles Falconer, who is still living.

3 The Hon. Captain George Falconer, R.N.; he *d.* in 1780, leaving a son, George Falconer, Esq.

Anthony-Adrian, 6th Earl Kintore, and 8th Lord Falconer, *d.* in 1804; and was succeeded by his only son, William, 7th Earl, who *d.* in 1812, when he was succeeded by his eldest son, Anthony-Adrian, present and 8th Earl.

KIRKCUDBRIGHT, BARON. (Maclellan.)

Peer of Scotland.

The name of Maclellan is of great antiquity in Scotland. Gilbert Maclellan obtained a charter of his lands from King David II.

William Maclellan of Bombie, had a charter of the land of Loch Fergus in 1471. His son, Sir Thomas Maclellan of Bombie, had two sons, viz:

1 Sir William, ancestor in the 4th degree of Sir Robert Maclellan, who was created in 1633, Baron of Kirkcudbright, to him and his heirs male whatever, and died without issue male in 1641.

2 Gilbert, from whom the present Lord is 10th in descent.

Sir Thomas Maclellan of Bombie, great-grandson of the above Sir William, *d.* in 1597, leaving three sons:

1 Sir Robert, the 1st Lord, created as above, and *d.* without issue.

2 William, father of Thomas, who succeeded his uncle, according to the terms of the patent, as 2nd Lord, and *d.* also without issue in 1647.

3 John, father of, 1 John, who succeeded as 3rd Lord, and *d.* in 1664, leaving one son, William, 4th Lord, who *d.* under age in 1669; 2 William; he had two sons, John, 5th Lord, who *d.* young, and James, 6th Lord, who *d.* in 1730; both suffered the title to fall into disuse. On the decease of the latter, the Peerage devolved on the descendant and heir male of Gilbert, 2nd son of the Sir Thomas Maclellan of Bombie, mentioned above.

From this Gilbert descended in the 6th degree, William Maclellan of Borness, who, on the death of the 6th Lord, became 7th Lord, as the nearest heir male under the patent, but failed to make good his claim; but John, his son and successor, 8th Lord, established his right to the title before the House of Lords in 1773; he *d.* in 1801, leaving two sons, Sholto-Henry, 9th Lord, his successor, who *d.* without issue in 1827, and Camden-Grey, present and 10th Lord, who succeeded his brother.

LAKE, VISCOUNT. (Lake.)

Peer of the United Kingdom.

The celebrated General Gerard Lake, who for his military services, especially in the command of the army in India, was created in 1804 Baron Lake of Delhi and Laswary, and of Aston Clinton, Co. Bucks, and in 1807 Viscount Lake, as aforesaid, was great-grandson of Sir Thomas Lake of Canons, Middlesex, Secretary of State to King James I. He *d.* in 1808, and was succeeded by his eldest son, Francis-Gerard, present and 2nd Viscount.

LANDAFF, EARL OF. (Mathew.)

Peer of Ireland.

This family, which derives its descent from David Mathew, great Standard Bearer to King Edward IV, was anciently seated at Llandaff, in Glamorganshire, and removed into Ireland early in the 17th century.

Francis Mathew, Esq., was created in 1783 Lord Landaff, Baron Landaff of Thomastown, Co. Tipperary; in 1793 Viscount Landaff; and in 1797 Earl of Landaff; he *d.* in 1806, and was succeeded by his eldest son, Francis-James, present and 2nd Earl.

LANESBOROUGH, EARL OF. (Butler.)

Peer of Ireland.

His Lordship's ancestor, John Butler, was seated at Waresley, Co. Huntingdon, in 1376. Sir Stephen Butler removed into Ireland in the reign of James I., and was grandfather of Francis Butler, Esq., who had two sons: 1 Theophilus, created in 1715, Baron of Newtown-Butler, Co. Fermanagh, with remainder to the heirs male of his father; 2 Brinsley, who succeeded his brother, and was created in 1728, Viscount Lanesborough; he *d.* in 1735, leaving the four sons following:

1 Humphrey, his successor, 2nd Viscount, created in 1756, Earl of Lanesborough; he *d.* in April 1768, having *m.* in May 1726, Mary, daughter and heir of Richard Berry, Esq., of Wardenstown, Co. Westmeath; by whom he had an only

son, Brinsley, 2nd Earl, who *d.* in 1779; and was succeeded by his eldest son, Robert-Herbert, 3rd Earl, to whom, in 1806, succeeded his only surviving son, Brinsley, present and 4th Earl.

2 The Hon. Thomas Butler, Governor of Limerick; he *d.* 16 Dec. 1753, having *m.* 11 June 1730, Mary, eldest daughter and heir of Duncan Cummin, Esq., and widow of John Ormsby, Esq., by whom, who *d.* 28 Dec. 1758, he was father of Mrs. St. Leger—see *The Peerage Volume.*

3 Hon. Robert, *m.* Mary Howard, sister of the 1st Viscount Wicklow.

4 Hon. John, *b.* 1707, *d.* 12 Dec. 1789; having *m.* 7 June 1735, the widow of —— Harrison, Esq., by whom he had the issue stated in *The Peerage Volume.*

LANGFORD, BARON. (Rowley.)

Peer of Ireland.

The family of Rowley was of Saxon origin, and settled in Ireland in the reign of King James I.

John Rowley *m.* Mary, eldest daughter and heir of Sir Hercules Langford, and by her was grandfather of the Right Hon. Hercules-Langford Rowley, whose wife, Elizabeth, only daughter of Clotworthy Upton, Esq., was created Viscountess Langford in 1766. They had issue:

1 Hercules, 2nd Viscount, on whose death in 1791, the title became extinct.

2 Clotworthy, who *d.* in 1781, leaving an only daughter Frances, heir to the Viscount, her uncle.

3 Jane, *m.* Thomas Taylour, Earl of Bective, by whom she had Thomas, present Marquis of Headfort; and Clotworthy, who, having *m.* Frances Rowley, his cousin above mentioned, assumed the name and arms of Rowley, was created in 1800, Baron Langford, of Summerhill, Co, Meath, and is the present Peer.

4 Catherine, *m.* Edward-Michael, 2nd Lord Longford.

LANSDOWNE, MARQUIS OF. (Petty-Fitz-Maurice.)

Peer of the United Kingdom and of Ireland.

Walter Fitz-Other, Castellan of Windsor in the reign of William the Conqueror, for whose descent see the pedigree of the Duke of Leinster, was father of Gerald Fitz-Walter, ancestor, by his eldest son Maurice, of the family of Fitz-Gerald, Duke of Leinster, and, by his 2nd son William, of that of Fitz-Maurice, Earl of Kerry.

Reymond, 2nd son of this William, was greatly instrumental in the conquest of Ireland in the reign of King Henry II.; he was father of Maurice, who obtained a large tract of land in the County of Kerry, and from whom his descendants adopted the surname of Fitz-Maurice. His son, Thomas Fitz-Maurice, 1st Lord of Kerry, Baron of Lixnaw, *d.* in 1280; his son, Maurice, 2nd Lord, *d.* in 1303, and was succeeded by his son, Nicholas, 3rd Lord, who *d.* in 1324, leaving two sons, successive Lords, viz.: 1 Maurice, 4th Lord, taken prisoner by Maurice, Earl of Desmond, for joining with the Irish and disturbing the peace of the country, and was starved to death in prison in 1339; 2 John, 5th Lord, who *d.* in 1348, and was succeeded by his eldest son, Maurice, 6th Lord, who *d.* in 1398; to him succceded in direct hereditary descent, Patrick, 7th Lord, who *d.* in 1410; Thomas, 8th Lord, he *d.* in 1469; Edmond, 9th Lord, *d.* in 1498; and Edmond, 10th Lord, who *d.* in 1543. The latter was father of four sons, who in the end all inherited the Barony, viz.:

1 Edmond, 11th Lord; he was created in 1537, Baron of Odorney and Viscount

of Kilmaule, which title became extinct upon his death in 1541, when the Barony of Kerry devolved on his next brother.

2 Patrick, 12th Lord, who *d.* in 1547, leaving two sons, successive Lords, Thomas, and Edmond, who both *d.* in their minority in 1549.

3 Gerald, 15th Lord, succeeded his nephew, and *d.* in 1550.

4 Thomas, 16th Lord; he was *b.* in 1502; and was a soldier in the Imperial service at Milan, when the rapid occurrence of deaths in his family called him to the succession, for which, however, he was indebted to the fidelity and enterprise of an aged dependant. One Gerald Fitz-Maurice entered, as next heir male, upon the family estates, and would probably have kept possession, but that the Lord Thomas's nurse, knowing where to find him, set out, accompanied by her daughter, on the journey, at that period both difficult and tedious; she sailed from Dingle, landed on the French coast, traversed that country, and reached Milan in safety, but died on her journey homewards. Lord Thomas, after much trouble and opposition, obtained his Peerage and estate. He did not, however, hold it more peaceably than had been usual with his ancestors. The English Governor holding him in some suspicion, intercepted the provisions destined for his castle of Lixnaw, and scarcely allowed him the means of subsisting his household, which so provoked his Lordship, that he rose in arms, and was with some difficulty subdued; but, through the intercession of the Earl of Ormonde, obtained his pardon; he *d.* in 1590. Patrick, 17th Lord, his eldest son and successor, waged continual war against the English, and having pulled down his castle of Beaulieu, lest it should fall into the hands of his enemies, *d.* in 1600, of grief for the loss of his castle of Lixnaw, which was taken by surprise. Thomas, 18th Lord, his eldest son, succeeded, and continued in rebellion to the end of the reign of Queen Elizabeth, whose Lieutenants reduced Listowell, his last remaining castle, took possession of all his estates, and drove him out of Kerry; he was excluded, with the Earl of Desmond and a few others, from every act of grace issued during the reign of Elizabeth, but obtained a full pardon from King James, with the restoration of his estates. He *d.* in 1630, and was succeeded by his eldest son, Patrick, 19th Lord, who *d.* in 1661. William, his eldest son and successor, 20th Lord, *d.* in 1697, and was succeeded by his eldest son, Thomas, 21st Lord, who, in 1723, was created Viscount Clanmaurice, Co. Kerry, and Earl of Kerry; he *d.* in 1741, having *m.* Anne, only daughter of the celebrated philosopher and mechanician, Sir William Petty, M.D., Secretary for Ireland to Oliver Cromwell, who, in that capacity, made a minute survey of all the forfeited and crown lands of Ireland, and acquired a large fortune by the per-centage allowed upon the survey; she was sister and heir of Henry Petty, created Earl of Shelburne in 1719; on whose death without surviving issue in 1751, the title became extinct. The Earl of Kerry had by her, besides other issue, two sons:

1 William, 2nd Earl, father of Francis-Thomas, 3rd Earl, who succeeded him in 1747, and on whose death without issue, 4 July 1818, his titles devolved on his cousin, the present Marquis.

2 John, appointed heir of his maternal uncle, Henry Petty, Earl of Shelburne, upon whose death he assumed the name and arms of Petty. He was created in 1751, Baron of Dunkerron, and Viscount Fitz-Maurice, and in 1753, Earl of Shelburne. In 1760, he was farther advanced to the dignity of the British Peerage, by the title of Baron Wycombe, of Chipping Wycombe, Co. Bucks, and *d.* in 1761, leaving two sons: 1 William, 2nd Earl, his successor; 2 The Hon. Thomas Fitz-Maurice, who *m.* Mary, present Countess of Orkney.—See *The Peerage Volume*, title Orkney.

William, 2nd Earl of Shelburne, is well known in the politics of the early part of the reign of George III.; having for a short time guided the helm of the state, he was displaced by the coalition of North and Fox, and never afterwards held any share in the administration. Having *m.* Lady Sophia Carteret, 6th daughter of John, 2nd Earl Granville, son of George, 1st Lord Carteret, by Lady Grace Granville, created Countess of Granville, aunt and co-heir of William-Henry, 3rd Earl of Bath, Viscount Lansdowne and Baron Granville; he was created in 1784, Viscount Calne and Calnstone, Co. Wilts, Earl of Wycombe, Co. Bucks, and Marquis of Lansdowne, Co. Somerset; he *d.* in 1805, leaving by his said 1st marriage, John-Henry, his successor, 2nd Marquis, who *d.* without issue in 1809; and by his 2nd marriage, with Lady Louisa Fitz-Patrick, daughter of John, 2nd Earl of Upper Ossory, Henry, the present nd 3rd Marquis, who succeeded his half brother.

LAUDERDALE, EARL OF. (Maitland.)

Peer of Scotland and of the United Kingdom.

This family is of Anglo-Norman lineage; the first of their ancestors on record is Thomas de Matulant, who *d.* 1228; his grandson, Sir Richard de Mantland, held the Barony of Thirlestane, and other property in the shire of Berwick, in the reign of Alexander III. 9th in descent from him was Sir Richard Maitland, of Leithington and Thirlestane, a Lord of Session and Keeper of the Privy Seal, who was employed in public offices for upwards of seventy years, under James IV., James V., Queen Mary, and James VI.; he *d.* in 1586. His two elder sons were, 1 William, a Lord of Session and Secretary of State; he was several times sent Ambassador into England, as the medium of communication between the two Queens, and was a staunch adherent of Queen Mary, in whose behalf he entered into an intrigue tending to her release, by means of her marriage with the Duke of Norfolk; after various differences with the successive Regents Moray, Marr, and Morton, he was at length proclaimed a traitor, and being taken in the Castle of Edinburgh when it surrendered to Morton's arms, he died by his own hand, to avoid a public execution, which, from his attachment to the cause of his Royal mistress, and the personal enmity of the Regent, he knew awaited him. He *d.* in 1573, in his father's lifetime, leaving one son, James, a Roman Catholic, who sold his estate to his uncle John, went abroad, and *d.* without issue. 2 Sir John Maitland, who, though forfeited in 1570 for his adherence to Queen Mary, afterwards rose high in the favour of James VI. He was a Lord of Session, Lord High Chancellor and Secretary of State, and was created Lord Maitland of Thirlestane in 1590; he *d.* in 1595, and was succeeded by his only son,

John, 2nd Lord, who was created Earl of Lauderdale, Viscount Maitland, Lord Thirlestane and Boltoun, in 1624, and *d.* in 1645, leaving three sons:

1 John, 2nd Earl, his successor; at the commencement of the civil war he joined the covenanters, was much trusted in the management of affairs, and endeavoured to bring about a pacification to the advantage of all parties; but failing in this object, he entered into the engagement for the rescue of the King in 1648, and went over to Holland to invite the Prince of Wales to join the army assembled for that purpose; meanwhile, the defeat at Preston destroyed all hopes from the confederation, and the Earl remained with the Prince, who now soon became King, till he repaired to Scotland; whither, and in his ill-fated expedition into England he accompanied his Majesty, and was taken prisoner at the battle of Worcester. He remained in confinement nine years; and after the Restoration, being high in the confidence of Charles II., he was nearly the supreme governor of Scotland, till falling under the displeasure of the Duke of York, he lost all his offices and influence. He was created Marquis of March and Duke of Lauderdale, 1672, and a Peer of England 1674, by the title of Baron of Petersham and Earl of Guilford; all which titles became extinct on his death, without issue male, 24 Aug. 1682.

2 Robert, whose male issue failed in 1664.

3 Charles, who succeeded his brother as 3rd Earl, and *d.* in 1691, leaving two sons: 1 Richard, 4th Earl, his successor, who *d.* without issue in 1695; 2 John, 5th Earl, who succeeded his brother, and *d.* in 1710.

Charles, 6th Earl; his eldest surviving son and successor, *d.* 15 July 1744, having *m.* Lady Elizabeth Ogilvie, eldest daughter of James, Earl of Findlater and Seafield, by whom, who *d.* 24 Sept. 1778, he had eight sons, who lived to maturity, viz.:

1 James, his successor, 7th Earl, who *d.* in 1789—see *The Peerage Volume.* He was succeeded by his eldest son James, present and 8th Earl; who, in 1806, was created Baron Lauderdale of Thirlestane, Co. Berwick, in the Peerage of the United Kingdom.

2 Hon. Charles, *d.* 28 Nov. 1795; having *m.* 1st, Isabel, daughter and heir of Sir Alexander Barclay, of Towie, and in consequence assumed the name of Barclay; she *d.* 23 Oct. 1761, leaving the issue stated in *The Peerage Volume.* He *m.* 2ndly, in April 1765, a daughter of Patrick Haldane, Esq., of Gleneagles; and 3rdly, 11 Feb. 1768, Janet, 3rd daughter of Sir Thomas Moncrieffe, Bart., who *d.* 6 Nov. 1799; he had no issue by the two last marriages.

3 Hon. and Rev. George, *d. unm.* Sept. 1764.

4 Hon. Colonel Richard, *b.* 10 Feb. 1724, *d.* 24 Aug, 1772; having served with the army in America, and *m.* an American lady, by whom he left the issue described in *The Peerage Volume.*

5 Hon. General Sir Alexander Maitland, Bart., *b.* 1725, *d.* 13 Feb. 1820; having *m.* 27 June 1754, Penelope, daughter of Colonel Martin Madan, by whom, who *d.* 22 Dec. 1805, he had, besides the surviving issue noticed in *The Peerage Volume,* a 2nd son, Lieut.-Colonel Augustus Maitland, of the 1st Foot-Guards, who was mortally wounded in an engagement near Egmont-op-Zee, where he commanded a battalion of the Guards, 6 Oct. 1799, and *d. unm.* the 21st of the same month.

6 Hon. Capt. Frederick-Lewis Maitland, R.N., *b.* 19 June 1730, *d.* 16 Dec. 1786; having *m.* 27 Aug. 1767, Margaret, daughter of James Dick, Esq., and heiress of the family of Makgill, of Rankeillour and Lindores, *b.* 16 Nov. 1749, *d.* 17 March 1825; they had, besides the issue described in *The Peerage Volume,* a younger son Robert, a Midshipman in the Royal Navy, who *d.* at Malta 2 July 1801, having served with the fleet in Egypt.

7 Hon. Patrick, *b.* 10 April 1731, *d.* 14 May 1797; having *m.* 29 Sept. 1774, Jane, 2nd daughter of Captain Maitland, and widow of John, 10th Earl of Rothes, by whom he left issue—see *The Peerage Volume.*

8 Hon. Colonel John Maitland, *d.* at Savannah of a fever brought on by his fatigues in the American campaign of that year, in which he had served with great distinction.

LE DESPENCER, BARON. (Stapleton.)

Peer of England.

Edward Despencer, 5th Lord, descended in the direct male line from Hugh, 1st Baron, by writ of summons in 1264, (for whose pedigree see Duke of Marlborough,) *m.* Elizabeth, daughter and sole heir of Bartholomew de Burghersh, summoned to Parliament as Baron de Burghersh in 1357. Thomas, their son, Earl of Gloucester, 6th Baron Despencer, and, in right of his mother, 3rd Baron Burghersh, was attainted and beheaded in 1400. Richard, his son and heir, who but for the attainder would have been 7th Lord, *d.* without issue in 1414.

Isabel, his sister and sole heir, had by her first marriage with Richard Beauchamp, Earl of Worcester, and 2nd Baron Abergavenny, an only daughter, Elizabeth; and by her second marriage with Richard Beauchamp, Earl of Warwick, a son, Henry, Duke of Warwick, whose issue failed in 1449; and a daughter, Anne, *m* to Richard Nevill, in her right Earl of Warwick, whose co-heirs are existing. The attainder being reversed in 1461, and the Barony of Despencer called out of abeyance, in favour of Elizabeth, the daughter and heir of the 1st marriage of the said

Isabel, Countess of Worcester and Warwick, she carried it with the Barony of Abergavenny to her husband,

Edward Nevill, 6th son of Ralph, 1st Earl of Westmoreland. Their great-grandson, HENRY NEVILL, 12th BARON LEDESPENCER, and 7th Baron Abergavenny, *d.* without issue male in 1587; and in 1603,

MARY, his daughter and heir, wife of Sir Thomas Fane, claimed and was allowed the Barony of Ledespencer, (that of Abergavenny being confirmed to Edward Nevill, the heir male of the last Baron.) Her son and heir, FRANCIS FANE, 14th LORD, was created Earl of Westmoreland, and the Barony of Le Despencer continued in his male descendants, till the death of JOHN, 20th LORD, and 7th Earl of Westmoreland, in 1762; when it fell into abeyance between his sisters, Lady Mary, who *m.* Sir Francis Dashwood, Bart.; and Lady Catherine, who *m.* William Paul, Esq., and had by him an only daughter and heir, Catherine, *m.* to Sir William Stapleton, Bart., who *d.* 27 June 1753, father by her of Sir Thomas Stapleton, Bart., father of the present LORD.

In 1763, the King called the Barony of Ledespencer out of abeyance, in favour of SIR FRANCIS DASHWOOD, 21st LORD, son and heir of Lady Mary; on his death in 1781, it again fell into abeyance between his sister and heir, Rachel, wife of Sir Robert Austen, Bart., and the present LORD. The abeyance was terminated by the death, 16 May 1788, of Lady Austen, the only surviving descendant of Lady Mary Dashwood, when SIR THOMAS STAPLETON, the present and 22nd LORD, succeeded to the title.

His Lordship is also the eldest co-heir of the Barony of Burghersh by writ, 1357; the other moiety of this Barony being in abeyance between the co-heirs of Anne, Countess of Warwick, daughter of ISABEL, Countess of Worcester and Warwick, by her 2nd marriage.

LEEDS, DUKE OF. (OSBORNE.)

Peer of England and of Scotland.

His Grace derives his descent from Sir Edward Osborne, eldest son of Richard Osborne, Esq., by Jane, daughter of John Broughton, of Broughton, Esq. He was apprenticed in his youth to Sir William Hewit, one of the most considerable merchants in London, whose only child, Anne, he had the good fortune to save from a watery grave in her infancy. The nursemaid playing with the child at an open window of his house on London Bridge, accidentally dropped it from her arms into the Thames; young Osborne leaped instantly into the river, and brought the infant safe to land. She grew up, and was given with a large estate in marriage to her preserver. He was knighted in 1582, when Lord Mayor of London, and *d.* in 1591. Sir Hewit Osborne, his son, *d.* in 1614, leaving a son, Sir Edward, created a Baronet in 1620; he was Vice-President of the Council to CHARLES I. for the North of England, under the Earl of Strafford, and on the breaking out of the great rebellion, was appointed Lieutenant-General of the King's forces in the North. SIR THOMAS, his son and successor, a zealous loyalist, co-operating in the King's restoration, filled several offices of trust in the administration under CHARLES II., till he rose, in 1673, to the post of Lord High Treasurer. He was created in the same year, Baron Osborne of Kiveton, Co. York, and Viscount Latimer of Danby, being descended, through his mother, a daughter of Thomas Walmesley, Esq., from the Nevilles, formerly Barons Latimer. In 1674, he was farther created Earl of Danby, Co. York; and in 1675, made a Peer of Scotland, by the title of Viscount Dumblane. He was accused of treating with France for a pension for the King, and became highly unpopular; was impeached of high treason, and, notwithstanding the precaution of procuring a pardon under the Great Seal, a bill of attainder was brought in by the Commons, and the Earl of Danby was committed to the Tower, where he remained for five years, when he was admitted to bail. He afterwards took an active part in bringing about the Revolution, and was in great credit with King WILLIAM and Queen MARY, by whom he was created Marquis of Carmarthen in 1689, and advanced in 1694 to the dignity of DUKE of LEEDS—having thus, in his own person, from a simple Baronet, passed through all the gradations of the Peerage to its summit. He *d.* in 1712, and was succeeded by his son PEREGRINE, 2nd DUKE, who *d.* in 1729. PEREGRINE, 3rd DUKE, his son, succeeded, and *d.* in 1731; he was succeeded by his son THOMAS, 4th DUKE, K.G. He *m.* Mary, youngest daughter and co-heir of Francis, 2nd EARL Godolphin, by Henrietta, Duchess of Marlborough, eldest daughter and co-heir of the great Duke of Marlborough; and dying in 1789, was followed by his eldest son, FRANCIS-GODOLPHIN, 5th DUKE. He *d.* in 1799; having *m.* LADY AMELIA D'ARCY, only daughter and heir of Robert, 4th Earl of Holderness, and heiress of the Barony of Conyers, by writ 1509; she was divorced from the Duke of Leeds, and afterwards *m.* John Byron, Esq., father (by another marriage) of the great poet Lord Byron; and on her death, in 1784, transmitted the Barony of Conyers to her son by her 1st marriage, GEORGE-WILLIAM-FREDERICK, present and 6th DUKE, K.G.

LEINSTER, DUKE OF. (FITZ-GERALD.)

Peer of Ireland and of Great Britain.

Walter Fitz-Other was Castellan of Windsor in the reign of William the Conqueror, but genealogists are disagreed as to his pedigree, which some deduce from Otho, a noble from Italy, who came into England with that King, and others from Othoere, a powerful Lord in the reign of King Alfred, whose ancestor was of Norwegian origin. This Walter Fitz-Other was, however, ancestor, by his sons William and Gerald, of the families, of Windsor, now represented in the female line by the Earl of Plymouth; and of Fitz-Gerald.

Gerald was father of Maurice, from whom the Duke descends, and of William, ancestor of the Marquis of Landsdowne.

This Maurice Fitz-Gerald, the eldest son, was one of the adventurers who, in 1169, undertook the conquest of Ireland under the guidance of Richard Strongbow, Earl of Pembroke. He obtained large grants of lands, among which was the Barony of Offaley, for his good services, and assumed the title of Lord Offaley; he *d.* in 1177. His eldest son, GERALD, was created BARON of OFFALEY in 1205, and dying in the same year, was succeeded by his son MAURICE, 2nd LORD. He was Lord Justice of Ireland, and on the defection of Richard Marshal, Earl of Pembroke, from the cause of King John, he waged battle with him, in which the Earl was defeated and slain. The Lord Offaley also obtained several victories over the Irish Princes; he *d.* in 1257, and was succeeded by his eldest son THOMAS, 3rd LORD, who *d.* in 1260, and was succeeded by his eldest son JOHN, 4th LORD, who was killed in 1261 with his brother Maurice, and MAURICE his eldest son, in a battle at Callan in Desmond, against Maccarthy More. His said eldest son, Maurice, left a son then nine months old, THOMAS, 6th LORD. The 4th Lord had several other sons, of whom Gilbert, his 2nd son, was ancestor of the Earl of Clare. THOMAS, 6th LORD, *d.* in 1296, leaving two sons: 1 JOHN, 7th LORD, his successor; 2 Maurice, created Earl of Desmond.

This Maurice, 1st Earl of Desmond, possessed considerable power and influence, and refusing to obey a summons to Parliament, he, once of his own authority, and again in conjunction with the Earl of Kildare, summoned a Parliament in opposition to that called by the Lord Justice in Dublin; he showed, however, that he had received injury from the Lord Justice, and had influence sufficient to procure his removal. He levied coigne, livery, and black-rents, after the Irish fashion, and making a distinction between English of blood and English of birth, almost separated himself from the English government; in this proceeding he was much outdone by his posterity, who, flourishing through six generations and sixteen successions, continually increased their power and greatness by encroachments upon the rights of government, till at length they acquired and retained the strange privilege, that the Earls of Desmond should never come to any Parliament or Grand Council, nor within any walled town, but at their own will and pleasure. Waging frequent war against the state, they were sometimes successful and sometimes overpowered; one of them, Thomas, the 8th Earl, was beheaded in 1467, but his estates and honours were restored to his son James, 9th Earl. Gerald, 16th Earl, one of the greatest subjects in Europe, was attainted in 1582, and forfeited his prodigious estate, which commanded nearly four counties, his lands, whereon were several strong castles, extending 110 miles in length. His son James, 17th Earl, was restored in blood and honours, but *d. unm.* in 1601, and with him ended the acknowledged line of the Earls of Desmond. The father of the 16th Earl had, however, by a former marriage, a son Thomas, older than Gerald, his successor; this Thomas he disinherited, and his son James, on the death of the 17th Earl, assumed the title, but *d.* in the Tower, without issue, in 1608; his brother John was afterwards called Earl of Desmond, and left an only son Gerald, called also Earl of Desmond, an officer in the Imperial army, who *d.* in Germany in 1632 without issue, and was the last who bore this title.

John, 7th Lord Offaley, elder brother of the 1st Earl of Desmond, having a personal quarrel with William Vesey, Lord of Kildare, Lord Justice of Ireland, laid his complaints before King Edward I., and challenged Vesey to single combat; the latter not approving this mode of settling the question, took refuge in France, when the King gave judgment in favour of the Lord Offaley, and granted to him the Lordship of Kildare and divers other lands thus forfeited by Vesey; in May 1316, his Lordship was created Earl of Kildare, and *d.* in September the same year. He was succeeded by his son Thomas, 2nd Earl, who *d.* in 1328, leaving two sons; Richard, 3rd Earl, the eldest, succeeded his father, and *d.* at twelve years of age in 1329, leaving the title to his only surviving brother Maurice, 4th Earl, Lord Justice of Ireland. He *d.* in 1390, and was succeeded by his son Gerald, 5th Earl, to whom, in 1410, succeeded his son John, 6th Earl; he *d.* in 1427, and was succeeded by his son Thomas, 7th Earl, Lord Deputy of Ireland; he *d.* in 1478, when his son Gerald, 8th Earl, succeeded.

The lives of all these nobles were passed in continual wars, sometimes with the Irish Chieftains, and sometimes with the English government, with various success, of course, but, upon the whole, with progressively increasing power, till this Gerald, 8th Earl, became so formidable, that the Kings of England considered that the safest means of retaining him and the whole of their Irish conquests in subjection, would be to delegate their authority to him; he was accordingly, at several times, thirty-three years chief-governor of Ireland, and once, in that capacity, levied actual war against King Henry VII. in aid of the impostor Lambert Simnel, professing to be the Earl of Warwick, son of George, Duke of Clarence, brother of King Edward IV., whom Henry retained, at this time, a close prisoner in the Tower. The Earl of Kildare, Lord Deputy, assisted at the coronation of this youth by the name of King Edward VI., which was performed with great solemnity, in 1487, by the Archbishop of Dublin, in Christ Church, Dublin, in presence of many Anglo-Irish nobles, who entertained a particular regard for the Prince thus represented, from his having been born amongst them when his father was Deputy of Ireland. The whole island followed the example of the capital, and not a sword was raised on behalf of Henry's crown; but when, emboldened by this success, they ventured on an invasion of England, assisted by two thousand Germans, furnished by the Duchess of Burgundy and some English malcontents, the army thus raised, and commanded by the Earl of Lincoln, experienced a total defeat at Stoke, in Nottinghamshire; Lambert Simnel was taken prisoner, and the Earl of Lincoln, together with Thomas Fitz-Gerald, Chancellor of Ireland, brother of the Earl of Kildare, was killed. Sir Richard Edgecombe, comptroller of the King's household, was sent into Ireland to receive anew the oaths of allegiance and fidelity; a general amnesty was granted; the Earl of Kildare made his submission; with many other of the chief nobles he was required to attend the King, who, after laying before them all the particulars of the imposture, as confessed by Simnel, and reproaching them that they would at last crown apes, dismissed them all with assurances of his favour upon their future good behaviour, and continued the Earl of Kildare as his Deputy. It was not long, however, before cause of fresh suspicion arose on the appearance of Perkin Warbeck, in the character of Richard, Duke of York; and the Earl, as a known adherent of the house of York, was removed from his high office. He now fell into some very irregular proceedings; was attainted of high-treason, and his motto, "Crom a Boo," with others of a similar nature used by some powerful families, was suppressed by law. He was again summoned to England to answer for the various misdemeanours he was alleged to have committed; when, accused before the King and Council of burning the church of Cashel, and expected to defend himself against the charge, he not only confessed the fact, but averred that he should never have burnt the church had he not believed the Archbishop was in it. While the Council was astonished at the boldness of this declaration, the King professed himself convinced, that a man of so open a character could not be guilty of the conspiracies charged against him; but the Bishop of Meath, his chief accuser, continuing to urge against him sundry important matters, the Earl waved the inquiry by asserting that he was not sufficiently learned to answer. The King thereupon required him to choose a counsellor, to which he consented, provided he was allowed to command the services of the good fellow he should name; the King assured him that he should, adding, it behoved him to choose very good counsel, for he doubted his cause was very bad. "I will choose," says the Earl, "the best counsel in England," and named the King himself, who, pleased with the freedom, undertook the cause. The Bishop, still persevering in his complaints, concluded with the observation, "You see what a man he is, all Ireland cannot rule him." "Then," replied the King, "it is meet that he rule all Ireland:" and so terminated this famous investigation. The Earl was sent back to Ireland, restored to his honours, estate, and vice-regal command, and from thenceforth conducted himself as a loyal subject, expending his restlessness upon the Irish in hostility to the English pale, over whom he gained several important victories, his very name being described as more terrible to the Irish than an army. In the year 1490, he received, as a present of great rarity and value, from Germany, six hand-guns, or muskets, with which his guard were armed when they stood sentinels before his residence of Thomas-Court. He was continued by King Henry VIII. in his office of Deputy, and *d.* in 1513, from the effect of a wound he had received in battle some time before, against the O'Mores of Leix. In his more advanced years, repenting of his former outrages against religion, he rebuilt the church of Cashel which he had formerly burnt.

He was succeeded by his son Gerald, 9th Earl, who was appointed Deputy of Ireland, in his father's room, and was eminently successful in reducing the Irish to subjection; being, however, vehemently opposed by the jealousy of the Anglo-Irish nobility, he was superseded, in 1519, by the appointment of Thomas Howard, Earl of Surrey, to be Lord Lieutenant of Ireland. A great feud breaking out between him and the Butlers, with the Earl of Ormond at their head, his Lordship, who had been reinstated in his office of Deputy in 1524, was summoned to England, in 1526, and committed to the Tower till he should clear himself of the offences imputed to him by Ormond; Cardinal Wolsey being opposed to him, it was not till 1530 that he obtained his release and returned to Ireland. Here he continued his hostilities against the Irish chiefs and the Butlers, and was again appointed Lord Deputy in 1532; but his proceedings tending rather to embroil the country than to its good government, he was again required to repair to England, with permission to name his Deputy in his absence. He appointed his son, Thomas, Lord Offaley, to this important office, and departed for England, furnishing all his castles with artillery and munition of war out of the King's stores. This act being construed as an intention of levying war against the King, and his affairs in England wearing an unfavourable appearance, a report was spread in Ireland that the Earl was beheaded, and that the same fate was intended for his son and brothers; the Lord Offaley, resigning his government, entered into open rebellion, laid siege to Dublin, engaged and defeated several detachments sent to its aid, and maintained a fierce war for several months, but was at length totally defeated near Naas, made prisoner, and with his five uncles sent to England, where all six were executed at Tyburn, 2 Feb. 1536. The Earl, his father, *d.* before him in the Tower, in Dec. 1534, oppressed with grief at the tidings of his inconsiderate rebellion, and with his son and brothers, was attainted of high-treason, by Act of Parliament, in May 1536. He left three sons; viz.

1 Thomas, Lord Offaley, whose unfortunate history has been related, but who succeeded his father as 10th Earl, the act of attainder not having passed till after his own decease.

2 Gerald, who being restored to the title, was 11th Earl.

3 Edward, father of Gerald, 14th Earl; and of Thomas, whose son George became the 16th Earl.

Gerald, 11th Earl, being but ten years of age at the time of his father's death, was preserved from the enmity of King Henry VIII., by the care of his female relatives, and of his tutor, Thomas Leverons, his father's foster-brother; but strict search being made for him in Ireland, he was conveyed to the Continent, and wandered from Court to Court, requisitions from England for his surrender still following him everywhere, till at length Cardinal Reginald Pole, a near relation of his mother (the Lady Elizabeth Grey, daughter of Thomas Marquis of Dorset) sent for him into Italy, and took charge of the completion of his education. After the death of Henry VIII. he returned te England, obtained from Edward VI. a grant of part of his estates; and, on his benefactor, Cardinal Pole's restoration to the country by Queen Mary's accession, was reinstated in all his honours and estates. In the reign of Queen Elizabeth, the act of attainder against his father, brother, and uncles was repealed. He proved a faithful servant of the Crown, and was extremely active in suppressing its Irish opponents. He *d.* in 1585, having had three sons, viz.

1 Gerald Lord Offaley, who *d.* before his father in 1580; leaving an only daughter and heir, Lettice, who was created Baroness Offaley for life; she *m.* Sir Robert Digby, carried considerable property into that family, and was mother of the first Lord Digby.

2 Henry, 12th Earl, who succeeded his father, and left a daughter, Bridget, *m.* 1st, to Rory O'Donel, created Earl of Tyrconnel; and, 2ndly, to Nicholas Barnewall, 1st Viscount Kingsland; he *d.* without issue male in 1597.

3 William, who succeeded his brother as 13th Earl; he was drowned in his passage from England to Ireland in 1599, and *d. unm.*

Gerald, 14th Earl, eldest son of Edward Fitz-Gerald, brother of the 11th Earl, succeeded. He *d.* in 1612, and was succeeded by his infant son Gerald, 15th Earl, who *d.* in 1620, in the 9th year of his age.

He was succeeded by his cousin George, 16th Earl, only surviving son of Thomas, brother of the 14th Earl; he was *b.* in 1611, and was consequently of the same age as the last Earl. His Lordship opposed the Irish rebels with all his power, and was a great sufferer in the troubles produced by their general insurrection in 1641. He *d.* in 1660, leaving two surviving sons:

1 Wentworth, 17th Earl, his successor; he *d.* in 1664, leaving an infant son, John, 18th Earl, who *d.* without issue in 1707.

2 Robert Fitz-Gerald, Esq., who having incurred suspicion from the government of King James II., was in confinement in Dublin Castle, when the news of the battle of the Boyne instantaneously set him at liberty, and operated a general revolution in the city. Mr. Fitz-Gerald, who was considered by the Protestants as a sort of martyr to their cause, immediately acquired a powerful influence over them, and by the energy of his measures, prevented all the excesses into which the two

parties were ready to break out, and preserved the peace of the city, for which he received the public thanks of King WILLIAM on his arrival in Dublin. He *d.* in 1698, leaving two sons: 1 George, who *d. unm.* very shortly after his father; 2 ROBERT, who succeeded as 19th EARL of KILDARE, and *d.* in 1744.

He was succeeded by his eldest surviving son JAMES, 20th EARL, who was created in 1747 Viscount Leinster of Taplow, Co. Bucks, in the Peerage of Great Britain; also, in 1761 Marquis of Kildare and Earl of Offaley, and in 1766 DUKE OF LEINSTER, in Ireland. He was *b.* 29 May 1722, and *d.* 19 Nov. 1773; having *m.* 7 Feb. 1747, Lady Mary Lennox, 3rd daughter of Charles, 2nd Duke of Richmond, who *m.* 2ndly, in 1774, William Ogilvie, Esq., and *d.* 27 March 1814; by this Lady the Duke had issue seventeen children, of whom his eldest son, George Earl of Offaley, *b.* 15 Jan. 1748, *d.* 26 Sept. 1765; his second son, William-Robert, succeeded him as 2nd Duke; his third son, Lord Charles-James Fitz-Gerald, *b.* 30 June 1756, was created in 1800, Baron Lecale of Ardglass, in the Peerage of Ireland, *m.* Aug. 1808, Julia, widow of Thomas Carton, Esq., and *d.* without issue 18 Feb. 1810, when the title became extinct; his seventh son, Lord Gerald, was lost at sea; and his eighth, Lord Augustus-Joseph, *d.* in 1771, at the age of four years; Lady Emily-Maria-Margaret, his eldest daughter, *b.* 15 March 1752, *d.* 8 April 1818; having *m.* 20 Aug. 1774, Charles Coote, last Earl of Bellamont, who *d.* 20 Oct. 1800, when the title became extinct; and his younger daughters, Lady Fanny-Charlotte-Elizabeth, Lady Henrietta-Catherine, Lady Caroline-Elizabeth-Mabel, Lady Louisa, and Lady Caroline, all *d.* young, or unmarried; for the remainder, who are living, or have left issue, see *The Peerage Volume.* His Grace was succeeded by his eldest surviving son, WILLIAM-ROBERT, 2nd Duke, to whom, in 1804, succeeded his eldest son AUGUSTUS-FREDERICK, present and 3rd DUKE.

LEITRIM, EARL OF. (CLEMENTS.)

Peer of Ireland and of the United Kingdom.

His Lordship's family is originally from France, where Albert Clements, one of his ancestors, was a Marshal in 1183. His descendants were settled in Ireland at the period of Cromwell's usurpation.

The Right Hon. Nathaniel Clements, Deputy Vice-Treasurer of Ireland, and a Teller of the Exchequer, by his marriage with Hannah, daughter of the Very Rev. William Gore, Dean of Down, was father of Robert Clements, Esq., created in 1783 Baron Leitrim of Manor Hamilton, Co. Leitrim; in 1793 Viscount Leitrim, and in 1795 EARL OF LEITRIM. He *d.* in 1804, and was succeeded by his eldest son NATHANIEL, present and 2nd EARL, who was created a Peer of the United Kingdom in 1831, by the title of Baron Clements of Kilmacrenan, Co. Donegal.

LEVEN AND MELVILLE, EARL OF. (LESLIE-MELVILLE.)

Peer of Scotland.

Galfrid de Maleville, who founded the church of Melville, in the reign of Malcolm IV., is the first of this family on record, but whether of Anglo-Norman, or, as it is said by some, of Hungarian origin, is not ascertained.

Sir John Melville of Raith, 14th from him, was one of the first who embraced the reformed religion. At the time of the war between King HENRY VIII. and the Scottish government, in the minority of Queen MARY, all correspondence being forbidden between the two kingdoms, a letter from this Sir John Melville to his son, then in England for his education, was intercepted, and the Catholic party then in power had him taken up, and upon this trifling incident, tried and executed for high treason in 1549. He left several sons, of whom the three eldest were,

1 John Melville of Raith, his successor, grandfather of JOHN, 3rd LORD, who was ancestor of all the Earls Melville.

2 Sir Robert Melville of Murdocarny, a Privy-Counsellor to King JAMES VI.; he was appointed Ambassador to England in 1562, and again in 1587, to endeavour to prevent the execution of Queen MARY. He discharged that commission with such fidelity and zeal, that Queen ELIZABETH, highly offended, threatened his life, and would have imprisoned him, but that his colleague, the Master of Gray, had sufficient influence with her to prevent this violation of the international law. He was created in 1616, BARON MELVILLE of Monymail, with remainder, failing his issue male, to the heirs male of John, his elder brother. He *d.* in 1621, leaving one son, ROBERT, 2nd LORD, who *d.* without issue in 1635.

3 Sir James Melville of Wallhill, Co. Fife, the well-known ambassador from MARY to ELIZABETH, a Privy-Counsellor to James VI. He *d*, in 1617, leaving male issue.

JOHN, 3rd LORD, son of John Melville of Raith, and grandson of John, elder brother of the first Lord, succeeded, on the extinction of the male issue of the first Lord, according to the provisions of the patent; he *d.* in 1643, and was succeeded by his son GEORGE, 4th Lord. Firmly attached to the Presbyterian worship, and weary with the oppression to which that profession was subjected during the reign of Charles II., he was in London, holding some clandestine intercourse with the Duke of Monmouth, when the detection of the Ryehouse Plot warned him to make a timely escape into Holland; from thence he accompanied the Duke of Monmouth on his fatal expedition to England in 1685, and had again the good fortune to escape on the discomfiture of that enterprise. He returned to England with King WILLIAM; his forfeiture was rescinded, and his estates restored; he was created in 1690, EARL of MELVILLE, Viscount of Kircaldy, Lord Raith, Monymail, and Balwearie; and he continued high in favour and office to the end of that Monarch's life, when he finally retired from public business. He *d.* in 1707. His marriage with the heiress of the Earldom of Leven, brought that title, of which some account must now be given, into his family.

Seventh in descent from George Leslie of Balquhain, 4th son of Sir Andrew Leslie of Rothes, ancestor of the family of Leslie, Earls of Rothes, was ALEXANDER LESLIE, 1st EARL of LEVEN, so created in 1641, with remainder to his heirs whatsoever. He early embraced the profession of arms, and by that excellent judge of military ability, Gustavus Adolphus, King of Sweden, was promoted to the rank of Field-Marshal, for his eminent services in the German wars; he continued, after that King's death, in the service of Queen Christina, reaping glory from his successful enterprizes, till invited into Scotland in 1639, by the Covenanters, to take the command of their rebellious army; he stormed the castle of Edinburgh, and brought the forces assembled at Dunse Law into the most efficient state of military discipline; but by the pacification which ensued, both parties agreed to disband. The peace was, however, of short duration; a fresh army was raised; General Leslie was appointed Commander-in-Chief; he invaded England in Aug. 1640, routed the royal army at Newburn, and obtained military possession of the counties of Northumberland and Durham; a cessation of hostilities was agreed upon, and a treaty followed, which was ratified in 1641, and General Leslie was created Lord Balgony and EARL of LEVEN. In 1643 he was appointed General of the Scotch forces, sent to the assistance of the English Parliament, and defeated the Royalists at Marston Moor in the following year; but when an army was raised in 1648, for the rescue of the King, the Earl of Leven refused to take the command; being, nevertheless, suspected of an intention to join that preparing for the assistance of Charles II. in 1651, he was surprised by a detachment from the garrison at Dundee, and carried prisoner to the Tower of London, but was released at the intercession of the Queen of

Sweden in 1654. He *d.* in 1661, having had two sons, who both *d.* before him: Gustavus, the eldest, without issue; and Alexander Lord Balgony, the youngest, leaving a son and a daughter, viz. ALEXANDER, 2nd EARL, and CATHERINE, at length COUNTESS of LEVEN, the wife of the 1st EARL of MELVILLE.

ALEXANDER, 2nd EARL, who succeeded his grandfather, *d.* in 1664; he left two daughters, who successively inherited his title, viz. MARGARET, 3rd COUNTESS, who *m.* in 1674, the Hon. Francis Montgomery, 2nd son of Hugh, 7th Earl of Eglintoun, but *d.* in minority, the same year, without issue; and CATHERINE, 4th COUNTESS, who *d. unm.* in 1706.

CATHERINE, her aunt, only daughter of Lord Balgony, succeeded her as 5th COUNTESS; she *m.* as before observed, GEORGE, 1st EARL of MELVILLE, and *d.* in 1713, leaving two surviving sons: DAVID, who succeeded her as 6th EARL of LEVEN, and his father as 2nd Earl of Melville; and James, who left male issue.

DAVID, 6th EARL, *d.* in 1728; he had two sons, of whom the eldest, George Lord Balgony, *d.* before him in 1721, leaving one son, DAVID, 7th EARL, who succeeded his grandfather, and *d.* in his 12th year; and ALEXANDER, the younger son, succeeded his nephew as 8th EARL in 1729, and *d.* in 1754, leaving two sons: DAVID, 9th EARL; and Lieut.-General the Hon. Alexander Leslie, who served with high distinction in the American war, and was second in command to Lord Cornwallis at the battle of Guildford in 1781; he *d.* in 1794, leaving one daughter, for whom see *The Peerage Volume.*

DAVID, 9th EARL, was *b.* 4 March 1722, and *d.* 9 June 1802; having *m.* 29 July 1747, Wilhelmina, posthumous daughter of William Nisbet, Esq., by whom, who *d.* 10 May 1798, he had the issue stated in *The Peerage Volume*, and ALEXANDER, 10th EARL, his successor, to whom, in 1820, succeeded his eldest son DAVID, present and 11th EARL.

LICHFIELD, EARL OF. (ANSON.)

Peer of the United Kingdom.

His Lordship's great-grandfather, Sambrooke Adams, Esq., of Sambrooke, Co. Salop, who *d.* May 1734, *m.* Janetta, sister and heir of the celebrated circumnavigator, Admiral GEORGE ANSON, created Baron Anson 1747, which title became extinct at his death, 6 June 1762; she *d.* 1771. The only surviving issue of this marriage was George Adams, Esq., who assumed the name and arms of ANSON, having inherited the property of his uncles, Lord Anson and his elder brother Thomas Anson, Esq., of Shugborough, Co. Stafford. He *m.* 5 Jan. 1763, the Hon. Mary Vernon, daughter of George, 1st Lord Vernon, *b.* 19 Dec. 1739, *d.* 11 Dec. 1821; by whom he had the following issue:

1 Mary, *b.* 8 Dec. 1763, widow of Sir Francis Ford, Bart., *b.* 15 Nov. 1758, *m.* 22 Jan. 1785, *d.* 7 June 1801.

2 THOMAS, who was created in 1806, VISCOUNT ANSON of Shugborough and Orgrave, Co. Stafford, and Baron Soberton of Soberton, Co. Hants; his marriage and issue are described in *The Peerage Volume.* He *d.* 31 July 1818, and was succeeded by his eldest son, THOMAS-WILLIAM, the present and 3rd VISCOUNT.

3 Anne, *b.* 22 Feb. 1768, deceased; having *m.* 20 Dec. 1792, Bell Lloyd, Esq.

4 Lieutenant-General Sir George, K.C.B., K.T.S., M.P., Colonel 4th Dragoon Guards, *b.* 12 Aug. 1769, *m.* 27 May 1800, Frances, daughter of the late John Hamilton, Esq., and sister of Sir Frederick Hamilton, Bart., *b.* 6 April 1781. They have issue: 1 George-Augustus, Lieutenant 11th Dragoons, *b.* 13 Aug. 1801, *d.* 10 May 1829, having *m.* 4 Dec. 1823, Miss Barbara Park. 2 Mary-Anne, *b.* 28 Jan. 1803, widow; having *m.* 17 Sept. 1823, Rev. Charles-Gregory Okeover, *b.* 1792, *d.* 1 Aug. 1826. 3 Francis-Harcourt, Lieutenant R.N., *b.* 2 April 1804, *d.* 20 July 1831. 4 Frances-Elizabeth, *b.* 13 April, *d.* 28 June 1805. 5 Frederick-Walpole, in the Hon. East

India Company's Military Service, *b.* 21 May 1806, *m.* 25 July 1827, Miss Catherine Hanson, and has issue. 6 Charlotte-Isabella, *b.* 26 April 1807, *m.* 29 March 1828, Edward-Richard Northey, Esq. 7 Theodosius Vernon, *b.* 8 Sept. 1808, *d.* 18 Jan. 1825. 8 Talavera-Vernon, *b.* 26 Nov. 1809. 9 Constantia, *b.* 11 Dec. 1810, *m.* 6 Oct. 1831, Robert-North-Colley Hamilton, Esq., eldest son of Sir Frederick Hamilton, Bart. 10 Sophia, *b.* 20 Oct. 1812. 11 Adelaide-Frances, *b.* 25 July 1814, *d.* 15 Jan. 1815. 12 Octavius-Henry-St. George, *b.* 28 Sept. 1817. 13 Thomas-Anchitel, *b.* 14 Oct. 1818. 14 Julia-Henrietta, *b.* 10 Nov. 1819. 15 Edward-Hamilton, *b.* 2 Dec. 1821.

5 Venerable Charles, Archdeacon of Carlisle, *b.* 20 Aug. 1770, *d.* 20 June 1827.

6 Lieutenant-General Sir William, K.C.B., Member of the Board of General Officers, created a Baronet in 1831; *b.* 13 Aug. 1772, *m.* 26 Jan. 1815, Louisa-Frances-Mary, only child of John Dickenson, Esq. They have issue: 1 John-William-Hamilton, *b.* 26 Jan. 1816. 2 Mary-Louisa, *b.* 5 Jan. 1818. 3 William-Vernon-Dickenson, *b.* 10 Feb. 1819. 4 George-Henry-Greville, *b.* 19 July 1820. 5 Anne-Georgina-Frances, *b.* 14 July 1822. 6 Louisa-Frances-Maria, 7 Archibald-Edward-Harbord, twins, *b.* 16 April 1826.

7 Rev. Henry, *b.* 19 Dec. 1773.

8 Edward, *b.* 28 April 1775, *m.* 21 Jan. 1808, Harriott, daughter of John Ramsbottom, Esq., *b.* 29 April 1786. They have issue: 1 Harriott-Mary, *b.* 31 Oct. 1803, *d.* 10 Sept. 1809. 2 Edward-John, *b.* 8 Feb. 1810, *d.* 30 April 1819. 3 Harriott, *b.* 19 Aug. 1811. 4 Charles, *b.* 20 Feb. 1813. 5 Edward-George, *b.* 7 April 1816. 6 Elizabeth-Mary, *b.* 6 April 1818, *d.* an infant.

9 Sambrooke, *b.* 18 Feb. 1778.

10 Rev. Frederick, Prebendary of Southwell, *b.* 23 March 1779, *m.* 2 May 1807, Anne, only daughter of the late Rev. Richard Levett; and has issue: 1 Ellen-Anne, *b.* 15 July 1808. 2 Mary, *b.* 3 Jan. 1810. 3 Frederick, *b.* 28 March 1811. 4 George-Edward, *b.* 14 May 1812. 5 Catherine-Louisa, *b.* 1 Jan. 1814. 6 Lucy-Frederica, *b.* 22 Sept. 1815. 7 Arthur-Henry, *b.* 10 Aug. 1817. 8 Thomas, *b.* 24 May 1820. 9 Georgiana-Frances, *b.* 9 Nov. 1823.

11 Catherine-Juliana, *b.* 27 Dec. 1780, *m.* 17 March 1807, Henry Stuart, Esq.

LIFFORD, VISCOUNT. (Hewitt.)

Peer of Ireland.

James Hewitt, Lord Chancellor of Ireland, of a gentleman's family in Warwickshire, was created in 1768, Baron Lifford of Lifford, Co. Donegal, and in 1781, Viscount Lifford; he was *b.* in 1709, and *d.* 28 April 1782; having *m.* 1st, the only daughter of the Rev. Rice Williams, D.D., who *d.* in 1765; and 2ndly Ambrosia, daughter of the Rev. Charles Bayley, of Knavestock, Co. Essex; by whom, who *d.* in March 1807, he had a son and two daughters, who all *d. unm.* By his 1st marriage he had four sons:

1 James, his successor, 2nd Viscount, who was succeeded in 1830, by his eldest son, James, present and 3rd Viscount.

2 Hon. William-Williams, who *d.* April 1798; having *m.* 16 Feb. 1774, Anne, eldest daughter of Thomas Strettell, Esq., by whom, besides the three daughters noticed in *The Peerage Volume*, he had two sons: William, who *d.* in 1824, and Thomas, who *d.* in 1807, both *unm.*

3 Joseph, one of the Judges of the King's Bench in Ireland, who *d. unm.* 1 April 1794.

4 The Hon. and Very Rev. John, Dean of Cloyne, who *d.* 14 May 1804; having *m.* Jane, daughter of Dr. Moore, by whom he had Mary, the late wife of the Hon. Major-General Henry King—see *The Peerage Volume*, title Kingston—and James, who *d.* in 1797, a Midshipman on board H. M. S. Nemesis.

LILFORD, BARON. (Powys.)

Peer of Great Britain.

William Powys, who lived in the reign of King Edward II., was ancestor of John Powys of Myvolt, Montgomeryshire, from whom Thomas Powys, created in 1797, Baron of Lilford, Co. Northampton, was 8th in descent. He *d.* in 1800; and was succeeded by his eldest son, Thomas, 2nd Lord, who *d.* in 1825, and was succeeded by his eldest son, Thomas-Atherton, present and 3rd Lord.

LIMERICK, EARL OF. (Pery.)

Peer of Ireland and of the United Kingdom.

Colonel Edmond Pery, of Stackpole, Co. Clare, grandfather of the 1st Lord Glentworth, *d.* in 1721; his son,

Rice-Stackpole Pery, Esq., *d.* in 1739, leaving two sons, viz.:

1 Edmund-Sexten Pery, Esq., Speaker of the Irish House of Commons, created in 1785, Viscount Pery of Newtown Pery, Co. Limerick; he was *b.* 3 April 1719, and *d.* 24 Feb. 1806, when his title became extinct; having *m.* 1st, 11 June 1756, Patty, youngest daughter of John Martin, Esq., who *d.* without issue in 1757; and 2ndly, 27 Oct. 1762, The Hon. Elizabeth Vesey, eldest daughter of John, 1st Lord Knapton, sister of Thomas, 1st Viscount de Vesci, and widow of Robert Hancock, Esq., by whom, who was *b.* in 1732, and *d.* 4 April 1821, he left the two daughters mentioned in *The Peerage Volume.*

2 William-Cecil, Bishop of Limerick, who was created in 1790, Baron Glentworth of Mallow, Co. Cork, and *d.* in 1794, when he was succeeded by his only son, Edmund-Henry, 2nd Lord, who was created in 1800, Viscount Limerick, of the County of Limerick, and in 1803, Earl of Limerick; also in 1815, a Peer of the United Kingdom by the title of Baron Foxford of Stackpole Court, Co. Clare, and is the present Earl.

LINDSEY, EARL OF. (Bertie.)

Peer of England.

Thomas Bertie, Esq., Captain of Hurst Castle, in the latter end of the reign of Henry VII., was father of Richard Bertie, Esq., who had the good fortune to marry Katherine, Baroness Willoughby de Eresby, widow of Charles Brandon, Duke of Suffolk, and daughter and heir of William Willoughby, 7th Lord Willoughby de Eresby. This Lady being a zealous supporter of the Reformation, had so much cause of alarm when the persecution of the Protestants became a favourite measure with the advisers of Queen Mary, that Mr. Bertie found it necessary to make a precipitate escape to the Continent, and they suffered the severest hardships, even to the necessity of taking refuge under the church-porch from the pitiless storm, during their compulsory travels. The Hansetown of Wesel afforded them the protection they requested, and there in a hired lodging, their son and heir was born, who, from the circumstances of his parents at the time, received the name of Peregrine. They were soon afterwards compelled to quit their retreat, in consequence of learning that a plot was on foot to seize them at Wesel; and they sought refuge in the territories of the Elector Palatine, where they lived in obscurity till their means of procuring the necessaries of life nearly failed them; in this emergency, it fortunately occurred that Sigismund II., King of Poland, heard of their distress, and hospitably invited them into his dominions; where he maintained them in security and ease, till the death of Queen Mary enabled them to return to their own country. Mr. Bertie *d.* in 1582, having survived his Duchess, on whose death in 1580, her son, Peregrine, claimed and was allowed the Barony of Willoughby de Eresby. He was much in favour with Queen ELIZABETH, served with distinction in her armies, and attained the rank of General; he *d.* in 1601, having *m.* Mary, daughter of John Vere, Earl of Oxford, and heir of her nephew, Henry, 18th Earl of Oxford, by whom he was father of ROBERT, 10th Lord Willoughby de Eresby K.G., his successor. In 1625, Lord Robert inherited from his cousin, Henry, 18th Earl of Oxford, the hereditary office of Lord Great Chamberlain of England, which, from the reign of HENRY II., had been possessed by that ancient and noble family, and in 1626, was created Earl of Lindsey. On the breaking out of the civil war, he was appointed General of the Royal forces, received his death wound, and was made prisoner at the battle of Edge Hill, 23 Oct. 1642, and *d.* the same night. Two of his eight sons also fell in the King's service before this fatal war was brought to a close. King CHARLES wrote a letter of condolence to his eldest son and successor, MONTAGUE, 2nd EARL, expressive of his high regard for his father's memory and grief for his loss. The 2nd Earl commanded the King's guards in several battles, and was wounded at Naseby; he attended upon the King to the last; and when he found that the rebels actually intended to murder their Sovereign, he, the Duke of Richmond, the Marquis of Hertford, and the Earl of Southampton, offered themselves to suffer in his stead, as the Counsellors who had advised all the measures imputed to him as criminal; their magnanimous proposition however answered no other purpose than that of procuring them the melancholy satisfaction of interring his remains. He *d.* in 1666, having *m.* 1st, Martha, daughter of Sir William Cockayn of Rushton, Co. Northampton, and widow of John Ramsay, Earl of Holdernesse; she *d.* in 1641, and he *m.* 2ndly, Bridget, Baroness Norreys of Rycote, widow of Edward Sackville, Esq., 2nd son of Edward, Earl of Dorset, and daughter and heir of Edward Wray, Esq., by Elizabeth his wife, daughter and heir of Francis, Lord Norreys of Rycote, and Earl of Berkshire. By his first marriage he had five sons: 1 ROBERT, 3rd EARL, his successor; 2 Peregrine, who *d.* without issue male; 3 Richard, and 4 Robert, who both *d. unm.*; 5 Charles, ancestor of the present Earl. By his 2nd marriage, the Earl had, besides other issue, a son James, Baron Norreys, of Rycote, and Earl of Abingdon, ancestor to the Earl of Abingdon.

ROBERT, 3rd EARL, *d.* in 1701, and was succeeded by his eldest son, ROBERT, 4th EARL, created Marquis of Lindsey in 1706, and Duke of Ancaster and Kesteven, in 1715; he *d.* in 1722, and was succeeded by his eldest son, PEREGRINE, 5th EARL and 2nd Duke, who *d.* in 1742; he left three sons, of whom the 2nd son, Lord Albemarle Bertie, *d. unm.* in 1765; the other two, both Dukes of Ancaster, were;

1 PEREGRINE, 6th EARL, and 3rd Duke, his successor, who *d.* 12 Aug. 1778, having *m.* 1st, 22 May 1735, Elizabeth, daughter and heir of William Blundell, Esq., and widow of Sir Charles-Gunter Nicol, K.B., who *d.* without issue in Dec. 1743; and he *m.* 2ndly, 7 Nov. 1750, Mary, daughter of Thomas Panton, Esq., by whom, who *d.* 19 Oct. 1793, he left the late Baroness Willoughby de Eresby—for whom see that title in *The Peerage Volume*—the present Marchioness Dowager Cholmondeley; and

ROBERT, 7th EARL, and 4th Duke, who succeeded his father; he was *b.* 17 Oct. 1756, and *d.* 8 July 1779, when he was succeeded in the Dukedom by his uncle BROWNLOW, 5th DUKE, in the office of Great Chamberlain, by his two sisters jointly, who exercise it alternately; and between whom the Barony of Willoughby de Eresby fell into abeyance, but was called out by the Crown in favour of the elder sister, Lady Priscilla-Barbara-Elizabeth, in 1780.

2 BROWNLOW, 8th EARL, 5th and last Duke of Ancaster, *b.* 1 May 1729, succeeded his nephew in 1779, and *d.* 8 Feb. 1809; having *m.* 1st, 6 Nov. 1762, Harriet, daughter and sole heir of George-Morton Pitt, Esq., who *d.* without issue, 23 April

1763; 2ndly, 2 Jan. 1769, Mary-Anne, youngest daughter of Major Peter Layard, who *d.* 11 Jan. 1804; by his 2nd marriage the Duke had a daughter, Lady Mary-Elizabeth, *b.* 24 July 1771, *d.* 10 Feb. 1797, Viscountess Milsington, see *The Peerage Volume*, title Portmore. On the Duke's death the titles of Duke of Ancaster and Kesteven, and Marquis of Lindsey, became extinct, and the Earldom devolved on

ALBEMARLE, 9th EARL, eldest surviving son of Peregrine Bertie, son of Charles, eldest son and heir of the Hon. Charles Bertie, 5th son of MONTAGU, 2nd Earl; he *d.* in 1818, and was succeeded by his eldest son, GEORGE-AUGUSTUS-FREDERICK-ALBEMARLE, present and 10th EARL.

LISBURNE, EARL OF. (VAUGHAN.)

Peer of Ireland.

Sir John Vaughan, whose ancestors had been seated at Trawscoed, in Cardiganshire, for many generations, was Lord Chief Justice of the Court of Common Pleas. His grandson, JOHN, was created in 1695, Lord Vaughan, Baron of Fethers, and Viscount Lisburne, Co. Antrim; his two sons, JOHN, who *d.* in 1741, and WILMOT, were successively 2nd and 3rd VISCOUNTS; the latter *d.* in 1766, and was succeeded by his eldest son, WILMOT, 4th Viscount, who was created EARL of LISBURNE, in 1776; he *d.* in 1800, leaving two sons: 1 WILMOT, 2nd EARL, his successor, who *d.* in 1820; 2 JOHN, who succeeded his brother, and is the present and 3rd EARL.

LISLE, BARON. (LYSAGHT.)

Peer of Ireland.

This family claims its descent from the ancient House of O'Brien in the Co. of Clare. JOHN LYSAGHT, Esq., was created BARON LISLE of Mountnorth, Co. Cork, in 1758, and *d.* 15 July 1781, having been twice married; 1st, in 1725, to Catherine, 3rd daughter and co-heir of Joseph Deane, Esq., by Margaret Boyle, sister of Henry, 1st Earl of Shannon, who *d.* 5 July 1743; and 2ndly, in 1746, to Elizabeth, only daughter of Edward Moore, Esq., who *d.* in Nov. 1788; by the first marriage his Lordship had issue, John, 2nd Lord, his successor; the Hon. Joseph Lysaght, who *d.* 8 Aug. 1799, having *m.* 3 June 1795, Hon. Henrietta St. Leger, eldest daughter of St. Leger, 1st Viscount Doneraile, and widow of John Godsell, Esq., who *d.* in April 1822; James, who *d. unm.*; and the two eldest daughters stated in *The Peerage Volume*; by the second, he had a son and daughter, who *d. unm.*, and Mrs. Travers, who also appears in *The Peerage Volume*. He was succeeded by his eldest son JOHN, 2nd LORD, who *d*, in 1798, and was succeeded by his eldest son, JOHN, present and 3rd LORD.

LISMORE, VISCOUNT. (O'CALLAGHAN.)

Peer of Ireland.

This ancient Irish family claims for ancestor, Callaghan, a Prince of Munster, renowned for his exploits against the Danes. Cornelius O'Callaghan, from whom his Lordship descends, was Lord of Poble Callaghan, in Munster, in 1594.

Cornelius O'Callaghan, Esq., a Member of Parliament, remarkable for his great abilities at the bar, who *d.* in 1761, was grandfather of Cornelius O'Callaghan, Esq., created in 1785, Baron Lismore of Shanbally, Co. Tipperary; he *d.* in 1797, and was succeeded by his eldest son, Cornelius, 2nd Lord; who was created in 1806, Viscount Lismore of Shanbally, Co. Tipperary, and is the present Peer.

LISTOWEL, EARL OF. (Hare.)

Peer of Ireland.

John Hare, Esq., his Lordship's grandfather, removed from the County of Norfolk into Ireland, and fixed his residence at Ennismore, early in the last century. His 3rd son, Richard, *d.* in 1792; having *m.* Margaret, daughter of Samuel Maylor, Esq., by whom he was father of William Hare, Esq., the present Peer; created in 1800, Baron Ennismore of Ennismore, Co. Kerry; in 1816, Viscount Ennismore and Listowel, Co. Kerry; and in 1822, Earl of Listowel.

LIVERPOOL, EARL OF. (Jenkinson.)

Peer of Great Britain.

Anthony Jenkinson, an eminent navigator and merchant in the reigns of Edward VI., Mary, and Elizabeth, was Ambassador from England to Constantinople and the Czar of Muscovy, and returning with a large fortune, vested it in lands in the counties of Oxford and Gloucester. Sir Robert Jenkinson, of Walcot, Co. Oxon, knighted in 1618, is supposed to be his descendant, his arms alluding to seamanship, corroborating the opinion; he was father of Sir Robert, who was created a Baronet in 1661, and appointed by the will of the celebrated Judge, Sir Matthew Hale, trustee of his estates and guardian of his grandchildren; he *d.* in 1677. Sir Robert, his successor, 2nd Baronet, *d.* in 1709, leaving two sons, viz.: 1 Sir Robert, 3rd Baronet, *d.* in 1717; he was grandfather of Sir Banks Jenkinson, 6th Baronet, on whose death in 1789, the Baronetcy devolved on the 1st Earl of Liverpool; and 2

Colonel Charles Jenkinson, who *d.* in 1750, having *m.* Aramantha, daughter of Captain Wolfran Cornwall, R.N., by whom, who *d.* in 1785, he had issue:

1 Charles, 1st Earl.

2 Colonel John Jenkinson, *d.* 1 May 1805, having *m.* Frances, daughter of Admiral John Barker, by whom, who *d.* 28 Aug. 1811, he had issue:

- 1 Charles, *b.* 23 Feb. 1779.
- 2 John Banks, D.D., Lord Bishop of St. David's, *b.* 2 Sept. 1781, *m.* 8 April 1813, Frances-Augusta, 3rd daughter of Augustus Pechell, Esq., and has issue.
- 3 George, *b.* 24 Feb. 1783, Lieut.-Colonel R.A., *d. unm.* 1823.
- 4 Robert-Henry, *b.* 8 June 1786, Lieutenant of Dover Castle, Registrar of the Excise, Receiver of the Customs.
- 5 Herbert-William, *d.* 13 Dec. 1817.
- 6 Fanny, *m.* 18 Jan. 1805, Sir William Boothby, Bart.
- 7 Anne-Maria, *m.* March 1810, Captain Fanshawe, R.N., and *d.* 13 Dec. 1818.

3 Elizabeth, *d.* 8 March 1809; having *m.* the Right Hon. Charles Wolfran Cornwall, who *d.* in 1784.

Charles, eldest son of Colonel Charles Jenkinson, was many years employed under the successive administrations of the reign of George III., and was especially distinguished for his knowledge of the finances of the country, of the principles of commerce, and of political arithmetic in general, on which subjects he has left several valuable tracts. He was created in 1786, Baron Hawkesbury, of Hawkesbury, Co. Gloucester, and in 1796, Earl of Liverpool. He *d.* in 1808, and was succeeded by his eldest son, Robert-Banks, 2nd Earl, who entered in very early life into the Government service, and rose through its various gradations, till, on the assassination of Mr. Perceval in 1812, he was appointed Prime Minister, which important office he held without interruption, and with the confidence of the nation, till a paralytic affection deprived the country of his talents in Feb. 1827, and terminated his life in Dec. 1828. He was succeeded by his only-surviving half brother, Charles-Cecil-Cope, the present and 3rd Earl.

LONDONDERRY, MARQUIS OF. (Vane-Stewart.)

Peer of Ireland and of the United Kingdom.

The Marquis claims his descent from the noble house of Stewart, Earl of Galloway, but separated before the creation of either Peerage. The first of the family who settled in Ireland was John Stewart, Esq., who, in the reign of Charles I., erected Ballylawn Castle, in the county of Donegal. His great-grandson, William Stewart, Esq., was active in his exertions in the Protestant interest at the period of the Revolution, and raised, at his own expense, a troop of horse for the relief of the city of Londonderry; his 2nd son, Alexander, succeeded at Ballylawn castle, on the death without issue of his elder brother Thomas, in 1740; he was *b.* in 1700, and *d.* 21 April 1781; having *m.* 30 June 1737, Mary, daughter of John Cowan, Esq., by whom, who *d.* 8 April 1788, he had, besides other issue, two surviving sons, viz.:

1 Robert, who was created in 1789, Baron Stewart of Londonderry, Co. Londonderry; in 1795, Viscount Castlereagh; in 1796, Earl of Londonderry; and in 1816, Marquis of Londonderry. He *d.* in 1821, and was succeeded by his eldest son, Robert, 2nd Marquis, better known as the celebrated Minister of State, Viscount Castlereagh; he *d.* in consequence of the exhaustion produced by unremitting attention to his complicated duties during a long and harassing session of Parliament in 1822; and was succeeded by his half-brother, Charles-William, present and 2nd Marquis, who, for his signal military services, had been created to the British Peerage in 1814, by the title of Baron Stewart, of Stewart's Court and Ballylawn, Co. Donegal. On occasion of his 2nd marriage with Lady Frances-Anne-Emily, daughter and heir of Sir Harry-Vane Tempest, Bart., by the present Countess of Antrim, in 1819, his Lordship assumed the name of Vane; and was created in 1823, Viscount Seaham, Co. Durham, and Earl Vane, with remainder to his issue male by his second wife.

LONGFORD, EARL OF. (Pakenham.)

Peer of Ireland and of the United Kingdom.

William de Pakenham was seated in Suffolk in the reign of King Edward I.; Edward Pakenham, his descendant, removed to Ireland in 1576; the 15th in descent from him was Thomas Pakenham, of Pakenham Hall, Co. Westmeath, who was created in 1756, Baron of Longford, and *d.* in 1766, having *m.* Elizabeth, daughter and heir of Michael Cuffee, Esq., by the sister and heir of Ambrose Aungier, 2nd Earl of Longford, [which title became extinct on his death in 1704;] she was created in 1785, Countess of Longford, and *d.* in 1794. They had issue: 1 Edward-Michael, 2nd Earl; 2 Hon. Robert, *d. unm.* in 1775; 3 William, *d.* young; 4 Hon. Sir Thomas, G.C.B., *b.* in 1757, for whose marriage and issue see *The Peerage Volume*; 5 Lady Elizabeth, *b.* in 1742, *d. unm.* in 1818; 6 Hon.

Frances, *d.* in 1772, having *m.* in June 1766, John-Ormsby Vandeleur, Esq., who *d.* in 1779; 7 Hon. Helena, *d.* in 1774, having *m.* in June 1768, William Sherlock, Esq., who *d.* in 1788; 8 Hon. Mary, *d.* in 1775, having *m.* in March 1770, Thomas Fortescue, Esq.

EDWARD-MICHAEL, 2nd EARL, their eldest son, succeeded his father in the Barony, and *d.* before his mother in 1792; when he was succeeded by his eldest son, THOMAS, who likewise succeeded his grandmother in the Earldom, and is the present Peer; he was created in 1821, Baron Silchester, Co. Southampton, in the Peerage of the United Kingdom.

LONSDALE, EARL OF. (LOWTHER.)

Peer of the United Kingdom.

This family is of great antiquity in the County of Westmoreland. Lord Crofton springs from a junior branch of it. Sir Gervasius de Lowther held a Knight's service of King Henry III. in 1217.

The 14th in descent from him was Sir John Lowther, who had three sons:

1 Sir John, his heir, created a Baronet of Nova Scotia in 1640, *d.* in 1675; he was father of,

- 1 Colonel John Lowther, who *d.* before his father; his son John was created Baron Lowther of Lowther, Co. Westmoreland, and Viscount Lonsdale, in 1696; he *d.* in 1700, leaving three sons, Richard, Henry, and Anthony, who all *d. unm.*, the latter in 1741; the two former were successive Viscounts, and the title became extinct in 1751, on the death of the 2nd son, Henry, 3rd Viscount.
- 2 Richard, grandfather of SIR JAMES LOWTHER, who succeeded to the Baronetcy on the death of the 3rd Viscount, and was created Baron Lowther of Lowther, and Baron of Kendal, Co. Cumberland, Baron of Burgh, Co. Westmoreland, Viscount of Lonsdale and Viscount Lowther, Co. Westmoreland, and Earl of Lonsdale, 1784; all which titles became extinct on his death without issue, 24 May 1802; but he was also created, in 1797, BARON and VISCOUNT LOWTHER of Whitehaven, Co. Cumberland, with remainder to the heirs male of the body of the Rev. Sir William Lowther, Bart., in which titles he was succeeded by the present Earl, son and heir of the said Sir William.

2 Sir Christopher, created a Baronet in 1641, which title became extinct, with his male issue, by the death of his grandson, Sir James, the 4th Baronet, in 1755.

3 Sir William Lowther of Swillington; he *d.* in 1687; his eldest son, Sir William, *d.* in 1705, having had eight sons, of whom only two left male issue, viz.:

- 1 Sir William, his successor at Swillington, created a Baronet in 1715, which title became extinct on the death of his son, Sir William, 2nd Baronet.
- 2 Christopher, who *d.* in 1718, leaving issue, Sir William, in holy orders, rector of Swillington; he succeeded to the estate of his cousin, Sir William, and was created a Baronet in 1764; he *d.* in 1788, and the titles of Viscount and Baron Lowther were entailed upon his issue male in 1797. He was succeeded in the Baronetcy by his eldest son, SIR WILLIAM, who also succeeded in 1802, as 2nd Viscount Lowther, was created EARL of LONSDALE, Co. Westmoreland, in 1807, and is the present Peer.

LORTON, VISCOUNT. (KING.)

Peer of Ireland.

His Lordship is the 2nd son of Robert, 2nd Earl of Kingston, and brother of the present Earl; he was created in 1800, Baron Erris of Erris, Co. Roscommon; and in 1806, VISCOUNT LORTON of Boyle, Co. Roscommon.

LOTHIAN, MARQUIS OF. (KERR.)

Peer of Scotland and of the United Kingdom.

The house of Kerr is of Anglo-Norman lineage. The Kers of Cessford, and the Kerrs of Fernihirst, from the latter of whom the present Marquis of Lothian descends, were the issue of two brothers who settled in Scotland in the 13th century, but which was the eldest is unknown.

Walter Ker of Cessford, who *d.* in 1501, had two sons: 1 Sir Robert, ancestor of the 1st Earl of Roxburghe, who *d.* without surviving issue male, in 1650; 2 Mark, whose son MARK KER was created EARL of LOTHIAN in 1606, with remainder to the heirs male of his body; he *d.* in 1609. ROBERT, 2nd EARL, his son, *d.* in 1624; having no male issue, he had obtained a confirmation of his title to the LADY ANNE, his eldest daughter, and the heirs male of her body; she *m.* William, eldest son of ROBERT, 1st EARL of ANCRUM.

Ralph Kerr, the first on record of the House of Fernihirst, settled in Teviotdale about 1330.

The 8th from him was Sir Andrew Kerr, of Fernihirst, who was much distinguished in the reigns of JAMES IV. and V. for his resistance to the power of England upon the borders, and particularly for his gallant defence of his castle of Fernihirst against the Earl of Surrey and Lord Dacre, to whom, after a long siege, he was compelled to surrender it in Sept. 1523. He *d.* in 1545, leaving two sons:

1 Sir John, who retook his castle of Fernihirst from the English, by storm, in 1549, and is accused of being accessory, with Sir Walter Kerr, to the nocturnal murder of Sir Walter Scott, of Branxholm, in the streets of Edinburgh, in 1552; he *d.* in 1562. His eldest son, Sir Thomas, was a loyal and active adherent of Queen Mary; he joined her at Hamilton, after her escape from Lochleven, in 1568; and the defeat of Langside having frustrated all hope of serving her in Scotland, he, in conjunction with Sir Walter Scott, of Buccleugh, carried fire and sword into England, in hopes of rendering her some assistance there; the Lord Hunsdon and the Earl of Sussex, in retaliation, demolished the castle of Fernihirst, and laid waste the adjacent country. He joined the gallant Kirkaldy in the defence of the castle of Edinburgh, whither he removed the charter-chest of his family, which, on the surrender of the fortress to the Regent Morton, was seized and never recovered. He was then obliged to take refuge in France, but was permitted to return with a full pardon as soon as JAMES VI. assumed the reins of government. In 1585, having, as Warden of the middle marches, met the English Warden on the borders, a fray took place, in which Sir Francis Russell, son of the Earl of Bedford, was killed; he was, to appease Queen ELIZABETH, committed to ward, in Aberdeen, where he *d.* in 1586. His youngest son was the celebrated and infamous favourite of King JAMES I., Robert Kerr, created Viscount Rochester in 1612, and Earl of Somerset in 1613; imprisoned in the Tower, and convicted, in 1616, of the murder of Sir Thomas Overbury, but pardoned in 1624; he *d.*, without issue male, in 1645; having *m.* Lady Frances Howard, the divorced wife of Robert Devereux, Earl of Essex. The eldest son of Sir Thomas Kerr, of Fernihirst, and brother of the Earl of Somerset,

was Sir Andrew, created, in 1622, LORD JEDBURGH, with remainder to his heirs male. He *d.* in 1628 without issue, and was succeeded by his next brother, SIR JAMES, 2nd LORD; he *d.* in 1645, and was succeeded by his son ROBERT, 3rd LORD, who obtained in 1670, a charter, limiting the title to William, Lord Newbottle, eldest son of ROBERT, 4th EARL, afterwards MARQUIS of LOTHIAN, and, after him, to the eldest son of the Earl of Lothian, for the time, as a distinct Peerage for ever. He *d.* in 1692, when the male line of Sir John, eldest son of the above Sir Andrew Kerr, of Fernihirst, became extinct, and the Barony devolved on the said WILLIAM, Lord Newbottle, eldest son of ROBERT, 4th EARL, afterwards 1st Marquis of Lothian.

2 Robert Kerr, of Ancrum, *d.* in 1588; his son and successor, William, was assassinated in 1590, by Robert Kerr, younger, of Cessford, when the disputes about seniority between the houses of Cessford and Fernihirst were at the highest. Sir Robert Kerr, his eldest son, was gentleman of the bedchamber to King Charles I., by whom he was created in 1633, EARL of ANCRUM, Lord Kerr, of Nisbet, Long-Newton, and Dolphingston, with remainder to his issue male by his 2nd marriage, failing which, to his heirs male. He was faithful to his Royal master throughout all his troubles, and after his murder, was compelled to take refuge in Holland; there, having sacrificed all his means in his Sovereign's cause, he passed the remainder of his days in solitude and poverty, all his afflictions being aggravated by the reflection, that his favourite son, the Earl of Lothian, had taken up arms in opposition to the sacred cause in which he himself was so severely suffering. He *d.* in 1654, leaving two sons; viz.,

By the 1st marriage.

1 WILLIAM, who *m.* the above-mentioned LADY ANNE, COUNTESS of LOTHIAN, and was created Earl of Lothian in 1631.

By the 2nd marriage.

2 CHARLES, who succeeded his father as 2nd Earl of Ancrum, and on whose death without issue, the title devolved on his nephew ROBERT, 4th EARL of LOTHIAN, and 3rd Earl of Ancrum, afterwards created MARQUIS of LOTHIAN.

WILLIAM, EARL of LOTHIAN, the eldest son, from the commencement of the differences between the King and Parliament, manifested great zeal for the Covenant, and was engaged in all the actions of the Scotch army till 1643, when he was sent on a mission to France, and, on his return, repaired to Oxford to give an account of his embassy to the King; here he was arrested on an unfounded suspicion of treachery, and confined for several months in Bristol Castle. In the following year he was joined with the Marquis of Argyll in command of the forces sent to oppose Montrose, but soon surrendered his commission. In 1648 he protested against the engagement for the rescue of the King, but as soon as the proposition for bringing his Majesty to trial became known, he was one of the commissioners sent from Scotland to remonstrate against any violence or indignity being committed upon his sacred person; on his return he received the thanks of Parliament for his honest, though ineffectual efforts, and for the solemn protest of abhorrence and detestation, which, in the name of the Scottish nation, he had made against the proceedings of the English rulers, and was soon after dispatched to invite King CHARLES II. into Scotland. He *d.* in 1675, leaving, by the COUNTESS of LOTHIAN, his consort, besides other issue, a son Charles, ancestor of the Kerrs of Abbotrule, still existing in the male line; and his eldest son and heir,

ROBERT, who succeeded his mother as 4th Earl of Lothian, and his uncle CHARLES, 2nd EARL, as 3rd Earl of Ancrum; he was created, in 1701, MARQUIS of LOTHIAN, and *d.* in 1703. WILLIAM, 2nd MARQUIS, his eldest son and successor, a libertine and without religion, was, however, a patriot, and an active supporter of the revolution. He *d.* in 1722, and was succeeded by his eldest son, WILLIAM, 3rd MARQUIS, whose 2nd son, Lord Robert Kerr, a Captain in the King's army, was killed at the battle of Culloden. The Marquis *d.* in 1767, and was succeeded by his eldest son, WILLIAM-HENRY, 4th MARQUIS; he commanded the cavalry on the left wing of the Royal army at the battle of Culloden, when his brother fell; he *d.* in 1775. WILLIAM-JOHN, his eldest son, 5th MARQUIS, succeeded, and was succeeded, in 1815, by his eldest son WILLIAM, 6th MARQUIS; to whom, in 1824, succeeded his eldest son JOHN-WILLIAM-ROBERT, present and 7th MARQUIS.

LOUDOUN, COUNTESS OF. (CAMPBELL-RAWDON-HASTINGS.)

Peeress of Scotland.

Sir Colin More Campbell, the common ancestor of the families of Argyll, Breadalbane, and Loudoun, was father of Sir Niel, who *d.* in 1316; and of Sir Donald, from whom, the 12th in paternal descent, was SIR HUGH CAMPBELL, created LORD CAMPBELL of LOUDOUN, in 1601, and *d.* in 1622. His only son George, *d.* before him in 1612, leaving a daughter and heir, MARGARET, BARONESS of LOUDOUN, who succeeded her grandfather.

From Sir Niel, eldest son of Sir Colin More, the 4th in descent, was Duncan, 1st Lord Campbell, who had two sons:

1 Archibald, ancestor of the Duke of Argyll.

2 Sir Colin; father of Sir Duncan, his eldest son, ancestor of the Earl of Breadalbane, and of John, his 2nd son, from whom descended in the 5th degree,

SIR JOHN CAMPBELL, who *m.* MARGARET BARONESS of LOUDOUN, abovementioned, and was created in 1633, EARL of LOUDOUN, Lord Farrinyean and Machline. In 1640, being engaged in active opposition to the Court, he was imprisoned in the Tower by the King's order, on account of a letter signed by him and other nobles to the King of France, imploring his assistance; he was however soon after liberated at the intercession of the Marquis of Hamilton. His Lordship took a principal part against the Royal authority in the troubles that ensued, till, having been one of the commissioners sent to treat with the King in the Isle of Wight in 1647, the result of that treaty proved to him and his colleagues, the Earls of Lauderdale and Lanark, that the party now in power in England, had ulterior objects in which the Scottish nation would never acquiesce, and the engagement for the King's rescue was immediately proposed and adopted; the Earl of Loudoun concurred in it, but, dissatisfied with his associates and their plans, soon withdrew. After the defeat of CHARLES II. he retired to the Highlands and joined Lord Glencairn and the Royalists, but, on their dispersion, submitted to General Monk. He *d.* in 1663.

JAMES, 2nd EARL, his eldest son, not concurring in the measures of Government under CHARLES II., went abroad, and *d.* at Leyden in 1684. Two of his sons left issue; viz.,

1 HUGH, 3rd EARL, his successor; he obtained a confirmation of his titles, with remainder to the heirs male of his body, remainder to the heirs whatsoever of the body of the 1st Earl. He *d.* in 1731, and his only son and successor JOHN, 4th EARL, who served in the army with great distinction against the rebels in 1745, and commanded in chief, the army opposed to the French in America, in the years 1756-7, *d.* without issue in 1782, when the issue of his father became extinct.

2 Lieut.-General Sir James Campbell, of Lawers, served in the army under the Duke of Marlborough, and, by his gallantry, contributed signally to the successful issue of the battle of Malplaquet. He was killed in the battle of Fontenoy, where he commanded the British horse, 30 April 1745. His only son, JAMES-MURE, succeeded as 5th EARL, and *d.* in 1780, leaving an only child, FLORA-MURE, present COUNTESS, now the widow of Francis Rawdon-Hastings, 1st Marquis of Hastings.

LOUTH, BARON. (Plunkett.)

Peer of Ireland.

This ancient family, of which Lord Louth is the chief, is of Danish extraction. Sir Hugh de Plunket came from England into Ireland in the reign of King Henry II., and was ancestor of John, living in the reign of Henry III., who had two sons, 1 John, ancestor of Oliver, 1st Lord Louth; 2 Richard, ancestor of the Earl of Fingall and Lord Dunsany.

Sir Oliver Plunkett, of Kilfaran, was created Baron of Louth, Co. Louth, in 1541; he was succeeded by his son, Thomas, 2nd Lord, who *d.* in 1574, leaving two sons: Patrick, 3rd Lord, his eldest son and successor, *d.* without issue male in 1575, and was succeeded by his brother Oliver, 4th Lord, who *d.* in 1607, and was successively followed in uninterrupted paternal descent by eight generations of Barons, to Thomas-Oliver, the present and 12th Lord, who succeeded his father, Thomas, 11th Lord, in 1823.

LUCAN, EARL OF. (Bingham.)

Peer of Ireland.

Of this ancient family, which is said to be of Saxon origin, was Sir John de Bingham, who was seated at Bingham's Melcomb, Co. Dorset, in the reign of Henry I. From him descended, in the time of King Henry VIII.,

Robert Bingham, whose eldest son Robert, continued the line at Melcomb, which still exists; and his 4th son,

George settled in Ireland; he had issue, Sir Henry Bingham, of Castlebar, Co. Mayo, eldest son, created a Baronet of Nova Scotia in 1632; and John, youngest son, ancestor of Lord Clanmorris.

Sir Charles Bingham, Bart., 4th in descent from the 1st Baronet, was created in 1776, Baron Lucan of Castlebar, Co. Mayo; and Earl of Lucan in 1795; he *d.* in 1799, and was succeeded by his only son, Richard, present and 2nd Earl.

LUDLOW, EARL. (Ludlow.)

Peer of Ireland and of the United Kingdom.

The family of Ludlow derive their surname from the town of Ludlow in Salop, where they were originally seated. William Ludlow, a branch of this family, took up his residence at Hill Deverell, Co. Wilts, in the middle of the 14th century. From him descended Stephen Ludlow, Esq., who settled in Ireland, and *d.* 1721. He was father of Peter Ludlow, Esq., who, by Mary, daughter and heir of Peter Ludlow, Esq. of Ardsalla, had issue, Peter, created in 1755 Baron of Ardsalla, Co. Meath; and in 1760 Viscount Preston and Earl Ludlow. He *d.* in 1803, leaving two sons, viz.: 1 Augustus, his successor, 2nd Earl, who *d. unm.* in 1811; 2 George-James, present and 3rd Earl, who succeeded his brother, and was created a Peer of the United Kingdom in 1831, by the title of Baron Ludlow.

LYNDHURST, BARON. (Copley.)

Peer of the United Kingdom.

Sir John-Singleton Copley, who had passed through the offices of Solicitor and Attorney-General, was advanced from the Mastership of the Rolls to be Lord High Chancellor of Great Britain in 1827, and was at the same time created Baron Lyndhurst of Lyndhurst, Co. Hants.;. he resigned the Great Seal in 1830, and was in 1831, appointed Lord Chief Baron of the Exchequer. His Lordship is son of John-Singleton Copley, Esq., R.A. who *d.* 9 Sept. 1815, by a daughter of Richard Clarke, Esq.; and has two sisters, one of whom *m.* Gardener Green, Esq., of Boston, in America.

LYNEDOCH, BARON. (Graham.)

Peer of the United Kingdom.

His Lordship is a branch of the family of the Duke of Montrose. Sir William Graham of Kincardine (10th in descent from William Graham, patriarch of the family,) *m.* 1st, Mariota, daughter of Sir John Oliphant, and had by her two sons, of whom Alexander, the eldest, was great-grandfather of the 1st Earl of Montrose, from whom the present Duke descends; and 2ndly, Mary Stewart, 2nd daughter of King Robert III., and relict of George, Earl of Angus, and by her had five sons, from the third of whom, William Graham, his Lordship is lineally descended. He is son of

Thomas Graham, Esq., of Balnagowan, who *d.* 6 Dec. 1766; by marriage with Lady Christian Hope, 6th daughter of Charles, 1st Earl of Hopetoun. He was created, in 1814, in consequence of his eminent military services, especially in the Peninsular War, Baron Lynedoch of Balnagowan, Co. Perth, and is the present Peer.

LYTTELTON, BARON. (Lyttelton.)

Peer of Great Britain and of Ireland.

His Lordship is paternally descended from the ancient family of Westcote, seated at Westcote in Devonshire; of whom Henry de Westcote held lands there in 1314.

Thomas de Westcote, a descendant of this Henry, *m.* Elizabeth, heiress of Thomas de Luttelton, of Frankley in Worcestershire, and assumed her surname, though their three younger sons continued the family name of Westcote. Their eldest son was the famous Judge, Sir Thomas Lyttleton, who *d.* in 1481; the 5th in descent from him was

John Lyttelton, Esq., of Frankley; who being a Roman Catholic, was induced by some gentlemen of that persuasion to join in the conspiracy against the government of Queen Elizabeth, which cost the Earl of Essex his life. He was convicted of high treason, though the evidence against him amounted only to his having joined the conspirators at Drury House, towards the close of a treasonable consultation. He was condemned to die, but the interest of Sir Walter Raleigh, procured by a considerable bribe, saved his life for a few months, and he *d.* of disease in the King's Bench prison, in 1601. All his estates were forfeited, but King James, soon after his accession, willing to ingratiate himself with the people, who retained great regard for Essex's memory, restored them to his widow and family. Muriel, his widow, daughter of Sir Thomas Bromley, survived him eight-and-twenty years; disencumbered his estates from the debts her husband's political enterprizes had created, and had the good fortune to breed up her children in the reformed religion. Her eldest son, Sir Thomas, was created a Baronet in 1618; he was active in the cause of King Charles I., and a member of the Oxford Parliament, but was taken prisoner by the rebels at Bewdley in 1643, and confined in the Tower of London till 1649, within which period his estates were sequestrated by Parliament, and his house at Frankley burnt to the ground by Prince Rupert, who had garrisoned it for the King, lest, on his being compelled to abandon it, the enemy should make the same advantage of it. He *d.* in 1649. His son and heir, Sir Henry, was arrested by Cromwell in 1654, and confined for seventeen months in the Tower, on suspicion of a design to subvert the Government, a large quantity of arms being discovered in a private room in his house at Hagley. He *d.* in 1693, leaving no issue, and was succeeded by his brother, Sir Charles, who was as much distinguished as his father and brother for his zeal in the Royal cause, during the continuance of the civil contests. He was in the town of Colchester when it was besieged by the Parliamentary forces, and on its surrender escaped to France. He was made prisoner in 1659, on the miscarriage of Sir George Booth's attempt upon Shrewsbury; but being shortly after released, was employed by the King as his medium of communication with those friends in England, who so materially facilitated the great work of the Restoration. He held office under Government during the reigns of Charles II. and James II., but resigned his employments at the Revolution, rather than take another oath of allegiance. He *d.* in 1714; having *m.* Christian, 2nd daughter of Sir Richard Temple, Bart., and sister of Richard, 1st Viscount Cobham, whose titles of Viscount and Baron Cobham, are entailed on her and her issue male, failing the issue male of her elder sister Hester, afterwards created Countess Temple, the wife of Richard Grenville, Esq., from whom the Duke of Buckingham, now Viscount Cobham, descends. By this Lady, besides two sons who *d.* young, Sir Thomas Lyttelton had issue:

1 George, created Baron Lyttelton in 1757. This elegant poet and most amiable man *d.* in 1773, leaving an only son, Thomas, 2nd Lord, a nobleman of great talents, but very profligate habits; he *d.* in 1779, when the title became extinct.

2 Charles, Bishop of Carlisle, *d. unm.* 1768.

3 Lieut.-General Sir Richard Lyttelton, K.B., *d.* without issue in 1770; having *m.* Rachel, daughter of Wriothesley, 2nd Duke of Bedford, and widow of Scroop, 1st Duke of Bridgewater.

4 William-Henry, created in 1776 Baron Westcote of Baltimore, Co. Longford, in the Peerage of Ireland; he succeeded to the Baronetcy on the death of his nephew, Thomas, Lord Lyttelton, and was created Lord Lyttelton, Baron of Frankley, in 1794. He *d.* in 1808, having had six sons, of whom only two survived him, viz. 1 George-Fulke, his successor, 2nd Lord, who *d. unm.* in 1828; 2 William-Henry, who succeeded his brother, and is the present and 3rd Lord.

MACCLESFIELD, EARL OF. (Parker.)

Peer of Great Britain.

The first certain ancestor of the Earl is Thomas Le Parker, a person of ample possessions in the reign of Edward III. The 8th in descent from him was Thomas Parker, who rose to the office of Lord High Chancellor in 1718, and was created in 1716 Baron Parker of Macclesfield, Co. Chester; and in 1721 Viscount Parker of Ewelme, Co. Oxford, and Earl of Macclesfield, Co. Cheshire, with remainder, failing his issue male, to his daughter Elizabeth, wife of William Heathcote, Esq., and her issue male. In consequence of which limitation, Sir William Heathcote of

Hursley, Bart, heir male of the said Lady Elizabeth, is next in succession to the Earldom, after the existing male descendants of the 1st Earl, who are described in *The Peerage Volume*. A numerous family of Heathcotes also descend in the male line from the said Lady Elizabeth, and are in remainder to the titles. The Earl was impeached in June 1725, on charges of corruption, tried by his Peers and found guilty; he was removed from his high office, and fined £30,000. He *d.* in 1332, and was succeeded by his only son George, 2nd Earl; this nobleman, who had passed several years on the Continent, was greatly instrumental in procuring the change of style in England, and gave considerable assistance in framing the Act of Parliament by which it was effected. He *d.* in 1764, and was succeeded by his eldest son, Thomas, 3rd Earl, who *d.* in 1795; when George, his eldest son, present and 4th Earl, succeeded.

MACDONALD, BARON. (Bosville-Macdonald.)

Peer of Ireland.

Somerled, of ancient Norwegian ancestry, Thane of Argyll, the patriarch of this family, early in the 12th century, acquired the Western Islands, by his marriage with Effrica, daughter of Olavus, King of Man; and assumed the designation of King of the Isles, which his successors held, independent of the Scottish Kings, till his great-grandson Angus acknowledged his subjection, and styled himself Lord of the Isles. This title continued in his heirs male, till Alexander, Lord of the Isles, 5th in descent from him, who had a maternal claim on the Earldom of Ross, having levied war against King James I., and burnt the town of Inverness, was totally defeated by the King in Lochaber, in 1429; on his humble submission his life was spared, but his honours and estates were forfeited; they were however restored in 1431; but his son John, Earl of Ross, having carried on a treasonable correspondence with Edward IV. King of England, again forfeited them in 1475; but was pardoned, and obtained a renewed charter of his estates and the title of Lord of the Isles to himself and the heirs male of his body, failing which, to Angus his natural son, on the extinction of whose descendants the title was suppressed. From Hugh, his brother, 2nd son of Alexander, Earl of Ross, the 6th in descent was Sir Donald Macdonald of Slate, who was created a Baronet of Nova Scotia in 1625, and *d.* in 1643. Sir James Macdonald, his son, joined the Marquis of Montrose in 1645, and sent some troops to the assistance of Charles II., when he marched into England in 1651; he *d.* in 1678. Sir Donald, his eldest son, left two sons:

1 Sir Donald, his successor, who joining in the rebellion of 1715, was attainted by Act of Parliament, and *d.* in 1718, leaving one son, Sir Donald, who *d. unm.* in 1720.

2 Sir James, who succeeded his nephew in the Baronetcy, and *d.* in 1723.

Sir Alexander Macdonald, only son and successor of Sir James, was almost the only person of consideration in the Western Isles who did not join the Pretender in 1745; he *d.* in 1746, leaving three sons, viz.

1 Sir James, who *d. unm.* in 1766.

2 Sir Alexander, who succeeded his brother, and was created Baron Macdonald of Slate, Co. Antrim, in 1776; he *d.* in 1795, leaving, besides other issue, for whom see *The Peerage Volume*,

   1 Alexander-Wentworth, his successor, 2nd Lord, who *d. unm.* in 1824.

   2 Godfrey, present and 3rd Lord, who succeeded his brother, and has assumed the additional surname of Bosville.

3 The Right Hon. Sir Archibald Macdonald, Lord Chief Baron of the Exchequer, *b.* 1747, *d.* 18 May 1826; having *m.* 26 Dec. 1777, Lady Louisa Leveson-Gower, eldest daughter of Granville, 1st Marquis of Stafford, by whom, who was *b.* 22 Oct. 1749, and *d.* 29 Jan. 1827, he left issue:

1 Louisa, *b.* 23 Aug. 1781.

2 Sir James Macdonald, Bart., M.P., a Clerk of the Privy Seal, and Commissioner of the India Board, *b.* 14 Feb. 1784, *m.* 1st, 5 Sept. 1805, Elizabeth, 2nd daughter of John Sparrow, Esq.; 2ndly, 10 Aug. 1819, Lady Sophia Keppel, eldest daughter of William-Charles, 4th Earl of Albemarle, who *d.* 29 Sept. 1824; 3rdly, 20 April 1826, Anne-Charlotte, youngest daughter of the Rev. J. S. Ogle. He has issue by his 2nd marriage, 1 Archibald Keppel, *b.* 15 Oct. 1820; 2 A son, *b.* 17 Oct. 1821.

3 Caroline-Diana, *b.* 7 July 1790, *m.* 28 May 1813, the Rev. Thomas Randolph, Prebendary of St. Paul's, Chaplain to the King.

MALMESBURY, EARL OF. (Harris.)

Peer of Great Britain.

His Lordship's ancestors have been for several generations gentlemen of the city of Salisbury. Sir James Harris, K.B., having sustained with great credit his high diplomatic stations of Minister Plenipotentiary, or Ambassador, to the Courts of Madrid, St. Petersburg, and the Hague, was created in 1788, Baron Malmesbury of Malmesbury, Co. Wilts; and in 1800, Viscount Fitz-Harris of Heron Court, Co. Southampton, and Earl of Malmesbury; he *d.* in 1820, and was succeeded by his eldest son, James-Edward, present and 2nd Earl.

MANCHESTER, DUKE OF. (Montagu.)

Peer of Great Britain.

The founder of the illustrious family of Montagu, was Drogo de Montacute, one of those noble warriors who came into England with William the Conqueror; he obtained considerable grants of land in the County of Somerset. Sixth in descent from him was Simon de Montacute, summoned to Parliament in 1300; he was father of William Lord Montacute, and grandfather of William, created Earl of Salisbury in 1337; to the beauty of whose Countess Catherine, daughter of William Lord Grandison, the gallantry of King Edward III. dedicated his noble institution of the Garter. He was father of William, 2nd Earl, K.G., grandfather of John, 3rd Earl, and great-grandfather of Thomas, 4th Earl of Salisbury, K.G., a series of heroes of whose exploits the annals of our history are the immortal records; the 4th Earl *d.* in 1428, and his only daughter and heir Alice, carried this Earldom by marriage, into the family of Neville; it was forfeited by the attainder of her son Richard Neville, the great Earl of Warwick and Salisbury, K.G., in 1471; his eldest daughter Isabel, having married George Duke of Clarence, brother of King Edward IV., the honours of this powerful house expired in a daughter of the blood Royal, Margaret Plantagenet, Countess of Salisbury, their daughter and eventual heir; who was created Countess of Salisbury in 1513, attainted in 1539, and beheaded in 1541, leaving a numerous issue by her husband, Sir Richard Pole, K.G.

It is not accurately decided whether the subsequent family of Montagu descended from Simon, a younger brother of John, 3rd Earl of Salisbury, or from James, a natural son of Thomas, the 4th Earl. One of these persons was ancestor of Sir Edward Montagu, Speaker of the House of Commons, of whose influence in that assembly King Henry VIII. had so high an opinion, that requiring, according to the arbitrary tenor of his government, the immediate passing of a bill of subsidies, which the Commons were unwilling to grant, he thus addressed Sir Edward Montagu, who was kneeling before him; "Get my bill to pass by such a time to-morrow, or by such a time this head of yours (laying his hand upon Sir Edward's head) shall be off." Sir Edward, considering the danger in which he stood under so imperious a Prince, exerted himself so effectually, that the bill passed by the time appointed. In 1537 he was constituted Lord Chief Justice of the King's Bench, and *d.* in 1557. Edward Montagu, Esq., of Boughton, Northamptonshire, his son and heir, left six sons, three of whom were,

1 Sir Edward, eldest son, his successor, created in 1621 Baron Montagu of Boughton; his son Edward, 2nd Lord, was father of Ralph, 3rd Lord, created in 1689 Viscount Monthermer, Co. Essex, and Earl of Montagu, and in 1705 Marquis of Monthermer, and Duke of Montagu; in his son John, 2nd Duke, who *d.* in 1749, the male line of the 1st Baron Montagu of Boughton became extinct. Mary, 2nd daughter, and at length sole heir of the 2nd Duke, *m.* George Brudenell, 4th Earl of Cardigan, and her eldest son John was created Duke of Montagu; his only daughter and heir, Elizabeth, conveyed the large estates of this branch of the house of Montagu into the ducal family of Buccleuch, and James, her younger son, is the present Lord Montagu of Boughton.

2 Sir Henry, (3rd son,) ancestor of the Duke of Manchester.

3 Sir Sidney, (6th son,) ancestor of the Earl of Sandwich.

Sir Henry Montagu, 3rd son of Edward Montagu, Esq., and grandson of the Lord Chief Justice, was bred to the bar, and became Lord Chief Justice of the King's Bench in 1616. He was for a short time Lord Treasurer of England, in the reign of James I.; he was created in 1620, Baron Montagu of Kimbolton, Co. Huntingdon, and Viscount Mandeville; and in 1626, Earl of Manchester. He was Lord Privy Seal under King Charles I., and *d.* in 1642; he left five sons, viz.:

1 Edward, 2nd Earl.

2 Walter, who professed the Romish religion, entered into a monastery in France, and was made Abbot of Pontoise; he was employed by the Queen to raise contributions for the Royal cause among the Roman Catholic gentry of England, and was arrested at Rochester when on such a mission in 1643, and kept a prisoner for four years; being then exiled and forbidden to return to England under pain of death, he retired to his abbey, and there entertained Prince Henry, Duke of Gloucester, whose education the Queen-mother had entrusted to his care.

3 James, *m.* Mary, daughter and heir of Sir Robert Baynard, of Lackham, Co. Wilts. He *d.* in 1665; having had twelve sons, of whom the eldest, who survived him, was James, his successor at Lackham, who *d.* in 1675. He left four sons, the two eldest of whom were, Edward, his successor, who *d.* in 1701; and James, who succeeded his brother at Lackham, and *d.* in 1747. He left three surviving sons:

1 James Montagu, Esq., of Lackham, who *d.* in 1790, leaving several daughters—for the survivors of whom, see *The Peerage Volume*—and two sons, viz.: James, his successor at Lackham, who *d. unm.* 12 July 1797; and Lieut.-Colonel George Montagu, *m.* Anne, daughter of William Courtenay, Esq., by Lady Jane Stuart, daughter of the 2nd Earl of Bute; he *d.* at his seat Knowle, Co. Devon, 19 June 1815, leaving George-Conway-Courtenay Montagu, Esq., present head of the collateral branch of this noble house, and two daughters, for all of whom see *The Peerage Volume;* he had also a son, Frederick, a Captain in the 23rd Foot, who was killed in the battle of Albuera, 16 May 1811.

2 Edward, a Master in Chancery, who *d.* in 1798, leaving a son Gerrard, deceased; for whose widow and issue, see *The Peerage Volume.*

3 Admiral John Montagu, *d.* in 1795, leaving—see *The Peerage Volume*—a daughter, Lady Thomas, and having also had the four sons following: 1 The Rev. John Montagu, D.D., *d. unm.* in 1818; 2 Sir George Montagu, G.C.B., *d.* in 1829, leaving a widow and issue—see *The Peerage Volume;* 3 James, Captain R.N., killed in Lord Howe's action 1 June 1794; 4 Edward, a Lieut.-Colonel of Artillery in the East India Company's service,

was killed at the siege of Seringapatam, 8 May 1799, leaving a widow and issue, for whom see *The Peerage Volume.*

4 Henry, Master of St. Catherine's Hospital, *d.* without issue.

5 George, who left, besides other issue, two sons, Edward and Charles; the latter, a statesman, a wit, and an author, was created in 1700, Baron Halifax, Co. York, with remainder, failing his issue male, to George, son and heir of his elder brother Edward. He was a Knight of the Garter, and was also created in 1714, Earl of Halifax and Viscount Sunbury; the latter titles became extinct on his death in 1715, when the Barony devolved on his nephew, George, created in 1715, Viscount Sunbury and Earl of Halifax; he *d.* in 1739, and was succeeded by his son and heir, George, last Earl of Halifax, K.G., a Secretary of State and 1st Lord of the Admiralty. He *d.* without surviving issue male in 1772, when all his honours became extinct.

Edward, 2nd Earl, eldest son of the first Earl, was called up to the House of Peers in his father's life-time, by the title of Lord Kimbolton; and was so forward in the first measures of opposition to the King's government, that he was accused by the Attorney-General before the House of Lords of high treason, at the same time with five Members of the House of Commons. The impeachment failed, and the Lord Kimbolton, who soon after succeeded his father as Earl of Manchester, took the command of the Parliamentary army, and was successful in all his actions against the Royal troops. Cromwell, however, his Lieut-General, taking advantage of the first check his arms experienced, in the King's relieving Donnington Castle, after the battle of Newbury, preferred an accusation against him before the House of Peers, in 1744, of having been backward in reducing the King's power; this had no immediate effect, but the self-denying ordinance of the following year, by removing from commands in the army all the Members of either House of Parliament, relieved Cromwell of a General who had hitherto been a great check upon his ambitious projects. His Lordship continued Speaker of the House of Lords, and in that capacity used his utmost endeavours to bring about a pacification upon moderate terms; but after the murder of the King, he never again sat in Parliament till the meeting of Peers in April 1660, when he was again called to the chair, and the restoration of King Charles II. was voted. As first Commissioner of the Great Seal and their Speaker, the Earl of Manchester was appointed by the House of Lords to offer their congratulations to his Majesty on his joyful entry into London, which he did in a memorable speech addressed to the King in the banquetting-house at Whitehall, on the 29th of May 1660, and received a most gracious reply. He *d.* in 1671, and was succeeded by his eldest son, Robert, 3rd Earl, who *d.* in 1682. He was succeeded by his son, Charles, 4th Earl, who was created in 1719, Duke of Manchester, and *d.* in 1722, leaving two sons, William, his successor, 2nd Duke, who *d.* without issue in 1739; and Robert, 3rd Duke, who succeeded his brother; he *d.* in 1762, and was succeeded by his eldest son, George, 4th Duke, to whom, who *d.* in 1788, succeeded his eldest son, William, present and 5th Duke.

MANNERS, BARON. (Manners.)

Peer of the United Kingdom.

Thomas Manners, the present Lord, is the 6th son of Lord George Manners-Sutton, 3rd son of John, 3rd Duke of Rutland, and is younger brother of Charles, late Lord Archbishop of Canterbury. He was appointed in 1807, Lord Chancellor of Ireland, and was at the same time created Baron Manners of Foston, Co. Lincoln.

MANSFIELD, EARL OF. (Murray.)

Peer of Great Britain and of Scotland.

The Earl is of the same family with the Duke of Athol. 9th in descent from Sir John de Moravia, was their common ancestor, Sir William Murray of Tullibardine, who *d.* about 1511, leaving his eldest son, William, from whom the Duke of Atholl descends, and Sir Andrew 2nd son, whose son

Sir David, was father of, 1 Sir Andrew, grandfather of Andrew, 1st Lord Balvaird, who *d.* in 1644; and 2

Sir David Murray, created Baron of Scone in 1608, and Viscount Stormont, in 1621, with remainder, failing his heirs male, to several heirs of entail. He *d.* in 1631, without issue, as did Sir Mungo Murray of Drumcairn, 2nd Viscount, 4th son of John, 1st Earl of Tullibardine, and James Murray, 2nd Earl of Annandale, who succeeded as 3rd Viscount, when, according to the entail, the Peerage devolved on

David, 4th Viscount, 2nd Lord Balvaird, son of Andrew, 1st Lord. He *d.* in 1668, and was succeeded by his son

David, 5th Viscount, who *d.* in 1731; of his six sons,

1 David, 6th Viscount, (eldest son,) was *b.* in 1689, and *d.* 23 July 1748; having *m.* 20 Jan. 1726, Anne, only daughter and heir of John Stewart, Esq., by whom he was father of David, 7th Viscount and 2nd Earl.

2 William, 1st Earl, (4th son,) the celebrated statesman and Chief Justice of the King's Bench; he was *b.* 2 March 1705, and *d.* 20 March 1793; having *m.* 20 Nov. 1738, Lady Elizabeth Finch, 7th daughter of Daniel, 6th Earl of Winchilsea, who *d.* 10 April 1784. He was created in 1776, Earl of Mansfield, Co. Nottingham, with remainder, failing the heirs male of his body, to Louisa, Viscountess Stormont, wife of his nephew, David, 7th Viscount, and her issue male by the Viscount; this Earldom is now enjoyed by the above Lady, mother of the Earl; but the 1st Earl obtained a renewal of his patent in 1792, with remainder to the said David, 7th Viscount, who succeeded him as 2nd Earl in 1793, and *d.* in 1796, when he was succeeded by his eldest son, William, the present and 3rd Earl.

MANVERS, EARL OF. (Pierrepont.)

Peer of the United Kingdom.

Robert Pierrepont, was created Baron Pierrepont of Holme-Pierrepont, Co. Notts., and Viscount Newark, Co. Notts. in 1627, and Earl of Kingston in 1628; Henry, his son, 2nd Earl, was created Marquis of Dorchester in 1643, which title became extinct on his death in 1680, but the Earldom devolved on Robert, 3rd Earl, grandson and heir of William, the Marquis's next brother; he *d.* in 1682, and was successively followed by his two brothers, William and Evelyn; the said Evelyn, 5th Earl, was created Marquis of Dorchester in 1706, and Duke of Kingston-upon-Hull in 1715; all these titles became extinct, 22 Sept. 1773, by the death of Evelyn, 2nd Duke, grandson and heir of the 1st Duke.

Charles, the 1st Earl Manvers, was son of Philip Medows, Esq., who *d.* Aug. 1781, by his marriage in May 1734, with Lady Frances Pierrepont, only daughter of William, Earl of Kingston, sister and heir of Evelyn, 2nd Duke of Kingston, who was *b.* 1711, and *d.* in Dec. 1795. His Lordship succeeded to the estates of the Duke, his uncle, on the death of his Grace's widow, Elizabeth, Duchess of Kingston, in Oct. 1788, when he assumed the name of Pierrepont. He was created in 1796, Baron Pierrepont of Holme-Pierrepont, Co. Notts., and EARL Manvers in 1806; he d. in 1816, and was succeeded by his eldest son, CHARLES-HERBERT, present and 2nd EARL.

MARLBOROUGH, DUKE OF. (SPENCER-CHURCHILL.)

Peer of England.

To dilate upon the services of John Churchill, the first and great Duke of Marlborough, K.G., which so long as the British name and nation last, will remain among our proudest remembrances, is the province of the British historian, and is a theme to which so limited a space as could be here allotted to it, would be altogether insufficient; taking it then for granted, that its merits are well known to every reader, it need here only be observed, that he was derived from a very ancient family, of which Roger de Coureil, a noble Norman, came into England with WILLIAM the Conqueror, and obtained from that Monarch grants of lands in the West of England. 14th in descent from this Roger, was Sir Winstan Churchill, who suffered from sequestration in the civil wars, as a strenuous partisan of the Royal cause. He d. in 1688; having had a numerous issue by his wife Elizabeth, daughter of Sir John Drake, Bart., of Ashe, in Devonshire, at which place, in consequence of the ruin of her husband's fortune, all her children were born. John Churchill, the 2nd but eldest surviving son of this family, was the hero whose talents, civil and military, raised him to the highest rank amongst the subjects of his native country, and acquired him an immortal fame throughout Europe. He m. Sarah, daughter and coheir of Richard Jennings of Sandridge, Co. Hertford—a lady of great abilities and excessive haughtiness, whose influence for some years held the mind of Queen ANNE almost in bondage, and enabled her to be eminently serviceable in promoting the political views of her husband at home, while he was conquering the enemies of the country abroad. Other influence however arose, which at length incited the Queen to cast off the subjection in which her haughty favourite had held her, and the downfall of the Marlborough and Whig party was the result. The Duchess d. 18 Oct. 1744. Their issue were:

1 John, Marquis of Blandford, b. 13 Jan. 1690, d. 20 Feb. 1703.

2 Lady HENRIETTA, m. Francis, 2nd Earl Godolphin, and succeeded her father as DUCHESS of MARLBOROUGH.

3 Lady Anne, m. Charles Spencer, Earl of Sunderland, and d. 15 April 1716, leaving issue, CHARLES, 3rd DUKE of MARLBOROUGH, and John, father of the 1st Earl Spencer.

4 Lady Elizabeth, m. Scroop Egerton, 1st Duke of Bridgewater, and d. 22 March 1714, without surviving issue.

5 Lady Mary, m. John, Duke of Montagu, and d. without issue male.

The Duke rose through all the gradations of the Peerage from his original rank of a simple gentleman; he was first created a Peer of Scotland, by the title of Lord Churchill of Eyemouth, Co. Berwick, in 1682, and was introduced to the Peerage of England in 1685, by the title of Baron Churchill of Sandridge, Co. Herts.; created Earl of Marlborough, Co. Wilts., in 1689; Marquis of Blandford and Duke of Marlborough, in 1702. After the death of his only son, all his English honours with the Manor of Woodstock and house and lands of Blenheim, were by Act of Parliament, in 1706, settled on his daughters according to their seniority of birth, and their issue male respectively. He d. 16 June 1722, and was succeeded by his eldest daughter,

HENRIETTA, DUCHESS of MARLBOROUGH, wife of Francis, Earl Godolphin; she d. 24 Oct. 1733, having survived her only son, William, Marquis of Blandford, who m. 25 April 1729, Maria-Catherine, daughter of Peter D'Jong of Utrecht, and d. without issue, 24 Aug. 1731. She left two daughters, Henrietta, m. to Thomas

Pelham Holles, Duke of Newcastle, and Mary to Thomas Osborne, Duke of Leeds. As the Duchess left no surviving issue male, the inheritance passed, according to the Act of Parliament, to the eldest son of her next sister, Anne, Countess of Sunderland, who was herself deceased.

The ancestors of the family of Spencer were of noble degree in Normandy before the Conquest. Robert Despencer, one of the Barons who came into England with William the Conqueror, was Steward or Despencer to that Monarch; his successors, William and Thurstan, enjoyed the same office under King Henry I., and from it the family derived a surname which speedily became famous in the English annals. Hugh, the 1st Baron Ledespencer, by writ of summons in 1264, was great-grandson of this Thurstan; he was appointed Grand Justiciary of England by the Barons, in opposition to King Henry III., and was killed at the battle of Evesham in 1265, fighting under Simon de Montfort, Earl of Leicester, against the assertors of the Royal authority. He was succeeded by his eldest son, Hugh, 2nd Lord Despencer, created in 1322, Earl of Winchester; and who, with Hugh Despencer the younger, his son, Earl of Gloucester, (in right of his wife Alianore, eldest sister and co-heir of Gilbert de Clare, Earl of Gloucester and Hertford, and niece of King Edward II.) occupy so large a space in the history of that reign; both the most powerful persons of their time, possessors of the greatest estates in England, and the unhappy favourites of an unhappy Monarch. How far the unpopular measures of King Edward might be attributed to these ministers, historians must decide; but certain it is, that with gratitude not always the consequence of court favour, they faithfully adhered to their Royal master through all the vicissitudes of his fortune. Both were put to death in 1326, by the Barons in arms against the Crown, without even the form of a trial—the father in October, having been delivered to his enemies by the garrison of Bristol, which city he was holding for the King, and the son in November, after a stout defence of the castle of Caerfili, which he at length surrendered upon capitulation, expressly guaranteeing the safety of his life. Hugh Despencer, his son and heir, was summoned to Parliament by King Edward III. in 1338; he *d.* without issue in 1349, and was succeeded by his nephew Edward, who by Elizabeth, daughter and sole heir of Bartholomew, 4th Baron Burghersh, left one son, Thomas, 6th Baron Le Despencer, who obtained the reversal of the act of Parliament by which his ancestors, the Earls of Winchester and Gloucester, had been attainted, after their deaths; and was created in 1397, Earl of Gloucester; he owed his elevation to King Richard II., and continued his allegiance to that Monarch after the superior fortune of Henry IV. had driven him from the throne; he took up arms for his restoration, in conjunction with many other nobles; but Henry obtained a premature knowledge of the conspiracy, met them with an irresistible force, and the Earl of Gloucester, who had taken refuge at Bristol, was given up by the citizens, attainted and beheaded in 1400. He left an infant son, Richard, on whose death in 1414, the male descendants of the first Baron Le Despencer became extinct. The Barony is now enjoyed by the heir-general of the 1st Baron.

From Geffrey Le Despencer, brother of Hugh, the 1st Baron, and also great-grandson of Thurstan, the patriarch of this family, descended, in the 18th degree, Sir Robert Spencer, created Baron Spencer of Wormleighton; he *d.* in 1627, and was succeeded by his eldest son, William, 2nd Lord, who *d.* in 1636. Henry, his son, 3rd Lord, was created Earl of Sunderland in 1643: though a very young man, he had heartily embarked in the cause of King Charles I., and lost his life in the battle of Newbury, 20 Sept. 1643, being then but twenty-three years of age. He left an infant son, Robert, 2nd Earl, K.G., who on attaining the age of maturity, was employed some years on foreign embassies, and recalled in 1679, to take the chief lead in the administration at home; from this time he retained his office of Secretary of State almost without intermission, till near the close of the reign of James II. His public life is marked with so many instances of change of policy, and apparently of change of principle, that though his abilities were confessedly great, history does not hold him in much respect. King William did not employ him in administration, and he *d.* in 1702.

He was succeeded by his son, CHARLES, 3rd EARL, K.G., who, as already noticed, *m.* Lady Anne Churchill, 2nd daughter of the 1st Duke of Marlborough; under the patronage of his father-in-law, he was introduced in a diplomatic character at several foreign courts, and was in 1706 appointed Secretary of State; he did not, however, long enjoy this office, for the Duke of Marlborough's power soon after began to give way under the Tory influence which marked the latter years of Queen Anne; he resigned in 1710, but was re-appointed under King George I., and held for a short time the situation of President of the Council; he *d.* in 1722, leaving, as noticed above, by Anne his Duchess, three surviving sons, viz.:

1 ROBERT, 4th EARL, his successor, who *d. unm.* 27 Nov. 1729.

2 CHARLES, 5th EARL, who succeeded his brother in 1729, and became 3rd DUKE, on the death of his aunt, Henrietta, Duchess of Marlborough, in 1733.

3 John, ancestor of the Earl Spencer.

CHARLES, 3rd DUKE, a General in the Army, was appointed in July 1758, to command the British forces sent to serve in Germany under Prince Ferdinand of Brunswick, but *d.* at Munster of a fever, in October the same year; he left three sons:

1 GEORGE, his successor, 4th DUKE, who *d.* in 1817, and was succeeded by his son, GEORGE, the present and 5th DUKE, who has assumed, by Royal sign-manual the additional name of CHURCHILL.

2 Lord Charles, *b.* 31 March 1740, *d.* 15 June 1820; having *m.* 2 Oct. 1762, the Hon. Mary Beauclerk, only daughter of Vere, Lord Vere, and sister of Aubrey, 5th Duke of St. Albans, by whom, who was *b.* 4 Dec. 1743, and *d.* 31 Jan. 1812, he left the issue stated in *The Peerage Volume.*

3 Lord Robert, *b.* 3 May 1747, *d.* without issue 23 June 1831; having *m.* 2 Oct. 1811, Henrietta, only daughter of Sir Everard Fawkener, K.B., widow of the Hon. Edward Bouverie, brother of William, 1st Earl of Radnor; she was *b.* Jan. 1750, and *d.* 17 Nov. 1825.

MARR, EARL OF. (ERSKINE.)

Peer of Great Britain.

Henry de Erskine was proprietor of the Barony of Erskine on the Clyde in the reign of Alexander II. The 6th from him was Sir Thomas Erskine, whose marriage with Janet, only child of Sir Edward Keith, Marischal of Scotland, by Christian, daughter of Sir John Menteith, by Lady Elyne Marr, daughter of Gratney, 11th Earl of Marr, eventually brought the Earldom into his family; his son, SIR ROBERT, assumed the title, and should have been 17th EARL, but did not obtain possession of the Earldom; and the date from which his descendants take precedence as Earls of Marr, according to a charter granted by Queen Mary, to JOHN, 5th LORD ERSKINE, and who should have been 6th Earl of this family, obliges us to reckon THOMAS, 1st LORD ERSKINE, son of this SIR ROBERT, as the 1st Earl.

The origin of this Earldom is lost in antiquity. Marticus, the 1st Earl on record, flourished in the reign of Malcolm Canmore; this male line failed in 1377, by the death of Thomas, 13th Earl, whose sister, Margaret, succeeded, and by William, Earl of Douglas, had issue: James Earl of Douglas, and 15th Earl of Marr, who *d.* without issue in 1388; and Isabel, who succeeded her brother; she *m.* 1st, Sir Malcolm Drummond of Drummond, who *d.* in 1403; and 2ndly, Alexander Stewart, natural son of Alexander, Earl of Buchan, 4th son of King Robert I.; the Countess *d.* without issue in 1419, when the Earldom should have devolved on SIR ROBERT

Erskine, of right 17th Earl, the heir of line as above stated; but King James I., then reigning, desirous to sap the foundations of a formidable Aristocracy, was endeavouring to unite the ancient Earldoms to the Crown, and seized this opportunity to require a surrender of the Earldom of Marr from Alexander Stewart, widower of the Countess; this Alexander, conscious that he possessed, at best, but a life interest in the Earldom, resigned it to the King, who re-granted it to him and his heirs male. Upon his death, without issue, in 1435, Sir Robert Erskine claimed the title, but was prevented from taking the estates, on pretence of the minority of King James II.; on his attaining the age of majority, the cause was heard in Parliament, and the Earldom decreed, in 1457, to the King, under various pleas, of which the chief was, his right as legal heir to Alexander, the last Earl, who was a bastard. The Earldom was after some years bestowed on John, 3rd son of King James II.; then on Cochrane, a favourite of King James III.; next on Alexander, 3rd son of King James III.; and lastly, on James Stewart, Prior of St. Andrews, a natural son of King James V. At length the rightful proprietor, John Lord Erskine, obtained permission from the Crown to have the question respecting the succession to the Earldom re-tried, and, after a lapse of one hundred and thirty years, obtained a verdict in his favour; upon which the Queen granted, in 1565, a charter to him and his heirs of the Earldom of Marr, with precedency from the year 1457; against which latter clause, the Earls of Marr have always protested, averring theirs to be the most ancient Earldom of Scotland.

Sir Thomas Erskine of Erskine, was father, as before stated, by Janet Keith, at length heiress of Marr, of Sir Robert Erskine, who claimed the Earldom, and should have been 1st Earl of this family; he *d.* however in 1453, before the Parliament had finally decided against him, leaving a son, Thomas, who was dispossessed of the Earldom by the decree of 1457, but had the title of Lord Erskine; as however the precedency of this title dates from that decree, this Thomas, Lord Erskine, must be reckoned as 1st Earl. He was succeeded by his only son, Alexander, 2nd Earl; whose son, Robert, 3rd Earl, was killed at the battle of Flodden, 9 Sept. 1513. His son and successor, John, 4th Earl, was entrusted with the keeping of the young King James V., whose favour he always retained; he *d.* 1552; his eldest son, Robert, Master of Erskine, was killed at the battle of Pinkie in 1547, in his life-time, and his 2nd son, Thomas, Master of Erskine, Ambassador to England, also *d.* before him; his 4th son, Sir Alexander, was father of Sir Thomas, created Earl of Kellie, and ancestor of all the succeeding Earls of Kellie, extinct in 1829; and his 3rd son, John, 5th Earl, succeeded, and obtained the recognition of his right from Queen Mary and the Parliament. Being Governor of the Castle of Edinburgh at the period of the birth of King James VI., his mother, Queen Mary, desirous to put the castle into the hands of the Earl of Bothwell, offered to commit the young Prince to the custody of the Earl of Marr, provided he would surrender the Castle. The Earl consented to these conditions, and conveyed the Royal child to the Castle of Stirling, of which also he was Keeper; peremptorily refusing to yield him up again to Bothwell, who used both artifice and force to recover possession of his person, but in vain; the Earl of Marr thus effectually preserving from the power of this ambitious man, a life of so much importance to the Scottish nation at that unquiet period, and from which have sprung all the succeeding Kings of Great Britain. The Earl was chosen Regent of Scotland on the death of the Regent Lennox, but *d.* in the following year, 1572, leaving to his successor, John, 6th Earl, the custody of the young King's person. The latter joined the Ruthven conspiracy in 1582, for obtaining possession of the King, who had now some years since assumed the reins of Government, for which he was attainted, but restored by Act of Parliament in 1585. He accompanied the King into England in 1603, and continued in favour to the end of James's reign; he *d.* in 1634, having had a grant of the Barony of Cardross to himself, his heirs and assigns, which he assigned accordingly to Henry his 3rd son, and his heirs male. He left eight sons, viz.:

John de Hope is
Magdalen, Queen of
chant, whose eldest s
Henry, was ancestor
Henry-Thomas Hope.

Thomas, the eldest
Sir John Hope of Cr
he was himself still
Session, of wearing
father should appear
1628, and *d*. in 1646.
Craighall, the present

Sir James Hope, of
grandfather of CHARL
Lord Hope, by Patent
to the heirs female of
William, 1st Marquis
his titles are claimed
William and Lady Ann
besides other issue, the

1 JOHN, 2nd EARL.

2 The Hon. Charles
1st, 26 July 1733, Cath
was *b*. 1 Dec. 1716,
Anne Vane, eldest dau
dissolved in 1757, and s
1st Lord Monson, and *d*.
of George Dunbar, Esq.
and his numerous desce
besides two named Charl

1 William, *b*. 17 Ma
daughter of Josep
elder children, w
Volume.

2 John *b*. 7 April 17
only daughter of
June 1767, he le
Session; 2 Lieut.-
Admiral Sir Willia
the military or nav

3 Brig.-General Henr
Sarah, daughter of

4 Capt. Charles Hop
daughter of Admira
the issue described
was *b*. 1790, and *d*.
Sibthorpe-John Haw

5 Rear-Admiral Sir G
marriages and issue

The 2nd EARL *d*. in 1781,

MASSEREENE, VISCOUNT. (Skeffington-Foster.)

Peer of Ireland.

Sir John Clotworthy was created in 1660, Baron of Lough Neagh, and Viscount of Massereene, both in the County of Antrim, with remainder, on failure of his issue male, to his son-in-law, Sir John Skeffington, husband of his only daughter Mary, and his issue male by the said Mary, and failing such, to the heirs general of Sir John Clotworthy. The Viscount *d.* in 1665, and Sir John Skeffington succeeded as 2nd Viscount; he *d.* in 1695, and was succeeded by Clotworthy, his son, 3rd Viscount, who *d.* in 1713; Clotworthy, his son, 4th Viscount, d. in 1738; his son and successor, Clotworthy, 5th Viscount, was created Earl of Massereene in 1756, and *d.* in 1757. He was father of Clotworthy, Henry, and Chichester, successive Earls; the last *d.* in 1816, when the Earldom became extinct. All the male issue of Sir John Skeffington, 2nd Viscount, failed, and Lady Harriet, only daughter and heir of Chichester, 4th Earl and 8th Viscount, succeeded as Viscountess, being heir-general of Sir John Clotworthy, 1st Viscount. She *m.* Thomas-Henry, 2nd Viscount Ferrard, and *d.* in 1831, leaving several children, of whom her eldest son, John, succeeded as 10th Viscount, and is the present Peer.

MASSY, BARON. (Massy.)

Peer of Ireland.

The family of Massey flourished in Normandy from the period of the conquest of that Province, by Duke Rollo, in 876; they derived their surname from the town and Lordship of Massey. After the Norman invasion of England, the Masseys were seated at Dunham Massey, in Cheshire; and the first of the family who settled in Ireland was General Hugh Massy; he held a military command in 1641, and was grandfather of Colonel Hugh Massy of Duntryleague, Co. Limerick, who was father of Hugh, created, in 1776, Baron Massy of Duntryleague, Co. Limerick, and of Eyre, 1st Lord Clarina; *see* that title.

Hugh, 1st Lord, *m.* 1st Mary, daughter and heir of Colonel James Dawson, of Bellinacourty, Co. Tipperary; and 2ndly, Rebecca, daughter of Francis Dunlap, Esq., of Antigua, and *d.* in 1788, leaving issue by his 1st marriage, 1 Hugh, 2nd Lord; 2 James, who assumed the name of Dawson, and *m.* Mary, daughter of John Lenard, Esq., by whom, who *d.* 26 May 1805, he was father of James-Hewitt Massy-Dawson, Esq., for whom see *The Peerage Volume.* His Lordship, by his 2nd marriage, had the issue stated as still surviving in *The Peerage Volume.* He was succeeded by his eldest son Hugh, 2nd Lord, who *d.* in 1790, and was succeeded by his eldest son Hugh, 3rd Lord, father of Hugh-Hammon, present and 4th Lord, who succeeded him in 1812.

MAYNARD, VISCOUNT. (Maynard.)

Peer of Great Britain.

It appears from the Roll of Battle Abbey, that Mainard accompanied William the Conqueror into England. From him descended John Maynard of Axminster, Co. Devon, who served under Edward the Black Prince in France. The 8th in descent from him was

Sir Henry Maynard, Secretary to the famous Lord Burghley; he *d.* in 1610, leaving six sons, four of whom *d.* without issue; the other two were,

1 William, created Baron Maynard of Wicklow, in the Peerage of Ireland, in 1620, and Baron Maynard of Estaines ad Turrim, Co. Essex, in the Peerage of England, in 1628; he *d.* in 1639, and was succeeded by his son William, 2nd Lord, who *d.* in 1698, and was succeeded by his son Banastre, 3rd Lord: he *d.* in 1718, leaving three surviving sons: Henry, 4th Lord, his successor, who *d. unm.* in 1742; Grey, 5th Lord, who *d.* also *unm.* in 1745; and Charles, 6th Lord.

2 Charles, *d.* in 1665; Sir William Maynard of Walthamstow, Co. Essex, his eldest surviving son, was created a Baronet in 1681, and *d.* in 1685; Sir William and Sir Henry, his sons, were successive Baronets; the latter *d.* in 1738, and was succeeded by his only son Sir William, on whom the titles of Viscount and Baron were entailed by the new patent of 1766; he *d.* in 1772, and was succeeded by his son Sir Charles, who also succeeded as 2nd Viscount in 1775.

CHARLES, 6th LORD, was created, in 1766, Baron Maynard of Much Easton, Co. Essex, and Viscount Maynard of Easton Lodge, Co. Essex, with remainder, failing his issue male, to Sir William Maynard, Bart., descended from Charles Maynard, Esq., the only brother, who left issue of William, 1st Lord. On the death of the 1st Viscount, 30 June 1775, the original English and Irish Baronies became extinct, and the titles of Viscount and Baron of the new creation devolved on SIR CHARLES MAYNARD, Bart., the 2nd Viscount, eldest son of Sir William Maynard, Bart.; he *d.* in 1824, and was succeeded by his nephew, HENRY, the present and 3rd VISCOUNT, son of his brother the Rev. Henry Maynard.

MAYO, EARL OF. (BOURKE.)

Peer of Ireland.

His Lordship derives his descent from the family of the Marquis of Clanricarde. Sir William de Burgh, grandson of Richard de Burgh, Lord of Connaught, who *d.* in 1203, was father of Sir William, ancestor of the Marquis of Clanricarde, and of Sir Edmund, the immediate ancestor of the Earl of Mayo, a younger branch of whose line was created to the Peerage, in 1627, by the title of Viscount Mayo, which became extinct 1767.

JOHN BOURKE, Esq., was created in 1776 Baron of Naas; in 1781 Viscount Mayo of Monycrower; and in 1785 EARL of MAYO. He *d.* in 1790, leaving two sons, JOHN, 2nd EARL, who *d.* in 1792, and JOSEPH-DEANE, 3rd EARL, father of the present and 4th Earl, by whom he was succeeded in 1794.

MEATH, EARL OF. (BRABAZON.)

Peer of Ireland and of the United Kingdom.

The surname of Brabazon is derived from the province of Brabant, from whence James Le Brabazon came to the assistance of William the Conqueror, in his descent upon England. The first of the family who settled in Ireland was Sir William Brabazon, Vice-Treasurer of Ireland, 12th in descent from the above James; he *d.* in 1552. SIR EDWARD, his eldest son, was created in 1618 LORD BRABAZON, Baron of Ardee, Co. Louth, and *d.* in 1625; he was father of WILLIAM, 2nd LORD, created in 1627 EARL of the County of MEATH; he *d.* in 1651, and was succeeded by his only son EDWARD, 2nd EARL, who *d.* in 1675, leaving three sons, who all succeeded to the Peerage; viz., 1 WILLIAM, 3rd EARL, he *d.*, without surviving issue male, in 1684; 2 EDWARD, 4th EARL, *d.* without issue in 1707; 3

CHAMBRE, 5th EARL; he *m.* Juliana, only child of the last Viscount Chaworth, and *d.* in 1715, leaving two sons, successive EARLS: viz., CHAWORTH, 6th EARL, who *d.* in 1763 without issue; and EDWARD, 7th EARL, who *d.* in 1772, leaving two sons: viz.,

1 ANTHONY, 8th EARL, his successor, who *d.* in 1790; and was succeeded by his eldest surviving son, WILLIAM, 9th EARL, who *d. unm.* in 1797, when his only surviving brother, JOHN-CHAMBRE, present and 10th EARL, succeeded; he was created, in 1831, Baron Chaworth of Eaton Hall, Co. Hereford, in the Peerage of the United Kingdom.

2 Hon. William, *b.* Aug. 1723, *d.* 29 Nov. 1790; having *m.* 10 May 1764, Catherine, daughter and sole heir of Arthur Gifford, Esq., by whom, who *d.* in 1776, he had the issue stated in *The Peerage Volume.*

MELBOURNE, VISCOUNT. (LAMB.)

Peer of Ireland and of the United Kingdom.

Sir Matthew Lambe, of Brocket Hall, Co. Herts., who was created a Baronet of Great Britain, and *d.* 6 Nov. 1768, was father, by Charlotte, only daughter of the Right Hon. Thomas Coke, and heir of her brother, George-Lewis Coke, Esq., of Sir Peniston Lamb, Bart., created in 1770, Lord Melbourne, Baron of Kilmore, Co. Cavan; and in 1781 VISCOUNT MELBOURNE; in 1815, he was also created a Peer of the United Kingdom, by the title of Baron Melbourne of Melbourne, Co. Derby; and *d.* in 1828, when he was succeeded by his eldest surviving son, WILLIAM, present and 2nd VISCOUNT.

MELVILLE, VISCOUNT. (SAUNDERS-DUNDAS.)

Peer of the United Kingdom.

His Lordship is a branch from the ancient family of Dundas, of Fingask—see the pedigree of Lord Dundas. Sir Archibald Dundas, of Dundas, 2nd son of James Dundas, of Fingask, who *d.* in 1436, was ancestor in the 4th degree of George Dundas, of Dundas, who had two sons: 1 Sir Walter, whose lineal representative is James Dundas, Esq., of Dundas, *m.* to a daughter of the late Viscount Duncan; and 2 Sir James Dundas of Arniston, father of Sir James Dundas of Arniston, who, early in the Civil War, signed the National Covenant; he lamented the violent measures to which the leading men of his own persuasion had recourse, but never would abjure his engagement. After the Restoration, he was appointed a Lord of Session, although he had not been bred to the law, from the high opinion entertained of his probity and abilities; but being required by Act of Parliament to subscribe a declaration that the National Covenant was an illegal association, which he would only concede so far as it led to actual rebellion, he refused compliance, and never took his seat on the bench; he *d.* in 1679. Robert, his eldest son, *d.* in 1727. His eldest surviving son,

Robert Dundas of Arniston, was Lord President of the Court of Session; he *d.* in 1753, leaving, besides other issue, three sons, viz.:

1 The Right Hon. Robert Dundas, also Lord President of the Court of Session; he *d.* 13 Dec. 1787; having *m.* 1st, 17 Oct. 1741, Henrietta, daughter of Sir James Carmichael; she *d.* 14 May 1755, and he *m.* 2ndly, Jane, daughter of William Grant, Esq. He had issue,

by his 1st marriage:

1 Elizabeth, *m.* 6 Sept. 1762, Sir John-Lockhart Ross, Bart., who *d.* 9 June 1790; she *d.* in June 1819.

2 Henrietta, m. 1 July 1731, Adam, 1st Viscount Duncan, and had issue.
3 Margaret, m. General John Scott, of Balcomie—see Viscountess Canning.
4 Anne, m. George Buchan, of Kelso, Esq.
by his 2nd marriage,
5 The Right Hon. Robert Dundas, late Lord Chief Baron of the Court of Exchequer in Scotland, b. 6 June 1753, d. 17 June 1819; having m. in May 1787, Elizabeth, daughter of Viscount Melville, and had issue, Anne, m. in 1819, John Borthwick, Esq.; Robert; Henry; and William-Pitt.
6 Lieut.-General Francis, m. and has issue.
7 The Right Hon William, Lord Register and Keeper of the Signet of Scotland.
8 Philip, late Governor of Prince of Wales's Island, d. 8 April 1807; having m. in 1803, Margaret, daughter of Sir John Wedderburn. Bart.
9 Grizel, d. 27 Sept. 1798; having m. 22 Sept. 1778, Robert Colt, Esq., of Auldhame, who d. Dec. 1779.
10 Janet, m. 1st, 8 Oct. 1782, John Hamilton, Esq., who d. without issue, 25 Dec. 1804; and 2ndly, 8 May 1827, George Dempster, of Skibo, Esq.

2 Lieut.-Colonel William Dundas, m. Mary, daughter of the Rev. Henry Bram. D.D., of St. John's, Antigua; by whom he left issue, 1 Anne, m. to James M'Neil, Esq.: 2 Mary, m. Major Cameron.

3 Henry, Treasurer of the Navy, President of the Board of Controul, and Secretary of State; all which offices he resigned on Mr. Pitt's secession in 1801: he was created in 1802, Baron Dunira, Co. Perth, and Viscount Melville of Melville, Co. Edinburgh. In 1806, an impeachment was instituted against him for malversation in his office of Treasurer of the Navy, of which he was acquitted after a solemn trial by his Peers. He d. in 1811, and was succeeded by his only son Robert, present and 2nd Viscount, who, in consequence of his marriage with a co-heir of Dr. Huck Saunders, sister of the Countess of Westmoreland, has assumed the additional name of Saunders.

MEXBOROUGH, EARL OF. (Savile.)

Peer of Ireland.

This is an ancient family of Yorkshire, and had been ennobled in two of its branches previous to the creation of the present Earldom; the Barons Savile of Pontefract, Co. York, created in 1628, Earls of Sussex in 1644, and extinct in 1671. and the Marquises of Halifax, created in 1668, extinct in 1700.

A third branch of the family, seated at Methley, Co. York, was represented in the reigns of Elizabeth and James I., by Sir John Savile, one of the Barons of the Exchequer; he left two sons, Sir Henry, created a Baronet in 1611, which title became extinct on his death; and John, whose grandson Charles Savile, Esq., of Methley, was father of Sir John Savile, K.B., created in 1753, Baron Pollington of Longford; and in 1766, Viscount Pollington of Terns, and Earl of Mexborough of Lifford, Co. Donegal. He d. in 1778, and was succeeded by his eldest son John, 2nd Earl, who d. in 1830, and was succeeded by his only son, John, present and 3rd Earl.

MIDDLETON, BARON. (Willoughby.)

Peer of Great Britain.

Sir John de Willoughby, a Norman Knight, had the Lordship of Willoughby in Lincolnshire, by gift of William the Conqueror; 6th in descent from him was Robert, summoned to Parliament in 1313, as Baron Willoughby of Eresby; he d. in

1316. John, 2nd Lord, his son, *d.* in 1349; and John, 3rd Lord, his son, in 1372; when he was succeeded by his son,

Robert, 4th Lord, who *d.* in 1396; he had issue, 1 William, 5th Lord, his successor; 2 Sir Thomas, whose great-grandson and heir, Robert, was summoned to Parliament in 1492, as Baron Willoughby de Broke; his male line failed in 1522, on the death of Robert, 2nd Lord, his son, and the Barony is now inherited by his heir-general.

William, 5th Lord Willoughby de Eresby, *d.* in 1409, leaving two sons: 1 Robert, 6th Lord, whose line failed in 1505; 2 Thomas, grandfather of

Sir Christopher Willoughby, who, besides other issue, had three sons:

1 William, who succeeded as Baron Willoughby de Eresby, and *d.* without issue male in 1525, when the Barony devolved on his only daughter, whose heir-general is the present Baron Willoughby de Eresby.

2 Christopher, whose only son, William, was created in 1547, Lord Willoughby of Parham, which title became extinct by the failure of his male line in 1779.

3 Thomas, Lord Chief Justice of the Common Pleas under King HENRY VIII.; he *d.* in 1545. The 5th in descent from him was Francis Willoughby, of Wollerton, Esq., a learned author, especially on natural history. He *d.* in 1672, aged thirty-seven, leaving two sons: 1 Francis, who was created a Baronet in 1677, with remainder to his brother, and *d. unm.* in his 20th year, in 1688; 2

THOMAS, who succeeded to the Baronetcy, and was created in 1711, BARON MIDDLETON of Middleton, Co. Warwick; he *d.* in 1729, leaving four sons of whom the two eldest were,

1 FRANCIS, his successor, 2nd LORD, who *d.* in 1758; he had two sons: FRANCIS, 3rd LORD, who *d. unm.* in 1774, and THOMAS, who succeeded his brother, and *d.* without issue in 1781.

2 Thomas, who *d.* in 1742; his sons who left issue were,

- 1 HENRY, 5th LORD, who succeeded his cousin in 1781; he *d.* in 1800, and was succeeded by his only son, HENRY, present and 6th LORD.
- 2 Francis, *m.* 25 May 1762, Octavia, daughter and co-heir of Francis Fisher, Esq., by whom he was father of Digby Willoughby, Esq., Commander R.N., present heir presumptive to the Barony.
- 3 The Rev. James Willoughby, who *d.* in March 1816; having *m.* 4 Nov. 1772, Eleanor, daughter and co-heir of James Hobson, Esq., by whom he was father of Henry Willoughby, Esq., of Settrington House, Co. York, and other issue—see *The Peerage Volume.*

MIDLETON, VISCOUNT. (BRODRICK.)

Peer of Ireland and of Great Britain.

George de Brodrick, ancestor of this family, came into England in the reign of WILLIAM the Conqueror.

Sir Thomas Brodrick, his descendant, had two sons, of whom Sir Alan, the eldest, continued the family at Wandsworth in Surrey; and Sir St.-John, the younger, going into Ireland during the troubles of 1641, had grants of land there, and settled at Midleton, Co. Cork; he was father of ALAN BRODRICK, Esq., Speaker of the House of Commons of Ireland; appointed Chief Justice of the King's Bench in Ireland in 1710, and afterwards Lord High Chancellor of that kingdom. He was created Baron Brodrick of Midleton, Co. Cork, in 1715; and VISCOUNT MIDLETON in 1717; and *d.* in 1728, when he was succeeded by his only surviving son, ALAN, 2nd VISCOUNT, whose only son, GEORGE, 3rd VISCOUNT, succeeded him in 1747, and *d.* in 1765. He was succeeded by his eldest son, GEORGE, present and 4th VISCOUNT, who was created in 1796, Baron Brodrick of Pepper Harrow, Co. Surrey, in the Peerage of Great Britain.

MILTOWN, EARL OF. (Leeson.)

Peer of Ireland.

Hugh Leeson, of a good family at Whitfield in Northamptonshire, settled in Ireland about 1680, and was grandfather of Joseph Leeson, Esq., created Baron Rusborough of Rusborough, Co. Wicklow, in 1756; Viscount Rusborough in 1760; and Earl of Miltown, Co. Dublin, in 1763. He *d.* in 1783, leaving Joseph, 2nd Earl, his successor, who *d. unm.* 27 Nov. 1801; Brice, 3rd Earl; and the other issue stated in *The Peerage Volume.*

Brice, 3rd Earl, who succeeded his brother in 1801, *d.* in 1807, and was succeeded by his grandson, Joseph, present and 4th Earl.

MINTO, EARL OF. (Elliot.)

Peer of Great Britain.

The family of Elliot of Stobs in Roxburghshire are said to have settled there in the reign of King James I. Gilbert Elliot, of Stobs, had six sons; of whom William, the eldest, was father of Sir Gilbert, created a Baronet in 1666, ancestor of the present Sir William-Francis Elliot, of Stobs, Bart., and of George-Augustus the celebrated General Elliot, whose title of Baron Heathfield became extinct by the death of his son Francis-Augustus, 2nd Lord, in 1813; and Gavin, the 4th son, was father of Sir Gilbert Elliot, a Lord of Session by the title of Lord Minto, who was created a Baronet in 1700, and was great-grandfather of Sir Gilbert, created in 1797, Baron of Minto, Co. Roxburgh, and in 1813, Viscount Melgund and Earl of Minto. His Lordship was appointed Viceroy of the Island of Corsica in 1795, he was afterwards Envoy Extraordinary to the Court of Vienna; and from 1807 to 1812, Governor-General of India. He *d.* in 1814, and was succeeded by his eldest son, Gilbert, the present and 2nd Earl.

MOLESWORTH, VISCOUNT. (Molesworth.)

Peer of Ireland.

This family was seated in the County of Northampton in the reign of Edward I. William Molesworth, of Helpston, Co. Northampton, was father of Robert Molesworth, who *m.* Judith, eldest daughter and co-heir of John Bysse, Lord Chief Justice of the Exchequer in Ireland, and was father by her of Robert Molesworth, Esq., of Edlington, Co, York; a man of talents and learning, who having been Envoy Extraordinary to the Court of Denmark, published an account of that country, much esteemed at the time, and was author of several other valuable pieces, chiefly political. He early distinguished himself by his zeal in the cause of the Revolution and having always warmly supported the Hanoverian succession in Parliament, was appointed to office under the Administration in the reign of George I., and was created Viscount Molesworth of Swords, Co. Dublin, and Baron af Philipstown King's County, in 1716; he *d.* in 1725, leaving seven sons, viz.

1 John, 2nd Viscount, who *d.* without issue male in 1726.

2 Richard, 3rd Viscount, who succeeded his brother, and *d.* in 1758, leaving issue, Richard-Nassau, 4th Viscount, his successor, who *d. unm.* in 1793; Mary, *m.* to Richard Rochfort, 1st Earl of Belvidere, whose title became extinct on the death of their son George, 2nd Earl, in 1814; Letitia, late wife of Col. James

Molesworth; and the three surviving daughters stated in *The Peerage Volume.*

3 William, *d.* in 1770; leaving three sons, viz.

1 Robert, who succeeded his cousin as 5th Viscount, and *d.* in 1813; leaving issue, William-John, 6th Viscount, his successor, who *d.* without issue in 1815; Robert, who *d.* in 1814, without issue male, leaving two daughters, one of whom survives; and the two daughters described in *The Peerage Volume.*

2 John, who *d.* without issue.

3 Richard, who *d.* in 1799; he was father of Richard-Pigot, the present and 7th Viscount, and of the other issue stated in *The Peerage Volume.*

4 Edward, *d.* in 1768; his two sons are mentioned in *The Peerage Volume.*

5 Walter, *d.* in 1773; he was married and had issue.

6 Coote, M.D. *d. unm.* in 1782.

7 Bysse, *d.* in 1779; for his issue see *The Peerage Volume.*

MONSON, BARON. (Monson.)

Peer of Great Britain.

John Monson, his Lordship's ancestor, was of East Reson in Lincolnshire in 1378; 7th in descent from him was Sir Thomas Monson of Carlton, Co. Lincoln, created a Baronet in 1611; he *d.* in 1641; leaving Sir John, his heir; and Sir William, created Viscount Castlemain, in Ireland, but degraded from his honours in 1661, for having assisted at the tribunal which condemned King Charles I.; he left no male issue.

Sir John Monson, 2nd Baronet, proved his loyalty throughout the civil wars, and suffered much loss on the King's behalf; he was succeeded by his grandson, Sir Henry, who was grandfather of Sir John, created in 1728, Baron Monson of Burton, Co. Lincoln; he *d.* in 1748; having *m.* Lady Margaret Watson, daughter of Lewis, 1st Earl of Rockingham, by whom he was father of 1 John, 2nd Lord, his successor; 2 Lewis, who assumed the name of Watson, and was created Baron Sondes in 1760. *See* Sondes.

John, 2nd Lord, *d.* in 1774, and was succeeded by his son John, 3rd Lord, who *d.* in 1806, and was succeeded by his son John-George, 4th Lord, to whom in 1809 succeeded his only son, Frederick-John, present and 5th Lord.

MONTAGU, BARON. (Montagu-Scott.)

Peer of Great Britain.

Henry-James Montagu-Scott, present and 2nd Lord Montagu, is the 2nd son of Henry, 3rd Duke of Buccleuch, by Lady Elizabeth Brudenell-Montagu, only surviving child of

George, 1st Lord, Duke of Montagu, and 4th Earl of Cardigan, who was created in 1786 Baron Montagu of Boughton, Co. Northampton, with remainder, failing his issue male, to his grandson, Henry-James Montagu-Scott, 2nd son of Henry, 3rd Duke of Buccleuch, by Elizabeth Montagu, his only daughter. The Duke was *b.* 26 July 1712, *d.* 28 May 1790, without surviving issue male; having *m.* 7 July 1730, Lady Mary Montagu, 2nd daughter and co-heir of John, Duke of Montagu, by Lady Mary Churchill, 4th daughter and co-heir of John, 1st Duke of Marlborough; she *d.* 1 May 1775.

MONTFORT, BARON. (BROMLEY.)

Peer of Great Britain.

HENRY, 1st LORD, grandfather of the present Lord, was son of John Bromley, Esq., of Horseheath, Co. Cambridge, by his marriage with Mercy, only surviving daughter and heir of William Bromley, Esq., of Holt Castle, Co. Worcester, of the same family. Which William Bromley was 16th in paternal descent from Sir Walter Bromleghe, who was seated at Bromleghe, Co. Stafford, in the reign of King JOHN.

HENRY BROMLEY, 1st LORD, was *b.* 20 Aug. 1705; was created in 1741 LORD MONTFORT, Baron of Horseheath; and *d.* 1 Jan. 1755; when he was succeeded by his son THOMAS, 2nd LORD; who *d.* in 1799, and was succeeded by his eldest son, HENRY, present and 3rd LORD.

MONTROSE, DUKE OF. (GRAHAM.)

Peer of Scotland and of Great Britain.

This noble family traces its descent from William de Graham, who settled in Scotland in the reign of King DAVID I., and obtained from him the lands of Abercorn and Dalkeith; from his eldest son Peter, several families of Grahams descend; and 9th in descent from John, his 2nd son, was Sir William Graham of Kincardine, whose eldest son Alexander was father of PATRICK, created BARON GRAHAM in 1445; and his 5th son William, was ancestor of Lord Lynedoch.

PATRICK, 1st LORD GRAHAM, *d.* in 1465, and was succeeded by his son WILLIAM, 2nd LORD; who *d.* in 1472, and was succeeded by his son,

WILLIAM, 3rd LORD, created in 1505 EARL of MONTROSE, and killed at the battle of Flodden, 9 Sept. 1513. His son WILLIAM, 2nd EARL, succeeded him, and *d.* in 1571; he outlived his eldest son Robert Lord Graham, who fell at the battle of Pinkie, 10 Sept. 1547, and to whom was afterwards born a posthumous son, JOHN, who succeeded his grandfather as 3rd EARL. He was appointed Viceroy of Scotland in 1604, and *d.* in 1608, when he was succeeded by his eldest son JOHN, 4th EARL: he *d.* in 1626, and was succeeded by his only son,

JAMES, 5th EARL, and 1st MARQUIS, K.G., commonly called the great Marquis of Montrose; he was *b.* in 1612, and completed his education, after his father's death, with great diligence; first making great proficiency in the learned languages, under preceptors in his own house, and afterwards spending several years abroad in acquiring the modern languages, and all the polite exercises of the age. He returned, remarkable for his accomplishments and the variety of his knowledge, but was not received at Court with all the distinction he expected; this rebuff, acting upon a vehement character, led him into opposition to the Government, and he was at first among the most zealous supporters of the Covenant; he fought always with success in several engagements, but the principles of his associates were little in unison with his ardent and chivalrous temper; he abandoned the cause, and retired to his own residence, some private rivalship with the Marquis of Hamilton preventing his immediately enlisting in the King's service. However, in 1643, he waited upon the King at Oxford, was favourably received, created Marquis of Montrose, and, from that time, devoted all the energies of his mind to the support of the Royal cause. No enterprize was too perilous, no exertion too arduous for his spirit and intrepidity. With what undisciplined troops the influence of his name procured him, he defeated large armies sent against him, and with little assistance from the immediate neighbourhood of his exploits, and no resources beyond it, he maintained a desultory war in the north of Scotland, till the unparalleled successes of his arms, and the confidence they inspired, placed him at the head of a considerable force with which he was enabled to march southwards, and even to obtain temporary possession of Edinburgh and Glasgow. Had the King's affairs now been in a state to afford effectual assistance, Scotland would doubtless have been reduced under the Royal authority; but Montrose's energetic character prompted him to advance, and the nature of the troops he led on rendered them liable to total dispersion on the first check; he was surprised and defeated at Philiphaugh on his march towards England, 13 Sept. 1645, and compelled, almost alone, to take refuge in the north. His exertions, however, soon placed him at the head of another army, but a command from the King caused him to disband it, and he retired to the continent. At Brussels the melancholy tidings of his sovereign's fate reached him, and he immediately repaired to the Hague to offer his services to CHARLES II., who gave him a commission to act as his Lieutenant in Scotland, and procured him the assistance of six hundred Germans. With these he landed in Orkney in the spring of 1650, and his army speedily increased to 1400 men. He then marched southwards, but was met at Invercharron, and totally defeated by Strachan, on the 27th of April. He was himself betrayed by Macleod of Assint, in whose house he had taken refuge, and delivered to General Leslie, who conducted him to Edinburgh, where, with every imaginable indignity, he was put to death; meeting the insults of his enemies with a calmness and magnanimity, and his end with an unfeigned cheerfulness, which true religion and the consciousness of a good cause only could impart. He was hanged on the 21st of May 1650, at the age of 38.

He left but one surviving son, JAMES, his successor, 2nd MARQUIS, who *d.* in 1669, and was succeeded by his son, JAMES, 3rd MARQUIS; he *d.* in 1684, when his son JAMES, 4th Marquis, succeeded; he was created in 1707, DUKE of MONTROSE, Marquis of Graham and Buchanan, Earl of Kincardine, Viscount of Dundaff, Lord Aberruthven, Mugdock, and Fintrie; all by patent, with remainder to the heirs male of his body, failing which, to the eldest heir female of his body without division. He *d.* in 1742; James, Marquis Graham, his eldest son, *d.* in his infancy; and David, Marquis Graham, his 2nd son, having been created in 1722, Earl and Baron Graham of Belford, Co. Northumberland, in the Peerage of Great Britain, with remainder to his brothers, Lords William and George Graham, *d.* also before him in 1731; Lord George, his youngest son, *d. unm.* in 1747; and WILLIAM, Marquis Graham, the only survivor, who had succeeded to his brother's British Peerage, also succeeded his father as 2nd DUKE; he *d.* in 1790, and was succeeded by his only son, JAMES, present and 3rd DUKE.

It is worthy of remark, that since the elevation of this family to the Peerage, the coronet has descended uninterruptedly, without one collateral succession, from father to son for a period of twelve generations; also that the wives of these noble Peers, the mothers of their successors, have been, without a single exception, taken from the daughters of the Peerage, and of the noblest families that adorn it.

MORAY, EARL OF. (STEWART.)

Peer of Scotland and of Great Britain.

The Earl descends from the same ancestor as the Earl of Castle-Stuart; viz., Walter, legitimated son of Sir James Stewart, 4th son of Murdoch, Duke of Albany, 3rd son of King Robert II. Andrew, Lord Avandale, son of Walter, was father of Andrew, 3rd Lord Avandale, ancestor of the Earl of Castle-Stuart; and of

Sir James Stewart of Beath, whose son, SIR JAMES STEWART, was created Lord Doun in 1581; his son, JAMES, 2nd LORD, *m.* Lady Elizabeth Stewart, eldest daughter and co-heir of the Regent, JAMES STEWART, created in 1561, Earl of Moray, natural son of King James V., and their son, JAMES, 3rd EARL, obtained, in 1611, a charter of the Earldom to himself and his heirs male.

Henry, 2nd son of the 1st Lord Doun, and brother of the 2nd Earl of Moray, was created in 1611, Baron of St. Colme, with remainder to his heirs male; his only son, James, 2nd Lord, succeeded him, and was succeeded by his cousin,

James, 3rd Earl of Moray; he *d.* in 1638; James, 4th Earl, his only son, succeeded him, and was father of Alexander, 5th Earl, and of Archibald, from whom descends James Stuart, Esq., of Dunlarn, and was succeeded, in 16[illegible], by his eldest son, Alexander, 5th Earl, who *d.* in 1700. James Lord Doun, his eldest son, *d.* before him, and Charles, and Francis, his younger sons, were successive Earls. Charles, 6th Earl, *d.* without issue in 1735, and Francis, 7th Earl, *d.* in 1739; his 3rd son Francis, has left a daughter, widow of the Bishop of Meath—see *The Peerage Volume*; his eldest son, James, 8th Earl, succeeded him; he *d.* in 1767, and was succeeded by his eldest son, Francis, 9th Earl; who was created in 1796, Baron Stuart of Castle Stuart, Co. Inverness, in the Peerage of Great Britain; he *d.* in 1810, and was succeeded by his eldest son, Francis, present and 10th Earl.

MORLEY, EARL OF. (Parker.)

Peer of the United Kingdom.

Edmund Parker, Esq., who was seated at North Molton, Co. Devon, in 1611, was ancestor in the 6th degree of John Parker, Esq., created in 1784, Baron Boringdon of Boringdon, Co. Devon; he d. in 1784, and was succeeded by his only son, John, 2nd Lord, who was created in 1815, Viscount Boringdon of North Molton, Co. Devon, and Earl of Morley, in the same County, and is the present Peer.

MORTON, EARL OF. (Douglas.)

Peer of Scotland.

Archibald de Douglas, grandson of Theobald, the Fleming, the 1st known ancestor of the House of Douglas, had two sons: 1 William, ancestor of the Duke of Hamilton, and Earl of Selkirk; 2 Andrew, whose great-grandson,

Sir John Douglas of Dalkeith, had two sons: 1 Sir James, great-grandfather of of James, 1st Earl.; 2 Sir Henry of Lochleven, from whom the 7th in lineal descent was William, 6th Earl, on whom, and his heirs male, the Earldom was entailed by charter, 1564; the present Earl is 7th in descent from him.

James Douglas, Lord Dalkeith and Aberdour, was created Earl of Morton in 1458; he was succeeded by his son, John, 2nd Earl; to whom succeeded his son, James, 3rd Earl; he *d.* in 1553, without issue male, having obtained in 1543, a Royal charter of the Earldom in favour of his son-in-law, James Douglas, brother of David, 7th Earl of Angus; David Douglas, his brother, (afterwards 7th Earl of Angus,) George Douglas, his father; Archibald, 6th Earl of Angus; Richard Douglas, brother of the Earl of Morton himself, besides several other substitutes and their heirs male respectively. In consequence of this settlement, the Earldom devolved upon

James Douglas, 4th Earl; son-in-law, of the 3rd Earl, son of George Douglas, of Pittendriech, grandson of George Master of Angus, and brother of David, 7th Earl of Angus. He was the principal actor in the murder of Rizzio in 1566, and was in consequence obliged to fly the kingdom. The influence of the Earl of Bothwell, however, obtained his pardon in the same year, and on his return he refused to concur with Bothwell in the proposed murder of Lord Darnley. In 1567, he entered into the association for the defence of the infant James, whom the malcontent nobles ad just proclaimed King, was appointed in the November following, Lord High Chancellor of Scotland, and in 1568, commanded the van of the King's army in the attle of Langside. In 1572, on the death of the Earl of Marr, the office of Regent f Scotland was conferred upon him, and he administered the Government in the ame of King JAMES VI. till 1578, when he resigned the Regency into the hands of e young King. Still, however, retaining an authority in the state which no other erson had influence or ability sufficient to wrest from him, his political enemies eeing no other means of ridding themselves of his ascendancy, accused him in Parliaent of being a party to the murder of Lord Darnley, and obtained his condemnation; which was immediately followed by his execution, 2 June 1581. He died with the enitence, resignation, and courage of a great man and a good Christian, leaving one f the most notable examples on record of the mutability of fortune.

He left no legitimate issue, and by his attainder his Earldom was forfeited. He ad obtained in 1564, a new charter, by which the Earldom was entailed, failing his ssue male, on Archibald, 8th Earl of Angus; William Douglas of Lochleven; Francis Douglas of Longniddry; William Douglas of Whittinghame; William Douglas and James his brother, sons of the deceased, Richard Douglas, brother of the 3rd Earl of Morton, and the heirs male of their bodies respectively; failing which, to his own legitimate heirs male for ever. But in consequence of his forfeiture, John Lord Maxwell, grandson of the 3rd Earl, through his 2nd daughter, obtained n June 1581, a charter of the Earldom; a general act of indemnity, however, passed in 1585, and a letter of rehabilitation of James Earl of Morton, issued under the Great Seal, which deprived Lord Maxwell of his title, by restoring the rights of the heir of entail.

ARCHIBALD, 8th Earl of Angus, and 5th EARL of MORTON, succeeded as the next substitute in the entail of 1564, but *d.* without surviving issue in 1588, when the Earldom devolved, according to the same charter, on SIR WILLIAM DOUGLAS of Lochleven, 6th EARL, descended from Sir Henry Douglas of Lochleven, mentioned above as younger son of Sir John Douglas of Dalkeith. Sir William Douglas of Lochleven, eldest son of the said Sir Henry, was father of the heroic Elizabeth Douglas, maid of honour to Queen Joanna, wife of King JAMES I.; who running to secure the door of the Royal apartment against the intrusion of the assassins of that King, unable to find the bar, thrust her arm into its place, but in vain; the murderers broke her arm, forced their way through, and accomplished their bloody purpose. Sir William was succeeded by his eldest son, Sir Henry, whose son, Robert Douglas of Lochleven, was killed in the battle of Flodden, in 1513. He was followed by his son and grandson, both Sir Roberts; the latter fell in the battle of Pinkie, in 1547.

SIR WILLIAM, his son, succeeded, and was the same mentioned above as successor to the 5th Earl; Queen Mary was committed to his custody at Lochleven Castle, in 1566; he *d.* in 1606, and was succeeded by his grandson WILLIAM, 7th EARL, only son of his eldest son Robert, who was lost at sea, on his voyage to Holland, in 1584, before his father's accession to the Earldom. This Earl, before the breaking out of the great rebellion, was one of the richest subjects in the kingdom; espousing the Royal cause with zeal, he advanced considerable sums for its support, disposing for that purpose of the noble property of Dalkeith and other estates, to the value of no less than £100,000 Scots of yearly rent. On the entire failure of the Royal arms, he retired to Orkney, and *d.* there in 1648. His eldest son Robert succeeded as 8th EARL, and *d.* also in Orkney, in 1649; his son WILLIAM, 9th EARL, *d.* without surviving issue in 1681, when the title devolved on JAMES, 10th EARL, second son of the 7th Earl; he *d.* in 1686, and was father of JAMES, 11th EARL, ROBERT, 12th EARL, and GEORGE, 13th EARL; the two former *d. unm.*, the first in 1715, and the second in 1730; GEORGE, 13th EARL, *d.* in 1738, and was succeeded by his eldest son,

JAMES, 14th EARL, who, being in France in 1746, was imprisoned in the Bastille for reasons never avowed, with his wife and child, and a sister of the Countess travelling with them; after three months' confinement they were released and permitted to proceed to England. He sold his large property in Orkney and Zetland to Sir Laurence Dundas; he was elected in 1764, President of the Royal Society, and *d.* in 1768, leaving two surviving sons:

1 SHOLTO-CHARLES, 15th EARL, his successor, who *d.* in 1774, and was succeeded by his only son GEORGE, 16th EARL; he *d.* without issue in 1827.

2 John, who *d.* in 1818; he was father of GEORGE-SHOLTO, the present and 17th EARL, who succeeded his cousin in 1827.

MOSTYN, BARON. (LLOYD.)

Peer of the United Kingdom.

John Lloyd, Esq., of Pontryffyd, Co. Flint, *d.* 2 May 1729, leaving, by his marriage with Rebecca, daughter and heir of William Owen, Esq., of Plasissa, Co. Monmouth, who *d.* in May 1724, besides other issue, two sons, viz.:

1 William, *m.* Frances, daughter and heir of Bell Jones, Esq., of Plasmaur, Co. Flint, by whom he was father of Bell Lloyd, Esq., of Bodsack, who, by Anne, daughter and heir of Edward Pryce, Esq., was father of EDWARD PRYCE, LORD MOSTYN, and other issue.

2 Sir Edward Lloyd, of Pengwern, Co. Flint, created a Baronet in 1778, with remainder to his nephew, Bell Lloyd, Esq.; he *d.* without issue, 26 May 1795, and was succeeded by his great nephew,

Sir Edward Pryce Lloyd, eldest son of the above Bell Lloyd. He was created in 1831, BARON MOSTYN of Mostyn, Co. Flint, and is the present Peer; he *m.* Elizabeth, 3rd daughter of the late Sir Roger, and sister and co-heir of the late Sir Thomas Mostyn, of Mostyn Hall, Barts.; and since the decease of the latter in 18.1, the Hon. Edward-Mostyn Lloyd, his Lordship's eldest son, has assumed the additional name of Mostyn.

MOUNT-CASHELL, EARL OF. (MOORE.)

Peer of Ireland.

This family descends from Thomas de Moore, who accompanied William the Conqueror from Normandy, held a command in the battle of Hastings, and settled in the West of England. Richard Moore was the first of the family who came into Ireland, and settling in the County of Clonmell, in the reign of King Charles I., was great-grandfather of STEPHEN MOORE, Esq., who was created in 1764, Baron Kilworth of Moore Park, Co. Cork, and in 1766, Viscount Mount-Cashell of Cashell, Co. Tipperary, and *d.* in 1766, leaving three sons, viz.:

1 STEPHEN, his successor, 2nd Viscount, who was created in 1781, EARL of MOUNT-CASHELL; he *d.* in 1790, and was succeeded by his eldest son, STEPHEN, 2nd EARL, who *d.* in 1822, and was succeeded by his eldest son, STEPHEN, present and 3rd EARL.

2 The Hon. William, *b.* 15 June 1738, *d.* 21 Nov. 1810; having *m.* Anne, daughter and co-heir of Digby Fowkes, Esq., by whom, who *d.* in March 1800, he had the issue given in *The Peerage Volume.*

3 The Hon. and Rev. Robert, *b.* 25 Nov. 1739, *d.* in April 1817; having *m.* Isabella, only daughter of Richard Odell, Esq., by whom he had several children; the survivors are stated in *The Peerage Volume.*

MOUNT-EDGECUMBE, EARL OF. (EDGECUMBE.)

Peer of Great Britain.

This family is denominated from their ancient residence, the Manor of Edgecomb, in Devonshire, whence, in the reign of EDWARD III., William de Edgecomb removed to Cotehele, in Cornwall.

His great-grandson, Sir Richard Edgecumbe, was a person of note in the reigns of EDWARD IV. and Richard III.; he joined Henry Stafford, Duke of Buckingham, in his rebellion against the latter Monarch, and was reduced, after its suppression, to great extremities; he had the good fortune to escape to Brittany, to the Earl of Richmond, in whose suite he returned to England, displayed great intrepidity at the battle of Bosworth, and was taken into the household and confidence of King HENRY VII. On the suppression of the Earl of Kildare's rebellion, he was sent into Ireland, to receive the renewed allegiance of the Irish nobility, and performed that difficult commission with great good fortune and address. He was afterwards frequently employed in political commissions by HENRY VII., and received from that Monarch, in reward for his many important services, large grants of land in Devonshire and Cornwall. He *d.* in 1489, and his estates devolved on his eldest son,

Sir Piers Edgecumbe; he was made a Knight banneret by Henry VIII. in his expedition into France, for his gallant behaviour at the battle of the Spurs. He *d.* in 1539; Sir Richard, his son and heir, built that splendid mansion at Stonehouse, in Devonshire, called Mount Edgecumbe, of which it is recorded, that the Duke of Medina Sidonia, the Commander of the Armada sent for the invasion of England, observing from the sea its noble situation, fixed upon it for his own, in his intended division of his conquest: the choice, at least, was creditable to his taste. His great-grandson, Colonel Piers Edgecumbe of Mount-Edgecumbe, firmly attached to the Church and King, endeavoured to support both in the civil wars to the utmost of his power and fortune; so great, indeed, was the enmity of the popular leaders against him, that Sir Alexander Carew, of Anthony, in Cornwall, was tried at Guildhall, condemned, and beheaded, solely upon a charge of corresponding by letter and personal conference with Colonel Edgecumbe; he *d.* in 1660. His eldest son, Sir Richard Edgecumbe, K.B., who *d.* in 1688, was father of

RICHARD, created in 1742, BARON EDGECUMBE of Mount-Edgecumbe, Co. Devon; he *d.* in 1758, and was succeeded by his eldest son, RICHARD, 2nd LORD, who *d. unm.* in 1761, and was succeeded by his only brother, GEORGE, 3rd LORD; he was created in 1781, Viscount Mount-Edgecumbe and Valletort, Co. Devon, and in 1789, EARL of Mount-Edgecumbe; he *d.* in 1795, and was succeeded by his only son, RICHARD, present and 2nd EARL.

MOUNTMORRES, VISCOUNT. (DE MONTMORENCY.)

Peer of Ireland.

This family claims its descent from Herve de Montmorency, Grand Butler of France; from whose elder son descended the French Barons of Montmorency, Dukes of Luxemburg, Beaumont, and Laval; his younger son, Geoffrey de Montmorency, was father of the branch which came into England with William the Conqueror, and settled in the Isle of Anglesey, from whence Hervey de Monte-Mariscoo and his brother Geoffrey went over to Ireland in the reign of HENRY II., and obtained grants of land in Wexford, Kerry, and Tipperary. Hervey *d.* without issue; and the descendants of Geoffrey came in time to bear the name of Morres, which the

Viscount and his relation, Viscount Frankfort, have exchanged, by Royal licence, for the original family name of De Montmorency.

Sir John Morres of Knockagh, was created a Baronet of Ireland in 1631, and *d.* in 1648. Sir Reymond, his son and successor, *d.* in 1650, leaving, besides other issue, two sons:

1 Sir John, his successor, whose issue male became extinct in 1794, by the death of Sir Nicholas Morres, 8th Baronet.

2 Hervey, whose son Francis had issue:

1 Hervey, created in 1756, Baron Mountmorres, of Castle-Morres, Co. Kilkenny; and in 1763, Viscount Mountmorres; he *d.* in 1766, leaving three sons: 1 Hervey-Redmond, 2nd Viscount, his successor, who *d. unm.* in 1797; 2 Francis-Hervey, present and 3rd Viscount, who succeeded his brother; 3 William-Mary, who was drowned near Dublin in 180[illegible], leaving a daughter.

2 Sir William-Evans Morres, created a Baronet in 1758; he was father of the two successive Baronets, Sir Heydock-Evans, and Sir William-Evans-Ryves Morres; on the death of the latter, in April 1829, the Baronetcy became extinct.

3 Redmond, father of Lodge-Evans, 1st Viscount Frankfort de Montmorency.

MOUNTNORRIS, EARL OF. (Annesley.)

Peer of Ireland.

This ancient family derive their surname from the manor of Annesley in Nottinghamshire, of which they were possessed before the Conquest. A younger branch settled at Newport-Pagnel in Bucks., whence Robert Annesley removed to Ireland in the reign of Queen Elizabeth; and was father of

Sir Francis Annesley, created a Baronet of Ireland in 1620; in 1622, he had a singular patent granted him of the dignity of Viscount of Valentia, Co. Kerry, to hold after the death of Henry Power, then Viscount Valentia, without issue, which title accordingly devolved upon him on that event occurring in 1642; but meanwhile he was created in 1629, Baron Mountnorris of Mountnorris, Co. Armagh. He was afterwards, in 1635, by an extraordinary act of power on the part of the Lord Deputy Wentworth, better known by his subsequent title of Earl of Strafford, sentenced to lose his head for an inconsiderate expression, construed by his judges into purpose of evil against the Lord Deputy; the sentence however was not executed, but he was kept a prisoner in Dublin Castle till April 1637, when the King's pardon was extended to him, and this affair was made one of the articles of impeachment against the Earl of Strafford in 1640. He seems to have been alienated from the Royal cause by this arbitrary act, but took no active part in the rebellion. He *d.* in 1660, leaving several sons; the Earl Annesley descends from Francis his 6th son.

Arthur, 2nd Viscount, his eldest son and successor, was among the loyal members who met in the Parliament summoned at Oxford in 1643; but the Royal cause having become almost hopeless, he was one of the five Commissioners appointed by the two Houses to settle the affairs of Ireland; and at length heartily concurred in the restoration of Charles II. In 1661 he was created Baron Annesley of Newport Pagnel, Co. Buckingham, and Earl of Anglesey, in the Peerage of England. He held the office of Privy Seal during many years of the reign of Charles II., and was removed from it in 1682, on account of the zeal with which he promoted the exclusion of the Duke of York from the throne. He *d.* in 1686, leaving, besides other issue, the three sons following:

1 James, 3rd Viscount, and 2nd Earl of Anglesey; he *d.* in 1690, and his three sons, James, John, and Arthur, successively inherited the title, and all *d.* without

male issue; Arthur, the youngest son, 6th Viscount and 5th Earl of Anglesey, *d.* in 1737.

2 Altham, created in 1681 a Peer of Ireland, by the title of Baron Altham of Altham, Co. Cork, with remainder, failing his issue male, to his younger brothers; he *d.* in 1699, and was succeeded by his only son James-George, 2nd Lord Altham, who *d.* an infant.

3 Richard, who succeeded his nephew as 3rd Lord Altham; he *d.* in 1701, leaving two sons:

1 Arthur, 4th Lord Altham, who *d.* in London in 1727; having *m.* in 1707 Mary, a natural daughter of John Sheffield, Duke of Buckingham, who *d.* in 1729. His Lordship was supposed to have died childless, and his brother thereupon assumed the title of Altham; but in the year 1743 a young man, calling himself James Annesley Lord Altham, introduced himself to Admiral Vernon in Jamaica, with so plausible a tale of his birth as the son of Lord and Lady Altham, that Admiral Vernon sent him to England with such representations in his favour as induced many persons of eminence and probity to support a suit, which was immediately commenced in the King's Courts in Dublin for the restitution of his rights. It was made to appear in evidence that he was born to Lady Altham at Dunmain in Ireland in 1715: that Lord and Lady Altham afterwards separated, his Lordship retaining the child; that Lady Altham being afterwards reduced to great distress, went to reside in London on the bounty of the Duchess of Buckingham: that Lord Altham, connecting himself with another woman, who considered the boy as an obstacle to her marriage, was by her induced to board him in the house of a poor person, and afterwards wanting to raise money upon his estates, which he could only do in conjunction with his next heir being of full age, found it convenient to disown the boy: that upon his Lordship's death the title was assumed by his brother and the child kidnapped, put on board an American ship, carried to the river Delaware, and there sold as a slave: and that it was not till after thirteen years of slavery that he found means to escape to Jamaica, where he made his case known to Admiral Vernon. All these circumstances and many others being established to the satisfaction of the jury, a verdict was given in his favour, which however was set aside upon a writ of error, and his claim was not decided when he *d.* 5 Jan. 1760, leaving two daughters and one son; the latter was *b.* 7 Jan. 1757, and *d.* 5 Nov. 1763.

2 Richard, who, as shown above, succeeded his brother as 5th Lord Altham, and on the death of Arthur, 5th Earl of Anglesey, and 6th Viscount Valentia, succeeded also to those titles; to all which, by the death of the young claimant in 1763, he acquired an indisputable right. He *d.* 14 Feb. 1761; having *m.* 1st, 24 Jan. 1715, Anne, daughter of Capt. John Prust, who *d.* without issue 31 Aug. 1741; and 2ndly, 15 Sept. 1741, Juliana, daughter of Cornelius Donovan, Esq.; she *d.* 20 Nov. 1776; (having *m.* 2ndly, Matthew Talbot, Esq.) This 2nd marriage, of which the first Earl of Mountnorris was the only issue, was disputed after the death of the Earl of Anglesey, when the House of Lords in England decided against it, and adjudged the English honours to be extinct; and the House of Lords in Ireland decided in its favour, and adjudged the Irish honours to his son Arthur, 8th Viscount, who was created in 1793, Earl of Mountnorris. He *d.* in 1816, and was succeeded by his eldest son, George, present and 2nd Earl.

MOUNT-SANDFORD, BARON. (SANDFORD.)

Peer of Ireland.

Theophilus Sandford, Esq., descended from a good family in Yorkshire, settled at Castlerea in the 17th century, and was ancestor of HENRY MOORE, Esq., who was created in 1800 BARON MOUNT-SANDFORD, of Castlerea, Co. Roscommon, with remainder, failing his issue male, to his brothers and their issue male; he *d.* in 1814, and was succeeded by his nephew, HENRY, 2nd LORD, only son of the Rev. William Sandford, his Lordship's next brother, who dying *unm.* in 1828, was succeeded by his uncle, GEORGE, the present and 3rd LORD, only surviving brother of the 1st LORD.

MULGRAVE, EARL OF. (PHIPPS.)

Peer of the United Kingdom and of Ireland.

Sir Constantine Phipps, appointed in 1710 Lord High Chancellor of England, *d.* in 1723. His son William married Lady Catherine Annesley, only child of James Earl of Anglesey, by his wife Lady Catherine Darnley, a natural daughter of King JAMES II. (who *m.* to her 2nd husband, John Sheffield, Duke of Buckingham, and was mother by him of the last Duke of Buckingham of that family. CONSTANTINE PHIPPS, Esq., their son and heir, was created in 1768 BARON MULGRAVE of New Ross, Co. Wexford, in the Peerage of Ireland; he *m.* 26 Feb. 1743, the Hon. Lepel Hervey, eldest daughter of John Lord Hervey, son and heir of the 1st Earl of Bristol, by whom, who *d.* in Feb. 1780, he had issue: Constantine-John, his successor, 2nd Lord; the Hon. Charles, a Captain in the R.N., who *d. unm.* 20 Oct. 1786; Henry, the late Earl; the Hon. Henrietta-Maria, *b.* 26 March 1757, *m.* 19 Aug. 1776, the Hon. Charles Dillon, afterward 12th Viscount Dillon, and *d.* 1 Dec. 1782; and two younger sons, for whom see *The Peerage Volume.* His Lordship *d.* 13 Sept. 1775, and was succeeded by his eldest son,

Constantine-John, 2nd Lord, who was created in 1790 Baron Mulgrave of Mulgrave, Co. York, in the Peerage of Great Britain, *b.* 30 May 1744, *m.* 20 June 1787, Anne-Elizabeth, youngest daughter of Nathaniel Cholmondeley, Esq., who *d.* 22 May 1788; by her he left an only daughter, who appears in *The Peerage Volume*, and *d.* without male issue 10 Oct. 1792, when the British Peerage became extinct, but the Irish Barony devolved on his next surviving brother HENRY, 3rd Lord. He was created in 1794 Baron Mulgrave of Mulgrave, Co. York, and in 1812 Viscount Normanby of Normanby, Co. York, and EARL of MULGRAVE; he *d.* in 1831, and was succeeded by his eldest son CONSTANTINE-HENRY, present and 2nd EARL.

MUNCASTER, BARON. (PENNINGTON.)

Peer of Ireland.

Gamel de Pennington, ancestor of this ancient House, was seated at Muncaster in Lancashire before the Conquest; from him descended, in the direct male line, Sir William Pennington of Muncaster, created a Baronet of England in 1676; his grandson Sir Joseph, who *d.* in 1793, was father of

1 SIR JOHN, created in 1783, BARON MUNCASTER, with remainder, failing his issue male, to his brother Lowther, and his issue male. His only son Gamel

3 Pennington, *d.* young; and his Lordship *d.* in 1813, when he was succeeded by his only brother,

2 LOWTHER, 2nd LORD; he *d.* in 1818, and was succeeded by his only son LOWTHER-AUGUSTUS-JOHN, present and 3rd LORD.

MUNSTER, EARL OF. (FITZ-CLARENCE.)

Peer of the United Kingdom.

Colonel GEORGE FITZ-CLARENCE, eldest son of his present Majesty by Mrs. Jordan, was created in 1831, EARL of MUNSTER, Viscount Fitz-Clarence, and Baron of Tewkesbury; with remainder, failing his issue male, to his brothers, the Lords Frederick, Adolphus, and Augustus Fitz-Clarence, and their issue male respectively.

MUSKERRY, BARON. (DEANE.)

Peer of Ireland.

His Lordship's ancestors were seated in Somersetshire, from whence Matthew, 3rd son of Matthew Deane, Esq., came into Ireland and settled at Dromore, Co. Cork; he was created a Baronet in 1709. SIR ROBERT-TILSON DEANE, Bart., created in 1781, Baron Muskerry of Dromore, Co. Cork, was 4th from him in direct male descent. He *d.* in 1818, and was succeeded by his eldest son JOHN-THOMAS-FITZ-MAURICE, 2nd LORD, who *d.* in 1825, and was succeeded by his only surviving brother, MATTHEW, present and 3rd LORD.

NAIRNE, BARON. (NAIRNE.)

Peer of Scotland.

His Lordship is a younger branch of the Duke of Atholl's family, and descended from LORD WILLIAM MURRAY; [4th son of John, 1st Marquis of Atholl;] by his marriage with the Hon. Margaret Nairne, only daughter and heir of ROBERT NAIRNE, of Strathord, who having been taken prisoner at Alyth, by the English army, in 1651, when concerting measures with the Earls of Crawford and Leven, and other noblemen, for raising an army for the invasion of England and the restoration of King CHARLES II., was committed to the Tower, and remained in custody there till 1660; was appointed a Lord of Session in 1661; and, in consideration of his sufferings in the cause of Royalty, and other merits, was created to the Peerage, in 1681, by the title of LORD NAIRNE, with limitation to the said Lord William Murray, and the heirs of his body by Margaret Nairne his wife.

He was succeeded by the said LORD WILLIAM, 2nd LORD, who did not take the oaths to Government, nor his seat in Parliament, after the Revolution; engaged in the Rebellion of 1715, in which his nephews, the Marquis of Tullibardine, and Lord Charles Murray, were also implicated, he was taken prisoner at Preston, sent to the Tower, attainted, tried, and condemned to death, but respited and afterwards pardoned. He *d.* in 1725, when, but for the attainder, his eldest son, JOHN, would have succeeded as 3rd LORD; his second son, Robert, *m.* Jean, heiress of the ancient family of Mercer of Aldie, and assumed her surname. He engaged in the Rebellion of 1745, and was killed in the battle of Culloden, which saved his estates from forfeiture. His eldest son, Colonel William Mercer of Aldie and Meikleour, *m.* Margaret Murray, heiress of Pitkeathly, and *d.* in 1790, leaving three daughters, of whom Jane, the eldest, was the 1st wife of George, late Viscount Keith, and mother of Margaret, now Baroness Keith, heiress of Aldie and Meikleour, who, in addition to her paternal name of Elphinstone, has assumed that of Mercer.

JOHN, 3rd LORD, was engaged with his father in the Rebellion of 1715, taken prisoner at Preston, and attainted, but pardoned; he engaged again in the Rebellion of 1745, and was included in the act of attainder of 1746. He passed the remainder of his life in France, and *d.* there in 1770, when his eldest surviving son, JOHN, should have succeeded as 4th Lord, but, in consequence of the attainders of his father and grandfather, never assumed the title, which was graciously restored under King GEORGE IV., by Act of Parliament, in 1824, to WILLIAM, his only surviving son, 5th LORD: he *d.* in 1830, and was succeeded by his son WILLIAM, present and 6th LORD.

NAPIER, BARON. (NAPIER.)

Peer of Scotland.

From John de Napier, who swore fealty to King EDWARD I., in 1296, descended, in the 11th degree, JOHN NAPIER, of Merchistoun, the celebrated author of the logarithms, who, after finishing his studies at the University of St. Andrews, and making the tour of Europe, returned to his house at Merchistoun, where he resided in privacy and retirement, chiefly inhabiting a small room at the top of the tower, and devoting his life to the study of the holy Scriptures and of mathematics; here he constructed the logarithms. He was looked upon by the common people as a warlock, and even the superior classes entertained ideas of his possessing a superhuman sagacity, and applied to him for the resolution of doubts which were beyond the reach of the ordinary powers of man. It is probable, indeed, that he amused himself by encouraging the popular belief of his skill in necromancy, that he might be the less interrupted in his meditations. He *d.* in 1617.

SIR ARCHIBALD NAPIER, his son and heir, was created LORD NAPIER of Merchistoun, in 1627, with remainder to his heirs male; he *m.* a sister of the great Marquis of Montrose, and taking a decided part in favour of the Royal cause, was imprisoned by the Covenanters, with his son the Master of Napier and others of his family, in Holyrood House, from whence the Master effected his escape, and joined the Marquis of Montrose; the rest of the family remained in closer confinement, first in the Castle of Edinburgh, and afterwards in the prison of Linlithgow, whence they were liberated by the Master of Napier after Montrose's victory of Kilsyth. Lord Napier accompanied the Marquis to the south, and, after the defeat of Philliphaugh, escaped with him into Atholl, where he *d.* in 1645.

His son ARCHIBALD, the gallant Master of Napier, succeeded as 2nd LORD, and devoted himself, with unlimited attachment, to the fortunes of his heroic uncle. He fortified the Marquis's house at Kincardine, and stood a siege against the army of General Middleton and a train of artillery, till the failure of water and provisions rendered capitulation necessary; he escaped before the surrender of the garrison, and rejoined Montrose. He went abroad with him, when the King recalled his commission, and, after the unfortunate issue of his second expedition, continued in Holland till his death, which took place before the Restoration in 1660.

ARCHIBALD, 3rd LORD, his son and successor, being the last heir male of the 1st Lord, procured, in 1677, an extension of the patent to his three sisters, with remainder to the heir male, failing which, to the eldest heir female, without division of each of them respectively. The issue of Jane, the eldest sister, failed in her son SIR THOMAS NICOLSON, 4th LORD, who succeeded his uncle in 1683, and *d. unm.* in 1686; and Mary, the youngest sister, *d. unm.*; MARGARET, the second, became 5th BARONESS; she *m.* John Brisbane, Esq., and had an only daughter Elizabeth, whose son

FRANCIS, succeeded his grandmother, in 1706, as 6th LORD. He was paternally descended from the family of Scott, Barts., of Thirlestane, and was 11th in descent rom Arthur Scott, of Howpaisley, in Eskdale; a junior, it is presumed, of the family of Scott, of Buccleuch. He *d.* in 1773, leaving a very numerous family, of vhom the four sons following have left issue.

1 WILLIAM, 7th LORD, who succeeded his father; he *d.* in 1775, and was suc·eeded by his eldest son FRANCIS, 8th LORD, who *d.* in 1823, and was succeeded by is eldest son, WILLIAM, present and 9th LORD.

2 Hon. Charles, *b.* 19 Nov. 1731, *d.* 19 Dec. 1807; having *m.* 1st 19 Dec. 1763, Grizel, daughter of Sir John Warrender, Bart., who *d.* without issue 15 Nov. 1774; and he *m.* 2ndly, 2 July, 1777, Christian, daughter of Gabriel Hamilton, Esq., by whom, who *d.* Feb. 1815, he has left the surviving issue stated in *The Peerage Volume.*

3 Hon. Major-General Mark, *b.* 30 Dec. 1738, *d.* 10 June 1809; having *m.* 1st, 24 Feb. 1761, Anne, daughter of John Nielson, Esq., by whom he had no surviving issue; he *m.* 2ndly, Margaret, daughter of Alexander Symson, Esq.; his surviving issue by her are described in *The Peerage Volume.*

4 Hon. George, *b.* 11 March 1751, *d.* 13 Oct. 1804; having *m.* 1st, 22 Jan. 1775, Elizabeth, daughter of Capt. Robert Pollock; and 2ndly, 27 Aug. 1781, Lady Sarah Lennox, 7th daughter of Charles, 2nd Duke of Richmond and Lennox, whose former marriage with Sir Thomas-Charles Bunbury, Bart., was dissolved, by Act of Parliament, 14 May 1776; she *d.* 20 Aug. 1826. His surviving issue by both marriages are described in *The Peerage Volume.*

Lord Sherborne is a younger branch of the original family of Napier, Lord Napier, but separated before the creation of the Peerage.

NELSON, EARL. (NELSON.)

Peer of the United Kingdom.

The name of Nelson is of considerable standing in the Co. of Norfolk, where his Lordship's family have long been patrons of the church of Hillborough, of which his grandfather was Rector; and have been connected by marriage with many families of distinction.

HORATIO, the 1st and great VISCOUNT NELSON, whose heroic exploits are too recent and too intimately connected with the most glorious pages of English history, to need recapitulation in a space far too limited to do them even a moderate degree of justice, was created in 1798, Baron Nelson of the Nile, and of Burnham Thorpe, Co. Norfolk, and Viscount Nelson in 1801; also, in 1801, BARON NELSON of the Nile, and of Hilborough, Co. Norfolk, with remainder to his father, the Rev. Edmund Nelson, and his heirs male; remainder to the issue male of his sisters Susannah and Catherine. On his Lordship's glorious death at Trafalgar, after a victory which finally swept the seas of every fleet inimical to Great Britain, the Viscounty, and the Barony of 1798, became extinct; but the Barony of 1801 devolved on his brother WILLIAM, the present EARL, who was advanced to the dignity of Viscount Merton and Trafalgar of Merton, Co. Surrey, and Earl Nelson of Merton and Trafalgar, with the same remainder.

NEWBOROUGH, BARON. (WYNN.)

Peer of Ireland.

This is an ancient Welsh family, of which Sir Thomas Wynn was created a Baronet in 1742; his grandson SIR THOMAS, 3rd Baronet, was created in 1776, BARON NEWBOROUGH; he *d.* in 1807, and having survived his only son John, was succeeded by his eldest grandson THOMAS-JOHN, the present and 2nd LORD.

NEWBURGH, EARL OF. (EYRE-LIVINGSTON.)

Peer of Scotland.

SIR JAMES LIVINGSTON, a Royalist of untainted principles and honour, was created in 1647, Viscount of Newburgh; and in 1660, by King CHARLES II., with whom he had resided abroad during the period of his exile, EARL of NEWBURGH, Viscount of Kinnaird, and Baron Livingston of Flacraig; with remainder to his heirs whatever. He *d.* in 1670, and was succeeded by his only son, CHARLES, 2nd EARL; and he, in 1694, by his only daughter, CHARLOTTE-MARIA, 3rd COUNTESS; she *m.* 1st. Thomas, eldest son and heir of Hugh, Lord Clifford, by whom she had no issue; and 2ndly, 24 June 1724, the Hon. Charles Radcliffe, brother of James, 3rd Earl of Derwentwater, with whom he engaged in the rebellion of 1715. The Earl was executed, and his title and noble estates forfeited; they have since been applied to the maintenance of Greenwich Hospital. Charles, his brother, was taken at Preston, tried for high treason, and condemned, but contrived to escape out of Newgate. He retired to France; and on the young Chevalier's landing in Scotland in 1745, embarked to join him on board the *Esperance* privateer, and was taken by the *Sheerness* man-of-war; he was thereupon committed to the Tower and beheaded in pursuance of his former sentence, 8 Dec. 1746. He left issue by the Countess of Newburgh, three sons and four daughters, of whom the two youngest sons, and the three eldest daughters *d. unm.* She *d.* 4 Aug. 1755, and was succeeded by her eldest son, JAMES-BARTHOLOMEW, 4th EARL, on whose death in 1786 his only surviving issue was ANTHONY-JAMES, 5th EARL, who *d.* in 1814, when FRANCIS-EYRE, the 6th EARL, succeeded, being eldest son of Francis Eyre, Esq., by Lady Mary Radcliffe, the 4th but only married daughter of the 3rd Countess. He *d.* in 1827, and was succeeded by his eldest son, THOMAS, the present and 7th EARL.

NEWCASTLE, DUKE OF. (PELHAM-CLINTON.)

Peer of Great Britain.

William de Villa Tancredi, Chamberlain of Normandy, had three sons: Osbert, Renebald, and William, who all accompanied William the Conqueror into England. The male line of Osbert failed in 1233. Among other lands granted by William to Renebald, was the Lordship of Clinton, in Oxfordshire, from which his descendants took their surname.

The 6th in descent from Renebald was John de Clinton, summoned to Parliament by writ 1299; from which period it is observable that his male descendants have sat uninterruptedly as Peers of Parliament to the present day; and that consequently, with the exception of the families of Berkeley and Neville, they are the oldest members of the House of Lords in the paternal line. The family of Courtenay, now Earl of Devon, is entitled to a similar distinction, but its misfortunes in the 16th century produced a long intermission of its rights.

To John, 1st Lord Clinton, succeeded, in direct paternal descent, a line of eight Lords, all men of considerable note in their time, and some of them particularly distinguished for the commands entrusted to them in the French and Scottish wars, and for their zeal on behalf of the House of York in the civil contests for the Crown.

EDWARD, 8th Lord Clinton, K.G., was thirty years Lord High Admiral of England; an elevation to which he arrived, not, as was frequently the case in those times, as the due meed of his birth and power, but through a series of active and important services in naval command. Queen ELIZABETH conferred on him, in

572, the dignity of EARL of LINCOLN. He *d.* in 1585, and was succeeded by his ldest son,

HENRY, 2nd EARL, who was also highly esteemed by Queen ELIZABETH, and owards the close of her reign, was one of the Commanders whom she employed to esiege the Earl of Essex in his house. He *d.* in 1616, leaving, besides other issue, hree sons, viz.:

1 THOMAS, 3rd EARL, who *d.* in 1619, and was succeeded by his eldest son, THEOPHILUS, 4th EARL. He took part with the Parliament against King CHARLES I., and, like most others of the same party, met with an ungrateful return for his services; the Commons impeaching him of high treason, for endeavouring to promote a treaty with the King. He *d.* in 1667, and having survived his son Edward, was succeeded by his grandson EDWARD, 5th EARL, and 12th Lord Clinton, K.G.; on whose death without issue in 1692, the Barony fell into abeyance between his aunts, the daughters of Theophilus, 4th Earl, and is now possessed by the heir-general of Lady Arabella, the 4th daughter, and the only one whose descendants survive. The Earldom devolved on FRANCIS CLINTON, 6th EARL, his cousin and heir male.

2 Sir Edward, whose eldest son, Robert, *m.* and *d.* without issue; and his 2nd son, Francis, was father of FRANCIS, who succeeded as 6th EARL.

3 Sir Henry Fynes-Clinton, who had five sons, of whom only Norreys, the third son, left male issue. This Norreys had six sons, the five younger left no known issue; but Norreys, the eldest son, was father of another Norreys, who *d.* in 1764, leaving by Martha, daughter of —— Thompson, Esq., two sons, viz. the late Rev. Dr. Charles Fynes-Clinton, and Kendall Fynes-Clinton, Esq., now living. The said Rev. Charles Fynes-Clinton, D.D., Sub-Dean of Westminster, eldest son of the third Norreys Fynes-Clinton, Esq., *d.* 13 Nov. 1827, leaving by Emma his wife, daughter of Job Brough, Esq., who *d.* 15 Aug. 1831, Henry Fynes-Clinton, Esq., and the other issue stated in *The Peerage Volume.*

FRANCIS, 6th EARL, grandson of Sir Edward Clinton, 2nd son of the 2nd Earl, *d.* in 1693, leaving two sons, viz.:

1 HENRY-FIENNES, his successor, 7th EARL, K.G., *m.* Lucy, daughter of Thomas, Lord Pelham, and sister of THOMAS, 1st DUKE of NEWCASTLE, and *d.* in 1728, leaving two sons, GEORGE, his successor, 8th EARL, who *d.* in 1730; and HENRY, 9th EARL, and 2nd DUKE of NEWCASTLE.

2 The Hon Admiral George Clinton, who *d.* in 1761, leaving one surviving son, Lieut.-General Sir Henry Clinton, K.B.; he *d.* 13 Dec. 1795, having *m.* Harriet, daughter and co-heir of —— Carter, Esq., by whom he had issue the present Lieut.-General Sir William-Henry Clinton, G.C.B., for whom see *The Peerage Volume*, and the late Lieut.-General Sir Henry Clinton, G.C.B., who *d.* without issue 11 Dec. 1829; having *m.* 23 Dec. 1799, Lady Susan Charteris, daughter of Francis, Lord Elcho, and grand-daughter of Francis, 6th Earl of Wemyss; she *d.* 17 Aug. 1816.

Sir Thomas Pelham, Bart., for whose pedigree see the Earl of Chichester, was created Baron Pelham of Laughton, Co. Sussex, in 1706; THOMAS, 2nd LORD, his son, the Prime Minister of King GEORGE I. and II., was created Viscount Pelham of Houghton, Co. Nottingham, and Earl of Clare in 1714; in 1715 Marquis of Clare, and Duke of Newcastle, Co. Northumberland; and subsequently, in 1756, DUKE of NEWCASTLE-under-Lyme, with remainder, failing his issue male, to Henry, Earl of Lincoln, son of his sister Lucy, Countess of Lincoln, and his issue male, by Catherine, his wife, eldest daughter and co-heir of Henry Pelham, deceased, and niece of the Duke; the Duke was also created in 1762, Baron Pelham of Stanmer, Co. Sussex, with remainder to Thomas Pelham, Esq., grandson of Henry Pelham, younger brother of Thomas, 1st Baron Pelham of Laughton. The Duke *d.* without issue, 17 Nov. 1768, when all his titles became extinct, except the Barony of Pelham of Stanmer, which devolved on the said Thomas Pelham, Esq., grandfather of the present Earl of Chichester; and the Dukedom of Newcastle-under-Lyme, which devolved on

Henry-Fiennes, 9th Earl of Lincoln, the 2nd Duke, K.G., son of Henry, 7th Earl, by the Hon. Lucy Pelham, daughter of Thomas, 1st Lord Pelham, and sister of the 1st Duke. He was *b.* 24 April 1720, succeeded his brother George, 8th Earl, 30 April 1730, and his uncle Thomas, 1st Duke, 17 Nov. 1768, and *d.* 22 Feb. 1794; having *m.* 16 Oct. 1744, Catherine, eldest surviving daughter and co-heir of the Right Hon. Henry Pelham, only brother of Thomas, 1st Duke, by whom, who was *b.* 24 July 1727, and *d.* 27 July 1760, he had, besides other issue, two sons, viz.:

1 Henry, Earl of Lincoln, *b.* 5 Nov. 1750, *d.* 22 Oct. 1778; having *m.* 22 May 1775, Lady Frances Seymour-Conway, 4th daughter of Francis, 1st Marquis of Hertford, by whom, who *d.* 11 Nov. 1820, he left issue:

1 Lady Catherine, *b.* 6 April 1776, *d.* 17 May 1804; having *m.* 2 Oct. 1800, William, Viscount Folkestone, now Earl of Radnor.

2 Henry, Earl of Lincoln, who was *b.* 23 Dec. 1777, *d.* 23 Sept. 1779.

2 Thomas, who having survived his brother and nephew, became Earl of Lincoln, and succeeded his father as 3rd Duke; he *d.* in 1795, and was succeeded by his eldest son, Henry-Pelham, present and 4th Duke, K.G.

NORBURY, EARL OF. (Toler.)

Peer of Ireland.

The family of Toler was originally of Norfolk, and settled in Ireland in the reign of Charles I. John, the late Earl, the celebrated Chief Justice of the Court of Common Pleas in Ireland, was the 2nd son (Daniel Toler, Esq., the eldest son, having *d.* in 1796, without issue male, leaving three daughters all married,) of Daniel Toler, Esq., of Beechwood, Co. Tipperary, by Letitia, daughter of Thomas Otway, Esq. His Lordship *m.* Grace, daughter of Hector Graham, Esq., who was created Baroness Norwood in 1797; he was himself created Baron Norbury in 1800, and was advanced to the titles of Viscount Glandine of Glandine, King's County, and Earl of Norbury, in 1827, with remainder to his 2nd son, Hector-John-Graham Toler, and his heirs male. His Lordship *d.* in 1831, and was succeeded in the Barony by his eldest son Daniel, 2nd Lord Norwood, and in the Earldom by his 2nd son, Hector-John-Graham, present and 2nd Earl.

NORFOLK, DUKE OF. (Howard.)

Peer of England.

Sir William Howard, Chief-Justice of the Common Pleas in the reign of Edward I., whose pedigree is variously deduced by different authorities, is the first certain ancestor of this noble House. The 4th in descent from him was

Sir Robert Howard, who *m.* Margaret, eldest daughter of Thomas de Mowbray, Duke of Norfolk, son of John, 4th Lord Mowbray, by Elizabeth, daughter and heir of John, Lord Segrave, by Margaret, daughter and heir of Thomas de Brotherton, Earl of Norfolk, and Earl Marshal of England, 5th son of King Edward I. On the death of John Mowbray, 5th Duke of Norfolk, grandson of John, 3rd Duke, brother of the above Margaret, the Baronies of Mowbray and Segrave devolved on Anne, his only daughter and heir; who dying without issue, they fell into abeyance between the heirs of her two great aunts, viz. this Margaret, wife of Sir Robert Howard, and Isabel, wife of James, 6th Lord Berkeley. The Barony of Mowbray was called out of abeyance in 1639, in favour of Henry, (7th Duke of Norfolk by descent) Earl of Arundel, Surrey, and Norfolk. The son and heir of Sir Robert Howard and Margaret his wife was,

John Howard, K.G., summoned to Parliament as Baron Howard in 1470, and created hereditary Earl Marshal of England and Duke of Norfolk in 1483; he was high in the favour of King Edward IV., and filled various offices of trust and honour throughout the reign of that Monarch, and of Richard III. He lost his life in the cause of the latter Prince at the battle of Bosworth-field, in 1485, and was subsequently attainted in Henry VII.'s 1st Parliament, and his honours forfeited.

Thomas, 2nd Duke, K.G., his eldest son, was created Earl of Surrey in 1483, at the same time that his father was created Duke of Norfolk. He fought with great valour at the battle of Bosworth, but was made prisoner, attainted, and confined for three years in the Tower; but afterwards liberated by Henry VII., restored to the Earldom of Surrey in 1489, and, distinguished by that Monarch's confidence, held the highest offices under his government, and that of King Henry VIII. He was Earl Marshal and Lord High Treasurer of England; in 1513, he had the command of the army which was assembled to meet the Scotch invasion under King James IV., and on the 9th of Sept. obtained that great and decisive victory at Flodden, in which the Scots King and so many of his nobles lost their lives. In memorial of this victory, Henry VIII. granted the Earl, as an augmentation to his arms, the inescutcheon charged with a demy lion within a double tressure flory counter flory, which is borne by all his descendants upon the bend in their shield. In the following year, 1514, he had a renewed patent of the Dukedom of Norfolk, and *d.* in 1524. This Duke had four sons, of whom only three left issue, viz.: 1 Thomas, (eldest son,) 3rd Duke; 2 Lord Edmund Howard, (3rd son,) Marshal of the Horse in the battle of Flodden field; he was father of Queen Catherine, 5th wife of Henry VIII., of three sons who all *d.* without issue, and of four other daughters, all married to private gentlemen; 3 Lord William, (9th son,) K.G., ancestor of the present Lord Howard of Effingham, and of the extinct Earls of Nottingham and Effingham.—*See* Lord Howard of Effingham.

Thomas, his eldest son, 3rd Duke, commanded in the North against the Scotch many years in his father's lifetime, bearing then the title of Earl of Surrey, to which he had been created; he continued in this command after he became Duke of Norfolk, and had also other important employments in the service of King Henry VIII.; who at length, towards the close of his reign, becoming jealous of the Duke's great power, which he imagined might be dangerous to his infant successor; having borne no good will to the family since the discovery of the dissolute manners of Catherine Howard, his fifth wife and the Duke's niece, before her marriage; and perhaps urged on by the Earl of Hertford and the Protestant party, who were desirous of arrogating to themselves the chief authority under the expected minority; caused him and his eldest son, Henry Earl of Surrey, the most accomplished nobleman of his time, and one of the earliest English poets, to be attainted on the most frivolous pretences; and the aged Duke had the misery of seeing his son beheaded, narrowly escaping the same fate himself by the opportune death of the King. He remained, however, a prisoner in the Tower till the accession of Queen Mary, who liberated him on the day of her first entry into London in 1553, and without any pardon or restitution in blood, allowed his titles, and put him in possession of his estates. He raised two hundred horse and six hundred foot for the suppression of Sir Thomas Wyat's rebellion; but these forces, after defeating Knivet, who was on his way to join Wyat, deserted from him, and went over to the rebels. He continued, however, his services in the suppression of the insurrection, and when it was accomplished, retired to his seat in Norfolk, and *d.* there in 1554, having seen the reigns of eight English sovereigns. He had two sons who survived their infancy, viz.:

1 Henry, before mentioned, Earl of Surrey, who was beheaded in 1547, leaving two sons: 1 Thomas, 4th Duke, who succeeded his grandfather; 2 Henry, K.G., created Earl of Northampton in 1604, a bad but fortunate man; he *d.* without issue in 1614, when the title became extinct.

2 Lord Thomas, created Viscount Bindon in 1559; he *d.* in 1582, leaving two sons, Henry, 2nd Viscount, and Thomas, 3rd Viscount, K.G.; the former *d.*

in whose service he was shipwrecked on a voyage from Ireland to France, in 1689; he left five sons, two of whom *d. unm.* the other three were . 1 Thomas, 11th Duke, who succeeded his uncle, and *d.* without issue in 17??, 2 Edward, 12th Duke, on whose death without issue, in 1777, the Earldom of Norwich, and Barony of Howard of Castle-Rising, became extinct; 3 Philip, *d.* in 1750; leaving one son Edward, whose death in 1767, was deeply lamented by the Duke, his uncle and the whole family, and two daughters, Winifred Lady Stourton, and Anne Lady Petre, between whom the Baronies of Mowbray, Furnival, Strange, Talbot, and Howard, fell into abeyance upon the death of Edward, 12th Duke, and continue in abeyance between their heirs; these ladies also became by the same event, co-heirs to one moiety of the Baronies of Segrave, 1264, Greystock, 1295, Botetourt, of Wemme, 1295, Giffard of Brimmesfield, 1295, and Dacre of Gillesland, 1482, Verdun, 1295, Braose of Gower, 1299, and Lisle 1357; to all which Baronies, by the intermarriages of his ancestors, the said 12th Duke was co-heir.

3 Philip, a Cardinal of the Romish Church, generally styled the Cardinal of Norfolk, and sometimes the Cardinal of England; he was Almoner to the Queen of Charles II., till the general objection to Popery in England induced him to return to Rome, where he was much consulted by the English Catholics in the reign of James II., to whom he always advised moderate measures, predicting the consequences of their precipitate proceedings. He *d.* at Rome in 1694.

4 Charles Howard, of Greystoke, Co. Cumberland; he *d.* in 1713, leaving one son, Charles, who *d.* in 1720; he was father of Charles, who succeeded as 13th, or, as he is more commonly called, 10th Duke, in 1777. He *d.* in 1786, and was succeeded by his only son, Charles, 14th Duke, who *d.* without issue in 1815.

5 Bernard Howard of Glossop, Co. Notts; he was father of Bernard, and grandfather of Henry Howard, Esqs., of Glossop, the latter, who *d.* in 1787, was father of Bernard-Edward, the present and 15th Duke, who succeeded in 1815.

NORMANTON, EARL OF. (Agar.)

Peer of Ireland.

The Most Rev. Charles Agar, Lord Archbishop of Cashell, and afterwards of Dublin, brother of James, 1st Viscount Clifden, (and son of Henry Agar, Esq., by Anne, sister of Welbore Ellis, created Lord Mendip, with remainder to his sister's sons—*see* Clifden,) was created in 1795 Baron of Somerton, Co. Kilkenny; in 1800 Viscount Somerton, and in 1806 Earl of Normanton, Co. Kilkenny. He *d.* in 1809, and was succeeded by his eldest son, Welbore-Ellis, the present and 2nd Earl.

NORTHAMPTON, MARQUIS OF. (Compton.)

Peer of the United Kingdom.

The ancestor of this family was Alwyne, of the race of the Saxon Earls of Warwick, and contemporary with Edward the Confessor, whose son, Turchil, was dispossessed of his Castle of Warwick by William the Conqueror; he assumed the name of Compton, from his Lordship of Compton, in Warwickshire.

Sir William Compton, 13th in descent from Alwyne, laid the foundation of the renovated fortune of his family, by the favour of King Henry VIII., in whose household he had been bred in the quality of Page, from the King's childhood and his own; he *d.* in 1528. Sir Henry Compton, his grandson, was summoned to Parliament, as Baron Compton, in 1572, and *d.* in 1589; William, his son and heir, 2nd Baron, K.G., was created Earl of Northampton, in 1618; he obtained a great fortune with his wife, Elizabeth, only daughter and heir of John Spencer, Lord Mayor of London, and *d.* in 1630, leaving an only son, Spencer, 2nd Earl; who, from the first appearance of hostility to King Charles's Government, devoted himself to its support in Parliament; and on the breaking out of the Civil War, repaired to his Majesty's standard at Nottingham, with a force of 2000 of the best disciplined troops that were in the army at the battle of Edge Hill. He secured the arms, ammunition, and garrisons, in the counties of Warwick, Stafford, and Northampton, and held those three counties in subjection to the King, till, on the 19th of March 1643, he fell in the battle of Hopton Heath, in which, with about 1000 soldiers under his command, he routed a force of more than double that number under Sir John Gell. He left six sons, of whom the five eldest were as actively and zealously engaged in the Royal cause throughout that unhappy war, as he had himself been in its commencement; Sir William, the third son, though liberated after having been made prisoner at Colchester, into which town he had thrown himself and his followers, as the last place in which he could serve the King, kept a constant correspondence with the King, and from that time to the Restoration, there was no plot or pretended plot in which he was not engaged. Henry, the 6th son, was too young to bear arms during the Civil Wars, and was bred to the Church; and, being in the reign of James II., Bishop of London, proved himself as zealous in the defence of the Protestant Church as his father and brothers had been in support of the Throne.

James, 3rd Earl, the eldest son, continued to exert his utmost abilities in support of the sinking cause of Royalty till nothing further could be done, when he was admitted to compound for his estates, and lived in retirement till the Restoration. He *d.* in 1681, leaving two sons: George, 4th Earl, his successor; and Sir Spencer, Speaker of the House of Commons, created in 1727 Baron Wilmington, and in 1730 Viscount Pevensey, and Earl of Wilmington; he *d. unm.* in 1743.

George, 4th Earl, the eldest son, *d.* in 1727; leaving three sons: viz.

1 James, 5th Earl, and 6th Baron Compton; he *m.* Elizabeth, 13th Baroness Ferrers of Chartley, grand-daughter and heir of Robert, 1st Earl Ferrers, and 12th Baron Ferrers of Chartley; she *d.* in 1741, and the Earl in 1754; when the Baronies of Ferrers of Chartley and Compton became united in their only surviving child, Charlotte, wife of George, 4th Viscount and 1st Marquis Townshend, and are now inherited by the Marquis Townshend, her grandson.

2 George, 6th Earl, who succeeded his brother as heir male, and *d.* without issue in 1758.

3 Charles, who *d.* in 1755; leaving two sons:

1 Charles, who succeeded his uncle as 7th Earl, and *d.* in 1763, leaving an only daughter, Elizabeth, now Countess of Burlington.

2 Spencer, who succeeded his brother as 8th Earl, and was succeeded in 1796, by his only son,

Charles, 9th Earl, created in 1812, Baron Wilmington of Wilmington, Co. Sussex, Earl Compton of Compton, Co. Warwick, and Marquis of the County of Northampton; he *d.* in 1828, and was succeeded by his only surviving son, Spencer-Joshua-Alwyne, present and 2nd Marquis.

NORTHESK, EARL OF. (Carnegie.)

Peer of Scotland.

In the reign of David II., John de Balinhard obtained a charter of the lands of Carnegy, from whence he took the name of Carnegy. Sixth in descent from Duthac de Carnegy, who was living in 1410, was David Carnegy of Panbride, who *d.* in 1598; he was father of,

1 Sir David, created in 1416 Lord Carnegy of Kinnaird, and in 1633 Earl of Southesk; he *d.* in 1658, leaving, besides other issue, the two sons following,

1 James, his successor, 2nd Earl of Southesk; to whom succeeded, in direct paternal descent, Robert, 3rd Earl; Charles 4th Earl; and James 5th Earl; the latter, engaged in the Rebellion of 1715, was attainted, and his estates and honours forfeited; he *d.* without surviving issue in 1729, when the male line of the 2nd Earl of Southesk became extinct.

2 Sir Alexander Carnegy of Pittarrow, created a Baronet of Nova Scotia, in 1663; he was father of Sir David, grandfather of Sir John, and great-grandfather of Sir James Carnegy, Baronets; the latter succeeded in 1729, as the male representative of this family on the death of the forfeited Earl of Southesk, and, but for the attainder, would have been 6th Earl; he *d.* in 1765, and was succeeded by his eldest son, Sir David, to whom succeeded in 1805, the present Baronet, Sir James Carnegie of Southesk, who but for the attainder, would be 8th Earl of Southesk.

2 Sir John, created Lord Lour in 1639; and Earl of Ethie, Lord Lour and Eglismadie in 1647; which titles were exchanged by patent, in 1662, for those of Earl of Northesk, and Lord Rosehill; he *d.* in 1667.

David, 2nd Earl, his eldest son and successor, *d.* in 1677, leaving besides other issue, two sons, whose representatives still subsist, viz:

1 David, 3rd Earl, who *d.* in 1688, and was succeeded by his son David, 4th Earl; he *d.* in 1729, leaving David, 5th Earl, who *d. unm.* in 1741, and George, 6th Earl, an Admiral; he succeeded his brother, and *d.* 22 Jan. 1792; having *m.* 30 April 1748, Lady Anne Leslie, eldest daughter of Alexander, 5th Earl of Leven and Melville, by whom, who *d.* 8 Nov. 1779, he had issue, 1 David Lord Rosehill—see *The Peerage Volume*. 2 William, 7th Earl; 3 James, who *d.* young; 4 Lady Elizabeth, *m.* James 3rd Earl of Hopetoun, and *d.* 18 Aug. 1793; 5 Lady Margaret, *d.* 15 March 1798; having *m.* 1780, Charles Watson, Esq., *b.* 17 Nov. 1740, *d.* 2 June 1804; 6 Lady Mary-Anne, *d.* 10 Aug. 1798; having *m.* 2 June 1797, Rev. John Kemp, D.D., *re-married* to Lady Elizabeth Hope, of Hopetoun, who *d.* 17 Sept. 1801; and 7 The Hon. Lieut.-Colonel George, whose marriage and issue are stated in *The Peerage Volume*. The 6th Earl was succeeded by his eldest surviving son, the distinguished Admiral, William, 7th Earl, whose gallant services at Trafalgar, where he was third in command, and on many other occasions, received the most honourable marks of approbation from his Sovereign and both Houses of Parliament; his Lordship *m.* Mary, daughter of William-Henry Ricketts, Esq., and niece of Earl St. Vincent, whose title of Viscount is in remainder to her male issue by the Earl of Northesk, failing the issue male of her only surviving brother, the present Viscount St. Vincent;—*See* St. Vincent. The Earl *d.* in 1831, and having lost his eldest son George Lord Rosehill, in his 16th year, a midshipman on board the Blenheim, bearing Admiral Troubridge's flag, when she sunk in the Indian Seas in Feb. 1807, was succeeded by his eldest surviving son, William-Hopetoun, present and 8th Earl.

2 Patrick Carnegy of Lour, Co. Forfar, ancestor of the only existing collateral branch, descended from the 1st Earl of Northesk; he *d.* in 1723, having been father of twenty children, most of whom *d. unm.* James, 11th son, was ancestor of a number of Carnegys in the County of Forfar and elsewhere. Patrick, his eldest son and successor at Lour, had five sons, of whom only one left issue, viz: Patrick, the eldest, who succeeded his father in 1723, and *d.* in 1799, leaving only one surviving son, Patrick, who *d.* in 1819, leaving a numerous issue, for whom see *The Peerage Volume*, and was succeeded by his eldest son, the present Patrick Carnegy, Esq., of Lour.

NORTHUMBERLAND, DUKE OF. (Percy.)

Peer of Great Britain.

The first ancestor of the original house of Percy was Mainfred de Percy, a Danish nobleman, who settled in Normandy before the Conquest of that province by Duke Rollo. The 6th from him was William de Percy, surnamed Alsgernons, or, with the whiskers, who came into England with William the Conqueror, and obtained large grants of lands in the counties of Lincoln and York, the latter being part of the forfeited estates of Cospatrick, Earl of Northumberland, a Saxon nobleman, whose daughter Emma he married, and who having levied war unsuccessfully against the Normans, was obliged to fly into Scotland; his male line was continued in England by the House of Neville, and in Scotland by that of Dunbar, Earls of Dunbar and March, now represented by the Earl of Home. The Lord William de Percy was a Baron of England, and founder of the famous Abbey of St. Hilda in Yorkshire; he *d.* about 1096. Alan, his son and heir, was father of William, 3rd Lord Percy, who having survived four sons, left his large patrimony to be divided between two daughters, his co-heirs, the Lady Maud, *m.* to William de Plessets, Earl of Warwick, without issue; and the Lady Agnes, in whose posterity the whole inheritance centred.

She *m.* Josceline de Louvaine, younger son of Godfrey I., Duke of Brabant, and brother of Adeliza, 2nd Consort of King Henry I.; he assumed the name of Percy and obtained from Queen Adeliza, his sister, a grant of the honour of Petworth in Sussex, formerly a member of Arundel, which was afterwards confirmed by King Henry II. He left by the Lady Agnes, besides other issue,

1 Henry, who succeeded him at Petworth, and *d.* before his mother, leaving a son, William.

2 Richard, who after the death of his father and brother got possession of the inheritance of his aunt, the Countess Maud, and subsequently of great part of that of his mother; he was one of the 25 Barons appointed in 1215 to enforce the observance of Magna Charta; he had long litigations with his nephew William respecting the succession to the family possessions, which was at length compromised, after a solemn hearing before King Henry III. in person, at Kennington in 1234, the estates being equally divided between the two parties during Richard's life, and the whole after his death being secured to his nephew, though Richard left male issue which failed in his grandsons.

Henry Lord Percy, great-grandson of William, was summoned to Parliament in 1299. He purchased of Anthony Beck, Bishop of Durham, the Barony of Alnwick in the Co. of Northumberland; he was appointed by King Edward I. Governor of Galloway and Ayr in Scotland, having signalised himself in the Scotch wars. He *d.* in 1315, and was succeeded by his son Henry, 2nd Baron Percy by writ, to whom in 1316 King Edward II. granted the lands in Northumberland of Patrick Dunbar, Earl of Dunbar and March (a male descendant of Cospatrick, Earl of Northumberland, above mentioned), who having been an adherent of England, had made his peace with King Robert Bruce, and was now in arms against Edward. He was one of the Barons who leagued to obtain the reform of abuses occasioned by the power of the Spencers, and was in 1327 appointed of the Council to King Edward III.; in 1328 he obtained a grant from that King of the Castle and Barony of Warkworth. He was in the battle of Hallidown Hill, and was on the subsequent day appointed Governor of Berwick. He continued to distinguish himself in the wars both in France and Scotland till his death in 1352.

Henry, 3rd Lord Percy, his son and successor, *d.* in 1368, having *m.* the Lady Mary Plantagenet, 6th daughter of Henry, 3rd Earl of Lancaster, grandson of King Henry III., by whom he had two sons:

1 Henry, 4th Lord, and 1st Earl of Northumberland.

2 Thomas, K.G., who throughout the reign of King Richard II. was employed in offices of high trust in France and England, and was a successful commander by sea and land; he was created in 1397 Earl of Worcester; HENRY IV. appointed him Ambassador to the French King, and gave him a military command in France; and afterwards made him his Lieutenant in Wales for the suppression of Owen Glendour's insurrection. Having never thoroughly approved the revolution which placed Henry on the throne, he took the opportunity of this Welsh war to declare for the rights of Edmund Mortimer, Earl of March; and entering into compact with Glendour, was joined by the forces of his brother and nephew; the gallant Hotspur was killed in the battle of Shrewsbury, and the immediate consequence was the total rout of this hitherto conquering army; the Earl of Worcester was taken prisoner and beheaded soon afterwards, in July 1402. He *d. unm.*

Henry, 4th Lord Percy, K.G., was distinguished in the French wars in the reign of King EDWARD III., but was at one time in danger of losing his life as a great favourer of the famous reformer Dr. John Wickliff; he was created Earl of Northumberland in 1377, by King RICHARD II., with remainder to his heirs general. About the year 1399, King RICHARD having suspicions instilled into him respecting his fidelity, sent him an order to attend him, which the Earl refusing to obey, he was proclaimed a traitor and banished the kingdom. Upon this he joined the standard of Henry Duke of Lancaster, not, as he averred, to depose the King, but to obtain a more equitable system of government. The Duke of Lancaster, however, was not to be restrained, and being successful against King RICHARD, chiefly through the assistance of the Earl of Northumberland, persuaded him to acquiesce in the transfer of the crown. But the jealousy which so naturally subsisted between a Monarch and a too powerful subject, in times when privilege and prerogative were not very accurately defined, threw the Earl of Northumberland again into rebellion. Having, with his gallant son Henry Hotspur, Lord Percy, defeated the Scotch at Homildon, and taken their leader, the Earl of Douglas, prisoner, he entered into an alliance with him, and assisted by some forces from Scotland and a great number of his own retainers, he proposed to join Owen Glendour and his brother, the Earl of Worcester, in Wales. He was, however, confined by indisposition at Berwick, when a battle was fought at Shrewsbury, by the rebel troops under Hotspur, against King HENRY's army, which ending in Percy's death and the total defeat of his party, the Earl was compelled to throw himself on the King's mercy, and was pardoned. Again in 1405 he was implicated in a project of treason, for which Thomas Mowbray, Earl Marshal, and Richard Scrope, Archbishop of York, were beheaded; the Earl of Northumberland, with young Henry Percy, his grandson and heir, took refuge in Scotland, and returning some time afterwards, raised a small force, with which he recovered some of his castles and Lordships, but being suddenly attacked by the Sheriff of Yorkshire with the posse-comitatus, was killed after a sharp fight on Bramham Moor, near Hazlewood, in February 1508; and being attainted, his estates and titles were forfeited.

Henry Lord Percy, K.G., his eldest son, commonly called Hotspur, commenced his career of glory at the age of 14; when at the storming of Berwick by his father he is said to have done so valiantly, that he deserved singular commendation; from that time he was foremost in every battle in which English prowess was engaged, and became so famous for his military skill and valour, that he is said by a foreigner, whose notes of that transaction are preserved in the Harleian MSS., to have been at the period of Henry IV.'s coronation, the most valiant and approved knight in England. At the battle of Otterbourne, in which James Earl of Douglas, the opposed commander, was killed, Hotspur was made prisoner by the Lord Montgomery, but paying an immense sum for his ransom, was speedily liberated. Many years after this, at the battle of Homildon, he took Archibald Earl of Douglas prisoner, and the fatal consequence of the association thereby produced, which ended in his death at the battle of Shrewsbury in July 1402, has been already described. He *d.* at 37 years of age, leaving an only son,

Henry, 2nd Earl of Northumberland; he was educated in Scotland with the greatest kindness and hospitality, under the Regent, Duke of Albany, and was recalled and restored to his honours and estates by King HENRY V., in 1414. During the wars of that King in France, he was left in charge of the eastern border against the Scotch, towards whom, in remembrance of their early kindness, he is said to have always acted with friendship and generosity; he had, however, his private feuds with individuals of that nation, and the battle of Pepperden, fought between him and William Douglas, Earl of Angus, with a small army of retainers on each side, and in which the latter had the advantage, is said to have given rise to the ballad of "Chevy Chase." The breaking out of the civil wars between the Houses of York and Lancaster enabled him to show, in his adherence to HENRY VI., the son of his Royal benefactor, another instance of his gratitude for past favours; and he was soon afterwards, 23 May 1455, killed in the battle of St. Albans, where the Lancastrian forces were routed, and the King himself made prisoner. He had nine sons, of whom three died young; two were in the Church, and the other four all fell in the Lancastrian cause; Sir Thomas Percy, 5th son, was created Baron Egremont in 1449, and was killed at the battle of Northampton, 1460, when his title became extinct; Sir Ralph Percy, 7th son, died at Hedgeley Moor, in 1464, fighting at the head of some forces raised by himself against the Yorkist General, Lord Montacute; he left male descendants who continued to the third generation; Sir Richard Percy, 8th son, was killed, with his eldest brother, the Earl of Northumberland, at the battle of Towton, in 1461.

Henry, 3rd Earl of Northumberland, was of the same age with King HENRY VI., and, at five years old, received the honour of Knighthood from the infant Monarch, who had himself just before been knighted by his uncle, the Duke of Bedford. After the decease of his father, whom he succeeded in title and estates, this Earl was the chief supporter of the Lancastrian interests in the north, till the bloody and decisive battle of Towton, 29 March 1461, in which, after fighting with unwearied courage for ten hours, he was killed, and victory declared for the Yorkists. He was attainted in the November following, by Act of Parliament, and his estates and honours forfeited. The Earldom of Northumberland was soon after conferred on John Neville, brother of Richard, Earl of Warwick and Salisbury. The Earl *m.* Eleanor, daughter and sole heir of Richard Poynings, who *d.* in his father's life-time, eldest son and heir of Robert, 5th Lord Poynings, by writ in 1337; this marriage brought the Barony of Poynings to the House of Percy, and it is erroneously supposed those of Fitz-payne and Bryan also, with which, however, this Eleanor had no direct connexion.

Henry, 4th Earl of Northumberland, K.G., their son and heir, being a minor at the time of his father's death, was committed a prisoner to the Tower, but was released by King EDWARD IV., in 1469; his father's attainder was reversed soon afterwards, and the Earldom of Northumberland, surrendered by John Neville, who was created Marquis of Montacute, was restored to him. He was appointed Warden of the East and Middle Marches, and, as such, had the chief command under Richard, Duke of Gloucester, of the army which invaded Scotland in 1482, and took the city of Edinburgh. King RICHARD III. sent to command the Earl to attend him with the forces of the north on the invasion of the Earl of Richmond, and he was on the field of battle at Bosworth; but, unwilling to lend his assistance to the King, withheld his troops from engaging, which acquired him the favour of King HENRY VII. He was killed, in 1489, in a tumult of the people, excited by King HENRY's imposition of some heavy taxes, from which the Earl had vainly endeavoured to dissuade him. From Josceline, his 4th son, descended a branch of Percys of Beverley, extinct in the senior line in the 4th generation, which continued, however, at Cambridge, in the junior line much longer, but is now extinct; the ancestor of this junior line was the Thomas Percy concerned in the Gunpowder Plot, grandson of this Josceline.

Henry-Algernon, 5th Earl of Northumberland, K.G., was also Lord Warden of the Marches; he was renowned for the splendour and hospitality of his manner of living, and was a generous patron of genius and learning. He *d.* in 1527, leaving three sons, of whom Sir Ingelram, the youngest, *d.* without legitimate issue in 1538; the two elder sons were,

1 Henry-Algernon, 6th Earl, K.G., the happiness of whose life was overshadowed by an early and ill-fated passion for the beautiful Anne Boleyn, the unfortunate wife of King HENRY VIII. Urged by the Royal mandate, the Earl, his father, compelled him to renounce the choice of his heart, and to marry a daughter of the Earl of Shrewsbury, from whom he separated himself without having had any living issue by her. The misfortunes which fell on his house by the attainder of his next brother, from whom its heirs descended, so affected him, that his constitution was unable to support the shock, and he *d.* 30 June 1537, the same month that his brother was executed, when the Earldom became extinct, on account of the attainder, as did the ancient Baronies by writ, of Percy created in 1299, and Poynings in 1337.

2 Sir Thomas Percy, who, unfortunately involving himself in Aske's rebellion, in 1536, was taken, tried for high-treason, condemned, and executed in June 1537, and afterwards attainted. He left two sons, Thomas and Henry, both Earls of Northumberland.

Thomas, 7th Earl of Northumberland, K.G., eldest son of Sir Thomas Percy, was created by Queen Mary, in 1557, Baron Percy, of Cockermouth and Petworth, Baron Poynings, Lucy, Bryan, and Fitz-Payne, with remainder, in default of issue male, to his brother Henry and his issue male, and Earl of Northumberland, with the same remainder; the estates of his family were restored to him, and he was appointed Warden of the Marches. Being a steady Catholic, he was disaffected to the government of Queen Elizabeth, and, after the miscarriage of several conspiracies, broke out in 1570 into open rebellion, in conjunction with the Earl of Westmoreland, for the avowed purpose of restoring the Roman Catholic religion in the country. He was attainted, and having taken refuge in Scotland, was delivered up by the Earl of Morton, and beheaded in 1572; he *d.* without issue male, but left four daughters, who, but for the attainder of their father and grandfather, would have been co-heirs of the ancient Baronies of Percy and Poynings.

Henry, 8th Earl, K.G., succeeded to the Earldom and the Baronies created in 1557, which, but for the limitation of the patent, would have been forfeited by his brother's attainder. He distinguished himself against the Scotch in the reigns both of Mary and Elizabeth, and, on his brother's rebellion, held true to his allegiance. But falling under suspicion, as a Catholic, of having plotted, with Francis Throckmorton and Lord Paget, for the liberation of the Queen of Scots, he was committed to the Tower, where he was some time afterwards found dead in his bed, shot in the breast with three pistol bullets, by his own hand, according to the verdict of a coroner's inquest. He *m.* Catherine, eldest daughter and co-heir of John Nevill, 4th Lord Latimer by the writ of 1432; co-heiress also to one moiety of the Baronies of Plaitz by writ 1317, and Lisle by writ 1357, which co-heirships have descended on their heir general the present Duke of Northumberland.

Henry, 9th Earl, K.G., their son and heir, was, at the commencement of the reign of King JAMES I., in high favour with that Monarch; but on the discovery of the Gunpowder Plot, in which his relative Mr. Thomas Percy was concerned, the Earl was supposed to be privy to it, and was, by the Star Chamber, condemned to pay a fine of £30,000, and to be imprisoned in the Tower for life—a sentence which clouded the remainder of his days; the payment of £20,000, which was exacted, greatly impairing his fortune, and an imprisonment of fifteen years materially injuring his health; he *d.* in 1632. He left two surviving sons, of whom

Henry, the younger son, was created Baron Percy of Alnwick in 1643, and was a zealous supporter of the Royal cause during the civil wars, till he was taken prisoner at Andover in 1645; after his liberation, being unable to attend his Royal master, who was himself a prisoner, and all hope of the restoration of his affairs being at an end, he went over to the Hague, and remained with the Prince of Wales, afterwards King CHARLES II., till his death in 1659, when his title became extinct.

Algernon, 10th Earl, K.G., the eldest surviving son of the 9th Earl, was Lord High Admiral of England, and one of King CHARLES's Ministers of State, till the discussions between the King and Parliament came to an open rupture, when he remained in the councils of the rebels, actuated probably by the unhappy persecution his father had so long endured. He was entrusted with the care of the King's children when they fell into the hands of the Parliament, and treated them with great respect and kindness; was wholly averse to the trial and murder of the King; and after that event he retired to his house at Petworth, where he resided till the Restoration, in which he concurred, and was afterwards of the Privy Council to King Charles II. He *d.* in 1668, and was succeeded by his only son,

Joseline, 11th Earl, who *d.* at Turin, on his travels, in 1670, in his twenty-sixth year, without issue male, when the Earldom of Northumberland, and the Baronies created by the patent of 1557, became extinct. He left an only-surviving child heiress to his large possessions,

The Lady Elizabeth Percy; she was *b.* 26 Jan. 1667, *m.* 1st in 1679, to Henry Cavendish, Earl of Ogle, son and heir of Henry Duke of Newcastle, who assumed the name of Percy, and *d.* in 1680; 2ndly, to Thomas Thynne, Esq., of Longleate, Co. Wilts, who was assassinated in 1682, by foreigners hired by Count Konigsmark, himself a pretender to the hand of the young heiress; and 3rdly, 30 May 1682, being thus twice a widow and the third time a wife, when little more than fifteen years of age, to Charles Seymour, 7th Duke of Somerset; she *d.* 23 Nov. 1722, and the Duke *d.* 2 Dec. 1748. They had thirteen children, of whom three daughters lived to marry; but only two sons survived the period of childhood, viz. Lord Percy Seymour, the 6th son, who *d. unm.* in 1721, aged twenty-five; and their son and heir,

ALGERNON SEYMOUR, Earl of Hertford, who was summoned to Parliament by writ in 1722, on the decease of his mother, upon the supposition that the ancient Barony of Percy had descended upon him, and he took the precedence of the writ of 1299; this Barony, however, if it had not been forfeited by the attainders of Sir Thomas Percy and his son, the 7th Earl, would be in abeyance between the representatives of the four daughters and co-heirs of that Earl; the writ, therefore, of 1722, created a new Barony in fee, descendible to the heirs general of Algernon, then Earl of Hertford, and afterwards 8th Duke of Somerset, and is the only Barony by writ inherited by the present Duke of Northumberland. He succeeded his father as Duke of Somerset in 1748, and was created in 1749, Baron Warkworth of Warkworth Castle, Co. Northumberland, and Earl of Northumberland, with remainder, failing his issue male, to his son-in-law, Sir Hugh Smithson, Bart., and the heirs male of his body by Lady Elizabeth, his wife, sole daughter of the said Duke of Somerset; he was also created Baron Cockermouth, and Earl of Egremont, with a special remainder—*See* Earl of Egremont. He *d.* in 1750, having survived his only son George, Viscount Beauchamp, a young nobleman of great promise, who *d.* on his nineteenth birthday, in 1744, while on his travels in Italy.

His only daughter and heir, the LADY ELIZABETH SEYMOUR, *b.* 5 Dec. 1716, *m.* 18 July 1740, Sir Hugh Smithson, Bart., of Stanwick, Co. York; she succeeded as BARONESS PERCY on the death of her father, to whom her husband succeeded as Earl of Northumberland and Baron Warkworth; he assumed the name of PERCY, and was created in 1766 Earl Percy and DUKE of NORTHUMBERLAND; and in 1784, Baron Louvaine of Alnwick, with remainder to Algernon Percy, his 2nd son, who succeeded to this Barony on his death, was created Earl of Beverley in 1790, and was father of the present Earl of Beverley. The Duchess *d.* 5 Dec. 1776, and was succeeded in the Barony of Percy by her son, HUGH, Earl Percy, K.G., who succeeded his father as 2nd DUKE of NORTHUMBERLAND, 6 June 1786, and *d.* 1 July 1817, when he was succeeded by his eldest son, HUGH, present and 3rd DUKE, K.G. His younger son, Lord Algernon Percy, was created Baron Prudhoe in 1816.

NORTHWICK, BARON. (RUSHOUT.)

Peer of Great Britain.

The family of Rushout, of which Thibault Rouault settled in France about 1[illegible] was originally English. From him descended Joachim Rushout, Lord of Gam[illegible], Marshal of France, whose eldest son, Adolph, was ancestor of a noble fam[illegible] in France; and his youngest son, John, was great-grandfather of John Rushout, who came into England in the reign of Charles I., was a merchant in London, and settled at Maylards, in Essex; he *d.* in 1653, leaving a son James, who was created a Baronet in 1661. He *d.* in 1698, leaving two sons:

1 Sir James, his successor, whose only son, Sir James, 3rd Baronet, *d.* in 1711 at nine years of age.

2 Sir John, who succeeded his nephew; he was leader of the opposition to the Walpole Administration, and was afterwards Treasurer of the Navy. He *d.* in 17[illegible] and was succeeded by his only son,

SIR JOHN RUSHOUT, who was created in 1797 Baron Northwick of Northwick Park, Co. Worcester, and *d.* in 1800, when he was succeeded by his eldest son JOHN, present and 2nd LORD.

NORWOOD, BARON. (TOLER.)

Peer of Ireland.

GRACE, the 1st BARONESS, daughter of Hector Graham, Esq., a descendant from the family of Montrose, by his marriage with Grace, daughter of Robert Maxwell Esq., brother of John, 1st Lord Farnham, *m.* John Toler, Esq., and when he was a Privy Councillor, and Solicitor-General of Ireland, was created BARONESS NORWOOD of Knockalton, Co. Tipperary, in 1797; he was appointed Attorney-General of Ireland in 1798, and Lord Chief Justice of the Common Pleas in 1800; and created BARON NORBURY, of Ballyorenode, Co. Tipperary, also in 1800. He was further created Viscount Glandine and Earl of Norbury in 1827, with remainder to his 2nd son, Hector-Graham Toler, who succeeded him in the Earldom in 1831; when the Barony of Norbury devolved on his eldest son DANIEL, the present and 2nd LORD, who had also succeeded his mother as BARON NORWOOD in 1822.

NUGENT, BARON. (NUGENT-GRENVILLE.)

Peer of Ireland.

His Lordship is the younger brother of Richard Duke of Buckingham and Chandos, and grandson of Robert, 1st Earl Nugent, in Ireland, who was created in 1766 Baron Nugent and Viscount Clare, and in 1776 Earl Nugent, with remainder to his son-in-law, George Grenville, Esq., afterwards Marquis of Buckingham. The Earl was *b.* in 1702; he *m.* 1st, 14 July 1730, Lady Emily Plunkett, 2nd daughter of Peter, 4th Earl of Fingal, she *d.* 16 Aug. 1731; he *m.* 2ndly, Anne,

laughter of James Craggs, Esq., and widow, 1st, of —— Newnham, Esq., and ndly, of John Knight, Esq., she *d.* in 1755; and he *m.* 3rdly, 2 Jan. 1757, Elizaeth, daughter of Henry Drax, Esq., Countess Dowager Berkeley, who *d.* 30 June 792. The Earl *d.* 13 Oct. 1788, leaving by his 3rd marriage two daughters: e left the whole of his property to his eldest daughter, the LADY MARY-ELIZABETH, Marchioness of Buckingham, and was succeeded in the Earldom by her husband, George Marquis of Buckingham, who assumed the additional name of NUGENT; the Marchioness was created in 1800 BARONESS NUGENT of Carlan's Town, Co. Westneath, with remainder to Lord George Nugent-Grenville, her 2nd son, and dying n 1812, was succeeded by LORD GEORGE, the present and 2nd Peer.

OAKLEY, BARON. (CADOGAN.)

Peer of the United Kingdom.

The Hon. GEORGE CADOGAN, the present Peer, is the second surviving son of Charles-Sloane, late Earl Cadogan, and brother and presumptive heir of the present Earl Cadogan; he was created in 1731, BARON OAKLEY of Caversham, Co. Oxford.

O'NEILL, EARL. (O'NEILL.)

Peer of Ireland.

The family of O'Neill descends from the ancient princes of Tyrone: its representative in the time of Henry VIII. was created Earl of Tyrone, on resigning the sovereignty. The branch to which the Earl O'Neill belongs has been seated for many generations at Shanes Castle, Co. Antrim. The Right Hon. JOHN O'NEILL, eldest son of Charles O'Neill, Esq., of Shanes Castle, by Catherine, 3rd daughter and co-heir of the Hon. Sir John Brodrick, eldest son of Alan, 1st Viscount Midleton, Lord Chancellor of Ireland, was created in 1793 Baron O'Neill, of Shanes Castle, Co. Antrim; and in 1795, VISCOUNT O'NEILL; he *d.* in 1798, and was succeeded by his eldest son, CHARLES-HENRY-ST.-JOHN, who was created in 1800 EARL O'NEILL, of Shanes Castle, Co. Antrim, and Viscount Raymond; and is the present Peer.

ONGLEY, BARON. (HENLEY-ONGLEY.)

Peer of Ireland.

ROBERT HENLEY, Esq., of the family of Henley, Co. Derby, assumed the name of ONGLEY, on succeeding to the estates of his great-uncle, Sir Samuel Ongley; and was created BARON ONGLEY of Old Warden in 1776. He *d.* in 1785, and was succeeded by his eldest son, ROBERT, 2nd LORD, who *d.* in 1814, when his eldest surviving son, ROBERT, present and 3rd LORD, succeeded.

ONSLOW, EARL OF. (ONSLOW.)

Peer of the United Kingdom.

Of this family, which took its surname from the Lordship of Onslow, Co. Salop, was Roger de Onslow, in the reign of Henry III.

Richard Onslow, Esq., Recorder of London and Solicitor-General, 8th in descent from him, was Speaker of the House of Commons in the reign of Queen Elizabeth; his grandson, Sir Richard Onslow, espoused the Republican party in the House of Commons, on the breaking out of the Parliamentary disputes with King Charles, and raised the regiment with which the Marquis of Winchester's house at Basing was besieged; but tired of all the evils which this ill-omened war brought in its train, he was one of those forty members whom the army took into custody for having carried, in Dec. 1648, a resolution in the House, "that the King's answer to the propositions of Parliament was sufficient ground for them to proceed upon the settlement of the kingdom's peace." He had no concern with the trial or condemnation of the King, but was one of the Select Committee who attended Cromwell in 1657, with the petition of that House, that he would assume the title and attributes of royalty, and delivered an oration to enforce it. At length, affected, together with nearly the whole nation, by an ardent desire to promote the restoration of King Charles II., he was in 1660, a member of the Convention Parliament which voted his recall. He *d.* in 1664, leaving six sons. Henry, his 2nd son, was ancestor in the 4th degree of General Denzil Onslow.

His eldest son, Arthur, was an active partisan and Member of Parliament, co-operating with his father throughout the troubles. He *m.* Mary, 2nd daughter and co-heir of Sir Thomas Foot, Lord Mayor of London in 1649, who was created a Baronet in 1660, with remainder to his said son-in-law, Arthur Onslow, Esq.; he *d.* in 1687, and was accordingly succeeded by Sir Arthur Onslow, 2nd Baronet. He *d.* in 1688, leaving two sons, viz.:

1 Sir Richard Onslow, Bart., his successor, chosen Speaker of the House of Commons in 1708; in 1714 he was appointed Chancellor of the Exchequer; and in 1716 was created Baron Onslow of Onslow, Co. Salop, and of West Clandon, Co. Surrey, with remainder, failing his issue male, to his uncle, Denzil Onslow, Esq. and his issue male, (which Denzil Onslow *d.* without issue;) failing which, to the issue male of his father; Sir Arthur Onslow, Bart.; he *d.* in 1717, and was succeeded by his only surviving son, Thomas, 2nd Lord; who was succeeded in 1740 by his only son, Richard, 3rd Lord, who *d.* without issue in 1776, when the male line of his grandfather, the 1st Lord, became extinct.

2 Foot Onslow, Esq. *d.* in 1710, leaving two sons:

1 The Right Hon. Arthur Onslow, thirty-three years Speaker of the House of Commons; he *d.* in 1768, leaving one son, George, who was created in May 1776, Baron Cranley of Imber Court, Co. Surrey; in October following he succeeded his cousin as 4th Lord Onslow, and in 1801 was created Viscount Cranley of Cranley, Co. Surrey, and Earl of Onslow, Co. Salop.

2 Lieut.-General Richard Onslow, who *d.* in 1760, leaving three sons, viz. 1 George, who *d.* in 1792; leaving a daughter Pooley, *m.* 1st to Rear-Admiral Sir Francis-Samuel Drake, Bart., and 2ndly, to Arthur Onslow, Esq.; she *d.* in 1822; also the Rev. George-Walton Onslow, and the Rev. Arthur Onslow, for both of whom see *The Peerage Volume.* 2 Admiral Sir Richard Onslow, G.C.B., who *d.* in 1817; for his widow and issue see *The Peerage Volume.* 3 The Very Rev. Arthur Onslow, Dean of Worcester, who also *d.* in 1817; and whose issue are described in *The Peerage Volume.*

George, 4th Lord Onslow, 1st Lord Cranley, and 1st Earl of Onslow, *d.* in 1814, and was succeeded by his eldest son, Thomas, 2nd Earl, who was succeeded in 1827 by his eldest son, Arthur-George, present and 3rd Earl.

ORFORD, EARL OF. (Walpole.)

Peer of the United Kingdom.

This family, which was in England before the Conquest, traces its descent from Reginald de Walpole, living about the time of the Conquest. The 18th from him was

Robert Walpole, Esq., of Houghton, Co. Norfolk, who *d.* in 1700, leaving, besides other issue, two sons viz.:

1 Sir Robert Walpole, K.G., twenty-one years Prime Minister to King George I. and King George II. On his retirement in 1742 he was created Viscount and Baron Walpole of Houghton, Co. Norfolk, and Earl of Orford, Co. Suffolk. He *d.* in 1745, leaving issue,

1 Robert, who was created in 1723 Baron Walpole of Walpole, Co. Norfolk, with remainder to his brothers and their issue male, in default of which to his father, Sir Robert Walpole, K.G., and his issue male, failing which, to the issue male of Robert Walpole, Esq., his grandfather. He succeeded his father as 2nd Earl of Orford in 1745. He *m.* Margaret, 14th Baroness Clinton, daughter and sole heir of Samuel Rolle, Esq., and *d.* in 1751, leaving by her, who *d.* in 1781, an only son, George, 3rd Earl, heir to all their titles; he passed many years in a state of mental alienation, and *d.* in 1791, when the Barony of Clinton devolved on the heir general, Robert-George-William Trefusis, Esq.; and his paternal honours on his uncle.

2 Sir Edward Walpole, K.B.; he *d. unm.* in 1784. He had three natural daughters, all now deceased, viz.: Maria, wife of James, 2nd Earl Waldegrave, and afterwards of the late Duke of Gloucester; Charlotte, wife of Lionel, 5th Earl of Dysart; and Laura, wife of the Hon. Frederick Keppel, Bishop of Exeter.

3 Horatio, 4th Earl of Orford, and 3rd Lord Walpole of Walpole; better known as the celebrated wit and author, Horace Walpole. He *d. unm.* in 1797, when all his titles became extinct, except the Barony of Walpole of Walpole.

2 Horatio, created in 1756, Baron Walpole of Wolterton, Co. Norfolk; he was Ambassador to the several Continental states during the whole period of his brother's ministry. He *d.* in 1757, leaving four sons, viz.:

1 Horatio, his successor, 2nd Lord, who succeeded as 4th Lord Walpole of Walpole, on the death of the 4th Earl of Orford in 1797; and was created in 1806 Earl of Orford; he *d.* in 1809, and was succeeded by his eldest son, Horatio, 2nd Earl, who was succeeded in 1822 by his eldest son, Horatio, present and 3rd Earl.

2 Hon. Thomas *b.* 25 Oct. 1727, and *d.* 21 March 1803; having *m.* 14 Nov. 1753, Elizabeth, eldest daughter of Sir Joshua Vanneck, Bart., and sister of Joshua, 1st Lord Huntingfield, by whom, who *d.* 9 June 1760, he had the issue stated in *The Peerage Volume.*

3 Hon. Richard, *d.* 18 Aug. 1798; having *m.* 22 Nov. 1758, Margaret, 4th daughter of Sir Joshua Vanneck, Bart., and sister of Joshua, 1st Lord Huntingfield, who *d.* 9 May 1818; for their surviving issue, see *The Peerage Volume.*

4 Hon. Robert, *b.* 1736, *d.* 19 April 1810; having *m.* 1st, 8 May 1780, Diana, daughter of John Grossett, Esq., by whom, who *d.* 24 July 1784, he had one son, the Rev. Robert Walpole—see *The Peerage Volume.* He *m.* 2ndly,

10 May 1785, Sophia, daughter of Richard Stert, Esq., by whom, who was *b.* 31 Oct. 1769, and *d.* 12 June 1829, he had the other issue stated in *The Peerage Volume.*

ORKNEY, COUNTESS OF. (Fitz-Maurice.)

Peeress of Scotland.

Lord George Hamilton, 5th son of William and Anne, 3rd Duke and Duchess of Hamilton, was created in 1796 Earl of Orkney, Viscount of Kirkwall, and Baron of Dechmont, with remainder to the heirs male of his body, failing which, to the heirs of his body whatsoever. He *d.* in 1737; having had three daughters, viz.:

1 Lady Anne, his successor, 2nd Countess.

2 Lady Frances, *m.* to Thomas, 3rd Earl of Scarborough, by whom she had issue. All her surviving descendants who appear in *The Peerage Volume*, under the title Scarborough, are in remainder to this Earldom, as are also the issue of her daughter Lady Frances, by Peter, 1st Earl Ludlow, who may be found in *The Peerage Volume*, under that title.

3 Lady Harriot, *m.* to John, 5th Earl of Corke and Orrery; the only descendants from her eldest son, Charles, Viscount Dungarvon, are the present Earl O'Neill and his brother, who therefore are in succession to this Earldom after the family of the Earl Ludlow; and from her only daughter, the Lady Elizabeth, wife of Sir Thomas Worsley, Bart., descended the late wife of the present Lord Yarborough, whose children—see *The Peerage Volume*—are therefore also in succession to this Peerage.

Lady Anne, the eldest daughter, succeeded her father as Countess of Orkney; she *m.* William O'Bryen, 4th Earl of Inchiquin, and *d.* in 1756, having had eight children, of whom she survived four sons and two daughters; Lady Anne, her 2nd daughter, *d. unm.* in 1808, and

Lady Mary O'Bryen, her eldest daughter, succeeded her as 3rd Countess; she *d.* in 1791, having *m.* her cousin-german, Murrough, 5th Earl of Inchiquin, created Marquis of Thomond, by whom she left an only surviving daughter,

Lady Mary O'Bryen, her successor, the present and 4th Countess, widow of the Hon. Thomas Fitz-Maurice, by whom she has had one son, John O'Bryen, late Viscount Kirkwall, who *d.* in 1820, leaving issue Thomas-John-Hamilton, the present Viscount Kirkwall, the Countess's heir apparent; and a 2nd son, the Hon. William-Edward Eitz-Maurice.

ORMONDE, MARQUIS OF. (Butler.)

Peer of Ireland and of Great Britain.

This noble family descends from Theobald, (son of Herveius Fitzwalter,) created by King Henry II., Chief Butler of Ireland, from which office his son Theobald assumed the surname of Butler.

Theobald Butler, great-grandson of the 1st Chief Butler, was father of, 1 Theobald, 5th Chief Butler, a Lord of Parliament, who *d.* without issue in 1290; 2 Edmund, Earl of Carrick; 3 Thomas, ancestor of Lord Dunboyne.

Edmund, his 2nd son, was created Earl of Carrick in 1315, for his services against Edward Bruce on his invasion of Ireland, the Earl being then Lord Justice of Ireland; he *d.* in 1321, leaving two sons, who had male descendants, viz.: 1 James, created Earl of Ormonde; 2 John, from whom the present Earl of Carrick descends.

JAMES, 2nd Earl of Carrick, eldest son of the 1st Earl, was created EARL of ORMONDE in 1328, and was succeeded by his son JAMES, 2nd EARL, who was Lord Justice of Ireland, and Lord Deputy to Lionel, Duke of Clarence, Lord Lieutenant of Ireland; he *d.* in 1382, and was succeeded by his eldest son,

JAMES, 3rd EARL, styled by some of the Irish annalists a mighty strong man, and head of the chivalry of Ireland, which kingdom he governed to the content of the King, and his good subjects. He *d.* in 1405, leaving two sons:

1 JAMES, 4th EARL, who was Lord Deputy of Ireland in the reign of HENRY IV., in which capacity he was godfather of George, Duke of Clarence, born in Dublin, the son of Richard Plantagenet, Duke of York; throughout the reign of HENRY V. he was Lord Lieutenant of Ireland, and maintained a successful war against the native Irish Princes. He was a proficient in history and antiquities, and persuaded the King to appoint a King of Arms for Ireland, at first called Ireland and afterwards Ulster; he also gave lands for ever to endow the College of Arms. On the death of HENRY V. he was superseded, but again appointed Lord Lieutenant in 1440; but removed on account of the jealousy of the Earl of Shrewsbury and other English Lords in 1446. He *d.* in 1452, leaving three sons successive Earls of Ormonde, viz.:

1 JAMES, 5th EARL, K.G., who had been created Earl of Wiltshire in 1449; he was knighted at six years of age, with some other young noblemen, by King HENRY VI., then aged five years, when that young Prince had just received his knighthood from his uncle, the Duke of Bedford. He was appointed Lord Lieutenant of Ireland in 1453, and, together with the Earl of Salisbury and others, undertook to guard the seas for three years, on receiving tonnage and poundage; under this commission, he fitted out five great ships at Genoa, in which he sailed to the Netherlands, to fight in behalf of King HENRY the fleet which the Earl of Warwick kept at sea for the benefit of the House of York. He commanded at the battle of Wakefield that wing of the army which surrounded and slew the Duke of York, in Dec. 1460, but was himself taken prisoner at the battle of Towton, in March 1461; was beheaded at Newcastle 1 May following, and was, with his brothers, attainted by Act of Parliament under King EDWARD IV. in November. He *d.* without issue, and was succeeded by his next brother,

2 JOHN, 6th EARL, restored in blood; he was perfect master of all the languages of Europe, and was employed in nearly all the continental courts, as his Ambassador, by King EDWARD IV.; who, himself an accomplished judge of such qualifications, pronounced him the goodliest knight and finest gentleman he ever beheld. He *d. unm.* in the Holy Land on a pilgrimage in 1478, and was succeeded by his only surviving brother,

3 THOMAS, 7th EARL; he was restored in blood, and the act of attainder against him and his brothers utterly abrogated in 1485, by the first Parliament of King HENRY VII. He was summoned to the English Parliament in 1495, as Baron Ormond of Rochford, and *d.* without issue male in 1515, when the Earldom devolved on the heir male, and the English Barony fell into abeyance between his two daughters and co-heirs, Anne, wife of Sir John St.-Leger, ancestor by her of the St.-Legers of Eggesford, Co. Devon; and Margaret, wife of Sir William Boleyn; the latter was mother of Sir Thomas Boleyn, created in 1527 Viscount Rochford, and in 1529 Earl of Wiltshire, with remainder to his heirs male, also Earl of Ormond in Ireland, with remainder to his heirs general. He *d.* in 1538, having survived his only son, George Boleyn, Viscount Rochford, who was attainted and beheaded, without issue male, in 1533. The Earl had two daughters, co-heirs of the Earldom of Ormonde; Anne, the wife of King HENRY VIII., and mother of Queen Elizabeth, on whose death in 1603 the abeyance terminated; and Lady Mary, wife of William Cary, Esq., mother of Henry Lord Hunsdon, and grandmother of George, 2nd Lord

Hunsden, whose daughter and sole heir, Elizabeth, *m.* Sir Thomas Berke-ley, and by him was mother of George, 18th Lord Berkeley, the direct ancestor of the present Earl Berkeley, who it should seem is the heir of the Earldom of Ormonde, created by the patent of 1529, to Thomas Boleyn, Earl of Wiltshire, and his heirs general.

2 Sir Richard Butler, whose son, Sir Edmund, *d.* in 1464, leaving three sons:

1 Sir James, who was attainted for siding, like the rest of his family, with the House of Lancaster; but the act of attainder was repealed under King EDWARD IV. His son, PIERCE, succeeded to the Earldom on the death of his kinsman, THOMAS, 7th EARL, in 1515; and became the 8th EARL.

2 Walter Butler, of Poolestown, the father of a numerous posterity, which flourished in the male line to the 7th generation. Sir Walter Butler, of Poolestown, his descendant in the 4th degree, was created a Baronet of Ireland, which title became extinct in 1723, by the death of his grandson Sir Walter, the 3rd Baronet.

3 John; he had two sons, 1 Pierce, whose son Richard Fitz-Pierce, *d.* childless; 2 John-Oge, whose son, William-Fitz-John-Oge, was attainted of felony, and executed in the reign of Queen Elizabeth.

3 James, ancestor of the Earl of Glengall.

PIERCE, 8th EARL, was created in 1527, EARL of OSSORY, in lieu of his Earldom of Ormond, to which King HENRY VIII. created Thomas Boleyn, Viscount Rochford, but the latter dying without issue male, the title of Earl of Ormond was restored to this Earl in Feb. 1539, by patent; he *d.* in Aug. the same year. He left two sons:

1 JAMES, 9th EARL, at whose suit an Act of Parliament, passed in 1541, confirming the Earldom of Ormond to him and his heirs male, against any ambiguities, arguments, or questions, that might arise to the contrary. He had been created Viscount Thurles, by patent, in 1537. He *d.* in 1546, being poisoned with thirty-five of his servants at a supper at Ely House, in Holborn; he left seven sons, of whom,

1 THOMAS, eldest son, and 10th EARL, succeeded; he was appointed Lord High Treasurer of Ireland in 1559, the first year of Queen ELIZABETH's reign, and continued in that high office to the end of his life, being employed in constant warfare against the Irish rebels. He *d.* in 1614, leaving no surviving issue male; his only daughter, Elizabeth *m.* 1st, her cousin, Theobald Butler, Viscount Tulleophelim, heir presumptive to the Earl, who *d.* without issue in 1613; and 2ndly, Sir Richard Preston, created Earl of Desmond, by whom she had an only daughter, Lady Elizabeth Preston, heir to her grandfather, the 10th EARL, who became wife of JAMES, Duke of Ormond, the 12th EARL.

2 Sir Edmund Butler left four sons, who all *d.* without legitimate issue male; though a claim was made to the Earldom after the death of the 10th EARL, by Pierce Butler, as son and heir of Pierce, Sir Edmund's eldest son. His claim, though a Commission was issued for its examination, appears to have failed. Theobald, the 4th and last surviving son, had the titles of Ormond and Ossory entailed on him, by patent in 1603, in default of issue male of THOMAS, 10th EARL; he was created in 1603 Viscount Tulleophelim, and *m.* the Lady Elizabeth, only daughter of EARL THOMAS; he *d.* in 1613, without issue.

3 John, who *d.* in 1570, leaving one son, WALTER, 11th EARL; he succeeded his uncle, EARL THOMAS, and *d.* in 1632, having survived his son Thomas, Viscount Thurles, who was drowned in his passage from England to Ireland, in 1619, leaving two sons, JAMES, 12th EARL, who succeeded his grandfather, and Sir Richard Butler of Kilcash, ancestor of the present Marquis.

2 Richard, Viscount Mountgarret, ancestor of the Earl of Kilkenny.

JAMES, 12th EARL, K.G., by marrying the Lady Elizabeth Preston, only dau.

and heir of the Earl of Desmond, and grand-daughter of the 10th Earl, termi-
.ed the unfortunate differences which had subsisted between his grandfather and
representative of his predecessors, and on account of which the great estates of
Earldom had been in sequestration. On the breaking out of the Irish rebellion 1641, the Earl was appointed Lieutenant-General of the King's forces in Ireland, d displayed the most indefatigible activity and undaunted resolution in dealing th the rebels; in April 1642 he gained a very signal victory over the Irish army mmanded by the Lord Mountgarret, at Kilrush, and was in consequence created arquis of Ormonde. He continued to pursue his successes, making the utmost nefit of them, and in March the following year, engaging General Preston at eat disadvantage, obtained, nevertheless, a complete victory, and had so entire an cendancy over the rebels, that on receiving information that the situation of the ing demanded his assistance, and the peace of Ireland, he speedily concluded an lvantageous treaty, which not only gave liberty to his own forces, but a subsidy to e King, and the co-operation of the Irish. He was then appointed Lord Lieutenant Ireland, and continued to hold that high office till the desperate state of the ing's affairs in England rendered it advisable to treat with the Parliamentary Com-issioners, to whom, by the King's direction, he surrendered, in 1647, the gar-isons of Ireland, and immediately left the kingdom, to join the Queen and Prince f Wales in Paris. In Sept. 1748 he returned to Ireland to make another effort for ie restoration of the Royal authority, and on receiving, with inexpressible grief, he intelligence of the murder of his Royal Master, he caused King Charles II. to e solemnly proclaimed, and received from him the continuation of his Commission s Lord Lieutenant. He used his utmost efforts to recover the kingdom to the Royal authority, but finding them ineffectual, he again left the kingdom and repaired o Paris. On the King's arrival there after the defeat of Worcester, he was sworn of the Privy Council, and continued from that time in attendance upon his person or in commissions for his service till the Restoration. He was created in 1660 Baron Butler of Lanthony, Co. Monmouth, and Earl of Brecknock in the Peerage of England, and in 1661 Duke of Ormonde in Ireland. He was re-appointed Lord Lieutenant of Ireland in 1661, and resigned that office in 1668; in 1677, he was a third time appointed to it, and with difficulty obtained permission to retire in 1682; when he was advanced to the dignity of Duke of Ormonde in the Peerage of England. The latter years of his life were clouded by the uneasiness with which he witnessed the course pursuing by King James II. towards his ruin, and his apprehensions of what might ensue are thought to have hastened his end; he *d.* in 1688, leaving a reputation for loyalty, ability in success, and constancy in adversity, equal if not superior to any which that era of agitation produced. He lost in the service of the crown, after deduct-ing all emoluments received, nearly £900,000, a sum incomparably greater at that time than, immense as it is, it can be considered at present. He had eight sons, of whom only three lived to maturity, viz.: 1 Thomas, Earl of Ossory; 2 Richard, who having purchased the Isles of Arran, was created in 1662 Baron Butler of Cloughgrenan, Vis-count of Tullogh, and Earl of Arran, in Ireland; and in 1673, in reward of the bravery he had displayed in the sea fights of that year against the Dutch, he was created a Peer of England, by the title of Baron Butler of Weston; he *d.* without issue male, in 1685, when all his titles became extinct; he left an only daughter and heir, the wife of Charles Lord Cornwallis, and mother of the first Earl Cornwallis, who was grandfather of the late Marquis and of the present Earl Cornwallis. 3 John, cre-ated in 1676, Baron of Agherim, Viscount of Clonmore, and Earl of Gowran, in the Peerage of Ireland, which titles became extinct by his death without issue, in 1677.

Thomas, Earl of Ossory, K.G., eldest son of the 1st Duke of Ormonde, was called to the House of Lords in Ireland, as Earl of Ossory in 1662, and took his seat above all Peers of that degree; he was Lieutenant-General of the army of Ireland; and a Rear Admiral, in which latter rank he gallantly commanded under Prince Rupert, in the three well-contested but indecisive sea-fights between the English and Dutch fleets in 1673, and in September hoisted his flag as Commander-in-Chief of the fleet in the absence of Prince Rupert. Peace being soon after concluded [illegible] [illegible] joined the Prince of Orange and gained great glory in [illegible] in the Netherlands. In 1679 he was summoned by writ to the [illegible] of Lords in England as Baron Butler of More Park, and there made a splen[illegible] [illegible] of his father's administration in Ireland, against the jealous accusations [illegible] Earl of [illegible]. He d. in 1680, to the regret of the whole nation and great grief [illegible] his noble father who, however, supported his loss with resignation and dignity. [illegible] [illegible] two sons, viz.

1 James, 2nd Duke of Ormonde, who succeeded his grandfather. He was [illegible] opposed to the despotic measures of King James II., and was one of the [illegible] who went over to William III. He attended that King into Ireland, [illegible] at the battle of the Boyne, and was afterwards detached to take possession [illegible] and protect that city from plunder. He afterwards accompanied the [illegible] and was taken prisoner at the battle of Landen, after receiving [illegible] wounds. He was appointed Lord Lieutenant of Ireland in 1702, and lived there [illegible] than had been ever before known; in 1711 he was appointed Captain General and Commander-in-Chief of all the land forces to be employed abroad and retained that distinguished, and to him most unfortunate, post, [illegible] [illegible] of the treaty of Utrecht; being withheld during the whole of this [illegible] from exerting his courage and abilities, by the express order of the Queen [illegible] [illegible] that he should neither fight a battle nor undertake a siege; obeying these orders, he remained in a state of inactivity, notwithstanding the remonstrances [illegible] Prince Eugene and the Allies; and when the accession of King George I. rest[illegible] to power the party opposed to the late peace, he was impeached for high treason [illegible] the Commons, for his conduct in the command of the army, at the same time [illegible] Lords Bolingbroke, Strafford, and Oxford were impeached for the prosecution [illegible] treaty. Party-spirit was now at its height; riotous assemblages, when the Duke's name was made a watchword of tumult, were common in London, and Ormonde [illegible] high-church was a popular cry; while the Duke himself was living in a style [illegible] magnificence, which contributed to inflame the revenge of his enemies. [illegible] the conclusion of the proceedings in the Commons, however, he saw that he had [illegible] chance of an impartial trial, and consulted his own safety by withdrawing from the kingdom. An Act then passed the two Houses, in August 1715, requiring him [illegible] Lord Bolingbroke to surrender by the 10th of September, or in default thereof [illegible] attaint them of high treason: the Duke neglected to do so, and the attainder [illegible] effect: and thus was the ruin of an illustrious family accomplished by party-spirit in the person of a brave, generous, and humane nobleman, to whom no crime was imputed but that of having obeyed the commands of his Sovereign. The Duke in great indignation immediately enterd the service of the Pretender, and thus clos[illegible] the door against any future restoration in his own person; an Act of Parliament however, past in 1721 to enable his brother, the Earl of Arran, to purchase his estate which he accordingly did. The Duke continued to reside abroad till his death without surviving issue, in 1745.

2 Charles, created in 1693 Baron of Cloughgrenan, Viscount of Tullogh, and Earl of Arran in the Peerage of Ireland, and Baron Butler of Weston, Co. Huntingdon, in the Peerage of England. He was a Lieutenant-General in the army, and held under Queen Anne several military offices, all which he resigned on her death. He would have succeeded to the Dukedom on the death of his brother, and should have been the 14th Earl. He *d.* without issue in 1758, when his titles became extinct. His estates he entailed on the male heir to the Earldom; who, the male issue of the 1st Duke being extinct, must be sought for in the descendants of his brother.

Sir Richard Butler of Kilcash. On the breaking out of the rebellion of 1641, Sir Richard joined with the Irish, was a reputed Lieut.-General among the rebels and Governor of the County of Waterford, and acted in that capacity with great vigour; he *d.* in 1701. His eldest son, Walter Butler, Esq., of Garryricken, *d.* the year before him, leaving three sons:

1 Thomas, who succeeded his grandfather at Kilcash; he was Colonel of a giment of horse in the service of King James II., and *d.* in 1738. John utler, Esq., of Kilcash, his only surviving son, succeeded to the estates of the arl of Arran in 1758, and should have been the 15th Earl; he *d.* without issue 1766.

2 John Butler, Esq., of Garryricken, whose only son Walter succeeded to the state, and should have been 16th Earl; his only son

John became Earl of Ormonde by the reversal of the attainder in 1791, and iould have been the 17th Earl; he *d.* in 1795, leaving the issue described in *'he Peerage Volume*; he was succeeded by his eldest son, Walter, 18th Earl, who as created Baron Butler of Lanthony, Co. Monmouth, in the Peerage of the 'nited Kingdom, in 1801, and Marquis of Ormonde, in Ireland, in 1816; he *d.* ithout issue in 1820, when both these titles became extinct, and he was succeeded n the Earldom by his next brother, James-Wandsford, present and 19th Earl, who lso was created a Peer of the United Kingdom in 1821, by the title of Baron)rmonde of Lanthony, Co. Monmouth; and Marquis of Ormonde, in Ireland, n 1825.

OXFORD, EARL OF. (Harley.)

Peer of Great Britain.

This family, of British or Saxon origin, possessed the Castle and Lordship of Harley, in Shropshire, before the Conquest. Sir John de Harley was seated there in the reign of William the Conqueror. 12th in descent from him was Sir Robert Harley, K.B., who sided with the Parliament in the civil war of the time of Charles I. His Lady, Brilliana, 2nd daughter of Edward Viscount Conway, heroically held out his Castle of Brampton for seven weeks against the Royal forces, in Aug. and Sept. 1643, when the greater part of the town of Brampton was burnt; the siege was raised, but she *d.* in the October following, and the Castle was soon after besieged again; it then surrendered after a gallant resistance by the servants only of Sir Robert, and was burnt to the ground, as was also his Castle of Wigmore, the loss in both amounting to not less than £50,000. The estate of Sir Henry Lingen, a Royalist, was afterwards laid under sequestration, and the profits granted to Sir Robert Harley, to make good his losses, but magnanimously restored by him to the widow of Sir Henry. In Dec. 1648 he was one, and his son, Col. Edward Harley, was another, of the forty-one Members of the House of Commons who were arrested and imprisoned by the army for having voted that the answer of the King to the propositions of Parliament was ground to proceed upon to the settlement of the kingdom's peace; he *d.* in 1656.

His son and heir, Sir Edward Harley, was a Colonel in the service of the Parliament, and was distinguished for his valour and abilities; in 1647 he was one of the eleven Members of the House of Commons impeached by the army for high treason, on account of their firmness in promoting a peace; he was then excluded the House, but being afterwards re-admitted, was made prisoner, with his father and the thirty-nine other Members, for the same cause. He was so active and instrumental in furthering the Restoration, that on his meeting Charles II. at Dover on the King's first landing there, he was appointed Governor of Dunkirk, and set out immediately to take possession of his government; but was displaced in 1661, before the town was put into the hands of the French; because the King apprehended from him a refusal to comply with the order for its surrender. He was elected a Knight of the Bath without his knowledge, while at Dunkirk, having previously refused a Peerage, lest his co-operation in the Restoration should be attributed to motives of personal ambition. At the Revolution he raised a troop of horse at his own expense, marched with them to Worcester, of which city he was immediately made Governor by the gentlemen of the county, and sent his two eldest sons to offer his services to the Prince of Orange, He *d.* in 1700, leaving, besides other issue, the two eldest sons above mentioned, viz.

1 Robert, who was educated at the private school of the Rev. Mr. Birch at Shilton in Oxfordshire; who, besides this young Harley, afterwards Lord High Treasurer, had under his care, at the same time, the future Lord High Chancellor Harcourt, Lord Trevor, Chief Justice of the Common Pleas, and ten Members of the House of Commons. After making his debut in politics by the offer of his own and his father's services; not obtaining so much consideration from the parties in power as he thought he deserved, and perhaps not altogether satisfied with the whig and presbyterian principles in which he had been educated, he became a staunch opponent of the Court measures; he was chosen Speaker of the House in the two last Parliaments of King William and the first of Queen Anne. In 1704 he was appointed Secretary of State, and resigned that office in 1708, having, while he held it, been instrumental in concluding the treaty of Union with Scotland. In 1710 on the overthrow of the Whig Administration, he was appointed Chancellor of the Exchequer, and was in the following year stabbed at the Council Board by the Marquis de Guiscard, a French Papist, then under examination upon a charge of treason, who received wounds and bruises in the scuffle that ensued, of which he died; and Mr. Harley, on his re-appearance after his recovery from his wounds, was congratulated by the House of Commons on his escape. In May 1711 he was created Baron Harley of Wigmore, Co. Hereford, Earl of Oxford, and Earl Mortimer, with remainder, failing his issue male, to the issue male of his grandfather, Sir Robert Harley, K.B.; and in the same month he was appointed Lord High Treasurer of Great Britain, in which office he continued till a few days before the death of Queen Anne in 1714; having been in 1712 elected a Knight of the Garter. In June 1715 he was impeached by the House of Commons for the part he had taken in forwarding the Treaty of Utrecht, then denounced as treasonable; he suffered a long and severe confinement in the Tower, but on trial by his Peers in July 1717, was unanimously acquitted. His Lordship took no farther part in public affairs; he possessed considerable learning himself, and was a great favourer and protector of learned men; he was an uncorrupt Minister, having made no addition during the period of his power to his patrimonial fortune; and suffered persecution with the intrepid consciousness of integrity, He *d.* in 1724, leaving an only son and heir, Edward, 2nd Earl; he made invaluable additions to the noble collection of manuscripts left by his father, and the whole were sold to the public by his widow, the Lady Henrietta Cavendish Holles, only daughter and heir of John Holles, Duke of Newcastle. He *d.* in 1741, leaving by her an only daughter and heir, the Lady Margaret Cavendish Harley, wife of William, 2nd Duke of Portland.

2 Edward Harley, of Eywood, Co. Hereford, Esq.; he *d.* in 1735, leaving a son,

Edward, who according to the limitation of the Patent, succeeded his cousin as 3rd Earl; he *d.* in 1755; leaving, besides other issue, the three sons following

1 Edward, 4th Earl, *b.* 2 Sept. 1720, succeeded 11 April 1755, *d.* 8 Oct. 1790, having *m.* July 1751, Susanna, daughter of William Archer, Esq., by whom, who *d.* 10 Nov. 1804, he had no issue.

2 John, Lord Bishop of Hereford, for whom see *The Peerage Volume*, father of Edward, the present and 5th Earl; who succeeded his uncle.

3 Thomas, Alderman of London; for whom see *The Peerage Volume*: he had issue, besides the two surviving daughters there mentioned, Martha, his eldest daughter, who *d.* in 1788; having *m.* George Drummond, Esq., of Strathallan, by whom she was mother of the present George-Harley Drummond, Esq., of Stanmore and Drumtochty, see *The Peerage Volume*, title Strathallan; Elizabeth, his daughter, who *d.* in 1824, having *m.* David Murray, Esq., of Elibank, by whom

ıe was mother of the present Rev. David-Rodney Murray; see *The Peerage olume*, title Elibank; and Margaret, his 5th daughter, who *d.* in 1830, having *m.* ıe late Sir John Boyd, Bart.

PALMERSTON, VISCOUNT. (Temple.)

Peer of Ireland.

Leofric, Earl of Mercia, who *d.* in 1057, (a descendant, as is supposed, of Leofric, Earl of Leicester in 716, under the Kings of Mercia,) husband of the famous Countess Godiva, had by her three sons, Algar Earl of Mercia, Montgomery, and Henry, named Del Temple, from his Manor of Temple, near Bosworth, in Leicestershire.

10th in descent from this Henry, was Peter Temple, Esq., of Stowe, who *d.* in 1577, father of two sons: 1 John, great-grandfather of Richard, created in 1718 Viscount Cobham; which title is now enjoyed by the Duke of Buckingham, as great-grandson and heir of Hester, his eldest sister; 2 Anthony, whose grandson, Sir William Temple, settled in Ireland, and was father of Sir John Temple, Master of the Rolls in Ireland, who *d.* in 1677 ;his son Sir John, Attorney General of Ireland, was father of

Henry Temple, created in 1722 Baron Temple of Mount-Temple, Co. Sligo, and Viscount Palmerston of Palmerston, Co. Dublin; and *d.* in 1757. Henry, his eldest son, *d.* before him in 1740, leaving an only son, Henry, 2nd Viscount, who succeeded his grandfather, and *d.* in 1802, when he was succeeded by his eldest son Henry-John, present and 3rd Viscount.

PANMURE, BARON. (Maule.)

Peer of the United Kingdom.

His Lordship is brother of the Earl of Dalhousie, and 2nd son of George, 8th Earl of Dalhousie, son of George Lord Ramsay, by Jane, daughter of the Hon. Henry Maule, brother of the 3rd and 4th Earls of Panmure.

The very ancient family of Maule is of French extraction, their name being assumed from the town and Lordship of Maule, eight leagues from Paris, which, together with the adjacent Barony of Panmure, had belonged to the Lords Maule for 400 years, when Roger, the last Lord, was killed in Hungary, fighting against the Turks in 1398. Guarin de Maule, a younger son of this family, accompanied William the Conqueror into England, and obtained from him the Lordship of Hatton, in Yorkshire, and other lands. His son Robert de Maule, came into Scotland with King David I. and obtained from that Monarch lands in Lothian; he *d.* about 1130. 16th in descent from him was

Patrick Maule, of Panmure, who accompanied King James I. into England. He was a Gentleman of the Bedchamber to King Charles, whom he attended throughout the civil war, fought in all the battles in which the King was engaged, and remained with him in his imprisonment till he was removed from him by order of the Parliament; having been created in 1646 Earl of Panmure, and Lord Maule of Brechin and Navar, in the Peerage of Scotland. He *d.* in 1661, and was succeeded by his eldest son George, 2nd Earl, who attached himself to King Charles II. while any hope of serving him remained, and made his peace with General Monk in 1652. He had three sons; viz.,

1 George, his successor, 3rd Earl, who *d.* without surviving issue in 1686.

2 James, 4th Earl, who succeeded his brother; having joined the standard of the Pretender in 1715, was taken at Sheriffmuir but rescued by his brother Harry. He

escaped abroad, was attainted of high treason, and his titles and estates were forfeited; offers of restoration were at different times made to him, but he never would take the oaths of allegiance to the House of Hanover, which he considered would be a revocation of those already due to his legitimate sovereign. He *d.* without issue in 1723.

3 The Hon. Harry Maule, who also engaged in the Rebellion of 1715; he *d.* in 1734, having had a numerous issue, who all *d. unm.* except one daughter Jean, the wife of George, Lord Ramsay. William Maule, his eldest son and successor in the Panmure estates, entered the army, and attained the rank of General. He was created in 1743 Earl of Panmure of Forth, and Viscount Maule of Whitechurch, in the Peerage of Ireland, with limitation of the honours to the heirs male of his body and those of his only surviving brother John. He *d.* in 1782, having made a settlement of his great estates on himself, his said brother John, and his nephew George, Earl of Dalhousie, in life-rent, and the 2nd, 3rd, and other sons of the Earl of Dalhousie, in fee. His brother having *d.* before him, he was succeeded by his nephew George, Earl of Dalhousie, on whose death in 1787 the large estates of the Earl of Panmure devolved, according to the settlement, on his 2nd son, the Hon. William Ramsay, who thereupon assumed the name and arms of Maule of Panmure, and was created in 1831 a Peer of the United Kingdom, by the title of Baron Panmure of Brechin and Navar, Co. Forfar.

PEMBROKE, EARL OF. (Herbert.)

Peer of England.

Some genealogists deduce this family from Herbert, a natural son of King Henry I., others from Henry Fitz-Herbert, Chamberlain to that King. He was father of Reginald, Peter, and Matthew, which last was ancestor of the family of the Earls of Winchilsea and Aylesford.

Sir William Herbert, 8th in descent from Reginald, the eldest son, was father of

1 Sir William Herbert, who for his valiant and effectual services to the House of York in the civil wars, received large grants of lands from King Edward IV. in Wales and elsewhere, estates forfeited by the Lancastrian party; he was summoned to Parliament in 1461, as Baron Herbert of Chepstow, and in 1468 was created Earl of Pembroke. In 1469 he marched northwards, at the head of 18,000 Welshmen, to suppress a powerful insurrection in the north in favour of the Lancastrians; he gave battle at Danes Moor, near Edgecote, in Northamptonshire, was utterly defeated, taken prisoner, and carried to Northampton, where he was beheaded by George, Duke of Clarence, and Richard Neville, Earl of Warwick, who had recently revolted from King Edward to join the Lancastrian standard. William, 2nd Earl, his son and successor, surrendered his title of Earl of Pembroke to King Edward IV., and was, in lieu of it, created Earl of Huntingdon; he *d.* without issue male, leaving a daughter and heir, Elizabeth, who carried the Barony of Herbert of Chepstow, into the family of Somerset, Duke of Beaufort.

2 Sir Richard, whose male line failed in 1801; he was ancestor to the Lords Herbert of Chirbury, and to the last Earl of Powis, of this family, whose sister and heir *m.* Edward, Lord Clive, the present Earl of Powis.

William, 1st Earl of Pembroke, eldest son of Sir William Herbert, left, besides William, 2nd Earl, a natural son, Sir Richard Herbert, whose son and heir,

Sir William Herbert, being of the household of King Henry VIII., obtained from that Monarch a grant of the house and site of the late monastery of Wilton, Wiltshire, and divers other lands in that and the other western counties. In 1551 he was created Baron Herbert of Cardiff, and Earl of Pembroke; he had two sons, 1 Henry, 2nd Earl; 2 Sir Edward, whose son and heir William, was ancestor

Earls and Marquises of Powis, which titles became extinct in 1748, on the death William, 3rd Marquis.

Henry, 2nd Earl, K.G., *d.* in 1601; he was father of William, 3rd Earl, .G. who *d.* without issue in 1630, and of Philip, created Baron Herbert of Shurld, and Earl of Montgomery, who succeeded his brother as 4th Earl of Pemoke, K.G.; he *d.* in 1650, and was succeeded by his eldest surviving son, ilip, 5th Earl, who *d.* in 1669, leaving three sons, successive Earls of Pemoke and Montgomery; viz., 1 William, 6th Earl, he *d.* without issue in 1674; Philip, 7th Earl, he *d.* without issue male in 1683; 3 Thomas, 8th Earl, .G., he *d.* in 1733, leaving, besides other issue, two sons, Henry, 9th Earl, and e Hon. William Herbert, father of Henry, 1st Earl of Carnarvon, and grandfather the present Earl of Carnarvon.

Henry, 9th Earl, eldest son of the 8th Earl, *d.* in 1751, and was succeeded by is only son Henry, 10th Earl; he *d.* in 1794, and was succeeded by his only son eorge-Augustus, 11th Earl; this much respected Nobleman *d.* in 1827, deeply mented by a numerous community, who, in the neighbourhood of his large estate Wilton, benefited by his constant residence among them as a most excellent landrd, and by the full employment which the improvements he was prosecuting around im furnished to the industrious poor. He was succeeded by his eldest son Robert-Henry, the present and 12th Earl of Pembroke, and 9th Earl of Montgomery.

PETRE, BARON. (Petre.)

Peer of England.

Sir William Petre, 5th in paternal descent from John Petre, whose widow Alice, *d.* in 1473, was Secretary of State to King Henry VIII., King Edward VI., Queen Mary, and Queen Elizabeth; he obtained considerable grants of church lands, and *d.* in 1572. His son John was created Baron Petre of Writtle, Co. Essex, in 1603, and *d.* in 1613; he was succeeded by his son William, 2nd Lord, to whom succeeded in 1637 his son Robert, 3rd Lord, who *d.* in 1638, and was father of William, who *d.* in 1683, without issue male; of John, who *d.* in 1684 without issue; and of Thomas, all successive Lords. Thomas, 6th Lord, the youngest son, *d.* in 1707, and was succeeded by his son Robert, 7th Lord; he *d.* in 1713, and was succeeded by his son Robert-James, 8th Lord, to whom, in 1742, succeeded his son Robert-Edward, 9th Lord, who *m.* Anne, 2nd daughter and co-heir of Philip Howard, Esq., brother of Thomas, 11th, and Edward, 12th Dukes of Norfolk, by whom he was father of Robert-Edward, 10th Lord, who succeeded him in 1801, and dying in 1809, was succeeded by his son William-Henry-Francis, present and 11th Lord.

His Lordship, as grandson and heir of Robert-Edward, 9th Lord, by Anne, 2nd daughter and co-heir of Philip Howard, Esq., brother of Thomas, 11th, and Edward, 12th Dukes of Norfolk, is co-heir (with Lord Stourton, as grandson and heir of William, 15th Lord Stourton, by Winifred, eldest daughter and co-heir of the said Philip Howard) of the Baronies, by writ, of Mowbray 1295, Furnival 1295, Strange of Blackmere 1308, Talbot 1331, and Howard 1470; also co-heir with Lord Stourton as above, of one moiety of the Baronies, by writ, of Segrave 1264, Greystock, Verdun, Boteler of Wemme, and Giffard of Brimmesfield, all 1295, Braose of Gower 1299, Lisle 1357, and Dacre of Gillesland 1482.

PLUNKET, BARON. (Plunket.)

Peer of the United Kingdom.

The Right Hon. William-Conyngham Plunket, successively Solicitor and Attorney-General for Ireland, the only surviving son of the late Rev. Mr. Plunket, of Dublin, was appointed in 1827 Lord Chief Justice of the Court of Common Pleas of Ireland, and created Baron Plunket of Newtown, Co. Cork, and is the present Peer.

PLYMOUTH, EARL OF. (Windsor.)

Peer of England.

William de Windsore, descended from William, son of Walter Fitz-Other, Castellan of Windsor, (ancestor of the Duke of Leinster and Marquis of Lansdowne) was summoned to Parliament in 1381, but *d.* without issue in 1384.

Andrews Windsor, descended from Sir Miles, brother of the said William, Baron Windsor, was summoned by writ in 1529, as Baron Windsor of Stanwell. Thomas, 6th Baron Windsor of Stanwell *d.* in 1642, leaving his two sisters, viz., Elizabeth (the elder,) wife of Dixie Hickman, Esq., and Elizabeth, (the younger,) *m.* 1st Andrew Windsor, Esq., and 2ndly to Sir James Ware, his heirs, between whom the Barony fell into abeyance, which was terminated by the Crown in 1660, in favour of Thomas Hickman, son and heir of the above-mentioned Dixie Hickman and Elizabeth his wife; he assumed the name of Windsor, and was created in 1682 Earl of Plymouth: he *d.* in 1687, having had, besides other issue, two sons; 1 Other, Lord Windsor, his heir apparent, who *d.* in his lifetime, leaving Other, 2nd Earl, who succeeded his grandfather; 2 Thomas, created Viscount Windsor in Ireland in 1699, and in 1711 Baron Montjoy of the Isle of Wight, in the Peerage of England; he *d.* in 1738, and was succeeded by his son Herbert, 2nd Viscount, at whose death in 1758, without issue male, his titles became extinct.

Other, 2nd Earl, who succeeded his grandfather, *d.* in 1727, and to him have succeeded, in direct paternal descent, Other, 3rd Earl, who *d.* in 1732; Other-Lewis, 4th Earl, who *d.* in 1771; Other-Hickman, 5th Earl, who *d.* in 17.., and Other-Archer, present and 6th Earl.

POLTIMORE, BARON. (Bamfylde.)

Peer of the United Kingdom.

The first of this family on record is Richard Baumfilde of Weston, Co. Somerset, in the reign of King John. 12th in descent from him was Sir John Bamfylde, of Haddington Park, Co. Somerset, created a Baronet in 1641; he was succeeded by his eldest son Sir Coplestone, who *d.* in 1691, and was succeeded by his grandson Sir Coplestone-Warwick; to whom, in 1727, succeeded his only son Sir Richard-Warwick, who *d.* in 1776, and was succeeded by his eldest son Sir Charles-Warwick Bamfylde, 5th Baronet, who, by Catherine, eldest daughter of Sir John Moore, Bart., was father of Sir George-Warwick Bamfylde, Bart., who succeeded him in 1823, was created in 1831 Baron Poltimore of Poltimore, Co. Devon, and is the present Peer.

POMFRET, EARL OF. (Fermor.)

Peer of Great Britain.

Thomas Ricards, alias Fermour, of Whitney, Co. Oxford, whose mother was the ıughter and heir of the family of Fermour, and his father was of the Welsh family Ricards, *d.* in 1485. His son, Richard Fermor, acquired great wealth as a merıant, but being a zealous Romanist, fell under the displeasure of King Henry III., for relieving his Confessor, Nicholas Thayne, when a close prisoner in uckingham gaol; and his whole fortune was confiscated under a præmunire; ome part of it, and amongst others his manor of Easton Neston, was restored to im by King Edward VI., and he *d.* there in 1552. The 4th in descent from him 'as Sir William Fermor, who served King Charles I. to the last with unshaken oyalty and honour, and was a severe sufferer by the sequestration of his estates. Ie *d.* in 1661.

His son, Sir William Fermor, was created in 1692 Baron Lempster, Co. Hereford; he *d.* in 1711, and was succeeded by his eldest son, Thomas, 2nd Lord, reated in 1721 Earl of Pomfret, Co. York; he *d.* in 1753, and was succeeded y his son, George, 2nd Earl; to whom, in 1785, succeeded his son, George, 3rd Earl; he *d.* in 1830, and was succeeded by his brother, Thomas-William, present and 4th Earl.

PONSONBY, BARON. (Ponsonby.)

Peer of the United Kingdom.

The Right-Hon. John Ponsonby, 2nd son of Brabazon, 1st Earl of Besborough, *d.* in 1787, having had, by the Lady Elizabeth Cavendish, 2nd daughter of William, 3rd Duke of Devonshire, a numerous issue; for those who lived to maturity, *see* Earl of Besborough, in this Volume. His eldest son, William-Brabazon, was created in March 1806, Baron Ponsonby of Imokilly, Co. Cork, and *d.* in Nov. following, when he was succeeded by his eldest son, John, present and 2nd Lord.

PORTARLINGTON, EARL OF. (Dawson.)

Peer of Ireland.

Marmaduke d'Ossone, the patriarch of this family, came into England with William the Conqueror; that branch of it from which his Lordship descends was settled at Spaldington, in Yorkshire, and his first ancestor who settled in Ireland was William Dawson, Esq., grandfather of William-Henry Dawson, created in 1770 Baron Dawson of Dawson's Court, Queen's County, and in 1776 Viscount Carlow; he *m.* Mary, daughter of Joseph Damer, Esq., of Came, Co. Dorset, and sister of Joseph, 1st Earl of Dorchester; he *d.* in 1779, leaving a numerous issue, of whom only one son, the Hon. and Rev. William Dawson, survives; he was succeeded by his eldest son, John, 2nd Viscount, who was created in 1785 Earl of Portarlington, and *d.* in 1798, leaving the issue described in *The Peerage Volume;* of whom his 2nd and 3rd sons, the Hon. Captain Henry Dawson, R.N., and the Hon. Lieutenant-Colonel George-Lionel Dawson, assumed the additional surname of Damer by Royal sign-manual in 1829. His eldest son John succeeded, and is the present and 2nd Earl.

PORTLAND, DUKE OF. (Scott-Bentinck.)

Peer of Great Britain.

Henry Bentinck, Heer Van Diepenham, in Overyssel, where his family had flo-rished for many ages, had three sons: Henry, his heir; Joseph, a General in the service of the States-General; and William, who was page of honour to King William III. when Prince of Orange, and accompanying that King into Englan. held the first place in his personal confidence and favour; he was created in 16.. Baron of Cirencester, Co. Gloucester, Viscount Woodstock, Co. Oxford, and Earl of Portland Co. Dorset; he was made a Knight of the Garter, and Groom of the Stole to the King; he commanded a Dutch regiment of horse-guards, with which he attended the King to Ireland in 1690, and was his Lieutenant-General at the batt.. of the Boyne; he attended the King in all his wars, and was constantly employed in public business throughout King William's reign, and was the last person the King spoke to at his death. The Earl afterwards led a retired life, and *d.* in 170.. besides two sons named William, who *d.* infants, he had three who survived him, viz.:

1 Henry, his successor, 2nd Earl and 1st Duke of Portland.

2 The Hon. William, created a Count of the Empire 29 Dec. 1732, *d.* 13 O.. 1774; having *m.* 1 June 1733, Countess Charlotte-Sophia-Hedwige-Eleonora, .. daughter and heir of Anthony, Count Aldenburgh, by whom, who *d.* 3 Feb. 1.. he had, besides other issue, two sons, viz.:

1 Christian-Frederick-Anthony, Count Bentinck Rhoon, who by his marriage with Mitje, eldest daughter of Baron Tuyll de Serooskerkin, who *d.* in N.. 1793, had, besides other issue deceased, the two sons stated in *The Peerage Volume.*

2 Captain John-Albert Bentinck, R.N., who *d.* in Sept. 1775, leaving by his marriage in 1763, with Renira-Saingert, 2nd daughter of Baron Tuyll de Serooskerkin, who *d.* in July 1792, Admiral William Bentinck, deceased, for whose widow and surviving issue see *The Peerage Volume*; a 2nd son John, a clergyman, who *d. unm.* in June 1804; also the two surviving daughters stated in *The Peerage Volume*, and a 3rd daughter, Henrietta-Elizabeth, the deceased wife of Admiral Sir George Martin, G.C.B.

3 Charles-John Count Bentinck, who *d.* 18 March 1779; having *m.* Lady Margaret, 2nd daughter and co-heir of William Earl Cadogan.

Henry, 2nd Earl, son and successor of the 1st Earl, was created in 1716 Marquis of Titchfield, Co. Southampton, and Duke of Portland; he *m.* Lady Elizabeth Noel, eldest daughter and co-heir of Wriothesley-Baptist, Earl of Gainsborough, .. of Edward, 1st Earl of Gainsborough, by Lady Elizabeth, eldest daughter and .. heir of Thomas Wriothesley, 4th Earl of Southampton; he *d.* in the island .. Jamaica in 1726, when he was succeeded by his eldest son, William, 2nd D.., K.G.; he *m.* Lady Margaret-Cavendish Harley, only daughter and heir of Edw.. 2nd Earl of Oxford, by Lady Henrietta-Cavendish Holles, only daughter and h.. of John Holles, Duke of Newcastle, by Lady Margaret, eldest daughter and co-.. of Henry Cavendish, 2nd Duke of Newcastle; he *d.* in 1762, leaving two so.. 1 William-Henry-Cavendish, his successor, 3rd Duke, K.G., who *d.* in 1.. and was succeeded by his eldest son, William-Henry-Cavendish, present and .. Duke, who has assumed the additional surname of Scott; and 2 Lord Edw.. Charles-Cavendish Bentinck, for whose widow and surviving issue see *The Pe.. Volume.*

PORTMORE, EARL OF. (COLYEAR.)

Peer of Scotland.

Sir Alexander Robertson, who was created a Baronet of England in 1677, and assumed the surname of Colyear, was father of SIR DAVID COLYEAR, who was created 1699 Lord Portmore and Blackness, and in 1703 EARL of PORTMORE, Viscount Milsington, and Lord Colyear; he *d.* in 1730, and was succeeded by his only surviving son, CHARLES, 2nd EARL, who *d.* in 1785, and was succeeded by his only surviving son, WILLIAM-CHARLES, 3rd EARL; to whom, in 1823, succeeded his eldest son, THOMAS-CHARLES, present and 4th EARL.

PORTSMOUTH, EARL OF. (WALLOP.)

Peer of Great Britain.

Four brothers, Englishmen, are mentioned in Domesday Book as possessors of Wallop, in Hampshire. From one of them descended Sir Robert Wallop, who *d.* in 1282, leaving an only daughter and heir *m.* to Peter de Barton. William, their son, was heir to his grandfather, and Richard, his son, assumed the name of Wallop, and was ancestor in the 12th degree of JOHN WALLOP, Esq., created Baron Wallop of Wallop, Co. Southampton, and Viscount Lymington, in the said county, in 1720; and in 1743 EARL of PORTSMOUTH; he *d.* in 1762, having survived his eldest son, John Viscount Lymington, who *d.* in 1749, leaving, besides other issue, two sons, whose descendants are still existing, viz.:

1 JOHN, 2nd EARL, who succeeded his grandfather, and *d.* in 1797; when he was succeeded by his eldest son, JOHN-CHARLES, present and 3rd EARL.

2 Hon Barton Wallop, who *d.* 1 Sept. 1781; having *m.* in 1771, Camilla-Powlett, daughter of the Rev. Richard Smyth, (by Annabella, daughter of William, son of Lord William Powlett, 2nd son of Charles, 1st Duke of Bolton,) by whom, who *d.* 29 Sept. 1820, he had issue,

1 Urania-Catherine-Camilla, *b.* 23 Nov. 1774, *d.* 31 Dec. 1814; having *m.* 26 March 1813, the Rev. Henry Wake.

2 Barton-William-Powlett, *b.* posthumous 24 Dec. 1781, *d.* Dec. 1824; having *m.* 21 Sept. 1807, Elizabeth, eldest daughter of —— Ward, Esq., by whom, who *d.* Nov. 1812, he left the three children stated in *The Peerage Volume.*

POULETT, EARL. (POULETT.)

Peer of England.

Hercules, Lord of Tournon, in Picardy, came to England with Geoffrey Plantagenet, 3rd son of King Henry, II., and having obtained the Lordship of Poulett, in Somersetshire, assumed his surname from that place. The 7th in descent from him was

Sir John Paulet, who had two sons; Sir Thomas, ancestor of the Earl; and William, ancestor of the extinct Dukes of Bolton and the Marquis of Winchester.

From Sir Thomas Poulett, the eldest son, descended in the 6th degree, Sir Amias Poulett, who after having been Ambassador from Queen ELIZABETH, to the French King, had the custody of Mary Queen of Scots committed to him during the last period of her unhappy imprisonment in England; he *d.* in 1588. JOHN POULETT, Esq., his grandson was created in 1627, BARON POULETT of Hinton St.

George, Co. Somerset; he was a loyal subject and active partisan of King Ch... I., and *d.* in 1649, when he was succeeded by his eldest son, John, 2nd Lord, ... also distinguished himself by his activity and zeal in the Royal cause; he *d.* ... and was succeeded by his eldest son, John, 3rd Lord, who *d.* in 1680. His ... son and successor, John, 4th Lord, K.G., was created in 1706 Viscount Hi... Hinton St. George, Co. Somerset, and Earl Poulett; he *d.* in 1743, and was ... ceeded by his eldest son, John, 2nd Earl, who *d. unm.* in 1764, and was succe... by his only surviving brother,

Vere, 3rd Earl, who *d.* in 1788, leaving two sons, viz:

1 John, his successor, 4th Earl, who *d.* in 1819, and was succeeded by his ... son, John, present and 5th Earl.

2 The Hon. Lieut.-General Vere Poulett, who was *b.* May 1761, and *d.* 15 ... 1812; having *m.* Miss Beecher, who *d.* 14 May 1799; their surviving issue ... stated in *The Peerage Volume.*

POWERSCOURT, VISCOUNT. (Wingfield.)

Peer of Ireland.

His Lordship's ancestors took their surname from the castle of Wingfield, ... folk, where they resided before the Conquest. The first of the family who ... into Ireland, was Richard Wingfield, created in 1618 Viscount Powerscourt, ... title became extinct 1634; his Irish estates devolved on his cousin, Sir Edw... Wingfield, whose grandson, Folliott, was created Viscount Powerscourt in 1... and also dying without issue, the title again became extinct in 1717. Edw... Wingfield, the heir male, succeeded to the estates, and was father of Ric... Wingfield, Esq., in whose favour the family honours were revived; he was cr... in 1743 Baron Wingfield of Wingfield, Co. Wexford, and Viscount Powers... of Powerscourt, Co. Wexford; he *d.* in 1751, leaving two sons, 1 Edward, his ... cessor, 2nd Viscount, who *d. unm.* in 1764; and Richard, 3rd Viscount, who s... ceeded his brother, and *d.* in 1788; he was succeeded by his eldest son, Ric... 4th Viscount, who *d.* in 1809, and was succeeded by his eldest son, Richard, ... Viscount, to whom, in 1823, succeeded his only son, the present minor ... Richard, 6th Viscount.

POWIS, EARL OF. (Clive.)

Peer of the United Kingdom and of Ireland.

The family of Clive has been seated in the County of Salop from the reign of K... Henry II.; they assumed their surname from the Manor of Clive, in that cou... From Henry, Lord of Clive, who, in the reign of King Edward II. *m.* Agnes, ... daughter and co-heir of Robert Huxleigh of Huxleigh, Co. Chester, descended in ... 15th degree, the celebrated General Robert Clive, created in 1761 Baron Cli... of Plassey, Co. Clare, in the Peerage of Ireland, in reward of the eminent serv... by which the British empire in India was protected in its most critical junctu... and placed above the reach of danger. His constitution, worn out by exertion in ... torrid climate of India, sunk on his return to his native land, and the infirmity of the body producing a corresponding depression of mind, caused the lamentable event by which he *d.* in 1774, when he was succeeded by his son Edward, ... Lord Clive, and present Earl Powis.

Sir William Herbert, son and heir of Sir Edward Herbert, 2nd son of William

Earl of Pembroke of the present creation, was created Baron Powis of Powis ...le, Co. Montgomery, in 1629; William, 3rd Lord, his grandson, was created of Powis, Co. Montgomery, in 1674, Viscount Montgomery, and Marquis of ...is, in 1687; all these titles became extinct in 1748, by the death of his grand- William, 3rd Marquis, whose only brother, Lord Edward Herbert, left a ...ghter and heir, Barbara, who *m.* Henry-Arthur Herbert, created Earl Powis.

...ir William Herbert, (next brother of William, 1st Earl of Pembroke of the ...ier creation, whose legitimate male line failed in his son, the 2nd Earl,) was ...ndfather of Edward Herbert, who had three sons, viz.:

Richard, who *d.* in 1597, leaving two sons;

1 Edward, the celebrated Lord Herbert of Chirbury, so created in 1629; which title became extinct in 1691, by the death of his grandson Henry, 4th Lord, whose 2nd sister and co-heir, Florentia, *m.* Richard Herbert, Esq., grandfather by her of Henry-Arthur, afterwards Earl Powis.

2 Henry, father of Henry, in whose favour the title of Herbert of Chirbury was revived in 1694; it again became extinct in 1709, on the death of his son Henry, 2nd Lord.

... Matthew, grandfather of Richard Herbert, Esq., who *m.* Florentia, sister and heir of Henry, 4th Lord Herbert of Chirbury; their grandson and heir, Henry-...hur, *m.* Barbara, niece and heir of William, 3rd Marquis of Powis, and was ...ated Baron Powis of Powis Castle, Viscount Ludlow, Co. Salop, and Earl Powis, 1748: all these titles became extinct in 1801, by the death of his son, George-...ward-Henry-Arthur, 2nd Earl; Henrietta-Antonia, daughter of the 1st Earl, and ...r of her brother, the 2nd Earl, *m.* Edward, 2nd Lord Clive, who was created in ...04 Baron Powis of Powis Castle, Co. Montgomery, Baron Herbert of Cher-...ry, Co. Salop, Viscount Clive of Ludlow, and Earl of Powis, Co. Montgomery, ...d is the present Earl.

3 Charles, grandfather of Arthur Herbert, created Earl of Torrington in 1689, ...ich title became extinct on his death in 1716.

PRUDHOE, BARON. (Percy.)

Peer of the United Kingdom.

Lord Algernon Percy, 3rd son of Hugh, 2nd Duke of Northumberland, only ...rviving brother of the present Duke, and heir presumptive to the title, was created 1816 Baron Prudhoe of Prudhoe Castle, Co. Northumberland; and is the pre-...nt Peer.

QUEENSBERRY, MARQUIS OF. (Douglas.)

Peer of Scotland.

Sir William Douglas, natural son of James, 2nd Earl of Douglas, (for whom *see* ...age 173 of this volume,) had a grant from his father of the Barony and Castle of ...rumlanrig, in the County of Dumfries, where his descendants continued to reside ...n honour, and exhibiting the valiant and restless spirit of the Douglases. His ...reat-grandson, Sir William Douglas of Drumlanrig, was killed in 1484, in the army ...f King James III., at the battle of Lochmaben, against the Duke of Albany and ...ames, 9th Earl of Douglas. Sir William Douglas, grandson of the last-named Sir ...William, was killed at Flodden Field in 1513; Sir William, his son, was engaged ...n the side of the King at the battle of Langside, and was grandfather of

George, Co. Somerset; he was a loyal subject and active partisan of King CHARLES I., and *d.* in 1649, when he was succeeded by his eldest son, JOHN, 2nd LORD, who also distinguished himself by his activity and zeal in the Royal cause; he *d.* in 16.., and was succeeded by his eldest son, JOHN, 3rd LORD, who *d.* in 1680. His only son and successor, JOHN, 4th Lord, K.G., was created in 1706 Viscount Hinton of Hinton St. George, Co. Somerset, and EARL POULETT; he *d.* in 1743, and was succeeded by his eldest son, JOHN, 2nd EARL, who *d. unm.* in 1764, and was succeeded by his only surviving brother,

VERE, 3rd EARL, who *d.* in 1788, leaving two sons, viz:

1 JOHN, his successor, 4th EARL, who *d.* in 1819, and was succeeded by his eldest son, JOHN, present and 5th EARL.

2 The Hon. Lieut.-General Vere Poulett, who was *b.* May 1761, and *d.* 15 March 1812; having *m.* Miss Beecher, who *d.* 14 May 1799; their surviving issue are stated in *The Peerage Volume.*

POWERSCOURT, VISCOUNT. (WINGFIELD.)

Peer of Ireland.

His Lordship's ancestors took their surname from the castle of Wingfield, in Suffolk, where they resided before the Conquest. The first of the family who removed into Ireland, was Richard Wingfield, created in 1618 Viscount Powerscourt, which title became extinct 1634; his Irish estates devolved on his cousin, Sir Edward Wingfield, whose grandson, Folliott, was created Viscount Powerscourt in 16.., and also dying without issue, the title again became extinct in 1717. Edward Wingfield, the heir male, succeeded to the estates, and was father of RICHARD WINGFIELD, Esq., in whose favour the family honours were revived; he was created in 1743 Baron Wingfield of Wingfield, Co. Wexford, and VISCOUNT POWERSCOURT of Powerscourt, Co. Wexford; he *d.* in 1751, leaving two sons, 1 EDWARD, his successor, 2nd VISCOUNT, who *d. unm.* in 1764; and RICHARD, 3rd VISCOUNT, who succeeded his brother, and *d.* in 1788; he was succeeded by his eldest son, RICHARD, 4th VISCOUNT, who *d.* in 1809, and was succeeded by his eldest son, RICHARD, 5th VISCOUNT, to whom, in 1823, succeeded his only son, the present minor Lord, RICHARD, 6th VISCOUNT.

POWIS, EARL OF. (CLIVE.)

Peer of the United Kingdom and of Ireland.

The family of Clive has been seated in the County of Salop from the reign of Henry II.; they assumed their surname from the Manor of Clive, in that county. From Henry, Lord of Clive, who, in the reign of King EDWARD II. *m.* Agnes, daughter and co-heir of Robert Huxleigh of Huxleigh, Co. Chester, descended, in the 15th degree, the celebrated General ROBERT CLIVE, created in 1761 BARON CLIVE of Plassey, Co. Clare, in the Peerage of Ireland, in reward of the eminent services by which the British empire in India was protected in its most critical juncture, and placed above the reach of danger. His constitution, worn out by exertions in the torrid climate of India, sunk on his return to his native land, and the infirmities of the body producing a corresponding depression of mind, caused the lamentable event by which he *d.* in 1774, when he was succeeded by his son EDWARD, Lord Clive, and present EARL POWIS.

Sir William Herbert, son and heir of Sir Edward Herbert, 2nd son of W..

heirs male of his body, which failing, to the younger sons of James, Duke of Queensberry, not succeeding to the dignity of Duke of Queensberry; these titles, together with his father's English titles, became extinct by his death without surviving issue male in 1778. He *m.* Lady Catherine Hyde, 2nd daughter of Henry, Earl of Clarendon and Rochester, celebrated for her beauty, wit, and sprightliness, by the great poets of the day, Pope, Swift, Prior, and Gay, the latter of whom she steadily supported.

2 Lady Jane, who *m.* Francis, 2nd Duke of Buccleuch, and was grand-mother of Henry, 3rd Duke of Buccleuch, who succeeded in 1810, as 5th Duke of Queensberry.

2 Lord William, created in 1697 Earl of March, Viscount of Peebles, Baron uglas of Neidpath, Lyne, and Manerhead, with remainder to the heirs male of his dy, failing which to the heirs male of the body of his father, failing which, to his ter the Lady Anne, and the heirs male of her body. He *d.* in 1705, and was ceeded by his eldest son, William, 2nd Earl of March, who *d.* in 1731; having Lady Anne Hamilton, Countess of Ruglen, daughter and at length sole heir of rd John Hamilton (4th son of William and Anne, Duke and Duchess of Hamil- n, *see* page 177 of this Volume,) who had been created in 1697 Earl of Ruglen, iscount Riccartoun, and Lord Hillhouse, with remainder to the heirs whatso- er of his body; she *d.* in 1748, and was succeeded by their only son,

William, 3rd Earl of March and Ruglen, who was *b.* 16 Dec. 1725, succeeded in 1778, as 4th Duke and Marquis of Queensberry; he *d. unm.* 23 Dec. 1810, when his titles of Earl of Ruglen, &c. became extinct; those of Earl of March, &c., devolved on the present Earl of Wemyss; those of Duke of Queensberry, &c., on Henry, 3rd Duke of Buccleuch, as heir of line of the 1st Duke, the heirs male of his body being extinct; and those of Marquis of Queensberry, Earl of Queensberry, Viscount of Drumlanrig, Lord Douglas of Hawick and Tibbers, entailed by the patents on the 1st Marquis, the 1st Earl, and their heirs male whatsoever, descended to Sir Charles Douglas, Bart., the present Marquis, the lineal representative of Sir William Douglas, 2nd son of William, 1st Earl, and the nearest heir male of the last Duke.

3 Lady Anne, *m.* to David, 3rd Earl of Wemyss; from which marriage Francis, present Earl of Wemyss and March, is 4th in paternal descent.

RADNOR, EARL OF. (Pleydell-Bouverie.)

Peer of Great Britain.

His Lordship is of an ancient and honourable family of the Low Countries, of which Laurence des Bouveries, driven from his home and his patrimony by religious persecution, took advantage of the liberal policy of Queen Elizabeth, which offered a safe asylum in this country to the Protestant refugees. His grandson, Sir Edward des Bouveries, an eminent Turkey merchant, was knighted by King James II., and *d.* in 1694, at his seat at Cheshunt. Sir William des Bouveries, his son, also a very eminent Turkey merchant, was created a Baronet in 1714; he *d.* in 1717, leaving, besides other issue, two sons, Sir Edward, his successor, who *d.* without issue in 1736, and

Sir Jacob, who in 1747 was created Lord Longford, Baron of Longford, Co. Wilts, and Viscount Folkestone of Folkestone, Co. Kent; he *d.* in 1761, leaving three sons, from all of whom there are surviving descendants, viz.:

1 William, his successor, 2nd Viscount.

2 The Hon. Edward Bouverie; he *d.* in 1810, having had, besides the surviving issue stated in *The Peerage Volume*, 1 Harriet-Elizabeth, *b.* 1771, *d.* 8 Aug. 1810, wife of the present Earl of Rosslyn. 2 Mary-Charlotte, *b.* 14 Nov. 1776, *d.* 19

Sept. 1816; having m. Aug. 1800, William Maxwell, Esq. 3 Jane, b. 15 Ju. 1781, d. 13 April 1805; having m. 16 Jan. 1802, the late Sir Francis Vi... Bart.

3 The Hon. Philip, who assumed the name of PUSEY; his widow and surviv... issue (four of his children d. young) are described in *The Peerage Volume*.

WILLIAM, 2nd Viscount, was created in 1765 Baron Pleydell-Bouverie of Co... hill, Co. Berks, and EARL of the County of RADNOR, with remainder of the Ea... dom, failing his issue male, to the issue male of his father, JACOB, VISCOUNT F... STONE, deceased. He was b. 26 Feb. 1725, and d. 28 Jan. 1776; having m. 1st, ... Jan. 1748, Harriet, only daughter and heir of Sir Mark-Stuart PLEYDELL, Bar... whom, who d. 29 May 1750, he was father of JACOB, his successor, 2nd EARL, whe... issue have all taken the name of Pleydell-Bouverie. The 1st Earl m. 2ndl... Sept. 1751, Rebecca, daughter of John Alleyne, Esq., who d. 4 May 1764, ... 3rdly, 22 July 1765, Anne, daughter of Sir Thomas Hales, Bart., and widow ... Anthony Duncombe, Lord Feversham, who d. without surviving issue by the E... 18 June 1795. By his 2nd marriage the Earl had three sons, William-Henry, Ba... tholomew, and Edward. The Hon. Bartholomew Bouverie only survives, but a... three married and had issue—see *The Peerage Volume*.

JACOB, 2nd EARL, eldest son and successor of the 1st EARL, d. in 1828, hav... had, besides the issue stated in *The Peerage Volume*, three daughters who d. you... and a son Laurence, b. in 1781, d. unm. in 1811. He was succeeded by his eld... son, WILLIAM, present and 3rd EARL,

RADSTOCK, BARON. (WALDEGRAVE.)

Peer of Ireland.

The Hon. Vice-Admiral WILLIAM WALDEGRAVE, 2nd son of John, 1st Ea... Waldegrave, was for his distinguished naval services created to the Irish Peera... in the year 1800, by the title of BARON RADSTOCK of Castletown, Queen's Cou...; he d. in 1825, and was succeeded by his eldest son, GRANVILLE-GEORGE, the pre... sent and 2nd LORD.

RANCLIFFE, BARON. (PARKYNS.)

Peer of Ireland.

Richard Parkyns, Esq., Barrister-at-Law, Recorder of the Towns of Notting... and Leicester, in the reign of Queen ELIZABETH, was great-grandfather of Sir Th... mas Parkyns, created a Baronet of England in 1681, who was grandfather of

Sir Thomas Parkyns, Bart., who was b. 8 Dec. 1727, and d. 17 March 18...; having m. 1st, April 1747, his cousin Jane, only daughter and heir of Thomas Pa... kyns, Esq., by whom, who d. 8 Dec. 1760, he had issue, THOMAS-BOOTHBY, 1st Lor...; Jane, late wife of Clement Winstanley, Esq.; and Elizabeth, late wife of Stephe... Charlesworth, Esq., deceased. He m. 2ndly, in 1765, Sarah, daughter of Dan... Smith, Esq., by whom, who d. 22 March 1796, he had Frederick-Cressy, Richard, Charlotte, and Sarah; and 3rdly, Miss Boultbee, by whom he had a son, Thomas, b. 4 Sept. 1797.

THOMAS-BOOTHBY-PARKYNS, Esq., the eldest son d. before his father in 1800, having been created in 1795 BARON RANCLIFFE, in the Peerage of Ireland. He was succeeded by his only son, GEORGE-AUGUSTUS-HENRY-ANNE, present and 2nd LORD.

RANELAGH, VISCOUNT. (Jones.)

Peer of Ireland.

Roger Jones, Esq., son of Thomas Jones, Archbishop of Dublin and Chancellor Ireland, was created in 1628, Viscount Ranelagh, Co. Wicklow, and Baron of van, Co. Meath; he *d.* the same year, leaving two sons:

1 Arthur, 2nd Viscount, who *d.* in 1669, and was succeeded by his only son chard, 3rd Viscount; he was created Earl of Ranelagh in 1674, and *d.* without ue male in 1711, when the Earldom became extinct.

2 Thomas, grandfather of Charles, 4th Viscount, who in 1759 claimed and was owed the titles of Viscount and Baron, which had remained dormant since the ath of Richard, Earl of Ranelagh; he *d.* in 1798, leaving two sons, Charles, 1 Viscount, his successor, who *d. unm.* in 1800; and Thomas, 6th Viscount, 10 succeeded his brother, and *d.* in 1820; when he was succeeded by his only rviving son, Thomas-Heron, present and 7th Viscount.

RANFURLY, EARL OF. (Knox.)

Peer of Ireland and of the United Kingdom.

The family of Knox is descended from Adam, the son of Uchtred, who, in the ·ign of Alexander II. King of Scotland, obtained the lands of Knox in Renfrew, om whence he assumed his surname. This branch of it settled in Ireland about ie period of the Revolution, and obtained estates in the County of Tyrone. Thoas Knox, Esq. was created Baron Welles of Dungannon, Co. Tyrone, in 1681, nd Viscount Northland, also of Dungannon, in 1791; he *d.* in 1818, and was ucceeded by his eldest son, Thomas, 2nd Viscount, the present Peer; who was reated Baron Ranfurly of Rampborlie, Co. Renfrew, in the Peerage of the United Kingdom in 1826; and in 1831, Earl of Ranfurly of Dungannon, Co. Tyrone, n the Peerage of Ireland.

RATHDOWN, EARL OF. (Monck.)

Peer of Ireland.

This family is descended from William le Moyne, or Monck, Lord of the Manor of Potheridge, Co. Devon, in 1066. He was ancestor of General Monck, who for his eminent services in the restoration of King Charles II., was created Duke of Albemarle; and of Charles Monck, cotemporary of the Duke, who settled in Ireland. From him descended in the fourth degree, Charles-Stanley Monck, Esq., created in 1797 Baron Monck of Ballytrammon, Co. Wexford, and in 1800 Viscount Monck; he *d.* in 1802, and was succeeded by his eldest son, Henry-Stanley, 2nd Viscount, the present Peer, who was created Earl of Rathdown in 1822.

RAVENSWORTH, BARON. (Liddell.)

Peer of the United Kingdom.

Thomas Liddell, who in 1607 purchased Ravensworth Castle, in the County of Durham, was grandfather of Sir Thomas Liddell, created a Baronet in 1642, a steady

Sept. 1816; having *m.* Aug. 1800, William Maxwell, Esq. 3 Jane, *b.* 15 Jan. 1781, *d.* 13 April 1805; having *m.* 16 Jan. 1802, the late Sir Francis Vincent Bart.

3 The Hon. Philip, who assumed the name of PUSEY; his widow and surviving issue (four of his children *d.* young) are described in *The Peerage Volume.*

WILLIAM, 2nd Viscount, was created in 1765 Baron Pleydell-Bouverie of Coleshill, Co. Berks, and EARL of the County of RADNOR, with remainder of the Earldom, failing his issue male, to the issue male of his father, JACOB, VISCOUNT FOLKESTONE, deceased. He was *b.* 26 Feb. 1725, and *d.* 28 Jan. 1776; having *m.* 1st, Jan. 1748, Harriet, only daughter and heir of Sir Mark-Stuart PLEYDELL, Bart., by whom, who *d.* 29 May 1750, he was father of JACOB, his successor, 2nd EARL, whose issue have all taken the name of Pleydell-Bouverie. The 1st Earl *m.* 2ndly, Sept. 1751, Rebecca, daughter of John Alleyne, Esq., who *d.* 4 May 1764. 3rdly, 22 July 1765, Anne, daughter of Sir Thomas Hales, Bart., and widow of Anthony Duncombe, Lord Feversham, who *d.* without surviving issue by the E. 18 June 1795. By his 2nd marriage the Earl had three sons, William-Henry, Bartholomew, and Edward. The Hon. Bartholomew Bouverie only survives, but three married and had issue—see *The Peerage Volume.*

JACOB, 2nd EARL, eldest son and successor of the 1st EARL, *d.* in 1828, having had, besides the issue stated in *The Peerage Volume,* three daughters who *d.* young, and a son Laurence, *b.* in 1781, *d. unm.* in 1811. He was succeeded by his eldest son, WILLIAM, present and 3rd EARL,

RADSTOCK, BARON. (WALDEGRAVE.)

Peer of Ireland.

The Hon. Vice-Admiral WILLIAM WALDEGRAVE, 2nd son of John, 1st E. Waldegrave, was for his distinguished naval services created to the Irish Peerage in the year 1800, by the title of BARON RADSTOCK of Castletown, Queen's County; he *d.* in 1825, and was succeeded by his eldest son, GRANVILLE-GEORGE, the present and 2nd LORD.

RANCLIFFE, BARON. (PARKYNS.)

Peer of Ireland.

Richard Parkyns, Esq., Barrister-at-Law, Recorder of the Towns of Nottingham and Leicester, in the reign of Queen ELIZABETH, was great-grandfather of Sir Thomas Parkyns, created a Baronet of England in 1681, who was grandfather of

Sir Thomas Parkyns, Bart., who was *b.* 8 Dec. 1727, and *d.* 17 March 1806, having *m.* 1st, April 1747, his cousin Jane, only daughter and heir of Thomas Parkyns, Esq., by whom, who *d.* 8 Dec. 1760, he had issue, THOMAS-BOOTHBY, 1st L. Jane, late wife of Clement Winstanley, Esq.; and Elizabeth, late wife of S. Charlesworth, Esq., deceased. He *m.* 2ndly, in 1765, Sarah, daughter of D. Smith, Esq., by whom, who *d.* 22 March 1796, he had Frederick-Cressy, Richard, Charlotte, and Sarah; and 3rdly, Miss Boultbee, by whom he had a son, Thomas, *b.* 4 Sept. 1797.

THOMAS-BOOTHBY-PARKYNS, Esq., the eldest son *d.* before his father in 1800, having been created in 1795 BARON RANCLIFFE, in the Peerage of Ireland. He was succeeded by his only son, GEORGE-AUGUSTUS-HENRY-ANNE, present and 2nd LORD.

Donald, his successor, 4th Lord, who *d.* in 1761, leaving two sons: George, Lord, who *d.* without male issue in 1768; and Hugh, 6th Lord, who succeeded brother, and *d. unm.* in 1797.

George, 3rd son; he *d.* in 1782, leaving Eric, the present and 7th Lord, who eeded his cousin in 1797, and other issue, for whom see *The Peerage Volume.*

REDESDALE, BARON. (Freeman-Mitford.)

Peer of the United Kingdom.

lis Lordship's father, John Mitford, Esq., was 20th in paternal descent from tthew, who was seated at Mitford Castle, Co, Northumberland, in the time of lliam the Conqueror. He *d.* in May 1762; having *m.* 13 Sept. 1740, Philaphia, daughter of William Reveley, of Newby, Co. York, Esq., (and 1st cousin Hugh, 1st Duke of Northumberland,) by whom, who *d.* 9 Jan. 1797, he had ue:

. William Mitford, Esq., of Exbury, Co. Hants, Colonel of the South Hants litia; *b.* 10 Feb. 1744, *d.* 10 Feb. 1827; having *m.* 18 May 1766, Frances, ighter of James Molloy, Esq., by whom, who *d.* 27 April 1776, he had issue:

1 William, *b.* 26 May 1767, *d.* Dec. 1790.
2 Frances, *b.* 22 June 1768, *d.* Aug. 1780.
3 Henry, Capt. R.N. *b.* 12 Sept. 1769, is deceased, having *m.* 1st, in 1796, Louisa, daughter of Anthony Wyke, Esq., who *d.* in May 1801; and he *m.* 2ndly, Mary, daughter of Hon. David Anstruther, [3rd son of Alexander, called 4th Lord Newark: she *m.* 2ndly, 13 April 1809, Iver-Spurgeon Farrer, Esq.;] he had issue by both marriages:

By the 1st,

1 Frances, *b.* 8 Aug. 1797.
2 Louisa, *b.* 21 Dec. 1798, *d.* 9 April 1826.
3 William Reveley, *b.* 7 June 1800, *d.* June 1801.

By the 2nd,

4 Henry-Revely Mitford, Esq., *m.* 28 Feb. 1828, Lady Georgiana-Jemima, daughter of Earl Ashburnham.

4 John, *b.* 25 May 1772, *m.* 12 Jan. 1808, Emily Street; they have issue.
5 Bertram, *b.* 1 Oct. 1774, *m.* 24 May 1806, Frances, 2nd daughter of John Vernon, Esq.

2 Mary, *b.* Feb. 1745, *d.* April 1800.
3 Sir John Mitford, appointed in 1802 Lord Chancellor of Ireland, and created Baron Redesdale of Redesdale, Co. Northumberland; he assumed the additional name of Freeman by Royal sign-manual in 1809, and *d.* in 1830, when he was succeeded by his only son John-Thomas, present and 2nd Lord.
4 Frances, *b.* April 1750, *d.* 19 June 1807.
5 Philadelphia, *b.* 1751.

RENDLESHAM, BARON. (Thelusson.)

Peer of Ireland.

This is originally an ancient and noble family of France. Theophilus de Thelusson, having escaped the massacre of St. Bartholomew, fled in 1572 to Geneva, where his descendants frequently filled the first offices in the magistracy, till

Peter Thelusson, Esq., (3rd son of Isaac de Thelusson, Ambassador from Geneva to the Court of Louis 15th.) settled in England about 1750; he was remarkable for supporter of King CHARLES I. He was succeeded by his grandson, Sir Thomas, whose son, Sir Henry, was succeeded by his grandson, Sir Henry, 4th Baronet, created Lord Ravensworth, Baron of Ravensworth, Co. Durham, in 1747, which title became extinct on his death without issue male in 1784, when the Baronetcy devolved on the son of his brother Thomas,

Sir Henry-George Liddell, Bart., who was *b.* 25 Nov. 1749, and *d.* 26 Nov. 1791, having *m.* April 1773, Elizabeth, daughter of Thomas Steel, Esq., by whom, who *d.* in Feb. 1811, he had, 1 THOMAS-HENRY, the present Peer, created in 1821, BARON RAVENSWORTH of Ravensworth Castle, Co. Durham; 2 The Rev. Henry-George Liddell, who is *m.* to Charlotte, 5th daughter of the Hon. Thomas Lyon of STRATHMORE, and has issue; 3 Elizabeth, wife of Brooke Richmond, Esq.; 4 Anne; 5 Charlotte-Amelia.

RAYLEIGH, BARONESS. (STRUTT.)

Peeress of the United Kingdom.

John Strutt, of Terling, Co. Essex, Esq., was descended from a brother of Sir Denner Strutt, who was created a Baronet in 1642, and was killed in the Civil War on the part of King CHARLES I., without male issue. Joseph-Holden Strutt, Esq., his son and heir, *m.* LADY CHARLOTTE-MARY-GERTRUDE FITZ-GERALD, 5th daughter of James, 1st Duke of Leinster, which Lady was created in 1821, BARONESS RAYLEIGH of Terling Place, Co. Essex, and is the present Peeress.

REAY, BARON. (MACKAY.)

Peer of Scotland.

This ancient family descends from Walter, supposed a junior of the House of Forbes, whose descendants for some generations bore no other surname than the patronymic Mack prefixed to their father's christian name. Donald, the great grandson of Walter, *m.* a daughter of Y Mackneill Ghika, by whom he had a son called Y, after his maternal grandfather. Donald, the son of Y, was called Macky, which from that time has been the surname of his posterity. The early history of this family, like that of all others of the north of Scotland at this barbarous period, is full of civil discords, petty feuds, and murders, veiled under the pretence of warfare; and it scarcely emerges from these lawless and obscure convulsions, before the creation of SIR DONALD MACKAY of Far, 9th in descent from the first Donald Macky, to the Baronetage in 1627; he was further created to the Peerage by the title of LORD REAY. He entered into the service of the King of Denmark, till the urgent wants of the Royalists in England called him home in 1644. He landed at Newcastle, with a considerable supply of arms and money from Denmark, all which were unfortunately taken when the town of Newcastle was stormed by the Scotch army; Lord Reay himself was made prisoner, and confined in the Tolbooth of Edinburgh, till released by Montrose after the battle of Kilsyth in Aug. 1645. On the subsequent dispersion of that hero's forces at Philiphaugh, Lord Reay returned home, and appears to have been protected by the remoteness of his situation from molestation by the prevailing party. He *d.* in Denmark in 1649, and was succeeded by his eldest son, JOHN, 2nd LORD, who after his father's death continued to support the Royal cause; he was taken prisoner by the Covenanters at Balveny in 1654. His eldest son, Donald, *d.* before him, leaving one son,

GEORGE, who succeeded his grandfather as 3rd LORD; he *d.* in 1748, leaving four sons, of whom Hugh, 2nd son, and Alexander, 4th son, *d.* without issue male. The other two were,

1 DONALD, his successor, 4th LORD, who *d.* in 1761, leaving two sons: GEORGE, 5th LORD, who *d.* without male issue in 1768; and HUGH, 6th LORD, who succeeded his brother, and *d. unm.* in 1797.

2 George, 3rd son; he *d.* in 1782, leaving ERIC, the present and 7th LORD, who succeeded his cousin in 1797, and other issue, for whom see *The Peerage Volume.*

REDESDALE, BARON. (FREEMAN-MITFORD.)

Peer of the United Kingdom.

His Lordship's father, John Mitford, Esq., was 20th in paternal descent from Matthew, who was seated at Mitford Castle, Co, Northumberland, in the time of William the Conqueror. He *d.* in May 1762; having *m.* 13 Sept. 1740, Philadelphia, daughter of William Reveley, of Newby, Co. York, Esq., (and 1st cousin to Hugh, 1st Duke of Northumberland,) by whom, who *d.* 9 Jan. 1797, he had issue:

1 William Mitford, Esq., of Exbury, Co. Hants, Colonel of the South Hants Militia; *b.* 10 Feb. 1744, *d.* 10 Feb. 1827; having *m.* 18 May 1766, Frances, daughter of James Molloy, Esq., by whom, who *d.* 27 April 1776, he had issue:

1 William, *b.* 26 May 1767, *d.* Dec. 1790.

2 Frances, *b.* 22 June 1768, *d.* Aug. 1780.

3 Henry, Capt. R.N. *b.* 12 Sept. 1769, is deceased, having *m.* 1st, in 1796, Louisa, daughter of Anthony Wyke, Esq., who *d.* in May 1801; and he *m.* 2ndly, Mary, daughter of Hon. David Anstruther, [3rd son of Alexander, called 4th Lord Newark: she *m.* 2ndly, 13 April 1809, Iver-Spurgeon Farrer, Esq.;] he had issue by both marriages:

By the 1st,

1 Frances, *b.* 8 Aug. 1797.

2 Louisa, *b.* 21 Dec. 1798, *d.* 9 April 1826.

3 William Reveley, *b.* 7 June 1800, *d.* June 1801.

By the 2nd,

4 Henry-Revely Mitford, Esq., *m.* 28 Feb. 1828, Lady Georgiana-Jemima, daughter of Earl Ashburnham.

4 John, *b.* 25 May 1772, *m.* 12 Jan. 1808, Emily Street; they have issue.

5 Bertram, *b.* 1 Oct. 1774, *m.* 24 May 1806, Frances, 2nd daughter of John Vernon, Esq.

2 Mary, *b.* Feb. 1745, *d.* April 1800.

3 SIR JOHN MITFORD, appointed in 1802 Lord Chancellor of Ireland, and created BARON REDESDALE of Redesdale, Co. Northumberland; he assumed the additional name of Freeman by Royal sign-manual in 1809, and *d.* in 1830, when he was succeeded by his only son JOHN-THOMAS, present and 2nd LORD.

4 Frances, *b.* April 1750, *d.* 19 June 1807.

5 Philadelphia, *b.* 1751.

RENDLESHAM, BARON. (THELUSSON.)

Peer of Ireland.

This is originally an ancient and noble family of France. Theophilus de Thelusson, having escaped the massacre of St. Bartholomew, fled in 1572 to Geneva, where his descendants frequently filled the first offices in the magistracy, till

Peter Thelusson, Esq., (3rd son of Isaac de Thelusson, Ambassador from Geneva to the Court of Louis 15th.) settled in England about 1750; he was remarkable for his great wealth and for the extraordinary will by which he bequeathed about £600,000 to trustees, to be laid out in the accumulation of landed property for the benefit of his eldest male descendant, when the last of his sons and their sons shall be dead; he was *b.* 27 June 1737, and *d.* 21 July 1797; having *m.* 6 Jan. 17— Anne, 2nd daughter of Matthew Woodford, Esq., and sister of Sir Ralph Woodford, of Carlby, Co. Lincoln, Bart.; by whom he had issue:

1 PETER-ISAAC THELUSSON, Esq., of Broadsworth, Co. York, created in 18— BARON RENDLESHAM of Rendlesham; he *d.* in 1808, and was succeeded by his eldest son JOHN, present and 2nd LORD.

2 George-Woodford, *b.* 2 March 1764, *d.* 30 Dec. 1811; having *m.* 30 April 1790, Mary-Anne, 3rd daughter of Philip Fonnereau, Esq., by whom he has issue:

1 Marianne, *b.* 11 Jan. 1791.

2 Georgiana, *b.* 6 Oct. 1795, *m.* 3 Feb. 1813, Henry-Hoyle Oddie, Esq.

3 Charles, *b.* 2 Feb. 1770, *d.* 2 Nov. 1815; having *m.* 15 Jan. 1795, Sabine, eldest daughter of Abraham Roberts, Esq., by whom, who was *b.* 31 March 1775, and *d.* 26 Feb. 1814, he had issue:

1 Charles, *b.* 31 Jan. 1797, *m.* 19 Oct. 1820, Mary, youngest daughter of George Grant, Esq., and has issue,

1 Charles-Sabine-Augustus, *b.* 5 March 1822. 2 Alexander-Dalton, *b.* 8 March 1824. 3 Frederick-George, *b.* 1 April 1825. 4 Seymour-Stuart, *b.* 26 Feb. 1827. 5 A son, *b.* 17 Jan. 1830.

2 Thomas-Roberts, *b.* June 1801, *m.* 17 Aug. 1822, Maria, 6th daughter of Sir Frances Macnaughten, by whom he has issue:

1 Sabina-Matilda, *b.* 9 June 1823. 2 Letitia, *b.* 17 Jan. 1825.

3 Adeline, *b.* 2 Jan. 1803.

4 Maria, *b.* 27 Feb. 1771, widow of the Hon. Augustus Phipps of MULGRAVE, uncle of the Earl of Mulgrave.

5 Anne, *b.* 25 Sept. 1774, *m.* 24 June 1801, Vice-Admiral William Windham.

6 Augusta-Charlotte, *b.* 2 Oct. 1776, *m.* 1st, 26 March 1799, Thomas-Champion Crespigny, Esq., who *d.* 2 Aug. 1799; and 2ndly, 3 Feb. 1827, Joseph Whatley, Esq.

RIBBLESDALE, BARON. (LISTER.)

Peer of Great Britain.

John Lister *m.* about 1312, Isabel, daughter and heir of John de Bolton; from which marriage Thomas Lister, Esq., was 15th in paternal descent; he had two sons:

1 Thomas, father of THOMAS LISTER, Esq., created in 1797 BARON RIBBLESDALE of Gisburne Park, Co. York; he *d.* in 1826, and was succeeded by his only son THOMAS, present and 2nd LORD.

2 Nathaniel, father of Thomas Lister, Esq., of Armitage Park, father of the present Lady Ribblesdale.

RICHMOND, DUKE OF. (LENNOX.)

Peer of England and of Scotland.

CHARLES, 1st Duke, K.G., on whom his Royal father conferred the surname of Lennox, was son of King CHARLES II. by Louise-Renee de Penencouet de Queronaille, whom he created in 1673 Baroness Petersfield, Co. Southampton, Countess of Fareham, Co. Hants, and Duchess of Portsmouth, for life; these titles became extinct on her death in 1734. Charles Lennox, her only son, *b.* 29 July 1672, was created in Aug. 1675 Baron of Settrington, Earl of March, and Duke of Richmond; and in Sept. following, Baron Methuen of Torbolton, Earl of Darnley, and Duke of Lennox, in the Peerage of Scotland. He *d.* in 1723, and was succeeded by his only son Charles, 2nd Duke, K.G., who *d.* in 1750; leaving two sons, viz. 1 Charles, 3rd Duke, K.G., his successor, who *d.* without issue in 1806; and 2 Lord George-Henry Lennox, who *d.* in 1805; leaving the three daughters stated in *The Peerage Volume*, and one son, Charles, 4th Duke, K.G., who succeeded his uncle in 1806, and *d.* in 1819, when he was succeeded by his eldest son Charles, present and 5th Duke, K.G.

His Grace is also Duke of Aubigny in France, a title which had been borne by the Dukes of Richmond and Lennox of the House of Stuart, and which was granted in 1684 by Louis XIV., King of France, to the Duchess of Portsmouth, with remainder to her son Charles Duke of Richmond and his heirs male.

RIVERS, BARON. (Pitt-Rivers.)

Peer of the United Kingdom.

John Pitt, Esq., Clerk of the Exchequer in the reign of Elizabeth, was father of Sir William, his eldest son; and of Thomas, 3rd son, ancestor of the Earl of Chatham.

The 5th in descent from Sir William Pitt was George Pitt, Esq., created in 1776 Baron Rivers of Strathfieldsaye; and in 1802 Baron Rivers of Sudley Castle, Co. Gloucester, with remainder, in default of issue male, to the issue male of his daughter Louisa, by Peter Beckford, Esq. His Lordship was *b.* in 1720, and *d.* 7 May 1803; having *m.* 4 Jan. 1746, Penelope, daughter and heir of Sir Richard Atkins, Bart., by whom, who *d.* 8 Feb. 1795, he had issue:

1 George, 2nd Lord, *b.* 19 Sept. 1751, *d.* 20 July 1828, when he was succeeded by his nephew, the present Lord.

2 Hon. Penelope, *m.* 1st Jan. 1767, Edward Earl Ligonier; this marriage was dissolved in 1772, and she *m.* 2ndly, in 1784, Capt. Smith.

3 Hon. Louisa, *d.* 4 May 1791, having *m.* 21 March 1773, Peter Beckford, Esq., by whom she had a daughter—see *The Peerage Volume*—and one son,

Horace-William Beckford, Esq., who succeeded his uncle as 3rd Lord, assumed for himself and his successors only the name of Pitt-Rivers, and that of Pitt for the rest of his issue: he was unfortunately drowned in 1831, and was succeeded by his eldest son George, the present and 4th Lord.

4 Hon. Marcia-Lucy, *b.* 29 March 1756, *d.* 5 Aug. 1822; having *m.* 23 July 1789, James Fox-Lane, Esq., who is also deceased.

RIVERSDALE, BARON. (Tonson.)

Peer of Ireland.

Benjamin Tonson, Esq. was Treasurer of the Navy in the reign of Queen Elizabeth. His descendant, Richard Tonson, Esq., settled at Spanish Island, Co. Cork, in the reign of Charles II., and was great-grandfather of William Tonson, Esq., who was created in 1783, Baron Riversdale of Rathcormac, Co. Cork; he *d.* in 1787, and was succeeded by his eldest son, William, present and 2nd Lord.

RODEN, EARL OF. (Jocelyn.)

Peer of Ireland and of the United Kingdom.

The patriarch of this family was Egidius de Jocelyn, a Nobleman of Brittany, wh came into England in the reign of Edward the Confessor.

His descendant, Sir Robert Jocelyn, created a Baronet in 1665, was father of Sir Strange, whose male issue failed in 1770, and of Thomas, father of Robert Jocely Lord High Chancellor of Ireland, who was created Baron Newport of Newport, C Tipperary, in 1743, and Viscount Jocelyn in 1755; he *d.* in 1756, and wa succeeded by his son,

Robert, 2nd Viscount, who was created Earl of Roden in 1771; he *m.* Lady Anne Hamilton, eldest daughter of James, 1st Earl of Clanbrassil, and sister a heir of James, 2nd Earl, on whose death, 6 Feb. 1798, the title became extinct; a by her had, besides Robert, 2nd Earl, his eldest son and successor, and the oth issue stated in *The Peerage Volume*, four daughters deceased, viz.:

1 Lady Harriet, who was *b.* in 1754, and *d.* in July 1831, the widow of Chichest 4th Earl of Massereene.

2 Lady Caroline, *d.* 7 Oct. 1831.

3 Lady Sophia, who *d.* in Oct. 1825; having *m.* 9 April 1798, James Arbuck Esq., who *d.* in 1824.

4 Lady Louisa, who *d.* 1 Sept. 1807, having *m.* 11 May 1800, the late Gener Leonard Orde.

RODNEY, BARON. (Rodney.)

Peer of Great Britain.

The first ancestor of this family on record is Walter Rodney, to whom the Empress Maud, daughter of King Henry I., granted lands in the countie Somerset, Devon, and Cornwall.

The gallant Admiral, Sir George-Brydges Rodney, K.B., was created a Baronet in 1764, and in 1782, in recompense of his distinguished naval servi was raised to the Peerage, by the title of Baron Rodney of Stoke Rodney, Somerset; he *d.* in 1792, and was succeeded by his eldest son, George, 2nd Lo who *d.* in 1802, and was succeeded by his eldest son, George, present and Lord.

ROKEBY, BARON. (Montagu.)

Peer of Ireland.

William Robinson settled at Kendal, Co. Westmoreland, in the reign of Hen VIII., and was great-grandfather of Thomas Robinson, Esq., Barrister-at-law, w had issue:

1 William, grandfather of Richard, Archbishop of Armagh, who was created 1777, Baron Rokeby of Armagh, with remainder, failing his issue male, t kinsman, Matthew Robinson, Esq., and his issue male; he *d. unm.* 10 Oct. 1794.

2 Sir Leonard, grandfather of the said

Matthew Robinson, Esq., of West Layton, Co. York, on whom the Peerage w entailed, and who *d.* in 1778, having had issue:

1 Matthew, 2nd Lord; he succeeded 10 Oct. 1794, and *d. unm.* 30 N 1800.

2 Thomas, who *d. unm.*

3 Morris Robinson, Esq., who *d.* 17 Oct. 1777; having *m.* Jane, eldest daughter of John Greenland, Esq., by whom, who *d.* 7 Sept. 1810, he had two sons: 1 Morris, 3rd Lord, who succeeded his uncle in 1800, and *d.* in 1829, *unm.*; 2 Matthew, who assumed the name of Montagu; he succeeded his brother as 4th Lord, and *d.* in 1831, when he was succeeded by his eldest son, Edward, present and 5th Lord.

4 Robert, who *d. unm.* in China.

5 The Rev. William Robinson, who was *b.* in 1728, and *d.* 8 Dec. 1803; leaving issue by his marriage in 1760, with Mary, daughter of Adam Richardson, Esq., besides the Lady of Sir Samuel Egerton-Brydges, Bart., who, as still living, is stated in *The Peerage Volume*, an elder daughter Mary, who *d. unm.*, and a son, the Rev. Matthew Robinson, who *d.* without issue 10 Aug. 1827.

6 John.

7 Charles Robinson, Esq., who *d.* 31 March 1807, leaving by his marriage with Mary, 2nd daughter of John Greenland, Esq., and widow of Richard Dawkes, Esq., who *d.* in June 1798, an only daughter.—See *The Peerage Volume.*

8 Elizabeth, who *d.* 25 Aug. 1800, widow of Edward Montagu, Esq. of Newbold-Vernon, Co. Leicester, son of the Hon. Charles Montagu, 5th son of Edward, 1st Earl of Sandwich; she left a large estate to her nephew Matthew, afterwards 4th Lord, who at her desire took the name of Montagu in 1776.

9 Sarah, *m.* George-Lewis Scott, Esq.

ROLLE, BARON. (Rolle.)

Peer of Great Britain.

George Rolle, of an ancient Dorsetshire family, was an eminent merchant of London, and having settled at Stevenstone, in Devonshire, *d.* in 1552; he was ancestor in the 5th degree of

John Rolle, Esq., whose eldest son Henry was created in 1748, Baron Rolle of Stevenstone, Co. Devon, which title became extinct on his death without issue in 1750; and his younger son, Denis, was father of John, the present Lord, in whose favour the Peerage was revived by the same title in 1796.

ROLLO, BARON. (Rollo.)

Peer of Scotland.

Rollo, the ancestor of this family, came into England with William the Conqueror; his descendant, Richard de Rollo, settled in Scotland in the reign of King David I.; and John de Rollo, from whom his Lordship's lineal descent is deduced, *d.* in the beginning of the 15th century. 8th in descent from him was Andrew Rollo, of Duncrub, a faithful adherent to the King in the civil war; he was created Lord Rollo of Duncrub in 1651. Sir William Rollo, his 5th son, was taken prisoner in Montrose's army at the battle of Philiphaugh, and executed at Edinburgh 28 Oct. 1645. James, 2nd son of the 1st Lord, succeeded as 2nd Lord, and *d.* in 1669, when his eldest son, Andrew, 3rd Lord, succeeded; he *d.* in 1700, and was succeeded by his only surviving son, Robert, 4th Lord; he assisted at the great council of the Jacobites in 1715, but forbearing to take up arms escaped forfeiture. He *d.* in 1758, leaving, besides other issue, two sons, successive Peers: 1 Andrew, 5th Lord, a distinguished military officer, who *d.* 1765, without surviving issue; and 2 John, 6th Lord, who succeeded his brother, and *d.* in 1783. He was succeeded by his son, James, 7th Lord, to whom, in 1784, succeeded his son John, present and 8th Lord.

ROMNEY, EARL OF. (MARSHAM.)

Peer of the United Kingdom.

This family takes its name from the town of Marsham, in Norfolk. Thom Marsham, an Alderman of London, who *d.* in 1624, was father of Sir John Marsh a zealous Royalist, who lost considerable property in the civil wars, and was cr a Baronet in 1663. His grandson, SIR ROBERT MARSHAM, 5th Baronet, was crea in 1716, BARON ROMNEY of Romney, Co. Kent, and *d.* in 1724. He was succe by his only surviving son, ROBERT, 2nd LORD, to whom in 1793, succeeded eldest surviving son, CHARLES, 3rd LORD; he was created in 1801, Visc Marsham of the Mote, and EARL of ROMNEY, and *d.* in 1811, when he was ceeded by his only son, CHARLES, present and 2nd EARL.

ROSCOMMON, EARL OF. (DILLON.)

Peer of Ireland.

His Lordship is of the same ancestry with the Lord Viscount Dillon—*see* that in this Volume; 9th in descent from Thomas Dillon, last Duke of Aquitaine of family was Gerald Dillon, of Drumrany, father of

1 Maurice, ancestor of Viscount Dillon.

2 Sir James Dillon, of Proudstown, whose son, Sir ROBERT, was father 1 Richard, ancestor of Sir Charles Drake Dillon, of Lismullen, Bart.; 2 Ger ancestor of Lord Clonbrook; 3 Sir James, great-grandfather of

SIR JAMES DILLON, who was created in 1619, Baron of Kilkenny West, and 1622, EARL of ROSCOMMON; he *d.* in 1641, leaving seven sons, viz.:

1 ROBERT, 2nd EARL, whose male line failed in 1746 on the death of the Earl.

2 Lucas, great-grandfather of ROBERT, 9th EARL; his male line also became tinct on the death of the 11th EARL, in 1816.

3 Thomas; 4 Christopher; 5 George; 6 John—from none of whom is there male issue.

7 Patrick, ancestor in the 5th generation of the present EARL.

ROBERT, 2nd EARL, the eldest son, succeeded his father; he *d.* in 1642, leav two sons:

1 JAMES, 3rd EARL, who *d.* in 1649, and was succeeded by his eldest son, WEN WORTH, 4th EARL, the celebrated poet, who *d.* without issue in 1684.

2 CARY, 5th EARL, who succeeded his nephew; he *d.* in 1689, and was succee by his son ROBERT, 6th EARL, who *d.* in 1715, leaving two sons: 1 ROBERT, 7 EARL, his successor, who *d.* without issue in 1721; and 2 JAMES, 8th EARL, succeeded his brother, and *d. unm.* in 1746, when the whole male issue of the EARL became extinct.

Lucas, 2nd son of the 1st EARL, left a son James, father of Patrick Dillon, Es who had, besides other issue, two sons, viz.:

1 ROBERT, who succeeded as 9th EARL, on the extinction of the male line o 2nd EARL, and *d. unm.* in 1770.

2 JOHN, 10th EARL, who succeeded his brother; he *d.* in 1782, and was suc ceeded by his only son, PATRICK, 11th EARL; on whose death without issue male 1816, the male line of Lucas, 2nd son of the 1st EARL, became extinct.

Patrick, 7th son of the 1st EARL, was father of James Dillon of Rath, whose elder sons were Edward and Michael; Edward left a son, Robert, who claimed t Roscommon title before the Irish House of Peers, but *d. unm.* Michael left a s

James, who was father of Michael Dillon, Esq., Captain in the County of Dublin Militia, who was killed by the Irish rebels at the battle of Ross, 5 June 1798; having *m.* Mary, daughter of the Rev. Richard Griffith, the only issue of which marriage was a posthumous son, Michael-James-Robert Dillon, in favour of whose claim, after a long and laborious investigation, the House of Lords decided 19 June 1828; he is the present and 12th Earl.

ROSEBERY, EARL OF. (Primrose.)

Peer of Scotland and of the United Kingdom.

This family derives its surname from the lands of Primrose, in Fife. Duncan Primrose was settled at Culross, Co. Perth, in the reign of Queen Mary. His great-grandson,

Sir Archibald Primrose of Carrington, was a zealous Royalist in the Civil War of King Charles I. He was taken prisoner at the battle of Philiphaugh in 1645, tried by the Parliament, and found guilty of high treason, but, by the intervention of the Marquis of Argyll, his life was spared; he was set at liberty in the following year in consequence of Montrose's capitulation, by which indemnity was granted to his followers, and permission to himself to quit the kingdom. Sir Archibald accompanied King Charles II. in his expedition into England, was created a Baronet in 1651, and had his estates sequestrated in consequence of the unfortunate result of the battle of Worcester. After the restoration of King Charles II. he was appointed Lord Register of Scotland, and constituted a Lord of Session by the style of Lord Carrington. He *d.* in 1679, leaving, besides other issue, the two sons following:

1 Sir William, whose son, Sir James, was created Viscount Primrose, Lord Primrose and Castlefield in 1703, which titles became extinct in 1741, on the death of his 2nd son Hugh, 3rd Viscount.

2 Archibald, created in 1700 Viscount of Rosebery, Lord Primrose and Dalmeny, to him and the heirs male of his body, which failing, to the heirs female of his body; and, in 1703 Earl of Rosebery, with the same limitation; he *d.* in 1723.

James, 2nd Earl, his only surviving son, succeeded to the Earldom, and in 1741 inherited the family estates and the Baronetcy, on the death of his cousin, Hugh, 3rd Viscount Primrose. He *d.* in 1756, and was succeeded by his only surviving son Neil, 3rd Earl, who was succeeded, in 1814, by his eldest son Archibald-John, present and 4th Earl; who was created in 1828 Baron Rosebery of Rosebery, Co. Edinburgh, in the Peerage of the United Kingdom.

ROSSE, EARL OF. (Parsons.)

Peer of Ireland.

Of this family which settled in Ireland early in the 17th century, were two brothers: Sir William Parsons Bart., appointed one of the Lords Justices of Ireland in 1641; and Sir Laurence, a Baron of the Exchequer of Ireland, ancestor in the 7th degree of the present Earl.

Sir Richard Parsons, grandson of Sir William, the elder brother, was created in 1681 Baron Oxmantown and Viscount Rosse; and his son Richard, 2nd Viscount, was created Earl of Rosse in 1706; these titles all became extinct in 1764, by the death of Richard, 2nd Earl, son of the 1st Earl.

Sir Laurence Parsons, the younger brother, was grandfather of Sir Laurence Parsons of Birr Castle, created a Baronet in 1677; his great-grandson, Sir Laurence, 3rd Bart., had two sons, viz.

1 Sir William, father of Sir Laurence, who succeeded him as 5th Baronet in 1791, and succeeded his uncle as 2nd Earl in 1807.

2 Laurence-Harman, created in 1792 Baron Oxmantown, Co. Dublin, with remainder, in default of male issue, to his nephew Sir Laurence Parsons, Bart.; Viscount Oxmantown 1795; and in 1806 Earl of Rosse, with the same remainder as the Barony; these titles, at his death, devolved on his nephew Laurence, the present and 2nd Earl, and that of Viscount became extinct.

ROSSLYN, EARL OF. (St. Clair-Erskine.)

Peer of the United Kingdom.

The Earl is a collateral branch of the Earl of Marr's family, being 4th in descent from Hon. Sir Charles Erskine of Alva, 4th son of John, 7th Earl of Marr; whose grandson Sir John Erskine, Bart., *m.* Catherine, 2nd daughter and eventually heir of Henry, 8th Lord Sinclair, which Catherine was the lineal representative of the ancient family of St. Clair of Rosslyn, formerly Earls of Orkney.

Sir William St. Clair, of Rosslyn, *m.* in the reign of King David II., Isabel, daughter and co-heir of Malise, Earl of Strathern, Caithness, and Orkney; their son Henry obtained the Earldom of Orkney, and was grandfather of William 3rd Earl, who surrendered his Earldom to the King, and had a grant in 1455, of that of Caithness, which he resigned to William, his son by a second marriage, from whom the present Earl of Caithness descends in the male line, passing over another William, the only son of his first marriage. This William, the elder son, was father of Henry, created Lord Sinclair in 1489; 5th in direct male descent from Henry, 1st Lord Sinclair, was John, 7th Lord, whose daughter and sole heir, Catherine, *m.* in 1659 John Sinclair, Esq., of Herdmanstown, and their son Henry succeeded his grandfather, as 8th Lord Sinclair; he obtained a confirmation of the dignity to his heirs male whatever. He was father of the two following Lords, and several other children, of whom Catherine, the 2nd daughter and eventual heiress of the property, (her elder sister's male issue having failed,) was the wife, as above described, of Sir John Erskine of Alva, Bart; but there are descendants still existing from three of her sisters. Their son, Lieut.-General Sir Henry Erskine, of Alva, Bart., *m.* Janet, daughter of Peter Wedderburn, Esq., of Chesterhall, Co. Midlothian, and sister of Alexander, 1st Earl of Rosslyn, and *d.* in 1765, leaving by her two sons; viz.,

1 Sir James-Sinclair Erskine, Bart, his successor, the present Earl.

2 John, who *d.* 10 Feb. 1817, having *m.* in Dec. 1802, Mary, 3rd daughter of Sir John Mordaunt, Bart, who *d.* 17 July 1821.

Alexander Wedderburn, 1st Earl, and Lord High Chancellor, was son of Peter Wedderburn, a Lord of Session, by the style of Lord Chesterhall; he was born 13 Feb. 1733, created Baron Loughborough of Loughborough, Co. Leicester, in 1780, and again in 1795 Baron Loughborough of Loughborough, Co. Surrey, with remainder to the heirs male of his sister Janet; also Earl of Rosslyn in 1801, with the same remainder. He *d.* 2 Jan. 1805; having *m.* 1st, 31 Dec. 1767, Betty-Anne, only daughter and heir of John Dawson, Esq., who *d.* 15 Feb. 1781; and 2ndly, 12 Sept. 1782, the Hon. Charlotte Courtenay, daughter of William, 1st Viscount Courtenay. The Earl was succeeded, according to the limitation of the patent, by his nephew Sir James-Sinclair Erskine, of Alva, Bart., the present and 2nd Earl.

ROSSMORE, BARON. (WESTENRA.)

Peer of Ireland.

His Lordship is 4th in descent from Warner Westenra, Esq., who settled in Ireland in the reign of CHARLES I.

ROBERT CUNINGHAME, 1st LORD, was *b.* 3 Aug. 1735, *m.* 29 May 1754, Elizabeth, 2nd daughter of Colonel John Murray, (and co-heir of her mother Mary, only daughter and heir of Sir Alexander Cairnes, Bart., widow, without issue by him, of Cadwallader, 7th Lord Blayney;) she *d.* 29 Sept. 1825. He was created in 1796 BARON ROSSMORE of Monaghan, with remainder, failing his issue male, to Henry-Alexander Jones, Esq., son of the Right Hon. Theophilus Jones, by Anne, sister to his Lordship's wife (and 4th daughter of Colonel John Murray,) and his issue male; (he *d. unm.* in the 1st Lord's lifetime;) failing which, to Warner-William Westenra, Esq., and Henry Westenra, Esq., sons of Henry Westenra, Esq., by Harriet, also sister to his Lordship's wife, (and 5th daughter of Colonel John Murray,) and their issue male. His Lordship *d.* in 1801, and was succeeded by WARNER-WILLIAM, the present and 2nd LORD.

ROTHES, EARL OF. (LESLIE.)

Peer of Scotland.

Bartholemew, a Flemish chief, settled in the reign of WILLIAM I., King of Scotland, at Lesley, in Aberdeenshire, from whence his posterity derived their surname. The 5th from him was

Sir Andrew de Lesley, whose eldest son, Norman, was great-grandfather of GEORGE, 1st EARL of ROTHES; and his 4th son, George, was ancestor, in the 4th degree, of Alexander, 1st Earl of Leven, whose grand-daughter Catherine, carried the Earldom of Leven into the family of Melville. *See* Earl of Leven and Melville in this Volume.

GEORGE LESLEY of Rothes, created EARL of ROTHES about 1458, survived his only son Andrew, Master of Rothes, and was succeeded by his grandson GEORGE, 2nd EARL. The latter, and his only brother William, were killed at Flodden Field in 1513; the Earl *d. unm*; his brother left two sons, GEORGE, who succeeded his uncle as 3rd EARL, and John. The 3rd EARL was one of those eight Commissioners from the Scottish Parliament to be present at the marriage of Queen MARY with the Dauphin of France, who so highly incensed the French government by their firm refusal of the crown matrimonial to the Dauphin, that three of their number who died in one night, 28 Nov. 1558, at Dieppe, of whom this Earl was one, were supposed to have been poisoned. His Lordship's eldest son, Norman, Master of Rothes, was the principal actor in the murder of Cardinal Betoun, for which he was found guilty of treason, and forfeited by Parliament in 1546; his father and John, his uncle, were tried as accomplices; the Earl was acquitted, but John Leslie was forfeited. The Master immediately entered the service of the French King, and was mortally wounded in 1554, in a battle between the French and Imperial forces near Cambray, where he had performed almost incredible acts of valour; he *d.* a few days afterwards, before his father, without issue.

ANDREW, 2nd son of the 3rd EARL, succeeded his father as 4th EARL; he had three sons, who left issue:

1 James, Master of Rothes, who *d.* before his father, leaving a son JOHN, 5th EARL, father of JOHN, 6th EARL.

2 Patrick, ancestor of the Lords Lindores, and of the Lords Newark; his male

line is extinct, and the title of Newark is claimed by John Anstruther, the heir-female of the first Lord Newark.

3 Sir John Leslie, whose present representative, John Leslie, of Lumquhat, Esq., claims the title of Lindores, as nearest heir male of the 1st Lord.

JOHN, 5th EARL, succeeded his grandfather and *d.* in 1641. JOHN, his only son, eleven years of age at his father's death, succeeded as 6th Earl; he carried the sword of state at the Coronation of King CHARLES II. in Scotland in 1651, and accompanying the King into England was taken prisoner at the battle of Worcester, but was liberated in 1655. In 1663 he obtained a confirmation of his titles by charter, granting them to himself and the heirs male of his body; which failing, to the eldest heir female of his body, without division, bearing the name and arms of Leslie, with several special limitations over. In 1667 he was appointed Lord High Chancellor of Scotland, and created Duke of Rothes, Marquis of Ballinbreich, Earl of Lesly, Viscount of Lugtoun, Lord Auchmoutie and Caskieberry, with limitation to the heirs male of his body; he *d.* 27 July 1681, without issue male, when the above titles became extinct, but the Earldom devolved on his eldest daughter.

MARGARET, 7th COUNTESS; she *m.* Charles Hamilton, 5th Earl of Haddington, and had two sons: JOHN, 8th EARL; and Thomas, on whom the Earldom of Haddington was settled by patent, and who was ancestor of the present Earl of Haddington.

JOHN, 8th EARL, her eldest son and successor, assumed the name of Hamilton; on the breaking out of the rebellion in 1715, his Lordship, with a detachment of the Scotch Greys, entered the town of Kinross, dispersed a party of the rebels who were about to proclaim the Pretender, and carried Sir Thomas Bruce, of Kinross, prisoner to Stirling. He was also distinguished for his gallantry in the battle of Sheriffmuir, where he commanded the horse volunteers. He *d.* in 1722, having had eight sons, of whom Andrew, the youngest and last survivor, became head of the Haddington branch of the House of Hamilton by the death of his nephew JOHN, 10th EARL of ROTHES, in 1773; but the Earldom of Rothes being entailed on the heir female, and that of Haddington being secured in the junior male line, Mr. Leslie, though he claimed the estates of Rothes, was entirely precluded from either inheritance; he *d. unm.* in 1776, when the Earl of Haddington again became the chief of his house. JOHN, eldest son of the 8th EARL, succeeded as 9th EARL, and *d.* in 1767, when he was succeeded by his only surviving son JOHN, 10th EARL, who dying without issue in 1773, was succeeded by his eldest sister.

JANE-ELIZABETH, 11th COUNTESS, *b.* 5 May 1750, *d.* 2 June 1810; having *m.* 1st, 1 Jan. 1766, George-Raymond Evelyn, Esq., who was father by her of GEORGE-WILLIAM, 12th EARL, and *d.* 23 Dec. 1770; the COUNTESS *m.* 2ndly, 30 Oct. 1772, Sir Lucas Pepys, Bart., M.D., and by him had the issue stated in *The Peerage Volume*, as half-brothers and sister of the 12th EARL; after the Countess's death, Sir Lucas re-married, 29 June 1813, Deborah, daughter of Anthony Askew, Esq., M.D., and *d.* 17 June 1830, when he was succeeded in his Baronetcy by the Hon. Sir Charles Leslie, his eldest son; all his issue by the COUNTESS having assumed the name of Leslie.

GEORGE-WILLIAM, 12th EARL, eldest son of the Countess, by her 1st marriage, succeeded his mother, and assumed the name of Leslie; he *d.* in 1817, having had six daughters, of whom only two survive—see *The Peerage Volume*. Amelia, 2nd daughter by his first marriage, and Julia and Georgiana, his two youngest daughters, *d.* young; LADY HENRIETTA-ANNE, his eldest daughter, succeeded as 13th Countess, and by her marriage with George Gwyther, Esq., who assumed the name of Leslie, left several children—see *The Peerage Volume*—of whom GEORGE-WILLIAM-EVELYN-LESLIE, present and 14th EARL, succeeded her in 1819.

ROXBURGHE, DUKE OF. (Innes-Ker.)

Peer of Scotland.

For the origin of the noble house of Ker, *see* the title of Lothian in this Volume.

Sir Robert Ker of Cessford, 10th in descent from John Ker, his first recorded ancestor, was at an early age appointed Warden of the Borders. In 1597, for some infraction of the border truce, he fell into the custody of the Archbishop of York, who writes of him to the Lord Treasurer Burleigh, "I understand that the gentleman is wise and valiant, but somewhat haughty and resolute." He was soon released and created a Peer, by the title of Lord Roxburghe. He held important official employments through the reigns of James I. and Charles I., and on the breaking out of the Rebellion adhered to the King. In 1616 he was created Earl of Roxburghe, Lord Ker of Cessford and Cavertoun; and having survived his two sons, William and Harry, both successively styled Lord Ker, he obtained in 1646 a new investiture of the titles, to himself and the heirs male of his body; failing which, to his heirs and assigns, to be nominated by himself: in 1648, he executed a deed of nomination, in favour of Sir William Drummond, 5th son of John, 2nd Earl of Perth, by Lady Jane Ker, eldest daughter of the said 1st Earl of Roxburghe, provided he married the eldest daughter of Harry Lord Ker; and after him, or failing this condition, the daughters of Harry Lord Ker, his son, deceased, and their heirs male successively; failing which, his own nearest heirs male whatsoever; he *d.* in 1650. His son, Harry Lord Ker, who *d.* before him in 1643, left four daughters; viz.:

1 Jane, *m.* to Sir William Drummond, who succeeded as 2nd Earl, assumed the name of Ker, and was ancestor of the Earls and Dukes of Roxburghe, to the death of William, 4th Duke, in 1805.

2 Anne, *m.* to John, 4th Earl of Wigtoun, without male issue.

3 Margaret, *m.* in 1666 to Sir James Innes of Innes, Bart., by whom she was mother of Sir Harry Innes, Bart., whose son, Sir Harry Innes, Bart., was father of Sir James, 5th Duke.

William, 2nd Earl, *d.* in 1675; he had four sons, of whom Robert, eldest son, succeeded as 3rd Earl; and John, 4th son, inherited the title of Lord Bellenden; besides other sons, he had John, 3rd Lord Bellenden, (father of Ker, 4th, and Robert, 6th Lord Bellenden; John, 5th Lord Bellenden, son of the 4th Lord, *d.* without issue;) and William, father of William, 7th Lord Bellenden, who succeeded as 4th Duke of Roxburghe.

Robert, 3rd Earl, going by sea to Scotland in 1682, with James Duke of York, was lost in the Gloucester frigate, when that vessel struck off Yarmouth, and the Duke of York narrowly escaped in his boat. He was father of Robert, 4th Earl, who *d. unm.* in 1696, and John, 5th Earl, who succeeded his brother. He was created in 1707 Duke of Roxburghe, Marquis of Beaumont and Cessford, Earl of Kelso, Viscount of Broxmouth, and Lord Ker of Cessford and Cavertoun, with remainder, failing the heirs male of his body, to the other heirs destined to succeed to the title of Earl of Roxburghe; he *d.* in 1741, leaving one son Robert, his successor, 2nd Duke, who *d.* 1755, and was succeeded by his eldest son John, 3rd Duke, K.G., he *d.* in 1804, and with him expired the male line of Robert, 3rd Earl.

William, 4th Duke, who succeeded, was descended as above, from John Lord Bellenden, 4th son of the 2nd Earl, and on his death in 1805 the whole male line of the 2nd Earl became extinct. After a tedious litigation, the House of Lords in 1812 decreed the titles to Sir James Innes, Bart., 5th Duke, the heir male as above recited of Sir James Innes, Bart., by the Honourable Margaret Ker, 3rd daughter of Harry Lord Ker, son and heir of the 1st Earl of Roxburghe. His Grace *d.* in 1823,

4th Lord, who *d.* in 1783, and was succeeded by his eldest son, James, 5th Lord. He *d.* in 1789, having had nine children, six of whom *d.* young or *unm.*, the three survivors are stated in the Peerage; he was succeeded by his eldest son, James, present and 6th Lord.

RUTLAND, DUKE OF. (Manners.)

Peer of England.

The name of Manners appears as of considerable note in the North of England, very soon after the Conquest. The first of his Grace's ancestors on record is Sir Robert Manners, Lord of the Manor of Ethale, in Northumberland, but at what date is unknown; Sir Robert Manners, 7th in descent from him, lived in the reign of King Henry III.

The 7th in descent from the last Sir Robert Manners, was another Sir Robert, who, in the reign of King Edward IV., obtained a large addition to his estates, and among other possessions the ancient seat of Belvoir Castle, in Lincolnshire, by his marriage with Eleanor, daughter, and at length heir of Edmund, 11th Baron Roos, by whom he had a son,

George, 12th Baron Roos, who *m.* Anne, sole daughter and heir of Sir Thomas St. Leger, by Anne Plantagenet, sister of King Edward IV., and was father by her of

Thomas, 13th Baron Roos, K.G., who succeeded his father in 1513, was created Earl of Rutland, in 1525, and *d.* in 1543; he had, besides other issue, two sons, viz.:

1 Henry, 2nd Earl, whose issue male failed on the death of George, 7th Earl.

2 Sir John Manners, whose eldest son, Sir George, was father of Sir John, who became 8th Earl.

Henry, 2nd Earl, Baron Roos, K.G., *d.* in 1563, leaving two sons:

1 Edward, 3rd Earl, Baron Roos, K.G., *d.* in 1587, without issue male, leaving an only daughter, Elizabeth, Baroness Roos, who *m.* William Cecil, son and heir of Thomas, 1st Earl of Exeter, and *d.* in 1591; leaving an only son, one year old at her death, William Cecil, who succeeded her as Baron Roos, and *d. unm.* in 1618.

2 John, who succeeded his brother as 4th Earl, and *d.* in 1588; three of his sons were successive Earls of Rutland, viz:

- 1 Roger, 5th Earl, the intimate friend of Robert Devereux, Earl of Essex, in whose insurrection in 1600 he was implicated and committed to the Tower, but released on the accession of King James I. in 1603.
- 2 Francis, 6th Earl, K.G., who succeeded his brother; he was created in 1616 Baron Roos of Hamlake, with remainder to his issue male; in 1618, he succeeded to the ancient Barony of Roos, on the death of William Cecil, Lord Roos, and *d.* in 1632, without issue male, when the new title of Roos became extinct; and the ancient Barony devolved on Katherine, his only daughter and heir, widow of George Villiers, 1st Duke of Buckingham, who *d.* in 1666, and was succeeded by her son George, 2nd Duke, on whose death in 1687 this Barony fell into abeyance between the two sisters of the 5th, 6th, and 7th Earls of Rutland, viz. Lady Bridget, wife of Robert Tyrwhitt, Esq.; and Lady Frances, wife of William, Lord Willoughby of Parham; the heir general of Lady Frances is the present Baroness de Roos, in whose favour the Barony was called out of abeyance in 1806.
- 3 George, 7th Earl, succeeded his brother, and *d.* without issue in 1641, when the Earldom devolved on the grandson of Sir John Manners, 2nd son of the 1st Earl.

John, 8th Earl, was succeeded in 1679 by his only surviving son, John, 9th

Earl, who had been summoned by writ to the House of Peers in 1679, a few months before the death of his father, as Baron Manners of Haddon; he was created in 1703 Marquis of Granby, Co. Notts., and Duke of Rutland; he *d.* in 1711, and was succeeded by his only surviving son, John, 2nd Duke, K.G., he *d.* in 1721 having had a numerous issue by two marriages; his 8th son, Lord Robert Manners, *d.* in 1782, leaving by his marriage with Mary, daughter of —— Digge, Esq., who *d.* in 1829, in her ninety-second year, two still surviving daughters, stated in *The Peerage Volume*, and two sons, General Robert Manners, who *d.* in 1823, and George Manners, Esq., who *d.* 1828, both *unm.*

John, 3rd Duke, K.G., succeeded his father; he *d.* in 1779; having *m.* Bridget only daughter and heir of Robert Sutton, Lord Lexington. His two younger sons, Lord Robert, who *d. unm.* in 1762, and Lord George, successively assumed the name of Sutton, on succeeding to the Lexington property. The latter *d.* in 1783, leaving a numerous issue, of whom the survivors, Lord Manners and Mrs. Dickins, will be found in *The Peerage Volume*. Louisa-Bridget, wife of the late Edward-Lockwood Percival, Esq.; Charlotte, wife of Thomas Lockwood, Esq.; and Mary, wife of the late Rev. Richard Lockwood, are deceased. John Manners, Esq. of Kellam, his eldest son, *d.* in 1826, leaving by Anne Manners, illegitimate daughter of his uncle, John, Marquis of Granby, the issue stated in *The Peerage Volume*; and the most Rev. Charles Lord Archbishop of Canterbury, his 2nd son, left by Mary, daughter of Thomas Thoroton, Esq., his surviving widow, a numerous issue, for whom see *The Peerage Volume*. John, Marquis of Granby, the Duke's eldest son, celebrated for his brilliant campaigns in Germany, *d.* in 1770 before his father, leaving two sons, Charles, 4th Duke, and the gallant Lord Robert Manners, Captain of his Majesty's ship *Resolution*, in the command of which he was mortally wounded, in the glorious engagement with the French fleet in the West Indies, 12 April 1782.

Charles, 4th Duke, K.G., succeeded his grandfather, and *d.* whilst Lord Lieutenant of Ireland in 1787, and was succeeded by his minor son, John-Henry, present and 5th Duke, K.G.

ST. ALBANS, DUKE OF. (Beauclerk.)

Peer of England.

Charles, the 1st Duke of St. Albans, K.G., on whom his Royal Father conferred the name of Beauclerk, was natural son of King Charles II., by the celebrated Mrs. Eleanor Gwin. He was *b.* 8 May 1670; created Baron of Heddington and Earl of Burford, both Co. Oxford, in 1676; and Duke of St. Albans in 1684. He was also appointed Hereditary Grand Falconer of England. He *m.* the Lady Diana de Vere, daughter and eventually sole heir of Aubrey de Vere, 20th and last Earl of Oxford of that noble family, created to the Earldom by the Empress Maude, and confirmed by King Henry II. in 1155. He *d.* in 1726, having, besides others who *d.* without issue, the five sons following:

1 Charles, 2nd Duke, K.G., who *d.* in 1751, and his issue male became extinct on the death of his son, George, 3rd Duke, 1 Feb. 1786.

2 Lord William, who *d.* in 1733; his only surviving son, Colonel Charles Beauclerk, *d.* in 1775, leaving one son, George, who succeeded his cousin as 4th Duke, on whose death, 15 Feb. 1787, the issue male of his grandfather Lord William became extinct.

3 Lord Vere, created in 1750 Baron Vere of Hanworth, in which title he was succeeded in 1781 by his only surviving son, Aubrey, who succeeded his cousin as 5th Duke; he *d.* in 1802, leaving besides a daughter, Lady Catherine-Elizabeth, who *d.* in 1803, wife of the late Rev. James Burgess, and the surviving issue described in *The Peerage Volume*, two sons, viz.:

1 AUBREY, 6th DUKE, *b.* 21 Aug. 1765, *d.* 12 Aug. 1815; having *m.* 1st, 9 July 1788, Mary, daughter of —— Moses, Esq., who *d.* 18 Aug. 1800; and 2ndly, 15 Aug. 1802, Louisa-Grace, 3rd daughter of John Manners, Esq. by Louisa, now Countess of Dysart; she *d.* 19 Feb. 1816. The Duke had issue by both marriages, viz.:

by the 1st marriage,

1 Lady Mary, Countess of Coventry.

by the 2nd marriage,

2 AUBREY, 7th DUKE, *b.* 7 April 1815, succeeded his father 12 Aug. 1815, and *d.* 19 Feb. 1816.

2 WILLIAM, 8th DUKE, who succeeded his infant nephew in 1816, and *d.* in 1825, when he was succeeded by his eldest son, WILLIAM-AUBREY-DE-VERE, the present and 9th DUKE.

ST. GERMANS, EARL OF. (ELIOT.)

Peer of the United Kingdom.

This family had flourished in the Counties of Devon and Cornwall for many generations before John Eliot, who was ancestor in the 8th degree of

EDWARD CRAGGS ELIOT, Esq., created in 1784 BARON ELIOT of St. Germans, Co. Cornwall; he *d.* 28 Feb. 1804, leaving three sons—see *The Peerage Volume*; 1 Edward, who *d.* before his father in 1797, without issue male; 2 JOHN, 2nd LORD, created in 1815 EARL of ST. GERMANS, with remainder, failing his issue male, to his brother William and his issue male; he *d.* without issue in 1823; 3 WILLIAM, present and 2nd EARL, who succeeded his brother.

ST. HELENS, BARON. (FITZ-HERBERT.)

Peer of Ireland and of the United Kingdom.

Herbert Fitz-Herbert, the ancestor of this family, came into England with William the Conqueror. From his descendant, William Fitz-Herbert, of Somersall Herbert, Derbyshire, William Fitz-Herbert, Esq., of Tissington, Co. Derby, his Lordship's father, was 15th in paternal descent. He *d.* in 1772, leaving issue by his marriage with Mary, daughter of Littleton-Poyntz Meynell, Esq., who *d.* in 1753,

1 Sir William Fitz-Herbert, *b.* 27 May 1748, created a Baronet in 1783, *d.* 30 July 1791; having *m.* 14 Oct. 1777, Sarah, only daughter of William Perrin, Esq., by whom, who *d.* in 1795, he had issue,

1 Sir Anthony-Perrin Fitz-Herbert, Bart., *b.* 21 July 1779, *d. unm.* 2 April 1798.

2 Charlotte, *b.* 20 June 1782.

3 Sir Henry Fitz-Herbert, present Baronet, *b.* 4 Aug. 1783, *m.* 27 Dec. 1805, Agnes, daughter of the late Rev. William Beresford, who was *b.* 23 April 1783. They have issue: 1 Selina, *b.* 22 Nov. 1806, *m.* 12 Aug. 1830, Francis Wright, Esq. 2 William, *b.* 2 June 1808. 3 Richard-Henry, Lieut. Rifle Brigade, *b.* 29 Oct. 1809. 4 Agnes-Louisa, *b.* 12 Sept. 1812, *d.* 12 Sept. 1817. 5 Alleyne, *b.* 9 May 1815. 6 Harriet-Maria, *b.* 31 Oct. 1816. 7 Anthony, *b.* 10 May 1818. 8 John-Knight, *b.* 27 March 1820. 9 Judith, *b.* 1 May 1821. 10 Frances-Rafella, *b.* 23 Nov. 1823. 11 A daughter, *b.* 3 Sept. 1828.

2 Selina, *b.* 31 Oct. 1751, *d.* 2 Jan. 1823; having *m.* Henry-Gally Knight, Esq., who *d.* 6 April 1808.

3 Alleyne Fitz-Herbert, Esq., who having been employed in some very important diplomatic missions, was created an Irish Peer in 1791, by the title of Baron St. Helens; in 1801, he was further created Baron St. Helens in the Isle of Wight, Co. Southampton, in the Peerage of the United Kingdom, and is the present Lord.

ST.-JOHN, BARON. (St.-John.)

Peer of England.

Hugh de Port, Baron of Basing, held fifty-five Lordships in Southampton, according to Domesday-Book, some of which descended to him from his ancestors before the Conquest. His great-grandson, Adam de Port, Baron of Basing, m. Mabel, daughter of Reginald de Aurevalle, by Muriel, daughter of Roger de St.-John, whose grandfather, William de St.-John, came into England with the Conqueror. William, their son, assumed the name of St.-John, and was Baron St.-John of Basing, which Barony is now in abeyance between the co-heirs of his great-grandson, John, Lord St.-John of Basing; of whom the Marquis of Winchester, whose ancestor was created Baron St.-John of Basing, is one. William St.-John, uncle of the said John, and grandson of William, the 1st Lord St.-John of Basing, was ancestor in the 7th degree of

Sir Oliver St.-John, who by Margaret, sister and heir of John, Lord Beauchamp of Bletsho, had two sons; 1 Sir John, great-grandfather of Oliver, created Lord St.-John of Bletsho in 1558; 2 Oliver, ancestor of Viscount Bolingbroke.

Oliver, 1st Lord, had, besides other issue, two sons; 1 John, 2nd Lord, who succeeded his father in 1582; he *d.* in 1596, without male issue, and the Barony of Beauchamp of Bletsho is now vested in the Duke of Gordon, the heir general of Anne, his only daughter; 2

Oliver, 3rd Lord, who succeeded his brother, and *d.* in 1618; he had, besides other sons,

1 Oliver, 4th Lord, his eldest son and successor, who was created Earl of Bolingbroke in 1624, and *d.* in 1646; he had four sons, of whom the two younger left no issue. Oliver, Lord St. John, the eldest, a man of dissolute habits, had accumulated so large a debt as to be compelled to fly the kingdom; till King Charles I. being informed of his situation, and that means could be found, if he were at home and at liberty, to pay his debts, and thereby to relieve many worthy persons who were securities for him, called him to the House of Peers. From the time of his taking his seat, he voted in every instance against the government; and when the disputes between the King and Parliament had grown into open war, he received a commission in the army of the Parliament, and was killed in 1642, in his father's lifetime, at the battle of Edgehill. He left three daughters, but no male issue. Sir Paulet, 2nd son, *d.* also before his father, leaving two sons: Oliver, 2nd Earl and 5th Lord, who *d.* without issue in 1688; and Paulet, 3rd Earl of Bolingbroke and 6th Lord St.-John, who succeeded his brother, and *d.* in 1711, when the Earldom became extinct.

2 Sir Rowland, whose son, Sir Oliver, was created a Baronet in 1660; he *d.* in 1661, and was succeeded by his son,

Sir St.-Andrew St.-John, Bart., who had besides other sons, 1 Sir St.-Andrew, whose son, Sir St.-Andrew, succeeded as 7th Lord, on the death of Paulet, 3rd Earl of Bolingbroke, and dying an infant in 1714, was succeeded by his uncle; 2 William, 8th Lord, who *d.* in 1720; and 3 Rowland, 9th Lord, who *d.* in 1722, both *unm.*; 4

John, 10th Lord; he *d.* in 1757, having had five sons, of whom three left

1 John, 11th Lord, who *d.* in 1767, leaving the three daughters described in *The Peerage Volume*, and three sons, viz.:

1 Henry-Beauchamp, 12th Lord, his successor; he survived his only son, Henry-Beauchamp, and *d.* in 1805, leaving four daughters, all married, for whom see *The Peerage Volume*.

2 St.-Andrew, 13th Lord, who succeeded his brother, and *d.* in 1817; he was succeeded by his infant son, St.-Andrew-Beauchamp, present and 14th Lord, who has now nearly attained his majority. The 13th Lord left also a 2nd son, William, who *d.* an infant; for his widow, re-married to Judge Vaughan, and his only daughter, see *The Peerage Volume*.

3 The Hon. Lieut.-Colonel George St.-John, *b.* 19 Oct. 1764, *m.* 10 May 1795, Lavinia, daughter of William Breton-Wolstenholme, Esq.; he was lost, with his Lady and four children, on his homeward passage from Bombay, in the *Prince of Wales* East-Indiaman, in 1804. Their two eldest sons, having been previously in England, are still living, and are described in *The Peerage Volume*.

2 The Hon. and Very Rev. St.-Andrew St.-John, Dean of Worcester; he was *b.* 28 Jan. 1732, and *d.* 23 March 1795; having *m.* in 1759, Sarah, daughter of Thomas Chase, Esq., by whom, who *d.* 29 Jan. 1806, he had issue, John-Francis-Seymour, who has assumed the name of Fleming, his 2nd son; St.-Andrew and Henry, his 3rd and 4th sons, who are all three living, with numerous families, and are described in *The Peerage Volume*; one daughter, Mrs. Barne, also living, and in *The Peerage Volume*; and two sons deceased, viz. Ambrose St.-John, Esq., his eldest son, who was *b.* 27 Sept. 1760, and *d.* 29 Nov. 1822; having *m.* 22 Feb. 1790, Arabella, daughter of Sir James Hamlyn, Bart., by whom, who *d.* 18 June 1805, he had the issue stated in *The Peerage Volume*; and Thomas St.-John, Esq., who *d.* in 1827, leaving issue by two marriages, for whom see *The Peerage Volume*.

3 The Hon. Capt. Henry St.-John, R.N., who was *b.* 1 June 1740, and *d.* 17 April 1780; leaving by his marriage with Mary, daughter of —— Schuyler, Esq., who *d.* 6 Nov. 1785, a son, Henry St.-John, Esq.—See *The Peerage Volume*.

ST.-VINCENT, VISCOUNT. (Jervis.)

Peer of the United Kingdom.

Swinfen Jervis, Esq., father of the late Earl St.-Vincent, was 7th in paternal descent from James Jervis, Esq., of Chatkyll, Staffordshire, in the time of Queen Elizabeth; he was *b.* Nov. 1703, and *d.* 21 Feb. 1771; having *m.* in 1727, Elizabeth, daughter of George Parker, Esq., who *d.* in March 1784. Their issue were,

1 William Jervis, of Meaford, Esq., who was *b.* in May 1728, and *d.* without issue 6 March 1813; having *m.* 28 May 1777, Jane, daughter of Thomas Hatsell, Esq.

2 The distinguished Admiral Sir John Jervis, K.B., who after a series of splendid services, fought the famous battle off Cape St. Vincent in Feb. 1797, in which he won his Peerage. He was created in June following Baron Jervis of Meaford, Co. Stafford, and Earl St. Vincent; and in 1801, Viscount St. Vincent, with remainder to his nephews, Captain William-Henry Ricketts, R.N., and Edward-Jervis Ricketts, Esq.; and to his niece, Mary, Countess of Northesk, and their heirs male respectively. The Earl was *b.* 20 Jan. 1735, and *d.* without issue 15 March 1823, when the Earldom and Barony became extinct. He *m.* 5 June 1783, Martha, daughter of Chief Baron Sir Thomas Parker, who *d.* 8 Feb. 1816.

3 Elizabeth, *m.* the Rev. —— Batewell, and *d.* without issue.

4 Mary, *m.* to William-Henry Ricketts, Esq., by whom she was mother of the late Captain William-Henry Ricketts, R.N., who assumed the name of Jervis, and

d. without male issue in 1805; of Edward-Jervis Ricketts, Esq., who has al-
assumed the name of Jervis, succeeded to the title of Viscount on the death of h
gallant uncle, and is the present Peer; and of Mary, now Countess-dowager
Northesk—for all of whom see *The Peerage Volume.*

SALISBURY, MARQUIS OF. (Gascoigne-Cecil.)

Peer of Great Britain.

Sir Robert Cecil, Secretary of State to Queen Elizabeth and King James I. and at length Lord High Treasurer, 2nd son of the celebrated Lord Treasurer Bu- leigh, and brother of Thomas, 1st Earl of Exeter, was created in 1603 Baron Ce of Essendon, Co. Rutland; in 1604, Viscount Cranbourne, Co. Dorset; and in 1605, Earl of Salisbury. He was a Knight of the Garter, and *d.* in 1612, when was succeeded by his only son, William, 2nd Earl, K.G. He *d.* in 1668, havi survived his eldest son, Charles, Viscount Cranbourne, whose eldest son, Jam 3rd Earl, K.G., *d.* in 1683. He was successively followed in the Earldom by son, grandson, and great-grandson, all named James. The 4th Earl *d.* in 16 the 5th Earl in 1728; and the 6th Earl in 1780. The latter was succeede his only son, James, 7th Earl, K.G., who was created Marquis of Salisbury 1789, and dying in 1823, was succeeded by his only son, James-Brownlow-Wi- liam, present and 2nd Marquis, who by Royal sign manual assumed the name Gascoigne, on his marriage with Frances-Mary, daughter and sole heir of Bamb Gascoigne, Esq.

SALTOUN, BARON. (Fraser.)

Peer of Scotland.

Alexander Abernethy of Saltoun and Rothemay, was created a Peer of Parli- ment in 1445, by the title of Lord Abernethy of Saltoun; he was father William, 2nd Lord, his successor, and James, 3rd Lord, who succeeded brother; he was followed in uninterrupted paternal descent by Alexander, 4 Lord, his son; William, 5th Lord; Alexander, 6th Lord; George, 7th Lo who *d.* in 1600; John, 8th Lord, and Alexander, 9th Lord, who *d.* in 16 With this latter expired the male line of the Lords Abernethy of Saltoun, and nearest heir was the son of Margaret Abernethy, eldest daughter of the 7th Lo by her marriage with Sir Alexander Fraser of Philorth, 12th in descent from Gilb Fraser, Sheriff of Traquair, in the reign of Alexander II. Their son

Alexander, 10th Lord Saltoun, consequently succeeded to the Peerage, as he of line. He advanced large sums in aid of the Royal cause in the civil wars; the command of a regiment in the expedition into England for the rescue Charles I. in 1648, and accompanied Charles II. to the battle of Worces whence he had the good fortune to escape into Scotland. He *d.* in 1693, in the year of his age, having survived his only son Alexander, Master of Saltoun, who in 1682, and his eldest grandson Alexander, who *d. unm.* in 1673.

William, 11th Lord, his 2nd grandson, succeeded him, and *d.* in 1715; leavi three sons, viz.

1 Alexander, 12th Lord, who *d.* in 1748; leaving two sons, Alexander, 1 Lord, his successor, who *d. unm.* in 1751, and George, 14th Lord, who succee his brother, and dying in 1781, was succeeded by his eldest son Alexand 15th Lord; to whom, in 1793, succeeded his eldest son, Alexander-Georg present and 16th Lord.

2 The Hon. William Fraser, who *d.* in 1727; having *m.* Lady Katharine-Anne Erskine, eldest daughter of David, 4th Earl of Buchan, by whom, who *d.* in 1733, he had an only son, William Fraser, Esq., of Fraserfield, who *d.* in 1788, leaving by his marriage with Rachel, daughter of the Rev. Hugh Kennedy, the numerous issue stated in *The Peerage Volume.*

3 The Hon. James Fraser of Lonmay, who by Lady Eleanor Lindsay, 3rd daughter of Colin, 3rd Earl of Balcarres, left an only son, William, who *d. unm.*

SANDWICH, EARL OF. (MONTAGU.)

Peer of England.

The Earl is a younger branch of the family of the Duke of Manchester.

Sir Edward Montagu of Boughton *d.* in 1602, leaving six sons, viz.

1 Edward, created Baron Montagu of Boughton in 1621; his male line failed in 1749, on the death of his great-grandson, John, 2nd Duke of Montagu; he is represented in the female line by the present Duke of Buccleuch.

2 Sir Walter Montagu of Houghton, Co. Northampton, who *d.* without issue in 1615.

3 Sir Henry, created Earl of Manchester, ancestor of the present Duke of Manchester.

4 Sir Charles Montagu of Cranbrook, Co. Essex, *d.* in 1625, without male issue, leaving three daughters, his co-heirs, who all left issue.

5 James, Bishop of Bath and Wells, and subsequently of Winchester; he *d. unm.* in 1618.

6 Sir Sidney Montagu, ancestor of the Earl of Sandwich. He was an opponent of the measures of King CHARLES I. in Parliament, till the contest between the two parties grew to a civil war; he was then committed to the Tower by the ruling powers, for producing in the House his Majesty's declaration that all persons taking up arms against him were traitors. He *d.* in 1644, and his eldest son Henry dying six months after him, Edward, the only surviving son, succeeded to the estate.

EDWARD MONTAGU, Esq., the surviving son of Sir Sidney, early took an active part in the civil war. He was in the rebel army in the battles of Marston Moor, Naseby and others, but seceded from Parliament when he found that body under the control of the army. He returned to the administration of public affairs in 1653, was soon after appointed a Lord of the Treasury, and joint Admiral of England; and having the command at sea at the time of Cromwell's death, he signified to the King, before the assembling of that Parliament which voted the restoration of the Royal family, that the fleet and himself were at his Majesty's disposal. For this service he was created in 1660 Baron Montagu of St. Neot's, Co. Huntingdon, Viscount Hinchinbroke, and EARL of SANDWICH. He was Vice-Admiral of England, and in that capacity served under the Duke of York in the great battle of Lowestoffe in June 1665; in Sept. the same year he beat a fleet convoying the Dutch East Indiamen, and took eight men of war. He was then appointed Ambassador Extraordinary, to conclude a peace with Spain, which he successfully accomplished. On the breaking out of the new Dutch war in 1672, he again fought under the command of the Duke of York in the great battle in Solbay, on the coast of Suffolk, on the 28th of May in that year; and was left in the *Royal James*, carrying 100 guns and 1000 men, to sustain the attack of the whole squadron of Van Ghent, aided by four fire-ships; after disabling, in this unequal contest, which he stood for many hours, seven of the enemy's ships and sinking three of the fire-ships, the *Royal James* was at last burnt by the fourth. The body of the Vice-Admiral was found on the 10th of June, and was afterwards interred, with every mark of honour, in Westminster Abbey. He left six sons, three of whom *d. unm.*; the other three were,

1 Edward, 2nd Earl.

2 The Hon. Sidney Montagu, who *m.* the daughter and heir of Sir Francis Wortley of Wortley, Co. York. For his posterity, *see* Lord Wharncliffe, in this volume.

3. The Hon. Charles Montagu, 5th son, father of James Montagu of Newbold-Vernon, Co. Leicester, Esq., who *d. unm.* in 1748, and of Edward Montagu, Esq., who succeeded his brother at Newbold-Vernon, and *d.* in 1775; having *m.* Elizabeth daughter of Matthew Robinson, Esq., of West Layton, Co. York. This celebrated literary Lady, author of the *Essay on the Genius of Shakspeare*, and other works, survived him till 1800, and left her large estates to her nephew, Matthew Robinson, Esq., who assumed the name of Montagu, and was the late Lord Rokeby.

Edward, 2nd Earl, *d.* in 1689, and was succeeded by his eldest son Edward, 3rd Earl, who *d.* in 1729; his only son Edward-Richard, Viscount Hinchinbroke, *d.* before him in 1722, leaving, besides other issue, John, his eldest son, who succeeded his grandfather as 4th Earl; he *d.* in 1792, and was succeeded by his eldest son John, 5th Earl; he was *b.* 26 Jan. 1744, and *d.* 6 June 1814; having *m.* 1st, 1 March 1766, Lady Elizabeth Montagu, only surviving daughter of George, 2nd and last Earl of Halifax, who *d.* 1 July 1768; and 2ndly, 25 April 1772, Lady Mary-Henrietta Powlett, eldest daughter of Harry, 6th and last Duke of Bolton, *b.* Oct. 1753, *d.* 30 March 1779; by his 2nd marriage he was father of George-John, his successor, 6th Earl, who *d.* in 1818, and was succeeded by his only son John-William, 7th Earl.

SANDYS, BARONESS. (Hill.)

Peeress of the United Kingdom.

Samuel Sandys, Esq., was created Baron Sandys in 1743, and *d.* 21 April 1770; he had seven sons, of whom

1 Edwin, 2nd Lord, the eldest and last surviving son, was *b.* in 1725, and *d.* without issue, 11 March 1797, when the title became extinct; and

2 Martin, (4th son,) *d.* 26 Dec. 1768; having *m.* 7 June 1760, Mary, only child and heir of William Trumbull, Esq., by whom, who *d.* in 1769, he had an only child, Mary, the present Baroness, widow of Arthur, 2nd Marquis of Downshire; she was created in 1802 Baroness Sandys of Ombersley, Co. Worcester, with remainder to her 2nd son Arthur-Moyses-William Hill, and his younger Brothers, and their heirs male successively; failing which, to her eldest son Arthur, present Marquis of Downshire, and his heirs male.

SAYE AND SELE, BARON. (Eardley-Twisleton-Fiennes.)

Peer of England.

Geoffrey de Say was summoned to Parliament in 1313; John, 4th Lord Say, his great-grandson, *d.* in 1382, leaving Elizabeth, his sister and heir; she *d.* without issue in 1399, and her co-heirs were the descendants of her two aunts, daughters and at length co-heirs of Geoffrey, 2nd Lord, viz.: 1 Idonea, wife of Sir John Clinton, whose heir general is the present Lord Clinton; and 2 Joan, wife of Sir William Fiennes, and mother of

Sir William Fiennes, who had two sons:

1 Roger, father of Richard Fiennes, who having *m.* Joan, grand-daughter of Thomas.

6th Baron Dacre, was summoned to Parliament as Baron Dacre: his heir general is the present Lord Dacre, between whom and Lord Clinton the Barony of Say, by writ 1513, is in abeyance.

2 James Fiennes, summoned to Parliament in 1447, as Baron Say and Sele, and afterwards, in the same year, created to that title, but it is uncertain whether with limitation to his heirs male; he was Lord High Treasurer in the reign of King Henry VI., and was beheaded in an insurrection of the Londoners, after a mock trial in Guildhall, in 1450. William, his son and heir, 2nd Lord, was killed at the battle of Barnet; and after him no summons was issued to his descendants, Henry, Richard, Edward, and Richard, the 3rd, 4th, 5th, and 6th Lords in direct lineal succession; Richard, 7th Lord, son and heir of the 6th Lord, obtained in 1603, a confirmation of this dignity to him and the heirs of his body; he *d.* in 1613. William, 8th Lord, his son, was created Viscount Say and Sele in 1624, which title became extinct in 1781, by the death of Richard, 6th Viscount, his last male descendant.

James, 2nd Viscount, eldest son of the 1st Viscount, succeeded him in 1662, and *d.* in 1674 without issue male, when the title of Viscount devolved on his nephew, and the Barony of Say and Sele by the patent of 1603, also that by writ 1447, unless afterwards limited by creation to the heirs male, fell into abeyance between his two daughters and co-heirs, viz.:

1 Elizabeth, who *m.* Sir John Twisleton, by whom she had an only daughter and heir, Cecil, wife of George Twisleton, Esq., and by him mother of Fiennes Twisleton, Esq., whose son John was father of Thomas, Lord Saye and Sele.

2 Frances, wife of Andrew Ellis, Esq., whose issue failed in 1715.

In 1781, Thomas Twisleton, Esq. claimed and was allowed the Barony; he *d.* in 1788, and was succeeded by his eldest son, Gregory-William, the present Lord, who in 1825 assumed, by two separate instruments under the Royal sign manual, the additional names of Fiennes and Eardley; the latter in consequence of his marriage with Maria-Marow, eldest daughter and co-heir of Sampson, late Lord Eardley.

SCARBOROUGH, EARL OF. (Lumley-Saunderson.)

Peer of England.

This family descends from Liulph, a nobleman of great note in the time of Edward the Confessor, who was stripped of his large possessions by the Normans; he *m.* Algitha, daughter of Aldred, Earl of Northumberland, (and sister to Cospatrick, ancestor of the Earl of Abergavenny, the Earl of Home, and Lord Dundas,) and was father, besides other issue, of Ughtred, whose son, Sir William, is styled de Lumley, from his castle of Lumley, in Durham. The 6th in descent from him was Ralph de Lumley, summoned to Parliament in 1384; he was killed at Cirencester in 1400, in a rebellion against King Henry IV. for the restoration of Richard II., and was attainted. Sir John Lumley, 2nd Lord Lumley, his son, was restored in blood, but was not summoned to Parliament; he distinguished himself in the French wars under King Henry V., and was killed at the battle of Baugy in 1421. Thomas, 3rd Lord, his son, was governor of Scarborough castle; he obtained in the first year of King Edward IV. the reversal of his grandfather's attainder, and received summons to Parliament; he was succeeded by his son George, 4th Lord, who, as well as his successors in the title, were all distinguished in the border wars between the Scotch and English nations; he *d.* in 1508, and was succeeded by his grandson, Richard, 5th Lord, eldest son of his son Thomas, who *d.* before him. Richard, 5th Lord, *d.* in 1510, leaving two sons:

1 John, 6th Lord, was one of the principal commanders of the vanguard in the battle of Flodden, and was in the fiercest of the fight, being opposed to the Earls of

of Lancaster, and made his chief seat at Sefton. He was ancestor in the 17th degree of

Sir Richard Molyneux, created a Baronet in 1611, and Viscount and Baron Molyneux of Maryborough, Queen's County, in 1628; he *d.* in 1632, leaving, besides other issue, two sons, Richard and Caryll, successive Viscounts; they both took up arms for King Charles at the commencement of the rebellion, raised a regiment of horse and another of foot, and were both in Oxford when it surrendered to the Parliamentary army. They joined King Charles II. when he marched into England from Scotland, and were with him at the battle of Worcester, from which they both escaped, and Richard, 2nd Viscount, dying soon after without issue. Caryl, 3rd Viscount, his brother and successor, was outlawed and excepted from Cromwell's act of grace. He *d.* in 1699, and was succeeded by

William, 4th Viscount, his only surviving son, who *d.* in 1717, leaving issue:

1 Richard, 5th Viscount, who *d.* without surviving issue male in 1738.

2 Caryll, 6th Viscount, who succeeded his brother, and *d.* in 1745, leaving three sons, viz.:

1 Richard, 7th Viscount, in holy orders of the Church of Rome, who was succeeded by his next brother.

2 William, 8th Viscount, who *d.* unm. in 1759.

3 Thomas, who *d.* in 1756, leaving an only son, Charles-William, who succeeded his uncle as 9th Viscount, was created Earl of Sefton in 1771, and *d.* in 1795, when he was succeeded by his only son, William-Philip, present and 2nd Earl, who was created a Peer of the United Kingdom in 1831, by the title of Baron Sefton of Croxteth, Co. Palatine of Lancaster.

SEGRAVE, BARON. (Berkeley.)

Peer of the United Kingdom.

William-Fitzhardinge Berkeley, the eldest son of Frederick-Augustus, 4th Earl Berkeley, by a marriage professed to have taken place with the present Countess Dowager, his widow, 30 March 1785, but disallowed by the House of Peers after a tedious investigation in 1811, was raised to the Peerage in 1831, by the title of Baron Segrave of Berkeley Castle, Co. Gloucester. The late Earl Berkeley, by his Countess after the alleged marriage of 1785 and before the acknowledged one of 1796, (of which Thomas-Morton-Fitzhardinge, the present Earl Berkeley, is the eldest son,) had, besides Lord Segrave, the following issue:

1 Captain Maurice-Frederick-Fitz-Hardinge Berkeley, R.N., *b.* 3 Jan. 1788, *m.* 4 Dec. 1823, Lady Charlotte Lennox, 6th daughter of Charles, 4th Duke of Richmond, by whom he has issue:

1 Frederica-Charlotte-Fitz-Hardinge, *b.* 15 April 1825.

2 Francis-William-Fitz-Hardinge, *b.* 16 Nov. 1826.

3 A daughter, *b.* 19, *d.* 22 April 1829.

4 A son, *b.* 19 April 1830.

2 Augustus-Fitz-Hardinge, *b.* 26 March 1789, *m.* Oct. 1815, Mary, eldest daughter of Sir John Dashwood King, Bart., M.P., and has a son, *b.* 10 July 1829, and other issue.

3 Maria-Fitz-Hardinge, *b.* 2 April 1790, *d.* young.

4 Henrietta-Fitz-Hardinge, *b.* 13 June 1793, *d.* young.

5 Francis-Henry-Fitz-Hardinge, *b.* 7 Dec. 1794.

SELKIRK, EARL OF. (Douglas.)

Peer of Scotland.

Lord William Douglas, 3rd son of William, 1st Marquis of Douglas, was created in 1646 Earl of Selkirk, Lord Daer and Shortcleuch; in 1660 he was created Duke of Hamilton for life, his wife Anne having succeeded her uncle as Duchess of Hamilton; and in 1688 he resigned the Earldom of Selkirk, which was granted, with the precedency of the former patent, to his 3rd son Lord Charles Douglas, and his issue male; which failing, to his younger sons, Lords John, George, Basil, and Archibald Hamilton, and their issue male; all now extinct, except the present Earl, descended from Lord Basil. The Duke of Hamilton, 1st Earl of Selkirk, *d.* in 1694, having had the seven sons following:

1 James, 4th Duke of Hamilton, whose descendant and heir male is the present Duke of Hamilton and Brandon.

2 Lord William, who *d.* in France without issue, probably before the patent of 1688.

3 Lord Charles, who in 1688 became 2nd Earl of Selkirk; he *d.* without issue 13 March 1739, and was succeeded by his next brother,

4 Lord John, created a Peer of Scotland in 1697 by the titles of Earl of Ruglen, Viscount Riccartoun, and Lord Hillhouse, with remainder to the heirs whatsoever of his body; he succeeded his brother Charles as 3rd Earl of Selkirk, and *d.* in 1744, without surviving issue male; his only child, who left issue, was Lady Anne, his eldest daughter, who succeeded as Countess of Ruglen; she was mother of William, 4th Duke of Queensberry, and 3rd Earl of Ruglen, on whose death without issue in 1810, that Earldom became extinct.

5 Lord George, created a Peer of Scotland in 1696, by the titles of Earl of Orkney, Viscount of Kirkwall, and Baron of Dechmont, with remainder to the heirs whatsoever of his body; he *d.* without issue male, in 1737, before his elder brothers, and was succeeded by his eldest daughter, Anne, who carried the Earldom of Orkney, by marriage, to the Irish family of O'Brien, Earl of Inchiquin; she was grandmother of the present Countess of Orkney.

6 Lord Basil, he was drowned in the autumn of 1701 in the Minnock, a small river of Galloway, when about to cross it with his brother the Earl of Selkirk, and other friends; a servant who rode forward to try the ford having been dismounted by the unexpected strength of the current, Lord Basil rushed in to save him, but his horse falling, both were carried away by the torrent before his brother or friends could render any assistance. He left two sons: William, the eldest, succeeded to his estate, and dying young soon after, was succeeded by his only surviving brother Basil Hamilton, of Baldron; he engaged in the Rebellion of 1715, was taken prisoner at Preston, after signalizing his valour in the battle, was tried for high treason, and condemned to death, but pardoned, and restored in blood by Act of Parliament in 1732. He *d.* in 1742, leaving an only son,

Dunbar, who succeeded his great-uncle John, Earl of Selkirk and Ruglen, as 4th Earl of Selkirk in 1744, and resumed his original family name of Douglas. On the breaking out of the rebellion in 1745 he exerted himself with the greatest zeal on behalf of the established government. He *d.* in 1799, having had issue, Sholto-Basil, Lord Daer, who *d.* an infant in 1760; Basil-William, Lord Daer, who *d.* in 1794 *unm.* in his thirtieth year, having given the highest hopes of talent and patriotism; John, who succeeded as Lord Daer; Dunbar, a Captain in the Navy; and Alexander, a Captain in the Army, who all three *d. unm.* at nearly the same time; David, and two daughters who *d.* young; Lady Isabella, who *d. unm.* 6 Sept. 1830; the three daughters named in the *The Peerage Volume;* and Thomas, 7th and youngest son, who succeeded his father as 5th Earl in 1799, and is remarkable for the settlement formed by him on Prince Edward's Island in the Gulph of St. Lawrence; he *d.* in 1820, and was succeeded by his only son Dunbar-James, present and 6th Earl.

7 Lord Archibald, *b.* 1673, and *d.* 5 April 1754, leaving three sons, of whom the 2nd and last survivor, the Rev. Frederick Hamilton, *d.* without surviving issue male in 1811.

SELSEY, BARON. (Peachey.)

Peer of Great Britain.

Edmund Peachey, Esq., of Eartham, Co. Sussex, descended from the ancient family of Peche, of Kingsthorpe, Co. Leicester, whose ancestor, Hamon Peche, was Sheriff of the Co. of Cambridge, in the time of King Henry III., was grandfather of Sir Henry Peachey, who was created a Baronet in 1736, with remainder to his brother John; he *d.* in 1737 without surviving issue male, and was succeeded by his said brother, Sir John Peachey, 2nd Baronet, who *d.* in 1744, leaving Sir John his successor, and Sir James, who succeeded his brother in 1768, and was created in 17.. Baron Selsey, of Selsey, Co. Sussex. He was *b.* 10 March 1723, and *d.* 1 Feb. 1808; having *m.* 19 Aug. 1747, Lady Georgiana-Caroline Scott, 2nd daughter of Henry, 1st Earl of Deloraine, by whom, who was *b.* Feb. 1727, and *d.* 13 Oct. 18.. he was father of John, 2nd Lord, his successor; to whom in 1816 succeeded his eldest surviving son, Henry-John, present and 3rd Lord.

SEMPILL, BARON. (Sempill.)

Peer of Great Britain.

Sir John Sempill was created a Peer of Parliament in 1494; he fell at the battle of Flodden in 1513, and was succeeded by his eldest son William, 2nd Lord, who *d.* in 1548. Robert, 3rd Lord, his eldest son and successor, took arms on behalf of King James VI. against Queen Mary, and was engaged in the battle of Langside, although his youngest son, John, who *m.* Mary, daughter of Alexander, .. Lord Livingstone, was, as well as his wife, among the Queen's most confidential servants; their son, Sir James Sempill, of Beltrees, was Ambassador to England in 1599, and an author of some note, as was his son Robert, and his grandson Francis; the latter, a steadfast adherent of the House of Stuart, sold Beltrees, but his line continued in his son and grandson, both named Robert, and the male descendants of this branch existed at least till 1789.

Robert Master of Sempill, eldest son of the 3rd Lord, *d.* before his father, leaving a son Robert, who succeeded as 4th Lord; he *d.* in 1611, and was succeeded by his eldest son Hugh, 5th Lord, who was father of Francis, 6th Lord, his successor in 1639, and Robert, 7th Lord, who succeeded his brother in 1644; he *d.* in 16.. leaving issue, 1 Francis, 8th Lord, who *d.* without issue in 1684; 2 Anne, *m.* to Francis Abercromby, of Fetternier, created in 1685 Lord Glassford, for life only; 3 Jean, *m.* to Alexander Sinclair, of Roslin.

On the death of Francis, 8th Lord, his eldest sister and heir, Anne, 9th Baroness, obtained in 1688 a renewal of the patent to herself, and Francis Abercromby, Lord Glassford, her husband, and their heirs male, remainder to their daughters and their heirs male, remainder to the eldest heir female, without division of their ... Their issue assumed the name of Sempill. They had, besides other sons, Francis, 10th Lord, who succeeded his mother, and John, 11th Lord, who both *d.* unm. ... Hugh, 12th Lord, who succeeded in 1716. He had the command of the left wing of the Royal army in the battle of Culloden, and *d.* in 1746, when he was succeeded by his eldest son JOHN, 13th LORD, to whom in 1782 succeeded his eldest son HUGH, 14th LORD, who *d.* in 1830, and was succeeded by his only surviving son SELKIRK, present and 15th LORD.

SHAFTESBURY, EARL OF. (ASHLEY-COOPER.)

Peer of England.

Sir John Cooper, of Rockbourne, in the County of Southampton, great-grandson of John Cooper, Esq., of Hertyng, who *d.* in 1495, was created a Baronet in 1622, *d.* in 1631, leaving by Anne, his 1st wife, daughter and sole heir of Sir Anthony Ashley, of Wimborne, St. Giles, Co. Dorset, Secretary at War in the reign of Queen Elizabeth, who *d.* in 1628, SIR ANTHONY-ASHLEY-COOPER, his eldest son and successor. This Sir Anthony succeeding in his childhood to a large estate, improved his natural abilities by a diligent application to his studies at Oxford, and afterwards at Gray's Inn, where he became conspicuous for his knowledge of the law. At the breaking out of the troubles he enlisted himself in the Royal party, but owing to some personal offences received from Prince Maurice, and afterwards from the King himself, Sir Anthony passed over to the Parliament. He however was so desirous of putting a stop to the civil contest, that his influence in the western counties gave rise to a third party denominated the Clubmen, which spreading over the country became very formidable both to the Royalist and Parliamentary army, with the avowed intention of compelling both to lay down their arms, and to submit their differences to the arbitration of a free Parliament convened for that especial purpose. The rapid successes of the Republican arms defeated this project. Sir Anthony vehemently opposed the usurpation of Cromwell, by whom he was secluded from his seat in Parliament, and, after his death, was very active and influential in promoting the Restoration of King CHARLES II. He was one of the deputation sent by the Parliament to request "that his Majesty would be pleased to return, and to take the government of the kingdom into his hands, where he would find all possible affection, duty, and obedience from all his subjects." Three days before the King's Coronation in 1661, he was created Baron Ashley, of Wimborne, St. Giles, Co. Dorset; he was a Minister of State through great part of CHARLES II.'s reign, and was one of the five ministers who, from the initials of their names, were styled by the Opposition the "Cabal." He was appointed Lord High Chancellor in 1672, and created Baron Cooper of Pawlett, Co. Somerset, and Earl of Shaftesbury. He was, however, so strong an opponent of Popery, and so little favourable to the succession of the Duke of York, that in 1673 he was, by the influence of the Duke, deprived of the Great Seal, and becoming a violent opposer of the Government, was thrown into the Tower in 1677, and there detained for a year on a charge of contempt of the authority and being of Parliament, and was only released at length upon acknowledging his offence on his knees at the bar of the House. In 1679 the feelings of the nation running high against Popery, he was for a short time made President of the Council, but again displaced for persisting in his opposition to the Duke of York's succession. In 1681 he was again committed to the Tower, and an indictment of high treason was preferred against him before the grand jury at the Old Bailey, charging him with being party to a conspiracy for forcibly preventing the accession of the Duke of York, seizing the King's guards, and compelling his Majesty to submit to such terms as the conspirators should prescribe; much was sworn against him by the false witnesses, so common at this period, but the grand jury, after duly weighing all the evidence, rejected the indictment. Finding the ruling powers now strongly excited against him, he quitted the theatre on which he had acted so conspicuous and eventful a part, and retiring to Amsterdam, *d.* there in 1683, leaving to history a character distinguished by extraordinary abilities, unrestricted in their public exercise by any bonds of political principle.

Anthony, his only son, 2nd Earl, succeeded; he *d.* in 1699, and was succeeded by his eldest son, Anthony, 3rd Earl, the author of the *Characteristics*, who *d.* in 1713. Anthony, 4th Earl, his only son and successor, *d.* in 1771; leaving two sons, Anthony, 5th Earl, who succeeded him, and *d.* without issue male in 1811, and Cropley, who succeeded his brother, and is the present and 6th Earl.

SHANNON EARL OF. (Boyle.)

Peer of Ireland and of Great Britain.

His Lordship is a branch of the family of the Earl of Cork and Orrery.

The three eldest sons of Richard, 1st Earl of Cork, were, 1 Richard, 2nd Earl of Cork, created Earl of Burlington, whose male line failed in 1735; 2 Lewis, Viscount Kinalmeaky, who *d. unm.* in 1642; 3

Roger, created Earl of Orrery, who left two sons: Roger, 2nd Earl of Orrery, from whom the present Earl of Cork and Orrery is 4th in descent, and

Henry, a zealous Protestant and supporter of the Revolution; he *d.* in 1693. His eldest surviving son, Henry, was created in 1756, Baron Boyle of Castlemartyr, Viscount Boyle of Bardon, Co. Cork, and Earl of Shannon, having been during twenty-three preceding years, Speaker of the House of Commons. He *d.* in 1764, having had six sons, of whom only two survived him, viz.: Richard, 2nd Earl, his successor, and Robert, (6th son,) who assumed the name of Walsingham; he was a Captain in the R.N., and was lost with all his crew, in the ship Thunderer which he commanded, in a hurricane in the West Indies, in Oct. 1779; leaving an only daughter, Charlotte, late Baroness De Ros, in her own right.

Richard, 2nd Earl, was created Lord Carleton, Baron of Carleton, Co. York, in 1786, and *d.* in 1807, when he was succeeded by his only surviving son, Henry, present and 3rd Earl.

SHEFFIELD, EARL OF. (Holroyd.)

Peer of Ireland and of the United Kingdom.

William de Howroyde possessed the lands of Howroyde, Co. York, in the time of Edward I. The first of his descendants who removed into Ireland, was Isaac Holroyd, Esq., who settled there in the reign of Charles II. He was great grandfather of John Holroyd, Esq. who, on succeeding to the estates of his mother's family, assumed the name of Baker. He was created in 1781 Baron Sheffield of Dunamore, Co. Meath, in the Peerage of Ireland, and in 1783, Baron Sheffield of Roscommon, also in the Peerage of Ireland, with limitation, in failure of his issue male, to his daughters and their issue male; in 1802, he was created a Peer of the United Kingdom, by the title of Baron Sheffield of Sheffield, Co. Sussex; and in 1816, Viscount Pevensey and Earl of Sheffield, in the Irish Peerage. He *d.* in 1821 and was succeeded by his only son, George-Augustus-Frederick-Charles, present and 2nd Earl.

SHERBORNE, BARON. (Dutton.)

Peer of Great Britain.

His Lordship is descended from the family of Napier, originally Lords Napier, but which title is now inherited by a junior branch of the family of Scott. His Lordship's ancestors separated from the pareht stock before the creation of the Peerage of Napier, and settled in Ireland.

James Naper of Loughcrew, Co. Meath, *m.* Ann, 2nd daughter of Sir Ralph Dutton of Sherborne, Co. Gloucester, Bart., and *d.* in 1716, leaving by her a son,

James Lennox Naper, Esq., who being appointed by will heir to his uncle, Sir John Dutton, Bart., assumed the name and arms of Dutton, (an ancient family, the Patriarch of which, Odard, came into England with William the Conqueror, and settled at Dutton in Cheshire, from whence his posterity derived their surname.) He *d.* in 1776, leaving issue:

1 James, created in 1784 Baron Sherborne of Sherborne, Co. Gloucester; he *d.* in 1820, and was succeeded by his only son John, present and 2nd Lord.

2 William, who assumed the family name of Naper, and *d.* 1 Dec. 1791; having *m.* 5 June 1787, Jane, daughter of Rev. Ferdinand-Tracy Travell, by whom, who *d.* in 1797, he had issue:

- 1 James-Lennox-William Naper, Esq., *b.* 18 Feb 1791, *m.* 3 May 1824, Selina, 2nd daughter of Sir Grey Skipwith, Bart., by whom, who was *b.* 26 March 1804, he has issue, James-Lennox, *b.* 5 Dec. 1825.
- 2 Jane, *b.* 5 Feb. 1792, *m.* 26 Sept. 1815, Sir George Cornewall, Bart., *b.* 16 Jan. 1774.

3 Ralph Dutton of Gressen Hall, Co. Norfolk, Esq., *b.* in 1755, *d.* without issue 25 Feb. 1804; having *m.* Miss Honor Gubbins, who *d.* in Jan. 1807.

4 Anne, *m.* Samuel Blackwell, Esq.

5 Mary, *m.* to Thomas Master Esq.

6 Frances, *m.* to Charles Lambert, Esq.

7 Jane, late wife of Thomas-William Coke, Esq.

SHREWSBURY, EARL OF (Talbot.)

Peer of England and Ireland.

This noble family is said to have been in England before the Conquest; but the first of the name on record is Richard de Talbot, a Baron in the reign of William the Conqueror. The 5th from him was Gilbert, Lord Talbot, who *m.* Guendaline, daughter and at length heir of Rhese ap Griffiths, Prince of South Wales; he *d.* in 1274. Richard Lord Talbot his son, relinquishing his paternal coat of arms, which was *bendy of ten pieces argent and gules*, assumed that of his mother and the Princes of Wales, her ancestors, viz.: *gules, a lion rampant within a bordure engrailed, or*; which is borne by his descendants to the present day; he *d.* in 1306. Gilbert Lord Talbot, his son and successor, received in 1331, the first summons to Parliament extant to any of his family, although there is abundant evidence that his ancestors had ranked as Barons of the realm from the period of the Conquest; before and after this Lord, the chiefs of this powerful and warlike family are named with distinction in all the feats of arms which fell within their sphere, and are frequently found in the great offices of State. From this period the descendants of Lord Gilbert have uninterruptedly enjoyed the dignity of the Peerage; he *d.* in 1346, and his title descended in the direct line to his son, grandson, and great-grandson, Richard, 2nd Lord, who *d.* in 1356; Gilbert, 3rd Lord, who *d.* in 1387; and *d.* in 1555, leaving two sons, GEORGE, 9th EARL, and John, father of JOHN, 10th EARL; 2 a second John of Salwarp, Co. Worcester, ancestor of the Earl Talbot and of Sir George Talbot, Bart.

GEORGE 4th EARL, K.G., son and heir of the 3rd EARL, was, like his ancestors, distinguished for his valour and loyalty, and was one of the chief nobles of the realm through the reign of King HENRY VIII. FRANCIS, 5th EARL, K.G., his eldest surviving son and successor, was successfully engaged in the Scottish wars; he *d.* in 1560, and was succeeded by his only surviving son,

GEORGE, 6th EARL, K.G.; a nobleman who is described as the richest and most powerful Peer of his time, but from which time the family may be said to have declined in consequence, chiefly perhaps from the circumstance of its lineal descent, hitherto uninterrupted, having from this period wholly failed; only in one instance afterwards the Peerage descended to the third generation, and even then those two successors were followed by a collateral line not issuing from the same ancestor. The fact is singular. In 1572 he was appointed Earl Marshal of England, and on the arrival of the Queen of Scots as a fugitive in this country, she was put under the custody of this Earl, from whom she received every attention consistent with the state of safe-guard in which he was compelled to detain her. He was not happy in his domestic circle; his second wife, a daughter and co-heir of John Hardwick, of Hardwick, Co. Derby, Esq., and, before her marriage with him, three times a widow, 1st of Robert Barley, Esq., who had bequeathed a large property to her and her heirs; 2ndly, of Sir William Cavendish, whose family was through her means raised to wealth and honours; and 3rdly, of Sir William St. Loe, whose large estates were also settled on herself and her issue; had a family of six children by her second marriage, to whose aggrandisement her influence over the Earl induced him to make concessions very unfavourable to his own interest and happiness and those of his children; while his own sons by a former marriage (he had no issue by the second) contributed to his cares by their disobedience and mutual dissensions. Thus deprived, by the necessity of perpetual watchfulness over his Royal charge, of the splendour of his public station, and prevented by internal uneasiness from taking refuge in domestic society, he was perhaps in a scarcely less enviable situation than his unfortunate prisoner herself; he was relieved after fifteen years of this painful trust, and *d.* in 1590; having survived his eldest son Francis Lord Talbot, who *d.* without issue in 1582; he left three sons, of whom Henry, the youngest, *d.* without issue male in 1596; and GILBERT and EDWARD were successively Earls of Shrewsbury, and both *d.* without male issue.

GILBERT, 7th EARL, K.G., *d.* in 1616, leaving three daughters, his co-heirs, of whom only the youngest, Lady Alathea, at length sole heir, left issue; she carried the Baronies of Talbot, Furnival, Strange of Blackmere, and her moiety of the Baronies of Verdon and Giffard of Brimmesfield, into the family of the Dukes of Norfolk; her co-heirs are the Lords Petre and Stourton.

EDWARD, 8th EARL, succeeded his brother as heir male, and *d.* without issue in 1618.

The descent of GEORGE, 9th EARL, from Sir Gilbert Talbot of Grafton, 3rd son of the 2nd Earl, has been already deduced; he *d. unm.* in 1630, and was succeeded by his nephew above mentioned.

JOHN, 10th EARL, *d.* in 1653, and was succeeded by his eldest surviving son FRANCIS, 11th EARL, who was killed in 1667, in a duel, by George Villiers, 2nd Duke of Buckingham, the paramour of his wife; he was succeeded by his eldest son CHARLES, 12th EARL, K.G., then but seven years of age, who on attaining the years of manhood, becoming intimately acquainted with Dr. John Tillotson, Archbishop of Canterbury, was by him pressed to a recognition of the errors of the Romish church; unable himself to refute the arguments of the Archbishop, he prevailed on his maternal grandfather, the Earl of Cardigan, to collect the defence of the Romish priests, which carrying to the Archbishop, he conveyed his answers again to his grandfather, and after two years close attention to this theological dispute, embraced Protestantism in 1681, at a period when the opinions he abjured were become un-fashionable through the influence of the Court. He had subsequently the satisfaction of converting his cousins, the Earl of Cardigan and his brother, from Popery. He was an active supporter of the Revolution, and was by King WILLIAM III. created Marquis of Alton, Co. Stafford, and Duke of Shrewsbury in 1694. Queen Anne on her death-bed delivered to him the staff of Lord Treasurer, just before resigned by the Earl of Oxford, his Grace being then Lord Lieutenant of Ireland, from whence he had been called to London, in consequence of the divisions among the ministry. This appointment contributed materially to the peaceable accession of King GEORGE I., whom his Grace immediately concurred in proclaiming. He d. in 1718, without issue, when the Dukedom became extinct, as did the male descendants of JOHN, 10th EARL. His Grace was succeeded in the Earldom by

GILBERT, 13th EARL, son of Gilbert, brother of the 10th Earl; he was a clergyman of the church of Rome. He *d.* in 1743; George, his brother, assumed the title, but died before him in 1733, leaving three sons, George, Charles, and Francis; for the issue of the latter, who *d.* in 1813, see *The Peerage Volume.*

GEORGE, 14th EARL, the eldest son, succeeded his uncle; he was *b.* 22 Dec. 17[illegible] and *d.* without issue 22 July 1787; having *m.* 21 Nov. 1753, the Hon. Elizabeth Dormer, daughter of John, 7th Lord Dormer, who *d.* 11 Aug. 1809.

CHARLES, 15th EARL, son of Charles, next brother of the 14th EARL, succeeded; he *d.* without issue in 1827, and was succeeded by his nephew,

JOHN, present and 16th EARL, son of John-Joseph, brother of the 15th EARL.

SIDMOUTH, VISCOUNT. (ADDINGTON.)

Peer of the United Kingdom.

Anthony Addington, Esq., of Trinity College, Oxford, M.D., was elected a Fellow of the College of Physicians in 1756; after practising for some years at London, he was obliged by ill health to retire into the country, and settled at Reading; he was *b.* 13 Dec. 1713, and *d.* 21 March 1790; having *m.* 22 Sept. 174[illegible] Mary, daughter and heir of the Rev. Haviland-John Hiley, by whom, who *d.* 7 Nov. 1778, he had issue,

1 HENRY, the present Peer, who having been Speaker of the House of Commons from the year 1789 to 1801, was in that year appointed First Lord of the Treasury and Chancellor of the Exchequer, and continued at the head of the Government till May 1804, during which period he concluded the peace of Amiens, and renewed the war with France. Since his resignation of the helm of State, he has held some office of importance under nearly all the Tory Administrations that have succeeded. In 1805 he was created VISCOUNT SIDMOUTH of Sidmouth, Co. Devon.

2 The Right Hon. John-Hiley Addington, *b.* Aug. 1759, *d.* 11 June 1818; having *m.* 25 Oct. 1785, Mary, daughter of Henry Unwin, Esq., by whom he has issue:

1 Haviland-John, *b.* 20 Nov. 1787.
2 Mary, *b.* 31 Dec. 1788.
3 Henry-Unwin, Envoy Extraordinary and Minister Plenipotentiary to the Court of Spain, *b.* 24 March 1790.

3 Anne, *d.* 12 June 1806; having *m.* 2 June 1770, William Goodenough, Esq., M.D.

4 Eleanor, *m.* 1 Aug. 1771, James Sutton, Esq., of New Park, near Devizes, by whom, who was *b.* 6 July 1733, and *d.* 6 July 1801, she was mother of a daughter and heir, Eleanor, late wife of Thomas-Grimstone Bucknall-Estcourt, Esq., M.P. for the University of Oxford.

5 Elizabeth, *d.* 26 June 1827; having *m.* in 1782, William Hoskyns, Esq., who *d.* 3 Feb. 1813.

6 Charlotte, *m.* 1 Aug, 1788, Right Hon. Charles Bathurst, Bencher of Lincoln's Inn.

SINCLAIR, BARON. (St.-Clair.)

The family of Sancto Claro, or St.-Clair, came into England from Normandy with William the Conqueror; two branches of it, those of Herdmanstown and Rosslyn, settled in Scotland in the 12th century. The St.-Clairs of Herdsmanstown derive their descent from Henry de Sancto Claro, vicecomes of Richard de Moreville, Constable of Scotland in 1162.

William, Earl of Orkney and Caithness, Chief of the Sinclairs of Rosslyn, resigned the Earldom of Orkney to King James III. in 1470, and in 1476 got a charter of that of Caithness, in favour of William, the eldest son of his 2nd marriage, passing over another William, the son of his 1st marriage; he also settled the lands of Roslin on Sir Oliver Sinclair, a younger son of his 2nd marriage, from whom descended the succeeding house of Sinclair of Roslin, the direct male line of which became extinct in 1778.

William St.-Clair, his disinherited eldest son, appealing to the laws, obtained by compromise with his younger brothers a good estate in the counties of Fife and Edinburgh. His son, Henry, was created a Peer of Parliament in 1489, and was killed at the battle of Flodden in 1513. He was succeeded by his son, William, 2nd Lord, to whom succeeded his son, Henry, 3rd Lord; the latter survived his eldest son, James, who was father of Henry, James, and Patrick, successively 4th, 5th, and 6th Lords. Patrick, 6th Lord, *d.* in 1615, and was succeeded by his eldest son, John, 7th Lord, who was taken prisoner at the battle of Worcester, and detained in custody till 1660; he *d.* in 1676. His only daughter and heir,

Catherine, who in 1659 *m.* John St.-Clair, Esq., of Herdmanstown, *d.* before her father in childbed in 1666; leaving three children, of whom Henry, 8th Lord, son of John and Catherine Sinclair, succeeded his grandfather the 7th Lord, and obtained in 1677 a confirmation of the dignity of Lord Sinclair, with the original precedency of 1489 by patent, with remainder to the heirs male of his body, failing which, to his heirs male whatever; but dying March 1723, the title became dormant in consequence of the attainder in 1715, of his eldest son John, who should have been 9th Lord; but who dying in 1750, and his brother James, 10th Lord, in 1762, both without issue, the title devolved on the heir male,

Charles Sinclair, eldest son of Matthew, brother of Henry, 8th Lord; neither he nor his son, Andrew, 12th Lord, who succeeded him in 1775, and *d.* the following year, assumed the title, but it was claimed by, and in 1782 adjudged to Charles, the present and 13th Lord, son of Andrew, who should have been 12th Lord.

SKELMERSDALE, BARON. (Bootle-Wilbraham.)

Peer of the United Kingdom.

His Lordship is 24th in lineal descent from Sir Richard de Wilburgham, Sheriff of Cheshire in 1259.

Richard Wilbraham, his Lordship's father, who *d.* 13 March 1796, assumed the name of Bootle, in consequence of his marriage, in 1755, with Mary, daughter and sole heir of Robert Bootle of Latham House, Co. Lancaster, Esq., by whom, who *d.* 10 April 1813, he had issue:

1 Edward Bootle-Wilbraham, Esq., the present Peer, created in 1828, Baron Skelmersdale of Skelmersdale, Co. Palatine of Lancaster. See *The Peerage Volume.*

2 Randle Bootle-Wilbraham, Esq., of Rode Hall, *b.* 10 Jan. 1773, *m.* 1st, 5 Dec. 1798, Letitia, daughter and heir of the Rev. Edward-Rudd Clerk, she *d.* 30 March 1805, and he *m.* 2ndly, 9 Feb. 1808, Sibylla daughter of Philip Egerton, Esq., & has issue by both marriages.

3 Anne-Dorothea, who *d.* in 1825, late Lady Alvanley. See that title in *The Peerage Volume.*

4 Mary, *d.* 13 Nov. 1784; having *m.* 26 Oct. 1780, William Egerton, Esq. of Tatton Park, Co. Cheshire.

5 Francisca-Alicia, *d.* 3 Sept. 1810; having *m.* 20 Dec. 1785, Anthony-Hardolph Eyre, Esq., of Grove, Co. Notts.

6 Sibylla-Georgiana, *d.* 22 Nov. 1799; having *m.* 16 June 1791, William Farrington, Esq., of Shaw Hall, Co. Lancaster.

7 Emma, *d.* 30 Nov. 1797; having *m.* 1 June 1794, the late Sir Charles Edmondstone, Bart.

8 Elizabeth, *m.* in 1821, the Rev. W. Barnes, Rector of Richmond, Co. York.

SLIGO, MARQUIS OF. (Browne.)

Peer of Ireland and of the United Kingdom.

Captain Richard Browne, supposed to be a junior of the family of Browne of Cowdray Castle, Co. Sussex, Viscounts Montague of England, settled in Ireland in the reign of Queen Elizabeth; Sir John Browne of the Neale, Co. Mayo, his grandson, was created a Baronet of Nova Scotia in 1636, and was father of

1 Sir George, his successor, ancestor of Lord Kilmaine.

2 Colonel John Browne, whose grandson, John, was created Baron of Mount Eagle, Co. Mayo, in 1760, Viscount Westport, Co. Mayo, in 1768, and Earl of Altamont in 1771. He *d.* 4 July 1776, leaving by Anne, eldest daughter of Sir Arthur Gore, Bart., and sister of Arthur, 1st Earl of Arran, who *d.* 7 March 1771, one daughter, Lady Anne, *m.* in 1763, to Ross Mahon, Esq., of Castle Gore, Co. Galway, and six sons, viz.:

1 Peter, his successor, 2nd Earl.

2 The Hon. Colonel Arthur Browne, who was *b.* 1731, and *d.* 21 July 1779; having *m.* Anne, daughter of John Gardiner, Esq., M.D., by whom, who *d.* in July 1807, he left the issue stated in *The Peerage Volume.*

3 Hon. George; he *d.* in July 1782, leaving by his marriage with Dorothea, daughter and co-heir of James Moore, Esq., one daughter, Margaret, *m.* 2 May 1785, to Dominick-Geoffrey Browne, Esq., of Castle-Margaret, Co. Mayo, who *d.* 8 May 1826.

4 Hon. James, a Serjeant at the Irish bar, *d. unm.* in Nov. 1790.

5 Hon. Henry, *d.* 28 July 1811 without issue; having *m.* a daughter of Sir Henry Lynch, Bart.

6 Hon. John, who *d.* 4 Aug. 1798; having *m.* 1st, Mary, daughter of — Cocks, Esq., by whom he had his two eldest daughters, Mrs. Browne and Mrs. Blake, mentioned in *The Peerage Volume*; he *m.* 2ndly, Rosalind, daughter of Eneas Gilker, Esq., by whom, who *d.* 30 April 1812, he had his son, Henry, and the two other daughters stated in *The Peerage Volume.*

Peter, 2nd Earl, *d.* 28 Dec. 1780; having *m.* 16 April 1752, Elizabeth, only daughter and heir of Denis Kelly, Esq., by whom, who *d.* 1 Aug. 1765, he had ssue, 1 John-Denis, his successor, 3rd Earl, created Marquis of Sligo in 1800; and Baron Monteagle of Westport, Co. Mayo, in the Peerage of the United Kingdom in 1806. He *d.* in 1809, and was succeeded by his only son, Howe-Peter, present and 2nd Marquis; 2 The Right Hon. Denis Browne, for whose widow and issue see *The Peerage Volume*; 3 Lady Anne, late Countess of Desart—see that title in *The Peerage Volume*; 4 Lady Elizabeth, who *d.* in Feb. 1795, having *m.* in Aug. 1786, her cousin Ross Mahon, Esq., created a Baronet in 1818; 4 Lady Charlotte Mahon, who survives. See *The Peerage Volume.*

SOMERS, EARL. (Cocks.)

Peer of the United Kingdom.

The family of Cocks was seated in the County of Kent as early as the reign of Edward I., and afterwards removed into the County of Gloucester.

Thomas Cocks, Esq., of Castle-Ditch, in the County of Hereford, left five sons, of whom only two left issue, viz.: 1 Thomas, father of the Rev. Thomas Cocks of Castle-Ditch, who left an only daughter and heir, Mary, *m.* in 1724 to her cousin, John Cocks, Esq.; 2

Charles Cocks, Esq., (5th son,) he *m.* Mary, eldest sister and co-heir of John Somers, Lord High Chancellor, created Lord Somers, Baron of Evesham, Co. Worcester, in 1697; which titles became extinct on his death in 1716; they had issue: 1 Catherine, who *d.* 13 June 1705; having *m.* James Harris, Esq., of the Close Salisbury, grandfather by a 2nd marriage of the 1st Earl of Malmesbury; 2 Margaret, who *d.* 10 Sept. 1761, having *m.* Philip Yorke, 1st Earl of Hardwicke and Lord High Chancellor; 3 James Cocks, Esq., of Bruckmans in Hertfordshire, who *d.* in 1750, leaving an only son, James, who *d. unm.* in 1758; 4

John Cocks, Esq., who *d.* 24 June 1771; having *m.* in 1724, Mary, daughter and sole heir of his cousin, the Rev. Thomas Cocks, by which marriage he became possessed of the family seat at Castle-Ditch; she *d.* 4 Feb. 1779. They had two daughters, who *d. unm.*, and ten sons, of whom six *d. unm.*; the other four were,

1 Sir Charles Cocks, created a Baronet in 1772; and Lord Somers, Baron of Evesham, Co. Worcester, in 1784; he *d.* in 1806, and was succeeded by his eldest son, John, present and 2nd Lord, who was created in 1821, Viscount Eastnor of Eastnor Castle, Co. Hereford, and Earl Somers.

2 Joseph Cocks, Esq., *b.* 24 Jan. 1733, *d.* 4 April 1775; having *m.* in 1758, Margaret, daughter of John Thorniloe, Esq., by whom, who was *b.* in 1734, and *d.* 31 Oct. 1774, he had issue:

- 1 Mary, *b.* 1759, *d.* 1785; having *m.* in 1782, William Russell, Esq., of Powyck, Co. Worcester, Barrister.
- 2 Margaret, *b.* 28 May 1773, widow, having *m.* 12 June 1798, Joseph Smith, Esq., *b.* 1757, *d.* 19 April 1822.

3 James Cocks, Esq., *b.* 22 June 1734, and is deceased, having *m.* 5 Nov. 1772, Martha, daughter of Vice-Admiral Charles Watson, by whom he had issue:

- 1 James Cocks, Esq., M.P.
- 2 Catherine, *b.* 18 July 1780, *m.* 17 Nov. 1800, Joseph Yorke, Esq. *See* Earl of Hardwicke.
- 3 Anne, *d.* 19 March 1810; having *m.* 21 Dec. 1802, the Hon. Reginald Cocks. See *The Peerage Volume.*
- 4 Elizabeth-Catherine *m.* Dec. 1810, Thomas Bradshaw, Esq.
- 5 Jane, *m.* 4 March 1807, the Rev. George Waddington.

4 Thomas-Somers Cocks, Esq., *b.* 3 Dec. 1737, *d.* 15 Nov. 1796; having *m.* 29 Aug. 1768, Anne, daughter of Alexander Thistlethwaite, Esq., by whom, who *d.* 25 Dec. 1817, he had issue:

1 Catherine; *m.* 23 Feb. 1802, James-Gladell Vernon, Esq., who is deceased.
2 Margaret-Sarah, *m.* 26 Oct. 1802, Vice-Admiral Sir James-Nicholl Morris K.C.B.
3 Maria, *m.* 11 May 1811, Vice-Admiral Sir William Hargood, K C.B.
4 Thomas-Somers Cocks, Esq., *m.* 24 Feb. 1813, Agneta, 5th daughter of the Right Hon. Reginald Pole-Carew, (by Jemima, only daughter and heir of the Hon. John Yorke, 4th son of Philip, 1st Earl of Hardwicke,) *b.* 13 May 1791; they have issue: 1 Jemima-Anne, *b.* 22 Nov. 1813. 2 Thomas-Somers, *b.* 5 Feb. 1815. 3 Reginald-Thistlethwaite, *b.* 6 Oct. 181.. 4 Charlotte-Agneta, *b.* 10 July 1818. 5 Charles-Lygon, *b.* 9 June 18.. 6 Walter-Carew, *b.* 10 March 1824. 7 Henrietta-Maria, *b.* 6 April 18..
5 Eliza-Jane, *m.* 13 Dec, 1824, Thomas-Raymond Barker, Esq.

SOMERSET, DUKE OF. (St.-Maur.)

Peer of England.

The family of St. Maur came into England with William the Conqueror, and settled in Monmouthshire; from whence they removed into Somersetshire, on the marriage of Sir Roger Seymour, with Cecily, eldest daughter of John, 2nd Baron Beauchamp of Hache, (by writ 1299,) and co-heir of her brother John, 3rd Lord.

Sir John Seymour, Knight-banneret, 6th in direct paternal descent from this marriage, *d.* 21 Dec. 1536, leaving by Margery, his wife, 2nd daughter of Sir Henry Wentworth of Nettlested, Co. Suffolk, Knight of the Bath, who *d.* in 1550, three sons and three daughters, viz.:

1 Edward, 1st Duke of Somerset.

2 Sir Henry Seymour, made a Knight of the Bath at the Coronation of King Edward VI. He *d.* in 1578, leaving a son, Sir John Seymour, who had three sons from whom there is no issue male remaining.

3 Sir Thomas Seymour, K.G. created in 1547 Baron Seymour of Sudley, Co. Gloucester, and soon after appointed Lord High Admiral. He *m.* the Queen-dowager Catherine, daughter of Thomas Parr, and widow 1st of John Nevile Lord Latimer, and 2ndly of King Henry VIII., to whom she was 6th wife; after her death, the Lord Sudley resumed his former object of marrying the Princess Elizabeth; and for his intrigues for that purpose, also for the purpose of obtaining possession of the King's person, and inducing him to govern without his council and for other designs for the subversion of the government as established by the late King's will, he was attainted by Act of Parliament, condemned unheard, and beheaded 10 March 1549. He left an only daughter, Mary, who *d.* an infant.

4 Jane, *m.* 20 May 1536, King Henry VIII., and *d.* 24 Oct. 1536, in childbed of her only son, King Edward VI.

5 Elizabeth, *m.* 1st, to Sir Anthony Oughtred, and 2ndly, to Gregory, Lord Cromwell.

6 Dorothy, *m.* 1st, to Sir Clement Smith, of Little Baddow, Co. Essex; and 2ndly to Thomas Leventhorpe, of Shingey Hall, Hertfordshire.

Sir Edward Seymour, K.G., the eldest son, brother of the Queen and uncle of King Edward VI., was created in June 1536 Viscount Beauchamp of Hache, Co. Somerset, in consideration of his descent, as above noticed, from the noble family of that name, and in 1537 Earl of Hertford, both with remainder to his issue male thereafter to be begotten. In 1547 he was created Baron Seymour and Duke of Somerset, with remainder to the heirs male of his body by Ann, his 2nd wife, failing which, to Sir Edward Seymour, his son by Catherine, his 1st wife, and his heirs male. He was appointed by King Henry VIII. Lord Great Chamberlain of England, and Lieutenant, in which latter capacity he invaded Scotland in 1542; and arking with two hundred sail, he landed at Leith, burnt and plundered that town nd Edinburgh, and returning into England by land, wasted Haddington, Dunbar, :c. on his march. He stood high in King HENRY's favour to the end of his reign, nd was by his will appointed one of the Council to young EDWARD. On the King's decease he repaired to his Royal nephew at Hertford, and conducted him to ondon, where he was unanimously elected by the Council Governor of the King's erson, and Protector of the kingdom during his minority. In the first year of his dministration he concluded a peace with France, that he might be enabled to direct ll his attention towards accomplishing the desirable union of the two kingdoms of his island by the marriage of the King to the infant Queen of Scots; but his nego- iations to this effect proving unavailing, he endeavoured to force the Scottish ation into compliance by an invasion—a method of wooing to which the Scotch ery naturally made vehement objections; their armed resistance, however, gave way at the battle of Pinkey, before the courage and conduct of the Protector, who obtained a signal victory, but was recalled from the scene of his successes by the necessity of securing his authority at home, against the intrigues of his brother, the Admiral. These were speedily suppressed by his death; but so great an accumu- ation of power as that now possessed by the Protector had never been enjoyed by a subject of this realm, especially by one who, notwithstanding his near relationship to the King, was not of the blood Royal, and it excited the jealousy of the nobility. A confederacy was formed against him, headed by John Dudley, Earl of Warwick, afterwards Duke of Northumberland, who himself, ruined by an excess of pros- perity, fell in an unsuccessful attempt at fixing the crown on the brow of his daughter-in-law, the Lady Jane Grey. The Duke of Somerset was unable to sup- port himself against their united machinations, but he did not wholly succumb at once; in 1549 he was deprived of his Protectorship, committed to the Tower, and his estates declared forfeited to the Crown; but he was liberated in three months, the chief of his property recovered, and a reconciliation effected in appearance between him and the Earl of Warwick, a marriage being solemnized between the Duke's eldest daughter and John Viscount Lisle, son of the Earl of Warwick, which the King graced with his presence. This feud, however, was not thus to be closed; dissen- tions again broke out; the Earl of Warwick, who procured a patent to raise him to the rank of Duke of Northumberland, possessed the political power, but the King favoured his uncle, and allowed him so much access to his person, that Northum- berland began to perceive, that unless he could effectually remove him, his own pre- eminence would not long exist. The Duke of Somerset was therefore impeached of high treason and felony; of the treason he was acquitted, but found guilty of felony, in an intention to murder the Duke of Northumberland, being a Privy Councillor; whether this accusation was founded in fact can no farther be ascertained than by the judgment of the Peers, but certain it is that no attempt had been made by Somerset upon the life of his rival; yet for this imputed intention he was con- demned to suffer death; and young Edward, though he had now attained an age when he was capable of acting to a certain extent for himself, was induced to permit the immolation upon the scaffold, for such a cause, of an uncle who had been so long in immediate attendance upon his person. He was beheaded in 1552, greatly lamented by the nation, and especially by the Protestants, whom he had warmly and steadily supported. His honours were forfeited. King EDWARD himself lived but eighteen months after this fatal event, and the troubles that ensued on his death, chiefly the result of Northumberland's intrigues, ended in bringing himself, the innocent instrument of his ambition, and others of his family, to the block.

EDWARD, Earl of Hertford, eldest son of the Protector by his 2nd marriage, who, according to the limitation of the patent, should have succeeded as 2nd DUKE, was by Queen Elizabeth, in 1559, created Baron Beauchamp of Hache, and Earl of Hertford. He fell into trouble, and was nine years detained a prisoner in the Tower, on account of his marriage with the Lady Catherine, daughter and heir of Henry when the male line of WILLIAM, 3rd DUKE, became extinct, as did the title of Marquis of Hertford. The Dukedom and other titles devolved on the male heir, grandson of

Francis, created in 1641 Baron Seymour of Trowbridge, brother of WILLIAM, 3rd DUKE. This Lord Francis *d* in 1664, and was succeeded by his only son, Charles, 2nd Lord Seymour of Trowbridge, who *d.* in 1665, leaving two surviving sons, viz.: 1 FRANCIS, his successor, 3rd Lord, who also succeeded, on the failure of the elder line, as 6th DUKE of SOMERSET; he was murdered at Lerice, in Italy, in 1678, by the vengeance of an Italian, for an affront offered to his wife, not by the Duke, but by some French gentleman with whom he was in company; he *d. unm.*, and was succeeded by his brother; 2

CHARLES, 7th DUKE, K.G., *m.* Elizabeth, only daughter and heir of Josceline, 5th Earl of Northumberland, and *d.* in 1748, leaving an only son, ALGERNON, 8th DUKE, who, uniting in his own person the blood and the possessions of his illustrious ancestors of the houses of Seymour and Percy, was, perhaps, the greatest subject his country has ever seen by hereditary right; he was summoned to Parliament in his father's lifetime as Baron Percy, in 1722, and created Earl of Northumberland and Earl of Egremont, each with a special limitation; he *d.* without surviving issue male in 1750, when the titles of Earl of Hertford and Baron Beauchamp of Hache, and Seymour of Trowbridge, became extinct; the Barony of Percy, by writ 1722, devolved on his only daughter and heir Lady Elizabeth, *m.* to Sir Hugh Smithson, Bart.; the Earldoms of Northumberland and Egremont descended according to the respective patents; and the Dukedom of Somerset and 1st Barony of Seymour, by the failure of heirs male of the 1st Duke by his 2nd marriage, devolved, according to the limitation of the patent, on

SIR EDWARD SEYMOUR, Bart., 9th DUKE, the 6th lineal descendant and heir male of Sir Edward Seymour, son of the 1st Duke, by his 1st marriage; whose posterity were thus put into possession of their birthright, after an exclusion in favour of a junior branch, which had continued for two hundred years. This Sir Edward Seymour, the son of the 1st DUKE, was restored in blood by act of Parliament in 1553, and *d.* in 1593; Sir Edward, his son, was created a Baronet in 1611, and *d.* in 1613; he was succeeded by his eldest son, Sir Edward, who expended £20,000 on improving and enlarging his ancient castle of Bury-Pomeroy, in Devonshire, which was afterwards laid in ruins by the Parliamentary army for the adherence of its owner and his family to the Royal cause; he *d.* in 1659. Henry, his 2nd son, served under the Marquis of Hertford, (3rd Duke of Somerset,) throughout the civil war, and being attached to the household of the Prince of Wales, was the bearer of the last messages which passed between the Prince and his Royal father; he left a son, Sir Henry Seymour, Bart., of Langley Park, Co. Bucks, who *d.* without issue in 1714. Thomas, 3rd son, and Sir Joseph, 6th son, of this Sir Edward, also left male issue.

Sir Edward Seymour, 3rd Bart., his eldest son and successor, was amongst the faithful and active adherents of King CHARLES I.; he *d.* in 1688, and was succeeded by his eldest son, Sir Edward, 4th Bart., who makes a conspicuous figure in the political transactions of his time. He was elected Speaker of the House of Commons in 1673; but when again elected to that office in 1679, though at the time a Privy Councillor and Treasurer of the Navy, the King three times refused to sanction his appointment. He opposed the Bill of Exclusion with forcible and efficacious arguments, but was a chief promoter of the Habeas Corpus Act, and at the Revolution joined the Prince of Orange. On the accession of Queen ANNE he was offered a Peerage, which, from motives of family pride, (for he is described as the proudest of men,) he declined, but procured the title of Baron Conway for his younger son. He *d.* in 1708, leaving two sons by his first wife, viz.: Sir Edward Seymour, his successor; and Lieut.-General William Seymour, who *d.* without issue in 1728; by his second wife, Letitia, daughter of Francis Popham, Esq., of Littlecote, Co. Wilts, and cousin of the 3rd Viscount Conway, in Ireland, he had six sons, on whom Lord

SOMERVILLE, BARON. (Somerville.)

Peer of Scotland.

Sir Walter de Somerville accompanied William the Conqueror into England; his grandson William settled in Scotland, in the reign of King David I.; 9th in descent from William was

Thomas Somerville, created a Peer of Parliament about 1424, and *d.* in 1445; William, 2nd Lord, his only son succeeded, and *d.* in 1455; he was succeeded by his eldest son John, 3rd Lord, whose younger son John, killed at the battle of Flodden in 1513, was ancestor of the Somervilles of Cambusnethan; his eldest son William, Master of Somerville, *d.* before him, leaving two sons, John, 4th Lord, who succeeded his grandfather, and *d.* without issue; and Hugh, 5th Lord, who succeeded his brother, and *d.* in 1549. James, 6th Lord, his eldest son and successor, joined Queen Mary at Hamilton in 1568, and was severely wounded in the battle of Langside; he *d.* in 1569, leaving two sons, of whom the younger was progenitor of a family of Somervilles still subsisting, and Hugh the elder succeeded him as 7th Lord; he *d.* in 1597, leaving two surviving sons, Gilbert, his successor, and Hugh, ancestor of the present Lord Somerville. Gilbert, 8th Lord, lived in a style of splendour so much exceeding his means, that he ruined his estate, and dying without male issue in 1618, left to his brother only an unportioned title.

Hugh Somerville of Drum, 2nd son of the 7th Lord, and who should have succeeded his brother as 9th Lord, never assumed the title; he *d.* in 1640, and was succeeded at Drum by a direct lineage of four generations of the name of James, none of whom assumed the rights of the Peerage. James, who should have been 10th Lord, *d.* in 1677; James, 11th Lord, in 1690; James, his eldest son, *d.* before him in 1682, leaving a son, James, at whose baptism, in 1674, his father, grandfather, and great-grandfather were present; he succeeded his grandfather in 1690, and should have been 12th Lord; he *d.* in 1709.

His son and successor, James, 13th Lord, claimed and established his right to the Peerage before the House of Lords in 1723, and *d.* in 1765, leaving two sons:

1 James, 14th Lord, his successor, who *d. unm.* in 1796.

2 The Hon. Lieut.-Colonel Hugh Somerville, who *d.* in 1795, leaving John, 15th Lord, who succeeded his uncle, and *d. unm.* in 1819; Mark, present and 16th Lord, and other issue stated in *The Peerage Volume.*

SONDES, BARON. (Watson.)

Peer of Great Britain.

Sir Lewis Watson, Bart., a zealous loyalist of the time of Charles I., was created Baron Rockingham of Rockingham Castle, Co. Northampton, in 1645, he *d.* in 1652, and was succeeded by his only surviving son,

Edward, 2nd Lord Rockingham; he *m.* the Lady Anne Wentworth, eldest daughter of Thomas, 1st Earl of Strafford, the unfortunate Minister of King Charles I. and *d.* in 1691, leaving by her, besides other issue, the two sons following:

1 Lewis, his successor, 3rd Lord Rockingham; he *m.* Catherine, daughter and at length sole heir of Sir George Sondes, K.B., of Lees Court, in Kent, created Baron of Throughley, Viscount Sondes, and Earl of Feversham; and was in consequence created in 1714 Baron of Throughley, and Viscount Sondes of Lees Court, Co. Kent, and Earl of Rockingham, Co. Northampton; he *d.* in 1724, having had,

besides two elder daughters, both married, and a younger son George, who *d.* unm. the following issue:

1 Edward, Viscount Sondes, who *d.* before his father, having *m.* Catherine eldest daughter and co-heir of Thomas Tufton, 6th Earl of Thanet, and 18th Baron De Clifford, by writ, by whom he left two sons, successive Earls of Rockingham, Lewis, 2nd Earl, and Thomas, 3rd Earl, who both *d.* without issue, the latter in 1746; and a daughter, Catherine, who *m.* Edward Southwell, Esq., by whom she was mother of Edward Southwell, 20th Lord De Clifford, in favour of whose descent through her that Barony was called out of abeyance in 1776.

2 Lady Margaret, (3rd daughter); she *m.* John Monson, 1st Lord Monson, and had issue, John, 2nd Lord Monson, and Lewis, 1st Lord Sondes.

2 Thomas, who succeeding by will to the estates of his uncle William, 2nd Earl of Strafford, assumed the name and arms of Wentworth, and was created Baron Malton in 1728, and Earl of Malton in 1734: in 1746 he succeeded his great-nephew Thomas, 3rd Earl, as 4th Earl of Rockingham, and was in the same year advanced to the dignity of Marquis of Rockingham; he *d.* in 1750, leaving one son, the only survivor of five, Charles, 2nd Marquis, his successor, who *d.* when Prime Minister in 1782, without issue; his eldest sister Anne *m.* William, 3rd Earl Fitz-William, and her son, the present Earl, has inherited the Wentworth estates, and assumed the surname of Wentworth.

Thomas, 3rd Earl of Rockingham, appointed his cousin, Lewis Monson, 2nd son of John, 1st Lord Monson, by the Lady Margaret Watson, heir to his estates, on condition of his assuming the name and arms of Watson; he was created in 1760 Baron Sondes of Lees Court, Co. Kent; *b.* 28 Nov. 1728, and *d.* 30 March 1795; having *m.* 12 Oct. 1752, Grace, 4th daughter and co-heir of the Right Hon. Henry Pelham, brother of Thomas, 1st Duke of Newcastle, who was *b.* in Jan. 1735, and *d.* 31 July 1777. Lewis-Thomas, 2nd Lord, their eldest son, succeeded his father, and *d.* in 1806, when he was succeeded by his eldest son Lewis-Richard, present and 3rd Lord.

SOUTHAMPTON, BARON. (Fitz-Roy.)

Peer of Great Britain.

Charles Fitz-Roy, brother of Augustus-Henry, 3rd Duke of Grafton, and 2nd son of Lord Augustus Fitz-Roy, 2nd son of Charles, 2nd Duke of Grafton, was created in 1780 Baron of Southampton, Co. Hants; he *d.* in 1797, leaving a numerous issue, for whom see *The Peerage Volume*, and was succeeded by his eldest son George-Ferdinand, 2nd Lord, to whom succeeded in 1810, his eldest son Charles, present and 3rd Lord.

SOUTHWELL, VISCOUNT. (Southwell.)

Peer of Ireland.

John Southwell, of Felix Hall, Co. Essex, M.P. for Lewes in the reign of King Henry VI., had two sons: 1 Robert, ancestor of the present Lord De Clifford. 2 John, from whom descended

John Southwell of Barham, Co. Suffolk, who removed to Ireland in the reign of James I.; his grandson Thomas, was created a Bart. in 1662, and was father of Sir Thomas, created in 1717 Baron Southwell of Castle Mattress, Co. Limerick; he *d.* in 1720, and was succeeded by his eldest son Thomas, 2nd Lord; he *d.* in

1760, and was succeeded by his eldest surviving son Thomas-George, 3rd Lord; he was created Viscount Southwell in 1776, and *d.* in 1780, when he was succeeded by his eldest son Thomas-Arthur, 2nd Viscount, who *d.* in 1796, and was succeeded by his eldest son Thomas-Anthony, present and 3rd Viscount.

SPENCER, EARL, (Spencer.)

Peer of Great Britain.

The Hon. John Spencer, 4th son of Charles, 3rd Earl of Sunderland [by Lady Anne Churchill, 2nd daughter and co-heir of John Churchill, the 1st and great Duke of Marlborough,] and brother of Charles Spencer, 3rd Duke of Marlborough, came into possession of the ancient family-seat at Althorpe and other estates of the Sunderland family, on the succession of his brother to the Marlborough inheritance; he also succeeded by will to a considerable property on the death of his grandmother Sarah, Duchess of Marlborough; he *d.* 20 June 1746; having *m.* Lady Georgina-Caroline, 3rd daughter of John Carteret, Earl Granville, by whom (who *m.* 2ndly, 1 May 1750, William, 2nd Earl Cowper, but had no issue by him, and *d.* in Aug. 1780,) he had one son,

John, created in 1761 Baron and Viscount Spencer of Althorpe, Co. Northampton, and in 1765 Viscount Althorpe and Earl Spencer; he *d.* in 1783, and was succeeded by his only son George-John, present and 2nd Earl, K.G.

STAFFORD, MARQUIS. (Leveson-Gower.)

Peer of Great Britain.

The family of Gower is of Anglo-Saxon origin, and was seated in Yorkshire at the time of the Conquest. The Marquis traces his pedigree from Sir Nicholas Gower, a Knight of the Shire for the Co. of York in the reign of Edward III. The 7th in descent from him was Sir Thomas Gower, of Stittenham, Co. York, created a Baronet in 1620. His eldest son and successor, Sir Thomas Gower, a steadfast adherent of King Charles I. *m.* 1st, Elizabeth, daughter of William Howard, of Naworth Castle, and sister of the 1st Earl of Carlisle, by whom he had no issue; and 2ndly, Frances, daughter and co-heir of Sir John Leveson, of Haling, Co. Kent, by whom he had two sons, Edward and William. Edward *d.* before his father; his only son, Sir Thomas, succeeded his grandfather, he was a Colonel in the army and *d. unm.* at the camp of Dunkalk, in Ireland, in 1689, when he was succeeded in title and estate by his uncle,

William, 2nd son of Sir Thomas Gower, assumed the additional name of Leveson on being appointed sole heir to his great-uncle Sir Richard Leveson, of Trentham, Co. Stafford, K.B., brother of Sir John Leveson, of Haling, his maternal grandfather; he *m.* Lady Jane Granville, eldest daughter of John, 1st Earl of that family, and at length co-heir of her nephew William-Henry, 3rd Earl; he *d.* in 1691. Sir John Leveson-Gower, his son and successor, was created in 1703 Baron Gower, of Stittenham, Co. York, and *d.* in 1709, when he was succeeded by his eldest son, John, 2nd Lord, who was created in 1746 Viscount Trentham, Co. Stafford, and Earl Gower. He *d.* in 1754, having been three times married, 1st to Lady Evelyn Pierrepont, 3rd daughter of Evelyn, Duke of Kingston, who *d.* in 1727; 2ndly, to Penelope, daughter of Sir John Stonehouse, Bart., and widow of Sir Henry Atkins, Bart., who *d.* in 1734; and 3rdly, to Lady Mary Tufton, daughter and co-heir of Thomas, Earl of Thanet, and widow of Anthony, Earl of Harold, son of Henry, Duke of Kent. He left issue, besides several daughters, all by the first wife, married into noble families, and other sons and daughters who *d.* young or *unm.*, the two sons following:

'AUL, his uncle and heir male, the 4th Earl, and who should have been 5th LORD, n whose death, without issue, in 1762 the Earldom became extinct. He was the ast male descendant of SIR WILLIAM HOWARD, Viscount Stafford, and 1st LORD; ut for whose attainder the Barony of 1640 would, on the extinction of his male eirs, have fallen into abeyance between the above three sisters of the 3rd Earl, and, n the decease of the Ladies Mary and Anne, would have emerged in the person f the LADY ANASTASIA STAFFORD-HOWARD, by right of inheritance 6th BARONESS; he *d.* in 1807, when

Sir William Jerningham, Bart, of Cossey Hall, Co. Norfolk, son of Sir George erningham, Bart., by Mary, daughter, and at length sole heir, of Francis Plowden, sq., by Mary, eldest daughter of John Stafford-Howard, 2nd son of the 1st Lord, ould, but for the iniquitous attainder of his ancestor, have become 7th Lord; hat attainder was reversed in 1824, in favour of his son SIR GEORGE-WILLIAM, he present and 8th LORD, and the title and precedence of daughter of a Baron as granted in 1831 to Charlotte-Georgiana, his only daughter.

The claim of the present Lord to the Barony created by patent in 1640, was allowed by the House of Peers 6 July 1825. His Lordship, who has assumed the additional name of STAFFORD, also claims the ancient Barony by writ 1299, but his ight to it has not yet been decided upon.

The family of Jerningham has been seated in the Counties of Norfolk and Suffolk, early from the time of the Conquest. Sir Henry Jerningham, 15th in descent from Jernegan, the first of the name on record, was created a Baronet in 1621, and was ancestor, in the 6th degree, of the present LORD.

STAIR, EARL OF. (DALRYMPLE.)

Peer of Scotland.

JAMES DALRYMPLE, Esq., of Stair, President of the Court of Session, 8th in descent from William de Dalrymple, who obtained the lands of Stair Montgomery, in Ayrshire, by marriage in 1450, was created in 1690 VISCOUNT of STAIR, Lord Glenluce and Stranraer; he *d.* in 1695, leaving five sons, viz.:

1 JOHN, his successor, 2nd Viscount and 1st EARL of STAIR.

2 The Hon. Sir James Dalrymple, created a Baronet in 1698; he had a numerous ssue, of whom the two sons following have left descendants:

1 Sir John, his successor, who *d.* in 1743; he had also a numerous issue, of whom only one son left issue,

Sir William Dalrymple, Bart., his successor; he *d.* in 1771, leaving issue,

1 Sir John Dalrymple, Bart., of Cousland and Fala, who *d.* in 1810; having *m.* Elizabeth, only daughter and heir of Thomas Hamilton-Macgill, Esq., by whom he had the present Lieut.-General Sir John HAMILTON-DALRYMPLE, Bart., and the other issue stated in *The Peerage Volume.*

2 Lieut.-Colonel William Dalrymple of Fordel; who *d.* in 1794, leaving Marton Dalrymple, Esq., deceased, and the other issue stated in *The Peerage Volume.*

3 General Samuel Dalrymple, for whom and Sir William's other surviving issue, see *The Peerage Volume.*

2 Robert Dalrymple, Esq., of Killock; he *d.* in 1765; his son, Admiral John Dalrymple, *d.* in 1798, leaving a son, Robert Dalrymple, Esq., of Killock, who is also deceased.

3 The Hon. Sir Hew Dalrymple of North Berwick, created a Baronet in 1698; he *d.* in 1737; having had, besides other issue:

1 Sir Robert, who *d.* before his father in 1734, having *m.* Johanna, daughter and heir of the Hon. Sir John Hamilton, [eldest son of John, 2nd Lord

Regent Duke of Orleans to the juggling pretences of the financier Law of Mississippi notoriety; he was recalled in 1720, and entering warmly into opposition to the Walpole administration, remained in retirement till its dissolution in 1742; when he was appointed Commander of the allied forces in Flanders with the rank of Field-Marshal. The following year, the King in person taking the command of the army, the Earl fought under his Majesty at the battle of Dettingen; but, finding his counsels slighted, and a preference shown on all occasions to the Hanoverian troops, resigned his command and retired. He *d.* in 1747, with the reputation of one of the most penetrating statesmen, and most experienced and brave warriors of his time; no less eminent in the Cabinet than in the field; of incorruptible integrity, and adorned by the finest accomplishments and manners. He was *m.* but left no issue. And his next brother and heir having *m.* Penelope, Countess of Dumfries, he obtained a renewal of his patent granting the Earldom of Stair to the second and every succeeding son of that marriage in tail male, and failing such issue, to William Earl of Dumfries, and his heirs male; conditionally that the two Earldoms should be separated so soon as there should be two sons descended of the said Earl to enjoy them.

2 The Hon. William Dalrymple of Glenmure; he *d.* before his elder brother in 1744, having *m.* Penelope, Countess of Dumfries, eldest daughter of Charles, Lord Crichton, and sister and heir of William, 3rd Earl of Dumfries; she *d.* in 1742: they had besides other issue, who all *d. unm.*, the following:

- 1 William, who succeeded his mother as 5th Earl of Dumfries, and on the death of his last surviving brother James, succeeded as 4th Earl of Stair, he *d.* without surviving issue in 1768.
- 2 James, who succeeded his uncle as 3rd Earl, according to the limitations of the renewed patent; he *d.* without issue in 1760, and was the last surviving male descendant of his father, except William, Earl of Dumfries, who, accordingly succeeded as 4th Earl; and on his death the title devolved on the descendants of the Hon. George Dalrymple, 3rd son of the 1st Earl.

3 The Hon. George Dalrymple of Dalmahoy; he *d.* in 1745, leaving two sons, viz.:

- 1 John, 5th Earl, who succeeded on the death of his cousin, William, Earl of Dumfries and Stair, and *d.* in 1789, leaving one son, John, 6th Earl, who had been Minister Plenipotentiary to the King and Republic of Poland, and was at the time of his accession to the Earldom, Envoy Extraordinary, and Minister Plenipotentiary at the Court of Berlin; he was *b.* 24 Sept. 1749, succeeded 13 Oct. 1789, and *d. unm.* 1 June 1821.
- 2 William, *b.* 1735, and *d.* 23 Feb. 1807; leaving one son, John-William-Henry, who succeeded his uncle, and is the present and 7th Earl.

STAMFORD, EARL OF. (Grey.)

Peer of England.

Anschetil de Grey, who is recorded in the Doomsday Book, but whose pedigree, whether Saxon or Norman, is uncertain, was the Patriarch of this noble family, one of the most ancient, most wide-spread, and most illustrious in the English Peerage his great-grandson, Sir John de Grey, was father of

Sir Henry de Grey, who had six sons, viz.:

1 Richard, whose grandson, Henry, was summoned to Parliament in 1299, as Baron Grey of Codnor, from whom the Lords Grey of Codnor continued, in lineal male succession, till the death of Henry, 7th Lord in 1496, when the Barony fell into abeyance.

2 Sir John; he *d.* in 1265, and was father of Reginald, summoned to Parlia-

1 Sir Thomas, who succeeded his grandfather as Baron Astley and Ferrars of Groby, and was created Marquis of Dorset; *see* below.

2 Sir Richard, taken prisoner by Richard Duke of Gloucester, while assisting the Earl Rivers, his uncle, in conveying the young King EDWARD V. to London, and beheaded by his orders in Pomfret Castle, without trial or accusation, in 1483.

2 Edward; he *d.* in 1491, having *m.* Elizabeth, sister and heir of Thomas Talbot, 2nd Viscount L'Isle, became in her right Baron L'Isle, and was created in 1483 Viscount L'Isle; his only son, John, 2nd Viscount, *d.* without issue male in 1512; and Elizabeth, daughter of the 1st and sister of the 2nd Viscount, becoming their eventual heir, carried the barony of L'Isle into the family of her husband, Edmund Dudley, whose son by her, John Dudley, Duke of Northumberland, became in her right Baron L'Isle.

3 Reginald, killed on the Lancastrian side in the battle of Wakefield in 1460.

Sir Thomas Grey, 7th Lord Astley, and 8th Lord Ferrars of Groby, K.G., was created Marquis of Dorset in 1475 by his step-father, King EDWARD IV; after whose death he was attainted under RICHARD III., and restored in blood in the first year of HENRY VII. He *d.* in 1501, having been twice married, 1st to Anne, daughter of Henry Holland, Earl of Exeter, by whom he had no issue; and 2ndly, to Cecily, only daughter and heir of William, 3rd Baron Bonville, (by writ 1449,) and maternally, 6th Baron Harrington, (by writ 1324;) they had, besides other issue, Lord Leonard Grey (their 6th son) created Viscount Garney in Ireland; but tried for some treasonable association with the Irish, attainted and beheaded on Tower-hill in 1541; and

Thomas, (their eldest surviving son,) who succeeded to the titles of his father and mother, 2nd Marquis of Dorset, K.G. He *d.* in 1530, leaving four sons, viz.:

1 Henry, 3rd Marquis, his successor, K.G., who in 1551 was created Duke of Suffolk; having *m.* Frances, daughter and co-heir of Charles Brandon, Duke of Suffolk, by Mary, Queen-dowager of France, daughter of King Henry VII. The Duke, having been induced by the Duke of Northumberland to enter into the plot for raising his daughter, the Lady Jane Grey, to the Throne, was attainted and beheaded in 1555, when the titles of Duke of Suffolk, Marquis of Dorset, Baron Astley, Ferrars of Groby, Harrington, and Bonville, became forfeited. By Frances his Duchess, who after his death *m.* Adrian Stokes, Esq., and *d.* without issue by him in 1563, he had three daughters, viz.:

1 The accomplished and unfortunate Lady Jane Grey, whom the ambition of the Duke of Northumberland elevated to the throne only to bring her to an untimely grave; she was *m.* to Lord Guildford Dudley, 4th son of the Duke of Northumberland, who suffered on the scaffold on the same day that she was beheaded, 12 Feb. 1555.

2 Lady Catherine Grey, the eventual heir of the Princess Mary, whose unfortunate marriage with the Earl of Hertford has been related in this volume—*see* title Somerset. She *d.* a prisoner in the Tower, where her two sons were born. The present representative of this marriage is Anna Eliza, Duchess of Buckingham and Chandos.

3 Lady Mary Grey; warned by the misfortunes of her sisters, she preferred security to honour, and *m.* Martin Keys, Esq., Serjeant-Porter to Queen ELIZABETH, and *d.* without issue.

2 Lord Thomas Grey, who after the proclamation of Queen MARY, joined in the insurrection of Sir Thomas Wyat, and was beheaded 27 April 1555.

3 Lord Leonard Grey, concerned in the same rebellion, and also beheaded in the Tower.

4 Lord John Grey, who after the execution of his three brothers, became the chief of this branch of the family, but could not inherit any of its honours on account of the attainder of his eldest brother, in whose person they were forfeited; he *d.* in 1564.

gossa, and in Sept. 1709 he entered Madrid, of which he took possession in the name of King Charles. But his triumphs were short. The Duke de Vendome assumed the command of the combined French and Spanish armies; the Castilians attached to King Philip abandoned Madrid and crowded to his standard; the armies of Charles were neglected both by the Governments of Vienna and London; General Stanhope retreated before a superior force, and being deserted by the German Commander, Prince Starhemberg, was surrounded at Brihuega at the end of November, and after a short but vigorous resistance, was compelled to surrender with his whole army, amounting to two thousand men. On the accession of King George I. he was appointed Secretary of State, and continued to hold a principal place in the Administration 'till his death. He was created in 1717 Baron Stanhope of Elveston, Co. Derby, and Viscount Stanhope of Mahon, with remainder, failing his issue male, to his kinsman, Thomas Stanhope, Esq., of Elveston, and to Charles and William, his brothers, and their heirs male respectively; they were sons of John Stanhope, Esq., grandson of Sir John Stanhope of Elveston, brother of the 1st Earl of Chesterfield. Of these three brothers, Thomas *d.* without issue, Charles *d. unm.*, and William was created Earl of Harrington, and was ancestor of the present Earl of Harrington, who, with all the male branches of his family, are consequently in remainder to this Peerage. He was farther created EARL STANHOPE in 1718, with remainder to the heirs male of his body. He *d.* in 1721, and was succeeded by his eldest son, PHILIP, 2nd EARL, who *d.* in 1786, and was succeeded by his only surviving son, CHARLES, 3rd EARL; this ingenious and scientific nobleman was succeeded in 1816 by his eldest son, PHILIP-HENRY, present and 4th EARL.

STOURTON, BARON. (STOURTON.)

Peer of England.

Of this family, which took its name from the town of Stourton, in Wilts, was Botolph Stourton, who, with his followers, defending the passes in the West against William the Conqueror, obtained from him the terms he required. He was ancestor in the 10th degree of

SIR JOHN STOURTON, created BARON STOURTON of Stourton, Co. Wilts; he *d.* in 1462. WILLIAM, 2nd LORD, his eldest son and successor, *m.* Margaret, 2nd daughter and co-heir of Sir John Chediock, co-heir with her sister Katherine, the wife of Sir John Arundel, of the Barony of Fitz-Paine, by writ 1299; Sir John, their father, being the son and heir of Sir John Chediock, who was son and heir of John Chediock, by Isabel his wife, sole daughter and heir of Robert, 5th Lord Fitz-Payne. The 2nd LORD STOURTON and Margaret his wife left three sons, JOHN, WILLIAM, and EDWARD, successive LORDS. JOHN, 3rd LORD, *d.* without issue male in 1484, and Anna, his daughter, *d. unm.* in 1533; WILLIAM, 4th LORD, *d.* without issue in 1522; and EDWARD, 5th LORD, *d.* in 1536, and was succeeded by his eldest son, WILLIAM, 6th LORD. His eldest son and successor, CHARLES, 7th LORD, was hanged at Salisbury in 1557, for having, with four of his sons, been concerned in a murder; he was succeeded by his eldest son, JOHN, 8th LORD, who *d.* in 1588, and was followed by his next brother, EDWARD, 9th LORD. To him succeeded, in 1632, his eldest son, WILLIAM, 10th LORD, who survived his eldest son Edward, a faithful adherent of King CHARLES I. in the civil war, and was succeeded by his grandson, WILLIAM, 11th LORD, only son of the said Edward. The 11th LORD *d.* in 1685, leaving, besides other issue, three sons: EDWARD and THOMAS, successive LORDS, who both *d.* without issue; and Charles, who, besides other issue, was father of CHARLES, 14th LORD, who succeeded his uncle, LORD THOMAS, in 1744, and *d.* without issue in 1753; and WILLIAM, 15th LORD, who succeeded his brother, and *d.* in 1781; he *m.* Winifred, eldest daughter and co-heir of Philip Howard, Esq., brother of Thomas, 11th, and Edward, 12th, Dukes of Norfolk, and co-heir with her [illegible] Lord Petre, of the Baronies by writ [illegible] in the house of [illegible] [illegible] succeeded his father as 16th Lord, and was succeeded [illegible] by his eldest son, William, present and 17th Lord.

[illegible] eldest son and heir of William, 15th Lord, by Winefrid, eldest daughter and co-heir of Philip Howard, Esq., brother of Thomas, 13th, and Edward, [illegible] co-heir with Lord Petre, as grandson and heir of Anne, [illegible] daughter of the said Philip Howard, Esq., of the Baronies by writ of Mowbray [illegible] and Howard 1470; [illegible] co-heir with Lord Petre as above, of the moiety of the Baronies by writ of Segrave [illegible] 1299, Lisle 1357, and Dacre [illegible]

[illegible] co-heir by the marriage above recited, of William, 2nd [illegible] of the Barony of Fitz-Payne, by writ 1299, to the [illegible] of which Barony Henry 8th Lord Arundell was heir; his co-heirs are [illegible] and [illegible] Clifford.

ST[illegible]WELL, BARON. (Scott.)

Peer of the United Kingdom.

His Lordship's father was William Scott, Esq., a merchant of Newcastle-upon-Tyne, who d. in Nov. 17[illegible], having m. Jane, daughter of Henry Atkinson, Esq., by whom, who was b. in 17[illegible] and d. 14 July 1800, he had issue,

1 Sir William Scott, the present Peer, who was appointed in 1788 Judge of the Consistory Court of London, and in 1798 Judge of the High Court of Admiralty; his Lordship is universally respected for his profound knowledge of the civil law, and for his luminous and discriminating decisions as a Judge; he was created in 1821 Baron Stowell, of Stowell Park, Co. Gloucester.

2 Henry, d. 8 Dec. 17[illegible], having m. Mary, daughter of John Cook, Esq., by whom, who d. 5 June 18[illegible], he had an only daughter, Mary, m. 8 July 1794, to [illegible] Forster, Esq.

3 John, Earl of Eldon, for so many years our exemplary Lord High Chancellor.

4 Barbara, twin with Lord Stowell; she d. unm.

5 Jane, who d. 8 May 18[illegible], having m. Sir Thomas Burdon, Knt.

STRADBROKE, EARL OF. (Rous.)

Peer of the United Kingdom.

The family of Rous existed in Suffolk before the Conquest. Sir John Rous of Henham Hall, Co. Suffolk, 11th in descent from Peter Le Rous of Dennington, Co. Suffolk, his first recorded ancestor, was created a Baronet in 1660. His great-grandson,

Sir John Rous, 5th Baronet, was *b.* in Feb. 1728, and *d.* 31 Oct. 1771; having *m.* in 1749, Judith, daughter of John Bedingfeld, Esq., who was *b.* 28 April 1730, *m.* 2ndly, 3 Nov. 1772, the Rev. Edward Lockwood,) and *d.* in Sept. 1794; by whom he had issue:

1 Sir John, his successor, who was created in 1796 Baron Rous of Dennington, Co. Suffolk, and Viscount Dunwich and Earl of Stradbroke, Co. Suffolk, in 1821.

2 Frances, late wife of Sir Henry Peyton, Bart., deceased.

3 Charlotte, who *d.* unm. in 1770.

4 Louisa Judith, late wife of John Birch, Esq., Deputy Governor of Chandernagore in the East Indies, where she *d.* in 1794.

STRANGFORD, VISCOUNT. (Smythe.)

Peer of Ireland and of Great Britain.

John Smythe, Esq., of a very ancient family in Wiltshire, was of Corsham, in that county, in the reign of Henry VIII.; his son Thomas was Farmer of the Customs to Queen Elizabath, settled at Ostenhanger, in Kent, and *d.* in 1591; leaving, besides other issue, the three sons following, viz.:

1 Sir John Smythe, who *d.* in 1608, leaving an only son, Sir Thomas, 1st Viscount Strangford.

2 Sir Thomas Smythe, Ambassador to Russia in 1604; he *d.* in 1625, having *m.* Sarah, daughter and heir of William Blount, Esq.; who *m.* 2ndly, Robert Sydney, 1st Earl of Leicester; his eldest son, Sir John, was father of Robert Smythe, Esq., of Bounds, near Tunbridge, who *m.* Lady Dorothy Sydney, eldest daughter of Robert, 2nd Earl of Leicester. This branch ended in 1777, by the death of Sir Sydney-Stafford Smythe, Lord Chief Baron of the Exchequer.

3 Sir Richard Smythe, of Leeds Castle, Co. Kent, who *d.* in 1628; his daughters became his co-heirs, on the death in 1632 of his only son, Sir John Smythe.

Sir Thomas Smythe, K.B., of Ostenhanger and Ashford, Co. Kent, *m.* Lady Barbara Sydney, 7th daughter of Robert, 1st Earl of Leicester, and was created in 1628 Viscount Strangford of Strangford, Co. Down; he *d.* in 1635, and was succeeded by his son, Philip, 2nd Viscount, who *m.* Lady Isabella Sydney, youngest daughter of Robert, 2nd Earl of Leicester, and by her, (who *d.* in 1663,) was father of Thomas, his successor, 3rd Viscount, who *d* in 1708; and was succeeded by his only son, Philip, 4th Viscount; to him succeeded in 1715, Endymion, his eldest surviving son, 5th Viscount, who *d.* in 1724, and was succeeded by his only son, Philip, 6th Viscount. He *d.* in 1787, when Lionel, his only surviving son, 7th Viscount, succeeded; he was succeeded in 1801 by his only surviving son, Percy-Clinton-Sydney, present and 8th Viscount, who in 1825 was created Baron Penshurst of Penshurst, Co. Kent, in the Peerage of the United Kingdom.

STRATHALLAN, VISCOUNT. (Drummond.)

Peer of Scotland.

The first of this ancient family who settled in Scotland is said to have been Maurice, a Hungarian, who accompanied Edgar Atheling and his sister Margaret into Scotland, and obtained from King Malcolm III. the lands of Drymen, from whence his posterity derived their surname. From him descended Sir Malcolm Drummond, who flourished in the reign of King William I. of Scotland; the 10th from him was

John, who was created Lord Drummond in 1488, and *d.* in 1519. His eldest son William, Master of Drummond, was executed in 1511 for setting fire to the Church of Monyvaird in which several of the Murrays, with whom he had a feud, and who had taken refuge there from an attack of Drummond's men, were burnt. He left a son Walter, who *d.* before his grandfather in 1518, leaving a son

David, who succeeded his great-grandfather as 2nd Lord; he joined the association at Hamilton in favour of Queen Mary in 1568, and *d.* in 1571, leaving two sons, viz.;

1 Patrick, 3rd Lord Drummond, who *d.* in 1600, leaving also two sons, viz.: James, 4th Lord, who was created Earl of Perth in 1605, with remainder to his heirs male whatsoever, and *d.* without issue male in 1611; and John, who succeeded

his brother as 2nd Earl of Perth. Throughout the troubles of the civil wars he was unshaken in his loyalty to King CHARLES, and *d.* in 1662, leaving, besides other issue, three sons:

1 James, 3rd Earl of Perth, who was taken prisoner at the battle of Philliphaugh; he *d.* in 1675, leaving two sons,

1 James, his successor, 4th Earl of Perth, who, adhering closely to King JAMES, and having suffered a severe imprisonment, followed by banishment for his loyalty to the abdicated Monarch, was by him created Duke of Perth. He *d.* in 1716, when his titles failed, his eldest son, James, Lord Drummond, having been attainted for his share in the rebellion of 1715; he escaped to France, and, on his father's death, assumed the title of Duke of Perth; he *d.* at Paris in 1730, leaving two sons: James, styled Duke of Perth, and Lord John Drummond, both attainted for joining in the rebellion of 1745. The Duke, escaping after the battle of Culloden, *d.* of exhaustion on his passage to France in 1746, in his thirty-third year, and his brother John *d.* in the following year, both without issue. Lords John and Edward, their uncles, younger sons of the 1st Duke, successively assumed the ducal title after the deaths of their nephews, and both *d.* without issue, the last at Paris in 1760. An Act of Parliament was passed in 1784 enabling the King to grant their forfeited estate to the legal heir and it was in consquence granted to James, late Lord Perth.

2 John, created in 1686 Earl of Melfort, with remainder to the issue male of his 2nd marriage, which failing, to his heirs male whatsoever; following King JAMES in his exile, he was by him created Duke of Melfort in 1690, and attainted by the English Parliament in 1695. He *d.* in 1714 at St. Germains, where for many years he had the chief administration of King JAMES's affairs. He was twice *m.* 1st to Sophia, heiress of Lundin, niece of the Duke of Lauderdale, whose family, against his will, brought up her children in the Protestant faith, and an exception was made in their favour in the act of attainder passed against him. James Drummond, of Lundin, his great-grandson by this marriage, having proved himself the heir male of the house of Perth, obtained in 1785 a grant of the estates of the Earl of Perth, in conformity to the Act of Parliament mentioned above, and was created in 1797, Lord Perth, Baron Drummond of Stob Hall, Co. Perth, which title became extinct on his death in 18[illegible]. He left an only daughter and heir, Clementina-Sarah, *m.* to the present Lord Willoughby de Eresby, who has assumed the name of DRUMMOND. But the titles of Melfort, but for the attainder, would have descended to the issue of the 1st Earl's 2nd marriage with Eupheme, daughter of Sir Thomas Wallace, and from this branch descends a still existing family, bearing the title of Duke Melfort.

2 Sir John Drummond, ancestor of the Right Hon. Sir William Drummond of Logiealmond, Knight of the Crescent, of literary and political notoriety.

3 William, 2nd Earl of Roxburghe, whose male line failed in 1805, on the death of William, 4th Duke of Roxburghe—*See* that title in this Volume.

2 JAMES, 2nd son of David, 2nd Lord Drummond, to whom the thread of this pedigree has at length arrived, the ancestor of the Viscount Strathallan, was educated with King JAMES VI., and was a great favourite of that Monarch, whom he accompanied to Perth on the memorable 5th of Aug. 1600, when the Earl of Gowrie and his brother were killed in an attempt upon his Majesty's life, and gave a clear deposition relative to that mysterious affair. He was created a Peer by the title of Lord MADERTY in 1609, and *d.* in 1623, leaving two sons, viz.:

1 JOHN, 2nd LORD, who with his two sons suffered considerably in the cause

of King CHARLES I., he was father of DAVID, 3rd LORD, who *d.* in 1684 without surviving issue male, and of WILLIAM, 4th LORD; the latter was created in 1686 VISCOUNT STRATHALLAN and Baron Drummond of Cromlix, with remainder, failing the heirs male of his body, to his heirs male whatsoever. He *d.* in 1688, and was succeeded by his only son WILLIAM, 2nd VISCOUNT, on the death of whose only son WILLIAM, 3rd VISCOUNT, in 1711, the issue male of the 1st Viscount failed.

2 James, also with his son Sir James, a loyalist in the civil war; the latter *d.* in 1675, leaving an only surviving son,

Sir John Drummond. He was outlawed in 1690 for his attachment to the abdicated family, and *d.* in 1707, leaving, besides a younger son Thomas, who was engaged in the rebellion of 1715, two elder sons, viz.:

1 WILLIAM, who succeeded as 4th Viscount on the extinction of the male descendants of the 1st Viscount in 1711; he engaged in the rebellion of 1715, and was taken at Sheriffmuir, but no proceedings took place against him; he also joined the young Chevalier in 1745, was left Commander-in-chief of his forces in Scotland, when he marched into England, and was killed at the battle of Culloden in 1746: he was attainted by Act of Parliament. Margaret, his wife, daughter of Lord William Murray, 2nd Lord Nairne, was committed to Edinburgh Castle in Feb. 1746, on account of her activity in the cause of the Chevalier, but was liberated on bail in November following. She *d.* in 1773; they had, besides three other sons, who *d. unm.*, the four following:

1 JAMES, who succeeded as 5th VISCOUNT, and having engaged in the rebellion of 1745, was attainted; he *d.* 22 July 1765, having *m.* Eupheme, daughter of Peter Gordon, Esq., by whom, who *d.* 5 July 1796, he left issue, 1 JAMES, his successor, who, but for the attainder, would have been 6th VISCOUNT; he was *b.* in 1752, and *d. unm.* 10 Dec. 1775; 2 ANDREW-JOHN, who should have succeeded his brother as 7th VISCOUNT; he was *b.* in 1758, and *d. unm.* 20 Jan. 1817; 3 Hon. Margaret, who *d.* in 1821; having *m.* in Dec. 1779, George-Augustus Haldane, Esq., of Gleneagles, who *d.* 26 Oct. 1799; 4 Hon. Elizabeth, who *d.* in July 1831, aged 76.

2 The Hon. William Drummond, (3rd son,) who *d.* 25 May 1772; having *m.* Anne, 2nd daughter of Major David Nairne, by whom, who *d.* 31 May 1782, he was father of JAMES-ANDREW-JOHN-LAURENCE-CHARLES, the present and 8th VISCOUNT, who, but for the attainder, would have succeeded in 1817 on the death of his cousin the 7th VISCOUNT, and was graciously restored to his honours under his late Majesty, by Act of Parliament, in 1824.

3 The Hon. Robert Drummond, of Cadlands, Co. Hants, Banker at Charing-Cross; (6th son;) he was *b.* in 1729, and *d.* 19 Jan. 1804; having *m.* in 1753, Winifred, daughter of William Thompson, Esq., who *d.* 2 April 1791. The numerous surviving descendants of this marriage are stated in *The Peerage Volume*.

4 The Hon. Henry Drummond, (7th son,) who *d.* 24 June 1795; having *m.* 21 March 1761, Elizabeth, 4th daughter of the Hon. Charles Compton, and sister of Charles, 7th, and Spencer, 8th Earls of Northampton, *b.* 13 Sept. 1744, *d.* 26 March 1819. They had an only son Henry, who *d.* before his father, 4 July 1794; and for whose surviving widow and issue, see *The Peerage Volume*.

2 Andrew Drummond, Esq. (5th but 2nd surviving son of Sir John Drummond,) the founder of the great banking-house at Charing Cross; he purchased the estate at Stanmore in Middlesex, and dying in 1769, in his 82nd year, was buried there; leaving an only son, John, who *d.* in June 1774; having *m.* 22 Dec. 1744 Charlotte, eldest daughter of Lord William Beauclerk, 2nd son of Charles, 1st Duke of St. Albans; by which Lady, who *d.* 7 March 1793, he had issue, 1 George Drummond, Esq., *b.* 15 June 1758, *d.* 6 March 1789; having *m.* 30 Nov. 1779, Martha, 5th daughter of the Right Hon. Thomas Harley of OXFORD, by whom, who was *b.* 10 May

1757, and *d.* 16 Aug. 1788, he had the three children stated in *The Peerage Volume.* 2 John, who survives—see *The Peerage Volume.* 3 Charlotte, *d.* March 1774; having *m.* 24 Nov. 1769, the Rev. Henry Beauclerk, only son of Lord Henry, 4th son of Charles, 1st Duke of St. Albans. 4 Jane-Diana, *d.* in 1790; having *m.* 7 April 1766, Richard-Bethel Cox, Esq.

STRATHMORE, EARL OF. (LYON-BOWES.)

Peer of Scotland.

John Lyon got from King DAVID II. the reversion of the Thanedom of Glamis; he was great-grandfather of PATRICK LYON, who was created LORD GLAMIS in 1445, and *d.* in 1459; his two eldest sons, ALEXANDER, who *d.* without issue in 1486, and John, who *d.* in 1497, were successively LORDS GLAMIS; the latter was succeeded by his son JOHN, 4th LORD, who *d.* in 1500; leaving issue, GEORGE, 5th LORD, who *d.* a minor in 1505, and JOHN, 6th LORD, who succeeded his brother.

The 6th LORD *d.* in 1528, having *m.* Janet Douglas, daughter of George, Master of Angus, and sister of Archibald, 6th Earl of Angus, who was, with Archibald Campbell of Kepneith, her 2nd husband, and her son LORD GLAMIS, and others indicted for designs, by poison or witchcraft, against the life of King James V. Campbell, in attempting to escape from the Castle of Edinburgh, was dashed to pieces against the rocks which form the base of that sublime edifice; the Lady was condemned for a witch, and burnt to death on the Castle Hill, 17 July 1537, displaying to an immense concourse of spectators a masculine firmness of mind worthy the house of Douglas, in a form of feminine grace and beauty. Her son JOHN, 7th LORD, still a minor, was also condemned to death, but his execution was respited till he came of age. Meanwhile the accuser, one Lyon, avowed his evidence to be false, and the LORD GLAMIS was released; he *d.* in 1558. Sir Thomas Lyon, his eldest son, was one of the principal agents in the raid of Ruthven in 1582; and the King's bursting into tears when Sir Thomas stopped him from passing the door, drew from him the exclamation, "No matter, better children weep than bearded men!" On the King's recovering his liberty the following year, Sir Thomas retired into England, and was forfeited, but was pardoned in 1586. At his death in 1594 the King remarked that the boldest and hardiest man in his dominions was taken away. JOHN, 8th LORD GLAMIS, his elder brother, and eldest son of the 7th LORD, was appointed Lord High Chancellor of Scotland in 1573, and in March 1578 was deputed by the nobility, who were tired of the administration of the Regent, Earl of Morton, to notify to the Earl that the King, though only in his 12th year, had resolved to take the government into his own hands. The Lord Glamis was accidentally killed in an encounter between his own followers and those of the Earl of Crawford at Stirling, on the 17th of the same month.

He was succeeded by his only son PATRICK, 9th LORD, who was created in 1606 EARL of KINGHORN, Lord Lyon and Glamis, and *d.* in 1615. He was succeeded by his eldest son JOHN, 2nd EARL; who sided with the Parliament in the civil war, he opposed the delivery up of the King to the English in January 1647, and *d.* in May the same year. He was succeeded by his only son PATRICK, 3rd EARL; who in 1672 obtained a charter of the Earldom to himself and the heirs male of his body, failing which, to such persons as shall be nominated by him, failing which, to his heirs male whatsoever, failing which, to his heirs and assigns whatsoever; and another charter decreeing that the Earls of Kinghorn should for the future be styled EARLS of STRATHMORE and Kinghorn, Viscounts Lyon, Lords Glamis, Tannadyce, Seidlaw, and Stradichtie; all the succeeding Earls are his male issue. He *d.* in 1695; leaving two sons, of whom the younger, the Hon. Patrick Lyon, was killed in the battle of Sheriffmuir, on the part of the rebels; and the elder, JOHN, 4th EARL, succeeded his father.

The family of the 4th EARL exhibited the extraordinary instance of six sons succeeding each other in their inheritance; they were, Patrick Lord Glamis, who *d.* in his 17th year; Philip Lord Glamis, who *d.* in his 19th year, both before their father; JOHN, who succeeded his father as 5th EARL, and was killed in the rebel army at the battle of Sheriffmuir, in 1715, *unm.*; CHARLES, 6th EARL, who in a quarrel between James Carnegy of Finhaven and John Lyon of Brigton, was accidentally killed by the latter in 1728; he *d.* without issue; JAMES, 7th EARL, who *d.* without issue in 1735; and THOMAS, 8th EARL.

The 8th EARL *d.* in 1753, leaving three sons: 1 JOHN, 9th EARL. 2 The Hon. James-Philip Lyon, who being in the service of the East India Company, was taken prisoner by Mir Cossim, Nabob of Bengal, and murdered at Patna, with several other British gentlemen, in 1763; he *d. unm.* 3 The Hon. Thomas Lyon of Hetton House, Co. Durham; he was *b.* in 1741, and *d.* 13 Sept. 1796; having *m.* 13 June 1774, Mary-Elizabeth, daughter of Farrer Wren, Esq., of Binchester, Co. Durham; by whom, who *d.* 31 May 1811, he left Mary, who *d.* 22 June 1803, having *m.* 1 Jan. 1799, Thomas Wilkinson, Esq.; and the other issue stated in *The Peerage Volume.*

JOHN, 9th EARL, succeeded his father, and *d.* in 1776, when he was succeeded by his eldest son JOHN, 10th EARL; who dying in 1820, was succeeded by his only surviving brother THOMAS, the present and 11th EARL.

STUART DE ROTHESAY, BARON. (STUART.)

Peer of the United Kingdom.

The Right Hon. SIR CHARLES STUART, G.C.B., many years British Ambassador at Paris, eldest son of the late Hon. Sir Charles Stuart, K.B., 3rd son of John, 3rd Earl of Bute, and great uncle of the present Marquis of Bute, was created in 1828 BARON STUART DE ROTHESAY of the Isle of Bute. *See* the title Bute in this volume.

SUFFIELD, BARON. (HARBORD.)

Peer of Great Britain.

William Morden, Esq., *m.* the daughter and heir of Harbord Harbord, Esq., of Gunton, Co. Norfolk; their son William took the name and arms of Harbord, on succeeding to his grandfather's estate in 1742; in 1744 he was elected a Knight of the Bath by the name of Sir William Harbord, and in 1745 was created a Baronet. SIR HARBORD HARBORD, his son and heir, was created BARON SUFFIELD of Suffield, Co. Norfolk, in 1786, and *d.* in 1810, when he was succeeded by his eldest son WILLIAM-ASHETON, 2nd LORD, who *d.* without issue in 1821, and was succeeded by his only surviving brother EDWARD, present and 3rd Lord.

SUFFOLK, EARL OF. (HOWARD.)

Peer of England.

Thomas, 4th Duke of Norfolk, was father, by his 1st marriage, of Philip, Earl of Arundel, ancestor of all the succeeding Dukes of Norfolk; and by his 2nd marriage, with Margaret, daughter and sole heir of Thomas, Lord Audley of Walden, he had Lord Thomas, and Lord William, ancestor of the Earl of Carlisle.

LORD THOMAS HOWARD, K.G., eldest son of the 2nd marriage, was summoned to ment till the Restoration. He had nine sons, of whom the four following succeeded or gave heirs to the title.

1 CHARLES, his successor, 2nd EARL of BERKSHIRE, *d.* without surviving issue male, in 1679.

2 THOMAS, 3rd EARL, succeeded his brother, and *d.* also without issue male, in 1706.

3 William, who had an only son, Craven, whose only son, HENRY BOWES, succeeded his great uncle as 4th EARL of BERKSHIRE, and on the failure of the elder branch in 1745, succeeded also as 11th EARL of SUFFOLK; he *d.* in 1757, having had three sons, of whom only the two following left issue:

1 William, Viscount Andover, who *d.* by a fall from his chaise, in his father's lifetime in 1756; leaving three daughters, of whom only one lived to marry, Frances, the wife of Richard Bagot, Esq., brother of the 1st Lord Bagot; and one son, HENRY, 12th EARL, who succeeded his grandfather, and *d.* in 1779. His posthumous son, HENRY, was *b.* 13th EARL in 1779, but lived only two days, when the title devolved on his great uncle, but Frances, his aunt, became heir to a great part of his property; Mr. Bagot, her husband, took the name of Howard, and they left an only daughter and heir, Mary, *m.* to the Hon. Fulke-Greville Upton, who has assumed the name of Howard, brother of Viscount Templetown.

2 THOMAS, who succeeded his great nephew as 14th EARL, and *d.* in 1783, without issue male, leaving an only daughter and heir, Lady Diana, the wife of Sir Michael le Fleming, Bart.

4 Philip, who *d.* in 1717; he had two sons; 1 James, who *d.* without surviving issue male, in 1722, and 2 Charles, a Captain in the Navy, lost in the *Swan* man-of-war, which he commanded in 1705, leaving an only son, Philip; he *d.* in 1741, having had four sons, of whom, JOHN, the 3rd son, and the only one who left issue, succeeded as 15th EARL in 1783, and *d.* in 1820; when he was succeeded by his only surviving son, THOMAS, the present and 16th EARL.

SUTHERLAND, COUNTESS OF. (LEVESON-GOWER.)

Peeress of Scotland.

WILLIAM, the first possessor of this very ancient Peerage, created about the year 1228, *d.* in 1248, and was succeeded by his infant son, WILLIAM, 2nd EARL, who having enjoyed the title seventy-seven years, *d.* in 1325, and was succeeded by his son, KENNETH, 3rd EARL, who was killed at the battle of Halidon Hill, in the cause of King DAVID II., in 1333. These Earls continued to succeed in direct paternal descent through five more generations, namely: WILLIAM, 4th EARL, who *d.* in 1470; WILLIAM, 5th EARL, who left a 2nd son, Kenneth, ancestor of George Sutherland of Forse, who, as heir male of the ancient Earls, claimed the dignity of Earl of Sutherland in 1766; ROBERT, 6th EARL, who *d.* in 1442; JOHN, 7th EARL, who *d.* in 1460; and JOHN 8th EARL. He *d.* in 1508, leaving a son and a daughter, viz.: JOHN, 9th EARL, who *d.* without issue in 1514; and ELIZABETH, on whom the succession devolved, and who was enfeoffed in the Earldom of Sutherland in 1515, being then the wife of Adam Gordon of Aboyne, 2nd son of George, 2nd Earl of Huntly.

ADAM GORDON had a charter of the Earldom jointly to himself and ELIZABETH his wife for life, and to the longest liver of them; the Countess *d.* in 1535, and the 10th EARL, her husband, in 1537. They both survived their eldest son, Alexander, Master of Sutherland, and were succeeded by their grandson, JOHN, 11th EARL, who was poisoned, with his wife, by the widow of his uncle, Gilbert Gordon, whose son, John, was next heir to the Earldom after Alexander, Master of Sutherland, the Earl's son. The Earl and Countess, with their son, were on a visit at Helmis-

TAAFFE, VISCOUNT. (TAAFFE.)

Peer of Ireland.

Of this family, which is of great antiquity in the Counties of Louth and Sligo, was John Taaf, Archbishop of Armagh in 1306.

SIR JOHN TAAFFE was created in 1628, VISCOUNT TAAFFE of Corran, and Baron of Ballymote, both in the County of Sligo, and *d.* in 1742, having had fourteen sons; of whom THEOBALD, the eldest son, was his successor, and ancestor of the succeeding Peers till 1757, when his male line became extinct; and William, the 8th son, was ancestor of the present Viscount.

THEOBALD, 2nd VISCOUNT, was created in 1662 Earl of Carlingford, Co. Louth, and *d.* in 1677, leaving four sons, viz.:

1 NICHOLAS, 2nd Earl and 3rd VISCOUNT, his successor, who *d.* without issue in 1690.

2 FRANCIS, the famous Imperial General, Count Taaffe; he succeeded his brother as 3rd Earl and 4th VISCOUNT, and *d.* without issue in 1704.

3 Dillon, whose issue male failed before the death of his brother.

4 John, who *d.* in 1689, leaving one son, THEOBALD-LAMBERT, 5th VISCOUNT, and 4th Earl of Carlingford, who succeeded his uncle, and *d.* without issue in 1738, when the Earldom and the male issue of the 2nd Viscount became extinct.

The inheritance then devolved to the heir male of William, 8th son of the 1st Viscount, the issue male of all the seven elder sons having become extinct; this William left an only son, Francis, whose only son, NICHOLAS, succeeded as 6th VISCOUNT, on the extinction of the elder line. He was a Count of the Holy Roman Empire, and a Lieutenant-General in the Austrian service, and possessed large estates in Silesia, Bohemia, and Upper Austria; he *d.* in 1769, and his eldest son, John, having *d.* before him in 1768, he was succeeded by his grandson RODOLPH, 7th VISCOUNT, to whom succeeded, in 1830, FRANCIS, his eldest son, the present VISCOUNT. The Viscount possesses the Lordships of Elischau in Bohemia, and of Wischenau in Moravia; he resides, as did his predecessors, in his Castle of Elischau, and enjoys a high station in the Austrian court.

TALBOT, EARL. (TALBOT.)

Peer of Great Britain.

This family is a collateral branch from that of the Earl of Shrewsbury.

John, 2nd Earl of Shrewsbury, had two sons:

1 John, 3rd Earl, whose male line became extinct in 1618, by the death of Edward, 6th Earl.

2 Sir Gilbert, whose son, Sir John Talbot, was twice married, and was father of

1 John, (by his 1st marriage,) grandfather of George, 9th Earl, ancestor of all the succeeding Earls of Shrewsbury.

2 Another John Talbot, Esq., (by his 2nd marriage,) who was great-grandfather of William, Bishop of Durham, father of 1 CHARLES 1st LORD and

2 Sherrington, grandfather of Sir George Talbot, Baronet.

CHARLES TALBOT, Lord High Chancellor, was created in 1733 BARON TALBOT of Hensol, Co. Glamorgan, and *d.* in 1737, leaving three sons:

1 WILLIAM, 2nd LORD, created Earl Talbot in 1761, and Baron Dynevor in 1780, the latter with remainder, failing his issue male, to his only daughter, Lady

Cecil, who accordingly succeeded to it on his death, 27 April 1782, when the Earldom became extinct.

2 John, father of John-Chetwynd, who succeeded his uncle as 3rd LORD; and was created in 1784 Viscount Ingestrie, Co. Stafford, and EARL TALBOT of Hensol, Co. Glamorgan; he *d.* in 1793, and was succeeded by his eldest son, CHARLES-CHETWYND, present and 2nd EARL.

3 The Hon. and Rev. George Talbot, D.D., who *d.* 19 Nov. 1785; having *m.* 4 Jan. 1761, the Hon. Anne Bouverie, 2nd daughter of Jacob, 1st Viscount Folkestone, by whom, who was *b.* 7 Oct. 1729, and *d.* 31 Dec. 1813, he left the issue stated in *The Peerage Volume.*

TALBOT AND MALAHIDE, BARONESS. (TALBOT.)

Peeress of Ireland.

MARGARET, widow of Richard-Wogan Talbot, Esq., late Member of Parliament for the County of Dublin, was created in 1831 BARONESS TALBOT of Malahide, and Lady Malahide of Malahide, Co. Dublin.

TANKERVILLE, EARL OF. (BENNET.)

Peer of Great Britain.

The family of Bennet was anciently seated in Berks. Thomas Bennet, of Chapcot, near Wallingford, was great-grandfather of Sir John Bennet, of Dawley, Co. Middlesex; who had issue,

1 Sir John Bennet, created in 1682 BARON OSSULSTON of Ossulston, Co. Middlesex; he *d.* in 1688, and was succeeded by his son, CHARLES, 2nd Lord and 1st EARL, ancestor of all the succeeding Earls—*see* below.

2 Henry, created Viscount Thetford in 1663, and in 1672 Earl of Arlington, with remainder of both titles, failing his issue male, to the heirs of his body; he *d.* in 1685, and was succeeded by his only daughter, Isabella, who *m.* Charles, 1st Duke of Grafton.

CHARLES, 2nd LORD, *m.* Mary, sole daughter and heir of Ford, 3rd Lord Grey of Werke, created in 1695 Viscount Grey of Glendale, and Earl of Tankerville, (one of his ancestors having been, by HENRY VI., created Earl of Tankerville in Normandy, which honour was forfeited by his grandson,) these titles became extinct by his death in 1701; and his son-in-law, CHARLES, 2nd LORD OSSULSTON, was created in 1714 EARL of TANKERVILLE, which honour has descended uninterruptedly, from father to son, upon CHARLES-AUGUSTUS, present and 5th EARL, through three intervening EARLS, all named CHARLES. The 1st EARL *d.* in 1722, the 2nd EARL in 1753; the 3rd in 1767; and the 4th EARL, who was succeeded by his eldest son, the present EARL, in 1822.

TEIGNMOUTH, BARON. (SHORE.)

Peer of Ireland.

Thomas Shore, Esq., of Melton, Co. Suffolk, his Lordship's father, was grandson of Sir John Shore of Derby, M.D.; he *d.* in 1759, having *m.* Miss Dorothy Shepherd, by whom, who *d.* 5 Nov. 1783, he had issue, JOHN SHORE, Esq., the present Peer, created in 1797 BARON TEIGNMOUTH of Teignmouth, and a 2nd son, the Rev. Thomas-William Shore, who *d.* 17 Feb. 1822, leaving issue.

TEMPLEMORE, BARON. (Chichester.)

Peer of the United Kingdom.

Lieut.-Colonel Arthur-Charles Chichester, eldest son of the late Lord Spencer-Stanley Chichester, 3rd son of Arthur, 1st Marquis of Donegal, and the only brother with issue of the present Marquis, was created in 1831 Baron Templemore of Templemore, Co. Donegal, and is the present Peer.

TEMPLETOWN, VISCOUNT. (Upton.)

Peer of Ireland.

The family of Upton was seated at Upton, Co. Cornwall, about the time of the Conquest. Henry Upton, 2nd son of Arthur Upton, of L'Upton, Co. Devon, went over to Ireland in 1598, and settled at Castle Upton, Co. Antrim; he was great-grandfather of Clotworthy Upton, Esq., created in 1776 Lord Templetown, Baron of Templetown, Co. Antrim; he *d.* in 1785, and was succeeded by his eldest son, John-Henry, 2nd Lord, who was created Viscount Templetown in 1806, and is the present Peer.

TENTERDEN, BARON. (Abbott.)

Peer of the United Kingdom.

Sir Charles Abbott, the upright and enlightened Lord Chief Justice of the King's Bench, who was created in 1827 Baron Tenterden of Hendon, Co. Middlesex, is the son of Mr. John Abbott, of Canterbury, who *d.* 14 Feb. 1795, by his marriage with Alice, only daughter and heir of Daniel Bunce, Esq., of Canterbury, who *d.* 8 April 1793. They had an elder son, John, a merchant of London, who was *b.* 8 July 1758, and *d.* 26 April 1828; having *m.* 21 May 1785, his first cousin Susan, daughter of Mr. James Abbott, by whom he has left issue; also a daughter Elizabeth, *m.* to John Matsell, Esq., of Great Yarmouth, merchant.

TEYNHAM, BARON. (Roper.)

Peer of England.

John Roper, of Well Hall, Eltham, and of St. Dunstan's, both in the county of Kent, was sixth in descent from Edwin Roper of Kent, with whom Philipot, in his visitation of Kent in 1619, commences the pedigree of this family; he had two sons:

1 William, *m.* Margaret, daughter of the upright Chancellor, Sir Thomas More, who suffered death on Tower Hill, under the tyranny of Henry VIII., for imputed treason; he *d.* in 1577, leaving by this Lady, so celebrated for her learning and filial piety, two sons, whose male issue flourished to the fourth generation, when the principal branch ended in heiresses.

2 Christopher, who was taken prisoner by the rebels in an attempt to suppress the insurrection of Sir Thomas Wyat against Queen Mary, but soon liberated on account of illness; his eldest son,

Sir John Roper, was created in 1616 Baron Teynham of Teynham, Co. Kent, and *d.* in 1618; his title descended uninterruptedly in the direct male line for four generations; CHRISTOPHER, 2nd LORD, *d.* in 1622; JOHN, 3rd LORD, in 1657, CHRISTOPHER, 4th LORD, in 1673; and CHRISTOPHER, 5th LORD, in 1688. The latter left three sons, successive Lords, namely: JOHN, 6th LORD, his successor, who *d.* in 1689, CHRISTOPHER, 7th LORD, who *d.* in 1697, both *unm.*, and

HENRY, 8th LORD, who *d.* in 1723, having *m.* three wives: 1st, Catherine, daughter of Philip Viscount Strangford; 2ndly, Mary, daughter of Sir John Gage of Firle, Bart.; and 3rdly, Lady Anne, daughter of Thomas Lennard, Earl of Sussex, widow of Richard Barrett-Lennard, Esq., and afterwards, in her own right, Baroness Dacre; she *m.* 3rdly, the Hon. Robert Moore, son of Henry Earl of Drogheda; by his second marriage he had no issue, but by the 1st and 3rd marriage he had the four sons following:

1 PHILIP, 9th LORD, *d. unm.* 1 June 1727, aged 19.

2 HENRY, 10th LORD, succeeded his brother, and *d.* 29 April 1781; leaving, besides other issue,

1 HENRY, 11th LORD, *b.* 7 May 1733, *d.* 10 Dec. 1786; having *m.* 1st, 2 June 1753, Mary-Wilhelmina, eldest daughter and co-heir of Sir Frances Head, Bart., who *d.* without issue in Oct. 1758; and 2ndly, Betty, daughter of —— Webber, Esq., and widow of Peter Mills, Esq., by whom, who was *b.* in 1726, and *d.* 4 Nov. 1793, he had the following issue:

1 Hon. Betty-Maria, *b.* 7 Aug. 1761, *d.* 1 March 1788; having *m.* Francis-Henry Tyler, Esq.

2 Hon. Catherine, *b.* 2 Aug. 1762, *d.* 1 Jan. 1829; having, after her sister's death, *m.* her brother-in-law, the above Francis-Henry Tyler Esq.

3 HENRY, 12th LORD, *b.* 3 March 1764, succeeded 10 Dec. 1786, *d.* 10 Jan. 1800.

4 Hon. Anne, *b.* Feb. 1765, *d.* in her youth *unm.*

5 JOHN, 13th LORD, *b.* 28 March 1767, succeeded 10 Jan. 1800, *d.* 7 Sept. 1784.

2 Hon. John, *b.* 20 June 1734, *d.* in Sept. 1780; having *m.* 21 March 1760 Anna-Gabriella, 2nd daughter and co-heir of Sir Francis Head, Bart., and widow of Moses Mendez, Esq.; she *d.* 11 Dec. 1771, having had an only son, which *d.* an infant.

3 Hon. Francis, for whom see *The Peerage Volume*; he *d.* in 1793, leaving issue, HENRY-FRANCIS, the present and 14th LORD, who succeeded to the title on the death of his cousin, and a daughter Charlotte.

4 Hon. Philip, *b.* 13 Oct. 1739, deceased; having *m.* in 1766, Barbara, 2nd daughter of Launcelot Lyttleton, Esq., by whom, who *d.* 10 April 1805, he left the issue stated in *The Peerage Volume.*

3 Hon. Charles, *d.* in 1754, having *m.* Gertrude, sister and co-heir of John Trevor, Esq., by whom he left issue,

1 Charles Trevor, who in 1786 succeeded his father's uterine brother as 19th Lord Dacre, and *d.* without issue 4 July 1794.

2 Henry, a Major in the army, killed in a duel in 1788.

3 Gertrude, who succeeded her brother as Baroness Dacre, *m.* Thomas Brand, Esq., and *d.* in 1819, when she was succeeded by her eldest son, Thomas, present and 21st Lord Dacre.

4 Hon. and Rev. Richard-Henry, *b.* 1723, and *d.* Nov. 1810; having *m.* 1st, Mary, daughter of William Chetwynd, Esq., who *d.* in Jan. 1758; and 2ndly, Mary daughter of Thomas Tennison, Esq., by whom he had the issue stated in *The Peerage Volume.*

THANET, EARL OF. (Tufton.)

Peer of England.

This family descends from Elfege de Toketon, living at Toketon, Co. Kent, in the reign of King John. His descendant, Simon de Tufton of Tufton, in Sussex, in the reign of King Richard II., was ancestor in the 5th degree of Sir John Tufton of Hothfield, Co. Kent, created a Baronet in 1611; he *d.* in 1624, and was father of

Sir Nicholas Tufton, created in 1626 Baron Tufton of Tufton, Co. Sussex, and in 1628 Earl of Thanet, Co. Kent; he *d.* in 1632, and was succeeded by his eldest son, John, 2nd Earl. Being a Royalist, he was obliged to compound with Cromwell's government for the restoration of his sequestrated estate, and *d.* in 1664, having *m.* Lady Margaret Sackville, eldest daughter and at length sole heir of Richard Earl of Dorset, by the Lady Anne Clifford, daughter and sole heir of George, 13th Lord De Clifford and 3rd Earl of Cumberland, by whom he left six sons: George, the youngest, *d. unm*, in 1670, of a wound received three years before in rescuing the Elector Palatine from an ambuscade; Nicholas, the eldest son, succeeded his father as 3rd Earl; and in 1678, by the death of his cousin, the Lady Alathea Compton, the other co-heir of the Barony, became, in right of his mother and grandmother, 15th Baron de Clifford, he *d. unm.* in 1679; John, 2nd son, succeeded his brother as 4th Earl and 16th Lord de Clifford, and dying *unm.* in 1680, was succeeded by his next brother, Richard, 5th Earl, and 17th Lord de Clifford; he also *d. unm.* in 1684, and was followed by Thomas, the 4th son, 6th Earl, and 18th Lord De Clifford, who *d.* in 1729, without surviving issue male, leaving five daughters and co-heirs, among whom the Barony fell into abeyance—*see* the title De Clifford in this Volume; Sackville, the 5th son of the 2nd Earl, *d.* in 1721, and his eldest son, Sackville, 7th Earl, succeeded his uncle in the Earldom; he *d.* in 1753, and was succeeded by his only surviving son, Sackville, 8th Earl, who *d.* in 1786, leaving, besides other issue, Sackville, his successor, 9th Earl, who *d.* without issue in 1825, and Charles, present and 10th Earl, who succeeded his brother.

THOMOND, MARQUIS OF. (O'Bryen.)

Peer of Ireland and of the United Kingdom.

This family descends from Brian Boirombe, King of all Ireland in 1002; whose ancestors had reigned in Ireland for many generations, and whose descendants continued Princes of Thomond, till, in the reign of King Henry VIII., Connor O'Brien, Prince of Thomond, left at his death an infant son, Donough, when his brother Murrough usurped his dominions, and, submitting himself to King Henry VIII., was created in 1543 Earl of Thomond for life, with remainder to his nephew Donough, who succeeded him.

Donough, 2nd Earl, was succeeded by his son Connor, 3rd Earl, who had issue, 1 Donough, 4th Earl, whose male line failed in 1741, by the death of Henry, 8th Earl; he had been created in 1714 Baron of Tadcaster, in the Peerage of Great Britain, which title became extinct by his death. 2 Daniel, created Viscount Clare, which title was forfeited by the attainder in 1691 of his great-grandson, Daniel, 4th Viscount; his male line and that of Connor, Prince of Thomond, father of the 2nd Earl, became extinct in 1774, by the death of Charles, who but for the attainder would have been 7th Viscount Clare, and 10th Earl of Thomond.

Murrough, 1st Earl of Thomond, was also created Baron of Inchiquin, with remainder to his issue male, and dying in 1551, this title descended in the direct male line through five generations: Dermod, 2nd Lord, *d.* in 1557; Murrough, 3rd Lord, in 1573; Murrough, 4th Lord, in 1597; and Dermod, 5th Lord, in 1624; he was succeeded by his son Murrough, 6th Lord, who was created Earl of Inchiquin in 1654; he *d.* in 1674, and was succeeded by his son William, 2nd Earl; he *d.* in 1692, in Jamaica, where he was Governor, and was succeeded by his son

William, 3rd Earl, who *d.* in 1719, leaving, besides other issue, two sons:

1 William, 4th Earl, who *d.* 18 July 1777, without issue male; leaving by his 1st marriage with the Lady Anne Hamilton, Countess of Orkney, an only surviving daughter, Mary, 3rd Countess of Orkney.

2 James, who had also, besides other issue, two sons:

1 Murrough, 5th Earl, created in 1801 Marquis of Thomond, with remainder failing his issue male, to his brother, Edward O'Brien, Esq., and his issue male; he *d.* without male issue 10 Feb. 1808; leaving by his marriage with his cousin, Lady Mary O'Brien, 3rd Countess of Orkney, an only daughter, Lady Mary, present Countess of Orkney.

2 Edward, on whom the Marquisate was entailed; he *d.* in 1801, and was father of William, the present Marquis, and other issue—see *The Peerage Volume*—to whom in 1809 his Majesty granted the title and precedence of sons and daughters of a Marquis.

William, the eldest son, present and 2nd Marquis, succeeded his uncle, according to the limitation of the patent, and was created in 1826 Baron, Tadcaster of Tadcaster, Co. York, in the Peerage of Great Britain.

THURLOW, BARON. (Hovell-Thurlow.)

Peer of Great Britain.

This is an ancient family, of the Co. of Norfolk.

The Rev. Thomas Thurlow, Rector of Ashfield, Co. Suffolk, *m.* Elizabeth, daughter and at length co-heir of Robert Smith, Esq., whose paternal name was Hovell, by whom he had issue,

1 Edward, who after passing through the minor gradations of legal rank, was appointed in 1778 Lord High Chancellor, which elevated office he retained till 1792, filling it with the great reputation which his superior mind, boldness of resolution, and remarkable sagacity, so justly merited; he was *b.* in 1735, created in 1778 Baron Thurlow of Ashfield, which title became extinct on his death, 12 Sept. 1806; and again in 1792, Baron Thurlow of Thurlow, Co. Suffolk, with remainder to the issue male of his brothers.

2 The Right Rev. Thomas Thurlow, D.D., Lord Bishop of Durham, *d.* 27 May 1791; having *m.* Anne, daughter of William Beere, Esq., who *d.* 7 Aug. 1791; they left, besides the issue mentioned in *The Peerage Volume*, an elder daughter, Amelia-Anne, who *d.* 8 Dec. 1809; having *m.* in July 1799, Lieut.-General Sir Edward Howarth, K.C.B., who *d.* 5 March 1827. Edward, the Bishop's eldest son, succeeded his uncle the Lord Chancellor, as 2nd Lord, and assumed the additional name of Hovell; he *d.* in 1829, and was succeeded by his eldest son, Edward-Thomas, present and 3rd Lord, a minor.

John Thurlow, Esq., *d.* 4 March 1782; leaving by his marriage with Josepha, daughter of John Morse, Esq., who *d.* 10 Dec. 1786, one son, the Rev. Edward-South Thurlow, for whom see *The Peerage Volume*.

TORPICHEN, BARON. (Sandilands.)

Peer of Scotland.

Sir James Sandilands had a charter from King David II. in 1336; 7th in descent from him was

Sir James Sandilands of Calder, who had two sons:

1 John, whose son James *d.* in 1577, and was father of James, 2nd Lord.

2 James, created in 1564 Baron Torpichen, with remainder to his heirs and assigns whatsoever; he *d.* without issue in 1596, and was succeeded by his great-nephew,

James, 2nd Lord, ancestor in the direct male line of all the succeeding Lords; he *d.* in 1617, and was followed successively by his two eldest sons, James, 3rd Lord, who *d. unm.* in 1622; and John, 4th Lord, who *d.* in 1637; he was also followed by his two elder sons in succession, namely, John, 5th Lord, who *d. unm.* in 1649; and Walter, 6th Lord, who *d.* in 1696, when he was succeeded by his eldest surviving son

James, 7th Lord, who was warmly engaged in the Royal army during the rebellion of 1715; he lost his eldest son James, a Lieutenant in the 44th regiment, in consequence of twenty-six wounds received at the battle of Preston, although he survived them four years; his Lordship *d.* in 1753, leaving, besides other surviving issue, the two sons following:

1 Walter, who succeeded as 8th Lord, and *d.* in 1765; his issue failed in 1815, on the death of his son and successor, James, 9th Lord.

2 The Hon. Robert Sandilands, who *d.* 16 May 1791; having *m.* Grizel, daughter and heir of Sir Thomas Kirkpatrick, Bart, by whom, who *d.* 10 Feb. 1776, he had one son, James, the present and 10th Lord.

TORRINGTON, VISCOUNT. (Byng.)

Peer of Great Britain.

Thomas Byng, seated at Wrotham in Kent, in the reign of Henry VII., was ancestor in the 6th degree of Admiral Sir George Byng, one of the greatest naval commanders we ever had before the immortal Nelson; devoting his whole time and application to any service committed to his management, from which no fatigue or indisposition could ever divert his attention; he was never unfortunate in any undertaking, nor miscarried in any expedition he was appointed to command. He was created a Baronet in 1715, and advanced for his distinguished merits to the honours of the Peerage in 1721, by the titles of Baron Byng of Southill, Co. Bedford, and Viscount Torrington, Co. Devon; he *d.* in 1733, leaving five sons, viz.:

1 Pattee, 2nd Viscount, who succeeded his father, and *d.* without surviving issue in 1747.

2 George, 3rd Viscount, who succeeded his brother, and *d.* in 1750, leaving two sons:

1 George, 4th Viscount, who *d.* 14 Dec. 1812; having *m.* 10 July 1765, Lady Lucy Boyle, 2nd daughter of John, 5th Earl of Corke and Orrery, *b.* 27 May 1744, and *d.* 18 March 1792, by whom, besides the two surviving daughters stated in the *The Peerage Volume*, he left the two following:

1 Hon. Georgiana-Elizabeth (2nd daughter), *b.* 24 Feb. 1768, *d.* 10 Oct. 1801; having *m.* 21 March 1786, Lord John Russell, now Duke of Bedford.

2 Hon. Emily, who *d.* 3 Sept. 1824; having *m.* 1 July 1800, Henry Seymour, Esq.—See *The Peerage Volume*, title Hertford.

2 JOHN, 5th VISCOUNT, who succeeded his brother; he was *b.* 11 Oct. 1740, and *d.* 8 Jan. 1813; having *m.* 3 March 1767, Bridget, daughter of Commodore Arthur Forrest, by whom, who *d.* 25 April 1823, he had, besides the issue described in *The Peerage Volume*, as uncles and aunts of the present Viscount, GEORGE, his eldest son and successor, the 6th VISCOUNT, who *d.* in 1831, and was succeeded by his eldest son GEORGE, present and 7th VISCOUNT, a minor.

3 The Hon. George Byng, Governor of Barbadoes; he had three sons, of whom Robert, 2nd son, was smothered in the black-hole at Calcutta, 20 June 1756; and John, the 3rd son, *d. unm.* 16 June 1764; George, the eldest son, was *b.* in 1735, and *d.* 27 Oct. 1789; having *m.* 5 March 1761, Anne, 2nd daughter of the Right Hon. William Conolly, by whom, who *d.* 3 Nov. 1805, he left the issue stated in *The Peerage Volume*.

4 The Hon. Admiral John Byng, whose life was sacrificed, after the unfortunate issue of his engagement with a French squadron off Minorca on the 19th May 1756, to the unmitigated severity of the 12th Article of War, which denounces death against every person who in time of action shall withdraw, keep back, or not come into fight, or who shall not do his utmost, through motives of cowardice, negligence, or disaffection. The court-martial expressly acquitted the Admiral of cowardice or disaffection, and made no mention of negligence, but condemned him to death; relieving their consciences by earnestly recommending him to the mercy of the Crown; this recommendation, however, was of no avail, though one of the Lords of the Admiralty, the Hon. Admiral John Forbes, father of the Countess of Clarendon and Lady Maryborough, conscientiously refused to sign the warrant for his execution; and Admiral Byng was shot on board the *Monarque*, in Portsmouth harbour, 14 March 1757.

5 The Hon. Edward Byng, *b.* in 1706; he was in an ill state of health, when his brother the Admiral was brought home a prisoner, and hastening to Portsmouth to visit him, was there seized, the morning after his arrival, with convulsions, and *d.* the same day at noon, 28 July 1756.

TOWNSHEND, MARQUIS. (TOWNSHEND.)

Peer of Great Britain.

The Patriarch of this family was Ludovic, a noble Norman, who came into England in the reign of HENRY I., and assumed the name of Townshend; the 11th in descent from him was Sir Roger Townshend, created a Baronet in 1617; he *d.* in 1636, leaving two sons: Sir Roger, who *d.* under age, and SIR HORATIO, who succeeded his brother; he was a minor during the reign of King CHARLES I., but put himself very forward in promoting the Restoration. He carried an address to the Parliament in Jan. 1659 from the County of Norfolk, demanding the restoration of the secluded Members, or the convening of a free Parliament; in that of 1660, which voted the Restoration, he represented the County, and was elected one of the twelve Commoners to carry over to the King the humble petition of the two Houses that he would be pleased speedily to return and take the government of the kingdom into his hands. He was created in 1661 Baron Townshend of Lynn Regis, Co. Norfolk, and in 1682 VISCOUNT TOWNSHEND, of Raynham, Co. Norfolk; he *d.* in 1687, and was succeeded by his eldest son

CHARLES, 2nd VISCOUNT, who throughout the reign of GEORGE I., and in the early part of that of GEORGE II., held a most distinguished station in the councils of the country. He retired from the administration in 1730 on account of the public and private jealousies which were daily increasing between him and his brother-in-law, formerly his warm friend and coadjutor, Sir Robert Walpole, neighbours in the country. Lord Townshend, the only Peerage family of the County of Norfolk, had long been accustomed to direct its politics, and now saw his influence superseded even there by the growing importance of the favourite Minister of the Crown; Rainham, long the seat of first consideration and splendour of the County, gradually sank beneath the rising magnificence and sumptuous hospitality of Houghton, while its noble owner, frank, impetuous, and overbearing, under the shadow of whose superior consequence his rival had risen into power, could not brook that independence of his dictates, and even contradiction to his projects, which Sir Robert Walpole now constantly displayed. He retired then with an unsullied character for integrity, honour, and disinterestedness, and after spending the evening of his life in rural occupations, never once visiting the capital lest he should be drawn again into the vortex of its intrigues, *d.* at Rainham in 1738. He was twice married; 1st, to Elizabeth, daughter of Thomas, Lord Pelham, and sister of Thomas, Duke of Newcastle; and 2ndly to Dorothy, sister of Sir Robert Walpole, 1st Earl of Orford; he had four sons by each marriage, of whom the three eldest of the 1st marriage, and the youngest of the second, left issue, viz.:

1 Charles, his successor, 3rd Viscount.

2 Hon. Thomas, *b.* 2 June 1701, *d.* 21 May 1780; having *m.* 2 May 1730, Albinia, daughter of Colonel John Selwyn, by whom, who *d.* in 1739, he was father of Thomas, 1st Viscount Sydney, and great-grandfather of the present Viscount—*See* that title in this Volume.

3 Hon. William, father of Charles, 1st Lord Bayning, and grandfather of the present Lord—*See* that title.

4 The Hon. and Very Rev. Edward, D.D., Dean of Windsor, 8th son, *b.* 11 May 1720, *d.* 27 Jan. 1765; having *m.* May 1747, Mary, daughter of General Price, by whom, who was *b.* 1732, and *d.* 14 Feb. 1816, he left the issue stated in *The Peerage Volume.*

Charles, 3rd Viscount, succeeded his father and *d.* in 1764, leaving two surviving sons, viz.:

1 George, 4th Viscount, and 1st Marquis Townshend.

2 The Right Hon. Charles Townshend, who, at the commencement of the reign of George III., acted a brilliant part in the Administrations of the time, and *d.* in the office of Chancellor of the Exchequer in 1767. The versatility of his political conduct acquired for him the nickname of *The Weathercock;* but his talents drew from the eloquent Edmund Burke, when summing up his character in the House of Commons, this spirited eulogium; "Perhaps there never arose in this country a man of more pointed and finished wit, and (where his passions were not concerned) of a more refined, exquisite, and penetrating judgment. He was the delight and ornament of this House, and the charm of every private society which he honoured with his presence. There are many young Members now present who never saw that prodigy Charles Townshend, nor of course know what a ferment he was able to excite in every thing by the violent ebullition of his mixed virtues and failings, for failings he undoubtedly had, but none which were not owing to a noble cause, to an ardent, generous, perhaps an immoderate passion for fame, a passion which is the instinct of all great souls." He *m.* Lady Caroline, eldest daughter and co-heir of John, Duke of Argyll and Greenwich, and widow of Francis, Earl of Dalkeith; by this lady, who was created in 1766 Baroness of Greenwich, with remainder to her male issue by him, and who *d.* in 1794, when that title became extinct, he left two sons, Thomas-Charles, and William-John, who both *d. unm.* before their mother, and one daughter, Anne, who *d.* in 1825; having *m.* 1st, Richard Wilson, Esq., from whom she obtained a divorce in 1798; and 2ndly, John Tempest, Esq.

George, 4th Viscount, was created in 1786 Marquis Townshend, of Rainham, Co. Norfolk; he was *b.* 28 Feb. 1724, and *d.* 14 Sept. 1807; having *m.* 1st, in Dec. 1751, Lady Charlotte Compton, 14th Baroness de Ferrers of Chartley, and 7th Baroness Compton, 3rd and only surviving daughter and heir of James, 5th

Earl of Northampton, who was *b.* 8 Aug. 1729, and *d.* 14 Sept. 1770; and 2ndly, 19 May 1773, Anne, 3rd daughter of Sir William Montgomery Bart., who was *b.* 6 Aug. 1753, and *d.* 30 March 1819. He had issue by both marriages; by the 1st, GEORGE, his successor, 2nd MARQUIS; Lord John, and Lord Frederick, for both of whom see *The Peerage Volume:* Lady Elizabeth, who was *b.* in Aug. 1766, and *d.* 21 March 1811, having *m.* 7 May 1790, General William Loftus, who *d.* 15 July 1831: one other son, Lord Charles, who *d. unm.* in 1796; and three daughters who *d.* young: by the 2nd marriage; the Duchess of Leeds, Lady Harriet de Blaquiere, and Lord James Townshend, for all of whom see *The Peerage Volume;* also Lady Honoria, and Lord William who *d. unm.*

GEORGE, 2nd MARQUIS, succeeded his mother in 1770 as 15th Baron de Ferrers of Chartley, and 8th Baron Compton, and was created in 1784 Earl of Leicester, in the patent of which Earldom he is styled Baron de Ferrers of Chartley, Baron Bourchier, Louvaine, Basset, and Compton. He succeeded his father in 1807, and *d.* in 1811, when he was succeeded by his eldest son GEORGE-FERRERS, present and 3rd Marquis.

The origin of the Barony of Ferrers of Chartley, is derived from the ancient family of Ferrers, of which Robert de Ferrers was created Earl of Derby in 1137, and Robert, his son, is styled Earl of Nottingham; these two Earldoms continued vested in the male heirs of the 2nd Earl, till Robert, 8th Earl, was dispossessed of them in 1265. JOHN FERRERS, his son and heir, was summoned to Parliament in 1299 as BARON FERRERS OF CHARTLEY, which Barony was inherited by his male descendants till the death in 1449 of EDMUND, 5th LORD, whose daughter and sole heir,

ANN, *m.* Walter Devereux, who was summoned to Parliament in her right as Baron de Ferrers of Chartley; their son, JOHN DEVEREUX, 7th LORD, *m.* Cecily, sister and at length heir of Henry Bourchier, Earl of Essex, and 6th BARON BOURCHIER, (by writ 1342;) WALTER, their son, 8th Baron Bourchier and de Ferrers of Chartley, was created Viscount Hereford, and was father of Richard, his eldest son, who *d.* before his father, leaving a son and heir, WALTER, 2nd Viscount; and of Sir Edward, his 3rd son, from whom the 5th and succeeding Viscounts Hereford descended. WALTER, 2nd VISCOUNT, was created Earl of Essex, which title became extinct on the death of his grandson, ROBERT, 3rd EARL, in 1646, when the Viscounty devolved, as above, on the heir male, and the Baronies fell into abeyance between his two sisters, Frances, wife of William Seymour, Duke of Somerset, whose present representative is Anne-Elizabeth, Duchess of Buckingham and Chandos, and Dorothy, wife of Sir Henry Shirley, Bart.

In 1677, the Crown terminated the abeyance of the Barony of Ferrers of Chartley, in favour of SIR ROBERT SHIRLEY, Bart., 12th LORD, eldest son of Sir Henry and Lady Dorothy Shirley; he was created Viscount Tamworth and Earl Ferrers, and *d.* in 1717, when the Earldom devolved on Washington, his 2nd, but eldest surviving son, and the Barony on ELIZABETH, his grand-daughter, sole daughter and heir of Robert, his eldest son.

She *m.* JAMES COMPTON, 5th Earl of Northampton, and 6th BARON COMPTON, by writ 1572, and *d.* in 1741, when the Barony of Ferrers fell into abeyance between her two daughters, but emerged on the death of Lady Jane, the eldest, in 1749, when LADY CHARLOTTE, the only surviving daughter, inherited it, as she did also in 1754 the Barony of Compton, by the death of her father the Earl of Northampton, when his Earldom devolved on his brother and heir male, George Compton, 6th Earl.

The Baroness *m.* George 4th Viscount, and 1st Marquis Townshend, and dying in 1770, was succeeded, as above, by her eldest son, the Hon. GEORGE TOWNSHEND, afterwards Earl of Leicester and 2nd MARQUIS TOWNSHEND, who was succeeded in 1811 by his eldest son, GEORGE-FERRERS, the present and 3rd MARQUIS, 2nd Earl of Leicester, 16th Baron de Ferrers of Chartley, and 9th Baron Compton.

TRAQUAIR, EARL OF. (Stuart.)

Peer of Scotland.

James Stuart, Earl of Buchan, 2nd son of Sir James Stuart of Lorn, by Jane, Queen-dowager of Scotland, (widow of King James I., and mother of King James II.,) had a natural son, James, who obtained a legitimation under the great seal in 1489, and was ancestor in the 4th degree of Sir John Stuart, who in 1628 was created Lord Stuart of Traquair, and in 1633 Earl of Traquair, Lord Lintoun and Caberstoun. Lord Clarendon says of him, that his integrity to the King was without blemish, and his affection to the Church so notorious, that he never deserted it, till both it and he were overrun and trodden under foot. He was taken prisoner at the battle of Preston in 1648, and sent under a strong guard to Warwick Castle, where he was confined four years; being at length released, he returned home, where he suffered extreme poverty, and *d.* in 1659. John, 2nd Earl, his only son, joined the Marquis of Montrose with a considerable body of horse in Sept. 1645, just before the battle of Philiphaugh, from which he escaped; but accompanying the Duke of Hamilton in his expedition into England in 1648, was taken also prisoner at Preston, but soon released. He succeeded his father in 1659, and *d.* in 1666; he was succeeded by his eldest son, William, 3rd Earl, who *d. unm.*, and was succeeded by his only surviving brother, Charles, 4th Earl. He *d.* in 1741, leaving two sons, Charles, his successor, 5th Earl, who *d.* without issue in 1764, and John, 6th Earl, to whom, in 1779, succeeded his only son, Charles, 7th Earl; he *d.* in 1827, and was succeeded by his only son, Charles, present and 8th Earl.

TRIMLESTOWN, BARON. (Barnewall.)

Peer of Ireland.

Sir Christopher Barnewall of Crickstown, whose younger brother John was ancestor of Viscount Kingsland, left two sons, viz.:

1 Sir Nicholas Barnewall, Lord Chief Justice of the Common Pleas in Ireland, whose descendant in the 6th degree, Sir Patrick, was created a Baronet of Ireland in 1622, and was ancestor of the present Sir Robert Barnewall, Bart., of Crickstown Castle, Co. Meath, the chief of this ancient family.

2 Robert, created in 1461 Baron Trimlestown, Co. Meath.

Christopher, 2nd Lord, his eldest son, succeeded him, and was succeeded by his eldest son, John, 3rd Lord, who *d.* in 1538, and was succeeded by his eldest son, Patrick, 4th Lord; he left two sons, Robert, 5th Lord, who *d. unm.*, and Peter, 6th Lord, who succeeded his brother, and dying in 1598, was succeeded by his only son, Robert, 7th Lord; he *d.* in 1639, having survived his eldest son, Christopher, who *d.* in 1622, leaving Matthias, 8th Lord, his eldest son, who succeeded his grandfather; and was succeeded by his eldest son, Robert, 9th Lord; he *d.* in 1689, leaving two sons, Matthias, 10th Lord, who *d.* under age in 1692; and

John, 11th Lord; he succeeded his brother, and *d.* in 1746, leaving, besides other issue, the two sons following:

1 Robert, (eldest son,) who succeeded his father as 12th Lord, and was succeeded by his only son, Thomas, 13th Lord, who *d. unm.* in 1796.

2 Richard, (3rd son,) father of Nicholas, 14th Lord, who succeeded his cousin, and was succeeded in 1813 by his only son, John-Thomas, present and 15th Lord.

TWEEDDALE, MARQUIS OF. (HAY.)

Peer of Scotland.

William de Haye, of Anglo-Norman lineage, who settled in Scotland in the 12th century, had two sons:

1 William, ancestor of the Earls of Errol, Hereditary High Constables of Scotland, extinct in the male line in 1717, and of the existing line of the Earls of Kinnoul.

2 Robert, ancestor in the 10th degree of JOHN HAY, who in 1488 was created a Peer of Parliament by the title of LORD HAY of Yester, and *d.* in 1509. He was succeeded by his eldest son, JOHN, 2nd LORD, who fell at the battle of Flodden in 1513. JOHN, 3rd LORD, his eldest son and successor, *d.* in 1543, leaving two sons, JOHN, the eldest, 4th LORD, and John, the younger, by a 2nd marriage, ancestor of the present Sir John Hay, Bart., of Smithfield and Haystoun.

JOHN, 4th Lord, eldest son and successor of the 3rd LORD, was taken prisoner by the English at the battle of Pinkie in 1547, sent to London and detained there in the Tower till the conclusion of peace; he *d.* in 1557, and was succeeded by his eldest son, WILLIAM, 5th LORD, who *d.* in 1576, leaving two sons, viz.: 1 WILLIAM, 6th LORD, who was engaged in the detention of King JAMES VI. at Ruthven Castle in 1582, and retired to the Continent the following year on the King's regaining his liberty, but returned in 1585, and was pardoned; he *d.* without issue male in 1591. 2 James, 7th LORD, who succeeded his brother, and *d.* in 1609; he was succeeded by his eldest son,

JOHN, 8th LORD, who was created in 1646 EARL OF TWEEDDALE, and *d.* in 1654, leaving two sons, JOHN, 2nd EARL; and the Hon. William Hay of Drummelzier, who *m.* the heiress of Whittinghame, and was father of Alexander Hay of Drummelzier and Whittinghame, who *d.* in 1789; his eldest surviving son, Robert Hay, of Drummelzier, Whittinghame, and Linplum, *d.* in the East Indies in 1807, having been nearly forty years in the Company's service at Bencoolen; he *m.* 7 Feb. 1767, Janet, eldest daughter of James Erskine, Esq., of Cardross, by whom, who *d.* 29 Aug. 1808, he left the issue stated in *The Peerage Volume.*

JOHN, 2nd Earl, the eldest son of the 1st EARL, succeeded his father; having previously been actively engaged in the civil wars. He join the standard of King CHARLES I. at Nottingham in 1642, retired in 1643, and was appointed to the command of a regiment in the service of the Scottish Parliament, at the head of which he fought against the Royalists at Marston Moor in 1644; had the command of the East Lothian regiment of twelve hundred men, raised in 1648 for the rescue of the King; and in 1651 garrisoned his house at Niedpath for King CHARLES II. He joined cordially in the Revolution, and was made Lord High Chancellor of Scotland in 1692; in 1694 he was created MARQUIS of TWEEDDALE, Earl of Gifford, and Viscount Walden; and *d.* in 1697, leaving, besides other issue, the three sons following, viz.:

1 JOHN, 2nd MARQUIS.

2 Lord David Hay, of Belton; he *m.* Dorothea, daughter of his cousin John Hay, of Newhall, and sister of GEORGE, 7th MARQUIS, and *d.* in 1727, leaving issue, James Hay, of Belton, who *d.* in 1798; he was father of Captain James Hay, R.N., of Belton.—See *The Peerage Volume.*

3 Lord Alexander Hay, of Spott, who *d.* in 1737; his son, William Hay, of Lawfield and Spott, was father, by Elizabeth, eldest daughter of Sir Robert Sinclair of Stevenston, Bart., of Robert Hay, Esq., now of Lawfield and Spott.

JOHN, 2nd MARQUIS, *d.* in 1713, leaving three sons, viz.:

1 JOHN, 3rd MARQUIS, his successor, who *d.* in 1715, leaving also three sons:

1 JOHN, 4th MARQUIS, who *d.* in 1762, and was succeeded by his only surviving son, GEORGE, 5th MARQUIS, who *d.* in his 13th year in 1770. His only surviving daughter, Lady Catherine, *m.* William Hay of Newhall, heir presumptive to the Marquisate, and *d.* in 1776, leaving an only daughter.

2 Lord Charles Hay, a Major-General in the army, *d. unm.* at London in 1760, when under arrest; having been sent home from America, by the Earl of Loudon, Commander of the forces there, to be tried by a court-martial, for expressing his dissatisfaction at the inactivity of the expedition to which he was attached.

3 GEORGE, 6th MARQUIS, succeeded his nephew, and *d. unm.* in 1787.

2 Lord John Hay, a Brigadier-General in the army, who acquired great honour in the campaigns in the Netherlands, and *d.* of a fever at Courtray in 1706.

3 Lord William Hay, of Newhall, *d.* in 1723, leaving, besides other issue,

1 John Hay, of Newhall, who *d.* in 1755, leaving issue,

1 William Hay, of Newhall, heir presumptive to the 6th MARQUIS, and a Major in the army, he *d.* in 1781; having *m.* 1st, in 1774, Lady Catherine Hay, only surviving child of JOHN, 4th Marquis, who *d.* in 1776, leaving an only child, Frances, heir to her mother, who *m.* in 1797, Charles Manners, now Tollemache, 3rd son of the Countess of Dysart, and *d.* in 1801, leaving issue; Major Hay *m.* 2ndly, in 1779, Mary, only daughter of William Nisbet, of Dirleton, and by her had an only child, George Hay, presumptive heir to the title, who *d.* 28 April 1783.

2 GEORGE, who succeeded as 7th MARQUIS, and *d.* in 1804, when he was succeeded by his eldest son, GEORGE, the present and 8th MARQUIS.

3 Edward Hay of Newhall, who assumed the additional name of MACKENZIE on his marriage with the heiress of the Earl of Cromatie.—See *The Peerage Volume.*

James Hay, Esq., Writer to the Signet; he *d.* in 1779, leaving issue.

Richard, who assumed the name of NEWTON on succeeding to the estates of that family, and *d.* in 1776, leaving the issue stated in *The Peerage Volume.*

TYRCONNEL, EARL OF. (CARPENTER.)

Peer of England.

This family is of great antiquity in the County of Hereford. John Carpenter, a Member of Parliament in the reign of Edward I., was ancestor of Lieutenant-General GEORGE CARPENTER, Governor of the Island of Minorca, who was created BARON CARPENTER of Killaghy, Co. Kilkenny, in 1719; he *d.* in 1731, and was succeeded by his only son, GEORGE, 2nd LORD, who *d.* in 1749, and was succeeded by his only son,

GEORGE, 3rd Lord, who was created Viscount Carlingford and EARL of TYRCONNEL in 1761; he was *b.* 26 Aug. 1723, and *d.* 9 March 1762; having *m.* March 1748, Frances, daughter and heir of Sir Robert Clifton, Bart., by whom, who *d.* 8 Nov. 1780, he had issue,

1 GEORGE, 2nd EARL, his successor, *b.* 30 June 1750, *d.* 15 April 1805; having *m.* 1st, 9 July 1772, Lady Frances Manners, eldest daughter of John, Marquis of Granby, (eldest son of John, 3rd Duke of Rutland,) *b.* 24 March 1753; this marriage was dissolved Oct. 1777, and she *d.* 15 Oct. 1792, having re-married 28 Oct. 1777, Philip Anstruther, Esq.; his Lordship *m.* 2ndly, 3 July 1780, the Hon. Sarah Hussey-Delaval, 6th daughter and co-heir of John, Lord Delaval, on whose death, 21 May 1808, that title became extinct, she *d.* 7 Oct. 1800, having had issue,

1 George, Viscount Carlingford, *b.* 4 April 1781, *d.* 20 July 1789.

2 Lady Susannah, *b.* 15 July 1784, *d.* 7 June 1827; late Marchioness of Waterford.

2 Lady Almeria, *b.* 20 March 1752, *d. unm.* 5 Oct. 1809.

3 Lady Elizabeth, *b.* 15 Aug. 1753; still living.

4 Lady Caroline, *b.* 20 Feb. 1755, *d.* 16 July 1826; having *m.* 28 April 1774, Sir Uvedale Price, Bart.

5 The Hon. Capt. Charles Carpenter, R.N., who *d.* in 1803, leaving two sons: 1 George, 3rd Earl, who succeeded his uncle, and entering as a volunteer into the Russian army at the period of the French invasion of Russia, *d.* at Wilna, in Lithuania, of excessive fatigue, 20 Dec. 1812; and

2 John-Delaval, present and 3rd Earl, who succeeded his brother.

VENTRY, BARON. (Mullins.)

Peer of Ireland.

The first of this family that settled in Ireland was Frederick-William Mullins, of Burnham, Co. Kerry, eldest son of William Mullins, of Burnham, Co. Norfolk, and great-grandfather of

Sir Thomas Mullins, created a Baronet in 1797, and in 1800 Baron Ventry of Ventry, Co. Kerry; he was *b.* 25 Oct. 1736, and *d.* 11 Jan. 1824; having *m.* 5 Oct. 1755, Elizabeth, daughter of Townsend Gunn, Esq., by whom, who was *b.* in 1735, and *d.* 19 Jan. 1823, he had 1 William-Townshend, 2nd Lord, his successor, who *d.* without surviving issue male in 1827—see *The Peerage Volume*; 2 The Hon. Townsend Mullins, who is deceased, leaving an only son, Thomas-Townsend-Arembero, who succeeded his uncle, and is the present and 3rd Lord; the surviving issue stated in *The Peerage Volume;* and two other daughters deceased, viz. the Hon. Arabella, who *d.* in Dec. 1821, having *m.* in Feb. 1780, Richard M'Gillicuddy, Esq.; and the Hon. Charlotte, who *d.* 29 April 1816; having *m.* 2 May 1792, Richard-Pierse Mahoney, Esq.

VERNON, BARON. (Venables-Vernon.)

Peer of Great Britain.

Richard, Lord Vernon, in Normandy, who accompanied William the Conqueror into England, is the Patriarch of this ancient family; from him desended Sir William Vernon, Constable of England, who *d.* in 1467, and was father of Sir Henry, Governor of Arthur, Prince of Wales. His descendant, Henry Vernon of Sudbury, Esq., *m.* Anne, only daughter of Thomas Pigot, Esq., by Mary, sister and at length sole heir of Peter Venables Lord Kinderton, by whom he had issue:

George Venables-Vernon, created in 1762, Lord Vernon, Baron of Kinderton; he was *b.* 9 Feb. 1709, and *d.* 2 Aug 1780; having *m.* 1st, 21 June 1734, the Hon. Mary Howard, 2nd daughter of Thomas, 6th Lord Howard of Effingham, who *d.* Feb. 1740; 2ndly, Dec. 1741, Anne, daughter of Sir Thomas Lee, Bart, who *d.* 22 Sept. 1742, by whom he had no issue; and 3rdly, 10 April 1744, Martha, 3rd daughter of the Hon. Simon Harcourt, sister of Simon, 1st Earl, and aunt of the two last Earls Harcourt, who *d.* 8 April 1794. His Lordship had by his 1st marriage,

1 George, 2nd Lord, who succeeded his father; he was *b.* 9 May 1735, and *d.* 18 June 1813, having *m.* 1st, 16 July 1757, Hon. Louisa-Barbarina Mansel, daughter and sole heir of Bussey, Lord Mansel, [whose title became extinct on his death, 29 Nov. 1750,] she *d.* without surviving issue in 1786; and he *m.* 2ndly, 25 May 1786, Georgiana, daughter of William Fauquier, Esq, by whom, who *d.* 31 May 1823, he had one

daughter who lived to maturity, the Hon. Georgiana Vernon, *b.* 9 Jan. 1788 *d.* 30 Sept. 1824, having *m.* the present Lord Suffield, by whom she left issue.

2 Hon. Mary, *b.* 19 Dec. 1739, *d.* 11 Dec. 1821; having *m.* 5 Jan. 1763, George Anson, Esq.—*See* Title Lichfield in this Volume.

By 3rd marriage.

3 Hon. Elizabeth, *b.* 21 Jan. 1746, *d.* 25 Jan. 1826; having *m.* 26 Sept. 1765, George-Simon, 2nd Earl Harcourt, who *d.* without issue, 25 April 1809; when he was succeeded by his only brother, William, 3rd Earl, on whose death without issue in 1830, the Archbishop of York succeeded to a large portion of his property.

4 Henry, who succeeded his brother as 3rd Lord, and *d.* in 1829, when he was succeeded by his only son, George-Charles, present and 4th Lord.

5 Hon. Martha, *b.* 25 Dec. 1751, *d.* June 1808.

6 Hon. Anne, still living.

7 Hon. and Most-Rev. Edward Lord Archbishop of York, who has assumed the name of Harcourt, and has a numerous issue—see *The Peerage Volume.*

VERULAM, EARL OF. (Grimston.)

Peer of the United Kingdom, of Ireland, and of Scotland.

Sir Capel Luckyn, Bart., of a good family in Essex, *m.* Mary, eldest daughter of Sir Harbottle Grimston, Bart., and sister of Sir Samuel, who dying without issue, left his estates to William, grandson of his sister by Sir Capel Luckyn; this William assumed the name and arms of Grimston, and was created in 1719 Viscount Grimston, and Baron of Dunboyne, Co. Meath; he *d.* in 1756, and was succeeded by his eldest surviving son, James, 2nd Viscount, who *d.* in 1773, leaving issue by Mary, daughter of John-Askell Bucknall of Oxney, Co. Herts, Esq., James-Bucknall, 3rd Viscount; William, who took the name and arms of Bucknall, and *d.* in 1814, leaving one surviving daughter, the Hon. Mrs. Berkeley Paget—see *The Peerage Volume;* the four surviving daughters stated in *The Peerage Volume*, and an elder daughter, Jane, who *d.* 3 Feb. 1829, having *m.* Thomas Estcourt, Esq., who *d.* in Sept. 1822, leaving by her one son, Thomas-Grimston Bucknall-Estcourt, Esq., the Member of Parliament for the University of Oxford, who has assumed the name of Bucknall.

James-Bucknall, 3rd Viscount, was created in 1790 Baron Verulam of Gorhambury, Co. Herts., in the Peerage of the United Kingdom, and *d.* in 1808, when he was succeeded by his only son, James-Walter, present and 4th Viscount, who was created in 1815 Viscount Grimston and Earl of Verulam; his Lordship succeeded to the Scotch Peerage of Forrester in 1808, in right of his mother.

George Forrester of Corstorphin, was created in 1633 Baron Forrester, with remainder to his heirs general; and, by a subsequent charter, (having no issue male,) with remainder to James Baillie, husband of his 4th daughter, Joanna, and the heirs of their marriage; failing which, to William Baillie, husband of his 5th daughter, Lillias, and the heirs of their marriage; which failing, to their heirs whatsoever. He *d.* in 1654, and was succeeded by James Baillie, 2nd Lord, who *d.* in 1679 without issue, by Joanna Forrester, his 1st wife, and was succeeded by his brother.

William Baillie, 3rd Lord, who *d.* in 1681; he was father, by Lillias, daughter of the 1st Lord, of William, 4th Lord, who *d.* in 1705, leaving George, 5th Lord, his eldest son, and John, his 6th son, whose only son, William, became 7th Lord, and *d.* 1763, when the male line of the 3rd Lord terminated.

George, 5th Lord, *d.* in 1727; he was father of George, 6th Lord, who *d.* without issue in 1748, and of two daughters: 1 Caroline, who succeeded as Baroness Forrester, on the extinction of the male line of the 3rd Lord, and *d.* 25 Feb. 1784; having *m.* Captain George Cockburn, R.N., by whom she had an only daughter and heir, Anna-Maria, 9th Baroness, who *d. unm.* 3 Dec. 1808; 2 Harriet, who *d.* 5 March 1795, having *m.* Edward Walter, Esq., by whom she had an only child, Harriet, who *d.* 8 Nov. 1786; having *m.* 28 July 1774, James-Bucknall, 3rd Viscount Grimston, by whom she was mother of James-Walter, the present Earl, who succeeded his cousin in this Barony in 1808.

WALDEGRAVE, EARL. (Waldegrave.)

Peer of Great Britain.

John de Walgrave, Sheriff of London in 1205, was son of Warine de Walgrave of Walgrave, in Northamptonshire. 10th from him, was Sir Edward Waldegrave, who being of the household of the Princess, afterwards Queen Mary, was committed to the Tower in the reign of King Edward VI., for refusing to forbid the celebration of Mass in her house; he had not, however, been confined much above a month, when, being seized with the quartan ague, he was entrusted to the custody of the Lieutenant of the Tower in a private house for his more easy cure, and six months afterwards obtained permission to return to his own house. The King lived not long after this; and the accession of Mary brought great advantage to her faithful servant. This prosperity was not, however, of long continuance; Mary died and Sir Edward was divested of all his employments by Elizabeth, and again thrown into the Tower, where he *d.* in 1561. Sir Edward Waldegrave, his grandson, was created a Baronet in 1643; though seventy years of age at the breaking out of the great rebellion, he loyally took up arms, performed good service to the King's cause in the West, and continued faithful to it to the last.

Sir Henry Waldegrave, great grandson of the last-mentioned Sir Edward, was created in 1686 Baron Waldegrave of Chewton, Co. Somerset; he *d.* in 1689, and was succeeded by his eldest son, James, 2nd Lord, K.G., created in 1729 Viscount Chewton of Chewton, Co. Somerset, and Earl Waldegrave, Co. Northampton; he *d.* in 1741, leaving two sons,

1 James, 2nd Earl, K.G., the friend and Minister of King George II.; he *d.* without issue male, in 1763, having *m.* Maria, 2nd daughter of Sir Edward Walpole, K.B., by whom, who was afterwards *m.* to the Duke of Gloucester, he left three daughters.

2 John, 3rd Earl, who succeeded his brother; he *d.* in 1784, leaving issue,

- 1 George, 4th Earl, who *d.* in 1789; leaving the issue described in *The Peerage Volume*; he was succeeded by his eldest son, George, 5th Earl, who was drowned in the Thames at Eton School in 1794, and was succeeded by his next brother, John-James, present and 6th Earl.
- 2 William, who was created Baron Radstock, and was father of the present Lord Radstock—*see* that Title.

WALLACE, BARON. (Wallace.)

Peer of the United Kingdom.

The Right Hon. Thomas Wallace, the only son of James Wallace, Esq., Attorney-General, who *d.* 11 Nov. 1783, by his marriage with Elizabeth, only daughter and heir of Thomas Simpson, Esq., of Carleton Hall, Co. Cumberland; was created in 1828, Baron Wallace of Knaresdale, Co. Northumberland, and is the present Lord.

WALLSCOURT, BARON. (Blake.)

Peer of Ireland.

His Lordship derives his descent from Richard Blake, who accompanied Prince John to Ireland in 1185, and whose services were rewarded by grants of lands in the County of Galway.

Joseph-Henry Blake, Esq., was created in 1800 Baron Wallscourt of Ardfrey, with remainder, failing his issue male, to the issue male of his father, Joseph Blake, Esq., for which issue, see *The Peerage Volume*; he *d.* without issue male, in 1803, and was succeeded by his nephew, Joseph-Henry, 2nd Lord, only son of Ignatius-Charles, next brother of the 1st Lord; he *d.* in 1816 *unm.*, and was succeeded by his cousin, Joseph-Henry, present and 3rd Lord, the eldest son of Colonel Henry-James Blake, second brother of the 1st Lord.

WALSINGHAM, BARON. (De Grey.)

Peer of Great Britain.

William de Grey appears to have been settled at Cavendish, Co. Suffolk, in the time of Edward I. Sir William De Grey retired in June 1780, from the office of Chief Justice of the Court of Common Pleas, and in October the same year was created Baron Walsingham of Walsingham, Co. Norfolk; he *d.* in 1781, and was succeeded by his only surviving son, Thomas, 2nd Lord, who *d.* in 1818; leaving, besides the issue described in *The Peerage Volume*, two daughters; Georgiana, who *d* 8 July 1806, and Augusta, *b.* 7 March 1780, who *d.* at Wisbaden, 2 Sept. 1830, both *unm.* His Lordship was succeeded by his eldest son, George, 3rd Lord, who being infirm from the effect of wounds received in the military service, was unfortunately burnt to death in his bed, 27 April 1831, when his Lady also met her death from a fall in endeavouring to escape from her bedroom-window. His Lordship was succeeded by his only brother, the Hon. and Rev. Thomas De Grey, present and 4th Lord.

WARWICK, EARL OF. (Greville.)

Peer of Great Britain.

William the Conqueror having dispossessed Turchil de Warwick, a Saxon nobleman, (ancestor of the Marquis of Northampton,) gave his lands and Castle of Warwick to Henry de Newburgh, 2nd son of Roger de Bellomonte, Earl of Mellent; from him the Earldom passed through six of his male descendants, to Thomas de Newburgh, who *d.* without male issue in 1242; when it devolved on heiresses, and finally, in 1267, on Isabel de Mauduit, daughter and at length heir of Alice, sister and at length heir of Henry, 5th Earl.

She *m.* William de Beauchamp, Baron of Elmly, by whom she had issue,

1 William, ancestor of the succeeding Earls of Warwick.

2 Walter de Beauchamp of Alcester, of whom hereafter.

From William de Beauchamp, Earl of Warwick, proceeded in direct succession from father to son, seven Earls of this family, the most powerful and illustrious in English history, and seated in their Baronial castle, which to the present day exhibits the finest specimen extant of the ancient fortified mansion. Henry, the last of them, was created Duke of Warwick in 1444; he *d.* without issue male, in 1445, and his infant daughter, Anne, Countess of Warwick, dying soon after, the inheritance devolved on

Richard Nevill, Earl of Warwick, the celebrated King Maker, son of Richard, Earl of Salisbury, by Anne de Beauchamp, sister of the Duke; Isabel, his eldest daughter, and at length sole heir, *m.* George, Duke of Clarence, brother of King EDWARD IV.; whose son, Edward, bore the title of Earl of Warwick, which was forfeited by his attainder in 1499. Margaret, his sister and heir, *m.* Sir Richard Pole, K.G.; the Marquis of Hastings is her eldest co-heir.

From Walter de Beauchamp of Alcester, 2nd son of William, Baron of Emley, by Isabel de Mauduit, Countess of Warwick, proceeded, in the junior male line, the Barons Beauchamp of Bletsho, (whose title, having passed by females through the families of St.-John and Mordaunt, now vests in the Duke of Gordon;) and in the senior, the Barons Beauchamp of Powycke, by writ 1447, whose male line failed about 1496, and Elizabeth the eldest daughter and co-heir of Richard, the last Lord. *m.* Robert, 2nd Lord Willoughby de Broke; their eldest son, Edward, left a daughter and heir, Elizabeth, who *m.* Sir Fulke Greville.

The family of Greville came into England at the conquest; and this Sir Fulke was 7th in descent from William Greville, who settled at Milcote in Warwickshire, in the reign of Richard II.

Sir Fulke Greville had, by Elizabeth Willoughby, two sons:

1 Fulke, whose son, the accomplished SIR FULKE GREVILLE, the friend of Sir Philip Sidney, and one of the brightest ornaments of the Court of our Maiden Queen. obtained from King JAMES I. a grant of Warwick Castle, which he found in a ruinous condition, and which at a vast expense he repaired and beautified. He was created in 1620 BARON BROOKE of Beauchamp Court, Co. Warwick, with remainder, failing issue his male, to Robert Greville, son and heir of Fulke, only son of Robert, his uncle; he *d.* without issue in 1628, assassinated by one of his own servants, and Margaret, his sister, became sole heir to the Barony of Willoughby de Broke, and eldest co-heir of the Barony of Beauchamp of Powycke; she *m.* Sir Richard Verney, ancestor, by her, of the present Lord Willoughby de Broke.

2 Robert, father of Fulke, whose son, ROBERT, succeeded as 2nd LORD, agreeably to the above limitation; educated by the 1st Lord as his heir, he nevertheless imbibed some wild principles of liberty which were certainly greatly at variance with the doctrines of the reign of ELIZABETH, and from the first symptom of disunion between the King and Parliament, he ranged himself in the most hostile position possible against all the measures of the Court; when these wordy broils grew to actual warfare, he was appointed Lieutenant-General under the Earl of Essex, and Commander of the Counties of Warwick and Stafford; and making his castle the principal stronghold of the Parliament in those parts, he engaged in the hottest of the war; he was mainly instrumental in the victory of his party at Edgehill, and was killed soon after in the assault of St. Chad's church at Lichfield, defended in the most gallant manner by the Earl of Chesterfield, 2 March 1643, being St. Chad's day; and having, as Lord Clarendon reports, that very morning prayed, "that if the cause he were in were not right and just, he might be presently cut off." He was followed in succession by three of his five sons, viz. 1 FRANCIS, 3rd LORD, who *d. unm.*; 2 ROBERT, 4th LORD, who *d.* without issue male; and 3

FULKE, 5th LORD, a posthumous son, who succeeded his brother in 1676, and *d.* in 1710; having had, besides two younger sons who *d. unm.*, the two following:

1 Francis, who *d.* eleven days before his father in 1710, leaving two sons, FULKE, who *d. unm.* in 1711, and WILLIAM, successive LORDS; the latter *d.* in 1727, and was succeeded by his only surviving son, FRANCIS, 8th Lord Brooke, and 1st EARL of WARWICK.

2 Algernon, father of Fulke Greville, Esq., of Wilberry, Co. Wilts, who *d.* in

1806, leaving by his marriage with Frances, 3rd daughter and co-heir of James Macartney, Esq., who *d.* in June 1789, Captain William Greville, R.N., and the other issue stated in *The Peerage Volume;* also Frances-Anne, who *d.* 23 Dec. 1818, having *m.* John, 1st Lord Crewe.

FRANCIS, 8th Lord, was created in 1746 Earl Brooke, and subsequently, in 1759, EARL of WARWICK, immediately after the extinction of the family of Rich, Earls of Warwick and Holland, eight descents of whom had enjoyed that title since their creation to it in 1618; he *d.* in 1773, and was succeeded by his eldest son, GEORGE, 2nd EARL Brooke and EARL of WARWICK to whom in 1816 succeeded his eldest son, HENRY-RICHARD, present and 3rd EARL.

WATERFORD, MARQUIS OF. (DE-LA-POER-BERESFORD.)

Peer of Ireland and of Great Britain.

The noble family of La-Poer, upon which a junior branch of the ancient house of Beresford has engrafted itself, descends from Sir Roger La-Poer, who in the reign of King HENRY II. accompanied Richard Strongbow, Earl of Pembroke, into Ireland, and for his services in that expedition was rewarded with divers grants of land in the conquered country. His descendants appear to have been Lords of Parliament, but the earliest summons extant is the writ of 1375, issued to NICHOLAS LORD LA-POER, the 8th in descent from this Sir Roger, and in virtue of which the Marquis of Waterford ranks as the 1st Baron by writ of the Irish Parliament. His grandson, Peter Lord La-Poer, *m.* the daughter of the Lord Decies, and by her had a son, Richard, created Lord Baron La-Poer of Curraghmore in 1535; he was slain in service against the Irish rebels about 1540. 5th in descent from him was RICHARD Lord La-Poer, who *m.* in 1673, Catherine, daughter and heir of John Fitz-Gerald, of Dromana and the Decies, Esq., and was created in the same year Viscount Decies and Earl of Tyrone; he *d.* in 1690, leaving two sons, John and James, Earls of Tyrone; John, 2nd Earl, *d. unm.* in 1693; and James, his brother and heir, the 3rd Earl, *d.* without issue male in 1704, when the Earldom became extinct; and it should be noted as remarkable of this ancient family, that during the lapse of more than five hundred years since they had been planted in Ireland, they had never suffered any forfeiture, having never once, though seated in a country continually disturbed by convulsions and civil wars, been engaged in any rebellion against the Crown of England; but had continued to enjoy the lands anciently granted to them, and to reside in the place at Curraghmore, in the County of Waterford, where they had first settled. James, 3rd Earl, left a daughter and sole heir, Catherine, who, as the lineal and chief representative of the family, claimed the ancient Barony of La-Poer; and it was resolved by the Irish House of Lords in 1767, that she had proved her claim, and was entitled to this Barony in fee; she was then the widow of MARCUS-BERESFORD, 1st EARL of TYRONE, of the new creation.

John de Beresford was seated at Beresford, in Staffordshire, in 1087; the 10th from him was John Beresford, Esq., father of

1 John, whose male line failed in the 4th generation, when the lands of Beresford were carried out of the family by an heiress.

2 Thomas, who had nine sons; the male posterity of the four eldest failed in the 2nd generation; Hugh, the 5th son, was ancestor of the Beresfords of Newtown Grange, Co. Stafford, now the eldest branch, and many others; the posterity of Robert, 6th son, terminated in females; Humphrey, 7th son, was great-grandfather of Tristram Beresford, Esq., who in the reign of JAMES I. settled at Coleraine, in the County of Londonderry; Sir Tristram Beresford of Coleraine, his eldest son, was created a Baronet in 1665; his great-grandson,

SIR MARCUS BERESFORD, 4th Baronet, *m.* 10 July 1717, the Lady Catherine De-

La-Poer, 13th BARONESS DE-LA-POER, only daughter and heir of JAMES, 3rd Earl of Tyrone, 12th LORD; he was created Baron Beresford of Beresford, Co. Tyrone, and Viscount of Tyrone, in 1720; and in 1746, EARL of the County of TYRONE; he *d.* 4 April 1763, and the Countess *d.* 27 July 1769; they had, besides other issue, the three sons following:

1 GEORGE, who succeeded as 2nd Earl, and was created a Peer of Great Britain in 1786, by the title of Baron Tyrone of Haverfordwest, Co. Pembroke; and in 1789 was advanced to the dignity of MARQUIS of WATERFORD, in the Peerage of Ireland; he was *b.* 8 Jan. 1735, and *d.* 3 Dec. 1800; having *m.* 18 April 1769, Elizabeth, only daughter and heir of Henry Monck, Esq., who *d.* 15 Jan. 1816. The Marquis was succeeded by his eldest son, HENRY, 2nd MARQUIS, who *d.* in 1826, and was succeeded by his eldest son, HENRY, present and 3rd MARQUIS, who will attain his majority on the 26th of April this year (1832).

2 The Right Hon. John Beresford, *b.* 14 March 1738, *d.* Nov. 1805; having *m.* 1st, 12 Nov. 1760, Anne-Constantia Ligondes, daughter of General Count de Ligondes, who *d.* 26 Oct. 1772; and 2ndly, 4 June 1774, Barbara, 2nd daughter of Sir William Montgomery, Bart., *b.* 12 May 1752, *d.* Dec. 1788. By his two marriages he had the numerous issue stated in *The Peerage Volume*, and several others, who *d.* young.

3 The Most Rev. William Lord Archbishop of Tuam, created Lord Decies.—See *The Peerage Volume*, title Decies.

WATERPARK, BARON. (CAVENDISH.)

Peer of Ireland.

Henry Cavendish, Esq., of Hardwick and Chatsworth, Co. Derby, elder brother of William, 1st Earl of Devonshire, *d.* without legitimate issue in 1616, but left an illegitimate son, to whom he gave Doveridge Hall, in the County of Derby, and a suitable estate; he was ancestor of Sir Henry Cavendish, who went over into Ireland with his relation, William, 3rd Duke of Devonshire, and was created a Baronet of England in 1755, he *d.* in 1776, and was succeeded by his son, Sir Henry, 2nd Baronet, who was *b.* 13 Sept. 1732, and *d.* 3 Aug. 1804; having *m.* 5 Aug. 1757, SARAH, only daughter and co-heir of Richard Bradshaw, Esq., who was created in 1792, BARONESS WATERPARK, Co. Cork, with remainder to her issue male by Sir Henry Cavendish; she *d.* 4 Aug. 1807, and was succeeded by her eldest son, SIR RICHARD CAVENDISH, 2nd LORD, who *d.* in 1830, and was succeeded by his eldest son, HENRY, present and 3rd LORD.

WELLESLEY, MARQUIS OF. (WELLESLEY.)

Peer of Ireland and of Great Britain.

The family of Cowley, or Colley, removed from Rutlandshire into Ireland in the reign of King HENRY VIII. Walter Colley was Solicitor-General for Ireland in 1537; the 7th from him was RICHARD COLLEY, Esq., who being appointed heir to the estates of his cousin, Garrett Wesley, or Wellesley, Esq., of Dangan Castle, Co. Meath, took the name of WELLESLEY; he was created BARON MORNINGTON of Mornington, Co. Meath, and *d.* in 1758; he was succeeded by his only son, GARRETT, 2nd LORD, who was created in 1760 Viscount Wellesley of Dangan, Co. Meath, and EARL of MORNINGTON; he *d.* in 1784, and was succeeded by his eldest son, RICHARD, 2nd Earl; he was created a Peer of Great Britain in 1797, by the title of Baron Wellesley of Wellesley, Co. Somerset, was advanced to the dignity of

MARQUIS WELLESLEY, in the Peerage of Ireland in 1799, and is the present MARQUIS. The 1st Earl was also father of William, Lord Maryborough, Arthur Duke of Wellington, the Hon. and Rev. Dr. Gerald-Valerian Wellesley, and Henry Lord Cowley.

WELLINGTON, DUKE OF. (WELLESLEY.)

Peer of the United Kingdom.

This illustrious hero, whose fame as a military Commander is written in indelible characters in the proudest pages of British history, was born, the Hon. Arthur Wellesley, 3rd son of Garrett, 1st Earl of Mornington, 1 May 1769; his first essay in active military service was made in Holland in 1794; in 1797, having purchased the Lieutenant-Colonelcy of the 33d Regiment, then on service in India, he accompanied his brother the Governor-General thither, and there laid the foundation of that renown which has since filled the world. He was eminently serviceable in the Mysore war, under the command of General Harris, and was appointed Governor of Seringapatam after the storming of that city. On the breaking out of the Mahratta war, he was appointed, with the rank of Major-General, to the command of a separate army within the Deccan, and in this command it was that his brilliant talents first shone upon the world, almost in their full splendour, in the skilful combinations by which, under the most adverse circumstances, he achieved the decisive victory of Assaye; that of Argaum, which followed, and the storming of the fortress of Gawilghar, ended the war, and earned for Major-General Wellesley the thanks of both Houses of Parliament, and the Order of the Bath.

Sir Arthur returned to Europe, and was appointed Chief Secretary of Ireland under the Vice-royalty of his friend the late Duke of Richmond, from which office he was called to a command in the expedition to Copenhagen, under Lord Cathcart, and materially contributed to its success.

In August 1808 he was sent to Portugal with a considerable force, and fought the battles of Roleia and Vimiera before the arrival of Sir Harry Burrard and Sir Hugh Dalrymple, who, by concluding the Convention of Cintra, destroyed a part of the advantages fairly to be expected from the courage of the army, and the skill of its Commander. The three Generals were summoned home, the command devolved on the brave but unfortunate Sir John Moore, and the Peninsula was evacuated by the British troops. An investigation into the whole of the Portuguese affair proved to the Government and to the nation, that Sir Arthur Wellesley was the General to lead the British army to victory, and his appointment to the command-in-chief of another expedition sent to Portugal followed in 1809. His brilliant passage of the Douro once more freed Portugal from the presence of the French troops, and the glorious, though indecisive conflict of Talavera ensued; in reward of which Sir Arthur was elevated to the Peerage in 1809 by the title of Baron Douro of Wellesley, Co. Somerset, and VISCOUNT WELLINGTON of Talavera and Wellington, Co. Somerset. All that consummate military skill could do against the prodigious superiority of force now opposed to the British General, was effected by the completion of the impregnable lines of Torres Vedras and the battle of Busaco. His defensive operations were completely successful, the enemy withdrew from the exhausted country, and the year 1812 opened with the capture of the important fortress of Ciudad Rodrigo. The year of restrictions on the functions of the Regency was now expired, and the first use made by the Prince Regent of the free exercise of his Regal powers was to raise the hero to the rank of Earl of Wellington, Co. Somerset. The fortress of Badajoz next fell, the victory of Fuentes d'Onores led the way to the glorious day of Salamanca, and the conqueror was created Marquis of Wellington; the siege of Cadiz raised, and the government of Spain restored to its capital, were the immediate fruits of this brilliant victory. The year 1813 was illustrated by the decisive victory of Vittoria, which won for the General a Field-Marshal's [illegible] of Pampeluna and San Sebastian, and the defeat of the French [illegible] of the Pyrenees, accomplished the deliverance of Spain, and the [illegible] saw the victor established on the territory of France. In 1814 [illegible] and Toulouse preceded the general peace, and, at its conclu[illegible] was raised to the Ducal dignity. Numerous votes of [illegible] Parliament, and the country, with a lavish hand, [illegible] the first man in the state so meritoriously won.

[illegible] honours on the British Commander, and [illegible] with the ... of the French armies and his chosen troops [illegible] his unrivaled glory: Napoleon returned from [illegible] Waterloo was fought and won, and Wellington's triumphs were [illegible]. England could do no more for the Duke and the Field-Marshal, but [illegible] laurels.

[illegible] so abundantly contributed, the Duke of Wel[illegible] Commander-in-chief, or Statesman at home, and very [illegible] has not ceased to devote his time and talents [illegible].

WEMYSS, EARL OF. (Wemyss-Charteris-Douglas.)

Peer of Scotland and of the United Kingdom.

Macduff, Thane of Fife, one of the most powerful subjects in Scotland, who over[illegible] and restored the throne to Malcolm III., was created Earl of Fife. [illegible] Earl, his descendant, had two sons, 1 Duncan, 5th Earl, from whom descended the succeeding Earls of Fife, till his male line failed in [illegible], and the Earldom, by the resignation of the Countess Isabel, daughter and heir of Duncan, [illegible] Earl, became vested in the crown; 2 Hugo, who obtained from his father the lands of Wemyss, Co. Fife, from which his descendants assumed their surname. The [illegible] was

Sir [illegible] Wemyss, of Wemyss, who d. 1544, leaving issue,

[illegible] Sir John, great-grandfather of [illegible], created in 1628 Lord Wemyss of Elcho, and in [illegible] Earl of Wemyss, Lord Elcho and Methel, with remainder to his heirs male for ever. His son David, 2nd Earl, obtained in 1672 a renewal of the patent, with the former precedency, with remainder to his youngest daughter Lady Margaret, and her heirs male; failing which to the heirs of entail contained in her contract of marriage. He d. in 167[illegible], and was succeeded by his daughter Margaret, [illegible] Countess.

2 James, from whom descended Sir James Wemyss of Caskyberry, who m. Margaret, [illegible] Countess. Her Ladyship d. in 1705, and was succeeded by her son David, [illegible] Earl, who d. in 1720, having m. Lady Anne Douglas, eldest daughter, and eventually heir of line of William, 1st Duke of Queensberry; and by her was father of

James, [illegible] Earl; he m. Janet, only daughter and heir of Col. Francis Charteris; and d. in 17[illegible], leaving issue by her,

1 David, Lord Elcho, who having engaged in the rebellion of 1745, was attainted, and d. in 17[illegible], without issue.

2 Francis, 6th Earl; he assumed the name of Charteris, on succeeding to the estates of his maternal grandfather; became Earl of Wemyss on the death of his brother Lord Elcho, and d. in Aug. 1808; having survived his only son Francis Lord Elcho, who d. in Jan. 1808; and whose only son Francis succeeded his grandfather, and is the present and 7th Earl. He succeeded also, on the death of William, 4th Duke of Queensberry, 23 Dec. 1810, to the titles of Earl of March, Baron of Neidpath, Lyne, and Munard, as heir of Lady Anne, daughter [illegible] William, 1st Earl of March, on whom and her issue male those titles, created

whom, and her issue male, these titles, created in 1697, were entailed by patent, and has assumed the additional name of DOUGLAS. His Lordship was created a Peer of the United Kingdom in 1821, by the title of Baron Wemyss of Wemyss, Co. Fife.

3 The Hon. James Wemyss of Wemyss, *b.* 6 March 1725, *d.* 10 May 1785; leaving by his marriage, Aug. 1757, with Lady Elizabeth Sutherland, daughter of William, 16th Earl of Sutherland, who was *b.* 23 July 1738, and *d.* 24 Jan. 1803, two sons, for whom see *The Peerage Volume*, and one daughter, Elizma, who *d.* in 1800, having *m.* the late Alexander Brodie, Esq. They had several other children, who all *d.* young or *unm.*

WENLOCK, BARON. (LAWLEY.)

Peer of the United Kingdom.

Thomas Lawley was cousin and heir of Sir John Wenlock, K.G., who was created Baron Wenlock of Wenlock, Co. Salop, in 1461, and was killed in the battle of Tewkesbury in 1471. This Thomas Lawley of Wenlock was ancestor in the fifth degree of Sir Thomas Lawley, created a Baronet in 1641, from whom in the 5th degree descends SIR ROBERT LAWLEY, 6th Baronet, who was created BARON WENLOCK of Wenlock, Co. Salop, in 1831, and is the present Peer.

WESTMEATH, MARQUIS OF. (NUGENT.)

Peer of Ireland.

Sir Gilbert de Nugent came into Ireland in 1171, and marrying Rosa, daughter of Hugh de Lacy, had with her the Barony of Delvin; he *d.* without surviving issue, but had two brothers: 1 Richard, who succeeded to the Barony, which was carried by his only daughter and heir into the family of Fitz-John; 2 Christopher, who was seated at Balrath; from him descended in the 5th degree, Sir William Nugent, who by marriage with Catherine, daughter and heir of John Fitz-John, recovered the Barony of Delvin; from them descended in the 6th degree

Richard, summoned to Parliament as Baron Delvin in 1486; he *d.* in 1537, and having survived his eldest son Christopher, was succeeded by his grandson RICHARD, 2nd LORD, who was created BARON DELVIN, by patent, in 1557; he *d.* in 1559, and was succeeded by his eldest son CHRISTOPHER, 3rd LORD, who in 1602 was succeeded by his eldest son RICHARD, 4th LORD, by writ, and 3rd by patent; he was created EARL of WESTMEATH in 1621, and *d.* in 1641, when he was succeeded by his grandson RICHARD, 2nd EARL, who *d.* in 1684; he was father of

Christopher, Lord Delvin, who *d.* before him, leaving three sons:

1 RICHARD, 3rd EARL, who *d. unm.* in 1714.

2 THOMAS, 4th EARL, between whose daughters and co-heirs the Barony by writ fell into abeyance; he *d.* without issue male in 1752.

3 JOHN, 5th EARL, who succeeded his brother, and dying in 1754, was succeeded by his eldest son, THOMAS, 6th EARL, to whom in 1791 succeeded his eldest surviving son, GEORGE-FREDERICK, 7th EARL. He *d.* in 1814, and was succeeded by his eldest son, GEORGE-JOHN-THOMAS, present and 8th Earl, who in 1822 was created MARQUIS of WESTMEATH.

WESTMINSTER, MARQUIS OF. (Grosvenor.)

Peer of the United Kingdom.

The ancestors of this noble family held the high rank of *Gros-Veneur* (from which they took their name) in the Duchy of Normandy, from its erection in 912, till the invasion of England, when Gilbert le Grosvenor and his uncle Hugh Lupus, accompanied King William. Robert, son of Gilbert, obtained lands in the Co. of Chester, from the said Hugh Lupus, Earl of Chester, and was lineal ancestor through six generations of Sir Robert le Grosvenor, who proved this pedigree before a Court of Chivalry in defence of his arms *azure, a bend or*, against Sir Richard le Scrope, who challenged them. The descent of Sir Robert was fully admitted, but the arms were adjudged to Scrope, and in conclusion Sir Robert le Grosvenor was recommended to bear *azure a garb or*, from the arms of the ancient Earls of Chester, which has ever since continued the cognizance of his descendants.

Sir Richard Grosvenor, 8th in descent from the above Sir Robert, was created a Baronet in 1622, and *d.* in 1645. Sir Richard, 2nd Baronet, his son and successor, was Sheriff of Cheshire in 1644, and raised the *posse comitatus* to oppose the Parliamentary army under Lord Fairfax, and his estate being in consequence sequestrated, he was ejected from his mansion at Eaton, and obliged to take refuge in the small house of a neighbour till the Restoration. He *d.* in 1664; and was succeeded by his grandson, Sir Thomas, three of whose sons, Sir Richard, Sir Thomas, and Sir Robert, were successive Baronets; the latter *d.* in 1755, and was succeeded by his eldest son,

Sir Richard, who in 1761 was created Baron Grosvenor of Eaton, Co. Chester, and in 1784 Viscount Belgrave, Co. Chester, and Earl Grosvenor; he *d.* in 1802, and was succeeded by Robert, his only son, present and 2nd Earl; who *m.* Lady Eleanor Egerton, only surviving daughter and heir of Thomas, Earl of Wilton, whose title was inherited in 1814, by his grandson, Thomas, the 2nd son of Earl Grosvenor.

WESTMORELAND, EARL OF. (Fane.)

Peer of England.

Howell ap Vane, of Monmouthshire, living before the Conquest, was ancestor in the 12th degree of John Vane, of Tudeley; whose 2nd son, Richard, was great-grandfather of Sir Thomas Fane, ancestor of the Earl; and his 4th son, John, was ancestor of the Marquis of Cleveland.

The above Sir Thomas Fane was attainted of high treason in 1554, for being concerned in Sir Thomas Wyatt's rebellion; he *m.* in 1574, Mary, Baroness Le De-Spencer, daughter and sole heir of Henry, Baron Abergavenny and Ledespencer, co-heir of the Barony of Burghersh, great-grandson of Edward Nevill, 6th son of Ralph, created Earl of Westmoreland in 1397, which title was forfeited in 1570, by the attainder of Charles, 6th Earl.

Their son Francis, was created Earl of Westmoreland and Baron Burghersh in 1624, and succeeded his mother as 14th Lord Le-De-Spencer in 1626; he *d.* in 1628, leaving several sons, of whom the two following were the eldest.

1 Mildmay, his successor, 2nd Earl; he *d.* in 1665, leaving two sons, viz.: Charles, 3rd Earl, his successor, who *d.* in 1691 without issue; and Vere, 4th Earl, who succeeded his brother, and *d.* in 1693; he left three sons, successive Earls, who all *d.* without issue; Vere, 5th Earl, in 1699; Thomas, 6th Earl, in 1736; and John, 7th Earl, in 1762; having, in 1733, been created Baron Cather-

lough in the Peerage of Ireland, which title became extinct at his death; and three daughters, Lady Susan, the youngest, *d. unm.* in 1735, and the Barony of Le-De-Spencer, upon the death of the 7th Earl, fell into abeyance between the two elder, Lady Mary Dashwood, whose descendants became extinct in 1788, and Lady Catherine Paul, whose heir-general is the present Lord Le-Despencer.

2 Sir Francis, who was Governor of Doncaster Castle, and afterwards of Lincoln, for the King in the civil wars; his 3rd son, Sir Henry, was father of Charles Fane, Esq., who in 1718 was created Viscount Fane and Baron Longhaire, in the Peerage of Ireland, which titles became extinct in 1782, by the death of Charles, 2nd Viscount, the only son who survived him. Sir Francis, eldest son of the above Sir Francis, was father of Francis Fane, Esq., of Fulbeck, in Lincolnshire; whose son and heir, Francis, *d.* in 1726, leaving three sons:

1 Francis Fane, Esq., of Fulbeck, who *d. unm.* in 1757.

2 Thomas Fane, Esq., of Brympton, in Somersetshire, a merchant in Bristol, who succeeded as 8th Earl in 1762, on the extinction of the issue of Mildmay, 2nd Earl.

3 Henry Fane, Esq., of Wormsley, in Oxfordshire, who *d.* in 1777, and was succeeded by his eldest son, John Fane, Esq., who was *b.* in 1751, and *d.* 8 Feb. 1824; having *m.* 30 Nov. 1773, Lady Elizabeth Parker, eldest daughter of Thomas, 3rd Earl of Macclesfield, by whom, who was *b.* 29 June 1751, and *d.* 10 June 1829, he has left the issue stated in *The Peerage Volume.*

Thomas, 8th Earl, *d.* in 1771, and was succeeded by his eldest son, John, 9th Earl, to whom in 1774 succeeded his eldest son, John, present and 10th Earl, K.G.

WHARNCLIFFE, BARON. (Stuart-Wortley.)

Peer of the United Kingdom.

His Lordship is the eldest son of the Hon. James Stuart-Wortley-Mackenzie, 2nd son of John, 3rd Earl of Bute, and brother of John, 1st Marquis of Bute.

The Honourable Sidney Montagu, 2nd son of Edward, 1st Earl of Sandwich, *m.* Anne, daughter and heir of Sir Francis Wortley, Bart., of a very ancient family seated at Wortley, Co. York, from the Conquest, and was obliged, according to the settlement of the Wortley estate, to take the name of Wortley. He had two sons, John, the younger, *d. unm.*, and Edward Wortley-Montagu, Esq., the elder, *m.* the celebrated Lady Mary Pierrepoint, daughter of Evelyn, Duke of Kingston, whose talents, wit, literary genius, and eccentricities, have made her fame as extensive as the English language; she *d.* 21 Aug. 1762, and Mr. Wortley Montagu *d.* in 1761. They had one son, Edward, who was disinherited, and *d.* without issue in 1776, and one daughter, Mary, on whom the Wortley property devolved; she was *b.* in Feb. 1718, *m.* John, 3rd Earl of Bute, and was created Baroness Mount-Stuart, with remainder to her issue male by the Earl; she *d.* 6 Nov. 1794, leaving a numerous issue.—*See* Earl of Bute in this Volume. Her 2nd son, the Hon. James Stuart, succeeded to her estate, and in consequence assumed in 1795, by the King's Royal sign-manual, the additional name of Wortley; to which, in 1803, he farther added by the same licence the name of Mackenzie, on succeeding his uncle, the Right Honourable James Stuart-Mackenzie, who *d.* without issue 6 April 1800, in the estates of Sir George Mackenzie of Rosehaugh, father of Agnes, wife of the 1st Earl of Bute, and his great-grandmother. He was *b.* 19 Sept. 1747, and *d.* 1 March 1818; having *m.* 8 June 1766, Margaret, daughter of Sir David Cunynghame, Bart., by whom, who *d.* 13 Jan. 1808, he had issue,

1 Mary, *b.* 23 Aug. 1769, *m.* 1 June 1813, the Right-Hon. William Dundas, nephew of Henry, 1st Viscount Melville.

2 JAMES-ARCHIBALD, *b.* Oct. 1776, who was created BARON WHARNCLIFFE in 1826, and is the present Peer.

3 Louisa-Harcourt, *b.* Oct. 1781, Countess of Beverley.

4 George, *b.* May 1783, *d.* 16 Sept. 1813.

WICKLOW, EARL OF. (HOWARD.)

Peer of Ireland.

This family has long been seated at Shelton, in the County of Wicklow.

Robert Howard, Lord Bishop of Elphin, *d.* in 1740; his eldest son, the Right-Hon. RALPH HOWARD, was created in 1778 Baron Clonmore of Clonmore Castle, Co. Carlow, and VISCOUNT WICKLOW in 1785. He *d.* 26 June 1789, having *m.* 11 Aug. 1755, ALICE, only daughter and heir of William Forward, Esq., of Castle Forward, Co. Donegal, who was created in 1793 COUNTESS OF WICKLOW, and *d.* 7 March 1807. Their eldest son, ROBERT, succeeded his father as 2nd Viscount, and his mother as 2nd EARL, and *d. unm.* in 1815, when he was succeeded by his next brother, WILLIAM, 3rd EARL, who *d.* in 1816, and was succeeded by his eldest son, WILLIAM, present and 4th EARL.

WILLOUGHBY DE BROKE, BARON. (VERNEY.)

Peer of England.

William, 4th Baron Latimer, (by writ 1299,) *d.* in 1380, leaving an only daughter and heir, Elizabeth, who was 2nd wife of John, 3rd Baron Nevill of Raby, (*see* Earl of Abergavenny,) by whom she had one son, John, who was summoned to Parliament as Baron Latimer, and *d.* without issue in 1430, and one daughter Elizabeth, sole heir to her brother, *m.* to Sir Thomas Willoughby, 2nd son of Robert, 4th Lord Willoughby de Eresby.—*See* Lord Middleton.

In 1432, George Neville, 5th son of Ralph, 1st Earl of Westmoreland, son and heir of John, 3rd Lord Nevill of Raby, by his 1st wife, Maud, daughter of Henry, Lord Percy, was summoned to Parliament as Baron Latimer.

But Robert WILLOUGHBY, great-grandson and heir of Sir Thomas Willoughby, by Elizabeth, sister and sole heir of John Nevill, 5th Lord Latimer, claimed his Barony, against Richard Nevill, 2nd Lord Latimer, under the new writ, grandson and heir of George Nevill, summoned in 1432; he did not, however, prosecute his claim, and was summoned to Parliament by writ in 1492, as BARON WILLOUGHBY de BROKE; he *d.* in 1502. ROBERT, 2nd LORD, his son and heir, *m.* Elizabeth, eldest daughter and co-heir of Richard, 2nd Lord Beauchamp of Powycke—*see* Earl of Warwick in this Volume—and *d.* in 1522; when the Barony of Willoughby de Broke fell into abeyance between his two grand-daughters, heirs of Edward, his eldest son, who *d.* before him; Blanche the younger daughter, *m.* Sir Francis Dawkey, but *d.* without issue, and Elizabeth, who after the death of her sister became the sole heir, *m.* Sir Fulke Greville; their eldest son, Fulke, was father of

1 Fulke, created Baron Brooke.

2 Margaret, heir to her brother; she *m.* Sir Richard Verney, and *d.* in 1631, leaving, besides other issue, her eldest son and heir, Sir Greville Verney, who *d.* in 1642; he left three sons, of whom George, the youngest, *d. unm.*; the two elder were,

1 SIR GREVILLE, who *d.* in 1668, leaving an only son, William, who *d. unm.* in 1683.

2 RICHARD, who became at length LORD WILLOUGHBY DE BROKE.

The Barony, however, remained dormant, till it was claimed by, and in 1696 allowed to, this RICHARD VERNEY, who should have been 10th LORD. He *d.* in

1711, and was succeeded by his eldest surviving son, GEORGE, 11th LORD, who *d* in 1728, leaving two surviving sons, RICHARD, his successor, 12th LORD, who *d.* without issue in 1752, and the Right Hon. John Verney, Master of the Rolls, who *d.* in 1741, leaving an only son, JOHN-PEYTO, who succeeded his uncle as 13th LORD. He *d.* in 1816, having had eleven children, of whom only three survived him, two sons and a daughter; JOHN-PEYTO, 14th LORD, his eldest son, succeeded, and *d. unm.* in 1820, when he was succeeded by his only surviving brother, HENRY-PEYTO, present and 15th LORD, who is the sole representative of the ancient Barons Latimer of the writ of 1299.

In the male line the family of Verney is very ancient; Sir Richard Verney, who *m.* Margaret Greville, and has been shown above to be ancestor in the 6th degree of the present Lord, was himself 15th in descent from Roger de Vernai, seated at Bromshulfe, Co. Stafford, grandson of William de Vernai, who is mentioned as living in 1119 and 1148, and was the son of another William de Vernai.

WILLOUGHBY D'ERESBY, BARON. (DRUMMOND-WILLOUGHBY.)

Peer of England.

Sir John de Willoughby, a Norman Knight, had the Lordship of Willoughby in Lincolnshire, by gift from William the Conqueror; he was ancestor in the direct male line of the present Lord Middleton.

Sir William Willoughby, his descendant in the 5th degree, *m.* Alice, sister and coheir of Walter, 2nd Baron Beke of Eresby; (by writ 1295;) their son, ROBERT, was summoned to Parliament as BARON WILLOUGHBY in 1313, and his successors were styled Barons Willougby de Eresby. He *d.* in 1316, and was followed in direct male descent from father to son by JOHN, 2nd LORD, who *d.* in 1349; JOHN, 3rd LORD, who *d.* in 1372; ROBERT, 4th LORD, who *d.* in 1396, and

WILLIAM, 5th LORD; he *d.* in 1409, leaving two sons:

1 ROBERT, 6th LORD, who *d.* without issue male, in 1452, leaving an only daughter and heir, JOAN, *m.* to RICHARD WELLES, son and heir of Leo, 6th Lord Welles, who had been attainted in 1461; he was summoned to Parliament in her right as BARON WILLOUGHBY, but beheaded by King EDWARD, IV., with his only son, Robert, for their adherence to the house of Lancaster, in 1469; he left an only daughter and heir, JOAN, *m.* to RICHARD HASTINGS, in her right 8th LORD WILLOUGHBY, he *d.* in 1503, and JOAN, his wife, *d.* also in 1505, without issue.

2 Sir Thomas, he was father of Sir Robert, whose son, Sir Christopher, *d.* in 1499, leaving WILLIAM, his eldest son, who succeeded in 1505, as 9th LORD WILLOUGHBY of ERESBY. Sir Christopher was also, by Christopher, his 2nd son, ancestor of the Lords Willoughby of Parham; extinct in 1779; and by Thomas, his 4th son, of the present Lord Middleton;—*see* that title in this Volume.

WILLIAM, 9th LORD, *d.* without issue male, in 1525, when the Barony devolved on his only daughter, KATHERINE; she *m.* 1st, Charles Brandon, Duke of Suffolk, widower of the Princess Mary, daughter of King HENRY VII., by whom, who *d.* in 1545, she had Henry, 2nd Duke of Suffolk, and Lord Charles Brandon, who both *d.* young on the same day, 14 July 1551; she *m.* 2ndly, Richard Bertie, Esq.; for her subsequent history and that of her descendants by Mr. Bertie, Barons Willoughby d'Eresby, Earls of Lindsey, and finally Dukes of Ancaster—*see* title Lindsey in this Volume; in which place they are described at length, it will, therefore, only be necessary here to state the succession of the Barony. PEREGRINE, their son and heir, 11th LORD, claimed and was allowed the Barony; he *d.* in 1601, having *m.* the Lady Mary Vere, daughter of John, Earl of Oxford, and Lord Great Chamberlain, by whom he was father of ROBERT, 12th LORD, his successor, 1st Earl of Lindsey, K.G., who inherited from his cousin, Henry de Vere, 18th Earl of Oxford, the office of

Hereditary Great Chamberlain of England, which had been enjoyed by that noble family since the reign of King HENRY II.; he *d.* in 1642, and was succeeded by his son MONTAGU, 13th LORD, 2nd Earl of Lindsey, who *d.* in 1666; he was followed by his son ROBERT, 14th LORD, 3rd Earl of Lindsey; and he in 1701, by his son ROBERT, 15th LORD, 1st Duke of Ancaster, who *d.* in 1722. PEREGRINE, his son and successor, 16th LORD, and 2nd Duke of Ancaster, was succeeded in 1742 by his eldest son PEREGRINE, 17th LORD, and 3rd Duke, who *d.* in 1778; leaving issue, 1 ROBERT, 4th Duke; 2 LADY PRISCILLA-BARBARA-ELIZABETH, the late BARONESS; 3 Lady Georgiana-Charlotte, present Dowager Marchioness Cholmondeley, and joint hereditary Great Chamberlain.

ROBERT, 4th Duke and 18th LORD, succeeded his father, and *d. unm.* 8 July 1779, when the Dukedom of Ancaster became extinct, the Earldom of Lindsey devolved on the heir male, (*see* that title in this Volume,) and this Barony fell into abeyance between his two sisters; it was called out 18 March 1780, in favour of LADY PRISCILLA-BARBARA-ELIZABETH, the late BARONESS, who was also co-heir with her sister, the Marchioness Dowager Cholmondeley, of one moiety of the ancient Barony of Beke. Her Ladyship *m.* PETER BURRELL, 1st LORD GWYDIR—see *The Peerage Volume*—and *d.* in 1828, when she was succeeded by her eldest son, PETER-ROBERT, the present and 20th LORD.

His Lordship's first known ancestor was Randulph de Burrell, living in the reign of Edward I.; 13th in lineal descent from him was

Peter Burrell, Esq., of Beckenham, Kent, who left two sons, viz.:

1 Peter, who *d.* in 1756; his 2nd son, Sir William, was created a Baronet in 1773, and was father of the present Sir Charles Merrick Burrell, Bart.; he was succeeded by his eldest son, Peter Burrell, Esq., also of Beckenham, who *d.* 6 Nov. 1775; having *m.* 28 March 1749, Elizabeth, daughter and co-heir of John Lewis, Esq., by whom, who *d.* 10 June 1794; he left issue; 1 PETER, 1st LORD GWYDIR; 2 Elizabeth-Amelia, widow of Richard-Henry-Alexander Bennett, Esq.; 3 Isabella-Susanna, *d.* 24 Jan. 1812, Countess of Beverley; 4 Frances-Julia, *d.* 28 April 1820, late Duchess of Northumberland; 5 Elizabeth, Marchioness Dowager of Exeter.

2 Sir Merrick Burrell, of West Grinstead Park, Sussex, a Governor of the Bank of England, created a Baronet in 1765, with remainder, failing his issue male, to his elder brother Peter Burrell, Esq., and his issue male. He *d.* without issue in 1787, and was succeeded by his great-nephew, the grandson of his said elder brother,

SIR PETER BURRELL, who was created to the Peerage in 1796 by the title of BARON GWYDIR of Gwydir, Co. Carnarvon. He *m.*, as above-mentioned, the BARONESS WILLOUGHBY D'ERESBY, and *d.* in 1820, when he was succeeded by his son PETER-ROBERT, 2nd LORD GWYDIR, and now 20th LORD WILLOUGHBY D'ERESBY, who having *m.* the Lady Clementina-Sarah Drummond, only daughter and heir of James, Lord Perth, representative of the Earls of Perth, (*see* Strathallan, p. 356,) took the surname and arms of DRUMMOND by Royal sign manual in 1807, and in 1829 the additional surname and arms of WILLOUGHBY, instead of those of Burrell.

WILTON, EARL OF. (EGERTON.)

Peer of the United Kingdom.

Reginald, 1st Lord Grey de Wilton, by writ 1295, for whose pedigree see the Earl of Stamford in this Volume, was father of John, 2nd Lord, who had two sons; Henry, 3rd Lord; and Roger, ancestor of the Barons Grey de Ruthyn, Earls of Kent, Marquises of Dorset, and Earls of Stamford. From Henry, 3rd Lord, proceeded the succeeding Lords Grey de Wilton, till the attainder in 1604 of Thomas, 15th Lord, whose sister and heir Bridget, *m.* Sir Rowland Egerton, Bart.; from this marriage descended, in the 5th degree,

Sir Thomas Egerton, created Baron Grey de Wilton in 1784, which title became extinct on his death, 23 Sept. 1814, without surviving issue male; he was also created in 1801 Earl of Wilton and Viscount Grey de Wilton, with remainder to the 2nd, and every succeeding son of his eldest and only surviving daughter, and their issue male respectively; he *m.* 11 Sept. 1769, Eleanor, daughter and co-heir of Sir Ralph Asheton, Bart., by whom, who *d.* 3 Feb. 1816, he had two sons and four daughters, who all died in their childhood except the eldest daughter, Eleanor, wife of the present Marquis of Westminster, and mother, by him, of Richard, Earl Grosvenor, heir apparent to the Marquis; Thomas, the present and 2nd Earl of Wilton, who succeeded his grandfather; and a 3rd son, Lord Robert Grosvenor.

WINCHESTER, MARQUIS OF. (Paulet.)

Peer of England.

Sir John Powlett, 7th in descent from Hercules—Lord of Tournon, *see* Earl Poulett, in this Volume, had two sons:

1 Thomas, ancestor, of Earl Poulett.

2 William, whose son, Sir John, *m.* Constance, eldest grand-daughter and co-heir of Sir Thomas Poynings, Lord St.-John of Basing, son of Lucas Poynings, by Isabel, daughter and at length heir of Hugh, Baron St.-John of Basing, (by writ 1299,) and by her was father of John Paulet, and grandfather of Sir John Paulet. The latter was father of

Sir William Paulet, K.G., Lord High Treasurer, created Baron St. John of Basing in 1539; Earl of Wiltshire in 1550; and Marquis of Winchester in 1551. A statesman and courtier, who, to use his own phrase, by being a willow and not an oak, rose to a high degree of rank and power, retained his prosperity to the end of a long life, and the favour of the crown through the various changes of politics which marked the successive reigns of Henry VIII., Edward VI., Mary, and Elizabeth. He *d.* in 1572, in the ninety-seventh year of his age, having lived to see one hundred and three of his own descendants. John, his eldest son, 2nd Marquis, succeeded; he *d.* in 1576, and was succeeded by his eldest son William, 3rd Marquis, to whom in 1598 succeeded his only son,

William, 4th Marquis. He entertained Queen Elizabeth with great splendour at Basing, and, by adopting a very magnificent style of living, brought himself into considerable pecuniary embarassment; he *d.* in 1628, leaving six sons, of whom only two had issue, viz.:

1 John, 3rd but eldest surviving son, his successor, 5th Marquis, who having garrisoned and stored his house at Basing as a place of support for the Royal forces, stood a siege in it, notwithstanding a treacherous attempt of his youngest brother, Lord Edward Paulet, to deliver it up to the enemy, from Aug. 1743 to 16 Oct. 1745, when in the general decline of the Royal cause, it was taken by storm after a most valiant and determined defence, and the Marquis was made prisoner with such of his garrison as survived the fight; ten pieces of ordnance and much ammunition were also taken by the conquerors, as Cromwell himself, who directed the assault, writes to the Speaker. The noble Marquis lived to see the Restoration, and was succeeded in 1674 by his eldest son, Charles, 6th Marquis, and 1st Duke of Bolton.

2 Lord Henry Paulet, 4th son, who left one son, Charles Paulet, Esq., of Anneport, Co. Hants, father of Francis Paulet, Esq., who by his marriage with Elizabeth, daughter of Sir Richard Norton, and heir of Sir John Norton, Bart., of Rotherfield Park, Co. Hants, had issue Norton Paulet, Esq., of Rotherfield, father of George, his only surviving son, who on the death of Harry, 6th Duke of Bolton, succeeded as 12th Marquis.

Charles, 6th Marquis, eldest son and successor of the 5th Marquis, was created

Duke of Bolton in 1689, and *d.* in 1699, leaving two sons, Charles, his successor, 2nd Duke, and Lord William, who left two sons, William, and Sir Charles-Armand Paulet, the latter *d.* in 1751 without issue; and William had one son, William, who *d. unm.*, and a daughter, Annabella, from whom descends Lord Bayning, who has assumed the name of William-Powlett.—*See* Bayning in this Volume.

Charles, 7th Marquis, and 2nd Duke of Bolton, K.G., *d.* in 1722, leaving three sons: Charles, 8th Marquis and 3rd Duke, K.G., who *d.* without legitimate issue in 1754; Harry, who succeeded his brother as 4th Duke; and Lord Nassau Paulet, father of Isabella, late Countess of Egmont, mother of the present Earl.

Harry, 9th Marquis and 4th Duke, *d.* in 1759, leaving two sons: Charles, his successor, 10th Marquis and 5th Duke, who *d. unm.* in 1765, leaving large estates to Jane-Mary, his natural daughter, whose husband, Thomas Orde, Esq., assumed the name of Powlett, and was created Lord Bolton in 1797—*see* that title; and Harry, 11th Marquis and 6th Duke of Bolton, who succeeded his brother, and *d.* 25 Dec. 1794, without issue male, when the Dukedom became extinct; he left three daughters, Lady Mary-Henrietta, late Countess of Sandwich, grandmother of the present Earl; Lady Katherine-Margaret, 1st wife of William-Henry, now Marquis of Cleveland, whose second son by her Ladyship, on succeeding to his grandfather's estates, has assumed the name of Powlett; and Lady Amelia, who is living *unm.*

The title of Marquis of Winchester devolved, on the death of the 6th Duke of Bolton, as shewn above, on George Paulet, Esq., of Anneport and Rotherfield, Co. Hants, 12th Marquis, descended from Lord Henry fourth son of the 4th Marquis. He *d.* in 1800, and was succeeded by his eldest son, Charles-Ingoldsby, present and 13th Marquis.

WINCHILSEA, EARL OF. (Finch-Hatton.)

Peer of England.

This family claims its descent from the same Henry Fitz-Herbert, Chamberlain to King Henry I., whose eldest son Reginald was ancestor, but by an illegitimate descent, of the Earl of Pembroke. His 3rd son, Matthew, was father of Herbert Fitz-Matthew, whose son, Herbert-Fitz-Herbert Herbert, otherwise Finch, is the first of the family who bore this surname, which is supposed to have been assumed from a marriage with an heiress, though the name of Herbert, alias Finch, was continued so late as the reign of King Edward IV.

Sir Thomas Finch, 9th in descent from Matthew Fitz-Herbert, joining with the Lord Abergavenny in 1553, drove Sir Thomas Wyat and his insurgents out of Kent. He was afterwards, in 1564, appointed by Queen Elizabeth Knight-Marshal of the forces in Newhaven, then besieged by the French, and was shipwrecked and drowned with the whole ship's crew and passengers, above two hundred persons, on his voyage thither. He *m.* Catherine, eldest daughter and co-heir of Sir Thomas Moyle, of Eastwell, Co. Kent, with whom he obtained that mansion, and by her had three sons, of whom Thomas, the youngest, *d.* without issue; the two elder were,

1 Sir Moyle Finch, created a Baronet in 1611, and *d.* in 1614, having *m.* Elizabeth, only daughter and heir of Sir Thomas Heneage, which Lady was created Viscountess of Maidstone, Co. Kent, in 1623, and Countess of Winchilsea in 1628; she *d.* in 1633, and was succeeded by their son, Thomas, 2nd Earl.

2 Sir Henry Finch, Lord Chief Justice of the Common Pleas, afterwards Lord Keeper, who, for the judgments he gave in the case of ship-money, incurred the displeasure of Parliament so greatly, that when affairs took a turn unfavourable to Royal cause, he was compelled to escape to Holland. He had been created

in 1640 Lord Finch of Fordwich, Co. Kent, which title became extinct on his death in 1661.

Sir Moyle Finch, the elder brother, had, by Elizabeth, Countess of Winchilsea, seven sons, of whom only the two following left issue, viz.:

1 Thomas, 2nd Earl, (2nd son,) he *d.* in 1639, and was succeeded by his eldest son, Heneage, 3rd Earl, to whom the charge of Dover Castle was committed by General Monck, previous to the restoration of King Charles II.; he was created in 1660 Baron Fitz-Herbert, of Eastwell, Co. Kent, and *d.* in 1689, having had twenty-seven children by four wives; of his sons, only the three following lived to bear his title or to give heirs to it.

1 William Viscount Maidstone; he was killed in the naval battle against the Dutch in 1672, leaving a posthumous son, Charles, who succeeded his grandfather as 4th Earl, and *d.* in 1712, without surviving issue.

2 Heneage, who succeeded his nephew as 5th Earl; he *d.* without issue in 1726.

3 John, who succeeded his brother, and also *d.* without issue in 1729, when the Barony of Fitz-Herbert and the male issue of the 2nd Earl became extinct.

2 Sir Heneage Finch, Recorder of London and Speaker of the House of Commons, who *d.* in 1631; leaving issue, Heneage, his son and heir, created a Baronet in 1660; in 1673 he was made Lord Keeper, and created Baron Finch of Daventry, Co. Northampton; in 1675 he was appointed Lord High Chancellor, and in 1681 created Earl of Nottingham; he *d.* in 1682, obtaining from Bishop Burnet the character of an uncorruptible Judge, impartial on the Bench, even against the King himself; filling the church livings with worthy men, and obliging all to residence; most eloquent in Parliament, on the Bench, and in conversation. He had ten sons, two of whom have left descendants still flourishing in the Peerage.

1 Daniel, 2nd Earl of Nottingham, his successor, who succeeded as 7th Earl of Winchilsea, on the extinction of the male issue of the 2nd Earl in 1729.

2 Heneage, 1st Earl of Aylesford, and ancestor of the present Earl.—*See* that title.

Daniel, 7th Earl of Winchilsea and 2nd of Nottingham, *d.* in 1730, leaving by Anne, only daughter of Christopher Viscount Hatton, and sister and heir of William the last Viscount, six sons, three of whom have succeeded or given heirs to the title, viz.:

1 Daniel, 8th Earl, K.G., who *d.* without issue male in 1769.

2 The Right-Hon. William Finch, who by Charlotte, daughter of Thomas Earl of Pomfret, and Governess to King George IV. and the Duke of York when infants, had one son, George, who succeeded his uncle as 9th Earl, was a Knight of the Garter, and *d. unm.* in 1826.

3 Edward, who assumed the additional name of Hatton, and *d.* 16 May 1771; having *m.* in 1746, Elizabeth, 3rd daughter and co-heir of Sir Thomas Palmer, Bart., by whom he was father of George Finch-Hatton, Esq., (see *The Peerage Volume,*) whose eldest son George succeeded his cousin, and is the present and 10th Earl, of Harriet-Frances-Charlotte, who was *b.* 19 Feb. 1752, and *d.* 11 June 1821, having *m.* Oct. 1781, Sir Jenison-William Gordon, Bart., K.C.B., who *d.* 9 May 1831, leaving considerable estates to the present Earl of Winchilsea; and of the surviving son and daughter, who will be found in *The Peerage Volume* as uncle and aunt of the Earl.

WINTERTON, EARL OF. (Turnour.)

Peer of Ireland.

Edward Garth, 1st Earl, assumed the name and arms of Turnour, being son of Joseph Garth, Esq., by Sarah, only daughter and heir of Francis Gee, Esq., by

Sarah, daughter and at length heir of Sir Edward Turnour, son of Sir Edward Turnour, Lord Chief Baron of the Court of Exchequer. He was created in 1761 Baron Winterton of Gort, Co. Galway, and in 1766 Viscount Turnour and EARL of WINTERTON; he *d.* in 1788, and was succeeded by his only son, EDWARD-GARTH, 2nd EARL, to whom succeeded in 1831, his eldest son, EDWARD, present and 3rd EARL.

WODEHOUSE, BARON. (WODEHOUSE.)

Peer of Great Britain.

Sir Armine Wodehouse, Bart., his Lordship's father, was 23d in descent from Sir Constantine Wodehouse, living in the reign of King HENRY I. He *d.* in 1777, having *m.* Letitia, eldest daughter and co-heir of Sir Edmund Bacon, Bart., by whom he had issue:

1 SIR JOHN, his successor, who was created in 1797 BARON WODEHOUSE of Kimberley, Co. Norfolk, and is the present Peer.

2 The Rev. Philip Wodehouse, who was *b.* May 1745, and *d.* 14 Feb. 1811; having *m.* 29 July 1775, Apollonia, daughter and co-heir of John Nourse, Esq., by whom, who *d.* 21 March 1817, he had issue,

1 Letitia, *m.* 9 June 1804, George-B. Mainwaring, Esq.
2 Elizabeth.
3 Lucy, *d.* 21 June 1829; having *m.* 26 June 1809, Edmond Wodehouse, Esq., M.P.—*See below.*
4 Lieut.-Col. Philip, *b.* 6 Aug. 1788.
5 Rev. Charles-N., Prebendary of Norwich, *b.* 8 Sept. 1790, *m.* 29 Dec. 1821, Lady Dulcibella-Jane Hay, eldest daughter of William, 16th Earl of Errol, and has issue: 1 Charles, *b.* 31 Dec. 1822; 2 James-Hay, *b.* 23 April 1824; 3 Isabella-Jane, *b.* 29 May 1825; 4 Elizabeth-Margaret, *b.* 7 May 1826.
6 Apollonia.

2 Thomas, *b.* 1747, is deceased, having *m.* 12 Sept. 1782, Sarah daughter of Pryce Campbell, Esq., and sister of John, 1st Lord Cawdor, by whom he left issue,

1 Edmond, M.P. widower, 21 June 1829, of Lucy, daughter of his uncle, the Rev. Philip Wodehouse—*see above*—by whom he has issue: 1 Philip-Edmond; 2 Sarah-Elizabeth, *d.* 21 June 1826; 3 Frances-Lucy, *d.* Oct. 1830; 4 Mary; 5 Edmond; 6 Lucy; 7 Charles-John; 8 Armine; 9 Campbell, *b.* 31 Jan. 1826.
2 Thomas, *b.* 13 Oct. 1788.
3 Lieut.-Colonel Nicholas, 50th foot, *b.* 18 Jan. 1790.
4 Rev. Nathaniel-Francis, *m.* 28 Sept. 1829, Georgiana, 3rd daughter of Hon. and Rev. William-Robert Capel, of Essex; they have issue, a daughter, *b.* 30 March 1831.
5 Mary.
6 Sarah.
7 Blanch.
8 Rachel.
9 Susan.
10 Isabel-Letitia.
11 Ellen.

WYNFORD, BARON. (Best.)

Peer of the United Kingdom.

Sir William-Draper Best, Lord Chief Justice of the Common Pleas, was created in 1829 Baron Wynford of Wynford-Eagle, Co. Dorset, and is the present Peer.

YARBOROUGH, BARON. (Anderson-Pelham.)

Peer of Great Britain.

Thomas Anderson, who came out of Scotland, and settled in Lincolnshire, was father of Sir Edmond Anderson, Chief Justice of the Common Pleas in the reign of Elizabeth; the 5th in descent from him was Francis Anderson, Esq., who *m.* Mary, eldest daughter of Charles Pelham, Esq., of Brocklesby, (a junior branch of the family of Pelham, now Earl of Chichester,) and sister of Charles Pelham, Esq., who *d. unm.*; their grandson Charles, father of the present Lord, having inherited the estates of his great uncle, assumed the additional name and arms of Pelham. He was created Baron Yarborough of Yarborough, Co. Lincoln, and *d.* in 1824, when he was succeeded by his eldest son Charles, present and 2nd Lord.

ZOUCHE, BARONESS. (Curzon.)

Peeress of England.

Roger le Zouche of Ashby descended from the Earls of Brittany, and whose predecessors had ranked as Barons of the realm in the reign of Richard I., *d.* in 1285, leaving two sons:

1 Alan, summoned to Parliament in 1299 as Lord Zouche of Ashby; he *d.* in 1314, leaving three daughters, his co-heirs, between whom the Barony fell into abeyance; they were,

1 Elene, *m.* to Nicholas, summoned to Parliament in 1314 as Baron St. Maur; and from them the Barony of St. Maur passed to their two sons, Thomas, 2nd Lord, and Nicholas, 3rd Lord; the latter *m.* Muriel, grand-daughter and heir of Richard, Baron Lovel of Kary, by writ 1348; and the two Baronies were successively inherited by their two sons Nicholas and Richard; the latter was father of Richard, 6th Baron St. Maur, and 5th Baron Lovel of Kary, and *d.* without male issue in 1409, leaving a daughter and sole heir, Alice, who *m.* William, 5th Lord Zouche of Haryngworth, to whom she carried the Baronies of St. Maur and Lovel of Kary, and her moiety of the Barony of Zouche of Ashby.

2 Maud, *m.* to Robert de Holand, who was summoned to Parliament in 1314 as Baron Holand; he was succeeded by his eldest son Robert, whose grand-daughter and sole heir *m.* John, 7th Lord Lovel, in whose descendants the Baronies of Lovel and Holand continued united for four generations, when Francis Viscount Lovel, K.G., was killed in the battle of Stoke in 1487, and attainted, leaving two sisters his co-heirs, between whom the Baronies of Lovel and Holand and his moiety of the Barony of Zouche of Ashby fell into abeyance, but on account of the attainder could not be inherited; they were, Joan, *m.* to Sir Bryan Stapleton, the heir of which marriage is Thomas Stapleton, Esq., who some time since claimed

the Barony of Beaumont; and Fridiswide, m. to Sir Edward Norris, the heir of which marriage is the Earl of Abingdon.

3 Elizabeth, a nun.

2 Eudo le Zouche, whose son and heir WILLIAM was summoned to Parliament in 1308 as LORD ZOUCHE of HARYNGWORTH; he *d.* in 1352, and was succeeded by his grandson and heir, WILLIAM, 2nd LORD, son and heir of Eudo, eldest son of the 1st LORD, who *d.* in his father's life time. From this WILLIAM, 2nd LORD, who *d.* in 1382, descended without interruption in the direct male line from father to son through nine successive generations, Lords Zouche of Haryngworth,

EDWARD, 11th LORD, who *d.* in 1625, leaving two daughters his co-heirs, Elizabeth and Mary; Mary, the younger daughter, m. 1st, Thomas Leighton, Esq., and 2ndly, William Connaid, Esq.; no descendants of the 2nd marriage have appeared, and her issue by Mr. Leighton have not been traced beyond the 2nd generation, and may be considered as extinct.

Elizabeth, eldest daughter, and probably at length sole heir of EDWARD, 11th LORD, m. Sir William Tate, and from them descended in the direct male line Bartholomew Tate, Esq., their great-grandson, who left issue,

1 Bartholomew Tate, Esq., who *d.* without surviving issue in 1776.

2 Catherine, m. Charles Hedges, Esq., and had two sons and two daughters; the sons both *d. unm.*, and Anna-Maria, the younger daughter, *d.* without issue, having m. the Hon. William Bateman; Susanna, the eldest daughter, and at length sole heir, m. Sir Cecil Bisshopp, Bart., and *d.* in 1791, leaving issue SIR CECIL BISSHOPP, Bart., in whose favour his late Majesty was graciously pleased to call this Barony out of abeyance in 1815.

3 Mary, m. Samuel Long, Esq.—*see* Farnborough in this volume—and had two sons, Robert and Edward, who both left issue; the three daughters and co-heirs of Robert the eldest son, were co-heirs, with the late Lord, of this Barony; they were,

1 Jane-Catherine-Sarah, m. to John Oliver, Esq., of Gray's Inn.

2 Mary-Charlotte, m. to Samuel-Scudamore Heming, Esq., and left a son, Samuel-George Heming, Esq.

3 Lucy-Anne, m. Thomas-Bayley Howell, Esq.

SIR CECIL BISSHOPP, Bart., summoned to Parliament in 1815, as Baron Zouche of Haryngworth, was also eldest co-heir of the Baronies of St. Maur and Lovel of Kary, and eldest co-heir of one moiety of the Barony of Zouche of Ashby. On his death in 1828 the Barony of ZOUCHE of Haryngworth again fell into abeyance between his two daughters and co-heirs, viz.: HARRIET-ANNE, the wife of the Hon. Robert Curzon; and Katherine-Annabella, the wife of Captain Pechel, R.N. —*see The Peerage Volume*—which abeyance his late Majesty was graciously pleased to terminate in 1829, in favour of HARRIETT-ANNE, the eldest daughter and co-heir, the present BARONESS.

MOTTOES OF ALL THE PEERS.

ALPHABETICALLY ARRANGED AND TRANSLATED.

N.B. BISHOPS AND PEERESSES USE NO MOTTOES.

Dieu et mon Droit. *God and my right.* The King.

A cruce salus. *Salvation from the cross.* e Mayo and l Downes.
A cuspide corona. *From a lance to a crown.* v Midleton.
A Deo et rege. *From God and the King.* e Chesterfield; e Stanhope; and e Harrington.
Æquabiliter et diligenter. *By equity and diligence.* Redesdale.
Æquam servare mentem. *To preserve an equal mind.* Rivers.
Æquanimiter. *Patiently.* Suffield.
A fin. *To the end.* e Airlie.
Agincourt. Wodehouse.
Ales volat propriis. *The bird flies to its own.* e Thanet.
Algiers. v Exmouth.
A ma puissance. *To my power.* e Stamford.
Amo. *I love.* d Buccleuch.
Anchor, fast anchor. Gray.
Animo et fide. *By courage and faith.* e Guilford.
Animo, non astutiâ. *By courage, not by craft.* d Gordon.
Antiquum obtinens. *Possessing antiquity.* Bagot.
Aperto vivere voto. *To live with will unfettered.* e Aylesford.
Appetitus rationi pareat. *Let the appetite be obedient to reason.* e Fitzwilliam.
Aquila non captat muscas. *An eagle does not catch flies.* Graves.
Astra castra, Numen lumen. *The stars are my camp, the Deity is my light.* e Balcarres.
At spes non fracta. *But my hope is not broken.* e Hopetoun.
Au bon droit. *To the best right.* e Egremont.
Auctor pretiosa facit. *The giver makes it more valuable.* e Buckinghamshire.

MOTTOES.

Audacter et sincere. *Boldly and sincerely.* e Powis.
Au plaisir fort de Dieu. *At the Almighty disposal of God.* e Mount-Edgecumbe.
Auspicium melioris ævi. *A pledge of better times.* d St. Albans.
Aut nunquam tentes, aut perfice. *Either never attempt, or accomplish.* d Dorset.
Auxilium ab alto. *Help from above.* e Roscommon; and l Clonbrock.
Avance. *Advance.* e Portmore.
Avancez. *Advance.* Hill.
Avi numerantur avorum. *I follow a long train of ancestors.* Grantley.
Avise la fin. *Consider the end.* m Ailsa.
Avito viret honore. *He flourishes in an honourable ancestry.* m Bute; l Stuart de Rothesay; and l Wharncliffe.
Aymez loyalté. *Love loyalty.* m Winchester; and l Bolton.

Bear and forbear. Langford.
Be fast. e Mexborough.
Be just and fear not. v Lifford.
Bella! horrida bella! *Wars! horrid wars!* Lisle.
Be mindful. Cawdor.
Benigno Numine. *By God's blessing.* e Chatham.

Candidè et constanter. *Candidly and constantly.* e Coventry.
Candidé securé. *Honesty is the best policy.* Lynedoch.
Cassis tutissima virtus. *Virtue is the safest defence.* m Cholmondeley; and l Delamere.
Cause caused it. Elphinstone; and Keith.
Cavendo tutus. *Secure in caution.* d Devonshire; and l Waterpark.
Che, sara, sara. *What will be, will be.* d of Bedford.
Chio che Dio vuole, io voglio. *What God wills, I will.* Dormer.
Clarior a tenebris. *More bright from obscurity.* e Miltown.
Cœlitus mihi vires. *My strength is from Heaven.* v Ranelagh.
Cœlum non animum. *You may change your climate, not your mind.* e Waldegrave.
Comme je fus. *As I was.* e Dudley.
Comme je trouve. *As I find.* m Ormonde,
Commit thy work to God. e Caithness.
Compositum jus fasque animi. *Law and equity.* Ellenborough.
Consequitur quodcunque petit. *He attains whatever he attempts.* m Headfort.
Consilio et animis. *By wisdom and courage.* e Lauderdale.
Consilio et prudentia. *By wisdom and prudence.* e Clancarty.
Constantia et virtute. *With constancy and valour.* e Amherst.
Cor unum, via una. *One heart, one way.* m Exeter; and l Mount-Sandford.
Courage sans peur. *Courage without fear.* v Gage.
Craignez honte. *Fear disgrace.* d Portland.
Crede Byron. *Trust Byron.* Byron.
Crescit sub pondere virtus. *Virtue grows under the imposed weight.* e Denbigh.
Crom a boo. *Crom (a Castle formerly belonging to the Fitz-Gerald family) for ever.* d Leinster.
Cruci dum spiro spero. *Whilst I have breath, I put my trust in the Cross.* v Netterville.

Data fata secutus. *Following his declared fate.* St. John.
Dat Deus incrementum. *God gives the increase.* Crofton.
De bon vouloir servir le roi. *To serve the King with good will.* e Tankerville; and e Grey
Decrevi. *I have resolved.* m Westmeath; and l Nugent.
Deed shaw. Ruthven.
Delectare in Domino. Poltimore.

Deo adjuvante fortuna sequatur. v Exmouth.
Deo adjuvante, non timendum. *God being my aid, nothing is to be feared.* v. Fitzwilliam.
Deo date. *Give to God.* Arundell.
Deo duce, ferro comitante. *God being my leader, and my sword my companion.* e Charlemont.
Deo non fortunâ. *From God, not fortune.* e Digby.
Deo, patriæ, amicis. *To God, my country, and my friends.* Colchester.
Deo, regi, patriæ. *To God, my king, and my country.* Feversham.
Depressus extollor. *I was depressed, I am exalted.* e Kilkenny.
Deum cole, regem serva. *Worship God, and serve the king.* e Enniskillen.
Deus Major columna. *God is the best support.* Henniker.
Dieu avec nous. *God with us.* e Berkeley.
Dieu ayde. *God assists.* v Montmorres; and v Frankfort de Montmorency.
Dieu defend le Droit. *God defends the right.* e Spencer; and l Churchill.
Disponendo me, non mutando me. *By disposing of me, not by changing me.* d Manchester.
Divini gloria ruris. *The glory of the heavenly mansions.* v Ferrard.
Dominus providebit. *The Lord will provide.* e Glasgow.
Dread God. v Kenmure.
Droit et avant. *Right and forward.* v Sydney.
Droit et loyal. *Just and loyal.* Huntingfield.
Dum spiro spero. *While I breathe I hope.* v Dillon.

En Dieu est ma fiance. *In God is my trust.* e Carhampton.
En grace affie. *On grace depend.* e Cardigan.
En la rose je fleurie. *I flourish in the rose.* d Richmond.
En suivant la vérité. *In following truth.* e Portsmouth.
Esperance en Dieu. *Hope in God.* d Northumberland; e Beverley; and l Prudhoe.
Essayez. *Try.* Dundas.
Esse, quàm videri. *To be, rather than seem to be.* e Winterton.
Esto quod esse videris. *Be what you appear.* Sondes.
Et decus et pretium recti. *The ornament aud reward of Virtue.* d Grafton; and l Southampton.
Et nos quoque tela sparsimus. *And we too have scattered arrows.* m Hastings.
Et vitam impendere vero. *Keep the truth at the hazard of life.* Holland.
Excitari non hebescere. *To be spirited, not inactive.* Walsingham.
Ex fide fortis. *Strong through faith.* e Beauchamp.

Faire mon devoir. *To do my duty.* e Roden.
Faire sans dire. *To act without words.* e Ilchester.
Famam extendere factis. *To extend fame by deeds.* v Galway.
Fama semper vivet. *Reputation lives for ever.* Ravensworth.
Fare, fac. *Speak, do.* Fairfax.
Fari quæ sentias. *Speak what you think.* e Oxford.
Fax mentis incendium gloriæ. *The torch of the mind is the flame of glory.* e Granard.
Fear God in life. Somerville.
Fear to transgress. e Clonmel.
Festina lentè. *Quick without impetuosity.* e Fingal; l Dunsany; Louth; and Plunket.
Fide et amore. *By faith and love.* m Hertford.
Fide et fiduciâ. *By faith and fortitude.* e Rosebery.
Fide et fortitudine. *By faith, and fortitude.* e Essex.
Fide, non armis. *By faith, not arms.* Gambier.
Fidei coticula crux. *The cross is the test of faith.* e Jersey; and e Clarendon.

Fideli certa merces. *A certain reward to the faithful.* e Morley.
Fidélité est de Dieu. *Truth is of God.* v Powerscourt.
Fidus et audax. *Faithful and courageous.* v Lismore.
Fiel pero desdichado. *Faithful but unfortunate.* d of Marlborough.
Fight. e Rosslyn; and l Sinclair.
Finem respice. *Look to the end.* e Darnley.
Firm. e Stair.
Firmior quò paratior. *I am stronger by being always prepared.* e Selkirk.
Flecti, non frangi. *To be bent, not broken.* v Palmerston.
Follow me. m Breadalbane.
Fortem posce animum. *Wish for a strong mind.* Saye-and-Sele.
Forte scutum salus ducum. *A strong shield proves the safety of the leaders.* e Fortescue.
Fortes fortuna juvat. *Fortune assists the brave.* Bloomfield.
Forti et fideli nihil difficile. *To courage and constancy nothing is difficult.* Muskerry.
Fortis cadere, cedere non potest. *The brave man may fall, but cannot yield.* m Drogheda.
Fortiter, fideliter, feliciter. *Boldly, faithfully, successfully.* e Rathdown.
Fortiter gerit crucem. *He bravely supports the cross.* e Donoughmore.
Fortuna sequatur. *Let fortune follow.* e Aberdeen.
Forward. m Queensberry, and e Castle-Stewart.
Foy pour devoir. *Faith for duty.* d Somerset.
Frangas, non flectes. *You may break, you shall not bend me.* m Stafford; v Granville.
Fuimus. *We were.* e Elgin; and m Ailesbury.
Furth fortune, and fill the fetters. d Atholl; l Glenlyon; and e Dunmore.

Gardez Bien. *Take care.* e Eglintoun.
Gardez ta foy. *Keep thy faith.* e Poulett; and l Kensington.
Gaudet tentamine virtus. *Virtue rejoices in trial.* e Dartmouth.
Gloria virtutis umbra. *Glory is the shadow of virtue.* e Longford.
God be my guide. e Glengall.
God send grace. e Erne.
Grace me guide. Forbes.
Gradu diverso, via una. *The same way, by different steps.* Calthorpe.
Gradescunt aucta labore. *They increase by labour.* Heytesbury.
Grata quies. *Rest is grateful.* Bexley.
Grip fast. e Rothes.

Hæc generi incrementa fides. *Ennobled for our fidelity.* m Townshend.
Haut et bon. *Great and good.* v Doneraile.
Honesta quàm splendida. *Honest things rather than splendid.* v Barrington.
Honestè audax. *Honourably bold.* Rancliffe.
Honor fidelitatis præmium. *Honour is the reward of fidelity.* Boston.
Honor virtutis præmium. *Honour is the reward of virtue.* e Ferrers; and e Cork.
Hora et semper. *Now and always.* e Pomfret.
Hostis honori invidia. *Envy is an enemy to honour.* e Harborough.
umani nihil alienum. *Nothing is indifferent to me which relates to man.* e Talbot.

I dare. e Carnwath.
I hope to speed. e Cathcart.
In Deo spero. *In God is my hope.* De Saumarez.
Indignante invidiâ florebit justus. *A just man will flourish in spite of indignant envy.* Brandon.
Ingenuas suscipet artes. *He fosters the polite arts.* Farnborough.
In God is all. Saltoun.

In hoc signo spes mea. *In this sign is my hope.* v Taaffe.
In hoc signo vinces. *In this sign thou shalt conquer.* e Arran.
In omnia paratus. *Prepared for every thing.* Dunally.
In portu quies. *In the haven is repose.* Skelmersdale.
Inservi Deo et lætare. *Serve God and rejoice.* e Wicklow.
In solo Deo salus. *Salvation in God alone.* e Harewood.
Intaminatis honoribus. *Unspotted honour.* St. Helens; and Henley.
In te, Domine, speravi. *In thee, O Lord, have I put my trust.* e Strathmore.
Integra mens augustissima possessio. *An honest mind is the most noble possession.* Blayney.
In utrâque fortunâ paratus. *In every situation prepared.* Combermere.
In utroque fidelis. *Faithful in both.* v Falkland.
In veritate victoria. *Victory is in truth.* e Huntingdon.
Invitem sequitur honor. *Honour follows against his will.* m Donegal; and l Templemore.

J'ai bonne cause. *I have good cause.* m Bath.
Jamais arrière. *Never behind.* e Selkirk; and l Douglas.
Je le tiens. *I hold it.* Audley.
Je me fie en Dieu. *I put my trust in God.* e Plymouth.
Je ne cherche qu'un. *I seek but one.* m Northampton.
Je n'oublierai jamais. *I shall never forget.* m Bristol.
Je pense. *I think.* e Wemyss.
Je pense plus. *I think farther.* e Marr.
Je suis prêt. *I am ready.* e Farnham.
Je vive en espoir. *I live in hope.* e Stradbroke.
Jour de ma vie. *The day of my life.* e Delawarr.
Judge nought. e Buchan; and e Traquair.
Judicium parium, aut leges terræ. *The judgment of our peers, or the laws of the land.* m Camden.

Keep thyself. Sempill.

Labore. *By labour.* Tenterden.
Labore et honore. *By industry and honour.* Rendlesham.
Labor ipse voluptas. *Labour itself is pleasure.* King.
La fortune passe par tout. *The vicissitudes of fortune are common to all.* Rollo.
Lamh dearg eirin. e O'Neil.
Laus Deo. *Praise be to God.* v Arbuthnot.
Lead on. Hotham.
Le jour viendra. *The day will come.* Durham.
Le roi et l'état. *The king and the state.* e Ashburnham.
Le roi le veut. *The king wills it.* De Clifford.
L'Esperance me comfort. *Hope comforts me.* Nairne.
Let Curzon hold what Curzon held. e Howe.
Libertas. *Liberty.* Carbery.
Libertas sub rege pio. *Liberty under a pious king.* v Sidmouth.
Libertè tout entière. *Liberty entire.* e Lanesborough.
Lock sicker. *Be secure.* e Morton.
Lord have mercy. v Strathallan.
Love—serve. e Shaftesbury.
Loyal devoir. *Loyal duty.* Carteret.
Loyal en tout. *Loyal in all things.* e Kenmare.
Loyal je serai durant ma vie. *I will be loyal during my life.* Stourton.
Loyauté me oblige. *Loyalty binds me.* e Lindsey.

Loyauté n'a honte. *Loyalty is never ashamed.* d Newcastle.

Magistratus indicat virum. *The magistrate shows the man.* e Lonsdale.
Magnanimiter crucem sustine. *Support afflictions with magnanimity.* Kenyon.
Malo mori quàm fœdari. *I had rather die than be disgraced.* e Athlone; v Kingsland; Trimlestown; and French.
Manu forti. *With a brave hand.* Reay.
Manus hæc inimica tyrannis. *This hand is hostile to tyrants.* e Carysfort and l Riversdale.
Manus justa nardus. *The just hand is as precious ointment.* v Maynard
Mediocria firma. *Firm in the middle state.* e Verulam.
Memor et fidelis. *Mindful and faithful.* Selsey.
Mens conscia recti. *A mind conscious of rectitude.* v Ashbrook.
Metuenda corolla draconis. *The collar of the dragon is to be feared.* m Londonderry.
Mihi cura futuri. *I am careful for the future.* Ongley.
Moveo et profiteor. *I proceed and am more prosperous.* v Northland.
Murus æneus conscientia sana. *A sound conscience is a brazen wall of defence.* e Scarborough.
Mutare vel timere sperno. *I scorn to change or fear.* d Beaufort.
My prince and my country. Harris.

Nec cupias nec metuas. *Neither desire nor fear.* e Hardwicke.
Ne cede malis. *Do not yield to misfortunes.* e Albemarle.
Ne cede malis, sed contrà. *Do not succumb to misfortune, but oppose it.* Garvagh.
Nec malè notus eques. *A well-known patrician.* v Southwell.
Nec rege nec populo, sed utroque. *Neither for the king nor for the people, but for both.* Rolle.
Nec temerè nec timidè. *Neither rashly nor fearfully.* m Cleveland; and e Bradford.
Nec timeo nec sperno. *I neither fear nor despise.* v Boyne.
N'oubliez. *Do not forget.* d Montrose.
Ne tentes, aut perfice. *Either attempt not, or accomplish.* m Downshire.
Ne vile fano. *Bring nothing base to the temple.* e Westmoreland.
Ne vile velis. *Incline to nothing base.* e Abergavenny; and l Braybrooke.
Nihil alienum. *Nothing foreign.* Dynevor.
Nil admirari. *To be astonished at nothing.* e Clare; and l Bolingbroke.
Nil conscire sibi. *Free from guilt.* e Winchilsea and Nottingham.
Nil desperandum. *Never despair.* e Blessington; and e Lichfield.
Nil nisi cruce. *There is no dependance but in the cross.* m Waterford; v Beresford; and l Decies.
Nobilitatis virtus non stemma character. *Virtue, not pedigree, should characterize nobility.* e Grosvenor.
Non generant aquilæ columbas. *Eagles do not bring forth doves.* Rodney.
Non hæc sine numine. *These things are not without the Deity.* v Clifden.
Non inferiora secutus. *Despising mean pursuits.* l Montfort.
Non quo, sed quomodo. *Not who, but how.* Howard de Walden; and Seaford.
Non revertar inultus. *I will not return unrevenged.* e Lisburne.
Non sibi, sed patriæ. *Not for himself, but for his country.* e Romney.
Non sine numine. *Not without Providence.* Gifford.
Numini et patriæ asto. *I stand to God and my country.* Aston.
Nunc aut nunquam. *Now or never.* e Kilmorey.

Occurrunt nubes. *Clouds will intervene.* e St. Germans.
Odi profanum. *I hate whatever is profane.* e Listowel.

Opera illius mea sunt. *His works are mine.* e Brownlow.
Ora et labora. *Pray and labour.* e Dalhousie.
Oublier ne puis. *I can never forget.* Colville.
Over fork over. m Conyngham.

Palmam qui meruit ferat. *Let him bear the palm who has deserved it.* e Nelson.
Palma non sine pulvere. *I have gained the palm, but not without labour.* e Liverpool.
Parta tueri. *You ought to defend what you have won.* Lilford.
Par ternis suppar. *The two are equal in antiquity to the three.* Northwick.
Patience passe science. *Patience surpasses knowledge.* e Falmouth.
Patientià vinces. *By patience thou shalt conquer.* Alvanley.
Patitur qui vincit. *He who conquers suffers.* Kinnaird.
Patria cara, carior libertas. *My country is dear, but liberty is dearer.* e Radnor.
Patriæ infelici fidelis. *Faithful to an unhappy country.* e Courtown.
Patriis virtutibus. *By hereditary virtues.* e Leitrim.
Pax in bello. *Peace in war.* d Leeds.
Per acuta belli. *By the stratagems of war.* e Tyrconnel.
Periculum fortitudine evasi. *By fortitude I have escaped from danger.* Hartland.
Per il suo contrario. *By its reverse.* m Anglesey.
Perimus licitis. *Death in a good cause.* Teignmouth.
Per mare per terras. *By sea and land.* e Caledon; and l Macdonald.
Perseverando. *By perseverance.* Ducie.
Per vias rectas. *By the right way.* Dufferin and Claneboyne.
Piè repone te. *Repose in pious confidence.* e Manvers.
Pollet virtus. *Virtue exalts.* Maryborough.
Porro unum est necessarium. *Moreover one thing is needful.* m Wellesley; and l Cowley.
Post prælia præmia. *Honours after battles.* Rossmore.
Post tot naufragia portum. *After so many shipwrecks, we find a harbour.* e Sandwich.
Pour bien desirer. *Desire good.* Dacre.
Pour y parvenir. *To attain the object.* d Rutland; and l Manners.
Præsto et persto. *I perform and persevere.* e Haddington.
Prend moi tel que je suis. *Take me such as I am.* And round the crest, Loyal à mort. *Loyal till death.* m Ely.
Prèt d'accomplir. *Ready to perform.* e Shrewsbury.
Prêt pour mon pays. *Ready for my country.* Monson.
Probitas verus honos. *Honesty is true honour.* v Chetwynd.
Pro Christo patrià. *For Christ and my country.* d Roxburghe.
Pro Deo et rege. *For God and the king.* e Rosse.
Prodesse quàm conspici. *Utility without ostentation.* e Somers.
Pro libertate patriæ. *For the liberty of my country.* Massy; and Clarina.
Pro Magna Charta. *For Magna Charta.* Ledespencer.
Pro rege et patrià. *For my king and country.* e Leven and Melville, and l de Tabley.
Pro rege et populo. *For the king and the people.* De Dunstanville.
Pro rege, lege, grege. *For the king, the law, and the people.* e Besborough, and l Ponsonby.

Quæ amissa, salva. *What has been lost is safe.* e Kintore.
Qualis ab incepto. *The same as from the beginning.* Grantham; and v Goderich.
Quem te Deus esse jussit. *What God commands you to be.* e Sheffield.
Quid verum atque decens. *What is just and honourable.* v Dungannon.
Qui invidet minor est. *He who envies is the inferior.* e Cadogan.
Qui pense. *Who thinks.* e Howth.

Qui uti scit, ei bona. *To him who knows how to use them, these things are good.* Berwick.
Quod potui perfeci. *I have done what I could do.* v Melville.
Quod sursum volo videre. *I am resolved to look at what is above.* e Dunraven.
Quo fata vocant. *Whither fate may call me.* Thurlow.
Quondam his vicimus armis. *We were once victorious with these arms.* Dorchester.

Ready, ay ready. Napier.
Rectè et suaviter. *Justly and mildly.* Scarsdale.
Renascentur. *They will rise again.* v Avonmore.
Renovate animos. *Renew your courage.* e Kinnoul.
Repetens exempla suorum. *Repeating the example of his ancestors.* Grenville.
Retinens vestigiæ famæ. *Retracing the achievements of an honourable ancestry.* Ribblesdale.
Ride through. Belhaven.
Right can never die. e Norbury; and l Norwood.

St. Vincent. Radstock.
Salus per Christum Redemptorem. *Salvation through Christ the Redeemer.* e Moray.
Sans changer. *Without changing.* e Derby.
Sans Dieu rien. *Nothing without God.* Petre.
Sans tâche. *Without stain.* v Gormanston.
Sapere aude. *Dare to be wise.* e Macclesfield.
Secundis dubiisque rectus. *Firm in every fortune.* v Duncan.
Sed sine labe decus. *Let your honours be without stain.* e Eldon; and l Stowell.
Semper eadem. *Always the same.* Forester.
Semper fidelis. *Always faithful* e Onslow.
Semper paratus. *Always ready.* Clifford.
Sequor nec inferior. *I follow, but not inferior.* l Crewe.
Serò sed seriò. *Late but in earnest.* m Salisbury, and m Lothian.
Servabo fidem. *I will keep faith.* Sherborne.
Serva jugum. *Preserve the yoke.* e Errol.
Servata fides cineri. *The promise made to my ancestor is now kept.* e Harrowby.
Si je puis. *If I can.* e Newburgh.
Si sit prudentia. *If there be but prudence.* Auckland; and St. Helens.
Sola juvat virtus. *Virtue alone delights me.* Blantyre.
Sola nobilitas virtus. *Virtue alone is true nobility.* m Abercorn.
Sola virtus invicta. *Virtue alone is invincible.* d Norfolk.
Solo Deo salus. *Safety in God alone.* Rokeby.
Soyez ferme. *Be firm.* e Carrick.
Spare nought. m Tweeddale.
Spectemur agendo. *Let us be seen by our actions.* Montagu.
Spero infestis; metuo secundis. *In adversity I hope, in prosperity I fear.* e Ludlow.
Spero meliora. *I hope for better times.* Torpichen.
Spes durat avorum. *The hope of my ancestors subsists,* e Rochford.
Spes mea Christus. *Christ is my hope.* e Lucan; and l Clanmorris.
Spes mea in Deo. *My hope is in God.* Teynham.
Spes tutissima cœlis. *Heaven is the safest hope.* e Kingston; and v Lorton.
Stand fast. e Seafield. .
Stant cætera tigno. *The rest stand on a beam.* e Aboyne.
Stare super vias antiquas. *I stand in the track of my ancestors.* Bayning.
Steady. Aylmer; and Bridport.
Strike. Hawke.
Suaviter et fortiter. *Mildly and firmly.* e Minto.
Suaviter in modo, fortiter in re. *Gentle in manner, but vigorous in the deed.* Newborough.

Sub cruce candidâ, *Under the fair cross.* e Egmont, and l Arden.
Sub cruce salus. *Salvation under the cross.* v Bangor.
Sub hoc signo vinces. *Under this sign you shall conquer.* v De Vesci.
Suivez raison. *Follow reason.* m Sligo; and l Kilmaine.
Suscipere et finire. *To undertake and to accomplish.* d Cumberland.

Tâche sans tâche. *A work without a stain.* e Northesk.
Templa quàm dilecta. *Temples how beloved.* d Buckingham and Chandos; and l Nugent.
Tenax et fidelis. *Persevering and faithful.* Carrington.
The noblest motive is the public good. e Bantry.
Think and thank. m Ailesbury.
Think on. Kirkcudbright.
Thou shalt want ere I want. Cranstoun.
Through. d Hamilton.
Thus. v St. Vincent.
Tiens a la vérité. *Maintain the truth.* De Blaquiere.
Tiens ta foy. *Keep thy faith.* e Bathurst.
Timet pudorem. *He fears shame.* v Down.
Timor Domini fons vitæ. *The fear of the Lord is the fountain of life.* Dunboyne.
Toujours prêt. *Always ready.* e Clanwilliam.
Toujours propice. *Ever propitious.* Cremorne.
Tout bien ou rien. *All or nothing.* Barham.
Tout vient de Dieu. *All things come from God.* Clinton.
Traditus, non victus. *Betrayed, not conquered.* Howden.
Trial by Jury. Erskine.
Triumpho morte tam vitâ. *I triumph in death as in life.* v Allen.
True to the end. e Home.
Tuebor. *I will defend,* v Torrington.
Tuum est. *It is your own.* e Cowper.

Ubi lapsus? Quid feci? *Whither am I fallen? What have I done?* e Devon.
Ubique patriam reminisci. *I have remembered my country every where.* e Malmesbury.
Ultra pergere. *To proceed further.* Lyndhurst.
Un Dieu, ung roy. *One God, one king.* Lyttelton.
Un je servirai, *One will I serve.* e Pembroke, and Montgomery, and e Carnarvon.
Un roy, une foy, une loy. *One king, one faith one law.* m Clanricarde.
Uni æquus virtuti. *Friendly to virtue alone.* e Mansfield.
Ut prosim. *That I may do good.* Foley.
Ut quocunque paratus. *Prepared on every side.* e Cavan.

Valet anchora virtus. *Virtue a sheet anchor.* Gardner.
Ventis secundis. *Prosperous winds.* v Hood.
Vérité sans peur. *Truth without fear.* Midleton.
Ver non semper viret. *The spring does not always flourish, or* Vernon *always flourishes.* Vernon.
Vertue vaunceth. *Virtue prevails.* Willoughby de Broke.
Vestigia nulla retrorsum. *Our footsteps are all advancing.* e Buckinghamshire.
Via trita, via tuta. *The beaten path is the safe path.* e Normanton.
Vigeur de dessus. *Strength is from above.* m Thomond.
Vigilantibus. *To the watchful* e Gosford.
Vigilate et orate. *Watch and pray.* v Castlemaine.
Vincit amor patriæ. *The love of my country prevails.* e Chichester; v Molesworth; l Muncaster; and l Yarborough.

INDEX TO THE PLATES.

INDEX TO THE PLATES.

N N

INDEX TO THE PLATES.

LONDON:

IBOTSON AND PALMER, PRINTERS, SAVOY STREET, STRAND.

Lightning Source UK Ltd.
Milton Keynes UK
173399UK00004B/25/P

9 781142 174538